INTERNATIONAL TRADE AND COMPETITION

CASES AND NOTES IN STRATEGY AND MANAGEMENT

McGraw-Hill Series in International Business and Economics

Chacholiades: International Economics
Davidson and de la Torre: Managing the Global Corporation: Case Studies in
  Strategy and Management
Yoffie: International Trade and Competition: Cases and Notes in Strategy and
  Management

INTERNATIONAL TRADE AND COMPETITION

CASES AND NOTES IN STRATEGY AND MANAGEMENT

David B. Yoffie

Graduate School of Business Administration
Harvard University

McGRAW-HILL PUBLISHING COMPANY

New York   St. Louis   San Francisco   Auckland   Bogotá   Caracas
Hamburg   Lisbon   London   Madrid   Mexico   Milan   Montreal   New Delhi
Oklahoma City   Paris   San Juan   São Paulo   Singapore   Sydney   Tokyo   Toronto

This book was set in Palatino by J.M. Post Graphics, Corp.
The editors were Kathleen L. Loy and Linda Richmond;
the production supervisor was Salvador Gonzales.
The cover was designed by Rafael Hernandez.
R. R. Donnelley & Sons Company was printer and binder.

INTERNATIONAL TRADE AND COMPETITION

Cases and Notes in Strategy and Management

1 2 3 4 5 6 7 8 9 0 DOC DOC 9 5 4 3 2 1 0

ISBN   0-07-072276-5

Library of Congress Cataloging-in-Publication Data

Yoffie, David B.
    International trade and competition: cases and notes in strategy and
    management / David B. Yoffie
       p.   cm. — (McGraw-Hill series in international business and economics)
    ISBN 0-07-072276-5
    1. International business enterprises—Management—Case studies.
  2. International trade—Case studies.   3. Comparative advantage
(International trade)—Case studies.   I. Title.   II. Series.
HD62.4.Y64   1990
658′.049—dc20   89-13471

About the Author

DAVID B. YOFFIE is an associate professor at the Harvard Business School. His first book, *Power and Protectionism*, explored the impact of government policy on international trade patterns. His subsequent writings on international trade, firm strategy, and public policy have appeared in a wide range of journals, including the *Harvard Business Review, International Management, California Management Review*, the *New York Times*, the *Wall St. Journal*, and many academic publications. Dr. Yoffie has been a consultant and an educator for many companies, including Alcan, Digital Equipment, General Electric, Honeywell, IBM, Lloyds Bank, McKinsey, and Nynex. In addition, he serves as a director of Intel Corporation.

For my wife, Terry

Contents

Preface

There have been dramatic shifts in the structure of international trade and international competition over the last decade. At the macro level, for instance, international trade has become relatively volatile. Growth in world trade was positive every year from the late 1950s until 1975, continuously outstripping the expansion in world GNP and averaging more than 7 percent growth. Since the first oil crisis, growth in international trade has varied widely, significantly underperforming the world economy in many years. The composition and patterns of international trade have also changed. Raw materials and agricultural products dominated world trade for most of the last two centuries, but growth in manufacturing exports has far outpaced commodity shipments in the past two decades.

Shifts at the macro level have been accompanied by competitive shifts and dramatic changes in world market shares by firms. Historically, dominant American firms have been increasingly challenged by Asian and European firms: in aerospace, Airbus captured about 25 percent of the world market in the late 1980s; in semiconductors, Japanese firms gathered almost 50 percent of the world market in 1988. The role of government has also become more and more extensive in international trade. While the Tokyo Round of trade talks reduced tariff barriers to their lowest level in the postwar period, nontariff barriers have been on the rise in industries ranging from steel and textiles to telecommunications and semiconductors. Moreover, governments in Europe and North America have been moving closer to the creation of economic blocs: in 1992, Europe is scheduled to have completed the reduction of all internal trade barriers; in the meantime, the United States has signed free trade agreements with Israel and Canada and has expressed interest in extending the concept to Mexico and other nations.

Managing these dynamic changes in international trade has always been a central piece of business strategy for European and Japanese firms, but has only recently been recognized as a significant issue for the U.S. government and the majority of U.S. companies. When international trade was a relatively insignificant portion of economic activity of the United States, only a few national and corporate leaders worried about the competitiveness of U.S. products and the ability of U.S. firms to manage the flow of goods and services across national boundaries. The enormous trade deficits faced by the United States in the 1980s changed this view. Learning how to exploit international competitive advantages, managing competition with imports, and understanding the role of government in affecting the terms of international competition are critical components of national and business policy.

This casebook was written to address these issues primarily from the perspective of general managers. Unlike other casebooks on international business which focus on managing global corporations, or textbooks on international trade which focus on abstract theory, this book seeks to blend theories of international trade with practical, managerial considerations, focusing on the central question of how international competition affects business strategy.

This casebook also seeks to plug one of the most serious gaps between economics departments and business schools. International trade has traditionally been a subject taught only in economics departments. The rationale behind this division of labor was that trade was seen by most managers as a simple precursor to multinational investment. Moreover, many economists were disinterested in the real world application of their theories. Cases on international trade were not especially useful. The premise of this book is that the strategic problems and opportunities associated with international trade warrant serious attention by managers and academics alike. Strategies for competing in international trade are both complex and distinct from strategies for purely domestic enterprises and from strategies for multinational firms. An additional premise is that the theories being developed in economics about trade, especially theories of trade in imperfect markets, do indeed have real world applications, which can benefit students of management.

ORGANIZATION OF THE BOOK

The idea of this book grew out of a second year elective course developed at the Harvard Business School entitled "Managing International Trade and Competition." The course, like this book, has three primary objectives:

1. To develop a conceptual framework for managers that will improve their ability to compete in international trade
2. To explore the multifaceted sources of advantages and disadvantages that firms can gain in international competition from country location, access to information, and government policies
3. To give students some institutional knowledge of international trade, specifically regarding the General Agreement on Tariffs and Trade, the Multi-fiber Arrangement, and U.S. trade law and U.S. trade institutions

The course framework has three pieces, which are reflected in the book's organization. The first element of the framework is to relate classical theories of trade to the actual practice of international trade by firms. For students unfamiliar with trade theory, or for students who want a review, the first two notes in Part 1 give an overview of traditional theoretical approaches to international trade in nontechnical language. The central thrust of this literature on comparative advantage and the sources of comparative advantage is that patterns of international trade—who exports what to whom—are determined by attributes of countries. From the managerial point of view, this suggests that the country you live in can provide advantages as well as disadvantages for competing internationally. The cases in Parts 2 and 3 then explore different types of advantages that can and should be exploited internationally and different types of country-based disadvantages which need to be overcome.

Attributes of countries, however, are not the whole story. First, most countries are not fortresses. Therefore, some advantages that may be inherent in a country's educational system or industrial base can be "exported" through movements in technology and information. Second, greater complexity, greater distances, diverse cultures, and so on, may create market imperfections. Imperfections of this type can produce opportunities for arbitrage. While many domestic markets adjust quickly to information imperfections, international markets are usually slower to adjust. Consequently, possessing superior information through international networks can be a source of advantage distinct from the attributes of your nation. Part 4 of the book explores one aspect of these informational advantages by looking at the strategy and operation of Japanese, U.S., and European trading companies.

The third piece of the framework is derived from literature in industrial organization, the new trade theories of strategic trade policy, and work in political economy. We know that theories of comparative advantage work reasonably well in undifferentiated, fragmented industries where firms have little market power and comparative costs are the fundamental determinant of competitive success. In the complex world of the 1980s and 1990s, however, imperfect markets and government policy can significantly affect the terms of competition between firms, industries, and nations. " 'New' Theories of International Trade" in Part 1 and "Note on Free Trade and Protectionism" in Part 5 provide a review of the conceptual literature. The cases in Part 5 then look at how national governments can affect international trade in practice. The cases explore three issues of particular importance: the role of import protectionism, the utility of export controls, and the consequences of regional economic integration.

Part 6 goes into depth on the role of government from a firm's perspective. The cases examine how various government trade policies, such as tariffs, quotas, voluntary export restraints, and so on, can affect the competitiveness of firms in basic industries; the impact of export controls on firm strategies; the role of subsidies in R&D intensive industries; and the management of domestic and international business-governments relations. A wide variety of industries were chosen to illustrate these topics, ranging from telecommunications, machine tools, and diesel engines to service businesses such as tourism and financial services.

Part 7 allows for a review of all the theoretical and managerial issues covered in the book. The first case on the global semiconductor industry explores how country advantages shift over time, the impact of shifting country advantages on national industries, and the role of information and technology in determining competitive advantage. The second case looks at the impact of government policies. And the third case examines the problems of devising competitive strategy for one firm in international trade where country-based, technology-based and government-based advantages are constantly changing.

ACKNOWLEDGMENTS

There are many people to thank upon the completion of any book, and this project is no exception. Professors Joseph Badaracco, David Collis, John Goodman, and Michael Porter, and post-doctoral fellow Heather Hazard, all colleagues of mine at the Harvard Business School, each wrote one case in this volume. The book would have been incomplete without their valuable contributions.

I am also indebted to several colleagues who taught the cases and gave me very useful feedback. Members of the teaching groups from two Harvard Business School courses—"Business, Government, and the International Economy" and "Competition and Strategy"—provided constructive comments on selected cases. I am especially grateful to Yair Aharoni from Duke University and Benjamin Gomes-Casseres, George Lodge, Michael Rukstad, Richard Rosenbloom, and Richard Vietor, all from Harvard Business School, who took added time to read many of the cases and offer advice.

A large number of companies provided access to their top executives. Without their help most of the cases in this book would not have been written. The companies include American Express, B-W Footwear, Cummins Engine Company, General Electric, Lotus Development Corporation, MG Services, Motorola, and Intel Corporation. Staff and executives from the Semiconductor Industry Association and the National Machine Tool Builders Association also gave generously of their time.

All of the funding for this book was provided by the Harvard Business School. The Division of Research under Professors Ray Corey and Jay Lorsch offered all the travel and logistical support any author could hope for; the Directors of Research in charge of overseeing my work, Professors Thomas McCraw and Michael Yoshino, were especially encouraging on my course development. Several research assistants also uncovered data, interviewed executives, and wrote, rewrote, and rewrote again large segments of this book. John Coleman played the most significant role, researching and writing drafts of many of the cases over a three-year period. Finally, this book would never have been completed without Cathyjean Gustafson. Not only did she prepare the final versions of each case, but her organizing skills and watchful eyes kept the project on track and kept the quality control at the highest level.

David B. Yoffie

INTERNATIONAL TRADE AND COMPETITION

CASES AND NOTES IN STRATEGY AND MANAGEMENT

PART ONE

Theories of International Trade

Note on Comparative Advantage

Why and when should nations trade? This two-part question has intrigued economists for centuries. Adam Smith theorized in 1776 that national real income could be maximized if a country specialized in its export sector and imported only those goods that others could make for less.[1] A nation had an *absolute advantage* in the production of a good if it could produce it more cheaply than other countries. The country should specialize in goods where it had an absolute advantage and export any surpluses. If a country had absolute advantages in all products, it should not trade at all.

Smith's theory was challenged in 1817 by David Ricardo and his theory of *comparative advantage*.[2] According to Ricardo, incentives for trade existed even when one country held an absolute cost advantage in all goods. If England produced cloth at a cost one-third of Portugal's,

and its cost of producing wine was one-half of Portugal's, then England should have specialized in cloth production because that was where its relative advantage was greater.[3] According to the theory of absolute advantage, England should export both cloth and wine; according to the theory of comparative advantage, however, England should export cloth and import wine, while Portugal should specialize in wine, the good in which it had the least comparative *disadvantage*. Ricardo argued that specialization maximized both countries' welfare. England charged a higher price (in units of wine) for its cloth in Portugal than it charged at home. But English cloth in Portugal was still cheaper than Portuguese cloth. Both countries got something from the deal. This situation is similar to the case of the Wall Street investment banker who also happened to be the city's best typist. Rather than do both activities, the investment banker should specialize in banking, where her comparative advantage was greater and income potential higher. Someone else should have been hired to do the typing, even though this employee would not be as productive as the banker.

This note was prepared by Research Assistant John J. Coleman, under the supervision of Associate Professor David B. Yoffie, as the basis for class discussion.

Copyright © 1986 by the President and Fellows of Harvard College. Harvard Business School case 9-387-023.

Ricardo's theory relied on a number of important assumptions. Pretrade prices were determined by relative labor productivity, not by demand, and the pattern of trade was completely determined by the technological differences between countries. While commodities faced a world market, "factors of production" (land, labor, and capital—the basic ingredients of all products) competed with each other only within national boundaries. Ricardo aggregated all these productive factors into a single unit. Every industry was assumed to use the same basic mix of factors and required factors of similar quality. These factors were, in effect, considered mobile between sectors at no cost. And because firms in this theory faced constant rather than increasing costs as they shifted their resources from one industry to the other, the logical result was that a country would shut down production of one good (wine, in England's case) in order to specialize its production in another product (cloth).

The classic trade theory developed by Smith and furthered by Ricardo implied that countries should trade freely.[4] Tariffs, as the figure below suggests, would have a negative effect on welfare, assuming there were no scale economies, no R&D or technological innovation, no transaction costs, and no market imperfections.

Under free trade, consumers enjoyed a surplus represented by the large triangle ACE. All those consumers who fell at points above point A on the demand curve were willing to pay more than the existing world price for the product but were able to buy at the world price. They were, in effect, saving the difference between what they would have been willing to pay and the world price. This difference, multiplied by the number of units that would have been purchased, was the total consumer surplus. After the tariff was imposed, the domestic price rose and the total consumer surplus declined to the triangle BCD. The loss to consumers, then, was area a + b + c + d.

For domestic producers, curve S_D represented a marginal cost curve as well as a supply curve. Producers' revenue was the rectangle marked by the intersection of lines extending from price and the quantity supplied at that price. Profit was marked by the area above the marginal cost curve; revenues below that curve paid for variable costs. When a tariff was imposed and the domestic price increased, domestic producers received new revenues marked by the areas a and b. Since b fell below the marginal cost curve and paid for variable costs, area a represented the gain to domestic producers from the imposition of a tariff.

The government's revenue gain from the imposition of a tariff was represented by the area c. The area between the domestic supply line and the domestic demand curve equaled the amount of imports that came into the country to meet consumer demand. After the government imposed the tariff, the supply from domestic producers increased and the supply from imports decreased. Total demand for the good at the new higher price also decreased. The rectangle c was the amount of the tariff multiplied by the new reduced demand for imports.

Reviewing these gains and losses, the classical theory reached the conclusion that the net effect of a tariff was negative. The losses by

Domestic Supply Curve/Marginal Cost Curve

Domestic Price with Tariff

Tariff

World Price

Domestic Demand Curve

consumers (area a + b + c + d) were partially offset by gains of producers and the government (areas a and c, respectively). Areas b and d were not offset by anyone's gain; they equaled the *net national loss* or deadweight loss resulting from the tariff. This has led classical economists to reach two particularly important conclusions regarding the impact of tariffs. First, tariffs usually lowered world well-being. Second, a tariff usually lowered the well-being of each nation involved, including the nation imposing the tariff. However, there were two exceptions to this second conclusion. A "nationally optimal" tariff could be imposed in a situation where a country had natural monopsony power and could affect the price at which foreigners supplied imports. In this case, the marginal cost at which society as a whole could buy imports was less than the price any one individual or firm would pay if acting alone in the absence of the tariff. The other exception consisted of "second-best" arguments that presented tariffs as a possibly useful way to overcome defects or "distortions" in the domestic economy.[5] Ultimately, these two exceptions depended on some alteration in the classic trade theory.

Economists after Ricardo generally accepted the idea of comparative advantage and free trade as valid. In fact, many of the articles of the General Agreement on Tariffs and Trade (*Exhibit 1*), the international regime which provided guidelines for world trade, were designed with Ricardo's theory in mind. While commitment to Ricardian logic has remained strong over time, economists have increasingly refined Ricardo's model by relaxing some of his assumptions.[6] The most important refinement of the Ricardian model was developed by Eli Heckscher and Bertil Ohlin.[7] Heckscher and Ohlin focused on two productive ingredients, or factors—labor and capital. The Heckscher-Ohlin theory, also known as the "factor proportions" or "factor endowments" theory, was based on two postulates: (1) commodities differed in how much labor or capital they required; i.e., they had differing *factor intensity;* and (2) countries differed in their supply of labor and capital; i.e., they had differing *factor abundance.* The theory assumed that all countries had the same technology, so labor productivity was considered equal. It ruled out scale economies due to the market size and also disregarded differences in tastes across countries. The proportions of labor and capital required to produce a given commodity were assumed to be the same across borders, and these productive factors were considered to be of identical quality in each country. Because labor and capital were assumed to have diminishing marginal productivity, it made little economic sense to push all productive resources toward the production of one commodity. The complete shutdown of production of the other good was unlikely. Finally, the Heckscher-Ohlin approach assumed "perfect markets, free trade, no transport costs, and complete international immobility of productive factors."[8]

The most important proposition resulting from the theory was that countries exported products that they were best suited to produce.[9] Plentiful supplies of capital provided a country with a comparative advantage in the production of capital-intensive goods. Capital-abundant countries, therefore, produced and exported capital-intensive commodities. These same countries imported relatively labor-intensive commodities.

Critics pointed out that several of these assumptions did not seem to reflect the reality of the international economy. For example, because of scale economies, a country might have decided to keep producing a particular good until the volume built up sufficiently to allow exploitation of these economies. The relevant scale economies could have been internal either to the plant or to external economies such as the size of the industry or the size of interdependent industries. The basic equality of knowledge and technology across countries implied by the theory suggested that innova-

GENERAL AGREEMENT ON TARIFFS AND TRADE: KEY PROVISIONS

PREAMBLE

Recognizing that their relations in the field of trade and economic endeavour should be conducted with a view to raising standards of living, ensuring full employment and a large and steadily growing volume of real income and effective demand, developing the full use of the resources of the world and expanding the production and exchange of goods.

Being desirous of contributing to these objectives by entering into reciprocal and mutually advantageous arrangements directed to the substantial reduction of tariffs and other barriers to trade and to the elimination of discriminatory treatment in international commerce.

Have through their Representatives agreed as follows:

ARTICLE I

General Most-Favoured-Nation Treatment

1. With respect to customs duties . . . and with respect to all rules and formalities in connection with importation and exportation . . . any advantage, favour, privilege or immunity granted by any contracting party to any product originating in or destined for any other country shall be accorded immediately and unconditionally to the like product originating in or destined for the territories of all other contracting parties. . . .

ARTICLE III

National Treatment on Internal Taxation and Regulation

1. The contracting parties recognize that internal taxes and other internal charges, and laws, regulations and requirements affecting the internal sale . . . should not be applied to imported or domestic products so as to afford protection to domestic production. . . .

ARTICLE VI

Anti-dumping and Countervailing Duties

1. The contracting parties recognize that dumping, by which products of one country are introduced into the commerce of another country at less than the normal value of the products, is to be condemned if it causes or threatens material injury to an established industry. . . . [A] product is to be considered . . . less than its normal value, if the price of the product exported from one country to another
   a. is less than the comparable price . . . for the like product when destined for consumption in the exporting country, or,
   b. in the absence of such domestic price, is less than either
      (1) the highest comparable price for the like product for export to any third country in the ordinary course of trade, or
      (2) the cost of production of the product in the country of origin plus a reasonable addition for selling cost and profit. . . .

CONTINUED

ARTICLE X

Publication and Administration of Trade Regulations

1. Laws, regulations, judicial decisions and administrative rulings of general application, made effective by any contracting party, pertaining to the classification or the valuation of products for customs purposes, or to rates of duty, taxes or other charges, or to requirements, restrictions or prohibitions on imports or exports or on the transfer of payments therefor . . . shall be published promptly in such a manner as to enable governments and traders to become acquainted with them. . . . The provisions of this paragraph shall not require any contracting party to disclose confidential information which would impede law enforcement or otherwise be contrary to the public interest or would prejudice the legitimate commercial interests of particular enterprises, public or private. . . .

ARTICLE XI

General Eliminations of Quantitative Restrictions

1. No prohibitions or restrictions other than duties, taxes or other charges, whether made effective through quotes, import or export licences or other measures, shall be instituted or maintained by any contracting party on the importation of any product of the territory of any other contracting party or on the exportation or sale for export of any product destined for the territory of any other contracting party. . . .

ARTICLE XIX

Emergency Action on Imports of Particular Products

1. **(a)** If, as a result of unforeseen developments and of the effect of the obligatins incurred by a contracting party under this Agreement, including tariff concessions, any product is being imported into the territory of that contracting party in such increased quantities and under such conditions as to cause or threaten serious injury to domestic producers in that territory of like or directly competitive products, the contracting party shall be free, in respect of such product, and to the extent and for such time as may be necessary to prevent or remedy such injury, to suspend the obligation in whole or in part or to withdraw or modify the concession. . . .

Source: The Contracting Parties to the G.A.T.T., *Basic Instruments and Selected Documents*, Vol. IV (Geneva 1969).

---

tion in knowledge and technology was as likely to occur in one country as another. But Raymond Vernon and Louis T. Wells argued that innovation played an important role in determining trade patterns. Vernon and Wells asserted that innovations tended to occur in some countries and not in others for certain kinds of goods, and that this innovation produced comparative advantage, at least for the short term.[10]

Another charge leveled against the Heck-scher-Ohlin theory was that it was static. Two of the theory's assumptions led to this criticism: the acceptance of the law of increasing costs and the implication that productive resources were found locally rather than created. According to this view, if some countries stuck to their "natural" advantages, then they might be stuck with second-best and second-rate economies. Furthermore, trade adjustments were assumed by the theory to operate smoothly at the margin; adjustments resulting from *major* changes in economic structure were not incorporated into the theory.[11] The Heckscher-Ohlin theory suggested that a country make the best of what it has rather than try to anticipate forthcoming changes in economic structure and build competitive strength in new and emerging industries. Yet many governments' industrial policies aimed at precisely those objectives.

The most significant empirical challenge to the Heckscher-Ohlin theory was leveled by Nobel Prize winner Wassily Leontief. In a seminal article, Leontief found that contrary to the expectations of the Heckscher-Ohlin theory, U.S. exports were, on average, *less* capital-intensive than were U.S. imports.[12] This finding, which became known as the "Leontief paradox," stimulated a number of alternative approaches to understanding the sources of comparative advantage. Nonetheless, the Heckscher-Ohlin theory has continued to be the foundation of international trade theory into the 1980s. Richard Caves and Ronald Jones concluded that despite problems with some of its assumptions and predictions, "the spirit of the Heckscher-Ohlin theory still remains to suggest that differences between countries in the endowment of broad classes of productive factors such as capital and labor will be reflected in differences in patterns of production and trade" (p. 132).

NOTES

1. *The Wealth of Nations*, Book 4, Chapter 2.
2. David Ricardo, "The Principles of Political Economy and Taxation," Chapter 7 in P. Sraffa (ed.), *The Works and Correspondence of David Ricardo*, Vol. 1. (New York: Cambridge University Press, 1953).
3. Relative cost indicates how much cloth England must forfeit in order to produce another unit of wine, and vice versa. England's absolute costs might be higher than Portugal's, but what are actually being compared are the cloth/wine exchange *ratios* within the two countries; i.e., which country has to exchange relatively less cloth to produce more wine?
4. This discussion of the treatment of tariffs in classic trade theory draws heavily on Chapters 6 and 7 of Peter H. Lindhert and Charles P. Kindleberger, *International Economics*, 7th ed. (Homewood, Ill: Richard D. Irwin, 1982).
5. See *Case 15*, "Note on Free Trade and Protectionism," for discussion on second-best arguments.
6. See, for example, Richard E. Caves and Ronald W. Jones, *World Trade and Payments: An Introduction*, 3rd ed. (Boston: Little, Brown, 1981); and Peter B. Kenen, *The International Economy*, (Englewood Cliffs, N.J.: Prentice-Hall, 1985).
7. Eli Heckscher, "The Effect of Foreign Trade on the Distribution of Income," originally published in Swedish in 1919. Reprinted in American Economic Association, *Readings in the Theory of International Trade* (Philadelphia: Blakiston, 1949), Chapter 13. Bertil Ohlin, *Interregional and International Trade* (Cambridge, Mass: Harvard University Press, 1933).
8. Robert E. Baldwin, "Determinants of the Commodity Structure of U.S. Trade," in Robert E. Baldwin and J. David Richardson, *International Trade and Finance: Readings*, 2nd ed. (Boston: Little, Brown, 1981), p. 5.
9. The other major conclusion was that commodity trade tended generally (but perhaps only partially) to eradicate international differences in wages, rents, and other factor returns. Free trade in commodities could, therefore, completely substitute for international mobility of capital and labor by driving wages and rents to equality for countries sharing the same technology. See Caves and Jones, 1981.
10. Raymond Vernon and Louis T. Wells, Jr., *The Economic Environment of International Business*, 4th ed. (Englewood Cliffs, N.J.: Prentice-Hall, 1986), pp. 85–87.
11. Bruce Scott, "U.S. Competitiveness: Concepts, Performance, and Implications," in Bruce R. Scott and George C. Lodge, eds., *U.S. Competitiveness in World Economy* (Boston: Harvard Business School Press, 1985).
12. Wassily W. Leontief, "Domestic Production and Foreign Trade: The American Capital Position Reexamined," *Economia Internazionale*, 7(1954):3–32.

Note on Sources of Comparative Advantage

The Heckscher-Ohlin factor-proportions theory of international trade stated that countries with plentiful capital and scarce labor would export primarily capital-intensive commodities and import labor-intensive commodities. After Wassily Leontief published data in the mid-1950s showing that U.S. exports were less capital-intensive than were U.S. imports, the Heckscher-Ohlin theory came under sharp scrutiny. By the late 1960s scholars had developed alternative explanations of the sources of comparative advantage in an attempt to explain the "Leontief paradox." This note reviews several of these efforts. If not factor proportions, then what?[1]

This note was prepared by Research Assistant John J. Coleman and Associate Professor David B. Yoffie as the basis for class discussion.

SKILLED LABOR

One influential response to the Leontief paradox emphasized the importance of skilled labor in the production of U.S. exports. Originally put forth by Leontief and Irving Kravis, the skilled-labor hypothesis was explored by a number of writers, most notably Donald Keesing.[2] According to these writers, the United States placed a strong emphasis on building skilled labor through education, on-the-job training, and health care. This emphasis raised the quality of the services performed and the decisions made by labor, management, professionals, and bureaucrats. Because the United States had relatively plentiful supplies of skilled labor, particularly in scientific and technical fields, U.S. exports should have embodied more skillful labor than U.S. imports.

Proponents of the skilled-labor approach presented various measures that indicated that U.S. exports made greater use of skilled labor than did U.S. imports. All these measures assumed that individual products were produced roughly the same way across borders, with similar amounts of labor, skilled labor, and capital.[3] Furthermore, these authors estimated that if the value of the education and training (so-called "human capital") was added to the value of the physical capital, the U.S. exports *were* capital-intensive and the Leontief paradox was reduced or reversed. Generally, then, this approach supported the Heckscher-Ohlin notion that a country produced and exported goods that heavily used what the country had, whether that be labor, land, or capital. The difference for an economist like Keesing was that he considered it necessary to abandon a simple *two-factor* approach (capital and labor) in favor of a factor-proportions approach that distinguished among different *types* of labor on the basis of skill.

R&D-ORIENTED INDUSTRIES

This explanation, developed by Keesing, William Gruber, Dileep Mehta, and Raymond Vernon, stressed that the United States gained an efficiency advantage from its R&D-oriented industries.[4] In the theory, R&D expenditures led to improvement of the machinery and technological processes used to manufacture goods, the quality of goods and services produced, and the managerial techniques utilized in organizing a business enterprise. This "knowledge capital" resulted in more efficient production.

Gruber, Mehta, and Vernon found that the most research-oriented industries in the United States featured high-employment concentration in the larger firms and economic domination by the larger firms. Surprisingly, however, these large-scale high-concentration industries were not particularly capital-intensive. Capital intensity did not explain the emergence of economies of large scale and barriers

to entry in these industries. Rather, successful product innovation and marketing required strong emphasis on R&D and resulted in scale economies and entry barriers. A firm that could spread its research risks over a large number of efforts stood a better chance of making a successful gamble. Moreover, these firms would be well-positioned to capitalize on economies of scale in sales, marketing, supplying spare parts, performing research to keep the product competitive, and so on. Studies showed that as R&D expenditures as a percentage of industry sales increased, so did U.S. export performance.[5] A high level of research was correlated with substantial U.S. trade surpluses. Since these industries were not capital-intensive, this explained why U.S. exports were less capital-intensive than U.S. imports.

NATURAL RESOURCES INDUSTRIES

Jaroslav Vanek and Muhammad Diab argued that the pattern of U.S. trade could be explained by considering the structure of natural resource industries.[6] This alternative began by assuming that the United States was relatively poorly endowed with natural resources and that their production in the United States, including mining and first-stage processing, was highly capital-intensive. Because natural resources were scarce in the United States, both natural resources and capital were conserved by not exporting natural resource products. The United States needed to import natural resource products which, when measured by U.S. production methods, were highly capital-intensive. Vanek found that on average natural resource products were twice as large a proportion of U.S. imports as of U.S. exports. Leontief also reexamined his original data and found that he could eliminate the famous "paradox" if he excluded natural resource industries from his analysis.

INTERNAL DEMAND

Staffan Burenstam Linder asserted that for manufactured goods, "the range of exportable products is determined by internal demand. It is a necessary, but not a sufficient, condition that a product be consumed (or invested) in the home country for this product to be a potential export product."[7] The internal demand had to be "representative" of national demands, meaning that a country would specialize in the production and export of those goods demanded by a dominant plurality of the population. (In the United States this meant products catered toward the middle and upper-middle income groups. In Saudi Arabia, representative demand did not include Cadillacs, even though some individuals owned those vehicles.) The reasoning behind this argument was that entrepreneurs pursued those profit opportunities of which they were most aware, which meant domestic needs. Exploitation of inventions was at first automatically geared to the home market. There was an easy access to crucial information between consumers and producers in the home market, the kind of information necessary for virtually any product's introduction when it went through a development and refinement period. With no home testing ground, the entrepreneur incurred heavy costs overseas to find this information.

An entrepreneur exported when the local market was insufficient for expansion and the entrepreneur realized that profits could be made abroad. According to Linder, "export is at the end, not the beginning, of a typical market expansion path."[8] This "typical" path could be altered if it was easy to gain awareness of foreign demand, if the product's availability didn't depend on inventive effort, and if little or no development work was needed. Linder concluded that trade would be heaviest between countries with similar demand structures, and since those demand structures depended on income, countries with relatively close per capita income and distribution of income would be particularly strong trading partners.

PRODUCT LIFE CYCLE

Trade cycle theory, an amalgam and extension of the R&D and internal demand approaches, was one of the few "dynamic" theories of trade to emerge following the Leontief paradox. Raymond Vernon and Louis T. Wells, primary architects of this theory, argued that U.S. goods went through a general cycle in which the United States gradually lost its trade advantage to foreign competitors.[9] In the final stage of the cycle, foreign competitors gained market share in the United States.

U.S. export strength at the outset of the cycle derived from the nature of the U.S. market. The high per capita income, high labor costs, and relatively plentiful capital in the United States pushed U.S. investment, innovation, and R&D toward labor-saving and luxury-oriented goods. It was not surprising, trade cycle theorists argued, that U.S. producers had a consistently higher rate of expenditure on labor-saving or high-income product development than did foreign producers. Inventors and entrepreneurs were sensitive to domestic demands in a way they couldn't be to foreign demand. And because of the size of the U.S. market, U.S. producers could take advantage of efficiencies from long runs.

As other countries gained in affluence, products that originated in the United States could be sold overseas, and U.S. firms would initially have great competitive advantages. U.S. producers possessed an input into the production process of these goods that was not accessible to foreign manufacturers—knowledge might have been protected because it required expensive "learning by doing" to increase efficiency. The problem for U.S. producers was that over time this knowledge of processes or products tended to depreciate and disperse. As industries matured, technology stabilized, and the United States would lose market share to countries with cheaper labor and newer productive facilities. As U.S. advantages in these products faded, however, new products, segments, and industries emerged to replace them. Trade cycle theorists argued that U.S. exports generally would be more labor-intensive than U.S. imports due to the innovative nature of the U.S. products. These products grew out of extensive labor-intensive R&D, as the R&D hypothesis suggested. Therefore, products tended to be more labor-intensive early in the product cycle, where the United States held a trade advantage. Cost-cutting through automation or mechanization became more important as an increasing number of producers were viable competitors.

INTRAINDUSTRY TRADE

By the mid-1970s intraindustry trade was a growing component of the trade between industrial nations. The Heckscher-Ohlin theory could not explain why a country like the United States might import products that it could also export. This gap in the Heckscher-Ohlin theory led Grubel to develop an alternative explanation of international trade.[10] Grubel argued that the most important industries produced "differentiated goods"—very close substitutes differentiated by style, quality, minor variations in performance characteristics, or brand name (e.g., automobiles, cigarette brands). Under the Heckscher-Ohlin theory, there were no incentives for trade between countries sharing these industries, but in the real world such trade did occur between countries at similar levels of development.

Grubel argued that this puzzle could be explained by dropping the Heckscher-Ohlin assumption of constant returns to scale. Scale economies, he argued, came not just from larger plants but from producing fewer differentiated goods within the same plant. The lower the number of differentiated products manufactured in each plant, the lower the per unit production costs. Since machines could be constructed specifically for long high-speed runs, and labor had to learn fewer tasks, it made sense for a firm to reduce the number of differentiated goods it produced. Different countries would specialize in alternative versions of a differentiated good. The products a country would specialize in depended on its physical environment, its history and culture, the quality of products demanded by the majority of the population, and the market size for technically sophisticated producer goods. For example, Sweden's highly developed program of publicly subsidized housing featured small apartments well-suited to a new type of furniture later known as "Scandinavian style." In the United States, on the other hand, a heavy "colonial style" of furniture emerged during the country's pioneer development, when neither space nor timber was scarce. Because each country had individuals whose tastes differed from the locally predominant choice, incentives existed for import and export of similar products. The wealthier a country, the more probable these tastes would be articulated and satisfied. The relative wealth of the United States meant that it was particularly likely that the United States would import large volumes of goods similar to those already produced domestically.

BEYOND COMPARATIVE ADVANTAGE

In the 1970s, the debate on why nations have comparative advantage in certain sectors and why they export particular products continued to rage. In reviewing these debates, two trade economists, Robert Baldwin and David Richardson, summed up the competing view of comparative advantage by suggesting that:

One should not conclude that relative factor proportions are not important in influencing trade patterns, but rather that such productive factors as human capital and natural resources must also be introduced into the traditional model. Furthermore, it is evident that temporary differences in technology, economies of scale, governmental trade policies, and other factors also play a significant role in determining the commodity structure of world trade. The task now is to ascertain the relative importance of these various elements from country to country and at different times.[11]

By the early 1980s, however, economists were becoming increasingly dissatisfied with state-of-the-art trade theory, especially the methodology and empirical research. Many of the revisions to Hecksher-Ohlin, such as the product life cycle or the Linder hypothesis on domestic demand, were qualitative in nature and not easily formalized mathematically. Empirical tests of many of the theories also proved weak. But, the most significant issue was that some scholars began to ask whether trade theorists were even asking the right questions. If comparative advantage was a meaningful concept, then trade should be greatest between *dissimilar* countries. Yet, since World War II, the majority of world trade took place between industrial nations, and those nations had become more *similar* over time. Moreover, the assumption in classical international trade theory that markets were perfect seemed less and less tenable. In a world of multinational corporations, huge economies of scale, and differentiation strategies by firms, it was possible that corporate strategies and government policies could influence global markets and the patterns of trade.

In response to these concerns, a new body of international trade theory began to emerge. Economists such as Krugman, Dixit, Brander, and Spencer devised methods for mathematically incorporating models of imperfect competition and game theory into the study of in-

ternational trade.[12] Business school academics, such as Michael Porter and Bruce Scott, also began proposing new theories that emphasized the role of industry structure and government policy (respectively).[13] While the theory of comparative advantage and factor proportions was far from dead in the late 1980s, holes in the Ricardian model appeared to be widening and deepening.

NOTES

1. For overviews of the alternative theories, see Herbert G. Grubel, *International Economics*, 2nd ed. (Homewood, Ill.: Richard D. Irwin, 1981), chap. 4; and Robert E. Baldwin "Determinants of the Commodity Structure of U.S. Trade," in Robert E. Baldwin and J. David Richardson, *International Trade and Finance: Readings*, 2nd ed. (Boston: Little, Brown, 1981), pp. 4–27.

2. Donald B. Keesing, "Labor Skills and Comparative Advantage," in Baldwin and Richardson, eds., *International Trade and Finance: Readings*, 1st ed. (Boston: Little, Brown, 1974), pp. 4–15; Irving Kravis, "Wages and Foreign Trade," *Review of Economics and Statistics* 38 (February 1956):14–30; R. Bharadwaj and Jagdish Bhagwati, "Human Capital and the Pattern of Foreign Trade: The Indian Case," *Indian Economic Review*, 2 (October 1967):117–142; Helen Waehrer, "Wage Rates, Labor Skills, and United States Foreign Trade," in Peter B. Kenen and Robert Lawrence, eds., *The Open Economy: Essays on International Trade and Finance* (New York: Columbia University Press, 1968).

3. One approach that didn't make this assumption was the "reversal of factor intensity" explanation. Basically, this approach assumed that at different prices for the factors of production, a product which was currently very capital-intensive to produce could become very labor-intensive. The United States could import goods made by capital-intensive methods at home but with labor-intensive methods abroad. Minhas collected production technique data for 24 different industries in 19 different countries. He found factor reversals in 5 industries. Grubel con-

cluded that while it seemed that factor reversals did indeed take place, it did not seem that there were enough of them to explain the Leontief paradox. See B.S. Minhas, "The Homohypallagic Production Function, Factor Intensity Reversals and the Heckscher-Ohlin Theorem," *Journal of Political Economy*, April 1962.

4. Keesing, "The Impact of Research and Development on United States Trade," in Kenen and Lawrence, pp. 175–189; William Gruber, Dileep Mehta, and Raymond Vernon, "The R&D Factor in International Trade and International Investment of United States Industries," in Baldwin and Richardson, 1st ed., pp. 16–33.

5. To illustrate the importance of these industries, consider that in 1982 the top 5 research-oriented industries in the United States accounted for 72% of U.S. exports of manufactured goods, 39.1% of U.S. total sales of manufactured goods, 89.4% of total U.S. R&D expenditures, and 74.6% of company-financed R&D. The 5 industries were transportation, electrical machinery, instruments, chemicals, and nonelectrical machines.

6. Jaroslav Vanek, "The Natural Resource Content of Foreign Trade, 1870–1955, and the Relative Abundance of Natural Resources in the United States," *Review of Economics and Statistics*, May 1959.

7. Staffan Burenstam Linder, "Causes of Trade in Primary Products versus Manufactures," in Baldwin and Richardson, 1st ed., pp. 43–54.

8. Linder, p. 45.

9. See Raymond Vernon, "International Investment and International Trade in the Product Cycle," in Baldwin and Richardson, 2nd ed., pp. 27–40; Louis T. Wells, Jr., "A Product Life Cycle for International Trade," in Baldwin and Richardson, 1st ed., pp. 34–43; and Wells, ed., *The Product Life Cycle and International Trade* (Boston: Harvard University Graduate School of Business, 1972).

10. See Grubel, *International Economics*, chap. 4; and "The Theory of Intra-Industry Trade," in Baldwin and Richardson, 2nd ed., pp. 51–60.

11. Baldwin and Richardson, "Introduction: Theories of International Trade," 2nd edition, pp. 3–4.

12. For the most accessible review of this body of work, see Paul Krugman, ed., *Strategic Trade Policy and the New International Economics* (Cambridge: MIT Press, 1986).

13. See Michael E. Porter, *The Competitive Advantage of Nations* (New York: Free Press, 1990); and Bruce Scott and George Lodge, eds., *U.S. Competitiveness and the World Economy* (Boston: Harvard Business School Press, 1985).

"New" Theories of International Trade

A new body of international trade theory emerged in the 1980s. The foundations of this theory were that competition in markets was *imperfect* and that firms and governments could act *strategically* to affect trade flows and national welfare. For many economists, this growing body of literature represented a radical departure from previous scholarship. Rigorous mathematical models were developed which questioned the heart and soul of classical comparative advantage. Respectable academic economists began asking whether unconditional free trade was a country's best policy choice.

This case reviews the background and central hypotheses of these "new" theories, which have also been called theories of strategic trade policy. The case looks at why many economists and policymakers thought alternative approaches were necessary, at what the contributions of industrial organization to this new theory were, and at what some of the tentative results in the 1980s were. The case ends with an overview of Michael Porter's book, *The Competitive Advantage of Nations*. Porter, like the strategic trade theorists, raised new questions about the value of classical comparative advantage and the role of firm and industry-level variables in determining who competes successfully in international trade.

CHANGES IN THE TRADING ENVIRONMENT

Several economic changes in the international trading system stimulated executives, policymakers, and theoreticians to revisit international trade theory in the 1980s. The first was growing economic interdependence among nations, especially the increasing importance of trade for the United States. The rapid growth of imports into the United States, for instance, meant that trade suddenly became a primary concern for executives and policymakers alike. For the first time, virtually all American com-

Dr. Heather A. Hazard prepared this case in collaboration with Associate Professor David B. Yoffie as the basis for class discussion rather than to illustrate either effective or ineffective handling of an administrative situation.

panies began facing serious foreign competition at home; at the same time, U.S. government policymakers found that policies for such diverse activities as antitrust or innovation could no longer be set in isolation from the world economy. Moreover, the possibility that foreign governments were providing assistance to their domestically based firms raised the question of whether the U.S. government should counter such assistance through its own initiatives. By the 1980s, some governments had demonstrated an ability to affect the welfare of Americans through policy actions.

The dramatic collapse in the U.S. trade position during the Reagan administration and its persistence into the late 1980s furthered interest in trade theory. Between 1980 and 1988, the U.S. share of world imports rose sharply from 13 to 16%, while exports fluctuated around 11%. As a consequence the current account moved from an annual surplus of $2 billion in 1980 to an annual deficit of $120 billion in 1988. If the trading system worked according to simple Ricardian logic, an exchange rate change would have quickly reduced the U.S. payment deficits and brought the world back into equilibrium. Throughout the 1980s, however, the empirical evidence indicated that a large and growing segment of trade was no longer driven by comparative advantage. Some countries were still observed to export primary and natural resource products which reflected their relative abundance of factors, but the pattern of trade in manufactures and services was less predictable. Contrary to the predictions that relied on the classical concept of relative factor proportions, countries could be observed importing, as well as exporting, goods and services in which they had a comparative advantage. This so-called **intraindustry trade**[1] took a dramatic jump during the 1980s after having remained steady during the 1970s.

Traditional predictions of trade patterns were further confounded by the emergence of huge scale economies in some industries and the growth of very large firms (usually multinationals) which dominated selected global markets. Classical theory assumed that firms did not have the power to affect prices. As long as there were many firms operating at arm's length, theory did not have to account for strategic behavior; all firms could be assumed to be price takers. But as industries became increasingly concentrated, with large firms capable of affecting the structure and conduct of the market, firms and governments had the opportunity to make strategic choices that could build competitive advantage in global markets.

Demand for Government Intervention

A second stimulus to the new trade theory was shifting political and policy dynamics. Rising demands for protectionism and growing pressures for regional trade blocs, especially in Europe and North America, led economists and politicians to search for solutions as well as justifications for their preferred policies.[2] In 1988, for instance, the United States and Canada signed a free-trade agreement that would eliminate virtually all restrictions to trade by 1998; and in 1985, European community governments passed the European Unification Act that would eliminate virtually all internal barriers by 1992. At the same time, however, demands for protection of the U.S. and European markets exploded. Mature industries continued lobbying for more protection, while normally free traders, such as semiconductors, telecommunications, and airframe firms, actively started to seek government assistance.

New Analytical Tools

While some economists had questioned classical trade theory for many years, they were never able to provide rigorous alternatives. As a result, theories such as the product life cycle, which incorporated ideas about imperfect competition, remained outside the mainstream of academic economics. In the late 1970s, however, some trade economists, most notably MIT's Paul Krugman, discovered that tools developed in the field of industrial organization could explain some of the anomalies in international trade.[3] Models of oligopolistic competition seemed particularly promising. Industrial organization theorists had developed new tools for analyzing **economies of scale, economies of scope, learning effects, R&D races,** and **technological spillovers.** (See *Appendix 1* for definitions of terms.) These tools could explain why it was sometimes beneficial for firms to engage in certain activities that otherwise did not seem feasible or rational. A few economists began to speculate that if these models of imperfect competition could be applied to international trade, we might better understand the new patterns of international flows.

ORIGINS OF THE NEW TRADE THEORY: INDUSTRIAL ORGANIZATION

While theories of trade under imperfect competition are a phenomenon of the 1980s, the roots of these theories can be traced back 150 years to when industrial organization (IO) first began describing how firms might behave when excess profits were available. One of the first major breakthroughs in IO came in 1838, when Augustin Cournot postulated that each firm chose to market the level of output that would maximize its own profits, assuming that the output of its rivals was fixed.[4] This led him to conclude that there was a stable price-quantity equilibrium in any industry, but that equilibrium depended upon the number of firms in the industry. (See *Appendix 2* for graphic representations of Cournot's thesis as well as price and quantity implications for alternative competitive conditions.) After the Great Depression, Chamberlin extended this line of analysis by postulating that firms expected their rivals to react to price and quantity changes in specific ways. Firms in an oligopolistic industry were expected to recognize their interdependence. In fact, they were expected to collude by setting prices at monopoly levels and dividing the market between them. The insights yielded by Chamberlin's original theory were limited, however, by the theory's inability to handle the critical differences among firms in their costs and market shares. Since firms in the real world did not have identical positions, conflicts could arise that would prevent producers from reaching their maximum joint profits.[5]

Building on Chamberlin's contributions, economists sought to develop new tools to understand how firms in oligopolistic industries could avoid myopic, aggressive behavior that would drive the industry away from joint profit-maximizing without resorting to formal collusive agreements. To solve this problem, a set of mathematical techniques known as **game theory** was applied.[6] The concept that firms could engage in zero-sum and positive-sum games[7] allowed industrial organization theorists to analyze (1) the conditions under which it would be profitable for firms to engage in specific types of behavior, (2) the conditions under which that behavior could in fact be expected, and (3) to what extent dominant firms would exhibit monopoly power.

These types of behavior were referred to as *strategic* because firms could consciously undertake them to capture control of markets and could anticipate the reactions of rivals to their actions. Among the types of strategic behavior firms could engage in were *dumping* (selling in markets below cost to develop economies of scale); *preemption* in R&D, product introduction, market penetration, etc. (moving before rivals to capture competitive advantage); and *predation* (incurring losses from price-cutting to drive rivals out of the marketplace).

CROSSING OVER FROM INDUSTRIAL ORGANIZATION TO INTERNATIONAL TRADE

An iconoclastic handful of trade theorists realized that there were reasons to be concerned with market imperfections and with strategic behavior in the international arena. The central proposition of the new trade theorists was that firms and governments could behave in strategically self-conscious ways in imperfect global markets and thereby affect a country's balance of trade and national welfare.

Trade policy theorists used the new tools from industrial organization as a springboard and adapted them for use in the analysis of international trade problems. The questions they posed were (1) should the U.S. government control access of foreign firms to domestic markets and (2) should the U.S. government promote the activities of domestic firms in global markets? Both questions were controversial because mainstream economists believed that government intervention in free markets would disrupt the general equilibrium of the economy as well as the efficient functioning of markets. The general equilibrium argument was that every industry competed with every other industry for resources. Therefore, if one industry received privileged access to resources, other industries would be deprived of these resources. The efficient markets argument was that resources would flow to their best use in a free market: government interventions would only distort these markets and lead to inefficiencies. So why intervene? The new trade theorists' answer was that through intervention, governments could encourage activities that generated *positive externalities*[8] and that *shifted profits*[9] from foreign economies to the domestic economy.

The positive externalities argument was concerned with situations where society could benefit from an action that might be too costly for an individual, rational firm to undertake. (In other words, a *market failure* occurred.) Suppose a firm's research and development activities would generate benefits for themselves and others (suppliers, customers, workers) in excess of the cost of the R&D, but the innovating firm's share of the benefits was inadequate to cover its costs. In such a case, it would make sense for the government to encourage the firm to undertake those activities, even if a subsidy (or protection) was required. The social benefits of the government's action outweighed the social costs. The new trade theorists had uncovered what many people had suspected of Japanese policy for decades; i.e., an activist trade policy could encourage domestic firms to undertake socially beneficial activities supporting a social agenda that would not necessarily be realized in a free market.

The profit-shifting argument was built on the assumption that a domestic government seeks to maximize *national* welfare, and not the welfare of the world or foreign consumers and producers. Based on the new trade theory, economists believed that governments could help domestic firms to capture profits that would otherwise accrue to foreign firms. Governments could use tax relief or subsidies, for example, to increase the profitability of private investments. If government policy facilitated domestically based firms to make a credible commitment to expand production facilities, foreign firms might be discouraged from expanding their own operations. The result would be increased market shares and profits for the domestic firms.

THE DEBATE OVER STRATEGIC GOVERNMENT INTERVENTION

The new trade theory offered fresh logic for using protectionism and subsidies to promote national welfare. While many of the policy debates surrounding this literature had clear mercantilist overtones, this was the first time that proponents of protection had a strong theoretical base to cite in their arguments. Elegant models were developed which explained why and under what conditions profits could be shifted from foreign firms to domestic firms, production runs could be lengthened (reducing marginal costs), the entry of domestic producers could be promoted, and external economies could be captured. The threat of market closure could also be portrayed as a negotiating position to force open protected foreign markets in this new light.

Other economists, however, countered that controlling market access was damaging in the long run because excessive numbers of domestic firms would be induced to enter into an industry by the prospect of earning above-average profits. Government policies could also inadvertently promote production inefficiencies, facilitate collusion among both foreign and domestic firms, and potentially redistribute income in undesirable ways (e.g., as surplus was shifted from consumers to producers through higher prices).

The difficulty in policy analysis was the calculation of the net benefit: exactly when did market failures occur and when did the benefits of intervention outweigh the costs? Few of the models offered strong support for government intervention. Economists found that the gains from strategic intervention were often small. In addition, if other governments intervened in retaliation, even these small gains might be wiped out.[10]

A second policy question raised in this debate was whether the government should promote the activities of domestic firms in global markets. The government had available a number of policy instruments including government procurement to stimulate domestic demand, production subsidies to lower the cost of goods and increase their competitiveness in international markets, and R&D subsidies to encourage U.S. firms to become leaders in in-

novation. Any government could use these instruments in a strategic manner to alter the competitive environment in favor of the entry of domestic firms.[11]

A simple example of a strategic trade policy would be the subsidization of research and development in an industry. By altering the payoffs to domestic firms, a government could attempt to discourage entry into the market by foreign firms and to preclude foreign firms from preempting the entry of domestic firms.

Applying the techniques of game theory, economists tried to show how such competitive government subsidies could alter competition in a business such as commercial aircraft. In the 1960s, for instance, several European aerospace companies were considering undertaking a joint venture (known as Airbus) into the market for the next generation of commercial aircraft frames. Suppose that Boeing, the largest American manufacturer, would have earned significant profits if it was the only producer. Further assume that Boeing and Airbus would have lost money if both produced. Finally, as-

FIGURE 1A

Payoffs in Competition between European and American Firms; No Subsidies. (American payoff in lower left of each box; European payoff in upper right.)

Europeans: Airbus

	Produce without Subsidy	Don't Produce
Americans: Boeing — Produce without Subsidy	−5 / −5	0 / 100
Americans: Boeing — Don't Produce	60 / 0	0 / 0

Europeans: Airbus

	Produce without Subsidy	Produce with Subsidy	Don't Produce
Produce without Subsidy	−5 −5	5 −5	0 100
Don't Produce	60 0	70 0	0 0

Americans: Boeing

FIGURE 1B
Payoffs in Competition between European and American Firms with European Subsidies Only.

sume that the opportunities and constraints facing Airbus were similar to Boeing's. Their payoffs could then be presented in a simple matrix, as illustrated in *Figure 1A*. Whichever manufacturer moved first would "win" because a follower would clearly destroy the market and cause both to lose money. If Boeing moved quickly and decisively, it could preempt Airbus's entry into the market.

The European governments could have foreclosed this opportunity to preempt by introducing a new alternative: provide a research and development subsidy to their domestic firm. This would have altered the payoffs to the firms in such a way that Boeing would have found entry unattractive, regardless of whether they led or followed (as illustrated in *Figure 1B*).

Thus, a government could attempt to discourage the entry of foreign firms through subsidies to its own firms. The strategic aspect of this policy was that the gains to the European firms were expected to be larger than the cost of the subsidy: even a modest subsidy might enable Airbus to capture large profits.[12]

But what about the ability of the U.S. government to retaliate with its own subsidy? If

this alternative had been introduced, then both firms could have ended up finding it attractive to produce aircraft (as illustrated in *Figure 1C*). In this example, the U.S. government could have intervened to subsidize the entry of Boeing. With these payoffs, both firms would have produced airplanes with subsidies but at net social cost.

The debate over the efficacy of competitive subsidies was intense in policy and academic circles in the 1980s. Advocates of government intervention suggested that promoting domestic firms in international trade could allow those firms to capture rents that would otherwise accrue to foreign producers, and facilitate firms' learning. The advocates also noted that traditional trade theory had assumed away these issues by assuming that imperfections were irrelevant for significant segments of trade, that profit sharing was irrelevant because the existence of rents was not acknowledged, and that the learning curve was not particularly important. Finally, advocates of this type of strategic trade policy focused on its dynamic character. By using iterative games, one could study the evolution of industries and competitive ad-

Europeans: Airbus

Americans: Boeing	Produce without Subsidy	Produce with Subsidy	Don't Produce
Produce without Subsidy	−5 (upper right) / −5 (lower left)	5 (upper right) / −5 (lower left)	0 (upper right) / 100 (lower left)
Produce with subsidy	−5 (upper right) / 5 (lower left)	5 (upper right) / 5 (lower left)	0 (upper right) / 110 (lower left)
Don't Produce	60 (upper right) / 0 (lower left)	70 (upper right) / 0 (lower left)	0 (upper right) / 0 (lower left)

FIGURE 1C
Payoffs in Subsidized Competition between European and American Firms: Both Subsidized.

vantage over time, while traditional models remained notoriously static. In the meantime, critics continued to argue that subsidies would distort the economy, bid resources away from other sectors, and run the risk of a trade war. If governments offer competing subsidies, the two firms might come out ahead, but consumers and national welfare in both countries could suffer.

EMPIRICAL RESEARCH

By developing clear, mathematical formulations, the new trade theorists gave strategic trade policy academic respectability. However, the models remained very tightly tied to narrow and unrealistic sets of assumptions, which reduced their usefulness for prescribing policy. To sort out which models were more or less robust, economists turned to empirical research.

Research on trade under imperfect competition faced daunting obstacles such as the lack of data. As a result, theorists mixed modeling techniques and relied on educated guesswork to set missing parameters.

The initial empirical findings were largely cautionary about the potential use of strategic trade policies. In the case of *trade protectionism*, the empirical research showed that gains from strategic beggar-thy-neighbor policies were likely to be small, even if other nations did not retaliate; if a trade war did result, then both countries might become net losers. For *trade liberalization*, gains were found to be significantly greater than those calculated using conventional models. The new increment in gains was due to the increased competition and the resulting rationalization in industries' structures: this rationalization effect had been neglected by the traditional models as a result of their assumption of perfect competition.[13]

IMPLICATIONS FOR TRADE POLICY

These empirical limitations of the new trade theory left theorists cautious about its application to real-world problems. What concerned economists most was that governments generally lacked sources of unbiased data upon which to base their decisions. Even when data was available there was a great deal of uncertainty about its veracity. Mistaken estimates could lead to misguided policies. A second concern was that few believed the models captured enough of the key elements of real-world behavior to provide a satisfactory guide to decision making. Even if the theory was refined sufficiently, it was unlikely that frontline policy analysts would have the time and resources necessary to build models of sufficient sophistication. Third, the sensitivity of the models to assumptions about the reactions of foreign firms and governments reduced the confidence of policymakers and academics in making prescriptions. R&D investment that was intended to be preemptive, as in the aircraft example, could also trigger an R&D subsidy war rather than preclude entry. And fourth, the complexity of the modeling could have made the policy process less transparent and, therefore, more difficult to monitor for fairness.

Given these hestitations, some new trade theorists concluded that governments would be wisest to follow a rule of "conditional, cooperative" trade initiatives. Unconditional cooperative strategies (such as "the United States will always support free trade regardless of the behavior of other countries") invited foreign governments to take a "free ride" at America's expense. Conditional strategies which offered the carrot of liberalized trade backed up by the stick of retaliation were considered the most likely to induce cooperation as the foreign response. Moreover, cooperative strategies avoided the potentially severe consequences of miscalculating the foreign response to a noncooperative move.

COMPETITIVE ADVANTAGE OF NATIONS

While trade economists in the 1980s were building formal models which relied heavily on insights from IO, business school academics were also applying insights from IO and business strategy to the field of international trade. Employing an empirical approach quite different from that of the new trade theorists, Michael Porter's research in *The Competitive Advantage of Nations* was perhaps the most extensive. Porter focused on the issue of why some nations' firms succeeded in international competition. His work was designed to guide both the decision-making of managers seeking competitive advantage in the global marketplace and the policy-making of government actors attempting to create a favorable business environment. While his aim was neither to prove nor to disprove any particular theory, he sought to go beyond traditional views of comparative advantage.

Porter posed three questions at the beginning of his research. First, why does a nation succeed internationally in a particular industry? Second, what is the influence of the nation on competition in specific industries and industry segments? Finally, why do a nation's firms select particular strategies? In answer to these questions, Porter began with four key premises:

1. The nature of competition and the sources of *competitive advantage* differ widely among industries (and even among industry segments).
2. Successful global competitors perform some activities in the *value chain* outside their home country and draw competitive advantages from their entire worldwide network rather than from just their home base.
3. Firms gain and sustain competitive advantage in modern international competition through innovation.
4. Firms that successfully gain competitive ad-

vantage in a industry are those that move early and aggressively to exploit a new market or technology.

The essence of Porter's argument was that attributes of a nation shaped the environment faced by domestic firms in ways that promoted or impeded the creation of competitive advantage. Four attributes were particularly important: factor conditions, demand conditions, the vigor of related and supporting industries, and the industrial structure (that determined the nature of domestic rivalry) combined with the cultural context (that determined corporate and personal goals). Nations were assessed within this framework to determine their likely ability to foster and maintain industries with international competitive advantage. (This framework is illustrated in *Figure 2.*) A favorable environment provided the basis for a nation's domestic industry to succeed in the global marketplace. Two other variables that Porter believed were important, but nonetheless auxiliary, were government actions and chance events.

FIGURE 2
The Determinants of National Competitive Advantage.

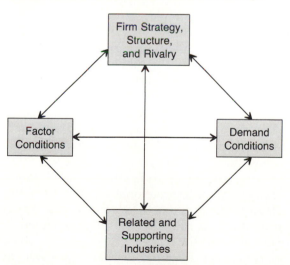

FACTOR CONDITIONS

Porter took the classical concept of *factor endowments* and revised it in two ways. First, he believed that a nation's endowment of factors played a more complex (and yet less complete) role in determining national competitive advantage than generally acknowledged. Second, he believed that endowments were dynamic and, consequently, could be upgraded, created, and specialized. His contention was that few factors were truly inherited; instead they were usually the product of investment. He also turned upside down the classical notion of factor abundance as a source of advantage by postulating that selective disadvantages in factors can contribute to a national industry's success by influencing strategy and stimulating innovation. Firms in nations with limited resources, for example, might learn to exploit factor mobility by convincing skilled labor to relocate or learn to acquire needed skills through foreign licensing or acquisition.

Porter divided factors into less aggregated categories than the traditional land/labor/capital split. He partitioned factors into human resources, physical resources, climatic conditions, knowledge resources, location, capital resources, and infrastructure. He also proposed a hierarchy of factors that distinguished between basic and advanced factors and between generalized and specialized factors. Basic factors required no action to develop or only relatively modest and unsophisticated social and private investment (e.g., some natural resources, climate, semiskilled and unskilled labor, location, and debt capital). Advanced factors, on the other hand, often required high, sustained levels of investment and included highly educated personnel and modern telecommunications infrastructures. A local supply of advanced factors was considered important to the ability of a national industry to achieve and maintain success because they were scarce locally and difficult to procure in global markets (or to tap via foreign subsidiaries). Moreover, advanced factors played an important role in the innovation process, which in turn needed to be integrated into a firm's overall strategy. Generalized factors could be deployed for use in a wide variety of industries (e.g., highway systems, markets for debt capital, and pools of skilled labor), while specialized factors could not (e.g., field-specific knowledge bases, highly specialized personnel, and tailored systems of infrastructure). Specialized factors were more likely to provide a basis for sustained competitive advantage because they were rarer, more difficult to cultivate, and less accessible.

Porter argued that nations had to engage in factor creation if their national industries were to sustain a dominant position in international competition. Nations needed to assist their domestically based industries by developing new pools of advanced factors and new pools of specialized factors. Thus, the renewal of investment in factor creation was required continuously. Particularly when industries had to overcome factor disadvantages, it was important that the domestically based industries had a long-term commitment to the industry, that adequate resources were available, and that domestic rivalry existed at a stimulating level. Given these conditions, domestically based firms would be spurred to look for sustainable advantages over local rivals, have the necessary fuel to undertake innovation, and be enabled to stay in the industry rather than shifting resources to another industry.

DEMAND CONDITIONS IN THE HOME MARKET

Demand conditions in the home market stimulate domestically based firms to bring new products to market. The sophistication of the products and the timing of their introduction depended heavily on the characteristics of domestic demand. Significant elements of demand conditions in Porter's framework were (1) the nature of domestic buyers' needs, (2) the size and pattern of growth of the domestic market, and (3) the mechanism by which domestic buyers' needs were communicated to foreign firms. In assessing demand conditions, it was important to account for the sophistication and fastidiousness of buyers, the timing of development of demands relative to buyers in foreign markets, the market size, the level of buyer concentration, the rate and pattern of growth, the level of uncertainty, the timing of market saturation, and the presence of domestic buyers in foreign markets. Tough consumers at home were a powerful stimulus to a strong internationally competitive position.

PRESENCE OF VIGOROUS SUPPLIER AND RELATED INDUSTRIES

The third element of the Porter framework was that home-based suppliers of inputs could create advantages for downstream industries in three important ways. Roughly paralleling the arguments in the strategic trade policy literature about positive externalities, Porter argued that suppliers could give downstream industries early, easy, rapid, and, sometimes, preferential access to the most cost-effective inputs. In addition, home-based suppliers provided an advantage in terms of ongoing coordination. Suppliers could gain early insights into the developing needs of downstream firms and tailor their product plans accordingly. Similarly, downstream firms would be able to alter their strategic plans to take advantage of supplier innovations.

The presence of horizontally related industries that were internationally competitive was also a source of competitive advantage in rough proportion to the technical interdependence. Since horizontally related industries could share or coordinate activities in the value chain or produce products that were complementary, international success in one industry could also pull through demand for the complementary products. This pull-through effect was believed to be the strongest at the beginning of an industry life cycle when the lead firms had an advantage in experience and knowledge. As followers proliferated, this advantage dissipated.

STRATEGY, STRUCTURE, AND RIVALRY

Without being uniform, firms nonetheless set goals, chose strategies, and organized themselves in nationally characteristic ways. Porter argued that these patterns had a profound influence on the process of innovation and international success. In many ways, the strength of domestic competitive rivalry was the most important factor in the Porter framework. The most successful industries, worldwide, were highly correlated with intense domestic competition which forced firms to push harder, innovate, and aggressively expand overseas.

Many variables determined the strength of domestic rivalry. *Managerial attitudes*, for instance, played an important part in the willingness and ability of firms to compete internationally. The goals firms set were most strongly influenced by the *ownership structure* and the motivation of owners. The goals of privately held corporations reflected many influences, but the goals of publicly held corporations often reflected the characteristics of the public *capital markets*. Domestic ownership structures and capital market conditions had three broad influences on the ability of a domestically based, publicly held firm to compete in global markets. First, a match between the goals of the owners or shareholders and the needs of the industry encouraged success. Second, national capital markets set different goals for different types of industries. Third, the influence of the capital markets was proportion-

ate to a firm's need for funds: thus, in industries where private ownership was infeasible, a domestically based industry could fail when capital markets set counterproductive goals. The *personal goals* of individuals in firms were influenced by the importance of financial remuneration, professional or technical pride, and attitudes toward risk-taking. The existence of vigorous domestic rivalry placed highly visible pressure on firms to innovate and to seek higher-order and more sustainable sources of competitive advantage.

Government Actions

Porter thought that the role of government policy in creating competitive advantage was inherently secondary. Government policies were held to be effective only in those industries where the underlying determinants of national advantage were already present. Government, he observed, could hasten or raise the odds of gaining competitive advantage (or slow or lower them), but it lacked the power to create advantage in the absence of other favorable conditions. Examples of government policies that frequently influenced the ability of local firms to compete abroad included foreign exchange controls limiting foreign direct investment, limitations on licensing technologies, restraints on the movements of domestic or foreign managerial personnel, and controls on international information flows. Such governmental policies biased the chances of firms to succeed internationally (and often in a negative fashion).

Chance Events

The second important auxiliary variable influencing the likelihood of success was chance. Chance events created turmoil in industries and the opportunity for new firms to enter and new countries to become players. A classic example of chance events influencing country advantage was Prohibition in America, facilitating the emergence of a liquor industry in Canada.

THE DETERMINANTS AS A SYSTEM

After defining his framework, Porter described the interrelationships among the determinants and variables. The complicated framework suggested that many other factors played roles in national competitive advantage, including the clustering of competitive industries and geographic concentration of related businesses. A staged model of development was also offered, suggesting that national economies generally move through four stages (factor-driven, investment-driven, innovation-driven, and wealth-driven), although not necessarily in strict progression.

IMPLICATIONS FOR GOVERNMENT POLICY

Porter based his prescriptions for government policy on a number of premises that differed from standard economic analyses. First, since firms competed, not nations, the policies of governments should be set to encourage an environment which creates competitive opportunities and pressures for continued innovations. Governments were discouraged from undertaking direct interventions. Second, sustaining national advantage demanded continuous innovation and change. Thus, governments were discouraged from resorting to policies that conveyed short-term, static advantages because they undermined innovation and dynamism. Third, some bases for national competitive advantage were more sustainable than others. As a consequence, governments were advised to encourage the development of specialized and advanced factors of production, superior product differentiation, and un-

served market segments. Fourth, national competitive advantage was created over decades, not over one- or two-year business cycles. Thus, the most beneficial government policies were the slow and patient ones, based on a long planning horizon, not on short-term economic fluctuations. Finally, a nation's firms and work force could not be relied upon to understand their own long-term self-interest. This meant that governments were encouraged to choose their policies without undue regard for the immediate comfort or desires of their constituents.

SUMMARY

By the end of the 1980s, relatively few scholars or practitioners accepted the theory of factor proportions and comparative advantage as an adequate explanation of the observed patterns of trade, particularly for manufactured goods traded among industrialized countries. To provide a new explanation, two very different types of research were undertaken. Trade economists developed a new set of theoretical tools for examining trade under imperfect competition and produced an eclectic basket of models. Despite a growing number of empirical studies, inadequate data continued to plague the field. In contrast to the trade theorists research, Michael Porter chose an inductive approach and built a complex framework for analyzing the competitiveness of nations.

While no definitive theory of international trade had yet emerged by the late 1980s, the decade produced significant advancement into new ideas and promising areas of research. Perhaps the only certain policy conclusion was that free trade had fallen from being considered an unequivocally superior policy to being the preferred policy of economists in an imperfect world. Academic research continued on work toward identifying the exceptions to this rule.

Short Definitions of Selected Aspects of Imperfect Competition

When there are static **economies of scale,** average costs decline with the scale of output. Economies of scale are closely linked to increasing returns to scale, but they are not synonymous. Increasing returns to scale is the technological basis for economies of scale, but contractual financial effects and price effects can also produce economies of scale.

Economies of scope exist where it is less costly to combine two or more product lines in one firm than to produce them separately. See John Panzar and Robert Willig, "Economies of Scope," *American Economics Review*, 74.2, 1981, pp. 268–272, for an exposition of ideas that they had developed at Bell Laboratories during the mid-1970s.

Learning effects are present when unit costs drop with *accumulated* volume. The intertemporal dimension of this effect differentiates it from static economies of scale and introduces the possibility of strategic behavior through the use of commitments to production. This theory was formalized by A. Michael Spence in "The Learning Curve and Competition," *Bell Journal of Economics,* 12.1, 1981, pp. 49–70.

Firms may be thought of as engaging in an **R&D race** with each other to secure supernormal profits. In such a race, firms will increase their expenditures on R&D in their attempt to be the first to obtain patents and to bring new products to market. See Chapter 10, "Research and Development and the Adoption of New Technologies," in Jean Tirole, *The Theory of Industrial Organization*, Cambridge, MA: MIT Press, 1989, for a general discussion. Gene Grossman and Carl Shapiro offer an interesting model of R&D races in "Optimal Dynamic R&D

Programs," *Rand Journal of Economics,* 1986, Vol. 17, pp. 581–593.

Technological spillovers refer to innovations occurring in one product line that can be taken advantage of in other product lines. Spillovers may occur within firms, within industries, and within or between nations. The more a firm can contain spillovers for its exclusive advantage, the more **appropriable** the rents from the innovation are.

Entry barriers can take many different forms, but their effect is to increase the difficulty of entry of new competitors to an industry and thereby protect the level of profits that can be earned in that industry. This strategic dimension of market structure was first developed extensively by Joe S. Bain in *Barriers to New Competition: Their Character and Consequences in Manufacturing Industries*, Cambridge, MA: Harvard University Press: 1956.

Supply and Demand Functions

"Competitive" Equilibrium

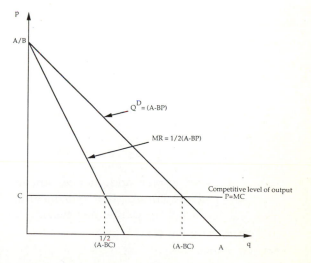

Assume:

Linear demand curves and, hence, linear marginal curves (that will have a slope twice that of the demand curves)

Constant marginal costs

No fixed costs

Therefore, under "perfect competition," we would expect

$$P = MC = C$$
$$q = A - BC$$
$$\pi = 0$$

But how does the perfectly competitive outcome compare with the outcome producers would choose if they could maintain collusion?

Collusive Equilibrium

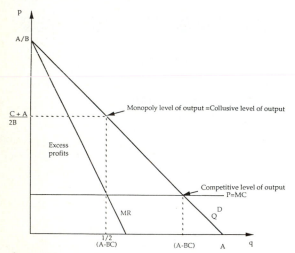

Assume:

n firms

Linear demand curves and, hence, linear marginal revenue curves (that will have a slope twice that of the demand curves)

Constant marginal costs

No fixed costs

Therefore, with perfect collusion, we would expect that

$$P > MC$$
$$q = \tfrac{1}{2}(A - BC)$$
$$\pi_{MAX}$$

and that each firm will produce $(A - BC)/2n$ of the total output, assuming symmetry.

Cournot Equilibrium

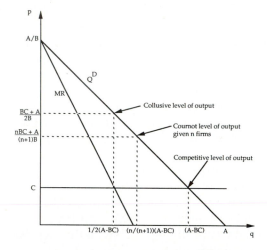

Under Cournot, the output level will be above that of the collusive outcome but below that of the perfectly competitive outcome. Given the assumptions of this model, total output will be $n/n + 1 (A - BC)$ and every firm will produce $1/(n + 1)$ share of the total output. As the number of firms, n, grows large, the output level will approach that of perfect competition.

NOTES

1. Herbert G. Grubel wrote the seminal article on this topic: "The Theory of Intra-Industry Trade" which was published in I.A. McDougall and Richard H. Snape, eds., *Studies in International Economics*, Amsterdam: North Holland Press, 1970. He followed this with Herbert G. Grubel

and Peter J. Lloyd, *Intra-Industry Trade: The Theory and Measurements of International Trade in Differential Products,* New York: Wiley, 1975. Later Paul Krugman reported on the results of empirical evidence of the existence of intraindustry trade and formalized the theory in "Intra-Industry Specialization and the Gains from Trade," *Journal of Political Economy,* 89.51, 1981, pp. 959–973.

2. The change in the political environment for U.S. trade policy-making is analyzed in David Yoffie, "American Trade Policy: An Obsolete Bargain?", in John Chubb, ed., *Can the Government Govern?,* Washington, D.C.: Brookings Institute, 1989, pp. 100–138.

3. For a fuller discussion of these changes, see Paul Krugman, ed., *Strategic Trade Policy and the New International Economics,* Cambridge, MA: MIT Press, 1986. Also see Paul Krugman's "Rethinking International Trade," *Business Economics,* April 1988, pp. 7–12, and "Is Free Trade Passé?", *Journal of Economic Perspectives,* 1.2, Fall 1987, pp. 131–144, for an easily accessible discussion of the revolution in trade theory and its implications for policy-making.

4. An alternative assumption is that rivals will hold their prices fixed, which is referred to as **Bertrand competition** as opposed to the quantity-based **Cournot competition.**

5. See F.M. Scherer, *Industrial Market Structure and Economic Performance,* Boston, MA: Houghton Mifflin, 1980, for a concise history of early industrial organization theory.

6. See John von Neumann and Oskar Morgenstern, *Theory of Games and Economic Behavior,* Princeton, N.J.: Princeton University Press, 1944, for the pioneering work in game theory.

7. A **zero-sum game** is a conflict among two or more actors in which the gains of any player can only occur at the direct expense of the other actors. Thus the focus is generally on how to claim the largest share of the pie (this, of course, is a function of the utility functions of the players, and neither benevolence nor vindictiveness is generally assumed). In **positive-sum games,** there are opportunities to increase the size of the pie through cooperation and the creative generation of solutions.

8. An example of a positive externality is the information the first oil company going in to drill in a new area generates about the likelihood that surrounding tracts do or do not hold oil. Because the incentives any individual company faces are distorted downward, they would not engage in the jointly optimal level of exploration. To overcome this distortion, firms holding tracts in a certain area can undertake joint exploration activities. An example of a negative externality is pollution: since the cost to the firm of undertaking the polluting activity did not accurately reflect the full social cost of that activity, they would tend to pollute too freely. The government can intervene to bring the private and social cost calculations in line by levying a fee on the polluting activity and causing the firm to internalize the social cost of its activities.

9. These imperfections could result in either insufficient or excessive levels of competition. If there was little rivalry, firms could exercise their market power to extract **rents** (i.e., profits above the level of normal economic returns required to keep resources in an industry) from consumers. Since consumers usually lost more than the producers gained, the society would incur a **deadweight loss.** On the other hand, if too many firms were competing in certain industries, they might fail to exhaust economies of scale.

10. See J. David Richardson, "Empirical Research on Trade Liberalization with Imperfect Competition: A Survey," Cambridge, MA: NBER Working Paper No. 2883, p. 1.

11. There was a burgeoning literature which attempted to distinguish the strategic implications of tariffs versus quotas versus voluntary export restraints. Each tool, under varying imperfect market conditions, could have positive or negative effects on welfare and trade. For example, since quotas restricted the supply of a good available, they functioned to drive up domestic prices and raise the market shares of domestic producers to the extent that domestic goods were substitutes. Some new trade theorists argued that quotas could promote exports in the presence of imperfect competition and economies of scale. The idea was that by shutting a market to

foreign producers, domestic producers would have a larger market share. As a consequence, they would be able to move down their average cost and learning curves. Assuming there were both static and dynamic economies of scale, firms were expected to capitalize on their learning in the protected home market, which would become a competitive advantage for serving foreign markets. For this outcome to be efficient, however, there would also have to be a mechanism for preventing excessive entry into the domestic industry in the short run. For examples of this type of analysis, see Alasdair Smith and Anthony Venables, "Trade and Industrial Policy under Imperfect Competition," *Economic Policy*, Vol. 1, pp. 621–660, 1986; Avinash Dixit, "Optimal Trade and Industrial Policies for the U.S. Automobile Industry," in Robert Feenstra, ed., *Empirical Methods for International Trade*, Cambridge, MA: MIT Press, 1988; Helpman and Krugman, *Trade Policy and Market Structure*, Cambridge, MA: MIT Press, 1989, Chapter 3; and Kala Krishna, "Trade Restrictions as Facilitating Practices," *Journal of International Economics*, Vol. 26, pp. 251–270, 1989.

12. Avinash Dixit points out, however, that in setting an R&D policy the negative common-pool externalities must be weighed against the positive spillovers and the cost of prospective failure must be considered as well as the prospective benefits of success. He also points out that corrective motives may lead to different policies than strategic motives. See Avinash Dixit, "International R&D Competition and Policy," in A. Michael Spence and Heather A. Hazard, eds., *International Competitiveness*, Cambridge, MA: Ballinger, 1988, pp. 149–171.

13. Debate remained, however, over the magnitude of the adjustment costs that could accompany such rationalizations.

SELECTED BIBLIOGRAPHY

Avinash Dixit, "An Agenda for Research," in Paul Krugman, ed., *Strategic Trade Policy and the New International Economics*, Cambridge, MA: MIT Press, 1986, pp. 283–304.

Avinash Dixit, "Optimal Trade and Industrial Policies for the U.S. Automobile Industry," in Robert Feenstra, ed., *Empirical Methods for International Trade*, Cambridge, MA: MIT Press, 1988.

Richard Harris, *Trade, Industrial Policy and Canadian Manufacturing*, Toronto: Ontario Economic Council, 1984.

Elhanen Helpman and Paul R. Krugman, *Trade Policy and Market Structure*, Cambridge, MA: MIT Press, 1989, pp. 117–131.

Kala Krishna, "Auction Quotas," NBER working paper, 1989.

Paul Krugman, "Import Protection as Export Promotion: International Competition in the Presence of Oligopoly and Economies of Scale," in Henry Kierkowski, ed., *Monopolistic Competition and International Trade*, Oxford: Oxford University Press, 1984, pp. 180–193.

Michael E. Porter, *The Competitive Advantage of Nations*, forthcoming (New York: Free Press, 1990).

Alasdair Smith and Anthony Venables, "Trade and Industrial Policy under Imperfect Competition," *Economic Policy*, Vol. 1, 1986, pp. 621–660.

PART TWO

Comparative Advantage and Corporate Strategy

Lotus Development Corporation: Entering International Markets

Events were moving rapidly at Lotus Development Corporation, the fastest-growing microcomputer software company in the United States. Lotus was in its twelfth month of accelerating growth in December 1983 when Jim Manzi, vice president of marketing, decided it was time to do something about international sales. "We've been getting bombarded with requests," he reported. "Overseas distributors have been calling to carry our product. We get customer support calls from France. There's been a flood of telexes from all over Europe. All these signs have been telling us that we need to get serious about international markets. That's why we hired Chuck Digate as our director of international operations two months ago. When we offered him the position, we suggested that he live in the United States for two years and then move overseas. His reply was 'You've got that exactly backward.' So we told him, 'Everything is up for grabs. The job is yours to make.' "

Digate's experience was in the hardware side of the microcomputer industry. After earning his MBA at Michigan, he held a number of positions at Texas Instruments (TI), including financial control management and consumer products marketing. He spent a year-and-a-half managing market research for all TI consumer products, managed 1000 salespeople in the company's home computer demonstration network, and in late 1982 was sent to the south of France as director of European operations for TI's home computer division. By the middle of 1983 the spectacular boom in home computers was waning; Digate thought it might be time to take on a new challenge in computer software. Starting with Lotus in December 1983, he immediately began working on an international business plan. Manzi would have to approve Digate's proposal before Lotus's international operations could begin in earnest.

BACKGROUND OF LOTUS DEVELOPMENT

Lotus was founded in April 1982 by Mitch Kapor, a former psychology student, who believed that "I was going to make my greatest contribution to the field of human services by leaving it." Kapor wrote the popular VisiPlot and VisiTrend programs, graphics and statistics companion items for the best-selling electronic spreadsheet, VisiCalc. When International Business Machines Corp. (IBM) announced it would enter the microcomputer marketplace with an advanced, powerful computer based on the 16-bit Intel 8088 microprocessor, Kapor saw an opportunity to create a more functional and easier-to-use spreadsheet and productivity tool. VisiCorp, the marketers of VisiCalc, rejected Kapor's plan, so Kapor decided to set up his own company to do the job. Kapor received $1.2 million by selling the rights to VisiPlot and VisiTrend and another $1 million in venture capital. In October 1982, Lotus announced 1-2-3, a software program for the IBM PC providing spreadsheet, database, and graphing capabilities. The program was conceived and developed by Kapor and Jonathan Sachs, Lotus's vice president of research and development. Sachs, an accomplished programmer who had a hand in three earlier spreadsheet projects, wrote much of the actual program code. Lotus booked $1 million in dealer orders for 1-2-3 at a major trade show in November. By this time Lotus has also amassed an additional $3.7 million in venture capital.

1-2-3 was shipped on time in January 1983, accompanied by a huge advertising and promotion campaign (*Exhibit 1*). The three-month campaign cost over $1 million, far beyond the reach of most microcomputer software companies. In addition, Lotus embarked on a major training program for computer store personnel and produced vast quantities of point-of-sales promotional literature. By March, 1-2-3 was the top-selling business program on the Softsel "Hot List" (a popular industry barometer published by a major software distributor), displacing VisiCalc from its long reign at the top. One industry observer remarked that "1-2-3 has single-handedly changed the face and direction of the personal computer software industry."

During the year, 1-2-3 was being adapted for other computers such as the Wang Professional Computer and Digital Equipment's Rainbow, which were also based on the same microprocessor as the IBM PC but not strictly compatible with it. Lotus explicitly stated it would not adapt its software (or write new software) for 8-bit machines, most notably the Apple II. The Company was also working on a follow-up product to 1-2-3 that would add integrated word processing and telecommunications capabilities (referred to internally as Lotus II). Lotus went public in October.

THE PERSONAL COMPUTER INDUSTRY, DECEMBER 1983

Hardware

The rise of the personal computer software industry paralleled the rise of smaller computers made possible by the development of integrated circuits and microprocessors and their rapid reduction in cost. By the end of the 1970s the markets for small home and business computers had grown substantially, and the 8-bit Apple II series and TRS-80 computers from Tandy/Radio Shack were the leading business microcomputers. Computers based on more powerful 16-bit microprocessors, specifically the IBM PC, hit the market in 1981. These machines typically processed data at least twice as fast as their 8-bit counterparts and could run much larger and more sophisticated programs; software on the IBM PC could access up to 640K bytes (characters) of memory.

IBM was fast becoming the "industry standard" in the business-oriented personal computer industry (*Exhibit 2*). *Business Week* (October 3, 1983) estimated that 75% of all personal computers in use in 1985 would be IBM PCs or PC-compatibles. Strong growth was expected in microcomputer hardware. A leading research firm expected the average number of microcomputers installed in *Fortune* 1300 companies to increase from 120 at year-end 1983 to 500 by December 1987. Another well-known firm estimated U.S. revenues for office personal computers would jump from $6 billion in 1983 to $20.7 billion in 1987 (and to $28.9 billion in 1989).

Software

Software was a billion-dollar industry by 1983; back in 1979 it was hardly on the map. A Dallas-based market research firm estimated that the U.S. personal computer software market would total $1.4 billion in 1983 and would grow to $8.1 billion by 1989. Basic productivity programs—word processors, spreadsheets, databases, and especially integrated programs that combined these functions—were expected to grow most rapidly. The lion's share of the market was oriented toward business programs (*Exhibit 4*).

The software market was no longer viewed as a cottage industry. As one industry observer put it, "The days of putting your program in a Baggie, stapling it, and selling it by mail are ending." Entering a new product on the market in late 1983 required an estimated marketing investment of $50,000 to $100,000. (By contrast, VisiCorp launched VisiCalc on a $500 budget in 1978.) Software distributors played an increasingly important role as the link between the thousands of software companies seeking space on retail shelves and the software retailers who invested $10,000 simply to stock an inventory of 75 to 100 titles. Distributors bought software at a 55 to 60% discount and then resold and shipped it to retailers at a 40 to 50% discount. Softsel, the largest distributor, screened 400 products a month and agreed to distribute perhaps 10 to 12. One industry observer warned that "the pipeline is only so big, and it's full." Indeed, many analysts in late 1983 perceived an oncoming software shakeout. A common estimate was that 60% of the industry volume in sales would be dominated by about a dozen companies, while the other 40% would be taken by smaller companies offering specialty programs.

COMPETITORS

Virtually all the major vendors in 1983 got to the top on the basis of one product and rarely competed with one another (*Exhibit 3*). But this situation was expected to change. Lotus's four primary competitors—VisiCorp, Microsoft, Micropro, and Ashton-Tate—were working on one fashion or another of integrated software products to challenge the market strength of 1-2-3.

VisiCorp marketed VisiCalc, developed in 1978 for the Apple II and considered a primary factor in that machine's success. Approximately 600,000 copies of VisiCalc had been sold worldwide for all machines by September 1983, but VisiCorp was struggling. Monthly sales of the relatively unchanged VisiCalc had decreased 75% from the beginning of the year, and sharp internal management disputes threatened to erupt into legal battles. VisiCorp was placing its hopes most strongly on VisiOn, an "operating environment" that provided users with "windows" through which to look at more than one program simultaneously and transfer data between them.

Microsoft, one of the oldest and most influential companies in the microcomputer software industry, was beginning to move strongly into the applications area, where it planned to release a line of independent products which would be highly compatible with each other. Microsoft had opened a European sales and marketing office in April 1982. Its products (operating system and languages) were translated into French and German, and the company made wide use of locals in its hiring. There were approximately 50 to 60 Microsoft employees in Europe. In August 1982 Microsoft began shipping its Multiplan spreadsheet program in the United States. Multiplan, which ran on a wide variety of 8-bit and 16-bit machines, did well in its first year but did not offer database or graphing functions. Microsoft was planning to introduce its applications line into Europe; Multiplan was sold by the company's European distributors and subsidiaries in 1983.

Micropro became a major player in the software industry on the basis of its extremely successful, multimachine word processor known as WordStar. The company was in the process of releasing a line of software programs that were to be compatible with WordStar but would be stand-alone products. Micropro had an installed base of 600,000 users and registered 15,000 WordStar sales per month. The firm had operations in 27 countries, more than any of its competitors, and had a particularly strong European presence. Over 20% of Micropro's revenue came from overseas.

Ashton-Tate's dBaseII was the dominant microcomputer database program in the business world. The company was expected to go public and was working on a highly integrated, mul-

tifunction product designed to compete with any new Lotus products on the high end. Ashton-Tate moved into Europe at the beginning of 1983, and translated programs were projected for year's end. Ashton-Tate worked through distributors (as many as 10 in a single country), did no product development or manufacturing in Europe, and used a high proportion of Americans in its operation. The company was considering OEM arrangements, offshore subsidiaries, and direct corporate selling.

INSIDE LOTUS DEVELOPMENT

By December 1983, 150,000 copies of 1-2-3 had been sold and revenues and earnings were increasing rapidly (*Exhibits 5a* and *5b*). 1-2-3 was still number 1 on the Softsel list. Part of the reason for this success was that Lotus was the first software company to use a dealer introduction kit for its product. The 1-2-3 kit was glossy, extensive, and high-quality. Lotus included a disk-based tutorial with 1-2-3 to teach buyers how to use the product. The tutorial was also sent to dealers who were encouraged to make copies for potential customers in their stores. Advertising and promotion totaled over $3.5 million for 1983, an amount far exceeding that spent by Lotus's competitors on any single product.

Manzi stressed that Lotus did not think of its markets in segments but, rather, considered 1-2-3's audience to be all business people and professionals whose jobs required the manipulation of quantitative data:

Obviously a number of groups—middle manager types doing financial analysis, consultants, accountants, economists—find the program useful. But, in reality, we haven't tried to identify these specific groups. We've advertised to the wide range of people who need to manipulate quantitative data and tie it into graphs and databases. Our message is uniform: 1-2-3 is fast, powerful, flexible, and integrated. People who can use the product buy it. So far we haven't had to worry about what specific types of people buy the product. All we've noticed is that people from large corporations have different problems than do independent professionals, and we try to reflect that in our service and support.

In general, Lotus downplayed price and stressed support and training. At $495 retail, 1-2-3 was more expensive than the VisiCalc ($250) and Multiplan ($275) spreadsheets, but was $200 less expensive than Context MBA, the first integrated program for the PC. Particularly with larger *Fortune* 2000 corporations— the one "segment" Lotus saw with distinct needs—Lotus helped train users and "train the trainers" in the corporation and provided extensive assistance in using Lotus's command language to tune the package for specific applications.

Lotus distributed 1-2-3 through four primary outlets. First, and most important, were retail computer stores, accounting for at least 80% of Lotus's sales. Larger stores (e.g., the Computerland chain) could purchase directly from Lotus; independent and smaller stores purchased 1-2-3 from Lotus's distributor, Softsel. The second outlet was "national accounts," direct selling from Lotus to large corporations. This channel provided less than 10% of Lotus's sales. The third distribution channel was through value-added resellers (VARs). VARs added value to 1-2-3 by packaging it with an additional product or providing special end-user support for specific or advanced applications. For example, one VAR provided the capability to load its proprietary database from an external mainframe computer onto individual personal computer workstations for use with 1-2-3. The VAR channel accounted for less than 10% of Lotus sales. The final outlet was third-party sales. Major companies such as Digital Equipment and Hewlett Packard participated in this channel. These companies packaged, printed, and promoted special versions of 1-2-3 adapted for their machines. They were responsible for supporting the product, which they sold through

their direct sales channels. Lotus retained the right to sell retail versions of 1-2-3 for these machines.

Another outlet for 1-2-3 existed, but it was not Lotus-approved. This consisted of sales through mail-order outlets, often available at from 25 to 50% off the retail price of 1-2-3. Lotus distributed no product to these so-called "grey market" dealers; they got their product mostly from authorized dealers looking for a quick infusion of cash. Lotus's policy was to discontinue relations with any dealer found selling to the grey market. Lotus did not, however, make any distinctions in customer service based on where the product was purchased. All registered owners of the product had equal access to support and service.

Lotus set up several regional retail sales offices to service dealers. Each dealer was sent a complete support kit containing sample product, advertising materials, point-of-sale items, and information to minimize ordering and stocking problems. Lotus sales representatives offered information, advice, demonstrations, and assistance. Training specialists conducted all-day training sessions with store personnel to familiarize them with 1-2-3's features and operation. Lotus also provided personnel and materials for dealer-sponsored promotions and customer seminars. The telephone support staff handled technical questions and product ordering on dedicated phone lines. These basic principles for aiding dealers were adapted for customers as well. Manzi pointed out that "management has stressed that the company's image and success depend directly on customer satisfaction with product support and product performance."

Human Resources

In December 1983 Lotus had 292 employees, 257 more than at the beginning of the year. Many employees were overqualified, but the company tried to provide these people with opportunities to move up while the company was growing rapidly. In an industry so young, it wasn't easy to attract highly technically trained applicants, so one found teachers in customer support and consumer products people in marketing. Janet Axelrod, Lotus's first employee and its vice president of human resources, believed the company was making a number of mistakes in the general area of hiring:

We get ripped off by headhunters and do a lot of expensive hiring by gut feeling. Keeping up with, even defining, departmental and personnel needs is a gigantic problem. We have to say "screw conventional wisdom" because almost all of it is bull for a company growing as fast as we are. Right now, there's no head count control at all. This just can't go on. Add new operations overseas? That's just nuts! My first reaction is: "Are you out of your mind?!"

Lotus, which was nonunionized, consciously tried to establish itself as a "progressive" employer. The company deliberately maintained itself in the top quartile of pay in the industry and had a generous and extensive benefits package. Axelrod defined the Lotus philosophy as fairness and justice are most important, employees at all levels have a right to speak their minds, every job has value, all people have a right to expect respect, the company is nothing without its employees, and diversity is best. "These values are important to me and the company," she observed, "and I have to insist that they'll be transferred overseas. But I'm not sure any of us knows the various cultures enough to do it."

Finance

In 1983 Lotus had no formal financial objectives, nor was any system in place to analyze potential new markets. Lotus had no real budget procedure but rather used more of a "wish list mentality," and there was no cost control

system in place. A general concern in finance was developing an infrastructure for a control system while coping with very rapid growth. Digate knew there was a long way to go in that regard: "Perhaps the ultimate irony is that we're still doing our general ledger on a [Tandy/Radio Shack] TRS-80."

Research and Development

Mitch Kapor was convinced that future success for Lotus meant undertaking research and development with an eye toward ongoing technological changes. If the company was going to enter a major new market (e.g., word processing), Kapor wanted to avoid entering "just this side of a major new technology." But Lotus also emphasized product development for the short term. The driving forces, according to Manzi, were to "keep the spreadsheet market, because that pays the salaries, leverage the spreadsheet market with add-ons, and keep poking around with the existing product."

Manufacturing

Once a software program was developed, written, and debugged, it was ready to be manufactured. Manufacturing involved two different processes—disk duplication and assembly of the diskettes, literature, binders, and so on. The various printing jobs (manuals, reference books, etc.) were done outside Lotus. Of Lotus's production costs, 80% was for materials, another 15% was overhead, and the last 5% was labor.

ENTERING INTERNATIONAL MARKETS

Lotus officials assumed from the start that business productivity software had a natural global market. Before Digate was hired, Lotus had thought about international issues but the situation was still "essentially a gigantic mess" according to Manzi. Lotus's first attempt at an international plan was a "weird psycholinguistics doctoral thesis. It was bizarre," Manzi laughed, "and needless to say it never went anywhere." Until Digate came aboard, no single person was really in charge of international business on a full-time basis.

Softsel had been Lotus's exclusive worldwide distributor since 1-2-3 hit the market, but Manzi thought the arrangement was unsatisfactory. Softsel did not provide end-user support and dealer support—services Lotus had stressed in the United States. Manzi wanted to resist the temptation to just take the U.S. version of 1-2-3 and "dump the product overseas." His first task, he said, was to "renegotiate everything." Manzi canceled Softsel's exclusive worldwide distribution rights and raised 1-2-3's price to Softsel by 20%. He didn't feel Lotus had to worry about access to distribution channels and saw no good reason to ignore or kill a French distributor, for example, simply to maintain the relationship with Softsel.

In the interim between changing the Softsel arrangement and hiring Digate, Lotus hired a small European consulting firm to do a study of the European market. The consulting firm put Lotus in touch with Reflex Ltd., which Lotus subsequently hired in September 1983 as its U.K. distributor. Reflex was responsible for a "mini-rollout" and some dealer training to take place in fall 1983. One person from headquarters was sent to Reflex to handle customer support. Lotus's first overseas subsidiary was also opened in September in Windsor, England. 1-2-3 had sold well in the United Kingdom even before these direct moves; Manzi estimated that by year's end $1 million of product had been sold there.

Manzi was looking to Digate for the answers to a series of important questions. What strategy should Lotus adopt toward overseas markets? Should Lotus move slowly or quickly? Where should Digate be stationed? How should international operations be organized? Several of these issues had caused debate at headquarters. The individual in charge of the Cambridge-based business development group argued strongly that international business development be under his purview. He felt that Digate should be reporting to him, not to Manzi. At the very least, he wanted international software development to be separate from any new international group. Similarly, the CFO had some international finance experience and wanted responsibility for Lotus's international finance. Manzi also sensed a bias among top managers in the company that senior managers should be based at headquarters. Manzi, on the other hand, wanted to see a completely separate international unit that would be self-sustaining. He wanted to leave Digate as much open field as possible. "Chuck inherited a big mess," Manzi said, "including loose promises and commitments made by people without the power to make them. I've made it clear to Chuck that he should not worry about Lotus politics or financial constraints affecting the international strategy."

One market Digate considered entering was Japan, but Japan posed enormous problems, including dominance of 8-bit machines, lack of a standard operating system, complex characters and symbols, and weak microcomputer penetration into corporations. The other major market was Europe. The market there was highly segmented by country, language, leading microcomputers, and business practices. Still, the market was growing; it stood at about half the size of the U.S. market, and many analysts expected its rate of growth to match or outpace the U.S. rate within the next few years (*Exhibit 6*). The level of development of the European market was considered by Digate to be 2 to 3 years behind the United States.

U.S. firms dominated the European personal computer market, holding three-fourths of the installed base of microcomputers in Western Europe. Part of the American advantage could be laid to the cash built from operating in the huge American domestic market. The IBM PC was introduced to the European market in 1983, and, although doing well, it had not achieved dominant market share (*Exhibit 7*). Digate estimated that IBM held perhaps 20% of the 16-bit market. But industry expectations were that IBM might be helped in Europe by the hardware shakeout going on in the United States and the failure of some West German companies. Analysts speculated that European businesses would begin to look for stable vendors, and IBM was considered nothing if not stable.

Different microcomputer firms dominated different countries. Triumph-Adler and Siemens did well in West Germany. Micral was expected to increase its share in France. Olivetti had a leading position in Italy. In Great Britain, the Victor Sirius, repackaged and distributed by a local firm, Applied Computer Techniques (ACT), had an estimated 90% of the sales of 16-bit machines for the 12 months from April 1982 to March 1983 (approximately 10,000 units). ACT also released a 16-bit hit of its own, known as the Apricot. Neither of these machines was IBM-compatible.

The segmented nature of the European market was even more apparent in software. Software companies had to deal with 13 countries and languages, contrasting business styles, different laws, regulations, and business practices which could make certain types of software (e.g., accounting or banking) extremely difficult to market throughout Europe. Applications programs were considered the most difficult to transfer, with systems and utilities programs somewhat easier. One sign that the European market was difficult was that European companies were seriously trying to gain a foothold in the American market, primarily because the market was huge and, compared to Europe, relatively homogenous.

No major European software firms had emerged in Lotus's 16-bit market. This was partly due to a lack of venture capital in Europe. Although there was some government support of fledgling software companies in Britain, and most European countries were concerned about their inferiority in large computer systems, Digate was not concerned about government protectionism because "there just isn't that much to protect." Tariffs on imported software were applied only to the value of the medium (diskettes and documentation, etc.) and not to the value of the software itself. In Britain an estimated 70% of the software sold was imported.

Digate believed that European buyers were driven by the same needs as U.S. buyers. "The *Fortune* 500 type companies are the trendsetters. And not only European companies: there are a large number of American multinational corporations in Europe, and our product is used at many of them in the U.S. These large European and multinational companies could be our gateway to the small- and medium-size businesses where the bulk of personal computer sales will be for the next 2 to 4 years." Despite the basic similarities between European and American buyers, one way buyers differed across Europe was the centralization of purchasing. "In the U.K. buying is dispersed like in the U.S. Outside the U.K. there is more centralized control by data processing managers, which makes for slower purchasing. Germany is particularly conservative in this regard."

Operating in Europe presented many challenges. Top managerial talent was hard to come by because of the relative immaturity of the industry. The European Community posted a 6% tariff on imported software, while manufacturing in Europe required an investment of $2.5 million to $3 million. Grey marketing—the undercutting of European dealers by U.S. distributors—posed yet another serious problem. And unauthorized copying of program disks (which had led Lotus to go to court in the United States) was known to be a real problem in parts of Europe. "Chuck tells me that the closer you get to the equator the more serious the problem becomes," Manzi joked. On the positive side, trouble with counterfeiting was relatively minor, and mail-order outlets were insignificant in Europe. Pricing didn't seem to be much of an issue; American software companies generally charged the U.S. price plus or minus 10% in dollars. Demand appeared to be price-inelastic.

Translation of 1-2-3 promised to be a major task. "First, we have to port for non-IBM hardware (i.e., write a series of drivers to support keyboards, screens, and other non-IBM system components). Then we have to translate the language, and I suspect that each translation will take from 9 to 12 months," Digate reported. 1-2-3 was not written with language translations in mind. "If we had only thought about going international 6 months earlier," Manzi noted, "we could have saved ourselves a lot of trouble." Text which would have to be translated was embedded in the computer code rather than being separated into specific modules. Lotus would have to "start from scratch," and that meant reading through the thousands upon thousands of lines of computer code. Beyond that was the problem of the translation itself. 1-2-3's user interface was highly dependent on full-screen layout, but it was highly unlikely that this interface could remain unchanged across national borders. Some things that could be expressed by one word in English might require two, three, or four words in another language. Even if a single word could be found, it might be too long. Differences in local currency, characters, and punctuation on dates, times, or decimals were not easily accommodated. In a sense, Digate observed, you were forced to create somewhat different products for the different markets. Even a small change such as requiring two screens rather than one to show a list of options could let a "bug" creep into a program. Furthermore, all the help screens in 1-2-3 (there were over 200) and the tutorial would need to be rewritten, requiring changes in screen layouts and fine attention to idiomatic language. And of course the extensive 1-2-3 documentation also required translation.

Digate sifted through these various issues while working up his international business proposal. Manzi received Digate's preliminary plan after entering international markets, reprinted in *Appendix 1*, two weeks after Digate joined the firm. Digate was clearly convinced that Lotus should act quickly. He stayed in Cambridge for only two weeks before moving to England to talk with dealers, headhunters, the distributor, and others knowledgeable about the European market. Manzi, in Cambridge, studied Digate's sketch of where Lotus should be headed internationally. Did this path hold the most promise for Lotus?

SAMPLE COPY FROM FIRST ADVERTISING CAMPAIGN

Meet 1-2-3—the remarkable new software package that puts more raw power at your finger tips than anything yet created for the IBM PC. 1-2-3 actually combines information management, spreadsheet, and graphing in one program that can instantly perform all three functions interchangeably and instantly at the touch of a key. That's power.

To explain: since 1-2-3's information management, spreadsheet and graphing functions reside in memory simultaneously, you can go from retrieval to spreadsheet calculation to graphing instantly, just by pressing a few keys. So now you can experiment and recalculate and look at data in an endless variety of ways. As fast as your mind can think up new possibilities. There's no lag between you and the computer. And that's a new kind of power—power that's greater than the sum of its programs.

Spreadsheet, graphing, information management all-in-one.

The spreadsheet function.

If 1-2-3 were just a spreadsheet, you'd want it because it has the largest workspace on the market (2048 rows by 256 columns). To give you a quick idea of 1-2-3's spreadsheet capabilities: VisiCalc's spreadsheet for the IBM PC offers 15 arithmetic, logical and relational operators, 28 functions and 32 spreadsheet-related commands. 1-2-3 has 15 operators, 41 functions and 66 commands. And if you include data base and graphing commands, it actually has 110!

In addition, 1-2-3 is up to 50 times as fast as established spreadsheets. With all the features you've ever seen on spreadsheets. 1-2-3 also gives you the capability to develop customized applications (with 26 macro keys) and lets you perform repetitive tasks automatically with one keystroke. If 1-2-3 were just a spreadsheet, it would be a very powerful tool. But it's much, much more.

The information management function.

Add to 1-2-3's spreadsheet a selective information management function, and the power curve rises at an awesome rate. Particularly since 1-2-3's information management capability reads files from other programs such as WordStar, VisiCalc and dBase II. So you can accumulate information on a limitless variety of topics and extract all or pieces of it for instant spreadsheet analysis. Unheard of before. Specific 1-2-3 information management features include sorting with primary and secondary keys. Retrieval using up to 32 criteria. 1-2-3 performs statistical functions such as mean, count, standard deviation and variance. It can produce histograms on part or all of the data base. 1-2-3 also allows for the maintenance of multiple data bases and multiple criteria.

The graphing function.

1-2-3 enables you to create graphs of up to six variables using information already on the spreadsheet. And have it on screen in less than two seconds! Once you've made a graph, three keystrokes will display it in a different form. If data on the spreadsheet changes, you can display a revised graph with one keystroke. This instant relationship of one format to another opens up a whole new application area. For the first time graphics can be used as a "what if" thinking tool!

For a full demonstration of 1-2-3's remarkable power, visit your nearby 1-2-3 dealer. For the name and address, call 1-800-343-5414 (in Mass. call 617-492-7171).

Lotus Devlopment Corporation, 55 Wheeler Street, Cambridge, MA 02138.

1-2-3 and Lotus are trademarks of Lotus Development Corporation. All rights reserved. WordStar is a registered trademark of MicroPro Inc. VisiCalc is a registered trademark of VisiCorp. dBase II is a registered trademark of Ashton-Tate.

EXHIBIT TWO

MICROCOMPUTERS INSTALLED IN U.S. CORPORATIONS

Percentage of sites with	1979	1980	1981	1982	1983[a]
Apple	16.8	24.7	42.0	39.0	23.6
DEC	...	...	...	1.7	5.7
IBM	...	...	...	13.1	35.4
Tandy	42.5	27.7	26.1	17.5	9.3
Others	40.7	47.6	31.9	28.7	26.0

[a]Estimate.
Source: Datamation, November 1983.

EXHIBIT THREE

ESTIMATED SALES FOR 1982 AND 1983

Firm	1982	1983
Microsoft	$33 million	$70 million
VisiCorp	36	53
Micropro International	28	51
Digital Research	22	46
Lotus Development	1	40
Ashton-Tate	8	35
Peachtree Software	9	21

Source: New York Times, October 16, 1983. © 1983 by The New York Times Company. Reprinted by permission.

EXHIBIT FOUR

THE U.S. MICROCOMPUTER SOFTWARE MARKET, 1983 ($million)

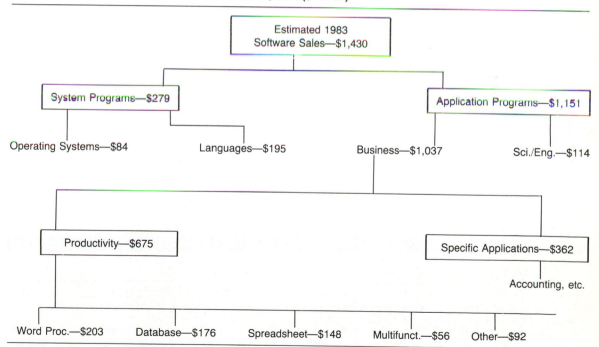

Source: New York Times, October 16, 1983.

EXHIBIT FIVE-A

CONSOLIDATED STATEMENT OF OPERATIONS, 1983 ($thousand)

	Q1	Q2	Q3	Q4
Net revenues	$ 4,787	$ 7,851	$16,465	$23,904
Costs and expenses:				
Cost of sales	812	920	1,933	3,133
Research and development	289	311	495	1,105
Sales and marketing	1,824	2,352	3,083	4,827
General and administrative	815	1,077	1,682	2,349
Total operating expenses	3,740	4,660	7,193	11,414
Income from operations	1,047	3,191	9,272	12,490
Interest income	44	50	112	738
Other income	1	3	167	317
Interest before provision for income taxes and extraordinary item	1,092	3,244	9,551	13,545
Provision for income taxes	529	1,571	4,843	6,772
Income before extraordinary item	563	1,673	4,708	6,773
Extraordinary item[a]	529	71	—	—
Net income	$ 1,092	$ 1,744	$ 4,708	$ 6,773
Net income per share:				
Income before extraordinary item	$0.04	$0.12	$0.35	$0.43
Extraordinary item	0.04	0.01	—	—
Net income per share	$0.08	$0.13	$0.35	$0.43
Weighted average common shares and common share equivalents outstanding	13,316	13,462	13,576	15,875
Key financial ratios (% of net revenues):				
Cost of sales	17.0%	11.7%	11.7%	13.1%
Research and development	6.0	4.0	3.0	4.6
Sales and marketing	38.1	30.0	18.7	20.2
General and administrative	17.0	13.7	10.2	9.8
Income from operations	21.9	40.6	56.3	52.3
Net income	22.8	22.2	28.6	28.3

[a]Utilization of a net operating loss carryforward.

EXHIBIT FIVE-B

CONSOLIDATED BALANCE SHEET, 1983 ($thousand)

	Q1	Q2	Q3	Q4
Assets				
Total current assets	5,112	8,585	17,544	72,631
Inc: Short-term investments	$ 910	$ 3,332	$ 5,136	$56,181
Accounts receivable	4,008	4,553	10,775	14,234
Inventory	107	553	978	1,846
Total assets	$6,042	$10,210	$20,612	$78,343

EXHIBIT FIVE-B

CONTINUED

	Q1	Q2	Q3	Q4
Liabilities				
Total current liabilities	1,168	3,541	9,141	19,183
Inc: Accounts payable	$ 777	$ 1,625	$ 1,946	$ 5,091
Accrued income taxes	—	1,442	6,208	12,796
Total liabilities	1,338	3,760	9,429	19,503
Stockholders' equity				
Inc: Common stock	139	141	141	166
Paid-in capital	4,686	4,715	4,715	45,547
Retained earnings	(54)	1,691	6,399	13,172
Total stockholders' equity	4,704	6,450	11,183	58,840
Total liabilities and stockholders' equity	$6,042	$10,210	$20,612	$78,343

EXHIBIT SIX

BUSINESS MICROCOMPUTER SALES IN WESTERN EUROPE (thousand units)

	1982	1986[a]
United Kingdom	80	180
West Germany	64	190
France	52	160
Italy	28	110

[a]Estimate.
Source: Mini-Micro Systems, April 1983.

EXHIBIT SEVEN

TOP TEN MICROCOMPUTER BRANDS IN WESTERN EUROPE, 1983[a]

Manufacturer	Market share %
Apple	19.2%
Commodore	18.7
IBM[b]	9.8
Olivetti[b]	7.0
Victor[b]	6.5
Hewlett-Packard[b]	4.6
Intertec[b]	3.0
Tandy	2.8
Digital[b]	2.4
Bull[b]	2.1

[a]Estimate.
[b]16-bit microprocessor.
Source: Mini-Micro Systems, May 1984.

APPENDIX 1

MEMORANDUM

TO: Jim Manzi
FROM: Chuck Digate
SUBJECT: Business Plan Attached

The summary business plan (below) for our European operations encompasses 1984 and a cursory look at 1985 in order to get a perspective of where we are going. The section on operations issues should be used as a basis for discussion with the management committee and myself upon my next visit to Cambridge. With respect to detailed marketing, sales, and finance plans, I haven't included them because they are still in process.

U.K. Business Plan

Organization   The attached chart [*Exhibit A*] shows the proposed organization and staffing plan. The U.K. Managing Director will also have responsibility for the site and for the Human Resources function for all Lotus employee residents in the U.K. Initial areas of organizational focus will be in Product Support and Corporate Accounts Sales. A Finance and Accounting function will also be developed immediately to enable revenue generation in the U.K. company.

Key Milestones   The organizational goals for the year are to be staffed with sufficiently trained personnel to enable direct sales to large accounts in late 2Q, to terminate Reflex's exclusive dealer distributorship in 3Q and to launch Lotus II by September using U.K. personnel for all marketing and sales and product support needs. We will spend $700,000 in the Lotus Ltd. launch campaign and expect to have 32 employees (20 exempt) by 4Q.

Germany/France Business Plan

Organization   Small marketing, sales and support staffs will be developed in these countries to support the Lotus name and our distributors.

Key Milestones   Selection and training of distributors will be completed by mid-2Q followed by the launch of 1-2-3 in English supported by a local language self-tutorial manual (being prepared in English).

General Start-up Procedures   Generally speaking, our distributors will adapt and translate promotional materials which will then be edited and approved by our in-house local marketing staff. In some cases, our advertising agencies will be commissioned to do this work. Initial training of distributors will be handled by U.K. personnel and then followed through by local staff and/or central European marketing staff as they come on board. Local software copyright laws and warranty issues will be incorporated in each country's product packaging *prior to shipment*. These processes will be managed by the manager of European marketing, who will be located in the U.K.

Minor Country Business Plan

Organization   The European Marketing Manager will assist in selecting distributors for these countries and in hiring appropriate Lotus staff—generally training and support personnel for 1984. A Northern European Marketing Manager based in Scandinavia will report to the European Marketing Manager, while the rest of Europe will be handled by a small staff in the U.K. Over time, business entities with full Lotus personnel will be established in three or four countries.

Key Milestones   Scandinavia will be started up first, due to reasonably widespread knowledge of English and 1-2-3 will be launched in English. The rest of Europe will not be supported by Lotus or its distributors until local language versions of Lotus II are available. The exception to this rule is the sale of English 1-2-3 to hardware manufacturers for their resale in volume to corporate accounts. The manufacturers will be trained by Lotus personnel from the U.K. and the U.S.

Operation Issues

Non-U.K. Versions of 1-2-3   A small team of temporary employees will be used to assemble product to be shipped outside the U.K. to hardware manufacturers who are selling into non-Lotus supported countries. This team will also prepare 1-2-3- products for shipment to Lotus distributors in Germany, France and Scandinavia.

EXHIBIT A

PROPOSED 1984/1985 INTERNATIONAL OPERATIONS ORGANIZATION

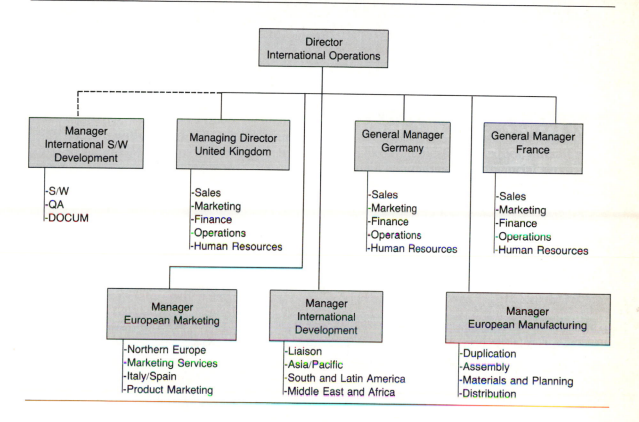

Lotus II   All local language versions of Lotus II will be manufactured in Europe from day one in order to maximize control over the language, legal and packaging problems. Initially, this process will be on a contract basis to U.K. vendors. Ultimately Lotus will bring this process in-house in a location that optimizes both Lotus' tax liabilities and operational control.

Transfer Pricing for 1-2-3   Transfer prices to the U.K. for both finished goods and bulk-packed product need to be established, taking into account the Lotus U.K. investments in marketing and development and the support Lotus will provide to other European countries for products that are packaged in the U.K. and shipped to Europe.

Corporate Structure in 1984   Branch offices will be established in all countries where Lotus has staff except for France and Germany, where subsidiaries should be established by 2Q84. These subs will begin generating local revenue when Lotus 1-2-3 is available in local packaging.

Rest of World in 1984   To the extent that American versions of either 1-2-3 or Lotus II are useful in other countries, product will be shipped directly from the U.S. Should versions be required that are available in Europe, product will be shipped from Europe. No subsidiaries will be established outside of Europe in 1984 with the possible exception of Australia. All Lotus staff will belong to Lotus U.S. branch offices.

Hattori-Seiko and the World Watch Industry in 1980

The production of watches was one of the oldest global industries, with a history of international competition dating back to before 1900. The industry had undergone some dramatic changes, however, and industry leadership had shifted several times. Hattori-Seiko, the world leader in 1980, was faced with the task of sustaining its position in a rapidly changing competitive environment.

This case describes the structure of the world watch industry, focusing on the industry's development and evolution in the three principal watch-producing countries: Switzerland, the United States, and Japan. The note separates the industry's recent history into three parts: (1) the period up to 1950, (2) the 1950s and 1960s, and (3) the 1970s.

EARLY INDUSTRY HISTORY

Until 1957, all watches were mechanical and spring-powered, based on the technology used in large clocks. The invention of the first watch is usually attributed to a German clockmaker in 1510. The Munich clockmakers largely ignored the new invention, however, and the craft of watchmaking advanced more rapidly in France and England during the 16th and 17th centuries. Miniaturization of parts and the de-

This note was prepared by Instructor Edward J. Hoff, under the supervision of Professor Michael E. Porter, as the basis for class discussion. Joseph Fuller, MBA '81, contributed substantially to the preparation of the note. The note also draws from Timex Corporation (6-373-080), prepared by Dr. Frederick Knickerbocker and Professor Hugo Uyterhoeven.

velopment of assembly techniques had been a major achievement in craftsmanship; designing and producing even smaller and thinner watches continued to be a major challenge. Watches were originally made to be carried in a pocket, usually on a chain.

The mechanical watch consisted of two groups of parts: the exterior visible elements—such as the case, crystal, dial, and hands—and the movement, which contained over 100 or more individual components. A mechanical watch movement consisted of an ebauche, comprising the winding mechanism and a gear train, and the regulating component, including the escapement wheel and hairspring, which controlled the rate at which the watch movement worked.

Mechanical watches could be divided into two broad types: jeweled-lever and pin-lever. More expensive watches contained jewels that tipped the teeth in the movement. Jeweled-lever watches were more complicated in construction than pin-lever watches and cost much more to produce. The number of jewels could range from 1 to 23 or more, and the cost of the watch rose with the number of jewels. Pin-lever watches used metal pins instead of jewel-tipped teeth, allowing the entire escapement mechanism to be greatly simplified. Pin-lever watches tended to be less accurate and to wear out faster than jeweled-lever watches but could be more rugged.

The quality of both jeweled-lever and pin-lever watches varied widely depending on the precision with which the parts were made and assembled. Improvement in accuracy was the principal focus of watchmakers, as they worked to improve the design and crafting of the movements. Accuracy was measured in minutes per month. Watchmakers also sought to make movements as thin as possible and to create elegant and stylish cases. The highest-quality watchmakers, especially the Swiss, encased their most accurate and thin movements in gold and other precious metals.

Production of mechanical watches was labor intensive and involved a high degree of hand-crafting. Immediately following World War II, the full production cost of a watch was divided into approximately 60% for labor, 20% for materials, 20% for depreciation. Construction of the movement required the most skilled labor, especially for jeweled-lever watches. Transportation costs added a small percentage above the production cost, depending on destination.

In the late 1940s, most watches sold for $25 to $100 ($150 to $600 in 1985 constant dollars). Approximately 60% of adults in industrialized countries owned a watch. Watches were often given as gifts, and handed down through several generations.

Watches were sold almost exclusively in jewelry stores and in some prestigious department stores. Jeweler margins on watches were 50%, comparable to margins on jewelry. Watches accounted for approximately 20% of both sales and profits for a typical jeweler. Jewelers serviced and repaired the watches they sold, and watch repair was a profitable business in its own right. Some watchmakers, particularly the Swiss, had sponsored training schools for their retailers.

THE SWISS WATCH INDUSTRY

The techniques of watchmaking were brought to Switzerland in the late 16th century by Protestant Huguenots fleeing religious persecution in France. Some Huguenots settled in Geneva, which for centuries had been a center of ornate jewelry making. Under the stern edicts of the Protestant leader John Calvin, who preached in Geneva in the mid-16th century, the jewelry trade had declined, and many jewelry makers quickly took up the new watchmaking trade. Genevan watchmakers began to encase their watch movements in precious metals.

In the mid- to late 18th century, several of the Geneva watchmakers moved to the Jura mountains of northwest Switzerland. This area was populated by farming families who were poor, but who had educated themselves through a closely knit system of community schools. These families, said to be characterized by stubborn independence that still carried into modern times, learned watchmaking from the Genevans and began to make a few watches each year during the winter months to supplement their farming income. The Swiss concentrated on making watches rather than clocks because watches were smaller and easier to transport from the mountains. To improve their craft, which they perceived as vital to continued independence and survival in the mountains, the Jura Swiss created an extensive system of apprenticeships and training programs.

In the late 18th century, the Jura Swiss also began designing their own high-precision machine tools to cut and form tiny parts. Most of these early machine tools were built in England, which was beginning to experience the Industrial Revolution. However, the watchmakers of London, who were considered the world's best at that time, saw these tools as a threat to their craft and persuaded Parliament to pass a law barring their use in England's watch industry. Also in the late 18th century, a Jura Swiss watchmaker invented the pin-lever design.

Individual Jura Swiss families began to specialize in the first half of the 19th century in response to advances in new powered machine tools for making parts. Some families concentrated on parts, while others assembled parts into finished watches. Sometimes, the Jura Swiss sold movements and parts to the Genevans, who then assembled them into watches. The Jura Swiss, however, retained a clearly separate identity from the Geneva firms, just as each canton (or province) retained a strong separate identity within the Swiss federal governmental system. With few changes, the industry retained this tiered structure up to the late 1960s.

Industry Associations

By 1900, the label "Swiss-made" had become a symbol of quality in watches, and the Swiss dominated watchmaking on a worldwide scale. However, Europe was hit by hard economic times in the early 1920s following the destruction and commercial disruptions caused by World War I. The Swiss watch industry saw its sales collapse and unemployment soar. In response to intense competition, over 2,500 separate Swiss firms organized themselves into three associations:

1. The Federation Suisse de Fabricants d'Horlogerie (*FH*): those firms assembling watches from component parts supplied by others plus a few firms with integrated manufacturing operations. These were the firms that actually sold watches in the marketplace.
2. *Ebauches SA:* 17 manufacturers of jeweled-lever ebauches grouped together into a trust.
3. The Union des Branches Annexes de l'Horlogeries (*UBAH*): the manufacturers of components other than ebauches.

Through these associations,[1] the Swiss jeweled-lever watch industry agreed to regulate the activities of its member firms. The agreements included the following provisions:

1. The members of Ebauches SA and UBAH agreed to sell components only to the members of FH.
2. In turn, the members of FH agreed, with one exception, to buy components only from member firms of Ebauches SA and UBAH. The firms in FH did reserve the right to buy foreign-made components, but they also agreed not to buy such components unless

---

[1]These associations involved the manufacture and sale of only jeweled-lever watches. Many Swiss, particularly in the Jura mountains, continued to make and sell the less expensive and accurate pin-lever watches.

they were priced more than 20% under the Swiss level.

3. The members of FH agreed to set their selling prices in accord with a complex inter-association pricing system and a markup formula. Ebauches SA and UBAH supplied the components at specified prices. The watch assemblers and integrated manufacturers established their prices using a standard markup above the association-determined manufacturing costs.

With the onset of the world depression in the early 1930s, the Swiss watch industry again saw sales plummet and sought aid from the Swiss government. In 1931, the Swiss government persuaded several watch assembly firms to join under one holding company, ASUAG. Many of the largest firms remained outside ASUAG. The government then agreed in 1934 to invest in a minority position in ASUAG and to provide the capital for it in turn to acquire the majority of shares of Ebauches SA and several of the leading component manufacturers. The watchmaking firms in ASUAG were grouped into the General Watch Company (GWC). Each of the member firms of ASUAG (whether a watch, movement, or part manufacturer) continued to operate as an independent profit center. FH remained an association of independent, private watch assembly and marketing firms.

Also in 1934, a Swiss federal statute ratified the industry's private controls and imposed new ones. In addition to the provisions above, the government statute required that Swiss firms obtain permits to manufacture and to export finished watches, movements, and components. Government regulations also controlled the transfer of permits and therefore of any mergers and acquisitions among Swiss watchmaking firms. Government approval was also required for the export of watchmaking tools and dies, engineering designs, and machinery.

Finally, foreign firms were prohibited from acquiring either the assets or equity of any Swiss watchmaking firms.

Immediately after World War II, the Swiss accounted for 80% of the world's watch production. The Swiss watch industry employed 80,000 people in 2,500 separate firms, accounting for approximately 10% of GNP. Over 95% of Swiss watches were exported, representing about 20% of total Swiss exports.

Sales and Promotion

Throughout the 1940s and early 1950s, most Swiss firms concentrated on making quality jeweled-lever watches. Swiss watchmakers channeled their promotional expenditures through organizations like FH into collective campaigns in overseas markets. The campaigns stressed the quality and reputation of Swiss-made watches. FH employed one New York advertising firm from 1947 to 1958 to direct its campaign in the United States. Annual expenditures were modest and allocated primarily to periodicals. A few of the larger independent watchmakers, such as Rolex and Omega, supplemented the industry's activities by promoting their own brands.

The Swiss industry sold watches exclusively through jewelry and department store retail outlets. Each individual company handled distribution and sales for its own watches. Most Swiss firms used wholesalers for these functions. Some of the larger Swiss firms established technical centers and after-sales service centers and sponsored watch-repair training schools in major foreign markets.

COMPETITIVE CHANGES: 1950–1970

The world watch industry grew rapidly in the 1950s and 1960s. Rising prosperity led to virtually all adults in industrialized countries owning a watch by 1970. Switzerland maintained the largest aggregate volume of watch production, though powerful forces were threatening its position by 1970.

Two new technologies were commercially developed and introduced during the 1950s and 1960s into the world watchmaking industry: the electric watch and the tuning fork watch. The development of the electric watch resulted from the successful miniaturization of batteries and electric motors. Electric current from a battery drove a tiny balance-wheel motor, which then turned a gear train and the hands of the watch. The accuracy of most electric watches was similar to that of high-quality mechanical watches.

The tuning fork watch represented a major technological advance. An electric current from a small battery caused a tuning fork to vibrate over 21,000 vibrations per minute. Gears converted these vibrations into the sweep of the hands on the watch face. Tuning fork watches could be accurate to within one minute per month.

The United States Watch Industry

During the first half of the 20th century, U.S. watch manufacturers found themselves competing with Swiss firms that had both lower labor rates and more highly skilled labor. Swiss wage rates were approximately one-half those in the United States for skilled labor. Following World War II, there were seven U.S. watch manufacturers: four made jeweled-lever watches, and three made pin-lever watches. In addition, more than 100 companies imported Swiss movements and assembled them in the United States. The late 1940s and early 1950s also marked some important changes in the U.S. market. Per capita disposable income was steadily increasing. At the same time, mass merchandising retail stores were emerging that provided new lower cost and more accessible

outlets for goods that had traditionally been sold through specialty stores. Commercial television was also expanding to become the most efficient and effective medium for the advertisement of many goods and services.

The early 1950s were characterized by growing Swiss dominance of the U.S. market. Swiss imports rose from 38% of U.S. consumption in 1949 to 58% in 1954. In 1954, the four U.S. jeweled-lever watch manufacturers petitioned the U.S. Tariff Commission (USTC) for tariff relief from Swiss imports, arguing that watch manufacturing technology was essential to American national defense. U.S. firms also contended that the Swiss enjoyed a cost advantage solely because of lower labor rates. Watch assemblers who imported Swiss movements countered that "the real basis of Swiss competition is in superior technology and marketing ability of that watch industry, not low wages of Swiss workers." The USTC concluded that, regardless of wages, one cause of the lack of U.S. competitiveness was the lack of specialized machine tool manufacturers who could supply the U.S. watch industry with the precision equipment that the Swiss had designed for themselves. The USTC agreed in 1954 to increase tariffs by 50% on watches with 1 to 17 jewels. The rate increased with the number of jewels, up to $10.75 per watch for the 17-jewel variety. The tariff on watches with no jewels remained at the prevailing rate of $0.50 per watch.

Most of the U.S. watch manufacturers either declared bankruptcy or exited the business during the 1950s and 1960s. A few remained in 1970, although most of them were unprofitable. At the same time that most U.S. firms were faltering, however, two U.S. companies emerged as notable successes.

Timex In 1950, the United States Time Corporation of Middlebury, Connecticut, introduced a line of inexpensive Timex watches to the U.S. marketplace. Since its inception, Timex had been guided by Joakim Lehmkuhl. Mr. Lehmkuhl, who had been born in Norway, though trained in engineering in the United States, fled his native country in 1940 in advance of the German army. In 1942, seeing the need for fuse timers for bombs, Lehmkuhl and a group of businessmen acquired a majority interest in the virtually bankrupt Waterbury Clock Company and converted the firm to fuse production. Prior to the war, Waterbury had manufactured the 41 Ingersoll pin-lever pocket watch which had since disappeared from the market.

After the war, as defense orders disappeared, Waterbury's sales fell from $70 million to $300,000. Lehmkuhl then reconverted his company to watch production. He said, "because it seemed the only thing to do." Lehmkuhl was convinced that a good, inexpensive watch could be produced by combining the precision tooling techniques used in making fuse timers with a high degree of mechanization. He gave Waterbury's engineers the task of designing a quality watch that could be truly mass-produced. Employing technology that came out of the World War II research effort, the engineers substituted new hard alloy bearings for jewels in the movement. This feature permitted the construction of pin-lever watches that would be the equal of many jeweled-lever models and better than any other pin-lever watches then available.

Lehmkuhl changed the company's name to U.S. Time and adopted the brand "Timex" for the new product line. The Timex watches introduced in 1950 were men's watches retailing at $6.95 to $7.95. They were designed with simple, tasteful styling and carried a one-year guarantee. Gradually, the company added watches with more features at slightly higher prices. In 1958, Timex introduced its first line of women's watches.

Initially lacking the resources for extensive promotion, Timex approached retail jewelers. Most jewelers were reluctant to handle the Timex line because of its low prices, pin-lever movements, and because the company offered only a 30% margin. As a result, Timex began to distribute its watches directly to 20,000 retail stores, 80% of which were drug stores. While watch turnover averaged 1.5 times per year in jewelry stores, Timex management claimed that its retailers would average a turnover of six times per year. Timex salespeople also displayed showmanship unheard of in the conservative watch business, slamming the watches against walls and dunking them in water to illustrate their shockproof and waterproof qualities. By the mid-1960s, Timex had gained distribution through almost 250,000 retail outlets.

Timex's advertising began on a small scale, limited mainly to magazines. In 1956, the company started the first extensive advertising on network television, and the annual budget for Timex advertising increased from $200,000 in 1952 to $3 million in 1959. The Timex TV commercials emphasized the product's durability and low cost. The "torture test" commercials made Timex renowned, first in the United States and then abroad, as the commercials featured former news commentator John Cameron Swazey showing Timex watches which, under varying circumstances, "took a licking and kept on ticking."

Manufacturing of Timex watches used mass production methods, employing relatively unskilled labor, and constant attention to production efficiency and quality control. The "simple but strict" production formula was based on (1) rigid standardization, with full interchangability of parts, (2) maximum mechanization to reduce human error and to minimize labor costs, and (3) centralized quality control. The company employed 500 tool makers who designed almost all the firm's production equipment. The product design was kept simple to permit mechanization and assembly processing. While Timex had four screws, other watches had as many as 31. The simple design and the riveted cases of the Timex watches made repairs impossible.

In the mid-1950s, U.S. Time began to expand both marketing and production overseas. The company maintained the same product design and production techniques for every market and plant. George Gelgauda, technical director in the 1950s, stated, "Parts fit together whether they are made here in Middlebury, Connecticut, or in Germany." The torture test advertising theme was also used in every market overseas. Overseas production was used to supply both Timex's new growing foreign markets and some of the watches that Timex sold in the burgeoning U.S. market.

The company continued to expand its product line, introducing a line of 17-jeweled watches in 1957 that retailed at $17.95. Despite predictions that Timex could not sell watches at this price through its network of retail outlets, the line was a success. In 1962, the company introduced a 21-jewel watch line, retailing at $21.95. As the Timex watches moved up in price range and quality, jewelers began to carry some of the company's line. In 1963, U.S. Time introduced a line of electric watches, retailing at $39.95, about half the price of the nearest competitor. These new watches were built with more simplified designs than any other jeweled-lever or electric watches then available.

Throughout the 1950s and 1960s (as well as the 1970s and early 1980s), U.S. Time remained a private company and did not publish its financial data. *Advertising Age,* reported, however, that 1961 sales and after-tax income for U.S. Time were $71.2 million and $2.9 million, respectively. The company had no debt and had financed all expansions in the 1950s out of earnings. It was widely believed that U.S. Time used far more assembly processing than any other watchmaker in operation.

By 1970, Timex (having changed its name from U.S. Time) had sales in the range of $200 million, approximately 20 plants scattered around the world, and 17,000 employees. Timex accounted for half the total unit sales of watches in the United States and was the world's largest watch manufacturer in number of units produced. (The U.S. market comprised 30% of the world market in 1970. In that year, Timex produced overseas approximately one-third of the watches that it sold in the United States.) The company had continued to bid on and perform U.S. defense contract work, particularly the development and manufacture of fuses and timing mechanisms. Defense contracts represented about 10 to 20% of Timex sales in 1970.

Bulova Bulova was the leading U.S. manufacturer of higher-quality, jeweled-lever watches. In the early 1950s all the company's watches were sold under the Bulova brand name and priced in the middle range of $25 to $75. Bulova sold only through jewelry and department stores through a direct sales force.

Bulova was also a U.S. defense contractor, bidding regularly on subcontracts that involved timing mechanisms and guidance systems for weapons. Defense work accounted for approximately 20 to 30% of Bulova's revenues during most of the 1950s and 1960s. This work usually required research in metallurgy and electronics.

Although the company had built some watch-manufacturing plants and research facilities in Switzerland in the early 1900s, most of its production in the 1950s was in the United States. Bulova suffered several difficult years during the early 1950s because of increasing Swiss imports, and was an active supporter in the petition filed with the U.S. ITC.

In 1959, Bulova made several strategic moves which changed the direction of the company. First, a Swiss engineer developed and patented a new tuning fork technology. The engineer tried unsuccessfully to interest the Swiss in the technology, so he sold the patent to Bulova.

Bulova brought the prototypes to the United States and miniaturized them by applying advanced electronics and metallurgical techniques. Bulova introduced a line of high-quality, tuning fork watches under the "Accutron" brand name in 1962, sold only through the most prestigious jewelers. By 1967, Accutron was the best-selling watch over $100 in the United States. Bulova had exclusive patents on the tuning fork technology until 1970.

In 1963, Bulova introduced the "Caravelle" line of low-priced jeweled-lever watches to meet the Timex challenge and the growing demand for low-priced watches. Bulova contracted with Japan's Citizen Watch Company to produce the movements for the Caravelle line, which Bulova then assembled and marketed in the United States. Bulova also granted Citizen a license until 1975 to assemble and sell the Caravelle line in Asia. The watches were inexpensive but of high quality. By 1968, Caravelle was the largest-selling jeweled-lever line in the United States. Bulova sold all three lines through a single direct sales force only to jewelers and department stores.

Bulova also expanded its manufacturing base around the world. The Accutron line was produced in the United States, the middle-priced Bulova line in Switzerland, and the Caravelle line in collaboration with Citizen Company in Japan. Management viewed its worldwide production system as a key competitive strength. Harry Henshel, president of Bulova, stated in 1970, "We've been able to beat foreign competition simply because we are foreign competition." Bulova's plants around the world were each dedicated to different product lines.

From 1960 to 1970, Bulova increased its international sales from 5 to 20% of total watch sales. Bulova introduced the different lines in different countries, and few countries other than the United States had all three lines. Bulova employed either a direct sales force or an exclusive distributor in the foreign markets that it entered. By 1970, Bulova had become the largest seller of watches in revenues in both the United States and the world overall (see *Exhibit 6*).

The Swiss Industry

With the 1954 increase of U.S. tariffs on jeweled-lever watches, Swiss watchmakers began to concentrate on selling either cheap pin-lever watches or highly expensive, ornate jeweled-lever watches to the United States. While the larger integrated Swiss watchmakers continued to concentrate on higher-quality, jeweled-lever watches, the smaller Swiss firms tended to move toward the production of pin-lever watches. With the rapid rise of worldwide Timex sales, Swiss pin-lever manufacturers expanded to try to gain a share of the growing demand. By the 1960s, Swiss pin-lever watches were being sold at low prices—some observers termed it dumping—in Asia as well as in North America. The watches were sold under little-known names solely through wholesalers or sometimes under inexpensive private labels.

In 1962, FH and ASUAG joined together to establish a research organization, the Centre Electronique Horloger (CEH). The initial goal was to develop a new time-determining device to compete with Bulova's tuning fork mechanism. The mission of CEH was to extend beyond the laboratory to the actual production of prototypes of new watches for the purpose of test marketing them. Once the prototypes proved themselves in the marketplace, the member firms of FH and ASUAG would engage in full-scale manufacturing and marketing. The CEH failed to develop an acceptable tuning fork technology that did not violate Bulova's patent. In 1968, Ebauches SA (part of ASUAG) entered into a license agreement with Bulova to manufacture and sell watches based on Bulova's tuning fork movement.

Swiss watch production continued to grow at a steady pace in the 1950s and 1960s, though the Swiss unit share of world watch production declined from over 80% in 1946 to 42% in 1970 (see *Exhibits 1* and *4*). Mounting pressures developed within the Swiss industry to eliminate the government and industry regulations of 1934. The regulations were eased in 1957 though little of significance was changed. Gradually from 1966 to 1981 the regulations were rescinded completely.

After the controls on manufacturing permits and mergers were removed, consolidation of the Swiss industry began to occur. Some watch assemblers merged to provide increased marketing clout for their individual brand names. The largest of the newly merged watch assembly firms was SSIH, which controlled the Omega and Tissot brands, among others. Other firms integrated backward into component manufacturing to enhance production efficiency and product development effectiveness. The number of Swiss watchmaking establishments declined from 1,927 in 1965 to 1,618 in 1970. Nevertheless, the number of people employed in the Swiss industry actually increased modestly between 1965 and 1970, from 83,922 to 89,448.

A study conducted for the FH in 1959 had recommended that individual Swiss firms advertise their own brand names, and not just the concept of Swiss-made. The study concluded that many consumers did not trust the jeweler and that the consumer "places his reliance on the advertised brand name." Few Swiss watchmakers followed this advice until 1970. FH also voiced concerns about whether the sale of cheap pin-lever Swiss watches on the world market during the 1960s had undermined the Swiss-made label.

The Japanese Industry

The Japanese watch industry had been concentrated since its inception in the 1880s. As the industry emerged from World War II there were three competitors: K. Hattori (which mar-

keted the Seiko brand), Citizen, and Orient, which accounted for 50, 30, and 20% of production, respectively, in 1950. All Japanese manufacturers made only jeweled-lever watches, using skilled labor commanding wages approximately one-eighth of those in the United States following World War II. At this time, the Japanese firms all sold their watches to the fast-growing domestic market exclusively through jewelry stores. Domestic demand for watches in Japan grew rapidly during the 1950s and 1960s. The Japanese industry remained concentrated with Hattori-Seiko, Citizen, and Orient comprising 60, 30, and 10% of the market, respectively, in 1970.

During the 1950s and 1960s, Timex, Bulova, and several of the largest Swiss firms had attempted to penetrate the growing Japanese market. While the Japanese government played little or no role in providing financing, underwriting research, or developing of export markets for Japanese firms, the government did impose tariffs and sales taxes on imported watches, which combined to add 70% to the price of such watches. The fragmentation of the Japanese retail channels also presented obstacles to the foreign watch firms. Imported watches accounted for less than 5% of the Japanese market in 1970.

Over the years the "big two" Japanese watch manufacturers had moved into the manufacture of products outside the timepiece field. By 1970 Seiko was producing desktop electronic calculators, high-speed printers for use with computers, miniature industrial robots, machine tools, electronic displays of various types, and information equipment. Citizen produced mechanical and electronic calculators, office equipment, and machine tools. In both cases, sales of nonwatch items represented a small part of the firm's total revenue.

Hattori-Seiko K. Hattori was the marketing company that sold the watches made by Seiko, a wholly owned design and manufacturing company. During the 1950s, Hattori's managers set the goal of eliminating the technological and styling gap that separated their products from Swiss watches, the industry standard. Although impressive progress had been made since the war, Seiko's movements remained bulkier, less accurate, and less reliable than Swiss watches. The disadvantage in styling was even greater. Hattori-Seiko also developed a policy of shifting product development from individual styles with their own unique movements to multiple styles based on common movement calibers.

Hattori-Seiko manufactured watches at two Japanese production locations, in Suwa and Tokyo. Management set out to upgrade manufacturing equipment but found that Japan's domestic tool manufacturers had little interest in producing custom equipment with such a narrow application. As a result, Seiko developed separate machine tool departments at both Suwa and Tokyo, charged with modifying purchased equipment to Seiko's specifications as well as producing customized equipment.

Seiko's management made a number of trips to the United States and Europe to study production methods used in other industries. Visits to American automobile plants proved the most influential, and Seiko's managers decided to use assembly-line techniques to enhance the productivity and the quality of their products. It was also decided to retain the policy of extensive vertical integration that had been adopted early in the company's history. Seiko was fully integrated into most watch components and maintained tapered vertical integration into those watch components for which it was not completely self-sufficient. All components were manufactured, either by Seiko or small suppliers, in plants grouped closely together around the assembly plants in Tokyo or Suwa.

By 1959, a healthy interdivisional rivalry had emerged between the Suwa and Tokyo plants. Hattori-Seiko created a new organization structure under which both companies maintained separate production, design, and research facilities. The two divisions sold all their output to Hattori. Hattori informed both divisions of its anticipated product needs. The two divisions then independently designed entire product lines from which Hattori selected models to be mass-produced for the market.

Hattori employed both a direct sales force and distributors to sell watches in Japan. Initially, Hattori believed that a sales force would be needed to overcome jewelry store resistance to accepting Seiko products. However, strong consumer demand and improvements in Seiko quality had brought extensive jewelry store acceptance. Hattori began to market a greater proportion and more of its sales through distributors, believing the higher expense of a sales force was not necessary. Hattori did not grant any exclusive distributorships and encouraged its distributors to compete with each other.

In the late 1950s, export sales comprised less than 5% of Hattori's unit sales. During the early 1960s, Hattori initiated rapid expansion of sales throughout Asia. By 1970, Seiko had become the leading watch brand in most Asian countries. In 1964, Hattori began selling in the United States, reaching a series of five-year agreements with 50 distributors, none of which were given exclusive territorial rights. Hattori also established ties with certain European distributors in the 1960s. A number of exclusive national agreements were reached with established wholesalers in Great Britain, Greece, Spain, Scandinavia, and France.

In 1967, Hattori dispatched a young executive, Hideaki Moriya, to New York to assume control of its American sales effort. Moriya recalled, "When I arrived, we had sales of $500,000, terrible brand name recognition, no advertising, and minimal influence over our distributors. To most of them, we were one item among the hundreds they handled." Moriya decided that Hattori would have to invest heavily in the U.S. market and would probably not realize a profit for seven to ten years. The initial investment was in television advertising, with the intent of building consumer brand recognition as well as support from the retail trade and the distributors.

Seiko Time, the U.S. subsidiary, also opened service centers in New York and Los Angeles. Retailers could send all repairs to these centers, avoiding the need for on-site servicing operations. Repairs were processed rapidly, often in less than five days. Retailers received a fee for their handling efforts. This program, coupled with the industry's lowest repair frequency, gave Seiko a reputation as the most reliable product available.

Moriya also moved to reorganize the U.S. distribution system. Moriya selected 20 distributors (of the original 50) that he thought had the strength and commitment to serve as "partners" with Hattori and granted them exclusive territorial distributorships. The distributors were asked to establish a fully independent company which would handle only Seiko products. The distributors would also have to contribute to the Seiko advertising campaign. Eventually Moriya reached agreement with 15 distributors on these terms.

Hattori-Seiko supplied all watches from Japan. Both Suwa and Tokyo invested heavily in automatic equipment that permitted Seiko to reduce labor to 35% of the full production cost of a watch in the late 1960s. Vertical integration of component manufacturing also permitted more rapid deployment of new technology and watch design. One industry observer estimated that the Japanese enjoyed a 15 to 45% variable cost advantage over the Swiss for jeweled mechanical watches in the mid-1960s.

During the late 1960s, Hattori initiated component fabrication and assembly operations abroad. Plants were located in Hong Kong (case manufacturing and mechanical watch assembly), Singapore (plate and wheel fabrication, assembly), and Malaysia (components). Workers at all three sites earned approximately one-third as much as did Japanese workers in the late 1960s and commanded fewer benefits and no guarantee of lifetime employment. Both Singapore and Hong Kong also offered extensive tax incentives and low corporate tax rates. In certain instances, older equipment was shifted from Japanese plants to these overseas facilities.

Citizen Citizen marketed almost 300 brands of mostly private-label watches throughout Asia and Europe. Its inexpensive, jeweled-lever watches were originally produced in vertically integrated plants in Japan. During the 1960s, Citizen aggressively built its own brand name while expanding outside of Japan. By 1970, the Citizen brand watch had become the second largest selling brand in most Asian countries. Furthermore, Citizen set up production facilities in several European countries in addition to establishing European distributorships. Citizen's agreement with Bulova kept it out of the U.S. market until at least 1975.

COMPETITIVE CHANGES: 1970–1980

A major new technology in watchmaking was introduced commercially during the 1970s, which resulted in the quartz watch. When an electric current was passed through a quartz crystal, the crystal could be stimulated to vibrate at a very high frequency and the oscillations converted into precise time increments. Quartz technology allowed the design of watches that were extremely accurate, measured in terms of seconds per year. Quartz also permitted miniaturization.

Unlike Bulova's tuning fork technology, the basic quartz technology was in the public domain and available to all competitors. The challenge for competitors in the watch industry was to devise product designs and production techniques to employ the technology.

Advances in integrated circuitry also permitted the digital display of time. Digital watches used liquid crystal displays (LCDs) or light-emitting diodes (LEDs). Because LEDs used considerable power in the display, the wearer had to press a button to illuminate the face of the watch. LCDs permitted the continuous display of the time, but were hard to read when first introduced. A quartz movement could also drive watches which retained the traditional face, hands, and gear train of so-called "analog" watches. Analog quartz watches involved a more complicated and delicate manufacturing process than did digital quartz watches, because they continued to contain critical moving parts that needed to be balanced and carefully fitted. Analog watches required more inspection and quality control during the assembly process.

Analog quartz watches contained fewer components and delicate moving parts than did jeweled-lever watches, permitting increased automation in the production process. The industry average variable costs of producing an analog quartz watch, according to the Swiss Watch Federation, had declined from approximately Swiss franc (SF) 100 in 1974 to SF 20 by 1979. This was almost as low as the variable costs of producing a high-quality mechanical watch, even though the quartz technology was far more advanced. Direct labor accounted for less than 20% of the full production cost of an analog quartz watch by 1979, as firms invested heavily in automated equipment.

The digital quartz watches contained no moving parts at all, permitting some watch manufacturers to install fully automated production lines (involving no assembly processing). LED display technology was the first developed, but consumers soon tired of pressing a button to read the time. LCD technology, with continuous display of time, often failed when initially introduced in 1973. By the late 1970s, however, many watch manufacturers had vastly improved the reliability and perfor-mance of LCD watches, and LCD technology began to dominate the digital segment.

Because digital quartz watches were based on microelectronic technology, many semiconductor firms—first American and later Hong Kong firms—were attracted to the growing watch market during the mid-1970s. Experience in the semiconductor industry had indicated a 30% decline in cost with each doubling in cumulative volume. The new entrants emphasized fully automated, low-variable-cost production processes, and the prices on digital quartz watches dropped dramatically, significantly below prices on analog quartz watches. Digital quartz watches were sold mainly through drug stores and catalog show rooms.

Many of the new entrants introduced digital quartz watches in plastic cases, which permitted a simpler production process and lower variable costs. Other watchmakers continued to emphasize metal cases as a point of differentiation. Quartz watches, both analog and digital, continued to vary widely in thinness, attractiveness, and style. Many jewelers grew reluctant to service these more complicated but less expensive quartz watches, and reliability became increasingly important for these retail outlets.

The world watch market grew significantly during the late 1970s. In the United States, adults who already owned a watch began to buy new ones for different occasions:

PERCENTAGE OF U.S. UNIT WATCH CONSUMPTION BY RETAIL PRICE

	$70 or less	$70 to $99	$100 to $299	$300 or more
1975	70.4%	12.7%	15.2%	1.7%
1979	74.3%	6.5%	15.4%	3.8%

Source: Jewelers' Circular Keystone.

The 1970s also saw a revaluation of currencies against the U.S. dollar, including the Swiss franc and the Japanese yen.

EXCHANGE RATES TO THE U.S. DOLLAR (annual average)

	(Fixed rate) 1950–70	1971	1972	1974	1976	1978	1980
Swiss Franc	4.373	4.1465	4.1466	3.5830	2.8859	2.2386	2.1810
Japanese Yen	360.0	350.4	329.2	351.3	342.4	263.5	295.1

Source: *International Monetary Fund Yearbook of Statistics.*

The Japanese Watch Industry

Hattori-Seiko Hattori had developed a quartz clock in 1956, approximately the size of a pickup truck, for use by television and radio stations. Despite the bulkiness of the existing quartz mechanisms, Hattori directed its engineers to develop smaller quartz technology. Each division was charged with different development tasks, all based on quartz. With the scheduling of the 1964 Summer Olympic games in Tokyo, Hattori management also decided to concentrate its research efforts in an effort to serve as the official timekeeper. Hattori management charged each division with different development tasks, all based on quartz technology. In 1963, Hattori filed its proposal to be the official timekeeper with the International Olympic Committee and won—against Omega and Longines, two highly respected Swiss watchmakers. This success gave Hattori management new determination. Hattori introduced the world's first quartz analog watch in 1969. Although the first Seiko quartz watch had to be withdrawn due to performance problems, a new line that proved technologically sound was introduced in 1971.

Hamilton Company, an old established U.S. watch manufacturer that had experienced difficulties since World War II, launched the new wave of digital quartz technology with the introduction of the Pulsar watch in 1972, featuring an LED readout. Digital watches proved initially more popular than the Seiko quartz analog watches. Nevertheless, Hattori management decided to cancel LED research and

to step up research into LCD technology. In 1975, Seiko introduced a new line of high-quality LCD quartz watches in most parts of the world, offering several unique features such as an alarm and the capability to record multiple time zones.

Hattori continued to grow profitably in Asia but registered losses in the United States and Europe despite rising revenues. Moriya, returning to the United States after a brief time in Japan, set out to revitalize the Seiko distribution network. In 1975, Moriya announced that (1) distributors' margins would be reduced from 22 to 20%, (2) Hattori would increase its U.S. advertising from $2 million annually in 1974 to $9 million annually by 1979, (3) Seiko U.S. distributors were to undertake a concerted effort to sell quartz watches, and (4) distributor sales targets for 1976 would be 60% above those in 1975. Seiko watches were sold in 15,000 jewelry and department stores.

Hattori-Seiko also undertook an extensive effort to convert most of its jeweled-lever production facilities to quartz—both analog and digital. By 1975, Hattori-Seiko had invested in plants to make integrated circuits, batteries, and LCD panels. Employees were retrained to work with the new technology. Seiko also increased its investment in robots and equipment for high-volume, automated production. These new Hattori production lines were each designed to produce, at minimum efficient scale, ranging from 100,000 to over 1,000,000 watches per year per line, depending on the type of watch. Management stated that a goal was to build manufacturing plants that could run without direct labor, except for inspection and quality control.

Analog quartz watches began to grow in popularity beginning in 1976 in most major markets. By 1979, approximately half the quartz watches sold in the world were analog and half digital. Over 80% of the digital watches sold in 1979 were LCD. Hattori-Seiko's product line shifted rapidly to quartz:

SHIFT TO QUARTZ TECHNOLOGY

	1975	1976	1977	1978	1979
Quartz as percent of world watches	3%	12%	18%	23%	31%
Quartz as percent of Seiko watches	20%	29%	45%	54%	72%

Sources: *Jewelers' Circular Keystone*, January 1980; Japanese Watch Association

By 1977 Hattori-Seiko had become the world's largest watch company in terms of revenues (see *Exhibit 5*), and Seiko had become the largest brand in the medium-price segment of the U.S. market.

Citizen By 1975, Citizen's manufacturing facilities were fully automated and almost fully integrated. It operated manufacturing/assembly plants in seven countries, including Japan, South Korea, Hong Kong, the United States, West Germany, and Mexico. After Citizen's contract with Bulova, Citizen undertook a major program to build up its own brand names in the United States. An industry observer was quoted as saying, "They make no bones about it. Citizen wants to overtake Hattori." Citizen introduced a high-quality quartz line in the United States and spent $9 million in 1979 for advertising. By 1979, the Citizen line was sold in 5,000 retail outlets, all jewelry and department stores. Citizen management stated that its policy was to avoid distribution through discount outlets "at all cost."

The U.S. Industry

By 1975, over 50 new companies, most based in the United States and all having expertise with integrated circuits, had started production of digital watches. Consumer demand for digitals had begun to grow in 1974, when National Semiconductor announced that it would sell an LED watch at $125, about half the prevailing price. Immediately afterward, Litronix, Texas Instruments, and Fairchild Camera and Instrument—all manufacturers of integrated circuits—introduced their own LED quartz watches. Each firm invested in high-volume, fully automated watch-manufacturing plants. These firms attempted to distribute their new watches through their existing sales forces for consumer electronics products—such as calculators and cameras—and through distributors to reach the types of outlets in which their products were not sold. Texas Instruments (TI) emerged as the most aggressive new entrant, introducing a line of LED quartz watches retailing at $19.95 in 1976. TI announced that it expected to bring its variable costs well below $10 per watch by 1977. Retail prices for all digital watches fell with TI's announcement.

Poor quality in digital watches, both for LED and particularly LCD models, plagued the market in 1975 and 1976. Consumer demand for inexpensive digitals waned in 1977, and capacity greatly exceeded demand. In 1977, TI dropped the price to $10. One by one, electronics firms exited, citing poor demand and distribution problems, and all but Texas Instruments had left the market by 1980. Texas Instruments continued to lose money on its watch business, and industry analysts expected TI to exit in the early 1980s.

Timex Timex had introduced in 1971 its first analog quartz watch retailing at $125, 60% under the least-expensive watch on the market at that time. Timex had no internal quartz crystal or integrated-circuit production capability, and purchased its quartz components from several suppliers. In explaining how Timex could market a watch at $125, Robert Mohr, executive vice president, stated:

Timex Corporation has a solid background of expertise in essentials like the design and manufacturing of miniature parts. In addition, the company has technology geared to vast production. In making millions of watches annually, we have developed watchmaking production capabilities unmatched anywhere in the world.[2]

Timex experienced management strife in the early 1970s over issues of succession, growth, and vertical integration. Fred Olsen, a Norwegian industrialist whose family had controlled 51% of Timex since they had financed Lehmkuhl's acquisition of the Waterbury company, removed Lehmkuhl as CEO in 1973. Olsen installed Ole Martin Siem, a former shipping company executive. Siem revised the company's objectives of aggressive growth, considering them risky. A former Timex executive stated, "Siem didn't want to hear about the Lehmkuhl era of up, up, up. He didn't even want to hear the name Lehmkuhl."[3]

In 1975, Timex introduced its first LED quartz watch, retailing at $89.95. Throughout the early and mid-1970s, Timex turned down numerous offers to form joint ventures or manufacturing partnerships with various semiconductor firms. In 1976, Timex introduced its first LCD quartz watch. Timex emphasized metal casings that required assembly-line production with low-skilled labor rather than the more highly automated processes for plastic casings. Timex continued to produce most of its watches outside the United States in the 1970s.

In the late 1970s, Timex lowered its prices for both digital and mechanical watches in response to the prices set by electronics firms for digital watches, but its quartz watches continued to retail for considerably more than those of TI. The majority of Timex's production in 1980 was still mechanical pin-lever watches. In 1980, Seiko surpassed Timex as the world's largest watch producer in units, as well as revenues, and the Timex share of the U.S. market had declined to approximately 33%. In the first quarter of 1980, Timex lost $10 million.

Bulova   Bulova had also introduced an analog quartz watch in 1972 under the Bulova name. Bulova purchased electronic components from outside suppliers. During the early 1970s, Bulova engineers remained skeptical of LED and LCD technology and the company avoided the digital watch market. In response to rapid market growth, Bulova introduced a line of LED quartz watches under the Bulova name in 1976 using purchased components. In 1977, Bulova had to write down the inventory of millions of obsolete LED watches, as the boom in that market had ended. Bulova began to introduce quartz watches under its premium Accutron brand name in 1975, beginning with analog watches and eventually adding LCD quartz watches in 1977.

After three years of significant losses, Loews Corporation purchased the Bulova Company in 1979. Loews Corporation had approximately $4 billion in annual revenues, primarily from its CNA insurance company and a network of movie theaters. Loews management announced in its 1980 annual report three primary objectives for the Bulova division:

1. Improved product innovation and a better product mix, including the final cessation of the production of tuning fork watches in Bulova's plant in Berne, Switzerland
2. Extensive production automation at the major plants in Switzerland

---

[2]*National Jeweler*, May 1972.
[3]*Business Week*, August 18, 1975.

3. A restructuring of the Bulova subsidiary's debt

The Hamilton Company   Hamilton was the only remaining U.S.-based watch manufacturer other than Timex and Bulova in the 1970s. The company was considered innovative and had introduced the Pulsar line of quartz watches in 1971, which were positioned in price below Bulova and Seiko but above Timex and the electronics firms. The company filed for bankruptcy in 1978; Hattori-Seiko purchased the rights to the Pulsar name, and SSIH purchased the remaining assets of the company.

The Swiss Industry

The Swiss had pioneered quartz technology in the late 1950s in the laboratory. The Centre Electronique Horloger (CEH), the Swiss research consortium which had been formed to examine tuning fork technology, had also undertaken in the 1960s to develop prototypes for quartz watches. FH had also formed in 1966 a laboratory for joint research in the fields of semiconductors, integrated circuits, and lasers with the Swiss company Brown Boveri, Landis & Cyr, and the Philips Corporation of the Netherlands. CEH had apparently achieved considerable progress in the 1960s, but Swiss firms did not commercially introduce quartz watches until much later in the 1970s.

Many Swiss watchmakers either consolidated or closed in the 1970s. Many of the consolidated companies failed to operate smoothly. A small number of companies, particularly those who manufactured less expensive watches, shifted production to non-Swiss sites, especially Hong Kong and Taiwan, to manufacture pin-lever or inexpensive jeweled-lever watches, which were marketed around the world based on price. Other companies increasingly turned to making only movements, which were then exported to Hong Kong to be encased and then reexported. Overall production of Swiss watches and movements and the number of establishments and employees in the Swiss watch industry declined (see *Exhibits 1, 2,* and *3*).

On the other hand, several Swiss watchmakers, who were all based in Geneva, emphasized highly accurate movements and expensive precious metal casings and focused on positioning their brands for the highest price segment of the market. These firms, such as Rolex and Omega, initiated extensive promotion campaigns in the United States that targeted the small but rapidly growing premium segment. Swiss firms continued to dominate this segment in 1980. Many of these watchmakers, most notably Rolex, remained committed to the traditional jeweled-lever mechanical movements, which the Swiss had made highly accurate and reliable, though somewhat less so than the best movements based on quartz technology.

New Entrants in 1980

A major new Japanese player had entered the market in 1978, Casio Inc., a joint venture between Casio Computer Company and Toyo Menka Kaisha Ltd., a leading Japanese trading company. Casio manufactured computers and consumer electronic goods. Casio's stated goal was to sell digital watches as consumer electronics products. The units were encased in plastic, like those of other electronic firms, but they were promoted as undamageable from sweat and marketed as joggers' watches. Casio began to sell its first model, the $39.95 model F-100, to electronics stores and sporting goods outlets. Neither type of outlet had tended to carry watches before. Casio rose to the number two spot in the under-$50 world watch market by 1980, behind only Timex. Casio diversified its line of low-cost watches in 1980 as its market share grew.

Hong Kong emerged in the late 1970s as the

fastest-growing watch production center in the world. Japanese, American, and Swiss watchmakers had all established plants in Hong Kong to take advantage of low-cost, highly skilled labor and low tax rates. Initially, Hong Kong production facilities tended to concentrate on mechanical watch production, while watchmakers tended to produce quartz watches in their home markets. However, several sizable Hong Kong semiconductor manufacturers began to produce low-cost digital quartz watches, which were then exported and sold at very inexpensive prices under little-known names or private labels. These watches were distributed almost solely through nonexclusive wholesalers and import/exporters. Other Hong Kong firms imported mechanical movements, primarily from Switzerland, and then assembled analog mechanical watches. However, by 1980, the nine largest Hong Kong semiconductor firms, which manufactured only digital quartz watches, had grown to account for more than half the 126 million watches (80.5 million watches fully made, with an additional 45.5 million watches assembled based on imported movements) that Hong Kong exported that year.

EXHIBIT ONE

ESTIMATED WORLD PRODUCTION OF WATCHES AND WATCH MOVEMENTS,[a] 1945–1980 (in millions)

	1945	1950	1955	1960	1965	1970	1975	1976	1977	1978	1978	1980
Switzerland	18.8	25.7	34.8	43.1	58.6	73.7	70.4	64.0	68.3	60.3	48.9	50.0
Japan	0.1	0.7	2.2	7.0	13.8	23.8	30.2	34.0	49.1	56.2	64.3	67.5
United States	1.8	9.7	8.4	9.5	13.6	19.4	27.3	29.0	28.0	27.1	20.4	12.1
Hong Kong	...	...	...	...	...	...	7.8	15.0	23.2	31.6	53.5	80.5
Others[b]	0.9	11.7	28.2	39.8	37.0	55.9	85.3	85.0	90.7	96.8	97.9	116.9
Approximate world watch production	21.6	47.8	73.6	99.4	123.0	172.9	221.0	227.0	259.3	272.0	285.0	327.0

[a]To avoid double counting, this chart accounts for the production of a complete watch or a watch movement. It does not include the placing of an imported watch movement into a casing.

[b] "Others" includes the USSR and People's Republic of China, which accounted for the production of 48 million and 33 million watches, respectively, in 1980. France, West Germany, East Germany, and the United Kingdom accounted for most of the remaining production.

Sources: Federation of Swiss Watchmakers; Japanese Watch Association; U.S. International Trade Commission; and U.S. Department of Commerce.

EXHIBIT TWO

WORLD PRODUCTION OF WATCH MOVEMENTS BY TYPE, 1975–1980 (in millions)

	1975	1976	1977	1978	1979	1980
Mechanical spring-powered movement production[a]						
Switzerland	69.0	60.3	63.8	54.5	40.9	38.0
Japan	26.9	26.5	36.4	36.5	31.9	17.0
United States	23.3	17.0	6.0	9.1	11.4	10.1
Hong Kong	7.5	14.0	17.2	14.8	14.0	1.0
Others	84.0	83.1	85.6	88.7	85.8	102.0
Total	210.7	200.9	209.0	203.6	184.0	168.1
Electronic movement production[b]						
Switzerland	1.4	3.7	4.5	5.8	8.0	12.0
Japan	3.3	7.5	12.7	19.7	32.4	50.5
United States	4.0	12.0	22.0	18.0	9.0	2.0
Hong Kong	0.3	1.0	6.0	16.8	39.5	79.5
Others	1.3	1.9	5.1	8.1	12.1	14.9
Total	10.3	26.1	50.3	68.4	101.0	158.9

[a]Includes both jeweled-lever and pin-lever spring-powered movements.
[b]Includes quartz, tuning fork, and battery-powered mechanical watch technologies.
Source: Federation of Swiss Watchmakers.

EXHIBIT THREE

NUMBER OF FIRMS AND WORKERS IN THE SWISS WATCH INDUSTRY, 1950–1980

	Number of firms	Managerial employees	Industrial workers	Home workers[a]	Employees
1950	1,863	10,052	43,119	7,068	60,239
1955	2,316	11,847	50,312	7,867	70,026
1960	2,167	13,510	51,617	9,089	74,216
1965	1,927	14,588	58,012	11,322	83,922
1970	1,618	17,307	58,738	13,403	89,448
1975	1,169	16,744	39,210	6,613	62,567
1976	1,083	15,314	34,677	5,191	55,182
1977	1,021	14,950	34,872	5,003	54,825
1978	979	14,692	33,613	4,364	52,669
1979	867	13,685	29,911	3,120	46,716
1980	861	14,155	30,018	2,825	46,998

[a]Home workers were self-employed. They were paid on a piece-rate basis for the crafting of a watch component or the assembling of a watch, under a contract with one of the larger Swiss watch firms.
Source: Federation of Swiss Watchmakers.

EXHIBIT FOUR

WORLD WATCH PRODUCTION, 1970

Millions of Watches and Watch Movements

Country	Production	Percent of world production	Exports	Exports as percent of production
Switzerland	73.7	42	71.4	97
Japan	23.8	14	13.7	58
USSR	21.5	12	1.8	8
United States	19.4	11	0.2	1
France	11.0	6	4.1	37
West Germany	8.2	5	4.1	50
Mainland China	5.0	3	—	—
East Germany	3.5	2	1.8	51
United Kingdom	3.2	2	1.0	31
Italy	2.6	1	0.6	23
Others	2.0	1	—	
Total	173.9		98.7	

Source: Federation of Swiss Watchmakers.

EXHIBIT FIVE

ESTIMATED REVENUE AND VOLUME OF WORLD'S TOP TEN WATCHMAKERS, 1977

	Watch revenue (millions)	Number of pieces (millions)
1. Hattori-Seiko (Japan)	$700	18.0
2. Timex (United States)	475	35.0
3. SSIH (Switzerland)	315	6.7
4. GWC (Switzerland)	230	7.5
5. Citizen (Japan)	180	9.0
6. Bulova (United States)	175	3.5
7. Orient (Japan)	140	3.0
8. Rolex (Switzerland)	90	0.2
9. SGT (Switzerland)	75	1.6
10. Texas (United States)	60	3.8

Jeweler's Circular Keystone estimated that total world watch production in 1977—including USSR, PRC, etc.— was 259 million units. Demand in the United States was approximately 60 million units.

Source: ERC Statistics International, London, England.

SELECTED FINANCIAL STATISTICS FOR BULOVA WATCH COMPANY, HATTORI-SEIKO, AND CITIZEN WATCH COMPANY

Bulova Watch Company: 1965–1978 (millions of dollars)

	1965	1966	1967	1968	1969	1970	1971	1972	1973	1974	1975a	1976	1977	1978
Net sales	$84.2	$99.8	$123.9	$129.8	$148.9	$158.7	$145.3	$148.8	$176.7	$213.8	$228.2	$204.7	$207.5	$203.1
Net income	2.8	3.2	3.9	4.5	5.9	6.6	6.2	3.9	6.5	8.3	1.1	(25.6)	(7.0)	(15.5)
Return on sales	3.3%	3.2%	3.1%	3.5%	4.0%	4.2%	4.3%	2.6%	3.7%	3.9%	0.5%	(12.5%)	(3.4%)	(7.6%)
Equity	41.3	49.4	46.4	50.0	57.6	64.8	70.0	72.2	70.4	81.1	81.1	54.9	49.8	34.3
Return on equity	6.8%	6.5%	8.4%	9.0%	10.2%	10.2%	8.9%	5.4%	9.2%	10.2%	1.4%	(46.6%)	(4.1%)	(45.2%)
Long-term debt	22.8	22.5	23.2	23.0	16.6	36.5	35.2	34.0	33.9	61.4	60.3	119.9	94.0	97.3
Long-term debt/debt & equity	35.6%	31.3%	33.3%	31.5%	22.4%	36.0%	33.5%	32.0%	32.5%	43.1%	42.6%	68.6%	65.4%	73.9%

Hattori-Seiko: 1968–1979 (billions of yen)

	1968	1969	1970	1971	1972	1973	1974	1975	1976	1977	1978	1979
Total sales	¥61	63	85	109	123	137	156	174	177	216	271	285
Export sales	NA	NA	NA	NA	NA	NA	NA	51	57	71	104	110
Net income	1.4	1.4	2.0	2.6	2.8	2.9	3.1	2.6	1.9	2.8	4.1	5.1
Return on sales	2.3%	2.2%	2.3%	2.4%	2.3%	2.1%	2.0%	1.5%	1.1%	1.3%	1.5%	1.8%
Return on assets	NA	NA	NA	5.0%	4.0%	3.9%	3.8%	3.0%	2.1%	2.5%	2.5%	3.5%

Citizen Watch Company: 1968–1979 (billions of yen)

	1968	1969	1970	1971	1972	1973	1974	1975	1976	1977	1978	1979
Total sales	¥19	22	31	34	29	35	43	51	47	60	71	83
Export sales	NA	NA	NA	NA	NA	NA	NA	20	23	27	38	45
Net income	NA	NA	NA	NA	1.3	1.6	1.8	1.8	1.2	1.8	3.2	4.5
Return on sales	NA	NA	NA	NA	4.4%	4.5%	4.2%	3.5%	2.6%	3.0%	4.5%	5.4%
Return on assets	NA	NA	NA	NA	3.6%	3.9%	4.1%	3.9%	2.2%	2.9%	4.2%	5.9%

aRestated to end fiscal year on March 31, 1975.
NA = not available.
Source: Bulova Annual Reports; Diamond's Japan Business Directory; Japan Company Handbook; and The Analyst's Guide.

The World VCR Industry

The origins of the modern videocassette recorder can be dated to September of 1951, when David Sarnoff, chairman of RCA, made a public speech challenging the technical staff of his company to develop "a television picture recorder that would record the video signals of television" within the next five years. Although RCA failed to be first, Sarnoff's challenge was met by Ampex Corporation, a small California engineering firm, which introduced the first commercially viable videotape recorder (VTR) in 1956. For the next 20 years, companies in various countries conducted R&D toward the goal of developing a video recorder for home use. Even though American companies invented the technology and dominated the world market for professional VTRs, Sony was the first company to mass-market home videocassette recorders (VCRs). By the mid-1980s, the consumer market was dominated by the Japanese. No U.S. firm manufactured VCRs, the Europeans were minor players, and Korean companies could only challenge Japan at the low end of the market.

THE EARLY MARKET

Before World War I, the world leaders in electronics were British and German firms. It was not until the 1920s that leadership shifted to the United States. The burgeoning domestic market for radio receiving sets in the thirties and government demand during WWII provided further catalysts to American dominance in electronics. The initial demand for video-recording did not emerge until television broadcasting began in 1946. By 1951, more than 11 million households in the United States had television receivers and close to 500,000 sets were being sold monthly. Television programs were broadcast live on a regional basis, but with coast-to-coast network broadcasting on the horizon, a means of time-delayed transmission was needed. At the time, audio signals were already being recorded and reproduced using magnetized tape. Engineers recognized that television signals could also be recorded on tape, but their greater frequency range posed technical difficulties (see *Appendix 1*). Although lab-

Research Assistant Ralinda Young Lurie prepared this note under the supervision of Associate Professor David B. Yoffie as the basis for class discussion. It is based, in part, on a research report prepared by Makoto Aoki and Katsuya Debari, Harvard MBAs, 1987.

oratories around the world experimented with various technologies, it was Ampex Corporation which emerged as the early winner.

Ampex[1]

The Ampex Corporation was an innovative engineering firm started in 1944. During World War II, the company made high-performance motors and generators for naval radar systems. After the war, management tried to leverage its military technology for the civilian marketplace. Their first product was a professional tape recorder inspired by a German Magnetophon, or magnetic tape recorder, which had been recovered from a German radio station in 1945. Ampex engineers mastered magnetic recording technology and developed a commercially successful line of audio recording equipment. The company also diversified into instrumentation equipment for scientific, military, and industrial applications. This market benefited from growing government spending in the United States for defense and space programs during the 1950s and 1960s. In all these fields, Ampex earned a strong reputation for developing innovative products which set standards for performance.

After the success of the company's initial entry into the civilian electronics industry, several Ampex engineers explored the idea of developing a videorecorder. An experimental model VTR (the VR-1000) was shown at a convention of TV broadcasters in 1956. Although not optimal in design, the VR-1000 was an immediate success: 100 of the $75,000 machines were ordered during the four-day convention. Recognizing the importance of the invention, Ampex aggressively sought to create an installed base in the broadcast market. By 1961, the company had sold almost 900 VTRs, about three-fourths of all videotape recorders in use. Nearly 300 of these machines were in service overseas. The company was also able to patent the fundamental VTR technology. This tech-

nology was so vital to the workings of all videorecorders that no other company was able to legally manufacture a VTR without a license from Ampex.

The four-head Ampex VTR system became the standard in the broadcast industry even though it was difficult to operate and maintain. In order to improve the product, Ampex widely crossed-licensed its patented technology with other firms. The possibilities for the technology seemed so great and the firm's position so strong that Ampex managers were not overly concerned about the competitive implications of transferring the technology. Thus the company entered into a cross-licensing agreement with RCA to achieve color recording. In exchange for its color patents, RCA was licensed to use the patented inventions embodied in the VR-1000 VTR. In 1959 Ampex also exchanged its technology for Sony's help in developing a VTR with transistorized circuits. Further cooperation with Sony ended after only two years due to a disagreement over royalty payments related to Sony's use of Ampex patents.

Ampex revenues boomed during the 1950s. Sales increased from $10 million in fiscal 1956 to almost $70 million by the end of fiscal 1960, while net earnings rose more than 1,000% during that five-year period. The company entered new markets including consumer audio equipment, magnetic recording tape, and computer memory products. Ampex also reorganized into five independent divisions in an attempt to maintain its entrepreneurial environment. However, the reorganization led to higher overhead costs which, along with flat VTR sales and increased competition, contributed to a net loss of $3.9 million on $70 million of sales in fiscal 1961. Ampex then hired a new CEO, William E. Roberts, who sought to reestablish Ampex's dynamic growth in revenues and profits by broadening the scope of its operations. In 1962, Roberts told security analysts that he planned to concentrate all of his efforts on "video, instrumentation and audio recording equipment, magnetic tape and computer memory products." He encouraged the development of unique, high-performance equipment for special applications while expanding the company's involvement in the consumer audio equipment market. By 1965, Ampex was marketing a full line of consumer audio products through retail stores and wholesalers across the United States. The company claimed to have 50% of the high-end market for audio tape recorders, while the Japanese dominated the low end. As Roberts commented in a 1967 *Business Week* article, "This prospect changes our whole format. Ampex has always been heavily oriented toward R&D and pushing out the state-of-the-art frontiers in magnetic recording. Now we're merchandisers too."

In the bull market environment of the 1960s, Ampex was one of the glamour stocks of Wall Street, trading at prices reaching 35 times earnings. Its record as a technological leader and its revenue and net profit growth of 18% per year, on average, provided Ampex with easy access to the capital markets. During this period, the company's invested capital rose at a compound annual rate of 26% as funding was needed for product development, plant construction, and the expansion of operations overseas. But Ampex continued to focus on the bottom line: Roberts wanted to maintain his stock price, so he continually pressured the organization for strong quarterly financial results in all product areas. Hence when margins got squeezed in 1968, Ampex reexamined its strategy. With competition rising in both the audio and video markets, the company commissioned an internal report which acknowledged the company's technical expertise but indicated that its manufacturing and distribution operations were weak. The report also recommended that Ampex actively pursue the consumer videorecorder market—a low-priority segment for Ampex during most of the 1960s. Ampex preferred to focus on expensive, higher-margin machines.

One outcome of the report was Instavideo, the Ampex response to the needs of the mass market (see *Exhibit 1*). Ampex had introduced a VTR for the consumer market once before in 1965. That black-and-white machine was perceived by consumers as too expensive and complicated to use. Instavideo, however, was a unique product for its time. It was lightweight, easy to use, offered many special features, and was capable of both playback and recording in monochrome or color. Instavideo was priced at $1,000 for the color recorder-player alone, with the camera available for an additional $500. It was a tremendous hit in 1970 when it was first introduced. Ampex's problem was that it did not have the requisite skills or facilities to manufacture a technologically sophisticated product in volume and at low cost. Given the company's cash-constrained position, Roberts decided to use the manufacturing capabilities of Toamco, Ampex's joint venture with Japan's Toshiba. Toamco, which was formed in 1964, was already manufacturing audio tape recorders and computer tape transports for sale by both companies. But Toamco also had no experience in manufacturing a complicated, low-cost, high-volume product. Nevertheless, Ampex prepared to produce Instavideo, building the manufacturing tools in the United States while making necessary changes in product design.

While the division prepared for a full-scale introduction of the videorecorder, the company experienced serious financial difficulties resulting from its aggressive expansion in the 1960s. A loss of $12 million was reported in fiscal 1971, and by fiscal 1972 its losses had grown to nearly $90 million. Roberts resigned and Ampex underwent a major restructuring, as plants were closed, businesses were discontinued, and operations were consolidated. In 1972, the new management at Ampex saw the Instavideo project as an ambitious venture beyond the dwindling resources of the company and terminated the project.

Ampex's U.S. Competition[2]

Ampex's primary U.S. competitor was RCA, which had one-third of worldwide VTR sales in the early 1960s. RCA was one of the world's great technological innovators. The company's legacy as a pioneer in the consumer electronics industry was symbolized by the firm's dominance of radio manufacturing prior to World War II: RCA had more than 2,000 patents pertaining to radio tubes and other kinds of wireless equipment. RCA also invested heavily in the development of electronic television receivers and sold more television-related goods in the late 1940s than the rest of the industry combined. As the leader in color TV technology, RCA received substantial license revenues from other manufacturers. Sarnoff stated publicly that he believed RCA was better off licensing technology and focusing on technological innovation for the U.S. market rather than aggressively seeking overseas markets for RCA hardware. When RCA technicians predicted that the market for color televisions would reach saturation by the mid-1970s, RCA explored home videoplayers as a means to extend its product line.

Several different research laboratories at RCA surveyed the existing forms of videorecording and playback equipment and undertook small, uncoordinated research projects to explore recording technologies and storage mediums. After rejecting the conventional approaches of using magnetic tape for a recording video system, RCA opted for a complex videoplayer, which it introduced under the name Selectavision in 1969. The first product was Selectavision Holotape. This videoplayer utilized lasers and holography for the first time in a consumer application. The exotic technology plus the use of low-cost materials was designed to produce a videoplayer priced well below the competition. However, Holotape's technical performance at its initial public demonstration in 1969 was poor. As more problems emerged

and as estimates of the cost of the system rose from $450 per unit to about $750, RCA opted to pursue other technologies. The ultimate choice was the videodisc—a high-risk approach which required revolutionary technological developments to make it work. RCA management chose this path because they wanted to reestablish their tarnished image as a technological leader. In the view of management, RCA had been humiliated by its computer battle with IBM, which resulted in a $250 million write-off in 1971. The videodisc, they hoped, would alter the market's perceptions.

The purpose of RCA's disc format videoplayer was to provide a reliable machine with a high-quality picture that could be purchased for less than $500. Recording was not considered to be necessary since the company planned to use its subsidiaries, NBC and RCA Records, to develop adequate software. After more than 15 years of development and an investment of about $200 million, RCA introduced the Selectavision VideoDisc in 1981. Sales were disappointing in the first year despite a $20 million investment in advertising. This translated into an advertising cost of approximately $200 for each player sold. In the VideoDisc's second and third years on the market, RCA temporarily boosted sales by drastically cutting prices. Dealers, however, were disappointed by the small margins compared to competing products and the burden of stocking prerecorded discs. By the spring of 1984, RCA announced it would discontinue production of the Selectavision VideoDisc and took a $175 million pretax write-off.

RCA's broadcasting rival, CBS, also tried to participate in the emerging video industry with its Electronic Video Recording (EVR) system. Conceived and developed at CBS Labs, EVR was designed to play back prerecorded programs using high-resolution photographic film. Introduced in 1968, the first videoplayers were targeted to institutional buyers for educational purposes, with the home market seen as three to five years in the future. Motorola had the exclusive license to produce the EVR players in the United States, while CBS would duplicate the cartridges. The *New York Times* and a number of film production companies signed agreements with CBS to produce new or convert existing programs to the EVR cartridge. Despite its $800 price tag and the high cost of producing cartridges, analysts were excited by the EVR system. Even though Motorola had trouble meeting its production schedules and programming was not readily available, the first EVR players were delivered in the fall of 1970. A year later, CBS announced it would no longer market the EVR, citing slow progress in developing the videocartridge market. CBS lost between $35 and $40 million.

The only other U.S. company accepting the videorecorder challenge was Cartridge Television, Inc. (CTI). Organized as a start-up in 1968 with approximately $7,000 of capital, CTI tried to develop and commercialize a videoplayer designed by a wholly owned subsidiary of a U.S. Volkswagen distributor. Its Cartrivision system offered a record and playback format. CTI went public in 1971, and its Cartrivision system reached retail outlets for the first time in 1972. The Cartrivision player-recorder hardware was sold to manufacturers of TV receivers and incorporated into their television consoles. Sears and Montgomery Ward marketed these combination TV/VCRs at prices well above $1,000. After the product encountered problems with hardware, tape quality, and software availability, CTI's largest shareholder (a diversified U.S. electronics firm) refused to provide additional operating funds, and CTI was forced to file for bankruptcy in 1973.

Although the basic technology pioneered by Ampex in the 1950s remained the industry standard into the 1980s, no American company succeeded in commercializing a videorecorder for the consumer market. Some observers speculated that this failure to play a leadership role in the videorecorder industry could affect U.S. involvement in subsequent applications of recording technologies relating to computers, communications equipment, and advanced personal electronics products, such as high-definition television (HDTV). America's best hope in this industry had been Ampex. But as Richard Rosenbloom and Karen Freeze of the Harvard Business School concluded in a major study of VCRs: "With the demise of Instavideo, American industry lost its best chance to participate in mass market for videocassette recorders. . . . The lessons inherent in Ampex's failure have . . . broader significance to American management."

DEVELOPMENTS IN JAPAN[3]

By 1955, Japan's economy had recovered to prewar levels. Japanese industrial planners identified electronics as a priority sector and encouraged the activities of consumer products companies through various government assistance programs. Faced with a small domestic market and very small homes that did not have space for many products, the industry initially grew through exports of low-volume specialty items. As Japanese firms mastered techniques of mass manufacturing and the technology of miniaturization, they created new consumer markets in the United States. Using transistors these companies pioneered small-screen TV receivers, low-priced radios and tape recorders, and compact stereo systems. Through the 1950s and 1960s, most American companies showed little interest in competing against Japan for these low-end consumer electronics products.

Even though television broadcasting did not begin in Japan until 1953, 54% of Japanese households owned TV sets by 1957. NHK (the Japanese national broadcasting corporation) imported an Ampex VR-1000 in 1958 and put the machine on display in Tokyo to encourage Japanese electronics companies to develop their own VTRs. Sony, in conjunction with the NHK

Lab, built a replica of the VR-1000. The machine was bulky and expensive, like the Ampex model, but the experience convinced Sony that a consumer videorecorder could be a logical extension of the company's product line.

Sony

Established in 1946 as a technology-driven consumer electronics company, Sony's basic philosophy was to develop innovative consumer products, which would often necessitate *creating* consumer demand. One of Sony's most significant early moves came in 1954 when the company bought a license to manufacture products using the transistor technology developed by Bell Labs. Transistors became the cornerstone of Sony's efforts to miniaturize products for consumer applications. Sony used transistors to manufacture and export high-quality, low-cost products ranging from portable radios to TVs. The company also distinguished itself from other Japanese companies with its marketing strategy. Even though Sony's distribution network in Japan was weak compared to some of its larger competitors (in the late 1970s, for instance, Sony had only 1,500 "Sony Shops," which was less than half the number for Matsushita), the company rarely sold its products on an OEM basis. Unlike most Japanese firms who entered the U.S. consumer electronics market by supplying OEM products to American mass merchandisers, Sony sought to create a worldwide reputation based on quality and a distinctive brand name.

Beginning in the late 1950s, Sony kept a project team working on a home videorecorder. The company's first VTR was designed for educational and industrial use. Introduced in 1962, it was one-fiftieth the size of the Ampex machine with a simpler recording system. American Airlines ordered 60 Sony machines for their in-flight movies. Almost a decade later in 1971, Sony introduced one of the first videocassette recorders (VCRs) for the consumer market. Like the American videorecorders and videoplayers, buyers found Sony's "U-matic" machines and cassettes too big and expensive. After some modifications, however, Sony sold the machine to industrial users. The company hoped that its learning from these institutional sales would lead to technological improvements and the development of lower-cost consumer products.

After CBS introduced its EVR system and RCA had announced Selectavision, Sony began to fear that these systems would threaten the future acceptance of magnetic tape VCRs for the home market. Sony therefore approached JVC and Matsushita, two of its biggest competitors, about establishing a Japanese industry standard around a new Sony technology which would reduce machine size. While the three companies agreed to share existing technologies, the competitors would only accept Sony's basic U-matic format, which remained too large for home use. Sony and JVC refused to cooperate or compromise on technology for smaller machines.

Matsushita and JVC

In the 1970s and 1980s, Matsushita was the largest Japanese manufacturer of home electrical products with the biggest chain of dedicated retail outlets in Japan. Its products were marketed under a number of brand names including National (domestic home appliances), Technics (audio equipment), Panasonic, and Quasar (both overseas brand names). Matsushita was considered to have expertise in marketing and distribution rather than product innovation. With an enormous sales network selling only Matsushita products, the company's primary objective was to ensure that its retail network of 18,000 "National Shops" and 12,000 cooperating stores were full with consumer appliances.

In 1953, Matsushita acquired 50% of the Victor Corporation of Japan (JVC), formerly a subsidiary of the Victor Company of America. JVC operated as an independent company with only financial ties to its parent. The company had proven expertise in audio and video technology, having produced Japan's first TV set in 1939, LP record in 1953, and stereo phonograph in 1958. By the early 1960s, JVC's product lines included TVs, radios, stereos, tape recorders, movie cameras, and electronic musical instruments, as well as office equipment. JVC and Matsushita, like Sony, began researching video recording in the mid-1950s; all three companies also competed in the commercial VTR market. However, while Sony made a modest profit in its VTR business, Matsushita and JVC lost money on most of their VTR projects. Despite the red ink, both companies continuously maintained VTR development efforts targeted toward the consumer. At JVC a special video home system (VHS) project team was put together in 1971 to develop a consumer VCR. The manager of the VHS project instructed his team of marketing, production, and design specialists not to ask what was technologically possible, but rather "to determine what consumers wanted in a home VCR and then to develop the technology to meet those requirements."

DEVELOPMENT OF THE CONSUMER VCR

It's no secret: cartridge television is on the way. Nobody knows exactly when it is coming, or exactly what it will bring, and nobody knows even approximately how big it will get to be; but the potential seems tremendous, both for all sorts of businessmen and for the great American television audience. (*Fortune*, June 1971.)

At the time of this article, there were approximately 40 companies working on various videoplayer systems involving four different and incompatible technologies. Over the next 15 years, the industry evolved from addressing the specialized requirements of broadcasters, to providing a general industrial and educational tool, to serving the consumer. VCRs were made smaller, lighter, and easier to use through the development of new recording technology and tape cassettes, experience in volume manufacturing of precision components, and semiconductor advances.

In the early 1970s, Sony identified 10 different ways of building a home VCR and created research teams to explore each of these alternatives. By mid-1974 a prototype, named Betamax, had been developed. Sony invested in a new plant facility to manufacture the Betamax, setting up a line capable of producing about 10,000 units per month. It also prepared the molds needed for mass production of the machine. The Betamax and Sony's marketing strategy was based on the idea of time-shifting. The company believed that consumers would primarily use a VCR to record TV programs for later viewing. In order to make the machine as compact as possible, Sony restricted the length of its recording capability, since the company believed that an hour of recording time was adequate to accommodate most television programming.

In the fall of 1974, Sony asked Matsushita and JVC to adopt Sony's Beta format. Both companies rejected the idea. Although Matsushita executives conceded that Sony had an excellent product, they cited Betamax's one-hour recording time as a major drawback. JVC was convinced of the superiority of its forthcoming VHS format (which was expected to deliver up to three hours of taping). Having failed to convince its Japanese competitors, Sony proceeded to market the Betamax in Japan in 1975 and in the United States a year later (see *Exhibit 2*). After the Betamax was introduced to the Japanese market, Hitachi approached Sony about licensing the Beta technology. Sony rejected the idea because of its uncertainty regarding Matsushita's response to an agreement with Hitachi and its concern that the Beta technology was not perfected.

JVC took a slightly different tack from Sony: it attempted to form an alliance of Japanese companies that would agree to accept the VHS as the standard format for the industry before it shipped its first product. A tentative alliance was developed with Matsushita, Hitachi, Mitsubishi, Sharp, Sanyo, and Toshiba. However, since VHS VCRs were not ready for mass production, Matsushita continued trying to market its own VX-2000 format VCRs and Sanyo and Toshiba introduced machines using competing technologies. The two warring camps, headed by Sony and JVC, approached Japan's Ministry of International Trade and Industry (MITI) in mid-1976, seeking mediation on the issue of standardization. Since neither company was willing to compromise, no agreement could be reached.

In October of 1976, JVC put its VHS format VCR on sale. Hitachi, which had entered into an OEM contract with JVC, was supplied with machines late in the year. Sharp also received shipments by early 1977. In January of 1977, Matsushita abandoned its VX-2000 VCR under pressure from its retail outlets which objected to the machine's poor picture quality and large cassette. Sony responded to JVC's growing coalition by seeking its own allies; Sanyo, Toshiba, and others soon joined the Beta group. The split of VCR manufacturers into two "families" affected the industry for the next 10 years (see *Exhibit 3*).

Akio Morita, chairman of Sony since its inception, proclaimed 1976 "the first year of the home VCR era" (see *Exhibits 4* and *5*). He predicted that the VCR would be the next major product in the consumer electronics industry after color television and promised that Sony would bet its future on the VCR. At the outset, Sony looked as though it would dominate the market. It distributed the VCRs not only to Sony-affiliated retailers but also to those affiliated with other manufacturers. In 1976 and 1977, the company maintained a market share of over 50%. Sony also aimed at expanding its market share among discount stores in metropolitan areas. By the end of 1977, almost 80% of the VCRs sold in the two biggest discount districts of Japan were believed to be the Betamax.

By the end of 1978, however, Matsushita replaced Sony as the share leader in VCR production with 35.8% of the market, while Sony's share dropped from 51.1% in 1977 to 27.9%. By 1988, the last chapter of the VHS-Beta battle was probably written: VHS had close to 95% of world sales, leading Sony to offer a line of low- and medium-priced VHS machines alongside its high-end Betamax.

THE U.S. VCR MARKET

Rather than produce VCRs, American firms opted to market the machines through OEM agreements with Japanese companies. In February of 1977, for example, Zenith announced that it would receive VCRs from Sony while Sanyo supplied Beta-format machines to Sears. In the same year, Magnavox and GTE Sylvania agreed to sell VHS-format VCRs manufactured by Matsushita. RCA reached an agreement with Matsushita which supplied RCA with VHS machines capable of recording for four hours. RCA made the request because "football games can easily go beyond three hours." The company aggressively marketed VCRs under its Selectavision name through its extensive distribution network. Priced at $1,000, the RCA VCR was about $300 less than comparable products while offering twice the playing time of other machines. RCA initially captured more than a quarter of the home VCR market in the United States (see *Exhibit 6*). Zenith, Sony, and other competitors had to follow RCA's lead by cutting prices (see *Exhibit 7*).

U.S. market penetration for VCRs rose from less than 2% in 1979 to more than 50% in 1987. This compared to a 31% penetration rate in Japan. The increasing sophistication of VCR devices along with the growing availability of prerecorded tapes stimulated sales. Analysts believed that 50% of VCR use in the United States was for prerecorded tapes. This compared to 75% in Europe and 5% in Japan, which did not introduce a rental system until April 1983. In both Japan and the United States, X-rated movies were the early mainstay of the market for prerecorded tapes. According to the *Wall Street Journal*, X-rated movies once accounted for up to 70% of rentals in 1978. In 1981, their share was down to below 50% of the $800 million rental tape market. The availability of rental tapes also influenced the consumer's choice of VCR hardware. In 1984 *Time* asserted that "the major disadvantage of buying Beta is that video rental stores often stock smaller inventories of prerecorded Beta cassettes."

THE EUROPEAN VCR MARKET

In 1972 Philips Corporation, the Dutch giant, marketed its first VCR. Developed for the institutional market, this machine enjoyed some success in Europe. Two consumer models were introduced in the mid-1970s. However, according to a Centre for Business Research report, these machines were "universally disliked because of [their] poor reliability—estimates have been given of 80% of the products being returned with faults." In addition, tapes were "notoriously difficult to obtain." The next consumer VCR developed by Philips was the V-2000. Japanese engineers considered the V-2000 to be an excellent product technologically, but its complex mechanism created manufacturing difficulties resulting in the machine selling for 20 to 30% more than comparable Japanese products.

In the early 1980s, the VHS format made up about two-thirds of the VCRs sold in Europe, Beta models represented almost a quarter of the market, and Philips' V-2000 accounted for a little more than 10%. Dissatisfied with European Community (EC) efforts to put a halt to the Japanese VCR "invasion," France decided to take matters into its own hands. On October 26, 1982, the French government announced that all imports of VCRs could be cleared only through Poitiers, an inland customs post with only a few inspectors. In addition, the French required foreign exporters to gain prior approval before they shipped to France. A few weeks after the French announcement, Philips and its VCR partner Grundig filed antidumping suits against Japanese VCR exporters. This was the largest antidumping suit in the history of Japanese-EC trade.

Instead of retaliating, Japan opted to negotiate a voluntary export restraint (VER) with Europe. The arrangement on VCRs, concluded in February of 1983, limited Japanese exports in 1983 to 4.55 million units and set restrictions on the price and Japan's overall market share. This European effort did "preserve" a domestic VCR industry—several European firms manufactured VCRs in the late 1980s. By 1988, however, European VCRs (including Philips) were produced under license from Japanese firms. Most Japanese VCR manufacturers had also set up assembly operations in Europe after 1982 (see *Exhibit 8*).

THE ENTRY OF KOREA

Korean consumer electronics companies had signed agreements licensing VCR technology from a number of Japanese companies in the early 1980s. All these agreements contained standstill clauses prohibiting Korean VCR exports to major foreign markets until 1985. According to the 1987 *Japan Electronics Almanac*, the vertically integrated Japanese firms as well as their suppliers had also "monopolize[d] almost all the development and production technologies . . ." (p. 171), especially in high-precision VCR components. This forced Korea to import between 40 and 60% of the components used in a Korean VCR.

When the Koreans entered the U.S. market in 1985, they sold inexpensive "promotional brands" usually on an OEM basis to mass merchandisers. The Japanese response was not to compete on price but instead to push higher value-added machines with extra features. U.S. retailers were reportedly apprehensive about the quality of the Korean machines, but by the end of 1985 they represented about 5% of all imported VCRs. The median price of a Korean VCR was approximately 30% below that of a Japanese VCR. As product quality improved in 1986, Korea became the second largest VCR exporter in the world with a 9% global share. More than half of Korean sales went to the United States.

THE NEXT FRONTIERS?

By the mid-1980s, the explosive market for VCRs began to slow. U.S. sales of VCRs in 1988 were expected to reach 10 million units, while Hitachi estimated that Asian firms had production capacity for the U.S. market of 17 to 18 million units. This led all large VCR firms to extend their product lines: JVC and its "family" introduced new, smaller camcorders as well as higher-resolution "Super" VHS systems; meanwhile Sony pushed a variety of new products, including 8-mm camcorders,* and 3-inch, flat-screen, pocketbook-sized 8-mm VCRs for watching movies on the subway or at your desk. Many companies also began selling integrated systems, with VCRs, TVs, and audio equipment bundled together.

The future of VCRs and video technology was uncertain in the late 1980s. In addition, the implications of Japan's dominance of VCRs for the electronics industries in the United States and Europe were widely debated. As new generations of video and information technologies were being prepared for market, observers wondered if the VCR story would be repeated.†

---

*Sony hoped that 8 mm would become the new standard: 8 mm, which could be used in a VCR with an adapter, offered higher quality and smaller size. Some observers speculated that Sony's purchase of CBS Records in 1986 was partly motivated by a desire to establish a captive distribution system for prerecorded tapes that would use Sony's format.

†In the late 1980s, some observers drew parallels between HDTV and VCRs. Japan, for instance, began development of HDTV in the late 1960s. Even though few HDTVs had been sold by 1988, Japanese firms had spent an estimated $700 million on HDTV R&D in the 1980s, while Europe had spent $220 million and U.S. firms virtually nothing. Estimates for the HDTV market ranged from $20 billion to $100 billion in annual sales by 2005. Like VCRs, which consumed approximately 12% of Japan's chip output and 5% of the world's semiconductors, HDTV would require huge volumes of sophisticated components, especially chips.

THE AMPEX INSTAVIDEO AND ITS 5-POUND CAMERA, 4.6-INCH CARTRIDGE, 1970–1971

Source: Reprinted form Richard S. Rosenbloom and Karen Freeze, "Ampex Corporation and Video Innovation," in Richard S. Rosenbloom, ed., *Research on Technological Innovation, Management and Policy*, vol. 2, 1985, Jai Press. Copyright © The President and Fellows of Harvard College.

EXHIBIT TWO

CONSUMER ELECTRONICS COMPANIES' SELECTED FINANCIALS ($MM)

RCA	1960	1965	1970	1975	1980	1985[a]
Sales	1,494.9	2,472.4	3,325.6	4,815.8	8,011.3	8,972.1
Net profit	35.1	116.7	91.7	110.0	315.3	369.1
NPP&E[b]	239.5	349.9	781.5	1,205.7	1,368.6	1,939.7
LTD	151.9	261.4	592.9	1,261.6	1,771.2	1,960.1
Equity	432.9	680.4	1,063.6	1,179.9	1,862.2	2,657.1
Total assets	815.5	1,269.4	2,936.1	3,728.4	7,147.6	6,705.0
Capital expense	NA	88.8	178.4	271.7	452.0	301.7
Depreciation	27.2	62.4	214.5	288.9	494.3	137.4

Matsushita	1960	1965	1970	1975	1980	1986
Sales	255.8	808.2	2,588.2	4,571.9	13,689.9	28,066.9
Net profit	29.1	39.4	195.7	104.6	584.9	1,004.1
NPP&E	37.6	192.7	323.6	577.9	1,458.8	3,440.2
LTD	8.8	83.9	94.9	125.4	276.0	866.6
Equity	66.1	257.1	898.9	1,889.9	5,128.8	13,321.2
Total assets	195.3	781.6	2,040.0	4,206.0	11,636.0	26,826.5
Capital expense	NA	NA	NA	117.3	610.4	937.7
Depreciation	NA	NA	65.0	93.2	304.9	1,013.4

Sony	1961	1965	1970	1975	1980	1986
Sales	52.3	104.6	414.4	1,062.8	4,231.1	5,764.4
Net profit	2.1	4.6	27.5	80.0	325.3	258.6
NPP&E	16.0	34.2	107.0	273.5	791.6	2,053.2
LTD	4.7	10.1	7.9	6.9	44.6	888.2
Equity	19.7	32.9	130.8	576.3	1,542.8	3,743.2
Total assets	56.7	124.5	445.0	2,005.3	4,158.4	8,951.5
Capital expense	NA	NA	35.2	40.7	230.9	581.1
Depreciation	1.4	3.0	13.9	35.1	117.1	486.5

Ampex	1960	1965	1970	1975	1980[c]	
Sales	68.1	153.5	296.3	244.9	469.0	
Net profit	4.0	7.7	13.7	10.3	34.7	
NPP&E	5.1	29.8	68.5	51.9	61.9	
LTD	5.8	33.1	150.7	140.9	77.4	
Equity	31.4	60.7	148.8	62.1	165.7	
Total assets	51.2	135.0	386.1	261.7	350.6	
Capital expense	NA	9.9	26.2	12.9	20.3	
Depreciation	NA	6.6	10.9	12.2	7.8	

[a]RCA Corp. was merged into the General Electric Co. in June 1986.
[b]Net property, plant, and equipment.
[c]In October 1980, an agreement of merger was reached between Ampex and Signal.
Sources: Annual reports, 10Ks, and *Moody's Industrial Manual.*

EXHIBIT THREE

ENTERING VCRs: MAJOR JAPANESE FIRMS

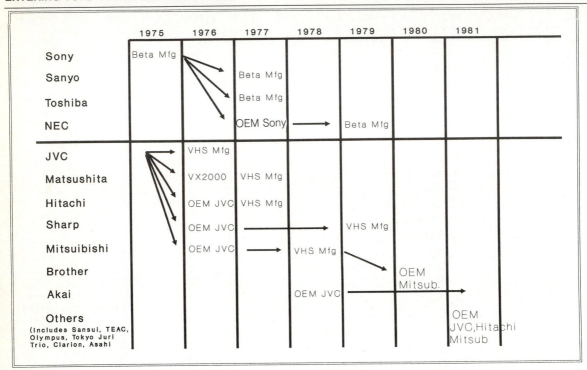

Source: Adapted from Nomura Research Institute data.

JAPANESE PRODUCTION AND EXPORT OF VCRs

(Hundred Million Yen; Thousand Units)

	Production		Exports		Domestic shipments	Exports by region		
	Units	Value	Units	Value	Units	U.S. units	EC units	Other units
1975	119	247	70	NA	NA	NA	NA	NA
1976	288	570	139	309	149	96	22	21
1977	762	1,260	402	659	360	329	31	42
1978	1,470	2,041	973	1,671	400	545	258	170
1979	2,199	2,961	1,671	2,223	480	680	522	469
1980	4,441	5,628	3,444	4,436	952	1,033	1,320	1,091
1981	9,498	10,867	7,355	8,535	1,547	2,367	2,854	2,126
1982	13,134	12,849	10,652	10,794	2,343	2,503	4,943	3,206
1983	18,216	15,139	15,237	12,607	3,658	5,440	4,647	5,150
1984	28,611	20,900	22,071	16,206	4,271	11,896	3,752	6,423
1985	30,581	19,111	25,475	15,841	4,006	15,922	3,261	6,292
1986	34,240	18,500E	27,689	NA	4,853	17,998[a]	3,018	6,673

[a]Value was approximately $4.4 billion (c.i.f.); sale of video cassettes was another $1.4 billion.
Source: Japan Electronics Almanac.

HOME VCR PRODUCTION SHARE IN JAPAN

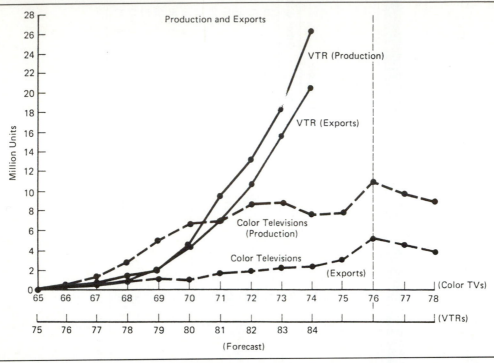

Source: EIAJ, NRI.

U.S. MARKET SHARES OF HOME VCRs AND VCPs[a] (1981–1986)

	Format	1986	1985	1984	1983	1982	1981
RCA	V	12.0%	13.8%	16.0%	16.0%	22.0%	28.0%
Panasonic	V	11.3	12.1	14.0	15.0	17.8	15.3
Fisher	V	6.8	7.7	6.0	5.0	2.0	
Sears	B/V	5.0	5.0	4.6	4.7	3.5	3.3
GE	V	5.0	5.0	5.0	5.5	5.0	3.3
Sharp	V	4.8	4.0	3.5	3.0	1.5	1.2
Sanyo	B	4.0	4.0	5.0	5.0	4.0	2.6
Magnavox	V	4.0	4.0	4.0	4.7	4.0	4.5
Mitsubishi	V	4.0	3.3	2.0	2.0	1.0	1.0
Zenith	B/V	4.0	3.5	3.0	2.6	4.1	6.0
Emerson	V	4.0	2.0	0.9			
JVC	V	3.5	3.6	5.0	5.0	4.1	3.9
Toshiba	B/V	3.5	3.1	1.5	1.2	1.0	1.5
Sony	B	3.1	4.8	6.5	7.0	13.0	14.2
Quasar	V	3.0	4.1	5.0	4.6	3.5	6.0
Hitachi	V	3.0	3.5	3.8	4.0	3.4	2.0
NEC	V	2.0	1.0	1.0			
Samsung	V	2.0	0.9				

[a]Firms with less than 2% included Goldstar, Penney, Montgomery Ward, Sylvania, Curtis Mathis, Radio Shack, Philco, Symphonic, Lloyds, and Canon.
Source: Television Digest.

EXHIBIT SEVEN

VCR UNIT FACTORY PRICES AND OUTPUT

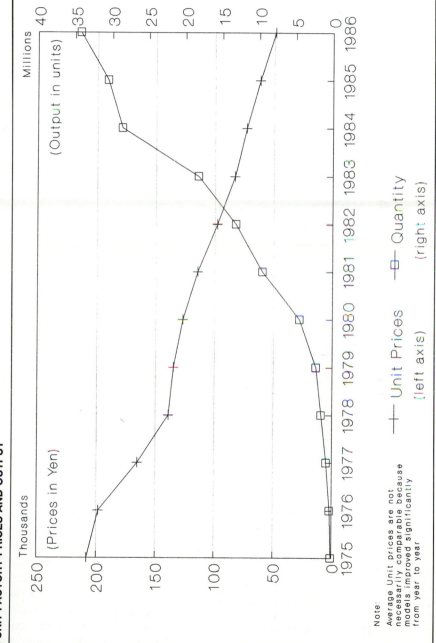

Note:
Average Unit prices are not
necessarily comparable because
models improved significantly
from year to year

Source: Japan Electronics Almanac, 1987.

EXHIBIT EIGHT

PROJECTED VCR PRODUCTION IN 1990 (percentage by region)

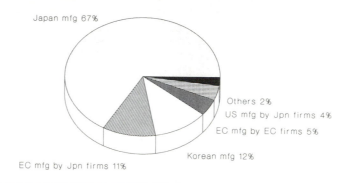

Japan mfg 67%

Others 2%
US mfg by Jpn firms 4%
EC mfg by EC firms 5%

Korean mfg 12%

EC mfg by Jpn firms 11%

Source: Japan Electronics Almanac, 1987.

APPENDIX 1

VCR TECHNOLOGY

In Margaret Graham's book *RCA and the Video Disc: The Business of Research*, she described the many ways to design a videoplayer system:

The videoplayer provided a means of storing, retrieving, and playing back visual and audio images through a television set. It was a more challenging achievement than audio because the amount of information involved was 200 times as great as that stored on a long-playing (LP) record.

The elements involved in any videoplayer included a high-density storage medium capable of accommodating the vast amount of information required in a manageable space, a mastering process capable of storing the information as a signal or an image on the medium, and an electronic retrieval device capable of detecting and playing the information back with high resolution comparable to other available visual-image technologies such as television and film.

Each element of the system could be approached in several possible ways. Media alternatives included film, magnetic or nonmagnetic tape, and hard vinyl discs, either grooved or ungrooved, of various sizes, coated or uncoated. Information could be stored in several different formats, but the main options were photographic images, optical images, or signals. The storage had to involve a mastering method, since the purpose was to replicate prerecorded programs many times over. This could be electromechanical, as in traditional audio recordings, photographic, electron beam, or optical, using a laser beam. The pickup device could be a magnetic head, an electromechanical needle in a groove, an electronic capacitance sensor, a piezoelectric needle (pressure pickup), or a laser optical device.

Although VCRs contained thousands of electronic components, the principal elements required for operation included (1) the recording medium and recording head, (2) the scanner and its transport mechanism, and (3) the electronic circuitry which processed the signals to and from the head as well as controlled the mechanical actions of the machine. VCRs, along with PCs, were also among the biggest markets for semiconductor memory products and other sophisticated semiconductor components.

Since video signals have a much higher and wider frequency range than audio signals, VCRs required a writing speed 100 times greater than was necessary for audio recorders. (The writing speed is the rate at which the recording head scans the medium.) The design of the scanner mechanism, therefore, represented a critical technical choice in the development of a VCR. Three scanner formats were developed as the industry evolved. In the first, the longitudinal scanner, a stationary recording head, scanned the magnetic tape as it passed by at a speed equal to the writing speed. This scanner format was used in the first VTR prototype developed by RCA. The second scanner design was the transverse scanner where the head rotated at the writing speed and scanned the tape crosswise as it passed the head at a rate much slower than the writing speed. The broadcast VTRs designed by Ampex operated with transverse scanners. The helical scanner was the third design which was the basis for the Beta- and VHS-format VCRs. With this format, rotating heads scanned the tape in a slanted pattern while the tape moved much slower than the writing speed.

Although Beta and VHS machines both used helical scanners, the formats were incompatible. The fundamental differences between the first Beta and VHS machines were their recording and playback capacities, cassette size, and tape-loading mechanisms. Sony continued to use the U-matic's loading format where the tape was wrapped around the head drum automatically when the cassette was loaded into the machine. This allowed for the rewind and fast-forward functions to be executed at high speeds. JVC's VHS cassette was about a third larger than the Betamax cassette. Its M-loading format pulled the tape past two small posts as opposed to the single large post in the U-matic system. Although Sony was familiar with the M-loading technique, having filed a patent on it in 1969, it felt that the two posts would create additional stress on the tape and would be prone to breakage. Most technical analysts assessed the performance of Beta VCRs as marginally superior to VHS machines. By 1988, however, the technical differences at the high end were insignificant.

NOTES

1. This section on Ampex draws heavily from Richard S. Rosenbloom and Karen Freeze, "Ampex Corporation and Video Innovation," in Richard S. Rosenbloom, ed., *Research on Technological Innovation, Management and Policy*, vol. 2, 1985, Jai Press.

2. This section draws heavily from Margaret Graham, *RCA and the Video Disc*, 1986, Cambridge University Press.

3. This section draws heavily from a note prepared in Japanese by Nomura Management School entitled (in translation) "Note on the VTR Industry, 1987 Edition," #N11-187-010. This section also draws from Richard S. Rosenbloom and Michael Cusumano, "Technological Pioneering and Competitive Advantage: The Birth of the VCR Industry," *California Management Review*, Summer 1987.

PART THREE

Comparative Disadvantage and Corporate Strategy

B-W Footwear

The President's decision to deny import relief to the footwear industry recognized that its contraction represents an adjustment to world market forces that are not a temporary but a permanent source of competitive pressure. Any efforts to reverse this process would be exceedingly expensive for American consumers and at the same time would deny market access to many debt-ridden developing countries.

1986 Economic Report of the President

For the second time in two years the Reagan administration had closed the door on import protection for domestic footwear manufacturers. Here was an industry that in 1968 had produced 640 million pairs of shoes in 1,000 plants employing 230,000 people. By the end of 1985 the industry's situation looked bleak: import penetration was over 70% of footwear sales and over 100,000 jobs had been lost.

Amidst this rather depressing situation, Robert Siff, chief executive officer of B-W Footwear Company, contemplated the future of his company. Siff was 61 years old and had been involved in his family's business since he graduated from Brown University in 1948. Now, 38 years later in June of 1986, he confided:

I have never seen the domestic shoe industry in such poor health. Import penetration was running at a rate of 81.7% through the first quarter of 1986, and every major footwear manufacturing firm is suffering. Even B-W, which has been outperforming virtually all of its domestic competitors, is having difficulty in this environment. For the first time in our company's history, we had a dramatic erosion of profits on domestically produced footwear in 1985. Which direction we should go in the next few years is a difficult question to answer.

THE U.S. FOOTWEAR INDUSTRY IN 1984

Demand for Nonrubber Footwear

In 1984, over 1 billion pairs of shoes were purchased in the United States (*Exhibit 1*), amounting to total producer sales of $8.6 billion. Sales

---

This case was prepared by Stewart C. Burton, MBA '86, and Associate Professor David B. Yoffie as the basis for class discussion rather than to illustrate either effective or ineffective handling of an administrative situation.

growth for the entire market had been relatively steady, with long-term demand for footwear being a function of the size and composition of the population. Within this broad market, changes in prices, incomes, and most important, styles, caused short-term demand to fluctuate considerably. Women's footwear accounted for over one-half of all consumption, primarily due to this segment's higher fashion-consciousness. Frequent styling changes resulted in a reduced product life for women's shoes, in contrast to men's, children's, and athletic footwear.

The market for footwear was highly segmented, reflecting the multitude of sizes, styles, materials, colors, and prices available to the consumer. Because of the diversity, less than 1% of an average shoe factory's yearly production was identical. This required a high degree of flexibility in the manufacturing process to meet the varied demand.

Evolution of the U.S. Footwear Industry

Footwear had been produced in the United States for over 200 years. Up until the early 1950s, the manufacturing process was characterized by relatively stable runs of few styles, providing some economies of scale to the larger manufacturers. With a growing market and negligible offshore competition, there was little cost pressure on domestic producers.

The industry began to change in the 1950s as Americans experienced rapid growth in their disposable incomes. Retailers demanded more and more styles to meet the growing needs of the consumer. As a result, manufacturers were forced to shorten production runs and provide a much wider line of fashionable footwear. With the profusion of fashions available, the risk inherent in making footwear also increased. Product obsolescence became a growing concern.

To compensate for the higher risk, domestic companies undertook certain strategies, including moving plants to low-wage states such as Tennessee, Arkansas, and Missouri. Others began purchasing smaller competitors, thereby increasing concentration in the industry (see *Exhibit 3*). Finally, many firms started to import lower-priced footwear, enabling them to augment their product lines and focus production on the more expensive and profitable mid- to upper-priced market segments.

Import penetration became significant in the late 1960s when foreign-priced footwear accounted for approximately 25% of consumption. Offshore competitors from the Far East were able to capitalize on the low wage rates in their countries and gain an absolute cost advantage over U.S. producers. Manufacturers from Taiwan and Korea came to dominate the lower end of the market by producing large quantities of inexpensive, less-fashionable shoes. These firms were able to capitalize on longer production runs because their product was less subject to fashion changes.

Domestic manufacturers retreated to the more expensive market segments throughout the 1970s but faced continued pressure at the top end from Italy and Spain. Italy had three educational institutions dedicated to training footwear designers; the United States had none. This lack of a domestic fashion center often meant that stylish foreign imports enjoyed a two- to six-month lead in fashionable offerings before U.S. producers could copy and diffuse the new styles. According to the General Accounting Office (GAO) in a study on the U.S footwear industry, domestic manufacturers were unwilling to forgo whatever economies could be achieved from longer production runs of less-stylish shoes.[1]

---

[1]Report to the Congress, *Slow Productivity Growth in the U.S. Footwear Industry—Can the Federal Government Help?*, U.S. General Accounting Office, February 25, 1980, p. 56.

Distribution

Footwear could be purchased in nearly 100,000 retail outlets across the United States; over three-quarters of all sales were accounted for by 25,000 shoe stores and 8,500 department stores. Retailers responded to consumer demands for fashion and price by sourcing footwear on a worldwide basis. The United States had no import quotas, but tariffs were above average: tariffs on men's leather footwear were approximately 8.5% ad valorem, and tariffs on women's leather footwear were approximately 10% to 15% ad valorem. All other things being equal, retailers preferred to buy domestically because delivery times were generally much shorter. Foreign shoes had to be ordered as much as nine months in advance, while U.S. manufacturers could generally deliver in four to eight weeks. Moreover, transportation time from overseas suppliers took approximately 30 days.

Domestic manufacturers capitalized on the greater profitability inherent in retailing by integrating forward. In 1984, Brown Shoe Company, the largest domestic shoe manufacturer, opened 134 outlets, bringing its total network to 1,902 units, while 60% of Genesco's total footwear business was accounted for by its retailing operations. The five largest retailers in the United States—Melville Corporation (Thom McAn), Woolworth Company (Kinney), Brown Group, Edison Brothers Stores, and Morse Shoe—together accounted for $4.7 billion in sales of the total industry retail sales of $22.1 billion. Concentration in shoe retailing had increased, with the eight largest firms accounting for almost 38% of total shoe store sales in 1982. These chains generally sold their own private-label brands in the lower- and middle-priced ranges, in contrast to independent shoe stores which sold more nationally branded footwear in the middle- and higher-priced segments.

Other channels included self-service stores (or discount houses) selling unbranded merchandise usually in the lowest-priced segments. Although these "off-price" stores were a relatively small part of the market, they were among the fastest-growing types of outlets. They sold nationally branded footwear but carried only a limited range of styles and sizes. Markups were smaller, reflecting a strategy of (1) locating in lower-rent areas, (2) reduced inventory-carrying charges, and (3) stricter returns policies. Their success in the bottom end of the market contributed to a deterioration in market position of the independent shoe retailers. The independents found themselves squeezed between the off-price outlets and the large retail chains who blanketed the best retail trading areas.

Department stores, accounting for approximately 13% of footwear volume, were being pressed by discount chains who sold name brands at reduced prices. Many department stores increased their private-label importing to obtain higher margins and to fight the discounters.

The Economics of Domestic Production

Because of the wide diversity of styles, sizes, and widths demanded by footwear consumers, the making of shoes differed markedly from that of a typical mass-produced good. Machines were used in all stages of the manufacturing process, but most operations were manually performed with low skill requirements. In fact, labor accounted for 28% of the selling price of the shoe—twice the proportion typical of all U.S. manufacturers (see *Exhibit 6*). Depending on the type of shoe produced, anywhere between 50 and 250 operations could be involved.

Although labor had been cited as the most important determinant of competitive advantage, raw materials actually made up more of the cost of a shoe. Typically, raw materials, principally leather, accounted for 45% to 50% of the selling price. The availability and price of leather varied widely, since rawhides were a by-product of the meat industry. Because the slaughter frequency did not match the demands of the tanneries and footwear industry, manufacturers were largely at the mercy of the vagaries of the demand for meat. Changes in demand for leather footwear could exercise a significant influence on the price of rawhide, due to the inelasticity of rawhide supplies. Finally, the United States was a major cattle-producing country, but foreign demand for hides on the world market could affect the domestic price for leather. Some of the largest U.S. footwear producers had integrated backward into the ownership of tanneries in order to exercise more control over this raw material.

A major concern for domestic manufacturers was the deterioration in the U.S. shoe component industry. Producers of various parts used in the marketing of a shoe (soles, heels, linings, and eyelets) had been exiting the industry as domestic footwear production declined. Observed one consultant, "As long as we keep 30% to 50% of the dollar volume [for domestic shoe firms], the component firms should survive. If we drop below the 30% level, the whole thing can crumble."

Domestic producers traditionally had limited access to the capital markets. Wall Street had not looked favorably upon the industry for years, resulting in few financing opportunities for smaller-sized firms suffering low returns. Besides poor profitability, many smaller firms were undercapitalized, limiting their ability to respond to market or technology changes.

The supply of machinery and equipment to the footwear industry had shaped much of its technological infrastructure. Up until 1954, United Shoe Machinery Corporation (U.S.M.) was almost the sole manufacturer of footwear technology. It followed a policy of leasing all shoe machinery and did not allow the manufacturer to purchase any of its equipment. Furthermore, U.S.M. put pressure on manufacturers not to use the machines of any other

company in combination with U.S.M. machinery. Because of the high cost and risk inherent in developing new machinery, U.S.M. had little incentive to develop radically new technologies, particularly when footwear producers were forced to use whatever U.S.M. would supply. As a result, the growth of productivity-enhancing machinery to help offset a rising labor cost disadvantage was inhibited. Antitrust actions by the Department of Justice resulted in a Supreme Court ruling in 1954 which prohibited many of U.S.M.'s policies. However, the company continued to be the major supplier of process technology to the industry.

Technology, a potential source of competitive advantage, was generally very simple, and whenever new processes were invented, they diffused rapidly throughout the world. Capital intensity in footwear manufacturing was low, with a ratio of fixed assets to total assets of 17%. Such a small capital requirement made entry and exit easy, a factor that was not lost on developing countries looking for new industries to provide employment.

Some shoe manufacturers relied on labor-saving equipment such as molding machines ($50,000 to $500,000 per machine) and computer-controlled stitching equipment ($6,000 to $75,000 per machine) to reduce labor costs. Injection molding of polyurethane material had increased, replacing several labor-intensive cutting, trimming, and finishing jobs. Another process, flow molding, could save up to 20% of the labor used in producing the shoe uppers but required skilled technicians to prepare the mold and cost approximately $55,000 per machine. This was most economical only for long production runs of vinyl footwear.

New computer-controlled laser-cutting techniques were available but required a large capital investment of $350,000 per machine, necessitating a well-financed company with access to the capital markets. Computer-aided design (CAD) saved time and money in designing the myriad of styles produced but offered few production efficiencies. According to the *1985 U.S. Industrial Outlook*, "The disparity in labor costs between many foreign suppliers and U.S. producers could be narrowed significantly with the application of new technology, especially robotics, but the large capital investment required is beyond the reach of many of the small- and medium-sized producers."

Further impediments to improving a lackluster productivity situation (*Exhibit 4*) through technological innovation were enumerated by the General Accounting Office in its 1980 study of productivity in the footwear industry. The GAO found the following obstacles to further automation:

1. The first companies to utilize the technological innovation take high risks because of the disruption of well-established manufacturing procedures.
2. Automated procedures implemented previously have not been flexible enough for manufacturers to respond to rapid style changes with short production runs. Shoes currently produced with automated machinery are usually part of long production runs and are therefore more standardized and less fashionable.
3. Technology was easily transferred abroad, eliminating any competitive advantage domestic manufacturers might temporarily achieve.

A government-commissioned series of consulting reports found that the management of many domestic footwear firms was often weak, lacking depth and experience. Footwear companies were unable to attract the type of management talent necessary to prosper. Exacerbating this problem was the general lack of adequate management information systems. Inadequate product accounting systems in many instances resulted in poor pricing decisions. Some consultants recommended consolidation of smaller firms through mergers or acquisitions.

Not only had the domestic footwear industry been buffeted by imports from low-wage countries, it also lagged behind European countries in the styling of footwear. American companies specialized in U.S. styles and did not attempt to match, for example, popular Italian fashions. As a result, retailers found U.S. manufacturers not responsive enough to market shifts and so resorted to imports to fill the fashion gap. Because small domestic producers had very limited access to styling suppliers, they were forced to wait two to six months to obtain a new styling sample. This lag, in an increasingly fashion-conscious market, prevented middle-of-the-season style changes and limited the responsiveness advantage inherent in domestic production. Most domestic producers were forced to compete largely in the middle-priced segment, abdicating the high-priced fashionable segment to Italy, Spain, and Brazil and the low-priced/high-volume end to Taiwan and Korea (see *Exhibits 5* and *10*).

The 400 companies in the footwear industry varied considerably in size, degree of vertical integration, and the extent to which they relied on imports to complement their product lines (see *Exhibit 3*). In 1984, fully 30% of total footwear imports were brought into the United States by domestic manufacturers themselves, an increase of 180% over 1980. Furthermore, some larger firms reduced domestic production costs by increasing their use of imported footwear components, particularly leather uppers. The high value of the dollar in the early 1980s had reduced the cost of foreign sourcing (see *Exhibit 8*).

Government Involvement with the Footwear Industry

A lengthy history of government interest in the footwear industry began in 1968 when President Johnson requested the Tariff Commission to study the impact of imports on domestic shoe companies. In 1969 the commission's report led to the creation of an Interagency Task Force to further review the economic conditions of the industry. On the basis of this report, the president initiated an escape clause investigation by the Tariff Commission under the Trade Expansion Act of 1962. Relief in the form of quotas or increased tariffs could be implemented by the president if the Tariff Commission judged that imports were a major cause of injury to the domestic industry. The commission, equally divided regarding the impact of imports, made no recommendation to President Nixon on the question of escape clause relief.

Late in 1975 the industry filed its first petition for import barriers under section 201 of the Trade Act of 1974. Although the International Trade Commission (ITC) recommended increased tariffs, President Ford limited government action to additional trade adjustment assistance and ordered the special trade representative to monitor footwear imports.

In late 1976 the Senate Finance Committee requested the ITC to undertake another investigation of footwear imports. The ITC again found the industry was suffering serious injury, which led President Carter to order the negotiation of Orderly Marketing Agreements (OMAs) with Taiwan and Korea. These four-year agreements were bilateral quotas based on the unit volume of imports. The OMAs cut Taiwan's and Korea's exports on nonrubber shoes by 22% in the first year and allowed for moderate growth over the next three years (see *Exhibit 11*). Carter further directed the Department of Commerce to institute a $56.3 million Footwear Industry Revitalization Program to provide retraining and promote industrywide adoption of new technology.

The OMAs expired in 1981, and the industry, with the support of the ITC, requested their extension. President Reagan nonetheless elected not to renew the OMAs. Three years later the Footwear Industries of America filed yet another petition for import relief. In contrast to its previous decisions, the ITC found that the domestic nonrubber footwear industry had not experienced "serious injury." The ITC found that the domestic industry was relatively profitable when compared with other manufacturing sectors. Analyzed in terms of value (as opposed to quantity), imports accounted for less than half of U.S. consumption and were concentrated in a unit price range substantially below the average for U.S. producers.

Again in 1985 the industry filed for import relief and was then supported by the ITC who found that substantial injury had occurred. According to the ITC report, conditions had changed since the last half of 1984 and imports were making serious inroads into the middle- and upper-price segments. The president again denied relief to the domestic manufacturers, stating that protectionism may increase the returns to existing producers but was unlikely to result in the reopening of already closed plants. However, the government did propose to ease merger restrictions in industries hurt by imports. This prompted Fawn Evenson of the Footwear Industry Association to respond, "If Brazil's wage scale is one buck an hour and ours is five bucks an hour, I don't think that merging two companies is going to get us back to a buck an hour."

Most government assistance to the industry had been reactive in nature and characterized by the GAO as "burial insurance." While some firms had depended on government actions to defend their market position, others sought to compete in new ways. Three such companies are profiled here.

COMPETITIVE PROFILES

Stride Rite Corporation

One of the most successful domestic competitors over the previous 10 years had been the Stride Rite Corporation. Under the leadership of Chairman Arnold Hiatt, the company had maintained a record of consistent profitability by concentrating on marketing brand names and integrating forward into retailing. Prior to Hiatt's arrival in 1969, the company was the leading producer of children's high-quality shoes. Since then, Stride Rite had acquired new product lines and added to its distribution capability by operating its own retail network ("Stride Rite Booteries," "Overland Trading Company" stores, and leasing departments in major chains such as Macy's, Jordan Marsh, and Neiman-Marcus). From 1973 to 1983, sales increased at a compound annual rate of 18%. In 1984, however, sales and earnings declined for the first time in years. The company was forced to write off twice as much inventory as usual in what Hiatt characterized as an "oversupplied" market. Moreover, one foreign and two domestic plants were closed, resulting in further nonrecurring charges.

Stride Rite had prospered by evolving from a production-oriented firm to one dominated by marketing considerations. The company added five new lines of footwear, including Sperry Topsiders, Keds sneakers, Grasshoppers, women's casuals, and Herman boots. After acquiring Topsider from Uniroyal in 1979, Stride Rite expanded distribution, added new lines, and increased advertising. The company stayed in the high-quality market segments, offering good products with excellent service to retailers. Over 1 million pairs of shoes were kept in inventory, enabling the firm to offer 24-hour service to its distributors. This inventory policy had substantial risk, however, which Hiatt noted: It invited obsolescence, even in children's footwear—a market which was becoming increasingly fashion-conscious.

In the children's market, according to Hiatt, Stride Rite made a "fetish" of service to the consumer. The company strove to be seen as a credible, quality-conscious shoe manufacturer, preferring to reach mothers through pediatricians than through children's television programs. Every child, when fitted with Stride Rite shoes, had a card filled out to facilitate the sending of a "size reminder note" three months later as the feet outgrew the shoes. In addition, Stride Rite sponsored "fitting seminars" for its salespeople to ensure their ability to provide professional service to children.

Although most of the company's leather footwear was still produced in the United States, Stride Rite was beginning to shift production overseas to lower-wage countries. Hiatt had stopped looking at manufacturing as a profit center. "The handwriting appears to be on the wall for domestic producers," he said. In fact, the company imported its leather uppers for Topsiders from Haiti, using its U.S. plant only to attach the sole. Retailing was emphasized as a necessity for survival in the future. In addition, the company would mitigate the cost advantage of its offshore competitors by maintaining its position in the top end of the market.

United States Shoe Corporation

In 1967 when 35-year-old Philip Barach became president of U.S. Shoe, the company was a small, sleepy footwear manufacturer seemingly destined to suffer the fate of many of its domestic competitors. However, during the past 10 years U.S. Shoe staged a remarkable turnaround. Sales rose to $1.7 billion and earnings to $53 million, sustaining a 15% compound annual growth rate in net income since 1974. The company became a recognized factor in specialty retailing while remaining one of the few significant domestic shoe manufacturers.

Barach was credited with much of U.S. Shoe's success. A 1955 graduate of the Harvard Business School, Barach decided in 1970 to diversify into specialty retailing by purchasing a chain of women's apparel stores. That first purchase—a small chain of 12 "Casual Corner" outlets—grew to over 600 units by 1974. Other acquisitions of small chains followed, and these grew to account for sales of $906 million and

40% of operating income. Totaling over 1,900 retail locations, U.S. Shoe operated 16 different specialty store formats, each targeted at a specific market segment. Chains included J. Riggins, Ups 'N Downs, Caren Charles, Pappagallo, and French Shriner. The company saw this format proliferation as a key to continued growth, given the slowing of shopping center development in the United States. Other future growth areas would include placing new store types in proven existing malls as well as in new shopping centers.

While increasing its women's apparel business, U.S. Shoe did not neglect its footwear operations. In 1969, the company's only business was moderately priced middle-of-the-road footwear, a slow-growth market with increasing import penetration. Barach expanded imports of high-fashion shoes until the company's imported footwear accounted for 60% of wholesale volume. Imports helped revitalize the company's traditional strength in higher-priced women's shoes such as Red Cross, Joyce, and Selby while adding fashion brands such as Liz Claiborne, Pappagallo, Evan-Picone, Capezio, Garolini, and Calvin Klein.

The company also expanded its footwear retailing. U.S. Shoe became a leader in developing "concept" stores (these usually owned by an independent merchant). For approximately $65,000, U.S. Shoe would set up a retailer in a small boutique that concentrated on selling one or two of the company's brands in every conceivable size and width. By 1984, U.S. Shoe had approximately 1,500 company-sponsored stores in operation. Moreover, the company owned over 500 stores that accounted for 9% of wholesale sales and, like the concept stores, largely targeted the middle- to upper-priced segments of women's shoes.

Interestingly, U.S. Shoe did not abandon domestic production of footwear. Since 1977 the company had invested over $12 million in its 18 factories to improve cost effectiveness and manufacturing flexibility. Robots, com-

puterized stitching equipment, compact conveyor systems, and computer-aided design techniques helped to increase worker productivity. Manufacturing employees were predominantly nonunion and earned just under the industry average when profit sharing was included in their per-hour compensation. The company maintained a strong domestic manufacturing base, which gave it flexibility to react quickly to changing market needs. Four to six times a year, new lines of footwear were developed by the company's designers, based on consumer buying patterns and European design trends. Although the new investment was important, Barach maintained: "I'll grant you, the new technology is more efficient, but as to why things have improved—out of 100 points I give the machines themselves 5. The real key is that they let us market quicker and better."[2]

Allen-Edmonds Shoe Corporation

Located in Belgium, Wisconsin, the Allen-Edmonds Shoe Corporation had undergone a remarkable transformation since 1980. At that time, the company was a 58-year-old family-owned enterprise that produced one of the best lines of men's dress shoes in the world but managed to lose $400,000 a year on sales of approximately $9 million. Four college friends headed by John Stollenwerk, all with no previous shoe manufacturing experience, purchased the firm and gave it a new marketing orientation. Stollenwerk tried to eliminate the "Allen who?" image, stating: "I had a lot of confidence in the product and the name. We needed to build on that reputation."[3]

The new managers increased advertising to over $1 million in 1984, placing ads in better-targeted, upscale publications like the *Wall Street*

---

[2]*Forbes*, March 16, 1981.
[3]*Business Week*, September 19, 1983.

Journal, *Fortune*, *Newsweek*, and *Omni*. In addition, a new advertising agency was hired to provide fresh ideas for the company's upmarket product positioning. This new strategy contrasted markedly with that of the previous owners who had spent the entire 1980 advertising budget of $50,000 on a full-page ad in *Life* magazine. Moreover, the company added a new line of lighter-weight dress shoes targeted at 25- to 45-year-old men. The company maintained its very high quality standards while adding a style orientation that appealed to younger, more fashion-conscious customers (a market segment it had previously neglected).

In carving out its own market niche, Allen-Edmonds eliminated all middlemen and went directly to its suppliers to be assured of high-quality raw materials. The plant was revamped by introducing a more efficient layout and more modern equipment. To improve further on the quality, Stollenwerk increased the compensation of the 250 nonunionized workers and cross-trained employees in a number of operations to combat boredom. When a 1984 fire completely destroyed the company's plant and inventory, its workers kept production going by setting up operations in an abandoned schoolhouse and working weekends in another shoe manufacturer's factory. Within two weeks, production was up to 1,000 pairs a week—approximately one-sixth of normal output. Insurance proceeds helped to finance a new 69,000-square-foot plant whose new equipment and more efficient layout were expected to help further quality.

Allen-Edmonds began to look overseas for sales. Stollenwerk attended numerous trade shows in Europe in order to convince distributors to handle his product. His persistence brought results: 10% of sales were exports to Italy, South Africa, and Singapore.

Further moves to strengthen the firm's market position included cooperative advertising with distributors and publishing a quarterly newsletter. The company offered a full line of inventory in all conceivable sizes and widths; over 56,000 pairs of shoes were kept in inventory, and Allen-Edmonds promised to ship all orders within 24 hours. The company's strategy paid off quickly. By 1981, sales had increased to $11.5 million and profits were made for the first time in five years. Sales continued upward to 1984 when they reached approximately $20 million.

B-W's Situation in 1986

Located in Webster, Massachusetts, B-W was among the most successful and profitable footwear firms in the United States over the past 30 years. Similar to Stride Rite, U.S. Shoe, and Allen-Edmonds, Robert Siff had found ways to thrive in the shoe business. With $35 million in sales in 1985, of which 60% was from imports, B-W had an excellent reputation for modern manufacturing and an ability to anticipate changes in the market (see *Exhibit 7*).

Siff's strategy had been to give customers whatever they wanted. He always sought to *lead* changes in the marketplace rather than *react*. Domestically, B-W manufactured men's medium-priced casual shoes (in the $25 to $50 range), golf shoes, and steel-toed safety footwear. In every one of his lines, Siff tried to give his products unique features. For instance, he pioneered the manufacturing of steel toes in different styles of casual footwear. For the first time, consumers who needed the safety of a steel toe could buy something other than a work boot.[4]

B-W attempted to capitalize on a number of advantages inherent in having a domestic production base. Delivery time on orders was

---

[4]Approximately 22 million steel-toed shoes were sold in the United States in 1985: 40% of the market for industrial use, 60% for other uses. The average retail price for B-W industrial shoes was $60; for nonindustrial shoes, $30.

speedier, approximately four to five weeks. In addition, the company manufactured a wide range of shoe sizes and widths, thereby filling a market segment that was uneconomical for low-cost offshore producers. (The company operated what was, in many respects, a job shop—producing footwear in short runs of 600 or more pairs.) Three full-time stylists were employed, enabling a speedy response to style changes. Thus, by concentrating on a few specialty market segments, by offering a better selection of sizes and widths, and by offering retailers much speedier delivery times, B-W was able to mitigate many of the inherent cost disadvantages of domestic manufacturing. Up to 1986, the company did not have its own branded lines, nor did it have any retailing outlets. Siff estimated a minimum cost of $5 million in advertising over a few years to establish a brand name.

Siff also recognized very early on that domestic production alone would be insufficient if B-W was to prosper. As early as 1954, long before most of his competitors, Siff began importing desert boots and sandals from Spain and Brazil. He recognized that his customers wanted these products, and it made more sense for him to import a sandal for $1.10 than to spend $5.00 to manufacture it in Webster. In the 1970s, Siff also pioneered importing from the newest source of cheap labor, the People's Republic of China. By 1974, B-W was the largest U.S. men's footwear importer from China. Siff eventually had to drop the Chinese as a supplier because it was taking between 12 and 18 months for delivery and because of enormous communications and quality problems (e.g., black shoes would be sewn with white stitches).

Much of B-W's historical success was attributed to Siff's ability to stay ahead of the competition on design, and especially to find the right mix of imports and domestic manufacturing—an important combination. The Webster operations lent product expertise to foreign exporters by designing shoes, making some of the dies and molds, and then shipping them overseas. In 1985, the company imported 10,000 to 11,000 pairs per day from Spain and several thousand additional pairs from Taiwan. B-W would also import men's shoes from Brazil, Italy, and the United Kingdom, shifting suppliers according to the best prices and styles. The company did not own any offshore facilities, preferring to subcontract. Although B-W had set up a corporate office in Taiwan to monitor factory production, Siff did not want to commit a significant investment overseas, due to the political uncertainties of expropriation and the difficulty of getting money out of certain countries.

In 1968, when the company's factory and adjoining headquarters were completely destroyed by fire, B-W had 400 employees. B-W then rebuilt a new air-conditioned facility which remained among the most modern in the industry. In 1986, B-W employed a predominantly female work force of 250 who manufactured approximately 2,400 pairs of shoes per day. At any one time, the plant was capable of producing 75 to 100 different styles.

Siff ran a very tight ship. He described his management style as a "team managment concept." Although Siff had final decision-making power, he listened closely to his three vice presidents of finance, sales/marketing, and operations and liked to reach a group consensus. The vice presidents were between 42 and 53 years old, and two of them had 20 years of experience at B-W. The collegial atmosphere and the wide-ranging responsibilities given to the vice presidents led to strong loyalty among top managers. In addition, Siff had an open door policy for everyone in the organization. He noted that "many of us here wear two hats. For example, I spend a great deal of time on the factory floor, taking at least two hours a day to handle any operations issues and to ensure that I have a good feel for the pulse of the organization. At the same time, I play an active role in marketing, design, and finance."

In many ways, B-W was in a very strong position in 1986. The firm was well-capitalized with no debt. It owned all its equipment, its plant, and its land in Webster. Some computerized stitchers and other modern equipment had been recently purchased and integrated into the production process. B-W also had good distribution for its products: sales went to discount houses, large retail chains such as Sears and J.C. Penney, and specialty chains like Florsheim and Nordstroms.

Yet the deterioration of the industry, which had hurt virtually everyone in 1986, was also being felt in Webster. The plant was operating at only 50% of capacity, forcing Siff to solicit more business from Sears and others in order to keep up production volumes. The company's supply lines were of particular concern: B-W was having increasing difficulty sourcing some essential footwear components. Siff also worried about attracting new management talent to B-W. He noted that "smart people know there is little future for manufacturing footwear in this country without a dramatic change in technology, labor costs, or a 30% fall in the dollar's value vis-à-vis the Taiwans and Koreas of the world."

Siff leaned back and considered his position. Was a large capital investment in new technologies worthwhile? Should he spend a few million dollars to brand a product or set up retail outlets? Should he give up on domestic production, relying exclusively on imports, or should he exit? If he were to leave now, he estimated that he would receive less than ten cents for every dollar invested in equipment. Siff was a man of numerous interests, and had been heavily involved in volunteer community work for many years. He was the director of a bank and several national philanthropic organizations. At the same time, he was a proud man with a lifelong commitment to the footwear manufacturing industry. For almost 25 years, Siff had been a director of the Footwear Industry Association. Yet importing was where B-W was making most of its money. Siff candidly explained that "without importing, we could not stay in business." Finally, his son and daughter, recent graduates from Brown University, were pursuing business careers. Should he encourage them to enter the family business? As Siff reflected about the future, he noted:

This is a tough business, but if you are a tough leader you can survive and prosper, as my situation at B-W illustrates. I also feel strongly that the government should see the light and give the industry some support. It is essential to have a manufacturing base in this country. We do not want to be a nation of "hollow corporations." We will never be able to maintain our standard of living if we only act as importers and employ people to work in Pizza Huts and McDonalds.

NONRUBBER FOOTWEAR: U.S. PRODUCTION, IMPORTS, AND EXPORTS
(millions of pairs)

Year	Production	Imports	Exports	Apparent U.S. consumption	Per capita consumption	Ratio of imports to consumption, %
1960	600.0	26.6	3.2	623.4	3.45	4
1965	626.2	87.6	2.5	711.3	3.66	12
1970	562.3	241.6	2.1	801.8	3.91	30
1971	535.8	268.6	2.1	802.3	3.86	33
1972	526.7	296.7	2.3	821.1	3.91	36
1973	490.0	307.5	3.6	793.9	3.75	39
1974	453.0	266.4	4.0	715.4	3.34	37
1975	413.1	286.4	4.6	694.9	3.22	41
1976	422.5	370.0	6.0	786.5	3.61	47
1977	418.1	368.1	5.4	780.1	3.54	47
1978	418.9	373.5	6.9	785.5	3.53	48
1979	398.9	404.6	9.3	794.2	3.53	51
1980	386.3	365.7	13.0	739.1	3.25	49
1981	372.0	375.6	11.2	736.4	3.21	51
1982	359.1	479.7	8.9	829.9	3.58	58
1983	344.3	581.9	7.5	918.6	3.92	63
1984	298.5	725.9	8.9	1,015.5	4.31	71

Source: U.S. International Trade Commission, *Nonrubber Footwear,* USITC Publication 1717, July 1985, Tables 5 and 11.

UNIT VALUE PER PAIR, 1984

Domestic producers	$13.13
Imports	6.41
Exports	11.09
Average wholesale price (all shoes)	$ 8.39

Source: U.S. International Trade Commission, *Nonrubber Footwear,* USITC Publication 1717, July 1985, Table 4.

NONRUBBER FOOTWEAR: PRODUCTION OUTPUT DISTRIBUTION (%)

Annual production	Percent of total output				Capacity utilization, %	
	1969	1975	1980	1984	1980	1984
Less than 200,000 pairs	2	2	2	2	61	37
200,000 to 499,999 pairs	8	7	6	6	81	68
500,000 to 999,999 pairs	14	12	9	11	71	70
1,000,000 to 1,999,999 pairs	24	14	16	15	56	56
2,000,000 to 3,999,999 pairs	15	15	16	15	78	77
4,000,000 pairs or more	37	50	51	51	85	74

Source: U.S. International Trade Commission, *Nonrubber Footwear,* USITC Publication 1717, July 1985, Tables 6 and 20.

EXHIBIT FOUR

Estimated hourly compensation for leather footwear (U.S. $)

	1980	**1984**
United States	5.67	7.32
Brazil	1.08	0.88
Italy	6.17	5.82
Korea	0.87	0.95
Taiwan	1.11	1.81

Productivity and total compensation, 1980–1984

	1980	**1981**	**1982**	**1983**	**1984**
Output per employee hour [index (1967 = 100)]	107	102	99	101	NA
Productivity (pairs per hour)	1.69	1.71	1.76	1.71	1.71
Hourly compensation (including benefits)	$5.27	$5.71	$6.16	$6.39	$6.74
Unit labor costs per pair	$3.12	$3.33	$3.51	$3.76	$3.94
Labor's share of average selling price (%)	27.6	27.2	27.5	27.9	28.1

Source: U.S. International Trade Commission, *Nonrubber Footwear,* USITC Publication 1717, July 1985, Table 28, p. A43, and Tables 37, 40, 43, and 45.

EXHIBIT FIVE

NONRUBBER FOOTWEAR, IMPORTS IN 1984

	Thousands of pairs	Percent
Taiwan	243,430	42
Korea	118,854	20
Brazil	64,391	11
Italy	56,355	10
Spain	26,706	5
Hong Kong	18,186	3
Philippines	7,632	1
China	7,162	1
Thailand	5,142	1
France	4,254	1
Other	29,739	5
Total	581,857	

Source: U.S. International Trade Commission, *Nonrubber Footwear,* USITC Publication 1717, July 1985, Table 50.

COMPARATIVE INCOME STATEMENTS
(thousands of pairs)

	Size of company					
	0–199 pairs	200–499 pairs	500–999 pairs	1,000–1,999 pairs	2,000–3,999 pairs	4,000+ pairs
Net sales	100.0%	100.0%	100.0%	100.0%	100.0%	100.0%
Cost of goods sold	78.2	78.0	79.8	77.6	78.8	77.7
Gross margin	21.8%	22.0%	20.2%	22.4%	21.2%	22.3%
S, G, & A expense	24.8	20.6	16.2	19.7	12.8	14.9
Operating income	NA	1.4%	4.0%	2.7%	8.4%	7.4%

Source: U.S. International Trade Commission, *Nonrubber Footwear,* USITC Publication 1717, July 1985, p. A59.

RATIO OF OPERATING INCOME TO SALES, %

Industry	1972	1977	1980	1981	1982	1983	1984
Nonrubber footwear	5.7	5.4	9.0	10.0	8.2	8.8	5.8
Textile mill products	5.3	5.6	5.2	5.4	4.5	6.3	NA
Nondurable goods	7.5	7.9	7.4	6.9	6.0	6.6	7.0
All U.S. manufacturing	7.8	8.1	6.8	6.7	5.1	5.9	6.8

Operating income = Income before taxes + interest.
Source: U.S. Senate Subcommittee on International Trade, 98th Congress, June 22, 1984, USITC Publication 1717, July 1985, p. A53.

COMPARISON OF OPERATING MARGINS OF VARIOUS-SIZED FOOTWEAR MANUFACTURERS, %

	1980	1984
Annual production volume:		
0–199,999 pairs	4.5	−3.0
200,000–499,999 pairs	3.6	1.4
500,000–999,999 pairs	7.8	4.0
1,000,000–1,999,999 pairs	7.1	2.7
2,000,000–3,999,999 pairs	10.7	8.4
4,000,000+ pairs	10.3	7.4
Market segment:		
Men's, boys'	9.9	7.4
Women's, misses	8.7	3.4
Children's, infants'	5.8	−0.1
Variety	7.4	6.9
Importing	12.5	11.1

Source: U.S. International Trade Commission, *Nonrubber Footwear,* USITC Publication 1717, July 1985, Tables 32, 34, and G3–G9.

FINANCIAL RATIOS OF A TYPICAL FOOTWEAR MANUFACTURER

	1980	1984
Sales to fixed assets	12.4×	12.5×
Debt to equity	69.0%	54.0%
Inventory turnover	4.4×	4.3×
Capital expenditures to net worth	6.9%	5.0%
Operating income to total assets	19.4%	12.9%
Operating income to net worth	32.9%	20.0%
Fixed assets to total assets	16.7%	15.0%

Source: U.S. International Trade Commission, *Nonrubber Footwear,* USITC Publication 1717, July 1985, Tables 32, 34, and G3–G9.

EXHIBIT SEVEN-A

B-W Footwear's Income Statements[a]
Year Ended December 31, 1984
(In Thousands)

Production	
Net sales	100.0%
Cost of goods sold	78.0
Gross margin	22.0
S, G, & A expense	14.8
Operating income	7.2

[a]These numbers should be compared with footwear companies with sales of 500,000 to 999,000 pairs of shoes in Exhibit 6.
Source: Company files.

EXHIBIT SEVEN-B

B-W Footwear's Financial Ratios

Sales to fixed assets	13.4 ×
Debt to equity	15.4%
Inventory turnover	2.79 ×
Capital expenditures to net worth	1.3%
Operating income to total assets	8.9%
Operating income to net worth	10.2%
Fixed assets to total assets	9.2%

Source: Company files.

EXHIBIT EIGHT

EXCHANGE RATE MOVEMENTS BETWEEN U.S. AND SHOE-IMPORTING COUNTRIES

	1980	1984
Taiwan:		
Nominal exchange rate index	100	91.8
Real exchange rate difference*	100	85.4
Korea:		
Nominal	100	69.7
Real	100	83.4
Brazil:		
Nominal	100	1.6
Real	100	103.5
Italy:		
Nominal	100	43.6
Real	100	63.1

*The real exchange rate is used to determine if changes in exchange rates have been affected by changes in inflation rates.

Real exchange rate index = nominal exchange rate index × foreign price index

U.S. price index

Source: U.S. International Trade Commission, *Nonrubber Footwear*, USITC Publication 171, July 1985, Tables K1–K4.

EXHIBIT NINE

SHOE RETAIL OUTLETS OPERATED BY LEADING PARENT

	1977	1984
Melville Shoe	2,458	3,372
Brown Shoe	1,240	1,308
Kinney Shoe	1,200	1,700
Genesco Incorporated	906	756
Edison Brothers Stores	900	1,226
Morse Shoe	823	1,105
Endicott Johnson Retail Division	768	828[a]
Shoe Corporation of America	751	749
Interco Incorporated	728	950
United States Shoe	586	625[a]
Volume Shoe	523	1,400
National Shoes	478	676[a]
Pic'N Pay	344	561

[a]1983 data.
Source: *Leather and Shoes*, July 1977, p. 44; July 1983, p. 48; November 1984, p. 35.

EXHIBIT TEN

IMPORT PENETRATION BY MAJOR MARKET SEGMENT, 1984

Segment	Price range	% imports	000s imports
Men's leather dress and casual	Under $10.01	82%	3,305
	$10.01–$18.00	41	7,293
	$18.01–$25.00	22	2,674
	$25.01–$38.00	15	1,256
	Over $38.00	21	517
Women's leather dress and casual	Under $9.01	76	11,898
	$ 9.01–$14.00	52	13,218
	$14.01–$24.00	55	28,287
	$24.01–$37.00	85	6,894
	Over $37.00	57	1,490
Women's vinyl dress and casual	Under $9.01	87	48,495
	$ 9.01–$14.00	28	4,574
	$14.01–$24.00	8	718
	$24.01–$37.00	100	194
	Over $37.00	100	37
Children's footwear	Under $5.01	64	11,322
	$ 5.01–$9.00	45	2,731
	$ 9.01–$13.00	31	1,025
	$13.01–$18.00	11	323
	Over $18.00	100	648
Athletic footwear	Under $6.01	82	14,393
	$ 6.01–$10.00	100	30,794
	$10.01–$17.00	97	39,375
	$17.01–$24.00	91	11,171
	Over $24.00	71	7,669

Source: U.S. International Trade Commission, *Nonrubber Footwear,* USITC Publication 1717, July 1985, Tables J4 to J6.

EXHIBIT ELEVEN

IMPACT OF OMAs

Volume of U.S. rubber and nonrubber footwear imports under the OMA, 1977–1980 (in millions of pairs)

	Total	Nonrubber	Rubber	OMA limit[a]
		Taiwan[b]		
1977	227.6	166.5	61.1	
1978	212.0	117.2	94.8	125
1979	178.6	124.8	53.8	131
1980	202.9	144.0	58.9	
		Korea		
1977	83.5	58.7	24.8	
1978	90.1	30.6	59.5	36.5
1979	66.1	24.3	41.8	37.5
1980	79.7	37.1	42.6	

Average unit value ($) of U.S. nonrubber imports, 1977–1980

Source	1977	1978	1979	1980	Percent change, 1977–1980
Taiwan	$2.08	$3.30	$3.49	$4.31	107
Korea	3.91	5.60	6.83	7.09	81
World average	4.34	5.51	6.00	6.28	45

[a]OMA quotas extended from June to June, not the calendar years shown.
[b]Excludes transshipped parts.
Source: U.S. International Trade Commission, *Nonrubber Footwear,* USITC Publication 1139, April 1981, Tables 1 and 3.

General Motors' Asian Alliances

In 1966, the General Motors Corporation (GM) stated that "unified ownership for coordinated policy control of all of our operations throughout the world is essential for our effective performance as a worldwide corporation." Twenty years later, GM had created joint ventures and other cooperative arrangements with a number of firms both in the United States and around the world. Among Asian firms, these tie-ups linked GM with Isuzu, Toyota, Suzuki, and Nissan; with the Daewoo Group in Korea; with Hitachi, the Japanese electronics giant; with Fanuc, a leading Japanese robotics maker; and with many smaller Japanese firms.

Cooperative arrangements were a familiar practice for Japanese and Korean firms but not for GM; hence GM's efforts in Asia are open to many interpretations. They could be viewed as a series of ad hoc solutions to pressing needs, as an extension to Asia of GM's practice of securing a range of suppliers to reduce risk and gain leverage—or perhaps as an embryonic American version of the Japanese enterprise groups.

The formation of these relationships took place against a backdrop of historic change, turbulence, and weakening performance at GM. In 1987, its market share in the United States had fallen to 36.5% and its car business earned less than $100 million (see *Exhibits 1* and *2*). GM was nearing the end of a multiyear, $40 billion investment in high technology and automation that had included the acquisitions of Electronic Data Systems (EDS) and Hughes Aircraft. Under Chairman Roger Smith, GM had also reorganized its car business into two large groups, one for smaller cars and one for larger ones, and had announced the creation of a new subsidiary, the Saturn Corporation, that would bring together state-of-the-art technology, innovative marketing and supplier arrangements, and a ground-breaking participatory relationship with the United Auto Workers (UAW).

Associate Professor Joseph L. Badaracco, Jr., prepared this case with the research assistance of Naomi Hasegwa as the basis for class discussion rather than to illustrate either effective or ineffective handling of an administrative situation.

This case describes the major relationships or groups of relationships that GM set up with Asian firms: (1) the Toyota joint venture, (2) partnerships with small Asian car makers (Isuzu, Suzuki, and Daewoo), (3) the Fanuc joint venture, and (4) alliances with companies that make parts and components.

TOYOTA

In 1983, GM and Toyota announced that they would create a 50-50 joint venture in California called New United Motor Manufacturing Incorporated (NUMMI), which soon became the most publicized and closely watched strategic alliance in recent U.S. history. Chrysler Chairman Lee Iacocca said, "It's a recipe for breaking the industry by 1990" and that Ford and Chrysler would again "be looking at bankruptcy or bailouts." The Federal Trade Commission (FTC), in response to such concerns, mounted one of the most *intensive efforts* in its history before finally approving NUMMI by a three-to-two vote.

Toyota contributed $100 million in cash to NUMMI, and GM contributed the same, including its plant in Fremont, California. A state-of-the-art operation when it opened in 1963, this facility had employed 7,000 workers in the late 1970s, but GM closed it in a cost-control and consolidation effort in the early 1980s. By then poor labor-management relations, high absenteeism, and alcohol and drug-related problems had handicapped its operations.

NUMMI would have its own board of directors, appointed in equal number by its parent firms, with Toyota choosing its president, chief executive officer, and other top officers. GM could assign no more than 16 executives to tours of duty at the plant at any one time. The plant's 2,100 employees would be members of the UAW.

NUMMI would manufacture approximately 200,000 cars a year. Its initial product was to be the Chevrolet Nova, a front-wheel-drive version of the Sprinter (a compact car Toyota had already been making and selling in Japan), to sell for about $7,500. NUMMI would be a stamping and assembly operation; Toyota would make the major components, including the drive train, in Japan; and other parts and components would originate in the United States. Under the FTC consent decree, the joint venture could not run beyond 1996.

The Toyota Group

Toyota is not simply a company but rather a confederation of firms more properly called the Toyota Group. As such, it is a common form of Japanese industrial organization known as enterprise groups, or *keiretsu*, which control roughly a third of Japan's industrial assets. Their distinguishing trait is the links among member firms, described by one economist as "a thick and complex skein of relations matched in no other industrial country."

Two sorts of *keiretsu* exist in contemporary Japan. One is a successor to the *zaibatsu*, the giant conglomerates that dominated the Japanese industrial landscape for most of the first half of this centruy. Mitsui, Mitsubishi, and Sumitomo were among the most famous and powerful *zaibatsu*. Their member firms included banks, insurance companies, light and heavy industrial firms, and overseas trading companies. The U.S. occupation following World War II broke up the *zaibatsu* to disperse their economic and political power, but after the occupation many of the original groups reemerged, though ties among member firms are now looser and more informal.

Toyota—along with Nissan, Hitachi, and other large Japanese manufacturing firms—represents the second kind of *keiretsu*. These manufacturers stand, in effect, at the apex of a hierarchy of firms. The dominant firm concentrates on assembly work and marketing; the next tier consists of primary suppliers. Toyota and Nissan make engine parts, brake parts, meters, chassis, and bodies; beneath them are secondary subcontractors that supply the primary suppliers. These rely, in turn, on a bottom tier of tertiary subcontractors. (As a result of its group affiliations, Toyota's level of vertical integration was approximately 30%; GM's was roughly 70%.) The Toyota Group includes thousands of tertiary suppliers, most of which are very small, who produce the simple "parts of parts" that secondary contractors and then primary suppliers use to maker their own products. The firms in each tier remain legally separate and are often small, owner-managed businesses. Their relationship with their parent company is semipermanent, and although it is unusual for such a relationship to be terminated or for one supplier to be replaced with another, it happens occasionally.

All tiers of this pyramid are connected through intricate arrangements, including minority equity ownership (Toyota owns 10 to 70% of many of its affiliated firms), interlocking directorates, and financial aid in the form of trade credits, loans, or credit guarantees given by the parent. The presidents of affiliated companies meet regularly. The peak firm may also lend personnel and offer technological guidance and exchanges. Above all, each tier in the hierarchy purchases a high fraction of its suppliers' outputs.

Some of these relationships originated during the 1950s when automotive firms and other manufacturers lacked the funds to invest in component operations. Moreover, wages and benefits were lower then among subcontractors, and few of their employees were assured lifetime jobs. Other groups had formed decades, even centuries, earlier, and their complex linkages did not wither away as these manufacturers became powerful and prosperous; relations within groups were refined, not replaced.

The Toyota Production System

Toyota had developed it *keiretsu* arrangements to a high degree of refinement. Its manufac-

turing took place almost entirely in Toyota City, a huge, intricately integrated complex of assembly plants and suppliers three hours away from Tokyo. Its *kanban*, or "just-in-time system," is another link among firms in the Toyota Group, and, according to one Toyota executive, it is "the essence of Toyota and its relationships." A *kanban* is simply a small paper or metal tag attached to a container of auto parts or components describing its destination, indicating what time it should arrive, and so forth. The phrase "just-in-time" refers to the notion that the component should arrive at the station where it is needed precisely *when* it is needed. Ideally, a firm's inventory consists only of a single unit of each part held until just the moment before it is used. In practice, the *kanban* system relies on very small inventory lots and resembles the daily-delivery system used to restock supermarket shelves.

The *kanban* inventory system reveals bottlenecks, lessens the need for managers and foremen, and permits a plant to shift product lines more quickly. Toyota executives also believe it gives members of the group a common interest in finding and anticipating problems and thus serves in focusing them on their joint concern—the manufacture of outstanding products. It is not, they stress, merely a system for highlighting problems or for figuring out which individuals should be held accountable for them. Though its mechanics are simple, the system's role within the Toyota Group is described in subtle, almost elusive ways: "a relationship from a spiritual point of view" and "intensely competitive but not unstable." Toyota's president called it an instrument of "harmony and communication."

As Toyota concentrated on and refined its production system during the 1960s and 1970s, the company grew more powerful, more ambitious, and yet perhaps more cautious. By 1986, Toyota's car and truck exports to the United States exceeded $10 billion, accounting for 25% of its sales and an even larger fraction of its profits. By 1987, its market share in Japan exceeded 50%. (Nissan, the next largest domestic firm, which had earlier been investing heavily in computers and robots, had less than 20% of the Japanese market.) Until the appreciation of the yen cut deeply into its operating profits, Toyota had become so profitable that its Japanese nickname was "the Toyota Bank," a reference to the $6 billion in liquid assets it had accumulated.

During the 1980s, Toyota's worldwide market share grew to 8%, making it the third largest auto firm (behind Ford and GM) in the world. Some speculated that the company's ambition for the 21st century was to overtake GM as the world's largest car producer. But Toyota generally let competitors make the first moves with new products. Nissan moved first into the sports car market with its Z series, and Honda developed vehicles that straddled the sports and family markets. (Later, Honda led the way into the high-priced market with its Acura line.) And, until it created NUMMI, Toyota, alone among Japan's three biggest car manufacturers, did not have an assembly plant in the United States.

NUMMI

NUMMI followed many of Toyota's established practices. Its workers, like Toyota's in Japan, were chosen only after intensive screening. The plant has only four job classifications in contrast to the hundred that existed previously at the Fremont plant, and workers have incentives (under a Pay for Learning program) to be trained for many jobs, not just one. Both Toyota and GM have made strong commitments to job security. Decision making has been delegated downward to small worker-led teams, and many of the first workers at the NUMMI plant visited Toyota City for extended training in the Toyota system. Toyota also implemented a just-in-time system and set extremely high quality-control standards for NUMMI suppliers. Though that caused antagonism among some U.S. suppliers, those who succeeded in

meeting Toyota standards often marketed themselves as "good enough to supply Toyota."

By the end of 1987, GM was trying to apply the lessons learned from NUMMI throughout its manufacturing system. It had created a Technical Liaison Office in California to document what it was learning about the NUMMI production system. GM plants in New Jersey and Delaware, which made the new Chevy Corsicas and Berretas, used a team approach derived from NUMMI, and GM based many of its plans for its new Saturn plant on the NUMMI experience. More than 3,000 GM employees were given one-day tours of the NUMMI facility. Finally, GM defended its 1987 contract with the UAW by arguing that its job security program and limits on plant closings were further investments in a genuinely cooperative relationship with the union. Under that contract, GM workers and managers would set up committees in every plant that would be given six months to report ways to improve productivity and quality.

Toyota had gained enough confidence from NUMMI to proceed with a $300 million auto plant in Canada and an $800 million auto plant in Kentucky; the latter would open in 1989 and produce about 200,000 Camrys each year.

The results at the NUMMI plant were mixed. GM's quality audits gave the plant extremely high ratings. Toyota was also impressed by the plant's quality and decided in 1987 to make 15,000 Corolla FX-16s at Fremont and sell them through its own dealers. Absenteeism had dropped to about 2%, compared with 22% during the old days at Fremont. Disappointment arose, however, from weak Nova sales, and in late 1987, NUMMI's production was cut from 600 to 400 cars per day. Factors contributing to this reduction included the marketing by Chevrolet of several cars such as the Suzuki and Isuzu vehicles and marketing decisions to do with the Nova, particularly its name. One auto analyst commented bluntly, "The previous Novas were not great cars." Also, Toyota had permitted GM to sell only a four-door vehicle, keeping the two-door hatchback for itself. The latter car, the Corolla FX, moved successfully through Toyota dealerships without the financial incentives amounting to several hundred dollars that GM had offered with the Nova during 1987.

Finally, press reports indicated clouds over the horizon at Fremont. *Business Month* wrote in June 1987: "GM and Toyota say the plant's a success, but it's no workers' paradise." The early excitement had ebbed, it reported, and workers were becoming worn out by the fast pace of operations (NUMMI used only a third as many workers as did comparable plants). Some had organized a dissident group called "The People's Movement" to oust the current union leadership in the 1988 election. GM and UAW officials dismissed some of these criticisms as union politics and stressed that NUMMI was trying to change adversarial attitudes embedded in GM labor relations for decades.

OTHER ASIAN CAR MAKERS

Isuzu

Isuzu's affiliation with GM began in 1971 when GM agreed to pay $56 million for a 34.2% interest in Isuzu. Under the agreement, that level of ownership would remain for five years; if for some reason GM did acquire more shares during that period, it could not vote them without Isuzu's permission. Four GM executives became members of Isuzu's board, but the agreement kept the posts of president and chairman in Isuzu's control. GM would assist Isuzu in designing, developing, and manufacturing cars; it would also distribute Isuzu products through its global network.

At the time of the agreement, Isuzu was encountering difficulties. In 1970, after experiencing problems in developing new trucks, its main product, Isuzu saw its market share fall from 36 to 20%; its passenger car sales were also low because of its weak sales network.

Isuzu had begun making cars in 1953 when it started assembling "knockdown" kits from a British supplier. This effort gave the company confidence, and in 1961 it designed and produced a diesel-powered car on its own. The car succeeded at first, but sales fell when nondiesel fuels became more abundant and when competitors' cars proved to be more comfortable and less noisy. During the next several years, Isuzu attempted tie-ups with Fuji Heavy Industries, Mitsubishi, and Nissan. None succeeded. After the liaison with Nissan fell through, Isuzu reached the agreement with GM that led to their partnership.

The GM deal raised Isuzu's capital from 25 to 38 billion yen, enabling Isuzu to build a parts factory. In 1972, Chevrolet began selling Isuzu's 1-ton truck in the United States, marketing it as the Chevy Luv. Chevrolet quickly sold 100,000 of the vehicles, and by 1973, Isuzu had almost doubled its exports (see *Exhibit 3*).

Isuzu's difficulties continued, however, and the company lost 8.7 billion yen in 1975. In 1976, Isuzu Finance Company, Isuzu's largest subsidiary, and General Motors Acceptance Corporation (GMAC) signed an affiliation agreement. GMAC purchased 51% of Isuzu Finance's stock, doubling its capital to 6 trillion yen.

Isuzu then set up several production and sales bases overseas: GM Pilipinas, a joint venture with GM in the Philippines to make Isuzu cars and components; a joint venture with Turkish partners in 1980 to manufacture and sell trucks; and a joint venture in Tunisia with GM and local partners in 1983 to assemble and sell Isuzu trucks and Opel cars. Also in 1983, Mesin Isuzu Indonesia (25% Isuzu ownership, 10% GM, and 8% C. Itoh) was established with three Indonesian automobile makers to make diesel engines. Later that year, plans for GM Egypt SAE (20% Isuzu and 31% GM) were announced to manufacture pickups and trucks to Cairo. Convesco Vehicle Sales (40% Isuzu and 60% GM) was also begun in Germany to market commercial vehicles in Europe, and Isuzu Motors Overseas Distribution Corporation (Isuzu 51%, GM 49%) was formed to sell Isuzu vehicles and parts through independent distributors (mostly also distributors of GM vehicles) in some 130 countries.

During the same period, Isuzu continued to build R&D and supply arrangements with GM. In 1981, Isuzu signed a seven-year parts supply contract with GM and another agreement to supply components to five GM subsidiaries, including Opel, in West Germany. Isuzu already had ties with Opel: in 1972, it had agreed with Opel and GM to purchase small-car technology.

In 1984, Isuzu began shipping a new vehicle, the Spectrum, to Chevrolet, which had invested $200 million in its development and sold it through its dealers. GM could get only 17,000 Spectrums in 1984, the maximum allowed under the voluntary restraints that the Japanese government had imposed on its automakers in 1981. Two years later, when Isuzu was permitted to ship 120,000 to the United States, 90% were sold through Chevrolet and the rest through Isuzu's own dealers. GM's purchases represented roughly 40% of Isuzu's total car and truck production.

In 1986, Isuzu and GM's Electronic Data Services unit (EDS) signed a five-year contract for upgrading Isuzu's telecommunications and engineering data processing capabilities in Japan and other countries: Isuzu would gain access to the worldwide telecommunications network EDS was creating for GM; EDS would also integrate Isuzu's CAD/CAM operations and engineering software. Later, EDS planned to study Isuzu's factory automation and flexible manufacturing systems for possible upgrading.

Finally, in February 1987, Isuzu formed a 10-year agreement to supply engines to Lotus, a wholly owned subsidiary of GM. In exchange, Isuzu would receive technology from Lotus—possibly an advanced suspension system—to use in a sports car called the Impulse, which Isuzu exported to Europe and the United States as a specialty car. Isuzu was also studying a proposal to sell Lotus cars in Japan. Later that year, GM and Isuzu created a 60-40 joint venture that would take over GM's unprofitable van operation in the United Kingdom.

Daewoo

One of four large Korean conglomerate groups, Daewoo had sales of $8.6 billion and profits of about $50 million in 1985. Its businesses included trade, construction, shipbuilding, industrial machinery, motor vehicles, electronics, telecommunications, textiles, aircraft parts, personal computers, and financial services.

GM's links with Daewoo began in 1972 when GM purchased a 50% share in Shinjin Industrial, a small Korean automobile maker, and established a joint venture with Shinjin called GM-Korea. Shinjin later pledged its shares to the Korea Development Bank, and in 1978 the Daewoo Group acquired these shares. Five years later, the company was rechristened Daewoo Motor Co.

GM and Daewoo announced in 1984 that they would produce small cars for sale in Korea and abroad, which represented a $427 million investment with each firm contributing $100 million and Korean banks and Japanese equipment leasing firms providing the remainder. The funds paid for new stamping, engine, and assembly plants with an annual capacity of 167,000 vehicles. This would raise Daewoo's passenger car capacity from 66,000 to 233,000, and of these, 80,000 to 100,000 cars would be marketed at about $5,000 in the United States as the Pontiac LeMans.

The LeMans is based on the Opel Kadett, chosen "European Car of the Year" in 1985. Plans for its production, evaluated by an international team of engineers from Daewoo, GM, and Adam Opel, included state-of-the-art technology, such as anticorrosive paint vats and automated spray booths for painting. The influence of Opel engineers was evident in a number of the production processes: an assembly line that tilted sideways for easier installation of brake, fuel, and exhaust parts and a one-piece assembly of the driver instrument panel, steering column, and wheel were innovations not found in American plants. The new plant also incorporated robots and other automated equipment to boost quality, including 18 welding robots manufactured by GM Fanuc and Italian welding robots that positioned body panels precisely during framing operations. Opel provided an engine suited to Korean driving conditions, and Pontiac and Opel adapted it for U.S. emissions requirements.

Because obtaining quality parts was a problem in Korea, Daewoo Precision Industries and GM's Delco Remy division formed Daewoo Automotive Components in 1984 to manufacture cranking motors, alternators, ignition distributors, and ignition coils at a new plant in Korea. In 1985, DHMS Industries, a joint venture representing a $100 million initial investment, was formed by Daewoo Precision Industries and three GM divisions (Delco-Moraine, Harrison Radiator, and Saginaw Steering), with Daewoo and GM providing $18 million each in equity. The new firm would make steering columns and gears, front axles, brakes, radiators, heaters, and air conditioner components.

Later in 1985, a Daewoo Group subsidiary, Korea Steel Chemical Co., and GM's Fisher Guide division created Koram Plastics with a total initial investment of $20.5 million to manufacture polyurethane bumpers, using an advanced injection-molding system.

In July 1986, Daewoo introduced the LeMans to the Korean market. Orders for the LeMans ran about 7,000 a month in contrast to 4,000 a month for comparable Hyundai, despite the LeMan's higher price. By the end of the year, Hyundai's share of the Korean market had been cut from 80 to 60%. Daewoo Motors, intending to increase production to 278,000 units in 1988, expanded its parts production for GM, and Daewoo's chairman stated that "by 1988, exports of parts will equal the value of cars— $1 billion annually."

Suzuki

Suzuki's ties with GM began in 1981 when the Japanese firm announced that it would sell a 5.3% interest to GM for $35 million. At the same time, Suzuki and Isuzu swapped roughly 3% of their shares with each other.

At the time of the GM deal, Suzuki had about 5% of the Japanese car market and was a leader among domestic motorcycle producers. In minicars, Suzuki ranked first in Japan (see *Exhibit 4*); its motor vehicles ranged from 500 to 1,000 cc; the 800- to 1,000-cc vehicles were exported. It exported fewer cars than its Japanese competitors because most were smaller than the minimum size allowable in Western markets. Suzuki, with GM's assistance, would design and produce a car greater than 550 cc that would satisfy U.S. emission and safety standards.

In 1983, Suzuki introduced the 1-liter Cultus to the Japanese market. Jointly developed with GM, the car was tailored to meet the requirements of GM's Chevrolet division. Although one automobile magazine concluded that "in terms of both technology and production costs, the new Cultus set standards comfortably ahead of anything which GM was capable of achieving," the car got a lukewarm reception in the domestic Japanese market. In 1984, Chevrolet began selling the Cultus in the United States as the Sprint and sold 60,000 in a fast-growing and highly competitive market.

Suzuki and Isuzu began pooling their distribution systems in 1985. Suzuki sold Isuzu cars and supplied Isuzu with minivans; Isuzu sold an Isuzu-badged version of the Suzuki Cultus 1-liter station wagon and planned to add other Cultus models. Japanese analysts speculated that joint manufacturing projects would follow these joint marketing efforts.

In 1986, Suzuki and GM announced that they would build a plant in Ontario, Canada, to assemble the Suzuki Cultus (Chevy Sprint) and the Suzuki Samurai at a rate of 120,000 and 80,000, respectively, per year. The 50-50 joint venture would begin production in 1989, and more than 60% of its parts would be procured locally. GM would receive 80% of the output and planned to export part of its share to the United States.

Nissan

Like Toyota, Nissan, the world's fourth largest auto maker, is an industrial group. Its share of Japanese auto production fell from 30% in 1975 to 20% in 1985, total production fell every year between 1980 and 1984, and profits fell from 96 billion yen in 1983 to 65 billion yen in 1986.

In 1984, GM's Holden's subsidiary in Australia began supplying panels to Nissan Australia for production of the Pulsar. Nissan then supplied Pulsars to Holden's, which sold these vehicles as the Astra. The next year, Nissan began supplying transmissions and jointly developed engines to Holden's. In 1986, after it realized the Australian government would not change its plan to consolidate carmakers in Australia from five to three, Nissan expanded its relation with Holden's, and in July, revealed that it would purchase 1.6- and 2-liter engines from GM Holden's.

In 1986, Nissan licensed the Daewoo Motor Company to produce the Vannette in Korea. Beginning in 1987, Daewoo would produce 30,000 vans a year to be sold first in Korea, but Daewoo expected to expand its output later and sell the vans in the United States through GM's sales network.

FANUC

GMFanuc Robotics Corporation (GMF) was created by GM and Fanuc, the Japanese controls and robotics company, with an investment of $5 million each. Its charter was to design, market, service, and develop factory automation robots. Technology would flow to and from GMF's parents, without royalties or licenses. GMF, whose headquarters and manufacturing facilities would be in Michigan, would have the exclusive right to sell robots made in Japan by Fanuc throughout North and South America, Australia, and New Zealand.

GMF grew explosively during its first five years. Its 1985 sales were more than triple those of its nearest competitor, Cincinnati Milacron's robotics division. Earning roughly $10 million on sales of $185 million in 1986, it claimed to be the number one robotics company in the world, with expected sales of $1 billion by 1990. Its robots, which cost from $12,000 to $150,000 each, painted, welded, assembled, sealed, and loaded, and they also unloaded heavy or awkward cargoes. GMF expected to move far beyond simple "duck-drinking water" robots that repetitively performed the same simple task at the same spot on the same product. Future robots would have sensory functions and use television cameras and laser beams or extend sensitive probes to locate objects, reducing the need for manufacturers to develop ways of aligning objects for robot processing. GMF held talks with machine vision companies in which GM had made equity investments, even though two of them competed directly with GMF on vision systems, and GM did joint research on robots with Comau in Italy and had plans to do so with Hitachi. Ultimately, GMF planned to become the world's largest seller of vision systems.

GMF built its record of achievement in an intensely competitive industry; about 70 firms competed in the $600 million U.S. robotics market. Some were giants, such as Hitachi and Matsushita, General Electric, IBM, and ASEA, but most were much smaller firms created in the late 1970s as a result of buoyant expectations in the field and abundant venture capital. Few firms were profitable. Margins evaporated because of price cutting and the high costs of customizing applications software to customers' needs. And the steep recession in the early 1980s forced many American firms to join Japanese robot builders—IBM with Sankyo Seiki,

Westinghouse with Mitsubishi Electric, and Bendix with Yasakawa Electric—making competition even fiercer.

GM executives gave several reasons for joining forces with Fanuc. First, as the largest U.S. user of robots, GM bought a third of those sold in the United States and expected to have about 14,000 by 1990. Along with tens of thousands of computers and computerized numerical control units (NCs), they formed the core of GM's high-technology manufacturing strategy. GM's aim was to make the company into a "21st century" firm. EDS, Hughes Aircraft, and the new Saturn subsidiary were also part of this effort. Second, GM was dissatisfied with some of its robotics vendors. Third, GM had developed some of its own robotics products and expertise and wanted to find a way to sell them. Fourth, GM was concerned that it might lose some of its robotics personnel and technology to other robotic companies.

Though the joint venture was begun within three months after initial contact, GM had carefully examined eight or ten potential partners and negotiated with two of them before settling on Fanuc, which had made a strong impression with its drive, aggressiveness, and entrepreneurial management, and enthusiasm for joining forces with GM. This pace of decision making was almost unheard of at GM but was quite natural for Fanuc, where Dr. Sieuemon Inaba, the chief executive, had installed in the product development lab a clock that ran at ten times normal speed.

Fanuc's History

In 1955, Fujitsu, the Japanese electronics and computer company, had placed Inaba in charge of a team of 500 engineers whose mission was to develop a factory automation business. Fujitsu spun off Fanuc in 1972, while retaining about 40% of its shares. Fanuc was Inaba's personal handiwork. Under him, it became the world's leader in computerized numerical controls, or NCs, electronic boxes that control the movements of machine tools such as lathes and milling machines. Widely recognized as the world's low-cost and quality leader, by 1980 it held 75% of the Japanese market and 50% of the world market for NC devices. Its operating profits were so high that potential investors were placed on a waiting list.

Fanuc's prowess in factory automation was demonstrated by the plant it opened in 1981. In its first year, this facility produced more than 100 robots and NCs a month with only 100 employees, one-fifth the work force of comparable firms. By 1986, Fanuc expected to quadruple the plant's output while only doubling its employment. The plant would run 24 hours a day, with NCs and robots producing NCs and robots.

Fanuc was an ultraworkaholic company, with 14-hour workdays ordinary for managers and researchers. Many lived in company dormitories and commuted home to see their families only on weekends. Managers earned as much as 50% more than their counterparts in Japan, and engineers as much as 30% or more. Inaba, a reclusive man with a reputation for blunt, sometimes dictatorial behavior, had been compared with Ian Fleming's Dr. No. Inaba ran Fanuc with military precision.

When Fanuc joined with GM, it was seeking to build its robotics business. In 1980, NC devices and systems accounted for about 90% of the firm's sales; robots, only about 3%. Inaba wanted to boost robot revenues to 15% of Fanuc's business within three years. NCs resembled the hardware used to control robots; therefore, Fanuc's high-volume NC output would support much larger R&D spending than that of its competitors. Three factors appeared likely to impede Fanuc's drive into robotics: the Japanese economy's slowdown in the early 1980s, competition of about 200 Japanese firms in the robot industry, and also, Inaba believed, Japanese robot technology. In 1983, he said:

I would like to stress that Japanese robot-making technology is not necessarily at the world's topmost levels. It is true that the Japanese makers have an overwhelming edge over Western counterparts in terms of commercialization and mass production, but we've lagged behind in basic research. U.S. and European firms keep ahead of us in the field of high-efficiency robots, such as the next-generation intelligent robot with visual functions, moving robots capable of walking around factories and offices on their own feet, and more sophisticated robots connected with CAD/CAM systems. Though Japan boasts itself as being a "robot kingdom" possessing more than 70% of all the robots in the world, they are mostly manual manipulator types and other low-grade ones handled by men with remote control machines.

GM was not Fanuc's first overseas partner. During the early 1970s, Siemens, the German electronics giant, marketed and distributed Fanuc's NC devices throughout the world and owned 5% of Fanuc's shares. By the early 1980s, however, Siemens' ownership had fallen to 1%, and Fanuc had built its own European marketing network, becoming Siemens' competitor. In 1982, Fanuc agreed with Korea's Kolon group to set up a joint robot-making company in Korea. During the 1970s, Fanuc had also licensed the manufacture of controls and motors to the Bulgarians and helped them build a production plant in Sophia. Since then Bulgaria had become the Eastern bloc's major supplier of machine tools for both civilian and military production. This Fanuc linkup led to controversy in the mid-1980s when an executive of the United States National Tool Builders Association returned from the Soviet Union and said he had seen advanced Fanuc controls used in Soviet machine tools plants. Inaba's response was that Fanuc adhered "faithfully" to the Ministry of International Trade and Industry (MITI) export controls.

GMF's Operations

GMF's president and CEO was Eric Mittelstadt, a career GM manager. Mittelstadt said that GM and Fanuc interfered little with GMF's day-to-day operations, commenting that "both parents felt the company should manage itself and live or die on the basis of the robotics industry, and I took the job on that basis." Mittelstadt reported to a board of directors consisting of himself, the GMF executive vice president, and four others, two from Fanuc and two from GM. The board met twice a year, with a very few additional, informal meetings involving board members. GMF's executive vice president, responsible for coordinating product development, was a former Fanuc executive. Aside from him, however, only two or three of GMF's employees were Japanese.

Supplier-Vendor Relations

GMF's working relationships with its parents fell into two broad categories—the first, a supplier-vendor one. Fanuc built all of GMF's robots in Japan, except for robotic painting systems that GMF manufactured in Michigan. During 1985, devices imported from Fanuc equaled roughly 25% of GMF's sales. The paint robot, and associated hardware and software systems, which Mittelstadt described as "perhaps the most far-reaching advance in this technology," accounted for half of GMF's 1985 sales. The remaining sales were value-added to the Fanuc-supplied robots, primarily application systems work.

GMF also had supplier-vendor relationships with its customers. In 1985 GM accounted for 85% of GMF's sales in dollars and 70% in units, though GMF had tried to reduce its dependence on the automobile industry and on GM. Some of GMF's remaining sales were to other automobile companies, including Ford, Chrysler, BMW, Daimler-Benz, and Volkswagen, but most were to a wide range of nonautomatic companies. More than 75% of GMF's customers were outside the automobile industry, but they accounted for only 15 to 20% of its sales.

Integrating robotics with other larger computer systems made GMF's relations with its customers complex. Robotics firms found that most of their work was costly systems design (writing software and fitting robots into existing production lines), not simply making and selling "naked robots" or machines without customized applications engineering. Said an industry executive, "Implementing robotics is not like plugging in your coffee maker." An industry rule of thumb was that the cost of a robot was only 30% of total installation costs. Moreover, the main goal of many robotics installations was not to eliminate direct labor costs. For many U.S. manufactured goods, the direct labor content was below 15% and sometimes as low as 5%. Hence, robotics and computer-integrated manufacturing created benefits mainly from automating the flow of information through a factory and reducing the costs (ranging as high as 50%) attributed to indirect labor, middle management, quality control, and other overhead.

Product Development

GMF's product development efforts were coordinated by meetings held four times a year and involving senior executives from both GMF and Fanuc. According to Mittelstadt, GMF spent "much more than our nearest competitor and possibly more than any of our worldwide competitors on R&D." Development projects were conducted by teams consisting of engineers from Fanuc, GMF, and sometimes GM, with engineers from both parents involved because GMF had access to robotics technology from both parents. Some projects concentrated on hardware, aiming at developing more economical and more specialized units; others on software, developing programming and communications languages. Perhaps the most extensive effort at GMF was the development of Karel (named for Czech playwright Karel Kapek, who coined the term "robot," the Czech word for "serf"), a programming language. It linked GMF robots, vision systems, and other devices to both

GMF and non-GMF products. Several Japanese engineers spent two years at GMF helping to develop the language so that Fanuc's robots could use it. Karel gained wide acceptance in the robotics industry and could become the industry-standard language.

In August 1986, GMF sharply cut its revenue forecast for the next year and announced it would reduce its work force by nearly a third. GM had canceled orders totaling nearly $90 million, or over a third of GMF's anticipated revenue for 1986, and there were capital constraints and frustration with some high-technology and automation efforts. GM's decision reverberated throughout the entire robotics industry. Estimates of total industry sales fell about one-third to roughly $400 million. Major U.S. companies, such as Cincinnati Milacron and Unimation, which had already lost some of their GM business to GMF, anticipated bleak years. GMF expected its sales to be down substantially, and Mittelstadt said, "We will do well to break even this year."

Fanuc agreed to the cut in GMF's work force, but press reports asserted that Inaba was frustrated with the company. *Business Week* said Inaba had complained that although GMF bought 75% of his robots, it caused 90% of his headaches; at the time, Fanuc's profits for 1986 were estimated to have fallen by 35%. The same article asserted that there was frequent bickering inside GMF about the lack of stock options and GMF's total reliance on Fanuc for robot components. These speculations were denied by both Dr. Inaba and Mr. Mittelstadt.

Events in 1986

Fanuc and General Electric announced in June 1986 that they would create a $200 million joint venture called GE-Fanuc Automation (GEF). *Fortune* described GE's willingness to join forces with Fanuc as a "surrender," as GE had been Fanuc's main competitor in NCs. The previous year, however, GE had lost at least $200 million in its effort to become an "automation supermarket." Under the joint venture, GE would stop making its own NC units and instead assemble Fanuc devices at a plant in Virginia. The venture would concentrate on control systems for automated production lines. GE executives expected the effort to earn a first-year profit of $250 million on worldwide sales. Denying capitulation to Fanuc, they asserted the venture was "a very natural marriage that is going to make one of the most competitive worldwide enterprises in the field."

The agreement would secure access for Fanuc to GE customers and personnel in engineering, service, and marketing. Fanuc also would have access to new products and technologies, such as programmable logic controllers and factory floor computers that GE had adapted after purchase from IBM and Digital Equipment. Cooperation between GEF and GMF was also expected. GEF would concentrate on NC products and systems, and GMF would concentrate on robotic products and systems, with the two cooperating on systems involving both areas. Finally, these arrangements—with both GMF and GEF—let Fanuc concentrate its efforts in NC and robotics hardware. The less profitable, much more difficult activity of customizing software would be done in conjunction with Fanuc's partners who would be closer to the customer requiring it.

PARTS AND COMPONENTS MAKERS

An executive of GM's Delco Electronics division in the late 1970s realized that the U.S. industry would soon face serious competition from Japan on the price, quality, and reliability of components. As a result, Delco made the first foray into Japan. By the mid-1980s, GM's total purchases had risen rapidly from a level of roughly $100 million in 1980. Even with the rising yen, GM continued to expand its purchases and open relationships with leading Japanese parts suppliers. Estimates placed GM's

1986 parts purchases—most made by Delco Electronics—at $350 million, an increase of 80% from 1985 and an amount not including GM's purchases from Isuzu and Suzuki or its transactions with Fanuc.

Hitachi

GM and Hitachi, the Japanese counterpart of GE in size and product range, first joined forces in 1982 when GM Delco Electronics announced that they would begin joint development of microcomputerized control systems for cars. An industrial group that makes electric appliances, industrial machinery, and power generation equipment, Hitachi from the late 1970s had expanded its auto parts production, an area it expects to grow rapidly with the incorporation of electronics. Hitachi already had similar projects with Isuzu and Suzuki. Later in the year, GM and Hitachi announced that they would begin joint development of robots for GM's plants: Hitachi would provide robot production technology and perhaps robots from Japan; GM would provide software.

In 1986, Hitachi and GM agreed to start cooperative development and production in five areas: car parts, electronic components, optical fibers, magnetic materials, other new products, and factory automation. The two firms set up joint project teams to investigate each area, with their first focus on car parts. Both firms would develop technology for car electronics and Hitachi would commercialize. Later, the two companies would turn to technology for computers and factory automation. At the same time, GM announced a long-term agreement to spend roughly $60 million a year buying electronic control systems for car engines from Hitachi's new plant in Kentucky.

Nihon Radiator

A member of the Nissan group, Nihon Radiator is one of Nissan's three major parts producers, and Nissan owns 34.7% of its shares. It earned profits of $20 million on its 1986 sales of $1 billion.

In 1986, Nihon Radiator and GM announced plans for Calsonic Harrison, a joint venture to produce next-generation (V5) compressors for air conditioners originally developed by GM's Harrison Radiator division. Calsonic would build a $60 million plant in Japan; production would start in 1987 and increase to 1 million units a year by 1990. Most of the plant's output would be exported to the United States. Nihon Radiator would gain access to GM's V5 compressor technology, considered to be the most advanced of its kind.

Atsugi

Atsugi Motor Parts, along with Nihon Radiator and Kanto Seiki, is one of Nissan's three main parts suppliers. Nissan own 37% of Atsugi's shares. Most of its sales are made to Nissan group companies, but the firm has gradually increased its sales to other carmakers, such as Fuji, Mitsubishi, Mazda, and Honda. Isuzu signed a parts contract with Atsugi in April 1986.

Atsugi began supplying GM with parts and accessories in 1981. In return, it received technical assistance. During the next several years, as demand for its main product, drive shafts, dropped because of the trend toward front-wheel-drive vehicles, Atsugi began to develop new products. In 1986, Nissan and Atsugi announced they would sell technology for their electronically controlled suspension system to Monroe, a major U.S. manufacturer of shock absorbers. Their system assesses road conditions with supersonic waves and then adjusts the suspension. Monroe would buy sensors from Nissan-related companies in Japan to produce the suspension system and then sell it to GM and other U.S. and Japanese automakers.

Kyoritsu

In 1981, GM announced it would buy Harada Industry's 20% holdings in Kyoritsu Hiparts, a wire-harness maker affiliated with Nissan. The other two investors in Kyoritsu are Hitachi Cable (40%) and Kanto Seiki (40%); the latter is 44% owned by Nissan.

Tachikawa Spring

Tachikawa, an automobile seat maker, is 20% owned by Nissan. In 1986, it agreed to supply its formed seat cover technology to GM through its U.S. partner, Hoover International, which will manufacture and supply seats to GM. Tachikawa's technology—not yet used in Japan or the United States—molds vinyl or cloth with heat into the desired shape, then attaches the cover to a cushion pad.

Akebono Brakes

Akebono, the largest Japanese brake manufacturer, has had relationships with U.S. companies since the early 1960s, when it accepted investments and technology from Bendix. In 1985, Akebono and GM's Delco-Moraine division announced a 50-50 joint venture, American Brake Industry, that would make drum and disk brakes and other brake parts in the midwest. The two firms would initially invest $50 million; customers would include GM's Saturn plant and other Japanese and American car manufacturers located in the midwest. The venture would develop next-generation brakes using electronics technology.

Akebono believed it had world-class technology and costs as much as 20% lower than for comparable products in the United States. GM's expertise in electronics was likely to become more important in the future—for anti-skid controls on braking systems, for example—and GM believed that its brake technology could be sold to Japanese auto companies and wanted a Japanese partner to help it develop this business.

NHK Spring

NHK Spring, a Japanese company, is the largest producer of auto suspension systems in the world. It is an independent company, without deep-rooted affiliations with any of the major auto firms, though Nissan, Isuzu, and Mitsubishi are among its major customers. Toyota owns shares of one of NHK's competitors. NHK Spring and Suzuki have a joint venture that makes seats for motorcycles and autos.

In 1985, U.S. automakers became interested in NHK's fiber-reinforced plastic (FRP) springs. FRP uses glass filaments to strengthen plastic springs, cutting their weight by 32 to 54 pounds. GM first used FRP springs from NHK on the Corvette and later on vans. GM's Inland unit and NHK announced that they would form a 55% NHK–45% GM joint venture in Japan to produce FRP auto suspension equipment; later it would produce electronic controls for suspension and related equipment. The two firms also agreed to establish joint ventures to manufacture car components in the United States, Western Europe, and elsewhere.

MANAGING THE RELATIONSHIPS

The critical links between GM and its component-making partners were between individual Asian firms and the GM divisions that they supplied. A GM executive observed that "in these activities, GM has equity participation, but manages the relationship in the context of vendor relations in general, with, perhaps, more technology transfer than in the usual vendor relation. There generally is no involvement in company management except in the component joint ventures." Divisions gave suppliers forecasts of their needs; lead time and accuracy

were especially important for large orders. Vendors also had to understand the new product plans of the divisions so that they could have equipment, capacity, engineering, and other resources ready. This was especially vital for complex components.

Roughly two-thirds of GM's Japanese suppliers had their own sales offices in the United States. Their reps called on GM divisions and could summon engineering support, either from the United States or from Japan, on short notice. At the same time, GM divisions like Delco and Harrison Radiator had managers based in Japan to help coordinate relationships.

For Isuzu and Suzuki, GM stationed personnel in Tokyo, including manufacturing, marketing, and engineering consultants, planners, procurement and distribution managers, industry analysts, and marketing and engineering specialists. At the Daewoo Motor Company, GM was represented by a career executive who lived in Korea and served as executive vice president of Daewoo Motor Company and as joint representative director and by other consultants.

These people were positioned to advise and assist, using any GM knowledge and experience. When new subjects arose between the parties involving knowledge proprietary to either, the exchange was usually covered by agreement, preceded by the proprietor party's consideration of whether or not to seek royalties or expense reimbursement. Various agreements or practices, formal or by precedent, govern the extent to which significant business decisions are shared. These agreements or practices are different between Isuzu and Daewoo Motor and are different between Isuzu and other Isuzu-GM affiliations.

Despite the importance of these relationships to the partners involved and efforts on both sides to manage them successfully, several problems arose. One was the NIH, or "not invented here," syndrome—engineers, marketing people, and managers had a tendency to prefer the ideas and products of their parent company rather than of their partner. Functional personnel on both sides also complained at times about the division of labor and opportunities, saying that activities or investment funds were being diverted to the partner or to a joint venture rather than given to them.

How each partner viewed the relationship also depended upon the market conditions it faced. When demand for a company's products was strong, its alliances didn't seem to matter very much. When demand was very weak, functional personnel and operating managers tended to concentrate almost exclusively on fixing their own company's problems, and paid much less attention to distant, overseas relationships. Only when demand fell into some intermediate zone were these relationships taken completely seriously. Changes in the relationship—such as a decision to develop a new product, or shifts in equity investments or operating control—exacerbated many of these tensions.

Finally, GM's dealings with its Asian partners were sometimes complicated by antitrust scrutiny in the United States. For example, the FTC required Toyota and GM to keep detailed logs describing discussions and transactions between the two companies. None of GM's other Asian relationships received this degree of scrutiny, but many of them required detailed discussions with the FTC or the antitrust division of the Justice Department, as well as continuing reports on the ventures.

EVENTS IN EARLY 1988

In January 1988, a GM vice president announced in Beijing an "initial step" in a "comprehensive China-GM program." GM said it would build light engines in cooperation with the Chinese government's auto company, as well as a foundry, an axle works, and operations making starter motors, distributors, and alternators. Press reports in Japan and the United States said that Fuji Heavy Industries of Japan, the maker of Subaru cars, would provide technology for the effort and that the partners would ultimately announce plans to make passenger vehicles in China, perhaps by 1990, in a $4.1 billion project.

In March, the *Wall Street Journal* reported that GM was considering a "radical cure" for falling sales of its imported and joint-venture subcompacts. Sales of the three cars had fallen 18% to 272,000 in 1987. It would create the first new nameplate—Geo—since the introduction of Pontiac in 1926. Chevrolet dealers would create separate display areas or even separate showrooms for updated and renamed models of the Nova, Sprint, and Spectrum, along with an imported Jeep-like, sports utility vehicle made by Suzuki. The reaction among GM dealers was reported to be very enthusiastic.

EXHIBIT ONE

GENERAL MOTORS IN 1988

Balance sheet data, 1976–1986 ($ millions)

December 31	Cash	Total assets	Long-term debt	Common equity	Return on equity
1987	4,706	87,422	4,313	32,989	10.8%
1986	4,019	72,593	4,325	30,444	9.7
1985	5,114	63,833	2,867	29,274	13.7
1984	8,567	52,145	2,773	23,959	18.4
1983	6,217	45,695	3,522	20,483	18.2
1982	3,126	41,398	4,745	18,004	5.3
1981	1,321	38,991	4,044	17,438	1.9
1980	3,715	34,581	2,058	17,531	NM*
1978	4,055	30,598	979	17,286	20.3
1976	4,625	24,442	1,070	14,102	20.6

Income data, 1976–1986 ($ millions)

Year ended December 31	Revenue	Operating income	Operating income/ revenue	Capital expendi- tures	Depreciation	Interest expense	Net income†	Net income/ revenue
1987	101,782	2,569	2.5%	7,057	6,113	1,631	3,551	3.5%
1986	102,814	1,431	1.4	11,712	6,594	954	2,945	2.9
1985	97,372	4,219	4.4	11,123	6,208	892	3,999	4.1
1984	83,890	4,700	5.6	6,047	4,966	909	4,517	5.4
1983	74,582	5,508	7.4	4,007	5,120	1,356	3,730	5.0
1982	60,026	5,512	9.2	6,212	4,551	1,415	963	1.6
1981	62,699	391	7.7	9,741	4,406	898	333	0.5
1980	57,729	(1,186)	5.2	7,762	4,178	532	(763)	NM
1978	63,221	6,485	15.1	4,564	3,036	356	3,508	5.5
1976	47,181	5,383	15.4	2,307	2,243	284	2,903	6.2

*NM—not meaningful.
†Includes earnings from GMAC and from EDS and General Motors Hughes Electronics after they were acquired.
Sources: Standard & Poor's Stock Reports, February 19, 1986, p. 978; and the 1985 and 1986 annual reports.

GM's SHARE OF THE U.S. MARKET

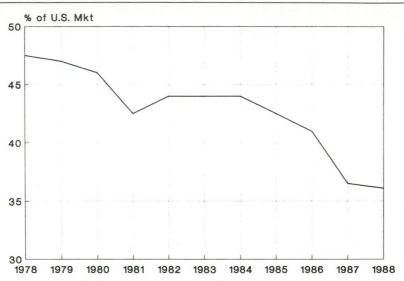

Source: *Wall Street Journal,* various issues.

GM's worldwide sales (units in thousands)

	Cars			Trucks and buses			Total		
	1987	1986	1985	1987	1986	1985	1987	1986	1985
U.S.	3,592	4,302	4,882	1,520	1,520	1,537	5,112	5,882	6,419
Canada	344	545	562	238	192	280	582	737	842
Overseas	1,857	1,783	1,762	214	234	282	2,071	2,017	2,044
Total	5,793	6,630	7,206	1,972	1,946	2,099	7,765	8,576	9,305

Source: General Motors annual reports.

EXHIBIT THREE

ISUZU SALES AND PROFITS
(In Millions of Yen)

Year ending October 31	Sales	Net income	% of Japanese production (in 1,000 units)	Total exports (1,000 units)
1967	149,336	4,480	3.6	
1971	197,539	(366)	2.3	17
1972	196,481	(3,440)	2.9	63
1973	262,593	2,415	3.1	60
1974	326,215	2,007	3.8	106
1975	356,302	(8,722)	3.5	113
1976	424,855	7,397	4.3	183
1977	468,758	6,182	4.0	167
1978	572,386	13,434	4.4	223
1979	635,442	12,643	4.4	214
1980	687,713	4,954	4.3	273
1981	727,410	8,510	4.1	259
1982	719,002	6,038	3.8	221
1983	684,624	5,285	3.5	201
1984	769,002	(17,725)	3.8	286
1985	1,016,250	13,384	4.8	408
1986	1,013,434	(3,979)	4.5	394

Source: Isuzu annual reports.

EXHIBIT FOUR

SUZUKI PERFORMANCE
(In Millions of Yen)

Year	Sales	Net profit
1975	87,723	996
1976	166,966	1,468
1977	215,960	3,314
1978	253,392	3,547
1979	271,517	3,451
1980	345,099	4,003
1981	457,779	4,793
1982	551,521	5,470
1983	542,319	6,590
1984	524,259	5,002
1985	580,841	6,027
1986	722,336	6,120

Source: Suzuki annual reports.

General Electric— Consumer Electronics Group

On December 12, 1985, GE Chairman Jack Welch announced the largest nonoil merger ever— General Electric Corp.'s $6.4 billion purchase of RCA. Among other businesses that would be combined as a result of the transaction were the two companies' consumer electronics divisions. Although the combined group would be the U.S. market leader (with a 23% share of the color television market and 17% of the VCR market), both divisions had recently experienced losses in the face of intense pressure from Japanese and Korean competitors.

Only eight months before the merger, Rick Miller had been promoted from his position as RCA's chief financial officer to head several RCA divisions including consumer electronics. To Miller's surprise, Jack Welch asked if he would assume control of the combined Consumer Electronics Group (CEG). Rick Miller accepted the offer while clearly understanding the difficulty of the challenge ahead—merging the two separate divisions and developing a strategy to restore the business to acceptable levels of profitability.

HISTORY OF THE TELEVISION INDUSTRY

United States

As the world leader in television set technology, RCA established the first American broadcast network (NBC) in 1939 to create demand for the new product. It began broadcasting only in New York City, and with the price of a TV set about half that of a car, by 1942 only 10,000 television sets had been sold. With postwar American affluence the popularity of television

Assistant Professor David J. Collis prepared this case with the assistance of Research Associates Richard Phelps and Nancy Donohue as the basis for class discussion rather than to illustrate either effective or ineffective handling of an administrative situation.

grew rapidly. By 1954 broadcast transmissions covered 90% of the nation, and by 1959 TV penetration of U.S. households reached 85% (*Exhibit 1*).

Despite the initial complexity of TV set manufacturing, 140 U.S. firms produced sets in 1950. This number fell to 35 by 1960 as television set technology matured during the 1950s. Of the five essential components of the television set (picture tube, cabinet, circuitry, chassis, and tuner), the picture tube represented the most complicated technology. Its manufacturing was highly automated, and an investment of $4 million was needed to set up an efficient black-and-white picture tube plant that produced 1.2 million units a year. Setting up an assembly plant that could produce 1 million black-and-white sets a year required an investment of approximately $5 million. Among the more profitable survivors by 1960 were those firms (RCA, GE, Philco, Motorola, Zenith, and Sears' Warwick subsidiary) that produced a full range of TV sets, radios, and appliances and sold and serviced them through department stores and independent servicing dealers. Marketing and service expenses averaged about 10% of sales.

In 1953 the FCC adopted RCA's all-electronic system as the industry standard for color television. Having only one serious rival (the Chromatron System of Paramount Pictures licensed to Sony), RCA orchestrated the introduction of color TV sets and broadcasting and had such a dominant patent position that in 1958 the Justice Department forced it to sign a consent decree giving competitors freer access to its technology. Despite disappointing color TV sales through the late 1950s, RCA invested heavily in color set production. Other producers refrained from making color sets and let RCA bear the burden of convincing a skeptical public to buy the product. More complex and expensive than their black-and-white counterparts, color sets required three times the number of components and cost consumers three to five times more. However, when color set

sales started to increase in the early 1960s, virtually every major player began to manufacture them. In 1964, before many producers had recovered their investment in color set production, RCA lowered its prices by over 20%, and by 1965 color TV sales exceeded black-and-white sales for the first time.

Major improvements took place in set design and production during the 1960s and 1970s. The move to solid state was completed, first with transistors and then with integrated circuits (ICs). This improved reliability substantially and reduced the need for repair and service. The use of ICs also enabled engineers to simplify sets and reduce component counts and the labor content of manufacturing. The best producers in the world went from multiple- to single-board chassis designs and reduced the number of components in a basic 19-inch set from 1,400 in 1965 to 400 by 1979 (*Exhibit 2*). Over the same period, the labor required to produce one TV set was reduced from 9 hours to less than 30 minutes, and the portion of assembly performed by automated insertion increased from 0% to close to 100%. Each redesign to incorporate new technology was expensive. In 1979, development costs for a new color TV model were estimated at $300,000 to $400,000, while retooling costs for each new model were about $1 million. Design costs for new color picture tubes were even higher.

Economies of scale in television set production were such that total production costs could be reduced approximately 5% for every doubling of volume between 50,000 to 250,000 sets per year. Above 500,000 units per year most experts believed that no further manufacturing economies were gained. Large scale was not necessary for automatic insertion, for example, which was feasible in plants with capacities of 100,000 color sets per year. In purchasing, cost savings existed primarily for ICs, where costs fell 25% for each doubling of volume and where supply shortages occurred periodically for firms not integrated into IC production.

Many U.S. manufacturers began to move production overseas between the years 1966 and 1973 to reduce costs. RCA, Sears, Zenith, Motorola, GTE, Magnavox, and Philco opened facilities in Mexico, Taiwan, and Singapore. By the mid-1970s, most black-and-white TV set production and the more labor-intensive portions of color TV production had been moved to low-wage countries, and many components were also sourced offshore.

Nevertheless, imports began to capture a greater share of the U.S. market during the 1970s, and American manufacturers lobbied for protection. An "orderly marketing agreement" (OMA) with Japan in 1977 marked the first of many ensuing legal attempts to restrict imports. The breach was quickly filled by Taiwan and Korea, and OMAs were subsequently negotiated with those two countries. In 1983, all OMAs lapsed and total imports doubled, with South Korea becoming the leading source of imports, followed by Taiwan (*Exhibit 3*). Major Japanese companies had since established U.S. production facilities.

Between 1960 and 1980, U.S. TV manufacturers had exited the industry at a rate of one per year. Among the larger producers, Motorola sold out to Matsushita in 1974, GTE-Sylvania bought Philco in 1974 and later sold its TV business to Philips, and the last independent tube maker, Westinghouse, closed in 1975. By 1980 more television sets were being manufactured in the United States by foreign firms than by American ones. Of the five U.S.-owned TV producers remaining, only three—RCA, GE, and Zenith—were of significant size (*Exhibit 4*).

Europe

Even though the European population exceeded that of the United States, sales of black-and-white sets did not exceed those of the United States until 1959, and sales of color sets not until 1974. TV sets were priced higher than in the United States, and Europeans tended to own them for a long time, keeping them meticulously serviced. The European market was fragmented by country, partly because there were three different standards for black-and-white television and two incompatible standards for color. Market penetration rates and distribution channels also differed by nation. Each manufacturer had therefore historically produced for its domestic market and handled its own distribution. When overcapacity emerged in the mid-1970s, after firms had rapidly expanded output to meet the peak color television set demand of the early 1970s and Japanese firms had entered the market for the first time, the European industry began to consolidate. Several manufacturers went out of business, while others merged or entered into joint ventures with the Japanese who, under the pressure of controls on licenses for European broadcast standards and import restrictions, had been setting up or acquiring manufacturing bases in Europe since 1970. By 1987 Philips and Thomson were the only major European manufacturers remaining.

Japan

Demand in the Japanese market was primarily for smaller sets since space was at a premium in Japanese homes. In the early 1960s, just as the Japanese domestic market became saturated with black-and-white sets and U.S. producers were turning their attention to larger color TVs, a new demand for small black-and-white TVs as a second set emerged in the United States. Japanese manufacturers, with experience in the miniaturization of components, started exporting small TVs to the U.S. market, selling them (with the exception of Sony products) under retailers' private labels. As the quality and low cost of the Japanese products became increasingly evident, U.S. manufacturers such as RCA, GE, and Zenith sourced

Japanese black-and-white sets for their product lines. In 1964, after RCA and Zenith had refused, Sears asked Toshiba to manufacture its private-label color sets. Sears provided Toshiba with the basic designs from its Warwick subsidiary and taught the company how to style its sets for the American consumer. Soon after, the major Japanese manufacturers began to establish their own distribution networks for color television sets in the United States.

Japanese producers were the first to move to solid-state sets employing ICs in the 1960s and were quick to adopt single-board chassis designs (with fewer connectors and lower materials costs), to automate insertion and testing, and to lower component counts, thereby saving labor and increasing reliability. These moves contributed to their reputation for high quality. In the mid-1970s, for example, while U.S. producer warranty call rates were about 12%, Japan's were about 3%.

Most Japanese producers opened U.S. production facilities after the mid-1970s partly because transport costs for large sets could outweigh the savings to be realized from assembly in Japan. Some manufacturers established plants where sets were assembled from imported kits. Others bought failing American companies, acquiring existing production facilities. Most of the Japanese producers, however, were not backward-integrated in the United States. For the elements of a television set that were expensive to transport, such as the cabinet, and the picture tubes (which faced a 15% import tariff), the Japanese sourced from American suppliers.

As sales of television sets by Japanese companies leveled off, growth in sales of video cassette recorders (VCRs) occurred. Japanese-made VCR sales doubled in each year from 1976 to 1981. Dominating the world market for VCRs with a 97% share, the Japanese exported 80% of their production and earned substantial profits. No U.S. company made VCRs—all sourced from Japanese manufacturers. Philips was the sole European producer of VCRs. Profits began to diminish for VCR makers in the mid-1980s as Korean and other Asian production began.

South Korea

South Korean manufacturers began small black-and-white set production in the 1960s with Japanese-licensed technology and a low-labor-cost advantage. They priced aggressively, mostly in the private-label business, outproducing Japan by 1979 and Taiwan by 1980. Producers built production capacity well in advance of sales and constructed facilities for the manufacture of essential components (picture tubes, glass bulbs, and picture masks). South Korea became a color TV producer in 1973, even though Korea had no color broadcasting of its own, when Japanese companies, prompted by the yen revaluation against the dollar, began using their Korean affiliates to export color TVs to the United States. Korean export volume increased dramatically after 1977 when Japanese exports to the United States were restricted by the OMA. By the 1980s, when all OMAs were removed, Korean and Taiwanese producers captured the low end of the TV market for black-and-white sets and small color sets. Expecting that the Chinese would begin exporting color sets by 1988, Korean firms began production of VCRs in 1981 with Japanese licenses for the Korean market only. After overcoming Japanese opposition, VCR exports began in 1985.

CURRENT STATE OF THE TV INDUSTRY

Technology

In 1987, advances in technology such as stereo sound, miniaturization, and modular components for home entertainment systems allowed firms to continually differentiate their products. Over the horizon loomed two more substantive innovations. High-definition television (HDTV), already developed by the Japanese at a cost of several hundred million dollars, yielded pictures with five times more detail than existing sets. U.S. TV manufacturers and the FCC (who would set the new industry standard) currently opposed HDTV introduction as it would make existing U.S. sets obsolete. The second innovation, digital TV, offered the possibility of simultaneous viewing and focused zooming, with quality and reliability much greater than present-day sets. Some of the digital TV features, such as split-screen capability, were currently available, though at an additional cost of $150 per set. Containing less than 10 ICs the price of digital sets would decline significantly if they became mass-produced. Liquid crystal display TVs, although still in the R&D stage, were a possible third major innovation. They used little power, were light in weight, and were slim enough to be hung on walls.

R&D expenditures varied among manufacturers, although it was difficult to discern how much a consumer electronics company spent specifically on televisions because most research took place in shared facilities. Nonetheless, it appeared that consumer electronics firms fell into three categories: companies that sold but did not manufacture TVs and spent nothing on R&D (Emerson), American and Korean producers that spent 1 to 5% of sales on R&D, and the Japanese and European producers that spent from 5% to 9% of sales on R&D and had steadily increased their expenditures through the 1980s. Absolute dollar expenditures for large manufacturers ranged from $120 million to $350 million per year.

Manufacturing

By 1987 U.S. and European producers had done much to imitate the Japanese manufacturing methods. RCA, for example, had reduced the average number of components in its TV sets to below 400, less than some Japanese producers. All producers had adopted single-circuit board designs and mechanized testing and had access to commodity electronic components, automated insertion equipment, and integrated circuits made by companies unassociated with TV set production. *Exhibit 5* displays a typical cost structure for TV sets in 1986. Successful producers operated production facilities in several countries and sourced components globally (*Exhibit 6*). Relative wage rates were an important determinant of the location of manufacturing operations. RCA estimated that in 1987 U.S. labor costs ranged from $9 to $15/hour compared to $14/hour in Japan, $2/hour in Taiwan and Hong Kong, $1.25/hour in Brazil and Korea, and $0.60 to $0.70/hour in Mexico and Malaysia. Plant minimum efficient scale was believed to be about 1 million sets per annum. A plant twice that size might save 3 to 4% of manufacturing costs. Transport cost for a small set from the Far East to the United States was 4% of total cost, and 7% for large sets.

Marketing and Distribution

The market share of the traditional retail channels, department and appliance stores, had diminished considerably by the 1980s with the success of consumer electronics superstores. These superstores sold cheaply and in high volume, stocked a large variety of brands, and ignored dealer territory. They now commanded over one-third of the retail market, responding to the increasing importance of price in consumer purchase criteria. Market research showed that for more than one-half of purchasers price was the most important factor in their decision to buy. The number of television set brands sold in the U.S. market, which had dwindled to 10 by 1976, had tripled to 30 by 1986, and average retail prices had declined at about 4% per year. VCR prices had declined 60% in the five years since 1981.

The market reach of the superstores, however, was not infinite. Since they required high-volume sales, they only existed in urban markets, leaving more rural areas to the traditional small dealer who offered only one or two brands. More conservative customers also preferred the intimate level of service found in small dealerships. All dealers could easily affect sales by manipulating a set's controls, so that the brand with the highest dealer margin had the best picture in the store. RCA executives claimed, for example, that only 50% of the customers who visited a store intending to buy RCA models ultimately did so.

Regional differences in the styling of television sets continued. The midwest favored large console sets in heavy "American" style wood cabinets. Urban areas demanded small table sets in streamlined "modern" cabinets. Superior style, performance, or technical features, such as the slimline cabinet or remote control, could lead to significant, if temporary, sales benefits for the innovating company (*Exhibit 7*). Most companies offered one-year warranties on their sets, and it was only the smaller brands that tried to lure consumers with three- to five-year warranties.

Expenditures on advertising and promotion by manufacturers to support their retailers averaged 1 to 2% of sales. The major producers spent $10 to $15 million on advertising in 1985, while the smaller Japanese and South Korean competitors spent from $1 to $4 million. Although all manufacturers sold to the same large chains, the number of independent dealers each distributed to differed. Emerson, for example, barely had any dealers of its own, while medium-sized manufacturers had over 1,000 dealers and larger companies (Sony and GE) had over 3,000. RCA served about 10,000 independent dealers. Offering a full line of consumer electronics to these dealers was important, since they relied on only a few producers to stock their stores.

To sell and distribute to the retail outlets, manufacturers either used their own sales forces and warehouse systems or relied on independent distributors. While independent distributors offered the service, local knowledge, and 24-hour delivery that a direct distribution network could not, it added another layer of cost and margin into the distribution chain. Different manufacturers used different mixes of direct and independent distribution channels, and no consistent pattern emerged except that the larger, urban retail chains were all dealt with direct. Total sales, marketing, and distribution expenses ranged from RCA's 6%, up to 10%.

COMPETITORS

United States

Zenith   In the 1960s Zenith built a reputation for quality claiming in its advertising that its sets were "handwired." It captured and held the number 2 position in U.S. TV set sales and the number 1 position in black-and-white sales until the 1980s. Zenith, however, had been slower than its competitors to convert to solid-state design and automated production techniques. Offshore facilities in Mexico and Taiwan constructed circuit boards, tuners, and small sets, while Zenith continued to make picture tubes and assemble large sets in the United States. From the 1970s, Zenith was the most persistent advocate of protection from Japanese and Korean imports. In the 1980s, Zenith's consumer electronics business was largely unprofitable, and it was diversifying successfully into personal computers (*Exhibit 8*).

Emerson   After purchasing the Emerson Radio brand name from an extinct company that had manufactured TVs in the United States until 1970, Emerson established an operation that consisted only of marketing and distribution. It purchased complete consumer electronic products from a variety of low-cost Asian suppliers under the Emerson brand name and pushed these products to large national chain retailers through a small sales force. Despite its minimalist character, Emerson was very profitable in the 1980s.

Europe

Philips Philips made the world's widest variety of electronic, lighting, communications, and electrical products and was the world's largest manufacturer of color TVs in 1987. A fully integrated worldwide TV manufacturer (including its own glass), Philips had over a fifth of the European TV market. It was the only European producer of VCRs (under license from JVC) and video and audio disc players (which it had invented). Evolving into a worldwide "federation of companies" spread over 60 countries, it centralized control over most engineering and R&D functions and decentralized country-level control over sales and marketing. North American (N.A.) Philips grew by acquiring the failing consumer electronics operations of GTE, Ford, and Magnavox. By the 1980s, it was the third largest producer in the United States, ahead of GE, with over 10% of the market. Fully integrated in TV manufacturing in North America, it assembled boards and chassis in Mexico and made its own picture tubes and cabinetry. In 1987, the parent Philips dissolved N.A. Philips as an independent entity in order to better coordinate its worldwide operations and exploit its size.

Thomson Thomson-Brandt was France's only significant consumer electronics manufacturer. Owned by the French government, it had diversified into other industries including defense and medical electronics. Starting in the 1970s, Thomson set out to increase its production scale and consolidate the European consumer electronics industry by acquiring GE's and GTE's failing European affiliates. By 1987 Thomson took over the German AEG Telefunken and the British Ferguson, and it boasted the second largest TV market share in Europe, behind Philips. Thomson was fairly open in its conviction that Europe could only support two profitable consumer electronics companies and advocated a revocation of national antitrust laws. Thomson possessed only minor operations outside Europe.

Japan

Sony Sony first entered the U.S. market in the 1950s, eschewing the policy of other Japanese companies that entered into OEM agreements with U.S. corporations. Unlike its Japanese competitors Sony used its own name on its products and was relatively undiversified outside consumer electronics. Notable among its few outside businesses were broadcast equipment (successful enough to push RCA out of that industry by the mid-1980s) and "software" (Sony purchased CBS records in 1987). With a reputation for innovation and quality, Sony charged premium prices for its products and spent 9% of sales on R&D. In technological leadership, Sony had many successes (the "Walkman" and the Trinitron color picture tube), but it also led the push to develop the unsuccessful Betamax format for VCRs. By 1987 Sony's TV operations in the United States were larger than in Japan. Sony's North American TV production was completely integrated (which was necessary because its picture tube was unique and not interchangeable with all other manufacturers' picture tubes), and it was using its U.S. base to export TVs to Latin America.

Matsushita In 1987, Matsushita was the world's leading manufacturer of consumer electronics products under the Panasonic, National, Quasar, and Technics names and Japan's foremost producer of consumer electronics and household appliances. The Japan Victor Company (JVC) was a 51% subsidiary. It was a technology "follower," reverse-engineering

Sony products and launching competing versions at a lower price within months of Sony's initial introduction. In the 1980s, Matsushita increased its effort to diversify out of consumer electronics (over 90% of its business) into office automation, communication equipment, and automated assembly equipment. Matsushita was second only to Philips in worldwide color TV market share. It made its own semiconductors and sold color picture tubes to other Japanese companies. Matsushita also aimed to manufacture more of its products near its end markets. Not yet fully integrated in the North American market, it bought some of its picture tubes from outside suppliers, as well as all of its cabinetry and glass. It also was discussing with Philips the possibility of opening a joint-venture facility for the production of picture tubes in the United States. Matsushita was badly hurt in the United States by the GE/RCA merger which resulted in the loss of the supply contract for GE's half-million set volume from a new facility it had built in Washington.

Korea

Lucky-Goldstar Sometimes called the General Electric of Korea because it dominated the electrical equipment industry there, the Lucky-Goldstar conglomerate was Korea's first TV set producer, and it held the largest domestic market share. Goldstar entered the U.S. television market in the late 1970s by supplying private-label sets to companies such as K mart and Emerson. By Goldstar's own estimate, it gained 5% of the U.S. color market through such arrangements. In 1981, Goldstar was the first Korean producer to build a production facility in the United States. Erecting a small factory in Alabama, it assembled Korean-made chassis with picture tubes purchased from N.A. Philips. To get around a 20% dumping tariff imposed on their imported sets in 1984, it increased production at the Alabama plant. In 1984, Goldstar produced almost 6 million black-

and-white and color TV sets (1 million of them in the United States), making it one of the world leaders in production volume. It mainly produced small, inexpensive sets which were purchased as second sets in the United States.

Samsung A large Korean conglomerate and trading company, the Samsung Group produced or traded a wide variety of products and accounted for 10% of South Korea's GNP. The Samsung Electronics division made color TVs, VCRs, audio gear, home appliances, some office equipment, and small computers. It was Korea's most integrated TV producer: Samsung Electronic Parts made components, Samsung Electronic Devices made picture tubes, and Corning Samsung (a joint venture with American Corning Glass) made glass. Starting out in a joint venture with Sanyo in 1969, Samsung began exporting to the United States in 1972 with a contract to supply black-and-white sets to K Mart and Sears. It began producing color sets in 1973 and bought out Sanyo's stake in 1977. By the mid-1980s Samsung maintained one plant in South Korea which would produce 3 million black-and-white sets, 1.5 million color sets, 4 million black-and-white picture tubes, 1.5 million color picture tubes, and 5 million glass bulbs, and had opened two overseas facilities in the United States and Portugal.

GE AND RCA

RCA was established after World War I at the government's request to be the U.S. developer and manufacturer of radios. It was jointly owned by GE, Westinghouse, and AT&T until the Justice Department forced its divestiture in the 1930s. RCA began selling household radio receivers in 1922 and began experiments with television in 1925. The company led in the development of black-and-white television before World War II. After investing heavily in R&D for color television, RCA made a decision to license its technology overseas rather than compete in foreign markets. This gave RCA annual royalties in the mid-1950s of $12 million on its 12,000 radio and TV patents. As color television set sales boomed in the early 1960s, RCA reaped the rewards of its position as the leading color TV producer and as the dominant supplier of picture tubes to the whole industry. As U.S. color TV demand matured in the 1970s, RCA lost market leadership to Zenith. It moved black-and-white production offshore and established picture tube joint ventures in Europe and the Far East. In 1974 it became the first U.S. manufacturer to fully convert to solid-state sets, and in 1979 it started color set production in Taiwan. Despite its U.S. market leadership in consumer electronics, RCA found profits hard to achieve in the competitive U.S. market of the 1980s. In 1985 a major reevaluation of the consumer electronics business was undertaken. The company decided that because of its importance to RCA (nearly one-half of the corporate revenues were attributable to consumer electronics), it would make a three-year commitment to the business.

GE, never a major player in the consumer electronics industry, was always a distant third in the U.S. market. As various attempts to gain greater market share and implement a global strategy failed and the Justice Department rebuffed an attempt to joint-venture all its television assets with Hitachi in 1977, GE decided to close its own manufacturing facilities and source all its sets from Japanese and Korean manufacturers. It was believed that the Consumer Electronics Group, comprising only 2.5% of GE's total revenues, was in business to keep the GE name in consumer view. Future exit had appeared likely before the merger in 1986.

The Consumer Electronics Group (CEG)

Rick Miller inherited a combined business with sales of $3.4 billion and net income of $8 million (exclusive of the very substantial royalty fees RCA still received from its technology licenses) (*Exhibit 9*). The product line included color televisions, color picture tubes, VCRs, and audio products. Market shares ranged from 23% in color televisions and 17% in VCRs down to 1 to 5% in the smaller telephone and audio equipment markets. In the newest consumer electronic product, camcorders, CEG's share was over 30%. Growth in the overall market had meant that the CEG sales volume had grown, even though its market share had declined since the early 1980s. However, declining real prices had led the group's revenue growth to level off.

While Rick Miller was evaluating Welch's offer, he visited GE's Major Appliance Group (MAG). Renowned within GE for its dramatic turnaround, the group had reversed a poor image for quality and durability to become the market leader on those dimensions and the low-cost producer. Models were redesigned to lessen the number of parts, facilitate assembly, and incorporate innovative technology. The main Louisville dishwasher plant, acclaimed as a "factory of the future," underwent investment of $30 million to become a highly automated factory. Management emphasized manufacturing quality and gave employees a direct voice in plant decision making via quality circles and worker committees.

With this experience in mind, Rick Miller studied reports written by teams of consultants that had worked for GE over the summer of 1986. One studied manufacturing cost competitiveness, a second examined marketing and distribution strategy, and a third had looked at the technology of current and future products. Miller incorporated this information into the development of his own strategy to be presented to Jack Welch. The basis of that strategy would be the reestablishment (within three years) of CEG as the lowest-cost manufacturer of mid- and large-size color TV sets delivered to the United States.

Organization

Miller's first task was to design an organization for the combined business and to choose his top management team. GE's old CEG structure reflected a divide between audio products (sourced in the Far East) and television products (manufactured by GE in the United States until 1985 and then sourced from Matsushita's U.S. facility). RCA's structure was more complicated, with four product divisions—picture tubes, parts and accessories, TVs, and VCRs—and separate marketing and sales groups. Picture tubes, for example, was a separate profit center that negotiated a transfer price with the television set division and was equally concerned with its external sales (which amounted to about half its total output). Miller's new organization was functional and decentralized decisions among product lines to lower levels, quickening response times required by the fast-moving Consumer Electronics business. It also made cost cutting easier to perform than in a profit center–oriented organization (*Exhibit 9*).

For senior management at CEG Jack Welch made available top GE managers. He encouraged Rick Miller to recruit the best and offered the title of GE vice president and whatever salary necessary to allow him to get those individuals. To head manufacturing Miller chose a former plant manager of GE's Portsmouth TV plant. To run R&D Miller retained the R&D head from RCA Consumer Electronics. He recruited the vice presidents of marketing and sales from GE's MAG. Several plant managers also came from Louisville to the Bloomington, Indiana, assembly plant. Former GE Consumer Electronics managers were retained to head all the staff functions except for HRM, where a GE veteran of the transportation equipment business with experience in downsizing facilities and negotiating with unions was hired. Jack Welch's only interventions were to ensure that a former GE employee ran the finance area and to approve all senior management salaries.

Manufacturing

Rick Miller, believed that CEG currently had 8 to 9% higher costs than its competitors. The new management therefore set a goal to reduce these costs by 20% over three years, at which time it estimated that it would have a 1 to 2% lower cost than anyone else delivering 19-inch sets into the U.S. market. To achieve an improvement of this degree a major restructuring was called for. With a goal of reducing plant fixed cost by one-third, plans were put in place to cut the 23 existing plants to 14, salaried personnel by 44%, and the number of hourly employees by 18%. Overall volume through the plants would also be increased by bringing in-house GE's one-half million large-set volume (from Matsushita's U.S. plant) and GE's small color set production to its Taiwan plant (from a Korean supplier). A limited number of components currently made in-house were to be outsourced, the sets were to be redesigned for easier manufacture, and the final assembly plant for large (over 15-inch) sets at Bloomington would be further automated. New equipment would replace 13 conveyor lines with five highly automated ones and would cut the need for hourly employees in half. GE also planned to invest in several $2 million auto insertion machines in order to come close to parity with the Japanese in automation and testing rates. Small sets would continue to be exclusively produced in the Taiwan plant.

In the past RCA had focused on production quantity rather than on quality so that yields were running at 87% for finished sets. Challenging the group to be the highest-quality producer by 1989, Miller set a target of 95% and implemented a Quality Leadership Process to train the work force in statistical quality control. In an effort to fundamentally change the culture at the plants and to communicate the magnitude and urgency of the cost problem, management met monthly with small groups of workers to discuss plans and problems.

Stressing its readiness to keep the work force informed and treating them as trusted members of the company, management abolished assigned parking spaces and separate canteens, encouraged worker suggestions, and distributed a newsletter/videotape of latest developments (which sometimes included projected cuts in personnel and plant closures). These changes were intended to help bridge the labor/management division and increase cooperation from the work force and the unions who agreed to substantial reductions in the number of job classifications.

Management also cited overhead labor as an area of critical concern. U.S. salaries remained much higher than Japan's, and even after the planned reductions that cut the manufacturing organization from nine to six layers, GE's overhead personnel numbers would be higher than their competitors'. Great emphasis was therefore to be placed on improving yields, reducing material handling costs, and designing more efficient production scheduling. A form of just-in-time inventory management was introduced, and changes in production scheduling to reduce the number of models manufactured in the plant at one time were implemented. The number of models CEG offered in its product range would continue to be larger than the Japanese, but the plan was to cut out old models as soon as new ones were introduced. When the GE set volume was brought back into the Bloomington plant, it was designed to be the same as the existing RCA models except for cosmetic differences. In the future, GE sets would be designed to be produced on the same assembly line.

Set redesign was already underway at RCA prior to the merger, and the 1985 component count for the basic 19-inch set was 490 for GE and 440 for RCA. The 1987 set was to have 380 components, only 35 more than the state-of-the-art Sharp set. This represented a substantial improvement over 1979 when GE had nearly 50% more components than the best Japanese competitor. All new designs also featured a single-board chassis.

Fewer changes were anticipated for the component plants. RCA was the largest domestic producer of wood cabinets and had a 10 to 20% cost advantage over other TV set manufacturers in the United States who either manufactured in-house or bought cabinets from independent suppliers. Similarly, RCA's scale in plastic cabinets provided the firm with a 7 to 12% cost advantage. The Indianapolis component plant and the Mexican and Taiwanese plants, which did subassembly work on tuners and chassis, were also cost-competitive, although some overhead might be saved by closing the Indianapolis plant and integrating the work into Bloomington.

Protected by a 15% tariff and having the advantage of being the only U.S. picture tube manufacturer vertically integrated into glass production, which saved an estimated 20% of glass cost, RCA was the low-cost producer of large picture tubes delivered into the United States. Nevertheless, because of RCA's poor process technology and outdated equipment, the Japanese and Koreans had a substantial f.o.b. cost advantage and a 20% greater yield in their Asian plants. The U.S. market also contained nearly 1 million units of excess picture tube capacity among the five producers in 1986 due to ongoing productivity improvements in existing plants. Moreover, Toshiba, in a joint venture with Westinghouse, intended to open a new 1 million capacity picture tube facility in the United States; the Korean producers had a capacity of over 2 million picture tubes priced competitively with RCA's (even after tariff and transportation costs), and Mitsubishi was planning expansion of its Canadian picture tube plant. Even with significant investment and work practice improvements, engineers agreed that RCA lacked the technical process knowledge to keep the picture tube plants competitive. Yet exit seemed inappropriate as all major competitors were integrated and close interaction with picture tube production was vital for set development. Placing the picture tube plants under manufacturing, with outside sales treated as incremental volume rather than as a separate profit center, was the first step to improve performance. The second step was to close the Syracuse picture tube plant, sell the assets to the mainland Chinese, and consolidate its volume into the Marion and Scranton plants. Beyond that the plan was uncertain since closing one of the two remaining plants would reduce the volume available for amortizing future picture tube development costs.

CEG's material costs looked favorable because RCA's purchasing department was recognized as a strategic asset. It had a single coordinated worldwide purchasing organization with representation in Europe and the Far East. The organization contracted with one or two suppliers worldwide that had the best product and lowest prices available. Some items, particularly raw materials like copper and plastic, were bought by a corporate pool at a discount, and some purchases such as cartons and packaging were shared with major appliances. Sourcing of finished products—VCRs came from Japan and Korea, all black-and-white sets were sourced in Korea—were handled by the same organization which maintained dual suppliers for nearly all products, a legacy of the different GE/RCA sources.

Total purchases of ICs were $15 million per annum. Diode and other electronic component purchases were over $30 million per annum. Even though RCA had a semiconductor design and manufacturing division outside Consumer Electronics, it was never closely involved in TV design. The division had an opportunity to compete for TV IC volume with some favoritism, but 80% of new IC designs had been sourced outside over the past five years. The standardization of many IC designs plus the proliferation of companies supplying them encouraged the TV set division to purchase outside for the lowest cost and to retain a choice for the one-quarter or so of ICs which remained specialized. Only for some advanced technol-

ogy features, such as integrated remote control of an audio and video system where no outside producer offered a custom IC, was integration believed to be valuable.

Marketing/Distribution

The consultants' postmerger study showed that the two companies' product lines would be complementary, not competing. RCA products carried an "upscale, middle America" image with an aura of technological leadership, while GE products were considered basic and purchased on the basis of price. For this reason, it was decided to keep both brands, enabling them to compete in almost all segments of the market. RCA products would continue to play the market leader with a technologically sophisticated image, while GE would be offered as a value brand. The product lines would, however, be culled to eliminate the more obvious overlaps.

Miller also decided to keep both the RCA and GE distribution systems and push both brands through each. RCA had channeled its products to dealers through a network of 35 independent distributors and only sold direct to national accounts. GE had sold direct to national accounts *and* independent dealers. Rather than trying to coordinate these different distribution channels at one level, Miller introduced a new regional structure to the marketing and sales organization. National accounts would be managed nationally, otherwise 12 regional managers would bear responsibility, sharing offices with the MAG regional sales organization. He would give each regional manager the latitude to determine pricing, promotion, product mix, and sales strategy appropriate for his region.

R&D/Technology

RCA's famous Sarnoff Labs, which had developed all the original TV set technology, had been donated to the Stanford Research Institute as part of the merger. Nevertheless, a $150 million contract guaranteed CEG continued access to the Lab's research for the next five years. As GE had decided to end all U.S.-based production in consumer electronics years before, the corporate facility in Schenectady, New York, no longer worked on consumer electronics research. On-going technical expertise therefore came mostly from RCA; in fact, only one engineer from GE's labs was brought to CEG.

Miller concluded that CEG could only lead in a few technological areas at any one time and would aim instead to be a fast technology follower. This would enable CEG to maintain its image in the minds of customers as a technology leader by always offering some unique features without requiring enormous expense. R&D would move from redesigning the whole set to adjusting the manufacturing process or the product's outer design. The one exception to this stability would come from high-definition TV which could require substantial development expenses. GE felt that Japanese attempts to obtain U.S. adoption of their HDTV standards could be delayed until its own HDTV system, which was fully compatible with existing sets, was completed after 1990. Total R&D expenditure was planned to be somewhat over $100 million per year.

Corporate Relations

Rick Miller insisted, as one of his conditions for accepting Jack Welch's offer to head CEG, that he retain an office in GE's Fairfield, Connecticut, corporate headquarters. Concerned that somewhere along the line CEG would disappoint GE and that a corporate financial officer or strategic planner would bring Jack Welch the news of "another month of disappointments in Bloomington," Rick Miller wanted to be in Fairfield to tell his side of the story and protect the business.

Welch's commitment to CEG had historically been limited: he had placed it outside the three-circle core he had announced for GE in 1984, and part of the purpose of the consultant's studies during 1986 was to honestly evaluate the option of divestment (*Exhibit 10*). Miller therefore asked for a visible commitment from Welch. In response, CEG was publicly classified as one of the support businesses for the core circles, and space was allocated to the group in the 1986 annual report. Welch also expressed his support for the new strategy and publicly appeared not to be considering divestment of the business. It was, however, understood that GE's commitment to the business was contingent on performance. Jack Welch had given CEG three years to meet GE targets of 15% ROI. Rick Miller's job was to reach the agreed performance level, and he was given a free hand to do so without interference or second guessing by corporate staff.

More practically, GE was able to offer CEG many shared services. Payroll processing, MIS, and accounting were contracted either to corporate headquarters or to MAG. The 1-800 Answer Center and the service network were shared with the other consumer products divisions. GE's facilities for management education and its in-house "Manufacturing Excellence Center" were also available to CEG. GE Credit Corporation would provide financial assistance for wholesaler inventories, dealer floor plans, and certain large consumer purchases for CEG, as it already did for MAG. It also reduced the finance charge by the fraction of a percent that a third-party financier would have earned as profit margin. All these overhead services, including legal, employee relations, and auditing, were implicitly charged for through the $30 million contribution CEG made to the corporate overhead, but many were irreplaceable and would not have been covered by the $5 to $10 million general and administrative overhead which CEG estimated that it would have required as a stand-alone enterprise.

The proposed CEG strategy would be slightly cash-positive on an operating basis. Capital investment requirements of about $100 million per annum would be met by reducing working capital and by the improvement in profitability. However, the write-offs and restructuring costs of plant closures could not be covered by CEG itself. Between $75 and $125 million would be needed over the strategy period to meet these exceptional expenses. GE, anticipating this problem, had written down the RCA assets at acquisition so that there would be no impact on the corporate income statement. Welch, however, agreed to cover the cash costs of the closures without it adversely affecting CEG's reported profitability.

Results

Early progress with the strategy reduced costs as rapidly as planned, but the market performance deteriorated in spring 1987. Hurt by the reorganization and the influx of many sales office managers to new areas, GE lost market share. Moreover, price cutting by the Koreans continued to depress market prices, pressuring margins. Rick Miller, prepared for this early setback, spent time in Fairfield assuring Jack Welch that remedial action was being taken. By early summer 1987 a market turnaround had begun while internal cost cutting and manufacturing investments continued apace.

In June 1987 Jack Welch returned from a trip to Europe and called on Rick Miller. Acknowledging that this was a "bombshell," he told Miller that GE was going to trade CEG to Thomson in return for an unspecified sum of money (rumored to be $7 to $800 million) and Thomson's Medical Electronics business. This would make Thomson the world's largest VCR and TV company and would make GE number 2 in the world in medical electronics.

Rick Miller listened to Jack Welch and then observed that he could not disagree with the decision. He would have argued vehemently about retaining consumer electronics only if he could have guaranteed that the busines would meet its ROI target. And he could not do that.

EXHIBIT ONE

COMPOSITION OF WORLD DEMAND

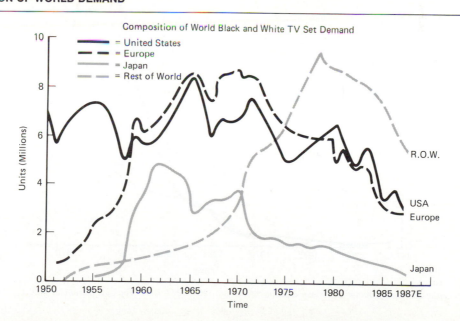

Composition of World Black and White TV Set Demand

(continued)

EXHIBIT ONE

CONTINUED

Composition of World Color TV Set Demand

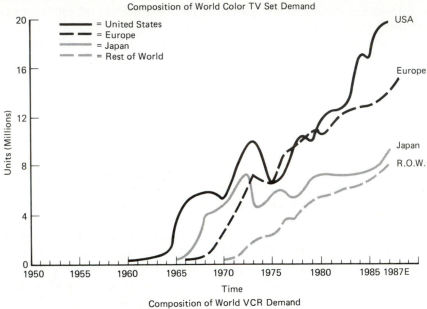

- ——— = United States
- – – – = Europe
- ——— = Japan
- – – – = Rest of World

Composition of World VCR Demand

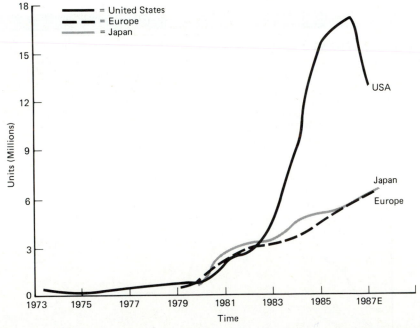

- ——— = United States
- – – – = Europe
- ——— = Japan

Sources: Japan Economic Journal; Japanese Electronic Almanac, 1964, 1967; NRI; Predicast Basebook 1966.

EXHIBIT TWO

MANUFACTURING ECONOMICS

	1965	1971	1977	1983	1987
Best Global Producer					
# Components	1,390	920	440	380	345
Direct Labor Hours	8.8	5.5	1.6	0.6	0.4
Automation (%)	0	0	65	90	100
Typical U.S. Producer					
# Components	1,240	1,150	620	450	380
Direct Labor Hours	7.6	6.0	3.0	0.9	0.6
Automation (%)	0	10	40	65	90

Source: Casewriter estimates, "Minding America's Business," I. Magaziner and R. Reich.

EXHIBIT THREE

U.S. IMPORTS OF TVs (complete sets, thousand units)

	1975 (B&W and color) Total	Color		
		1980	1985	1987
Japan	1,787	424	2,142	621
Korea	283	292	845	1,914
Taiwan	2,264	303	1,767	2,650
Singapore	—	74	233	491
Malaysia	—	—	789	902
Hong Kong	—	—	NA	229
Europe	3	36	2	11
Mexico	—	—	138	1,690
Total	4,337	1,129	5,916	8,508

	Black and white		
	1980	1985	1987
Japan	333	670	477
Korea	1,876	2,980	2,791
Taiwan	3,221	1,005	561
Singapore	112	5	32
Malaysia	—	N/A	12
Hong Kong	16	30	142
Europe	1	7	3
Mexico	—	33	2
Total	5,559	4,730	4,020

Source: U.S. Commerce Department.

Color TV market shares, %

United States	1973	1978	1983	1984	1985	1986	1987
RCA	20	20	20	19	18	18	17
Zenith	23	21	19	18	17	16	15
Philips	0	12	11	10	10	10	10
Matsushita	2	8	8	9	8	8	7
GE	6	7	8	8	7	6	6
Sears	8	9	7	7	7	6	6
Sony	4	7	7	7	6	6	6
NEC						1	2
Samsung						2	2
Gold Star						2	1
Others	37	15	20	22	27	25	28

Japan	1978	1985		Europe	1976	1986
Matsushita	26	27		Philips	25	21
Sony	17	17		Thomson-Brandt	4	18
Toshiba	15	16		Japanese Companies	8	14
Hitachi	14	15		Grundig	12	13
Sanyo	7	8		ITT	8	9
Sharp	3	7		Sabra/Luxor	4	5
Mitsubishi	5	6		Blaupunkt	4	4
Others	13	4		AEG Telefunken	6	
				Thorn	6	
				Others	23	16

United States VCR market shares, %

	1981	1982	1983	1984	1985	1986	1987
RCA	28	22	16	16	14	12	17 (GE/RCA)
Matsushita	21	21	20	19	16	11	13
Sanyo	3	6	10	11	12	11	11
Philips	7	7	8	7	6	6	6
GE	3	5	6	5	5	5	
Sears	3	4	5	5	5	5	5
Zenith	6	4	3	3	3	4	4
Sony	14	13	7	7	5	3	3
Emerson						4	4
Gold Star						1	3
Samsung						2	3
Others	15	18	25	27	34	36	34

United States black-and-white TV market shares, %, 1986

Samsung	13
Sanyo	11
RCA	10
Matsushita	10
NAP[a]	9
Zenith	9
Sony	5
GoldStar	5
Others	28

[a]NAP includes Magnavox, Sylvania, and Philco.
Sources: BIS Mackintosh; *TV Digest; Appliance; Market Share in Japan; Electronic World; Wall Street Journal.*

EXHIBIT FIVE

1986 TYPICAL COST STRUCTURES

Total cost structure, %		Manufacturing cost breakdown, %			
		19-in plastic cabinet set		25-in wood cabinet set	
Manufacturing	75–80	Total components and material	77	Total components and materials	79
Sales and marketing	6–9	Cabinet	7	Cabinet	15
		Picture tube	38	Picture tube	26
R&D	3–5	% of which is glass	11	% of which is glass	9
		Circuitry	13	Circuitry	14
G&A	9	Other	19	Other	24
		Hourly labor	10	Hourly labor	7
Margin	1–3	Fixed overhead	13	Fixed overhead	14
Total	100	Total	100	Total	100

Source: Case writer estimates.

EXHIBIT SIX

1987 GLOBAL CONFIGURATION

	Worldwide color TV					U.S. color TV				
			Level of integration					Level of integration		
	1975 sales (M units)	Production capacity (M units)	ICs	Picture tube	Glass	Facility opened	Production capacity (M units)	Picture tube (M units)	Glass	Cabinet
NV Philips	2.8	6.2	x	x	x	1974	2.2	2–3		x
Matsushita	3.1	4.7	x	x	x	1974	1.5			
Sony	1.8	3.8	x	x	x	1972	0.9	1		
GE/RCA	0.5 & 1.3	3.2	x	x	x	—	3.0	5	x	x
Toshiba	1.4	3.2	x	x	x	1978	1.5	1 (planned)		
Hitachi	1.4	3.1	x	x	x	1979	0.2			
Thomson	0.3	3.0	x	x	x	NA				
Lucky-Goldstar	NA	2.0	x	x	x	1974	0.9			
Zenith	1.6	2.0	x	x			2.0	2–3		x
Sanyo	1.5	1.8	x			1979	1.1			
Sharp	0.9	1.7				1983	0.5			
Samsung	NA	1.5	x	x	x	1978	0.5			
Mitsubishi	NA	1.0		x		1978	0.5	0.6		

EXHIBIT SEVEN

PRICE RANGES, FEATURES, AND RELIABILITY OF 19- TO 20-INCH COLOR MODELS
(One Month's Data, 1987)

Brand	Price range, $	Features[a]	Reliability[b]
Emerson	119–?	Low	NA
Portland (Daewoo)	149–250	Low	NA
Hitachi	149–409	Low	9
Magnavox	180–305	Medium	23
General Electric	190–290	Low	20
RCA	190–330	Medium	17
Panasonic	230–330	Low	11
Mitsubishi	230–410	High	8
Sony	235–460	High	9

[a]Case writer's judgment of low, medium, and high number and quality of features based on *Consumer Report* data.
[b]Repair index. High numbers represent a high need for repair.
Sources: Consumer Reports; RCA.

EXHIBIT EIGHT

COMPANY FINANCIALS ($ millions)

	1982	1983	1984	1985	1986
GE					
Total sales	$27,189	$27,677	$28,931	$24,252	$36,725
Net income	1,790	2,002	2,239	2,277	2,492
Assets	21,409	23,047	24,555	26,162	34,591
R&D, % of sales					3.8
Consumer products sales	3,558	3,422	3,466	3,220	4,654
Consumer products oper. income	306	309	533	425	577
RCA					
Total sales	$ 8,862	$ 7,605	$ 8,671	$ 8,972	
Net income	216	227	341	359	
Assets	5,811	6,182	6,772	6,705	
R&D, % of sales	2.3	2.8	2.8	2.8	
Consumer products sales		1,802	2,188	1,992	
Consumer products oper. income	73	87	21	147	
Zenith					
Total sales	$ 1,239.2	$ 1,361.3	$ 1,716.0	$ 1,624.7	$ 1,892.1
Net income	(24.3)	46.3	63.6	(7.7)	(10)
Assets	672.9	739.0	908.9	927.3	1,235
Consumer electronic sales	1,045	1,099	1,269	1,142	1,212
Consumer electronic oper. income	NA	NA	NA	NA	Loss

(continued)

CONTINUED

	1982	1983	1984	1985	1986
Emerson					
Total sales	$ 88	$ 95	$ 183	$ 357	$ 566
Net income	25	3	9	13	13
Assets	42	47	67	155	179
Consumer electronic sales	88	95	182	356	563
Consumer electronic oper. income	5	2	15	32	28
Sony					
Total sales	$ 4,489	$ 4,681	$ 5,316	$ 6,003	$ 7,911
Net income	185	126	301	309	250
Assets	4,999	5,185	5,519	6,115	8,657
R&D, % of sales	6.9	8.0	7.9	7.8	9.2
Matsushita					
Total sales	$22,390	$24,469	$28,961	$30,998	$28,066
Net income	963	1,121	1,462	1,511	1,004
Assets	19,470	21,169	25,406	26,775	26,826
R&D, % of sales	4.1	4.4	4.2	4.8	5.5
Video equipment sales	8,154	8,811	10,591	11,596	9,219
Video equipment oper. income	NA	NA	NA	NA	NA
Philips					
Total sales	$16,110	$16,219	$16,811	$18,236	$25,097
Net income	162	227	348	279	463
Assets	16,225	16,876	17,042	15,984	23,087
R&D, % of sales				6.7	7.6
Consumer electronics sales	4,393	4,088	3,880	5,082	7,675
Consumer electronics oper. income	NA	(69)	(130)	10	295
Thomson					
Total sales		$ 6,519	$ 6,561	$ 6,719	$ 9,711
Net income		(141)	(2)	(302)	(257)
Assets	NA	7,290	8,065	8,394	
R&D, % of sales	6.3	5.6	5.4	6.0	
Consumer electronics sales		1,887	1,747	1,781	2,384
Consumer electronics oper. income	NA	NA	NA	NA	NA
Lucky-Goldstar					
Total sales	$ 2,143	$ 3,218	$ 4,196		
Net income	64	54			
Assets	1,669	2,540		NA	NA
Electronics sales	1,161	1,405			
Electronics oper. income	154	183			
Samsung Group					
Total sales	$ 5,826		$ 6,207	$ 8,603	$ 9,368
Net income	27		72	62	95
Assets	4,641	NA	4,171	5,113	5,987
Samsung electronics sales			2,093	2,736	3,525
Samsung electronics oper. income	NA		70	64	275

CEG 1986 ASSETS, SALES, AND INCOME ($ million)

	Net assets	Sales	Net income
Color TV		1,352	(11)
Picture tubes		343	0
VCR and camcorder		1,170	30
Audio		246	(1)
Telephone		63	2
Other		212	(12)
Total	900	3,386	8

ORGANIZATION GE/RCA CONSUMER ELECTRONICS BUSINESSES IN 1985

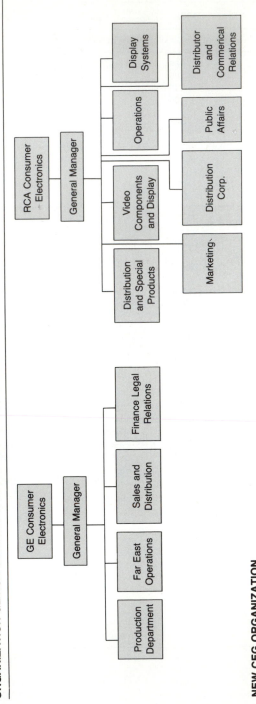

NEW CEG ORGANIZATION

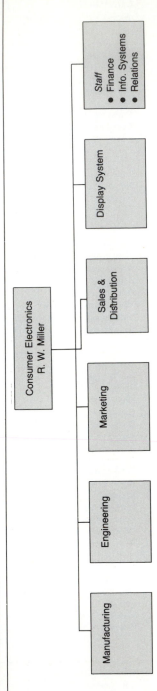

144

EXHIBIT TEN

RETURN ON ASSETS, 1986

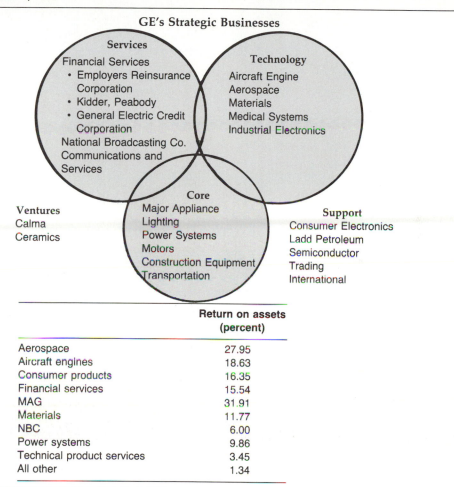

GE's Strategic Businesses

Services
Financial Services
- Employers Reinsurance Corporation
- Kidder, Peabody
- General Electric Credit Corporation
National Broadcasting Co.
Communications and Services

Technology
Aircraft Engine
Aerospace
Materials
Medical Systems
Industrial Electronics

Core
Major Appliance
Lighting
Power Systems
Motors
Construction Equipment
Transportation

Ventures
Calma
Ceramics

Support
Consumer Electronics
Ladd Petroleum
Semiconductor
Trading
International

	Return on assets (percent)
Aerospace	27.95
Aircraft engines	18.63
Consumer products	16.35
Financial services	15.54
MAG	31.91
Materials	11.77
NBC	6.00
Power systems	9.86
Technical product services	3.45
All other	1.34

PART FOUR

Intermediation and International Trade

Japan's Sogoshosha

The sogoshosha have developed along two paths. Mitsui, Mitsubishi, and, to a lesser extent, Sumitomo started out as small, general trading firms dealing in diverse products and services. . . . The other path was followed by firms like C. Itoh, Marubeni, Tomen, Kanematsu, Nissho-Iwai, Nichimen, and the now-defunct Ataka. Following World War II, they were transformed from specialized trading firms (senmonshosha) into sogoshosha.

TWO PATHS

The process by which these two paths converged during the post-World War II era was, in part, a response to the external economic pressures that caused trading firms to pursue both large size (economies of scale) and diversification of products and services. Even the legendary regrouping of Mitsui and Mitsubishi, after their dismantling into hundreds of

small specialized trading firms as required by the antitrust policies of the Allied Occupying Forces after World War II, can also be explained by the external economic pressures that forced them to choose between extinction and survival.

First, in the mid-nineteenth century, fear of the ulterior motives of the Western powers occupied the minds of Japanese political leaders, especially when they learned the brutal results of the First Opium War (1839–1842) started by the United Kingdom against Japan's mentor, China. When the political and industrial leaders of Japan's new regime later learned of the unequal treaties of international trade signed by the feudal Tokugawa Shogunate with the Western powers between 1854 and 1860, these memories rushed back. The fear of Western powers drove Japan almost instinctively to avoid foreign direct investment as an expedient way of obtaining the five necessary inputs for Japan's industrial development, namely, (1) capital, (2) technology, (3) access to foreign exchange (export markets), (4) managerial skills, and (5) ideological commitment to industrial growth. Armed with this innate nationalistic attitude, further fueled by the humiliating memories of unequal treaties with the Western powers, Japan evolved a strategy to rely on the

This case, prepared by Associate Professor David B. Yoffie and updated by Research Associate Richard Phelps, was excerpted from Yoshi Tsurmi, *Sogoshosha: Engines of Export-Based Growth* (Montreal: Institute for Research on Public Policy, 1980), as the basis for class discussion.

West only for manufacturing technology. Japan's leaders agreed that they would select the requisite technologies to be brought into their country. This goal and Japan's concerted efforts to catch up industrially with the West came to be widely shared, not only by political and industrial leaders but by the Japanese at large.

Second, after having decided to proceed alone, the leaders of Meiji Japan [as this era (1867–1912) is customarily referred to] turned to the one resource that the country had in abundance—her people. At first, almost as an act of faith, the Meiji leaders in business and government assumed that hard work, along with improved technical skills and knowledge instilled in the Japanese population, would augment their scarce ingredient—capital (machinery). It is no coincidence, therefore, that Japan instituted compulsory primary school education for both boys and girls at public expense in the early 1870s. This was almost two decades earlier than the leading power of the West at the time, the United Kingdom. While emphasizing this bottom-up approach for improving human resources through widespread promotion of primary schools and selective and limited development of colleges and universities, both government and business circles sent educators and engineers abroad to seek scientific knowledge, technology, and an exposure to different economic and political institutions and foreign markets. This research-and-retrieve policy of Japan was reinforced by another expedient tactic. Japan invited teachers, engineers, and technicians from abroad on sessional contracts and matched them with Japanese counterpart trainees. Both the government and business circles were willing to allow young trainees who returned from abroad and those trained in Japan to perform important tasks. The youthful recipients of this new knowledge and skill responded early to challenge.

Third, and most important, Japan needed to devise a specific strategy to catch up with the West. The mastery of necessary industrial and commercial tasks had to be accomplished in less time than had been taken by her Western competitors. The engineering, industrial, and institutional skills necessary for the performance of these tasks also had to be acquired quickly. How was Japan able to shorten the required time period?

EMERGENCE OF THE SOGOSHOSHA AND SENMONSHOSHA

. . . A short history of the sogoshosha and senmonshosha is invariably tied to the development of Japan's modern industries and industrial structure. Japan's means of paying for new imported manufacturing technology shaped the growth of both the sogoshosha and the senmonshosha. The first sogoshosha in the modern period was Mitsui & Co., established in 1876 as a separate trading firm of the House of Mitsui. Its major export item was coal and its major import items, cotton and spinning machines. Later, as Japan was able to export cotton cloth, Mitsui began to export this product to Korea, Manchuria, and China in direct competition with British cotton fabrics from India. In addition to its trading activities at home and abroad, Mitsui often took the initiative in creating various manufacturing subsidiaries. By guaranteeing the purchase of manufactured products, Mitsui helped create infant manufacturing industries. As Mitsui *Zaibatsu*, an industrial combine, developed its manufacturing and mercantile activities, Mitsui & Co. also grew. By 1911, Mitsui was handling about 29 percent of Japan's exports of raw silk, 96 percent of her coal exports, and 40 percent of her cotton yarn exports, as well as 51 percent of her raw cotton imports and 38 percent of her machinery, rolling stock, and other manufactured goods.

Another prototype sogoshosha, the Mitsubishi Corporation, was created in 1889 as the marketing arm of the Mitsubishi Group. It trailed Mitsui, however, in terms of trading volume.

Starting out with coal exports to China, Mitsubishi Corporation added pulp and paper, beer, sheet glass, and other manufactured goods of the Mitsubishi Group to its export list. During World War I, like other Japanese trading companies, Mitsubishi became a real sogoshosha by adding rice, wheat, sugar, tea, fats, fertilizer, lumber, cement, and pharmaceutical products to its export list. It also opened offices in London, New York, and Peking. Mitsubishi emerged from the economic boom of World War I as the second largest sogoshosha, with Mitsui as the leader.

The growth of the cotton spinning industry in Japan triggered the creation of senmonshosha dealing in cotton, cotton yarn, and fabrics at home and abroad. C. Itoh, established in 1907, was one of the senmonshosha that began by specializing in cotton yarn exports. After 1920 C. Itoh opened overseas branches in Peking, Manila, New York, and Calcutta, joining Mitsui and Mitsubishi in the direct export of cotton yarn and cloth to key Japanese export makers.

The growth of the Japanese cotton spinning industry made it imperative to import raw cotton from Texas, Latin America, India, and Africa. Rather than purchasing cotton through foreign trading firms, the Japanese trading companies opened their own purchasing offices in the key world cotton exporting locations. In this way, the Japanese cotton spinning industry was assured of guaranteed purchases of vital raw materials at prices competitive with those charged Japan's competitors, the United Kingdom and India.

The preceding accounts provide a number of useful pointers. . . . Any firm can expand its business territory by starting as an import or export senmonshosha with a limited product line. However, if it happens to become a sogoshosha, it would have a better chance of entering import-export trade activities if it chose products that its country must import en masse or export in increasing quantity. The firm should

continue to add goods and services demanded by its clients at home and abroad. In addition, the growth-oriented trading company can improve its chances of becoming a sogoshosha by importing machinery, technologies, and raw materials that the newly created industries require and by guaranteeing purchases (distribution) of products of infant manufacturing industries.

CONCENTRATION AND DIVERSIFICATION: A ROAD TO SOGOSHOSHA

For the first half century after the 1870s, Japan's exports were dominated by raw silk yarns while her imports were dominated by raw cotton. As Japan developed manufacturing industries, her export and import composites shifted to reflect her industrial structures. The relative importance of silk yarns and cottons in Japan's international trade lasted well into the 1930s.

These two commodities share two intrinsic characteristics which led them to speculative price fluctuations at home and abroad. These are the once-a-year harvest (like other annual crops such as soybeans) that is susceptible to climatic changes and insect and disease damage and the possibility of massive stockpiling by harvesters and traders. Price speculation dominates these two commodity markets. The senmonshosha and sogoshosha dealing in these two commodities required a large capital base in order to ride out violent price fluctuations. Smaller trading firms lacking bankers' support gradually disappeared from the cotton and silk trade.

In order to stabilize their earnings (particularly with regard to the cotton spinning industry), senmonshosha, such as Gosho, Nichimen, Tomen, and C. Itoh, and sogoshosha, such as Mitsui and Mitsubishi, tied raw cotton importation for cotton spinning firms to the trading firms' exclusive purchase of manufacturers' woven yarns and cloths, for both domestic and international distribution. In this way, the small- to medium-sized senmon-shosha, specializing in either the import of cotton or the domestic or international distribution of cotton yarns, were eliminated from the scene.

By the dawn of World War II, the survivors of the turmoils of prewar trading activities had emerged. These were the forerunners of today's sogoshosha. Japan's defeat in World War II resulted in the breaking up of her large sogoshosha such as Mitsui and Mitsubishi by the Allied Occupying Forces under General MacArthur. The importing-exporting activities of the senmonshosha were also shut down.

From the end of the 1940s through the 1950s, many senmonshosha, including the fragments of Mitsui and Mitsubishi, groped their way once again toward concentration and diversification. How did this metamorphosis from senmonshosha to sogoshosha occur? The answer lies in the ways in which these trading firms adapted themselves to the specific industrial policies of postwar Japan and to the recurrent economic cycles of upswings and downturns in the Japanese economy.

The initial adaptation was necessary immediately after the war, when the Allied Occupying Forces rationed Japan's imports and exports. In order to obtain products for resale in Japan, many senmonshosha competed with one another, bidding for products outside their traditional lines of business. The requisite trading skill was simply the clerical ability to process documents for importation, subsequent warehousing, and distribution of goods. Few special trading or marketing skills were required. One senmonshosha's experience in handling cotton yarns, for instance, was directly transferable to the handling of the rationed wheat flour. When direct involvement in international trade by Japanese trading firms was resumed with the permission of the Allied Forces in 1947, many senmonshosha, which by

then had handled such diverse products as fertilizers, foods, machinery, or industrial raw materials, emerged as contenders for sogoshosha dealings in a wide range of products.

The second adaptation was necessary during the acute dollar (foreign exchange) shortage which plagued Japan even when the Japanese trading firms' direct participation in foreign trade was permitted from 1947 to 1948. The Japanese government carefully rationed important economic resources—foreign exchange, capital funds, and technology—among targeted industries. By rationing the scarce foreign exchange among trading firms for designated imports, the government was able to control not only the amount but also the kinds of imports. In order to obtain their ration of foreign exchange, the senmonshosha, which now included literally hundreds of segments of the former Mitsui and Mitsubishi operations, competed for manufacturers' import orders.

The scrambling for manufacturers' orders was countered by the senmonshosha's ability to conclude barter trade, a practice encouraged by the Japanese government and even rewarded with further allocations of foreign exchange to successful senmonshosha. Ammonium sulfate fertilizer was traded (exported) for crude sugar imports; iron slabs and whale oil were bartered for industrial raw materials and foods; imported crude oil was traded for galvanized iron sheets, nails, and rubber products; and raw cotton was exchanged for barbed wire. In order to survive, trading firms had to develop internal abilities adequate to effect barter trade. This pressure drove a number of scattered senmonshosha to merge, while the remaining ones gradually diversified their products and services.

Encouraged by barter trade, in 1953 the Japanese government instituted the linking trade policy. This policy held that imports of specific lucrative products and raw materials were tied to exports of specific heavy and chemical manufacturers, designated as vital to the postwar recovery of the Japanese economy. Import licenses for such lucrative consumer goods as bananas, whiskey, and crude sugar were given to the trading firms which had already met the export targets for ships, rolling stock, and machine tools. The export of ships was particularly subsidized through this linking practice, for both shipbuilders and their export agent trading firms were allowed to split the profits from crude sugar imports. Lasting well into the late 1950s, the linking policy naturally precipitated the diversification of goods and services handled by one trading firm. The quest of senmonshosha for sogoshosha was fueled even more by this policy. It also further cemented the traditional demarcation of tasks between manufacturing and trading firms. In addition, the policy prevented any single-line product manufacturer from commencing his own exporting and importing activities. The dependence of traditional manufacturing firms on trading firms became complete during this immediate postwar era.

The third stage in this metamorphosis from senmonshosha to sogoshosha was born in response to the recurring booms and busts of the postwar business cycles. These business pressures motivated the old atomistically scattered pieces of Mitsui and Mitsubishi to merge initially with one another and later to reemerge as reborn sogoshosha. From 1949 to 1963, the Japanese economy experienced six severe business downturns. Each downturn destroyed the weaker senmonshosha and precipitated a concentration and diversification among the remaining trading firms.

Throughout this period, trading firms were usually earning, at best, an average of 2 to 3 percent on their sales. The average collection time for their accounts receivable was well over 110 days. Most firms had already borrowed from banks more than ten times the amount of their shareholder's equity. The financial solvency of trading firms was, accordingly, squeezed in any tight-money situation. At each business downturn, therefore, weaker senmonshosha were absorbed by stronger ones. Banks encouraged such mergers in order to protect their investments and loans. It was no accident that Mitsui Bussan and Daiichi, the last two contending firms of the old Mitsui, agreed to a merger in 1959 in the midst of an economic downturn.

By the mid-1960s, thirteen sogoshosha remained: Mitsui, Mitsubishi, Marubeni, C. Itoh, Sumitomo, Nissho, Iwai, Tomen, Nichimen, Kanematsu, Gosho, Iida, and Ataka. Mergers later created Nissho-Iwai, Kanematsu-Gosho, and Marubeni-IIda, thus reducing the lineup to ten sogoshosha. The Nissho-Iwai tie-up was a harbinger of Ataka's subsequent demise and of other mergers among trading firms. Iwai had long overcommitted itself to a single country fraught with political and economic instability—Indonesia. When the Indonesian economy neared bankruptcy toward the end of the 1950s, Iwai had to be rescued by Nissho. A trading firm's greater involvement in overseas ventures than in ordinary export-import trade signaled that its failure would further precipitate the absorption of weaker sogoshosha by stronger ones. Ataka's fall in 1977 was triggered by its unwise investment in the ill-fated oil refinery by Come-By-Chance, Newfoundland. . . .

The Japanese economy cannot be expected to grow at the two-digit rate familiar to Japan watchers during the 1960s and the early 1970s. Leading sogoshosha have long been intensifying their direct involvements in large-scale ventures abroad. Therefore, it appears that the concentration and diversification processes, characteristic of Japan's trading companies since development of sogoshosha in the nineteenth and twentieth centuries, are still alive, and further consolidation can be expected.

SOGOSHOSHA AS MARKET INTERMEDIARIES FOR THE DOMESTIC AND INTERNATIONAL DISTRIBUTION OF JAPANESE MANUFACTURING FIRMS

. . . [S]ogoshosha are characterized by a substantial involvement both in domestic distribution of goods and services and in export and import transactions on behalf of diverse Japanese firms. The sogoshosha's trading strength is at its best in this latter area. Sogoshosha are specialists not only in the export-and-import business. These activities are closely linked with distributional activities in various product and service markets in Japan. This profile separates sogoshosha from literally thousands of "specialized" (senmonshosha) trading firms, which often specialize either in domestic distribution or in the export or import of a limited product line. These senmonshosha are very much akin to domestic wholesale distributors or to the many import or export firms found around the world.

The sogoshosha's deep involvement in both domestic and overseas business activities should surprise no one. After all, import-and-export activities are vital for a country like Japan whose Gross National Product has grown by using her foreign trade sector as the trigger for her industrial expansion. Without extensive networks of domestic distribution, the sogoshosha would be unable to find diverse export products from suppliers scattered all over Japan.

As can be readily demonstrated, the composition of exports of Japan has been shifting dynamically over time, reflecting the changes in Japan's manufacturing industries' international competitive strength. What was exportable from Japan one year becomes unexportable the next when lower-wage countries take over labor-intensive and standard manufactured goods in the world market. Accordingly, sogoshosha must have their "sensor tentacles" for seeking exportable products stretched throughout the country. They must also be aware of importation of food items, industrial raw materials, and machinery. These imports are often used, in turn, to produce exportable products. The sogoshosha's foreign networks of market intelligence, which identify products and technologies required by Japanese and foreign firms, can function well only when sogoshosha are closely linked to domestic distribution channels of diverse commodities and products.

THE SOGOSHOSHA'S CORPORATE ORGANIZATION AS EXAMPLES OF ECONOMIES OF SCALE

. . . Since the sogoshosha trade in goods, services, and information, one would expect that their size results partly from the growth in international trade. The larger the number of their employees—scattered inside and outside Japan—the greater would be the opportunity to seek and obtain business deals.

Expansion requires initial investment in office space, communication hardware, basic clerical staff, and personnel for the opening of a new office location and its links with the sogoshosha headquarters. Once this initial fixed investment is made, however, the incremental costs of seeking new business opportunities and of striking deals are rather small, as compared to the size of business deals.

A simple arithmetical illustration demonstrates the above point. For every additional "contact point," the permutations of all existing contact points increase in number exponentially. In other words, the increase in contact points is represented by an arithmetical progression (that is, 1, 2, 3, 4, . . .), whereas the concomitant increase in the possible combinations of business exchanges among the contact points is represented by a geometric progression (that is, 2, 4, 8, 16, . . .). Accordingly, the larger the number of existing contact points, the greater the potential for striking business deals among them. The greater the number of contact points of sogoshosha, the larger are the inflows of funds generated from exponentially increasing business contacts. Accordingly, the big get bigger, and the smaller struggle unsuccessfully to catch up.

The fact that the sogoshosha have thrived through information trading is best illustrated by noting the care with which each built and updated worldwide communication networks among contact points, customers, and affiliates. The sogoshosha always adopted the best available hardware for communications. In 1876, when Mitsui & Co. was established, for instance, the company immediately started using its own private code for telegrams inside Japan to facilitate trading of information. With the availability of international telegram services a few years later in 1881, Mitsui immediately began using its own private telegram code in English.

In 1979, for example, Mitsui was using four computerized centers: Tokyo, covering all Asia; New York, spanning North and Latin America; London, encompassing Europe and Africa; and Sydney, covering Oceania. The Bahrain subcenter handles the special communication needs of the Middle East. These centers are now connected with one another by satellites. Approximately 50 offices in Japan and 130 overseas offices in 77 countries are linked by privately leased channels, and their combined length is sufficient to encircle the world ten times. These systems operate around the clock because somewhere around the world the sogoshosha's offices, customers, and affiliates are working. Furthermore, political, social, economic, or climatic change is occurring which affects the sogoshosha's worldwide activities. These computer-controlled telex networks are supplemented by telephone networks and by mail. The mail handling of Mitsui headquarters, alone, is usually about one-tenth of the communications handled by telex networks. Its mail volume is larger than that handled by a Japanese city with a population of over 125,000.

In fact, to visualize the internal workings of sogoshosha, a large exchange should be imagined in which tens of thousands of brokers are attempting to close complex deals for their clients. Each broker (trader) submits his bids to other traders in the same market and stays alert for potential business deals submitted by other traders. Active participation requires each broker to cultivate and continually seek clients.

Today, this marketplace consists only of communication networks of computer-controlled telex systems, telephones, mail, and intense face-to-face negotiations. It was not surprising to find employees of sogoshosha, even after hours, swapping information and striking deals among fellow employees of the same firm. All these employees are operating within an intricate matrix of simultaneously represented products and geographical areas. Their business deals can only be consummated when their product-and-area interest matrix is matched with a comparable matrix held by other brokers and clients.

A typical organization chart, drawn to identify job titles, office layout, and hierarchical positions of respective employees, cannot capture the essence of the dynamic market-style matrix of the sogoshosha's organizational activities.

ORGANIZATIONAL FLEXIBILITY OF SOGOSHOSHA

. . . [S]ogoshosha's internal workings must be sufficiently flexible to enable a quick adjustment to violent national and international market uncertainties. Since the sogoshosha are serving both domestic and foreign clients, they can only cope with these sudden shifts by helping firms make necessary adjustments to new technologies and business environments rather than by expediently ditching yesterday's faithful clients. This interdependency between client firms and the sogoshosha must be carefully managed. A balance must be found somewhere between quickly dropping one client and sinking slowly with another—the recalcitrant client who refuses to change.

FINANCIAL STRUCTURE OF THE SOGOSHOSHA

If the balance sheets of any of these nine leading sogoshosha were checked, it would be immediately obvious that each sogoshosha has frequently taken short-term loans from banks. Each has, in turn, reloaned this money to, or invested it in, its own affiliate firms and clients. Indeed, "relendings" or "reinvestments" by sogoshosha to small- or medium-sized clients constitute anywhere between 30 to 40 percent of each sogoshosha's total outstanding debt at any given time. More important, the annual amount of each sogoshosha's write-offs for bad debts often total anywhere from 30 to 50 percent of its annual profits in economic recessions and 15 to 30 percent in economic booms.

The sogoshosha act as financing channels for small- to medium-sized manufacturing and sales firms. Large banks choose to allow the sogoshosha to absorb financial risks of loans or investments in firms which are financially too weak to borrow directly from commercial banks in Japan. In turn, the sogoshosha use their "financial clout" to provide venture capital, working capital, and even long-term loans and investments to prospective clients.

The apparent high debt-equity ratios of the sogoshosha (for that matter, the same ratios for any Japanese firm) should be revised downward. The bulk of these firms' debt is loaned by commercial banks, insurance firms, or trust banks holding common voting shares in the sogoshosha. Accordingly, the loans which are extended by the banks with ownership interest in their client sogoshosha are tantamount to "preferred stock" for which the interest is tax-deductible.

In 1978, for the nine leading sogoshosha, combined ownership by commercial banks and other financial institutions ranged on average from about 21 percent for Mitsubishi and Nichimen to 37 percent for Kanematsu-Gosho. Likewise, short-term loans, which fall due within one year, are perpetually rolled over by bank creditors. These short-term loans are equivalent to long-term loans with short-term (lower) interest rates.

This is the financial structure of the sogoshosha whose profits are extremely sensitive to short-term interest rate policies of the Bank of Japan. . . . [A] one percentage point decline in the interest rate easily *doubles* each sogoshosha's net profit. About 85 to 90 percent of each sogoshosha's annual expenses could be considered "fixed" expenses—interest payments, write-offs for bad debts, and personnel expenses under the celebrated job security of the lifetime employment system for sogoshosha professionals. Accordingly, it is not only the high debt-equity ratios but also the high fixed-cost ratio of each sogoshosha's annual expenses that make it vulnerable to slight declines in its business volumes. These are the elements in the financial structure of each sogoshosha which keep its personnel alert to business growth potentials and to shifts in the business environment. Since gross profit margin on sales is usually less than 2 percent for any sogoshosha, the sogoshosha thrive on the flow of goods and services, not on the stock of assets. They are vulnerable, therefore, to sudden mishaps and miscalculations of expensive projects both domestically and overseas.

PROFILE SYNTHESIS

. . . The manner in which respective sogoshosha attempt to retain these functional advantages vis-à-vis their client firms is an outgrowth of the sogoshosha's current and future strategies of growth and survival. The ways in which general trading firms, which started out as "specialized" trading firms, have successfully sought to obtain and expand these vital functions demonstrate the economic bases of the sogoshosha's existence. Furthermore, the means whereby these vital functions are internalized by the sogoshosha over a period of time provide basic prescriptions for other nations wishing to develop their own sogoshosha as the engines of both international and domestic trade.

TERRITORIAL KNOWLEDGE

The first distinct advantage of the sogoshosha is territorial knowledge of both domestic and international markets. In reality, this market information is neither free nor easily available to all business entities involved in different markets. Even if such information were freely available to all participants in each market, there is no telling whether it would be evaluated, processed, and finally translated into business opportunities by everyone in an identical and uniform manner.

The real barrier to entry to both nationwide and international trade, as perceived by dominant regionally oriented, small- to medium-sized manufacturing and trading firms, is ignorance of existing market opportunities. This lack of knowledge is multiplied by the firms' inability to evaluate even available market information outside familiar territories. Companies, like the individuals who compose them, simply do not venture outside their own territories. They perceive the unknown and the uncertain as the most risky and fearful business ventures.

By accumulating, internally, the relevant "territorial information" concerning business opportunities, clients, distribution contacts, trading procedures, and finances, sogoshosha have built up a team of professional traders with intracompany communication channels to translate this territorial knowledge into business opportunities for their clients. A client's

risk perceptions are effectively reduced because he is dealing with familiar firms and individuals. The sogoshosha's ability to update and promptly process territorial knowledge of domestic and foreign markets is the source of their distinct expertise for which their clients are willing to pay well.

ECONOMIES OF SCALE

Second, in order to accumulate and process proprietary knowledge of market territories, sogoshosha thrive on both dynamic and static economies of scale. Static economies of scale of sogoshosha come from their national and worldwide network of market contacts. After the one-shot investment in large-scale informational networks is made, any incremental costs of processing territorial information are marginal to both sogoshosha and their clients. Accordingly, those small- to medium-sized firms in Japan and elsewhere that are too financially and managerially weak to have their own market contacts points even in the most vital places need merely link up with the vast informational networks of sogoshosha for a small fee. This fee covers only incremental costs and incremental contributions to the sogoshosha's overhead. Often even the largest manufacturing firms choose to utilize sogoshosha's informational and distribution networks for the purpose of cultivating uncertain markets and also to service domestic and international markets not readily covered by their own distributional networks.

The dynamic economies of scale of the sogoshosha spring from both the organizations' and the individual's cumulative ability to identify, screen, process, and translate into business opportunities the political, economic, social, and even climatic occurrences that befall domestic and international markets. These cumulative abilities to translate market information into clients' business opportunities come from the process of learning by doing that takes place inside sogoshosha. The accumulated experience of the sogoshosha's past successes and failures is passed on to their recruits, who in turn join the internal efforts to augment the trading companies' "informational stock." Therefore, long years of experience can be transmitted to both new and old personnel in condensed packages of relevant territorial knowledge.

Both the dynamic and static economies of scale of the sogoshosha's information trading are often best applied to the reduction of shipping costs of goods for the sogoshosha's clients. Since the sogoshosha deal in diverse commodities and, more important, at diverse locations, they can charter vehicles, freighters, aircraft, trains, barges, and other modes of transportation and fill them by pooling goods supplied by many clients. In this way, clients do not have to pay any premium for guaranteed and timely handling of their cargo. Even if the sogoshosha do not charter a whole vehicle, or another mode of transportation, they can often negotiate a bulk discount for volume shipping. By guaranteeing return traffic to a freight firm, the sogoshosha can obtain favorable freight costs from transportation firms eager to fill their shipping capacity.

A LARGE INTERNAL MARKET

Third, the sogoshosha's large internal market is another distinct advantage seldom imitated by specialized trading or manufacturing firms. Since sogoshosha deal in a variety of goods and services for clients scattered throughout the country and the world, they can effectively barter goods and services among themselves. This ability permits the sogoshosha to generate new business even when a single manufacturing firm with a limited product line finds it difficult to locate customers. The sogoshosha can receive, for instance, crocodile hides and animal fats as payment in kind for sewing machines exported to remote places in Africa. Sewing machine firms would usually refuse this business opportunity because they ordinarily lack the ability to resell crocodile hides and animal fats for anything less than totally depressed prices. For the sogoshosha, this might be a bizarre but, nonetheless, routine transaction. They would pay the supplier of the sewing machines in cash and find appropriate customers somewhere in the world for the crocodile hides and animal fats. Check any leading sogoshosha for examples. There are even instances in which a supertanker is swapped for fresh grapes. All these transactions would be internally processed so that the suppliers of both the supertanker and the fresh grapes could be paid in cash by the sogoshosha.

FINANCING

Financing services round out the preceding three distinct advantages of sogoshosha. Although the sogoshosha charge interest rates reflecting their borrowing costs, plus some handling charges and marginal commissions, these charges tend to be far less than the costs of alternative financing. More often than not, the borrowers do not have access to ready funds (in this case, their costs of borrowed funds are prohibitively high). In particular, the sogoshosha can borrow from the most advantageous sources today in international capital markets and can channel these funds to any client throughout the world.

In this way, sogoshosha not only absorb the financial risks and potentially higher costs of borrowing for their clients but, more important, they absorb the risks and costs associated with foreign exchange transactions. The diverse and vast internal swapping of goods and services within given sogoshosha permits the firms to balance one kind of foreign exchange risk with another using various international currencies. The larger the sogoshosha's volume of worldwide trade, and the more diverse a sogoshosha's handling of foreign currencies, the greater is its ability to absorb financial risks, including foreign exchange transaction risk for its clients. Sogoshosha have, of course, been consciously accumulating the expertise for currency handling and channeling of necessary working capital and investment funds for their clients.

SCENARIOS FOR SOGOSHOSHA OBITUARIES

Unsolicited obituaries for sogoshosha are written from time to time by Japanese and foreign sogoshosha watchers. In fact, each time the Japanese economy strikes a snag, doomsday prophecies for sogoshosha appear, only to be proven wrong once again by the sogoshosha's phoenixlike comebacks. Between 1978 and 1979, the Japanese economy was again squeezed externally by the fluctuating yen, by rising protectionist sentiment abroad against Japanese products, and by inroads made by developing countries such as Korea and Brazil into the standard manufactured goods export market once dominated by Japan. Today, the obituaries for sogoshosha are increasingly being read aloud.

EXHIBIT ONE

SOGOSHOSHA SHARE OF JAPAN'S IMPORT'S AND EXPORTS IN SELECTED RECENT YEARS

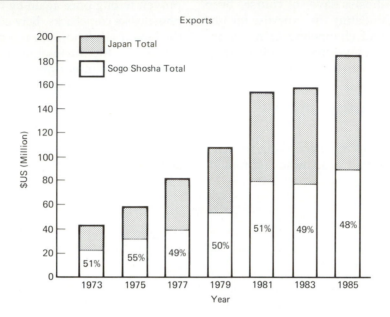

Exports

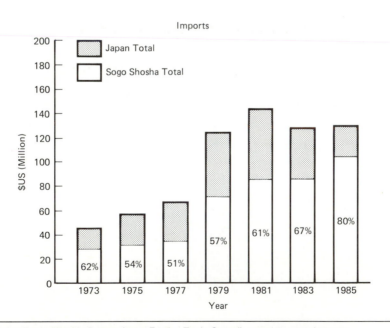

Imports

Sources: *Japan Foreign Trade Monthly Report;* Japan Foreign Trade Council; company annual reports.

EXHIBIT TWO

SALES IN THE POSTWAR PERIOD ($ million)

	C. Itoh	Kanematsu-Gosho	Marubeni	Mitsubishi	Mitsui-Bussan	Nichimen	Nissho-Iwai	Sumitomo	Toyo Menka
1950	191	139	141		75	125	91	39	130
1955	554	399	585	748	610	341	324	147	313
1960	1,505	737	1,696	1,782	1,771	843	862	543	768
1965	3,137	1,455	3,190	4,047	4,219	1,607	2,244	1,372	1,768
1970	7,111	2,353	7,532	11,360	10,461	2,482	5,193	4,732	3,844
1975	18,970	7,777	19,414	30,796	26,568	5,708	13,336	18,562	8,066
1979	30,069	9,349	28,740	40,500	38,318	8,199	19,143	26,806	9,789
1980	39,282	12,234	37,181	53,488	49,681	10,151	25,576	33,692	14,548
1981	48,637	13,426	46,274	63,321	57,551	11,867	29,918	43,866	14,911
1982	49,702	13,167	46,523	59,174	53,284	11,837	29,944	44,174	14,968
1983	52,612	14,537	48,993	62,700	59,591	13,728	33,770	47,826	16,495
1984	54,728	14,703	49,815	63,333	58,828	13,898	32,828	48,984	17,080
1985	59,497	15,854	57,329	69,429	62,975	16,708	36,145	55,642	19,032
1986	90,746	24,478	84,776	96,716	92,537	26,961	53,731	84,776	28,484
1987[a]	108,992	28,610	102,180	115,804	108,992	29,973	64,714	103,542	37,466

[a]Estimates.
Sources: Japan Company Handbook; company annual reports.

EXHIBIT THREE

PROFITS IN RECENT YEARS ($ million)

	C. Itoh	Kanematsu-Gosho	Marubeni	Mitsubishi	Mitsui-Bussan	Nichimen	Nissho-Iwai	Sumitomo	Toyo Menka
1979	10.23	0.56	20.23	73.93	51.26	5.22	13.52	35.10	7.06
1980	12.08	0.53	42.36	85.68	59.89	6.84	19.38	44.59	7.14
1981	20.56	0.55	44.81	92.94	50.73	7.38	0.72	50.75	7.85
1982	20.20	0.47	21.26	85.14	(60.94)	6.56	22.65	62.74	7.47
1983	12.95	0.50	1.46	76.79	43.57	5.82	33.51	72.40	8.07
1984	14.38	0.51	15.74	85.61	26.01	6.18	24.39	78.72	9.28
1985	22.92	0.77	34.65	97.90	21.95	8.58	18.24	88.15	10.83
1986	41.79	11.94	35.82	143.28	32.84	12.84	29.85	125.37	19.16
1987[a]	47.68	13.62	34.06	136.24	37.47	13.62	30.65	136.24	20.44

[a]Estimates.
Sources: Japan Company Handbook; company annual reports.

MARKET SEGMENT SALES BY COMMODITY IN 1985

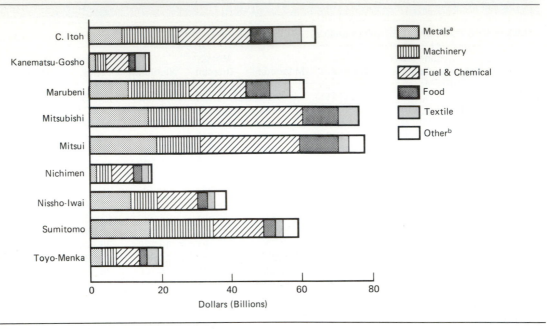

Dollars (Billions)

[a]Includes construction for C. Itoh and Nissho-Iwai.

[b]Includes construction for Mitsui, Nichimen, Sumitomo, and Toyo-Menka. Nissho-Iwei places chemicals in "other," not in "fuel." Lumber/forest products included in "other" when relevant.

MARKET SEGMENT SALES BY TYPE OF TRADE IN 1985

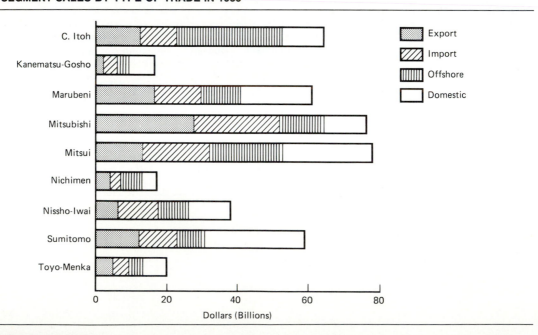

Dollars (Billions)

Source: Company annual reports.

COMPARISON OF ASSET AND LIABILITY DEPLOYMENT OF SELECTED BALANCE SHEET ITEMS AND SELECTED INCOME FIGURES IN 1986

(Percentages of Total Assets and Liabilities)

	Mitsui	Mitsubishi	Toyota	Nippon Steel	Matsushita
Current assets	70.9%	69.3%	51.7%	46.7%	55.9%
Cash and current deposits	11.5	6.1	14.3	7.2	20.1
Customer credit	46.5	46.1	15.5	12.5	12.7
Inventory	6.4	5.2	6.2	20.8	13.4
Fixed assets	29.1	30.7	48.3	53.3	44.1
Tangible fixed assets	3.7	3.9	23.9	43.7	12.8
Investments	24.6	25.4	24.0	9.3	26.8
Current liabilities	69.7	67.2	29.4	47.2	31.2
Accounts payable	35.9	34.2	10.7	13.2	9.6
Short-term loans	30.5	28.4	3.3	19.6	4.3
Long-term liabilities	26.7	25.8	4.9	35.4	19.1
Long-term debt	26.1	24.8	.1	18.4	3.2
Reserves	1.4	1.6	4.2	2.7	6.3
Equity	2.2	5.4	61.5	14.7	43.4
			(in $ million)		
Total sales	92,537	96,716	39,683	16,032	27,317
Cost of goods sold	90,663	94,744	32,195	13,046	18,677
SGA expenses	1,407	1,556	4,496	1,349	6,777
Net income	33	143	2,066	221	979
Reserves	67	80	197	585	221
Employees	11,889[a]	14,125	82,620	65,001	135,881

[a]1984 figure.

Source: Japan Company Handbook; company annual reports.

EXHIBIT SEVEN

TOP NINE TRADING COMPANIES' OWNERSHIP INTEREST IN OVERSEAS MANUFACTURING VENTURES, 1980

Equity participation, %	Mitsui	Mitsubishi	Marubeni	C. Itoh	Others[a]	Total ventures by ownership	
						No.	%
1–9	40	27	20	22	75	184	26.9
10–29	62	44	50	47	124	327	47.9
30–49	21	16	17	22	24	100	14.7
50	0	6	6	1	3	16	2.3
51–79	3	2	2	3	9	19	2.8
80–100	5	1	5	4	11	26	3.8
	(2)[b]	(0)	(3)	(3)	(3)	(11)	
Not available	0	2	3	0	5	10	1.5
Total ventures by company	131	98	103	99	251	682	100.0

[a]Others: Sumitomo, Nissho Iwai, Kanematsu, Tomen, Nichimen.
[b]The figures in parentheses show number of 100% ownership included in the 80–100% category.
Source: "Japan's General Trading Companies: Merchants of Economic Development," *OECD,* Paris, 1984.

General Electric Trading Company, 1985

Tak Argentinis, the vice president of General Electric Trading Company (GETC) had to present a plan for his group at an upcoming board meeting in May of 1985. Argentinis had been vice president at GETC since its inception in July 1982. As an engineer, he began his career at GE in its management training program. He subsequently worked in a variety of positions including manufacturing, engineering, marketing, finance, plant management, and field service. After transferring to GE's International Sector, he was appointed manager of Countertrade, Barter and Consortia, a forerunner of GETC. Eventually, Argentinis became responsible for laying down much of GETC's organizational structure and business policy.

That organizational structure was being tested in 1985 as GE's worldwide countertrade obligations exploded. Argentinis had to find a solution for managing this increased volume of obligations as well as for dealing with the growing diversity of products that GETC was expected to handle. GETC lacked trading expertise in commodities such as agricultural goods, oil, processed foods, and textiles—product groups that were important to the countries that imposed countertrade obligations on GE. One option was for Argentinis to use subcontractors to fulfill part or all of this expected increase in countertrade. Alternatively, he could hire additional traders in existing product groups and create new departments for the new product areas.

This case was prepared by Assistant Professor David B. Yoffie with the assistance of Merle Gehman, John McCormack, and Ralph Monforte, all MBAs '85, and Research Assistant Feisal Nanji as the basis for class discussion rather than to illustrate either effective or ineffective handling of an administrative situation.

Copyright © 1985 by the President and Fellows of Harvard College. Harvard Business School case 9-386-103.

General Electric

In 1984, General Electric Corporation was a highly diversified firm with sales of $28 billion and after-tax earnings of $2.3 billion. GE conducted operations in 15 business categories which it divided into three segments: core, high-technology, and services. Its core strategic business units (SBUs) were GE's more established businesses and had been part of GE for decades. There were six such SBUs: lighting, major appliance, motor, turbine, construction equipment, and transportation. The SBUs in its high-technology sector were industrial electronics, medical systems, engineering materials, aerospace, and aircraft engines. The final major segment at GE was its services group which included financial, information, construction and engineering, and nuclear. Three businesses were classified outside these three segments and served the entire company: Semiconductor, Ladd Petroleum, and GETC. (See *Exhibit 1.*)

Many business analysts have perceived GE as a company with vision and a leader in American industry. In the late 1960s, for example, GE's approach to cost controls was rapidly duplicated by firms of all sizes. Similarly, when GE implemented its strategic planning process in the early 1970s, other companies tried to emulate GE's method of analyzing new markets and allocating resources. Most business observers believed that GE was continuing its leadership role in the 1980s. This speculation was based in part on the election of Jack Welch as GE's new chairman in 1981. Welch was renowned at GE for his bold, vigorous, and risk-taking approach to management in GE's Materials SBU. As chairman, he would no longer reward managers for being cautious and operating on fixed and predetermined schedules. Rather, GE's new philosophy was to reward those who took chances and made bold moves in a true entrepreneurial spirit. Welch remarked that "admittedly, the older philosophy was strong and rigid enough to prevent major mistakes, yet I believe it also stifled enterprise and stunted innovation." In the words of GE corporate planner and Harvard MBA Michael Carpenter, "This new philosophy essentially meant thinking through the fundamental keys to the success of a business. What is the competition doing, how do the economics work, how do you create competitive advantage, and how do you nail the other guy?"

Two of Welch's highest priorities were the modernization of plants and investment, and research and development. This would be true for core businesses as well as high-technology SBUs. GE emphasized increasing productivity through automation and better product quality for the core sector. This modernization, automation, and streamlining process was aimed at making every division occupy a leadership position in world market share. Welch noted that "our strategy to become the most competitive enterprise in the world will only work if we are number 1 or number 2 in market share in every business we are in. Where a business has the potential to achieve such a position, we will support it vigorously to attain that status. Where it doesn't, we must divest." Welch also tried to change the way GE would measure success: "I try to measure people not on some internal numbers, but on how they are doing against their environment. We sometimes measure our managers in the old systems of management by numbers. Yet, some of the businesses we are losing money in were managed by better managers who were fighting a tougher, more competitive environment."

This competitive outlook extended to the world markets where GE had become increasingly dependent on foreign sources of revenue. GE was among the largest diversified exporters of American manufactured goods. While single-product companies, such as Boeing, sometimes topped the list of U.S. exporters, GE traded in 360 of the 400 or so International Trade Commission export classifications. Yet Welch wanted to make the company even more international in orientation: "I think more than anything we are trying to see ourselves in everything we do as being world competitive in cost, quality, and service. We accept the reality that we are going to have to cut costs, do more offshore sourcing and make more offshore investment, enter creative alliances and joint ventures, and step up our marketing efforts to be more competitive in international markets."

History and Status of GETC

GE's growing interest in global competition in the late 1970s prompted then-chairman Reginald Jones to carry out an intensive look at its international operations. After two years of study, a group recommended that GE establish its own trading operations. The group believed that a trading company at GE could fulfill three functions: it could serve as a general trading company, promoting GE and non-GE exports of medium-technology goods such as appliances, electrical pumps, and drives; it could fulfill GE's countertrade obligations (discussed below) at minimum risk and cost to the company; and it could bolster GE's overseas sales by offering international trading services to GE's customers.

Chairman Welch gave the final go-ahead to establish General Electric Trading Company (GETC) in January 1982. By the following July, GETC became an independent subsidiary, initially capitalized with approximately $20 million. Its initial staff of 250 had the capability of dealing in 28 languages. GETC would be supported by 765 GE distributors, sales representatives in 140 countries, and 750 export support staff workers in GE's Manhattan office. The subsidiary began with two divisions: Sales and Marketing, and Countertrade, Offset and Barter (COB). Each was run by a GETC vice president, with Tak Argentinis heading COB. Sales and Marketing's main activity was to export and service GE goods in the medium-tech-

nology area. Most of the initial staff of 250 were from GE's international distributor operations, and sales personnel were from medium technology SBUs. GE executives hoped that reorganizing those people under GETC would significantly boost GE exports. In addition, GETC's charter called for aiding the exports of small American manufacturers of medium-technology goods that did not directly compete with GE. The objective was to enlist companies that could deliver products within a matter of months—products such as pumps, compressors, and fans rather than locomotives. GE's pitch to American manufacturers was that GE not only had extensive experience in traditional export activities, but that it also could perform special trading programs such as countertrade.

The role of the newly created COB division was to assist SBUs in negotiating and fulfilling countertrade obligations. (For definitions of countertrade, see *Appendix 1*.). Since GE purchased $12 billion of materials, goods, and services every year, it potentially had more to offer in countertrade deals than most manufacturing companies, worldwide. (In fact, GE's ongoing international purchases were already generating 50% of the company's countertrade credits.) As GE's countertrade obligations rose from 1982 to 1984 (see *Exhibit 2*), the COB division grew rapidly (see *Exhibit 3*). GETC's Sales and Marketing unit, however, experienced serious problems by early 1984. It had not increased GE's medium-technology exports, nor had it generated much business for non-GE exports. Thus in the fall of 1984, the Sales and Marketing function was dissolved. Most of the employees that had fallen under GETC's wing reverted to their SBUs, or to a "pooled" sales force under GE's overseas area divisions.

GETC ORGANIZATIONAL STRUCTURE

GETC's COB group was divided into two sections: Trade Development and Trading. Trade Development had three major functions: negotiated countertrade agreements with foreign countries on behalf of GE's SBUs, set the fee which GETC would charge that SBU, and ensured that all exports generated by GETC would be registered with the respective governments' countertrade committees. Not surprisingly, the issue of fees was one of the most contentious within General Electric. Since SBUs were required by corporate policy to use GETC, they wanted the lowest possible fees. What GETC charged depended on a variety of factors, such as:

1. Type of product: steel, for example, was easier to trade than electric fans.
2. Difficulty of the transaction: for example, most products that could be handled within GE or within the United States required less work than products sold to third parties.
3. Product price, availability, and quality: if the best-quality products were not available, GE would have to buy lower-quality goods which may not have a readily available market. In addition, goods were frequently not available at "fair" market prices, and some exporters in Eastern European and developing nations also charged a premium for using their goods to count in a countertrade transaction.
4. Number of trader hours needed to fulfill a transaction.
5. Dollar volume of transaction: in some circumstances, higher volumes would reduce unit costs.
6. Penalties for late or nonfulfillment. Generally, SBUs maintained both the commercial and financial risk of nonperformance. But if GETC assumed this responsibility, the added risk would be reflected in the price. On the other hand, GETC retained the risk of the trading transactions required to perform the contract.

The actual rate was computed using a computer algorithm incorporating the above variables. Fees ranged from 2 to 8% of the coun-

tertrade transaction, but GETC generally charged between 4 and 6%.

A subset of Trade Development was Advance Trade Development (ADT). ADT's mission was to develop "proactive" trading solutions, which meant assisting SBUs in identifying potential opportunities in a particular country in advance of a sale. If an SBU wanted to sell to a country that did not want to allocate its foreign exchange for GE products, ADT would look for ways to demonetize the transaction in order to help generate the sale. ADT's first step was to produce an in-depth country study which analyzed environmental and business conditions. ADT would then suggest GETC's possible role in enhancing GE sales and its ability to handle any COB obligations.

Once ADT helped to find a customer and the Trade Development group assisted in negotiating a contract, GETC's Trading Group would take over. Whenever possible, GETC tried to utilize GE's huge internal market to satisfy obligations. GETC traders would try to match GE's internal needs with the countertrade demands of the various governments. Occasionally, GETC ran into resistance from Corporate Purchasing and SBUs, which would express concerns about quality controls, prices, and disrupting established supplier relations.

When the internal market could not absorb the countertrade products, traders would look for third markets. By early 1985, GETC had 46 traders conducting transactions in five product categories (see *Exhibit 3*). Argentinis' policy was to hire traders from inside GE who had an engineering degree, an MBA, and were fluent in at least one other language. He felt that this enabled GETC to have the expertise needed to handle complex products, to understand the fundamentals of business, and to be sensitive to different cultural environments. GETC also employed trade specialists responsible for arranging shipping, insurance, and letters of credit. Traders were further supported by trade administrators in countries where GE had obligations. They ensured that countertrade contracts were being fulfilled as required.

While the five product groups conducted transactions independently of each other, GETC essentially traded in two business classifications: commodities and manufactured goods. The commodity groups' approach to trading was different from the manufactured groups' approach. G. William LaRosa, manager of the electrical/electronics group, saw his group's role as a provider of an elaborate sales function. He stated that manufactured goods were difficult to trade since specifications were often complex and the key to making a sale was obtaining a satisfactory relationship between a customer and a supplier. Therefore, traders of manufactured goods had to be more creative than the typical "middleman." They might have to arrange financing, provide a distributor network, or offer complete manufacturing facilities so that a supplier could produce custom-made products. In line with GETC policy, transactions were back-to-back; i.e., a buyer would be lined up before GETC entered the deal. Argentinis generally did not allow speculative transactions. If a trader wanted to take a position and hold inventory, he/she would have to have approval of the department general manager. If the trade involved more than $1.0 million the divisional general manager had to review the deal.

Typically the customer (i.e., a foreign government) preferred companies such as GE to export industrial products. Moreover, the customers usually became more sophisticated over time, demanding that GE take specific goods and add value locally. Some customers, however, allowed companies to fulfill obligations with commodity purchases—a relatively high-risk business for GETC. Although explicit limits were set on each trader's exposure, Mr. J. Urioste, manager of the metals and mineral commodity group, would instruct his traders to speculate and hold positions in certain commodities. Argentinis had set specific policy

guidelines and different levels of review and approval for these transactions in order to contain the risk within an acceptable level.

By early 1985, GETC's trading operations could be divided into roughly three equal parts. One-third of all GETC's trades were done to fulfill existing countertrade obligations; one-third of the trades were in countries identified by ADT as potential, future countertrade obligations; and the remaining third was trade in noncountertrade countries designed to help generate volume and profit for the organization. In fiscal 1984, Argentinis reported that "GETC had helped GE SBUs win $1.3 billion in export orders with $80 to $100 million net income, but GETC had lost approximately $5 million on about $150 million in trade volume. This was largely because we had underestimated our fee rate to the SBUs." Corporate headquarters wanted GETC to break even by 1986.

Countertrade and GETC, 1985

By the end of 1984, Argentinis' main concern was the anticipated rise of GETC's COB obligations. Countertrade had become a very important component in the overseas sales of aircraft engines, transportation equipment, gas and steam turbines, and medical equipment—all markets facing intense international competition. In the last three years, $2.5 billion in GE export orders had been subject to COB obligations. GETC was officially responsible for 40% of the transactions, while the remainder would be handled by the SBUs. However, if the volume and number of countries that imposed countertrade increased, then GETC's responsibilities would probably grow to 80 to 100% of the obligations. (See *Exhibit 2*.) The actual obligation, which could accumulate to as much as $15 billion, would depend on SBU sales overseas and the percentage of GE obligations GETC would incur.

A major complication facing Argentinis was

that many countries required GE to export goods which GETC could not presently handle. GETC had no internal mechanism for dealing with products such as agricultural commodities and oil. In addition, the trend in countertrade in many countries was to require firms to export fewer traditional products and more value-added goods, such as processed foods and textiles. If GETC projections were accurate, then as much as 55% of the goods GE would need to trade in 1993 would be in products where GETC had no expertise. (See *Exhibits 4* and *5.*)

Before deciding how GETC should handle this problem, Argentinis wanted to compare GETC's performance against the performance of competitive trading companies and find out if subcontracting would be cost-effective. A team was put together that examined how GETC compared with some of the large Japanese trading companies (known as sogoshosha) and the American firm of Phillip Brothers. Their report is excerpted below, and the comparison of performance indicators is displayed in *Exhibit 6.*

Japanese Trading Companies The general trading companies of Japan were starkly different from GETC in 1985 by virtue of their sheer size and diversity. Yet comparisons with the sogoshosha were important because GETC was trying to duplicate many of their functions, albeit on a smaller scale. While some Japanese trading firms dated back to the early 1600s, the role of Japanese traders in the Japanese economy did not become significant until the late 19th century. From the advent of the Meiji era through the early 1970s, the Japanese trading companies grew to handle between 50 and 70% of their country's total imports and exports. Japanese domestic companies relied on the sogoshosha to identify markets, procure raw materials, arrange for shipment and warehousing, finance inventories, and market finished products. Since the large general trading companies had vast information networks with personnel and offices in literally thousands of locations around the globe, they offered their clients services which no individual manufacturing firm could duplicate. Most sogoshosha also realized significant economies of scale in procuring and distributing bank loans.

The cost structures at a typical sogoshosha made it essential to maximize transaction volume. Japanese trading companies were highly leveraged, and their return on sales was minuscule by American standards. (See *Exhibit 6.*) In addition, most costs—personnel, office, and communication—were fixed, and the incremental expense of an individual transaction was small. Hence, as world trade slowed in the early 1980s, most sogoshosha suffered. By the end of 1983, trading income was only half of investment income. Furthermore, the sogoshosha did not fully recover as world trade picked up in 1984 and early 1985. The sogoshosha's trading base was in bulk products that required relatively little aftermarket service. Since Japanese firms had increasingly shifted their manufacturing toward more sophisticated, higher value-added goods, they preferred to export directly rather than work through a trading company.

Phillip Brothers Phillip Brothers was an American company that claimed to be the largest pure commodity trader in the world. Known as Phibro, it competed directly against the sogoshosha in the trading of 150 different commodities ranging from crude oil and precious metals to fertilizers and agricultural products. Phibro's size allowed it to buy, ship, insure, warehouse, and distribute commodities at a cost lower than most producers and end users. Unlike the sogoshosha, however, Phibro was primarily in the business of maximizing trading profits rather than building long-term client relationships. Phibro was renowned as a risk-taking company: it hired a relatively small number of very high priced traders (top traders would make more than $1.5 million per year) that specialized in large-scale arbitrage. A copper specialist enjoyed telling the *Wall Street Journal*[1] that his "favorite deal was when I bought $750,000 worth of copper from a company and sold it back to the European branch of the same firm. I got it there more cheaply and at a profit for Phillip Brothers."

Phibro grew with terrifying speed in the 1970s, from $1.2 billion in 1971 to almost $30 billion by 1984. Most of the growth came from diversification into new product areas. Yet the 1982–1983 recession hurt Phibro in much the same way it damaged the sogoshosha. Although Phibro was somewhat more flexible than Japanese traders since it did not have a life employment system, it also had a high fixed-cost organization that was dependent upon volume. By early 1985, Phibro was retrenching: the slow recovery in world commodity markets forced the company to fire hundreds of traders and led to the resignation of the top management.

GETC and Subcontractors

Other American companies approached their countertrade obligations differently from GE. Some manufacturers subcontracted all their countertrade commitments to specialists like Phibro or Mitsui, while others maintained only limited capabilities to handle their obligations in-house. For example, FMC Corporation, one of the largest manufacturers of mobile armored vehicles, had a countertrade group which was a cost center and part of its procurement division. The group looked for ways to substitute existing suppliers for suppliers in countries where the firm had countertrade commitments. If the countertrade obligation could not be satisfied in-house, a subcontractor would be hired. Combustion Engineering, by contrast, had a small trading group that functioned as a cost center at the corporate staff level. A few

[1]August 18, 1981.

highly trained professionals negotiated COB transactions but relied almost exclusively on outside traders to fulfill COB obligations. Finally, companies such as Douglas Aircraft and General Motors had countertrade profit centers ranging from 10 to 30 people that would look for the cheapest way to handle a deal, either through sales within the corporation or by using outside contractors.

If GETC was going to follow any of these models, Argentinis needed to know exactly what subcontractors could do for the company and at what cost. Argentinis' team found that subcontractors could potentially perform four major functions for GETC: negotiate on behalf of the SBU, find appropriate countertrade products, deliver the product to end users, and ensure that GE would obtain countertrade credit from the government. GETC could have one or more of these functions performed by subcontractors. The team also found that three different types of firms were available: full-service firms, such as Phibro, Sears World Trade, and Metallgesellschaft, that would perform all the functions; procurement assistance firms that could buy particular products; and outside distributors that would deliver the products to end users.

GETC sent a survey to large full-service and procurement assistance firms, inquiring about their capacity to assist GE with two existing countertrade contracts in Spain and Turkey. Since GETC regularly used outside distributors, and embedded distribution costs in their price, they were not polled. The team chose Spain and Turkey because they represented the diversity of products and trade volumes that GETC was likely to face over the next decade. The $317 million that GE had to export from Turkey would be similar to GE's requirements in other developing countries, and the $204 million obligation in Spain was analogous to GE's situation in many industrialized countries. Both commitments were spread over ten years. (See *Appendixes* 2 and 3.)

Full-Service Firms The survey found that full-service firms would undertake all the stages of a transaction, from proposal writing to obtaining final credit from a government's countertrade committee. Although fees could be negotiated, the range was 4 to 6% of the total transaction. Full-service firms were either a division of a major trading company or the trading arms of banks. By virtue of their size, and the fact that they traded without restricting their efforts to specific countries, most of these firms could complete a countertrade transaction faster than GETC, which was restricted by its charter to focus on specific countries. A deal which might take GETC 12 months could be completed in 3 months by a full-service trader. However, most full-service firms preferred to work on a "best-effort" basis. This meant that if the countertrade country imposed a penalty for delay of shipment or nonfulfillment, the principal (GE) would have to pay the penalty. If the subcontractor offered performance guarantees, then the fees would be 2 to 5% higher. The firms which responded to the survey reported that they could each handle between 30 and 50% of GE's annual obligations in Spain and Turkey, leaving GE with the problem of managing several competitors at any given time. (See *Exhibit 7*.)

Procurement Assistance Firms Procurement assistance (P.A.) firms were specialists in particular commodities. After GETC negotiated a contract, it might want to use a P.A. firm to buy specific commodities that GETC could not handle internally. The survey found that P.A. firms were widely available at reasonable costs for countries that offered commodity products. Fees ranged from 1 to 10%, depending on the commodity, the country, and the time frame. In metals, for example, ten traders indicated that they could buy between $5 and $20 million annually in Turkey or Spain at a fee of approximately 1%. Petroleum products could also be handled by P.A. firms for 1%, and they could fulfill an obligation in 2 months that would take GETC 12 months. Since P.A. firms traded continuously with a variety of buyers and suppliers, they could respond faster than GETC, which primarily focused on filling countertrade orders. Procurement assistance in other products, such as chemicals and processed foods, were significantly more costly, and procurement assistance was virtually nonexistent or very expensive in differentiated products. P.A. firms were most helpful in trading goods that had well-established markets. These firms were reticent about taking products that did not have a proven sales history from a particular country.

Argentinis' Dilemma

Having heard the results of the survey, Argentinis had to decide what to recommend to his board of directors at their upcoming meeting. The decisions regarding GETC's mission, size, breadth of products, and relationship with outside subcontractors would have a lasting impact on GETC's future.

EXHIBIT ONE					
	1984	**1983**	**1982**	**1981**	**1980**
Summary of industry segments performance					
Revenues ($ million):					
Consumer products	3,858	3,741	3,943	4,202	3,998
Major appliances	3,650	3,078	2,751	3,132	3,012
Industrial systems	4,274	4,228	4,705	5,364	4,907
Power systems	6,010	5,878	6,093	6,015	5,703
Aircraft engines	3,835	3,495	3,140	2,950	2,660
Materials	2,241	2,060	1,791	2,050	1,877
Technical products and services	4,803	3,823	3,546	3,005	2,424
Financial services	448	397	286	239	193
Natural resources	609	1,579	1,575	1,722	1,374
Corporate items and eliminations	(792)	(598)	(638)	(825)	(625)
Total	28,936	27,681	27,192	27,854	25,523
Net earnings ($ million):					
Consumer products	228	163	146	225	241
Major appliances	223	156	79	82	104
Industrial systems	73	84	148	212	218
Power systems	486	439	384	242	223
Aircraft engines	251	196	161	149	141
Materials	262	182	148	189	170
Technical products and services	232	210	218	144	99
Financial services	336	285	203	145	126
Natural resources	117	301	318	284	224
Corporate items and eliminations	72	8	12	(20)	(32)
Total	2,280	2,024	1,817	1,652	1,514
Summary of international operations (all industry segments)					
Revenue outside U.S. ($ million):					
Foreign operations and licensing	4,448	5,509	6,100	6,509	5,816
U.S. exports to external customers	3,255	3,639	3,312	3,681	3,781
Total	7,703	9,148	9,412	10,190	9,597
Net earnings	419	668	680	574	639

Source: GE Annual Report, 1984.

COUNTERTRADE, OFFSET AND BARTER: STATUS, DECEMBER 1984 ($ million)

Country	Total obligations	GE SBU portion	GETC portion	GE SBU balance	GETC balance	Cumulative projected obligations, 1993
Romania	175	9	166	6	93	0
Spain	305	101	204	101	193	430
Canada	728	728	0	175	0	620
Turkey	475	157	318	157	316	261
Israel	161	80	81	80	80	285
Australia	111	111	0	99	0	623
Korea	23	23	0	15	0	443
Brazil	14	2	12	1	0	1,957
Sweden	600	300	300	300	268	321
Italy	33	33	0	18	0	635
Switzerland	30	30	0	0	0	145
Poland	12	12	0	6	0	0
China	9	9	0	8	0	2,051
Netherlands	5	5	0	0	0	106
Pakistan	5	5	0	5	0	0
Yugoslavia	4	4	0	4	0	0
United Kingdom	16	0	16	0	0	0
Other	102					7,407[a]
Total	2,808	1,609	1,081	975	950	15,284

[a]The largest countries in this group include France ($1,085), United States ($930), Mexico ($1,214), Saudi Arabia ($741), India ($602), and Indonesia ($511).

Source: Company documents.

EXHIBIT THREE

Product group performance and characteristics ($ thousand)

	Machinery, tooling, and equipment	Chemicals, oil, construction materials	Electrical/ electronics	Metals and minerals	Industrial products and components
Sales 1984	4,455	32,860	13,375	48,080	2,335
Contribution margin	545	630	1,620[a]	1,680	210
Base costs:					
Selling	1,050	1,600	2,125	1,420	890
Overhead	575	760	865	690	435
Operating margin/(loss)	(1,080)	(1,730)	(1,370)	(430)	(1,115)
Forecasted sales volume (1985)	9,600	50,000	24,600	95,200	10,600
Annual GE purchases	400,000	600,000	750,000	800,000	400,000
Total no. of employees	17	21	25	20	12

Product classifications by product group

Machine tools	Construction materials	Electronics		Low-medium technical goods
Plastic equipment and tooling	Fertilizers and heavy chemicals	Computer systems	Raw materials	Manufactured goods involving testing
Cutting tools	Organic chemicals	Medical and scientific instruments	Engineered products	
Capital equipment	Oil products	Electrical	Nonferrous metals and ores	
	Forestry products		Specialty metals	

GETC performance indicators ($ million)

	1983	1984[b]	1985[c]
Trade volume	136.7	151.9	230.0
Contribution margin	4.6	7.9	14.9
Base costs:			
Selling	4.3	9.3	13.2
Finance and general	0.4	1.0	1.5
Corporate assessments	1.5	2.6	4.7
Total base costs	6.2	12.9	19.4
Gross margin	(1.6)	(5.0)	(4.5)
Number of employees	55	125	125

(*continued*)

EXHIBIT THREE

CONTINUED

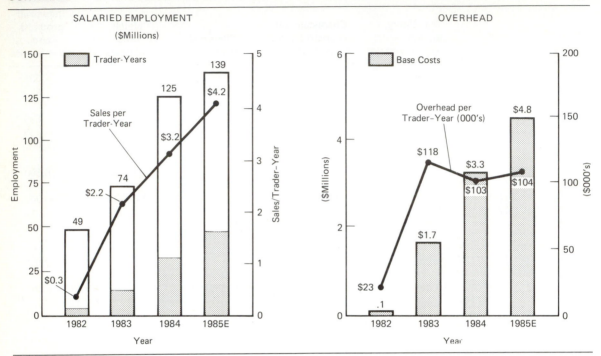

SALARIED EMPLOYMENT ($Millions)

OVERHEAD

aExcludes $1.4 million write-down on semiconductor inventory.
bEstimate.
cProjection.
Source: Company documents.

EXHIBIT FOUR

DISTRIBUTION (%) of WORLD TRADE BY COMMODITY (1993 FORECAST)

1.	Food products	17
2.	Agricultural raw materials	5
3.	Fuels and combustibles	27
4.	Ores and metal	10
5.	Chemical products	6
6.	Machinery and equipment	15
7.	Other manufacturing	19

Categories 1–3: Non-GETC products as of 1984.
Categories 4–7: GETC products as of 1984.
Source: U.N. International Trade Statistics, 1984.

SAMPLE OF COUNTRIES ENGAGING IN COUNTERTRADE AND KEY ALLOWABLE PRODUCTS

Countries	GETC products					Non-GETC products			
	Metals and minerals	Chemicals and construction materials	Electrical/ electronics	Machinery and tooling	Industrial (castings, machine parts, etc.)	Energy products (LNG, coal, oil)	Rubber textiles, agricultural products, leather goods	Services	Miscellaneous industrial and construction
E. Europe	X			X	X				
Brazil	X	X	X	X	X	X	X		X
Canada								X	
Malaysia						X	X		X
Italy				X				X	
Australia	X		X					X	X
South Korea	X	X	X	X	X		X	X	
Spain	X		X	X	X			X	
Netherlands								X	
Sweden			X				X	X	
Israel	X		X	X	X		X	X	X
People's Republic of China	X	X	X	X	X	X	X	X	X
Philippines									
Thailand				X			X		
United Kingdom							X		X
India		X				X	X	X	
Indonesia		X				X	X		
Argentina	X	X				X	X		
Taiwan	X	X				X			
Turkey	X						X		
Singapore									
Iran	X	X				X	X		
Algeria	X	X				X	X		X
Egypt								X	
Nigeria						X	X		

Source: Company documents.

EXHIBIT SIX

TRADING COMPANY PERFORMANCE COMPARISONS (selected data)

	Mitsubishi			Mitsui			C. Itoh		
	1984	1983	1982	1984	1983	1982	1984	1983	1982
Income data $ millions (¥224; $1):									
Trading transactions	70,604	70,013	69,800	71,914	70,056	68,947	60,105	57,187	56,740
Gross trading profit	1,338	1,278	1,440	1,532	1,508	1,618	1,241	2,167	1,054
Selling, general, and administrative expenses	1,080	1,055	1,041	1,102	1,088	1,003	21	1	23
Net income	119	113	152	39	30	5	958	898	
Trading profit/sales, %	1.89	1.84	2.06	2.18	2.15	2.35	2.06	2.04	1.85
No. of employees (only 1983 figures available)		14,000			12,000			10,000	
Balance sheet data:									
Current assets	17,866	17,425	15,492	17,656	16,827	15,403	15,746	14,375	12,692
Total assets	25,252	24,614	22,399	25,060	24,771	22,454	20,114	18,436	16,514
Current liabilities	17,640	16,786	14,722	18,062	17,335	15,519	16,117	14,183	12,374
Long-term debt	5,488	5,770	5,664	5,963	6,398	5,910	3,462	3,700	3,577
Equity	1,902	1,856	1,811	904	916	909	387	400	409

	Phillip Brothers		
	1984	1983	1982
Income data ($ millions):			
Sales	28,911	28,200	24,308
Earnings before taxes	260	307	222
Pretax profit/sales, %	0.90	1.13	0.91
Selling, general, and administrative expenses as % sales	3.03	0.90	1.00
No. of employees (only 1983 figures available)		3,700	
Balance sheet data:			
Current assets	57,815	41,217	38,777
Total assets	58,370	42,017	39,669
Current liabilities	55,313	39,079	37,134
Long-term debt	651	698	766
Equity	2,406	2,240	1,769

Sources: Corporate annual reports.

EXHIBIT SEVEN

Full-service firms

Type	Cost, % transaction	Capacity[a]	Service level
GETC	4% Spain	100%	Best effort–SBU
	7% Turkey		Pays penalty
Trading companies:			
Turkey	6%	30%	Best efforts
Spain	[c]		Best efforts
Banks' countertrade arms:			
Turkey	5–6%	50%	Best efforts
Spain	4–5%	25%	Best efforts[b]

Procurement assistance firms

Product area	Cost, % transaction	Capacity[d]	Response time
Metals	1–5%	$5–20 million	3 months
Petroleum products	1%	$10–15 million	2 months
Chemicals	8%	$1–5 million	6 months
Processed foods	5–10%	$10–30 million	1 month
Electrical equipment		Expertise not available	

Turkey

Metals	NA	$1–5 million	3 months
Petroleum products	1%	$25–50 million	2 months
Chemicals			
Processed foods	5–10%	$5–10 million	1 month
Electrical equipment		Expertise not available	

[a]Capacity denotes ability of subcontractor to handle GE obligations in terms of percentage.
[b]Best-effort basis indicates an unwillingness to assume penalties for nonfulfillment.
[c]Respondents not active in Spain.
[d]Capacity in terms of annual dollar volume.

APPENDIX 1

DEFINITIONS OF COUNTERTRADE

Countertrade is an umbrella term encompassing a wide range of barterlike activities in international trade. Countertrade is best defined as any transaction where the sale of a good or service into a country is linked to the export of other goods or services from that same country. Hence countertrade includes activities such as barter, counterpurchase, compensation, offset, and switch trading. Definitions for each of these forms of countertrade are described below.

Barter

Barter has been around since the beginning of commercial transactions. In international barter deals, a buyer insists on payment in goods rather than in cash. Most barter deals are one-time transactions covered by a single contract. The goods are usually exchanged simultaneously or within a short period of time. Examples of international barter include exchanges of weapons for crude oil between the Soviet Union and oil exporters in the Middle East and the exchange of Vietnamese rice for French wheat.

Counterpurchase

Counterpurchase is one of the most prevalent forms of countertrade: a seller delivers its goods to a country and agrees to purchase and export products equal to some, all, or more of the value of the original sale. Unlike pure barter, counterpurchase contracts are usually specified in a currency and employ traditional financing. Counterpurchase deals are divided into two contracts: one covers the original export and the other the obligation to counterpurchase goods or services. An example of a counterpurchase deal was Hawker Siddeley's $20 million sale of railroad cars to Indonesia in 1983. Hawker Siddeley was paid by Indonesia with traditional trade finance, but the company agreed to buy approximately $20 million of Indonesian products, ranging from rubber to cement.

Compensation

While counterpurchase tends to involve two independent transactions, a *compensation* deal involves an exporter taking a related good as partial or full payment. In a compensation arrangement, a seller of capital goods or technology agrees to buy products that are produced from its own equipment. Compensation agreements are generally long-term, and they have been common in East-West trade and military sales for decades. An example is Levi Strauss's sale of a blue jeans factory to Hungary. In partial payment, the American company agreed to take output from the plant—up to 500,000 jeans per year—which it would market in West Europe and North Africa.

Offset

Offset is a term frequently used in the aerospace industry to describe a mixture of different types of countertrade obligations. Typically, offset contracts are divided into two types: direct and indirect. Direct offset involves a combination of direct investment and compensation trade: in direct offset deals, firms are required to make local purchases of supplies as well as make investment in the customer country in industries related to the end product. In an airplane deal, for instance, the seller may be asked to buy local airplane parts. The firm must find a local supplier or make investments to create a parts industry. These investments are often in the form of joint ventures with local companies. Indirect offset is another term for counterpurchase.

Switch

Switch trading is a highly specialized form of countertrade. Switch trading is based on trying to smooth out problems associated with clearing agreements. A clearing agreement, which is most frequently found between European countries and less developed countries, calls for the exchange of fixed amounts of goods between two nations. Payments for these transactions are typically made in local, nonconvertible currencies. An importer pays for foreign goods by putting local currency into a "clearing account" at a local bank. Then a domestic exporter can withdraw the local currency as payment for his/her shipments. In theory, the accounts are suppose to be "cleared" or balanced, usually at the end of the year. Switch traders serve two purposes: they try to resolve unbalanced accounts and in the process help multinationals sell products to a clearing partner. The essence of switch trading is to buy nonconvertible currency and clearing rights from one country at a discount, then sell the currency and import rights to a third party such as a multinational.

Turkey: Indirect Offset Requirements

- Total obligation: $317.7 million
- Fulfillment period (1984–1994):
  10 years + 3 grace
- Performance schedule

Years	Incremental achievement	Total achievement
1986	5%	5%
1988	15	20
1990	25	45
1992	25	70
1994	30	100

- Export activities:

  Goods or services produced or provided and paid in foreign currencies in Turkey.

  The investment of capital and/or any reinvested profits generated therefrom.

  Marketing assistance program(s).

  Transfer of technology.

  Joint venture or partnership.

  All transactions are to be credited in "then-year dollars," and the exchange rate shall be the official dollar/lira exchange rate at the time of the transaction completion.

  Qualifying transactions are classified into one of the two groups. Group 1 transactions include capital investments, joint ventures, and technology transfers. Group 2 includes *all* other transactions, including the purchases of goods and services from a Turkish company. Achievement of 10% Group A and 90% Group B is required.

- Liquidated damages. If, after the grace period, a shortfall exists, liquidated damages will be applied.

Spanish F-404 Offset Program Specs (commerical or indirect portion only)

- Total obligation: $204 million (1981$)
- Fullfillment period (1983–1993): 10 years + 3 grace
- Export/activities restrictions:

  Offset exports to be "incremental."

  40% of obligation to be fulfilled with offsets involving technologies characteristic to developed countries.

  Tourism activity will be an eligible offset transaction up to a maximum of 10% of total offset obligation.

  Non-U.S. dollar transactions to be converted into U.S. dollars at rate exchange quoted by the Chase Manhattan Banks at transaction date.

  All transactions to be credited in January 1981 dollars. Index to be used will be the CPI for urban wage earners and clerical workers as published by the U.S. BLS.

  Exports to the United States will be subject to an added-value factor. That is, only the Spanish ingredient (materials, labor, energy, etc.) will be credited against offset obligation.

  Offset credits to be awarded on FOB Spain Port unless Spanish flag vessels are used. In this case, transportation expenses will also receive offset credit.

  No restriction insofar as industry type is concerned other than those mentioned above.

- Liquidated damages. If there is a shortfall at the end of the grace period, liquidated damages will be assessed as follows:

  7.5% of shortfall on first 30% of offset obligation

  5.0% of shortfall on next 40% of offset obligations

  2.5% of shortfall on the last 30% of offset obligations

MG Services

"If you want to deal with large companies like General Electric, at the end of the day what you need is credibility," said Siegfried K. Hodapp, president of Metallgesellschaft Corp. (MG Corp.), as lunch was being cleared away at the Racquet and Tennis Club. He was speaking about his company's countertrade subsidiary, MG Services Company (MGS), which had grown rapidly in the difficult trading environment of the 1980s. "One of MGS's advantages is that our people are deal makers and not just traders, so we're able to provide a whole package of services."

Countertrade (CT) was an umbrella term describing situations where the import of goods or services into a country was linked to exports from that country (see *Exhibit 1*). Although CT had been relatively rare since World War II, it exploded during the early 1980s. MGS had been formed in 1983 amidst the crush of banks, trading houses, and multinational manufacturing concerns trying to grab a share of the burgeoning market.

By 1986, however, countertrade growth was slackening. Hodapp explained that "large corporations were selling fewer projects; governments were not mandating countertrade as often as they had in the early 1980s; and many of the new countertrade projects had become 'plain vanilla' operations, not requiring the same creative skills. As a result, our profit margins have been squeezed."

Hodapp believed that MGS had a creative staff with many options. "We could extend our product base, expand geographically, or even try to capture every countertrade deal in the world," he said, listing several options. "But we have to develop a sustainable advantage. I see our presence in different markets and activities as a form of trading in participations," Hodapp continued, pointing out that MG Corp. was also expanding beyond its traditional trading base in metals into trading oil and U.S. government securities. "This allows us to diversify our risks and be well placed to take advantage of an upsurge in any sector. We're seeking commodities and areas where we can be a major player but we're still small and have to operate independently of Frankfurt."

This case was prepared by Research Assistant Eugene Salorio and Associate Professor David B. Yoffie as the basis for class discussion rather than to illustrate either effective or ineffective handling of an administrative situation.

BACKGROUND OF METALLGESELLSCHAFT

MG Corp. was the U.S. subsidiary of Metallgesellschaft AG, one of West Germany's largest firms and a world leader in the trading, mining, and process engineering of nonferrous metals. Founded in Frankfurt in 1881 as a metal trader, MG.AG soon integrated into both mining and processing metal ores and subsequently expanded into the manufacture of semifinished metal products and chemicals. Mining and smelting investments in Australia and the United States came next, followed by establishment of overseas trade agencies. Long-term supply contracts and mining joint ventures with financially weak foreign firms, plus provision of financing, insurance, and technical assistance to both suppliers and customers, completed a global network.

Within 30 years MG.AG was a world leader in the metals industry and was cited by Lenin as a "monster of monopoly capitalism." Although the firm's overseas assets were expropriated after World War I, it quickly replaced its international network. One of its mainstays during this interwar era was the Lurgi engineering division, which designed, engineered, and supplied plants for a wide variety of industrial mineralogical processes; the USSR was a major client.

After World War II Metallgesellschaft's overseas assets were again expropriated by the victorious allies, and the company's new rebuilding effort concentrated on erecting a domestic fixed asset base; finance and trading were treated as ancillary activities. MG became a traditional German company known for excellence in metals manufacturing. It was managed by German nationals who generally spent their lives in MG.AG, working their way up through the company ranks.

By the late 1970s, MG.AG had again expanded internationally, with mining and manufacturing operations from Canada and Mexico to Australia and Papua, New Guinea. In 1982, however, the firm reported its first loss in over 30 years (see *Exhibit 2*). In response, the company slashed its work force and closed or sold several money-losing manufacturing operations. A decision was made to refocus the com-

pany on its original prewar businesses: metals mining and processing, trading, and engineering services. One of the major proponents of the new strategy was Dr. Heinz Schimmelbusch, at the time head of MG.AG's U.S. subsidiary (MG Corp.) and formerly corporate planning director at Frankfurt headquarters. It was under his aegis that MG Corp. moved into a variety of new areas such as trading oil, gold, and financial instruments. Schimmelbusch also broke with company tradition by hiring Siegfried Hodapp, a 12-year veteran of Citibank with no metals trading background. The hiring of Hodapp underscored Schimmelbusch's commitment to redirect MG.AG.

Schimmelbusch believed that MG.AG could become "a raw materials service company that can utilize every aspect of a complex transaction as a separate business opportunity." In 1981, as an example, he negotiated a $100 million mining deal with the Chinese government that entailed MG's raising the external funding, providing technical assistance in production and product quality, a long-term marketing agreement, and a trilateral China-MG-USA repayment schedule with the U.S. lenders. He returned to headquarters in 1984 in the dual roles of managing director and head of the raw materials division, which quickly grew to 62% of corporate sales.

COUNTERTRADE IN 1983 AND THE FORMATION OF MG SERVICES

Schimmelbusch's original mandate to MG Services was to assume the character of a "deal maker" in countertrade. MG.AG's countertrade experience had largely originated from Lurgi buyback or barter deals that were handled by the commodity traders on product desks. Schimmelbusch, however, felt that many export-oriented manufacturing companies encountering CT regulations in LDC markets were anxious to lay off their countertrade obligations on a third party. Few manufacturers, Schimmelbusch believed, wanted to buy and sell unknown products or be burdened with possible penalties that could show up as contingent liabilities on their balance sheets.

Even though MG.AG had no prior experience in marketing such services, it established a new subsidiary in New York that would assume CT obligations for American, European, and Asian clients. Schimmelbusch and Hodapp believed that MG Service would have great strength because it could work through the more than 1,000 MG.AG trade representatives in 50 worldwide locations. The idea was to put together an entire package for companies exporting to difficult markets, including the "software" of countertrade documentation. MGS would help firms navigate through the maze of often vague or conflicting regulations on timing, value, eligible products, and the perceived risk associated with failure to perform a CT obligation. The key was to make it a low-overhead service organization, to be "brain- and relationship-intensive" in contrast to MG.AG's other high-fixed-cost businesses.

Countertrade in 1983

For most of the postwar period, CT was largely forced upon firms selling capital goods to Eastern Europe. An array of boutique-type firms, specialized banks, traders, and subcontractors centered in Austria and Switzerland grew to service these specific transactions. In 1981, however, Indonesia instituted a 100% counterpurchase requirement for all foreign suppliers selling more than $775,000 to Indonesian government agencies or state-owned enterprises; noncompliance carried a 50% penalty. The Indonesian government's stated goals were to diversify exports, especially toward labor-intensive manufactured goods, and cut down on imports. Petroleum and natural gas exports did not count toward countertrade fulfillment, and natural resource goods had to be shipped to new markets.

The announcement was greeted with great scepticism, as no nonsocialist country had successfully imposed large-scale countertrade requirements on anything except military sales in more than 30 years. Critics stated that Indonesia's need for critical imports would force it to waive the requirements, and that corrupt government officials could easily be bribed to suspend the obligations on major transactions. International institutions like the IMF claimed that such practices distorted trade patterns based on comparative advantage, thereby diminishing global welfare.

Neighboring countries and other LDCs, however, observed the Indonesian experiment closely. While some feared that increased Indonesian raw materials exports might cut into their own export markets, others wondered if CT programs might not improve their own trading positions in international markets. Malaysia, for instance, copied Indonesia by mandating that CT offers be evaluated as part of any foreign bid on a government tender; it soon thereafter bartered $50 million in timber and palm oil for South Korean patrol boats and exchanged tin and rubber for $2 million of Yugoslavian electrical equipment. Such practices spread rapidly with numerous variations. Colombia, New Zealand, Israel, South Korea, and Greece, among others, institutionalized CT requirements. (See *Exhibit 3A* for details on Colombia's program and *3B* for Pakistan's program.)

Setting Up Shop

Hodapp and Schimmelbusch saw this rapid spread of CT as an opportunity to be capitalized on immediately. They quickly hired three CT specialists away from competitors to form MG Services. They were given three objectives: to make MGS a stand-alone profit center, to enhance the trading profits of existing businesses, and to provide an in-house service to support the manufacturing and exporting divisions of MG.AG, principally Lurgi. Offices were opened in New York, London, and Hong Kong.

The three professionals, who were recruited as a team, were all Americans in their 30s with varied backgrounds. George Horton, who had an MBA in international finance from the University of Michigan, had helped form Motors Trading (a GM subsidiary) before starting the CT unit at Citibank in 1981. The second had been a CT and trade finance specialist for Merban (a boutique trading firm that was subsequently purchased by Continental Grain); the third, Thomas Gottlieb, got a graduate degree in political science, then spent 2 1/2 years in First Chicago's China group before joining Citibank as its Asia region CT representative. For them, the move to MG Services was a chance to pursue CT with the support of a large firm offering "traders, capital, reputation, commitment, and the ability to move the product," in the words of George Horton. "When we walk into someone's office and say 'We have the answer to your trading problems,' it definitely helps to have the name of a major multinational behind you. They want to know that you're going to fulfill." MG Services' strength, said Horton, "was our dedication to CT; CT was our only business. While we were flexible abut financing and holding products, the banks had no commitment to CT. Banks primarily saw CT as a marketing tool for capturing other trade finance transactions like letters of credit or foreign exchange. In addition, the banks did not know how to gauge CT risk. If you walk down the hall at a bank and say you're long sterling, no one get excited. If you say you're long bananas, all hell breaks loose."

MG Services was capitalized at $100,000 with $750,000 budgeted for overhead in the first year. Their compensation terms were a guaranteed salary plus a bonus based on profits. The initial objectives were to establish MG Service's name, develop a client base, and educate MG.AG internally on the new approach to CT. Finan-cially, they projected to break even in the first year or to realize a small loss. By the third year, they expected to be handling $50 to $75 million yearly in CT, with a gross profit margin of about 3%; three more professionals would then be added to the staff.

Size of the Market

By the time MGS was formed, some sources claimed that as much as $600 billion (roughly 30%) of world trade involved CT. Horton, however, thought that the OECD's 1983 estimate of $80 billion was much closer. The OECD estimates, which included significant government-to-government deals, were broken down as follows:

	$ billion	% of trade involved
Industrial countries trade with:		
East Europe	$15.6	15
Oil exporters	4.3	2
Other LDCs	16.6	5
Among each other	15.7	2
Developing countries trade with:		
East Europe	14.2	30
Among each other	12.5	10

The First Year

MGS signed its first deal in January 1983, only four weeks after being formed. The firm arranged to fulfill a countertrade obligation on a "best-efforts" basis for a Korean firm which had exported steel to Indonesia. Since MGS assumed no risk on the deal, its fee was relatively low; they performed by exporting rubber and wood products which were sold both inside and outside MG.AG. Their next customer in March was a Japanese trading company facing a 50% penalty for nonperformance on a $30 million Indonesian CT obligation. MG Services took over the entire obligation in return for a 6.5 to 7% premium, the going rate at the time. MGS purchased and exported Indonesian rubber and wood at world market prices; some of this was later sold back to another arm of the same Japanese company.

The Hong Kong manager, Tom Gottlieb, spent most of his time in Indonesia during the first year trying to determine the key players and master the regulations on timing, payment, and documentation. "There were a lot of manufacturing and trading companies that could have purchased the rubber or wood," he later commented. "But they were reluctant to assume the perceived risks. When they finally entered the market in 1984 and 1985, the only way they could differentiate themselves was by cutting price." MGS' strategy was to underwrite obligations which it would then syndicate to different traders inside and outside of MG.AG. MGS would offer the traders a fee that varied from a high of 3% to a low of 1/4% as an inducement for their help. At first, MGS sought to pass to the traders the full risk associated with nonperformance; subsequently MGS decided to pay lower fees and retain the risks. Initially there was some friction between MGS and MG Corp. traders. The traders didn't really understand CT; moreover, government requirements were often vague. Hodapp often acted to smooth the relationship, until standards were developed for splitting the CT fees. These standards gave the traders the right of first refusal on any export deal and established a formula for fulfilling obligations. Hodapp set country limits for total CT obligations over a given time period and took great interest in the first deal in any new country, preferring that it be done on a best-efforts basis. Limits were set on how much each MG Corp. trader could get involved with MGS, to minimize each's exposure if the other failed to perform.

For the longer-term (multiyear) export obligations MGS found it was impossible to fulfill all the obligations in-house. "Imagine," said George Horton, "putting a salesman in a room with a copper trader. The salesman says his company is selling a major project to Peru with a 10-year barter arrangement and needs a fixed price offer for copper over this period. But the copper trader would only offer a fixed price for the next 30 seconds, so they weren't able to speak the same language. Only someone like MGS can provide the software and skills to bridge these worlds."

By the end of its first year, MGS had fulfilled over $50 million in CT obligations and was expanding so quickly that additional people were needed. Experienced traders from Phibro and Greficomex (a Continental Grain-Credit Lyonnais joint venture) were added, and the firm opened offices in Frankfurt, Bucharest, and Toronto.

CONTINUED GROWTH OF MG SERVICES

As they developed experience in the CT market, MGS found that its most productive activities were largely marketing-oriented: making personal calls, visiting prospective clients, and trying to establish close working relations with a core group of companies. One of the persistent problems they encountered was a low "kill ratio"; no matter how well known MGS became, they had to actively pursue many deals in order to close only a few. As MGS' overhead grew, this problem became especially vexing: it had little bread and butter to support its growing global network. MGS found that its success ratio was better when the government requirements for CT were solid and well-enforced. As a solution to this problem, the firm considered soliciting governments directly with the proposition of advising them on setting up CT programs that would have a less inhibiting effect on trade. They also actively pursued non-CT opportunities where import and foreign exchange restrictions made trade more difficult, or where U.S. multinationals were unable to convert overseas subsidiaries' local currency earnings into dollars for repatriation back to the United States. MGS would take the local currency earnings, buy products, export them, and convert the proceeds from their sales back into dollars for payment to the U.S. parent (see *Exhibit 1*).

MGS also began providing a fully integrated advisory service to major customers on how to negotiate their CT responsibilities with foreign governments, with MGS assuming these obligations for its usual fee. According to George Horton, the service was geared to "helping companies commit to the lowest obligation possible while still beating out the competition." One example of such a deal involved a consortium bidding for an equipment deal in Eastern Europe. MGS was hired by the American consortium member, whose portion of the bid was about $50 million. The Eastern Europeans were pressing for the successful bidder to assume a 100% counterpurchase obligation, and wanted a substantial portion of this to be limited to manufactured metal goods. The American firm hired MGS to take over its portion of the obligation as well as to assist in the countertrade negotiations. The final deal required two separate contracts: one between the American firm and the East European government determining the specific obligations, and the other between the American firm and MGS to determine the latter's obligations and compensation, including its fee if the American firm's consortium did not win the contract.

In the negotiation with the Eastern Europeans, the major points at issue were the percentage of the total contract price that would carry CT obligations, determination of whether the contract's base value would include transportation and local labor costs or only the FOB price, and specification of the required blend of products. The latter point was particularly important, since it would determine not only the ease with which products could be sold but also the particular Eastern European government ministry with which MGS would have to deal. From its previous experience in the country, MGS knew that the degree of flexibility and international trade experience varied widely among the different ministries.

MGS' payment for the negotiation portion of the deal was structured on a straight-fee basis; a contingent contract for the CT obligations was then added, specifying MGS' fee structure for the different classes of goods whose export might ultimately be required as a result of the negotiations and a winning contract bid. Thus, MGS' ultimate fee when the American firm's consortium won the bid was a blended rate: a 10% commission on the portion of the $50 million that required exports of manufactured metal products and machinery, and a 6% commission on the portion that could be fulfilled by exports of raw materials or consumer goods. MGS met its obligation by exporting steel, cement, clothes, fabric, aluminum, ball bearings, refrigerators, and tractors, obtaining a 1 to 2% gross margin on the total contract amount; the balance of the commission was used as an inducement to get Europeans and Americans to purchase the Eastern European products.

By mid-1986 MGS had contracted for over $600 million in CT obligations and had a staff of 40 with 26 professionals. New offices were opened all over the world with exclusive agents in a dozen countries (*Exhibit 1*). The Beijing office, known as Carvex, was actually an independent operation that had only recently been purchased from Louis Dreyfus. Its function was to assist U.S. firms interested in investing in or trading with China, both of which required extensive knowledge of local regulations and familiarity with local officials.

NEW JOINT VENTURES

MG.AG's management had long realized the importance of allies in being able to offer a broad array of services to potential customers. Former MG.AG chairman Karl Ratjen had been a firm believer that giant companies like MG.AG would increasingly find themselves as minority partners in joint ventures. In 1981 he stated, "In doing business nowadays, financial power is declining in importance, whatever certain multinational managements may think. What is coming to count more is expertise in technology and competence in human relations."

In late 1984, Schimmelbusch extended this concept to MGS by selling a 50% interest in MG Services to Louis Dreyfus & Cie., a $10 billion privately owned, vertically integrated global French grain trader and agribusiness concern. The fit seemed ideal: there was little overlap between the two giants' product lines, and the traditional Louis Dreyfus business philosophy of maintaining flexibility, minimizing fixed asset investments, and seeking outside partnerships to diversify risks and tap into additional expertise blended well with MG.AG's current strategic direction.

Shortly thereafter, MG Services entered into a joint venture with the First Boston Corporation. The new venture, known as FB/MG, was designed to advise multinational corporations and government agencies on developing and structuring innovative project financing packages. First Boston, one of the world's leading project finance advisors, would arrange long-term financing, while MGS would handle any goods or commodities delivered in payment.

First Boston prided itself on being a complete "financial engineer"; the link with MGS gave it the ability to help its clients by acting as a principal in handling goods. Like its rival Phibro-Salomon, it would be able to handle all aspects of a project contract being negotiated by one of its major corporate customers, or to convert blocked overseas earnings into dollars via a CT transaction. The potential now existed for First Boston to take the initiative in suggesting to a developing country that a joint venture be set up for a particular project which the country badly needed. First Boston would handle the financing, one of its clients would provide the technical expertise, and MG Services would be responsible for handling the export sales of the goods to foreign buyers.

While First Boston had long-term hopes for its joint venture, Dreyfus' goals were more immediate. Gerard Louis Dreyfus, president, stated that oversupply in world grain markets was creating competitive problems in selling to traditional customers, who were insisting on CT. But rather than do the activity in-house, he preferred to purchase an interest in an outside firm since "CT was an activity that was fundamentally different than trading commodities," especially since it would involve goods with which the in-house traders were not experienced.

THE COMPETITIVE ENVIRONMENT IN 1986

"CT competition has thinned out, although there are still always three or four firms trying to do any decent deal," said George Horton (see *Exhibits 4, 5,* and *6*). "Sears World Trade went out of business and the U.S. banks largely dropped out. Many multinationals didn't recognize the costs associated with CT, underbid on projects, and then put the CT obligations on their books, but haven't performed. So there's a growing international book of unfilled offset obligations that will become more important as their completion dates approach." Indeed, the function of many in-house units had been scaled back as the CT market matured; their mission was now largely restricted to helping their divisions unload products internally and coordinate efforts with countertraders.

"We think CT is going to become more complicated," Horton stated. "There are going to be more countries that use CT as a means to slow import growth." At the same time, CT business in some countries was becoming increasingly concentrated. "You can't be a broker in CT anymore, there is no room," a Centrobank professional stated. "You can only compete as a principal." "Our attitude hasn't changed at all," an MGS competitor commented. "All that has changed is the fee we charge. At the beginning of 1983 it was 7 to 9%. Now it's between 1 and 2%. . . . Because the risks are lower we are happy to charge less." Among the poorest countries, however, barter was growing and risks were increasing (see *Exhibit 7*). The challenge for countertraders was the ability to extract cash crops after imports had gone in.

DIVERSIFICATION

Back in his office down the hall from both MGS and MG Corp. commodity traders, Hodapp considered MGS' options for growth. "There will always be countries that want to do CT. One of our advantages is that we always have transactions going through the system, which gives us both market intelligence and name recognition. In businesses like East European clearing and switching, you have to cultivate state trading agency contacts. You can't just walk in and do a deal. That's why Carvex, our Beijing office, is such an opportunity; foreign MNCs are going to need a lot of help in dealing with the Chinese government." Hodapp exuded confidence about the future of MGS.

Hodapp pointed toward the changing faces within MGS as an illustration of the firm's dynamic character. Of the original threesome that started MGS, only Horton remained. The London-based director was asked to resign in mid-1986 for personal reasons, and the following November Gottlieb became an outside director for MGS while he pursued venture capital opportunities in Asia. Hodapp was dismayed by Gottlieb's departure because CT in Asia had been the foundation of MGS' initial success. However, Hodapp noted that most CT deals in Asia in late 1986 required less innovation than in the past; many of MGS' creative CT dealings had been copied by competitors. Since this made it possible for a more specialized person to negotiate CT deals, MGS decided to incorporate in both Korea and Japan, utilizing existing infrastructure to manage their contracts.

In a separate move in early 1986, Hodapp hired a trade finance specialist, Joe Rinaldi, away from Phibro. Hodapp had long been looking to expand into trade finance, and at last he felt that he found the right person. In addition, he hired a banking specialist and former McKinsey consultant, Ruth Eliel, from Chase Manhattan to run the new MG Finance, a newly licensed deposit-taking entity in Hong Kong. Both were initially hired as senior vice presidents. Rinaldi and Eliel were independent and entrepreneurial: Hodapp tried to maximize their potential by giving them a great deal of leeway during their first year. While MG Finance was largely created to provide the financing group with a banking vehicle (e.g., MG Finance could post standby letters of credit for CT transactions and other financial deals), Rinaldi thought the major opportunity for MGS was to become a classical merchant banker that was transaction- and product-oriented.

"We are doing financing that is commodity-driven," continued Rinaldi, "which marries two worlds that don't know each other. With our information networks, our perceptions of the risk involved will often differ from the market because our experience and contacts will actually make the risk lower. We can structure transactions that banks will not touch." Rinaldi gave an example of such a transaction being planned to generate some initial income from the First Boston joint venture. "The idea was to open the U.S. capital markets to LDC borrowers. A special-purpose company could be formed to borrow on these markets; it would in turn relend the money to the LDCs who would provide physical commodities as collateral. First Boston and FB/MG might then underwrite the special-purpose company's loans based on MGS' ability to market the collateral if the borrower were unable to repay. We would do this type of paper in conjunction with political risk insurance and would try to get the World Bank involved since they want to see financial markets open up to LDCs. The FB/MG partnership would be profit-based on its ability to assume the performance or collateral risk that would otherwise have gone to the lender."

Rinaldi hoped that MGS could replicate and then expand what he had done at Phibro. One such alternative mentioned by Rinaldi was debt-equity conversions in countries such as Brazil. MGS' plan was to find a foreign investor interested in putting money in a debt-ridden country. MGS would get government clearance to swap bank debt for local currency as well as arrange to buy the debt from a bank at a discount. The debt would then be converted into an equity investment by MGS' client, usually for a project that generated exports in commodities MG.AG handled. Rinaldi felt that MGS could also go long and short on such deals by buying the bank debt prior to finding an investor. One debt-equity conversion had already been completed in East Asia, and Rinaldi hoped to expand this business. A prerequisite to the successful completion of such deals would involve the building of a database on the holders of debt.

OPTIONS

The new faces and skills both broadened and complicated MGS' strategy. In the past three years, MGS had built an impressive global network: new high-priced professionals further raised MGS' operating costs just as the core business was being squeezed. Hodapp had to consider whether product diversification alone was the answer and to what extent MGS would gain a competitive edge by bundling these products together. Should MGS become a one-stop shopping center for supporting MNCs in difficult transactions? Should it try to become the exclusive countertrader for a select group of large companies with big obligations? Should MGS maintain its countertrade position in all markets, even if there are narrow margins, or should MGS shrink the countertrade opera-

tions? Hodapp also wondered if MGS could or should be integrated into MG Corp. trading operations as a staff/support function.

"Sigi's real challenge," noted Joe Rinaldi, was "getting the right people and designing proper reward systems." Schimmelbusch had once described the Metallgesellschaft management style in a magazine interview as essentially people-oriented, based on three principles: decentralization, realization of individual potential, and recognition that authority is not a matter of establishing a hierarchy but of competence. Horton endorsed this philosophy: "Our people have to be hungry," he said "and able to close a deal rather than just talk to people about one." Horton also wondered about how the emerging MGS would differ from the original MGS.

Hodapp, however, remained confident that these issues could be easily managed. As a first step, he realigned responsibilities. As of November 1986, three former SVPs were promoted to executive vice presidents: an SVP in Frankfurt (Heinrich Binder) took over all operational responsibility for CT, Carvex, and Eastern Europe; Horton left the day-to-day CT deals to take charge of a group (one to two professionals) to pursue "special projects and really go after the big deals"; and Rinaldi become responsible for all trade finance activities. Each would report directly to Hodapp. Furthermore, Hodapp noted that "I want MGS to remain small with a low overhead because a few specialists in our field can generate high income off the invested capital. I doubt that MGS will ever grow beyond 50 professionals, but I don't see that as a problem since what traders want to do is. trade, not move up the ladder and assume managerial roles. If people want a predictable career in management, then they should go into banking. We do not have to worry about hierarchy and managerial conflicts here. As long as we provide our people with all the support they need to trade, and as long as we compensate them according to their performance, we will accomplish our goal."

MGS

Changes in the ways international business is conducted are making it increasingly difficult for companies to achieve their export goals. Our objective at MG Services is simple — we aim to assist you to compete more effectively in this environment.

To meet this objective, however, numerous obstacles to trade must first be overcome:
— *Many less developed countries have shortages of foreign exchange*
— *International banks are increasingly unwilling to finance foreign buyers*
— *Many developed countries are erecting trade barriers to protect their local industries*
— *Overseas buyers are imposing various forms of countertrade and offset*
— *Government regulations and priorities are constantly evolving*

To overcome these hurdles, MG Services has developed a team of international trade specialists strategically based around the world who design and implement comprehensive solutions to your trade problems. Since each transaction is unique, the first task is to identify the constellation of problems our clients confront. Only then can we engineer an effective strategy. To be successful, these strategies must be tailor made:
— *Creating short term trade finance paper*
— *Designing a debt settlement program to recover lost assets*
— *Underwriting a countertrade obligation to purchase a basket of local products*
— *Arranging a financing structure by guaranteeing a long term purchase commitment*
— *Developing new trade channels for export products*

The international trade specialists at MG Services have diverse backgrounds in trade, marketing, finance, law and countertrade. These skills, combined with a global information network perfected over 100 years by our parent companies, gives MG Services the capabilities to design the complex international trade programs needed to compete effectively today. With primary offices in New York, Toronto, London, Paris, Frankfurt, Hong Kong and Beijing, MG Services is also represented in all major markets including such countries as: Argentina, Australia, Brazil, Colombia, Greece, India, Indonesia, Japan, Korea, Malaysia, New Zealand, Nigeria, Pakistan, the Philippines, Romania, Thailand, Turkey and Venezuela.

MG Services is a partnership between the Metallgesellschaft Group of Frankfurt, West Germany and the Louis Dreyfus Group of Paris, France. The principal lines of business for Metallgesellschaft, or MG as it is known, include mining, processing, marketing and trading of industrial products and raw materials — metals, ores, petroleum products, crude oil and chemicals — as well as semi-finished products, engineering services and automotive products. MG, through its more than 20,000 employees, has created a comprehensive global network of purchasing capabilities and contacts. This integrated system today has consolidated revenues of over US$5 billion on a trading volume of approximately US$22 billion.

Louis Dreyfus' traditional business activities include the international merchandising and trading of bulk agricultural commodities including grains and oil seeds, sugar, livestock and meats, fibres and cotton, as well as processed products such as industrial alcohol, compound feed and dairy products. It is also active in shipping as well as manufacturing and processing of various industrial products. Louis Dreyfus also has a major global trading network which, when combined with MG, provides representation in over 30 countries. Annual trading volume for both companies totals over US$40 billion.

Through these groups, MG Services has coordinated transactions ranging from US$1 million to US$1 billion dollars in value. Highlights of sales we have facilitated include:

(continued)

CONTINUED

Canadian power station to East Europe

Korean transportation equipment to Latin America

Swiss equipment to New Zealand

Japanese railroad machinery to Indonesia

United States oil service products to Brazil

Latin American debt settlement

German capital goods to the Philippines

French telecommunication system to Korea

Combining the extensive trading networks of its parent companies and their subsidiaries as well as its own affiliated companies, MG Services is uniquely positioned to offer its clients complete access to global trade opportunities for their products through its full range of services, including planning, structuring, negotiating and underwriting complex countertrade and financing transactions.

COUNTERTRADE

PLANNING

Management at all levels must be familiar with countertrade techniques in order to recognize promising prospects. More specifically, financial executives must thoroughly understand the risks and costs of countertrade and how they relate to overall profitability of international transactions. Marketing directors must be trained to distinguish between promising opportunities and hidden problems. Senior management must orchestrate the participation of several different business divisions in the development of complex transactions.

MG Services advises clients how to use countertrade as a tool to increase exports of products, equipment and services. We assist senior management, marketing directors, purchasing directors and financial executives to meet the challenges presented by countertrade and to exploit the business opportunities it provides innovative companies.

MG Services enables clients to plan for and be prepared to take advantage of specific business opportunities as well as to assess their likelihood of success.

STRUCTURING

MG Services assists clients to structure comprehensive countertrade packages for specific transactions, including:

forfaiting
barter
counterpurchase
offset
switch
clearing agreements
debt settlement
trade finance

For example, we can assist exporters sell their products to customers who either demand payment in kind (barter) or that they purchase a similar value of products from that country (counterpurchase). The exporter may not be able to absorb the products offered in barter or counterpurchase transactions within its own organisation.

In such cases, MG Services assists the exporter develop an optimal structure for each transaction, ideally

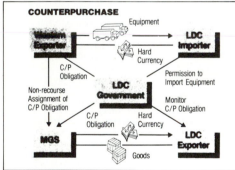

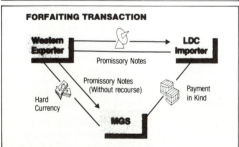

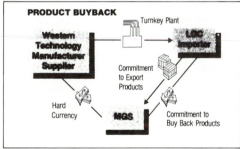

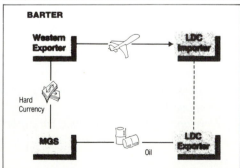

Source: Company documents.

METALLGESELLSCHAFT—SUMMARY OF OPERATIONS, 1974–1984

	Fiscal year ending September 30									
	1975/ 76	1976/ 77	1977/ 78	1978/ 79	1979/ 80	1980/ 81	1981/ 82	1982/ 83	1983/ 84	1984/ 85
Sales, DM mill	6,226	6,930	7,117	7,891	9,047	10,474	9,741	9,791	10,491	11,207
Foreign portion thereof, %	39	44	47	53	47	57	59	54	47	52
Additions to fixed assets, DM mill.	153	196	234	190	189	215	230	171	167	190
New investments in affiliates, DM mill.	15	23	21	35	78	130	38	139[a]	73	63
Depreciation of fixed assets, DM mill.	155	161	180	208	236	194	192	185	217	174
Reduction of investments in affiliates, DM mill.	26	2	2	4	13	0	17	9	70	20
Net book value of fixed assets on Sept. 30, DM mill.	715	745	790	766	713	729	700	620	567	561
Investments in affiliates on Sept. 30, DM mill.	196	137	154	185	211	339	359	488	490	509
Long-term loans receivable on Sept. 30, DM mill.	65	47	44	33	29	44	40	64	53	45
Share capital on Sept. 30, DM mill.	210	210	210	210	240	240	240	240	240	280
Additional paid-in capital and appropriated retained earnings on Sept, 30, DM mill.	324	340	349	347	401	412	417	385	432	548
Net profit for the year[b] DM mill.	18	41	24	20	42	34	(19)	25	25	61
Dividend declared, DM/share	5.00	5.00	4.00	4.00	5.00 +1.00	4.00	· · ·	· · ·	· · ·	6.00[c]
Number of employees, Sept. 30	26,053	27,678	27,342	27,283	27,220	26,829	23,757	22,123	21,985	21,384
Personnel costs (excluding pension costs), DM mill.	944	1,065	1,126	1,200	1,287	1,343	1,370	1,235	1,255	1,313
DM1.00 in U.S. cents (av)	· · ·	· · ·	50	54	55	44	41	39	35	35

[a]Net new investments
[b]( ): net loss
[c]Recommended dividend.
Source: Annual reports.

COLOMBIAN COUNTERTRADE RESTRICTIONS

Imports requiring barter or a 100% offsetting countertrade arrangement:
   Foodstuffs: olives, capers, cherries, cinnamon, cumin, sparkling wine, cognac, brandy, vodka, whiskey
   Photocopiers, photographic and microfilm equipment
   Machinery: elevators, milking machines, sewing machines, chainsaws, typewriters, electronic scales
   Adhesive tape
   Calculators and cash registers
   Tractors and campers
   Automobile air conditioners
   (These goods accounted for $300 million in imports in 1984.)

Traditional exports not valid for barter or countertrade:
   Foodstuffs: coffee, sugar, cotton, bananas,[a] flowers,[a] tobacco,[b] cocoa, sesame, rice, snails, oysters, shrimp, confections
   Ferronickel
   Precious metals and stones
   Textiles
   Coals

[a]Not valid if exported to traditional markets; valid if exported to new markets.
[b]Valid only if a domestic surplus exists.
Source: Countertrade in Columbia, Harvard Business School case 4-385-304.

EXPORTABLE ITEMS UNDER PAKISTANI COUNTERTRADE AGREEMENT

Item	Maximum export value, $ million
Cotton	4.0
Molasses	2.0
Urea	2.0
Naphtha	1.0
Rice	5.0
Fruits and vegetables	1.5
Tobacco	0.25
Fish	0.50
Cotton textiles	15.0
Wool and products	2.0
Leather products	5.0
Nonelectrical machinery	2.5
Electrical machinery	0.50
Transport equipment	1.0
Engineering goods	0.50
Chemicals and pharmaceuticals	1.0
Petrochemicals	0.50
Minerals	1.0
Gems and stones	0.50
Handicrafts	1.0
Miscellaneous manufactures	3.0
Total	50.00

Source: Tradefinance Asia, April 1986, p. 25.

COUNTERTRADE RETHINK IN INDONESIA

While London countertraders remain enthusiastic about countertrade in Indonesia, a rethink is going on within the office of the junior minister for the promotion of domestic investment, Ginandjar Kartasasmita—the man who first aggressively pushed the Indonesian counter purchase scheme. Begun in January 1982, the counter purchase policy has resulted in US$1.4 trillion of obligations, $876 billion of which had been realised by 30 September 1985.

"But we now think it is not as effective as we used to think," says Ginandjar in an aboutface from his early promotion of the trade. He stressed that there is little chance of the policy being abolished and simply that it is being applied with much more caution and discrimination. "We still have not abandoned this policy but we use it selectively now, very selectively."

The change in attitude is explained in terms of the difficulties in ascertaining whether countertrade is in addition to normal trade. Ginandjar comments that countertrade may actually be replacing other trade. If it is not, there is the threat that it may be competing with non-counter purchase deals. This means, in the end, that no improvement in Indonesia's exports is achieved, only a difference in the way transactions are made.

"We want to quantify exactly which products we will deal with in counter purchase," Ginandjar says. Although more deals are being confirmed, Ginandjar concludes that "we are not pursuing this as aggressively as before."

Meanwhile, firms that have taken a large share of the counter purchase work in Indonesia see no reason to scale down or alter their trading in any way. They remain pleased at the efficiency of the Indonesian system and are generally ignoring the rumours of a scaling down in the programme which, they say, have been circulating for up to 18 months.

"We know they are questioning the policy," comments Thomas Gottlieb, managing director of Metallgesellschaft Services. "But we have no idea when or if a change will occur."

Realisation of counter purchase obligation (US$ million)*

Supplier's country of origin	Counter purchase obligation	Realisation of counter purchase obligation	Rest of counter purchase obligation not yet realised
Japan	285.07	177.58	139.30
United States	104.47	98.38	10.69
West Germany	390.98	243.49	147.89
Singapore	88.40	57.54	34.13
Holland	38.17	35.86	9.09
Canada	212.15	67.91	144.25
South Korea	63.99	53.13	11.62
England	77.89	29.29	48.78
Rumania	61.95	61.97	
France	23.63	14.26	9.70
Hong Kong	16.90	9.60	7.39
East Germany	6.58	2.26	4.32
Sweden	1.76	2.16	
Australia	20.80	6.28	14.62
Italy	9.59	1.12	8.47
Malaysia	2.36	2.38	
Austria	22.18	2.46	19.77
Panama	1.01	0.50	0.53
Mexico	1.26	· · ·	1.26
Yugoslavia	6.69	· · ·	6.69
Switzerland	1.53	0.10	1.42
Belgium	1.62	· · ·	1.62
Poland	4.91	10.54	
Total	1443.89	876.81†	621.54

*By supplier's country of origin and confirmation letter issue.
†Including surplus of obligation of several suppliers with the amount of US$54.44. Position as at 30/09/85.
Source: Vaudine England, *Tradefinance Asia*, January 1986, p. 10.

U.S. EXPORT TRADING COMPANIES

American banking's fascination with trading company affiliates has cooled somewhat in recent months, but new ones still continue to come on stream. The October 1982 passage of the Export Trading Company (ETC) Act was a landmark policy change, breaching the historic US wall between banking and commerce. Yet the law was adopted in an atmosphere of such grandiose hopes and naïve rhetoric that it was sure to generate disappointment.

That has been the case, not so much among the banks themselves, who always felt it was a longer-term strategy, as within the international business community, which has been quick to criticize the lack of dramatic results so far.

The ETC law determined that ETCs had to earn at least 51 per cent of their income from exporting. But the banks could not have faced a worse time to get into exporting. Burdened with a high-flying dollar, the USA chalked up a $148.5bn trade deficit last year. 1986 may not be much better and the Latin American market, always a mainstay of American exporters, has shrivelled under its debt problem.

Here is an overview of how some of the 40 banks are using their ETCs.

Money centre banks

• Bankers Trust International Trading Company (New York) is building a niche in 15–20 targetted countries, focussed on countertrade in oil (till recently), and has pursued some offset deals. It has also become active in Turkish trade.

Its first president, Stephen Sohn, resigned after a disagreement about strategy. His successor Jeffrey Glibert spent over six years with Bankers Trust in London doing commodity trade finance. Its London operation is run by Paul Fletcher, formerly a trader with Gargill Metals. A Hong Kong office is planned this year and there are also plans for a Sao Paolo office. "Brazil is the only market in Latin America with a big industrial base." says Glibert. Trading has been mostly in commodities and light manufacturers.

Naïve rhetoric and grandiose hopes were sure to disappoint

• Chase Manhattan (New York) has pursued a broad range of business services in its ETC. Chase Trade has pointedly steered clear of countertrade or trade finance related business. Both have stayed firmly within the bank.

Most significant has been a leading operation in the Foreign Sales Corporation (FSC) field, the US export tax incentive vehicle. Chase provides management services in the Virgin Islands for over 350 major US corporations, making it one of the two leading firms in this field.

Another important ETC operation is providing cargo insurance through a master policy. The trading unit has also taken title, worked closely with the bank's countertrade unit, and done some of these deals itself. It had 22 employees last year. Its president, Michael Rice, previously ran Chase's factoring operation.

• Citibank (New York) is now in a retrenchment phase with its trading affiliate Citicorp International Trading Services (CITC). Current strategy is to focus more on trade finance and less on physical trading (unless the latter is tied to trade finance). CITC has tried practically everything, ranging from countertrade to market development. But reportedly it has yet to make a profit.

Its more successful operations have been acquisitions. For example, it bought American Technology, a sales representative operation in China for oil drilling equipment. That firm has few staff but high sales. And CITC has done a joint venture with Li and Fung Group, which does warehousing in Hong Kong, Macao, and Beijing. CITC has imported ethanol from Brazil too. Its most recent move is acquisition of Anglo American Aviation, 35-year-old Los Angeles exporter of aircraft spares, which it has placed within Citicorp AIR, a specialist firm associated with the ETC.

• Bank of America (San Francisco) has reversed strategy totally, and now performs entirely as a trade finance organization under president Dan Cecchin, a countertrade specialist. The ETC, BankAmerica World Trade (BAWT), is back in the main bank building where it focuses on countertrade, forfaiting, and other non traditional trade finance operations. Cecchin maintains BAWT has completed more countertrade deals than any other bank, including China and Latin America and a blocked funds deal in Yugoslavia.

Forfaiting is new for the bank, and the ETC puts the deals together, with the bank holding the paper, depending on its appetite at any one time, selling the rest through its correspondent network. Its countertrade role is to find products and buyers, purchasing without recourse. It is not a consultancy, preferring to get directly involved and using the bank's global network. The ETC puts together Eximbank/FCIA packages too, using forfaiting or countertrade to arrange the required 15 percent downpayment.

Source: Euromoney Trade Finance Report, March 1986, pp. 37–38.

"Phibro is hiring"

For the last few years Philipp Brothers, the world's most famous trading house, has been hard at work generating bad news. It turned really sour a year ago, when 600 planned staff cuts were announced. What worried Phibro staff was that no one knew where. And rather than face the axe many left of their own accord. Kaines, Pru Bache, MG Services, to name a few, are stuffed with ex-Phibro men.

Some may have jumped ship too soon. Phibro's two leading lights, its 33-year-old chairman Marti Kaufman and its president Henry Schachar, have decided that countertrade and trade finance are money spinners.

"Both are very keen and are willing to give full backing," says Tony Frizelle, Phibro's new managing director for trade finance and countertrade. Frizelle has been brought in from Phibro Canada, where he is still president, in charge of negotiations for a $550m barter deal with Nigeria.

This backing has unleashed a recruitment drive. Advertisements are popping up in the financial press. Headhunters (after finding out what countertrade and trade finance are) are making discreet phone calls.

So far, only three people have joined Phibro. Thiery Semo joins this month as an East European specialist, based in London. He was with Greficomex before working freelance. Last month Terry English moved into the New York office from Continental Grain. Another recruit there was Mark Katz. He arrives from Phibro's Los Angeles office, but worked before for Sears World Trade. Katz's brief is to sell Phibro to US companies facing offset demands. "There's a $4bn market out there," says Frizelle.

But apart from these moves the recruitment drive has had limited success. Frizelle is still looking for the following specialists. He wants two "senior people" in London responsible for trade finance and countertrade. Three vacancies are on offer in New York: a senior countertrader and two trade finance specialists. One of the trade finance recruits will, according to Frizelle, be a "trader" pushing forfaiting and debt swaps, among other techniques.

Phibro's new operation will be different from the old. Countertrade will not be a separate profit centre. "In the past there was friction between traders and countertraders. Now there is one bottom line" says Frizelle.

He also has this to say about who should apply. "Basically we are looking for entrepreneurs. That means people who can make a lot of money for us. We are looking for people who can write a minimum of $50m worth of business a year."

And Frizelle has a heart warming message for all those thinking of applying. "We are not looking at cost, but the return. We are not scared of paying well."

Source: Euromoney Trade Finance Report, October 1986, p. 72.

EXHIBIT SEVEN

VOEST INTERTRADING SLIPS DOWN THE OIL WELL

The biggest and most aggressive of the world's specialist countertraders has collapsed. Last month the entire board of VOEST-Alpine, Austria's state-owned steel and plant manufacturer, was sacked after the company revealed horrendous losses, totalling Asch5.7bn ($322m).

Nearly half the losses, Asch2.4bn ($135m), came from VOEST's countertrading subsidiary, VOEST-Alpine Intertrading (VAIT). Its board, led by the ambitious Gernot Preschern (a man reported to have said: "L'Intertrade, c'est moi"), has also been sacked.

The events at VAIT will make many countertrading companies, oil traders and exporters question the wisdom of oil based countertrade deals.

But VAIT's loss figures are estimates. Auditors still have to unravel the numerous forward contracts that VAIT signed on the oil market. These and an Iranian oil barter deal still outstanding could reveal even larger losses.

How could this have happened at VAIT, a company which made its name as one of the giants of oil barter? Citing oil speculation as the single major cause may be only half the truth. VAIT regularly speculated on the oil markets, just as other oil trading companies do. VAIT speculated because it had to. In the company's 1984 results, a third of its oil business was ascribed to countertrade deals, in particular two huge oil barter deals with Iran and Nigeria.

It was with VAIT's most recent (and current) Iranian deal that things began to go wrong. But the real problem may have been that once losses began to occur, VAIT's management was incapable of adapting to the changes undermining the company.

VAIT's demise lies in its origins. Formed in 1978, it began with a staff of six. VAIT's brief was to take on the countertrade commitments from turn-key projects built by its parent.

Under the driving leadership of Gernot Preschern, VAIT became a trading house employing around 250 people worldwide, claiming to trade in products as basic as steel, grain and coal, and as esoteric as gentlemen's suits. By early 1985, its turnover was larger than that of its parent. On oil trading alone, VAIT had a bigger turnover than Austria's state owned oil company.

Negotiations for the first major deal with Iran began at the end of 1981.

Vienna's trade banks were keen to act as intermediaries in such a deal. In bidding they proposed an oil barter arrangement which would finance Iran's imports.

But then the talks ran aground. The Viennese banks were worried about the risks they ran in accepting too large a sized deal. Their limits ranged between $40m–$50m. Iran wanted commitments from the banks to take a minimum of $100m worth of crude oil, with an option on a further $100m.

When the banks refused, VAIT eagerly accepted. Since then, several more deals have followed, the last in April 1985 valued at $2bn. VAIT also signed a $200m barter deal with Nigeria last year.

The first Iranian deal was a coup for VAIT. It made the Viennese countertraders, reputed for their flair, look stuffy.

The concept behind the Iranian deals was simple, at least on the surface.

VAIT bought oil from the Iranians at the official government selling price (gsp). VAIT then sold the oil on the spot market, returning 25 per cent of the gsp value directly to the Iranians.

The remaining 75 percent was placed in an escrow account—called a Treuhandkonto—held in the name of Iran's central bank, Bank Markazi Jomhourie Islami. The account is at the Vienna headquarters of the Bank für Arbeit und Wirtschaft AG (BAWAG). VAIT then marketed the credits vigorously to exporters selling to Iran. The arrangement worked like this.

The exporter invoiced VAIT, which in turn presented its own invoice to the Iranians, adding a service charge. Bank Markazi then opened an irrevocable letter of credit in favour of VAIT. On receipt of this, VAIT instructed BAWAG to assign the letter of credit, minus VAIT's charges, in favour of the exporter.

VAIT's strategy was that the service charges' would recoup the losses it made from buying gsp priced oil, but selling it on the spot market at lower prices.

But there was a serious problem which VAIT had to overcome. Each deal ran for a specified period, usually a year. At the end of the period money still in the escrow account, but unused, had to be returned to Iran. The arrangement worked so long as the Iranians kept buying goods through the deal and this did not become a serious problem until the middle of 1985.

Last year VAIT began overreaching itself. Its 1984 results showed that margins were perilously thin and that trading in oil made up 83 percent of its business. Its 1984 profits of Asch140m ($8m) represented little more than 0.1 per cent of turnover.

The turning point appears to have been last year's

EXHIBIT SEVEN

CONTINUED

$2bn deal with Iran. It was then that the major flaw in the agreements revealed itself. The control over imports lay with Iran.

At the same time falling oil prices increased the pressures on VAIT. "It was naive to construct an agreement in which Iran could choose the products." says an oil consultant.

VAIT needed a high volume of exports to Iran if it was to avert huge losses. As spot oil prices fell (VAIT was still buying at gsp rates) VAIT had to increase its service charges, making the scheme even more difficult to sell to exporters.

In April 1985, VAIT's charges were broken down as follows: 9 per cent to cover the oil price difference, plus a handling fee of 1 percent. By September 1985 the price had risen to 15 percent, while the most recent quote given was 16 per cent. In comparison, the current cost of confirming a 360 day letter of credit to Iran is about 10 per cent.

The reaction of one European pharmaceuticals exporter, which turned down a VAIT offer in August last year, was typical.

"We thought that we would require more help at the Iranian end. Intertrading were just providing a financial conduit. There was no assistance in Iran with the various ministries to get the imports approved. Also, the costs VAIT were charging reduced our margins to unacceptable levels."

The time limit on the $2bn Iranian deal expires at the end of next month, February 1986. But last summer it became obvious that VAIT had to market the Iranian credit more aggressively if it was to avoid a major loss.

At this point its staffing weaknesses became crucial. Beneath the high profile Preschern, and his deputy Siegfried Purrer, middle management was thin. As a state owned company, VAIT could not afford the high salaries experienced countertraders earned. "VAIT pay is low by international standards," says one ex employee. Consequently many of its staff were young and inexperienced, and turnover was high. In addition top level management control was lax.

Source: Euromoney Trade Finance Report, January 1986.

Note on Trade Finance

Trade finance involves the provision of credit and risk management services for international goods transactions. Participants include private firms, commercial banks, state-owned enterprises, and government agencies as well as insurance firms and capital market investors. Trade finance can be used as a source of working capital by the exporter or as a means of securing immediate payment upon shipment. Alternatively, trade finance can be a method of providing funds to the buyer so that he can make prompt payment on export to the supplier.

Traditional trade finance indicates clearly which party bears which risks during each stage of the transaction. Essentially, the supplier wants the security of prompt and full payment in (usually) her home currency. Standing in the way are the commercial risk of the buyer, the political risk of war or government-mandated foreign exchange inconvertibility, foreign exchange or currency risk if the sale is not de-nominated in the exporter's home currency, and the risk of damage to the goods themselves while in transit. Instruments therefore exist to enable buyers and sellers to transfer their risks to third-party intermediaries.

In addition to providing liquidity, trade finance instruments in the 1980s have also become tools for managing risks as well as competitive weapons. Since the advent of floating foreign exchange rates in 1973, foreign exchange (FX) risk management has been a critical feature of international business operations. Managers have to worry that exchange rates may fluctuate between the time a contract is agreed to, shipment is made, and payment is due to be received. If a contract is denominated in a foreign currency that unexpectedly depreciates against the exporter's home currency during the time between contract agreement and payment, the seller could suffer a loss. Buyers, however, may be reluctant or unable to pay in the supplier's home currency or other convertible currency. In slack world markets where numerous suppliers have unused plant capacity, sellers can be forced to accept payment in undesirable currencies in order to secure a contract.

Under these circumstances trade finance becomes a competitive tool for companies and

This case was prepared by Research Assistant Eugene Salorio under the supervision of Associate Professor David B. Yoffie as a basis for class discussion.

nations. Buyers are offered subsidized interest rates, better disbursement terms, payback grace periods, or long-term repayment schedules. Government agencies subsidize lenders, provide both funds and insurance, and assume a portion of the risks and costs as a means of encouraging exports. In so doing, they enable local firms to offer better terms to prospective foreign borrowers.

TRADITIONAL METHODS OF TRADE FINANCE

The traditional methods of export financing and payment are often classified according to the portion of risk born by the exporter:

1. Those where the exporter bears all the risk:
   a. Consignment
   b. Sales on open account
   c. Draft/documents for collection
   d. Secured bank overdraft
2. Those where the exporter bears some of the risk:
   a. Government export guarantee programs
   b. Credit insurance
3. Those where the exporter passes on all risk to a financing institution or bank:
   a. Confirming house facilities
   b. Buyer credits
   c. Export leasing

Exporter Risk

In a consignment transaction, the exporter ships the goods to the buyer with the understanding that the latter will make a best effort to sell the goods and then forward payment to the exporter after deducting for expenses and sales commission. The exporter is thus exposed to FX, commercial, political, and other risks. Under an open account sale, the exporter ships the goods to the buyer and then bills him, with the buyer promising to make payment on a mutually agreeable date. Under a secured bank overdraft, the exporter pledges her receivable from the buyer as collateral for receiving a short-term credit line from her bank. In the case of documents for collection, the exporter draws a draft (essentially a document demanding payment) on the importer and forwards it along with the shipping documents to the importer via the importer's bank. The shipping documents, which provide title to the goods, are given to the importer by the bank only after his formal recognition ("acceptance") that the draft drawn against his account constitutes a valid debt. This is called a documentary draft, since it involves the delivery of shipping documents to the buyer at the time of his acceptance. There are also so-called clean drafts, which are drawn on parties without any accompanying documents; these are most commonly used for nontrade remittances.

The terms of the draft negotiated at the time of the original contract can call for either immediate or delayed payment. In the latter case the draft (also known as a bill of exchange) can in some cases be sold at a discount to a local financial institution. Under this arrangement, however, the exporter must reimburse the lender if the buyer eventually defaults. Documents for collection are normally used when the parties know and trust each other and want to avoid third-party fees or commissions.

Shared Risk

Under a shared-risk arrangement, a third party (usually in the exporter's home country) will assume a portion of the risk as a means of both earning income and facilitating the sale. For example, private insurance firms offer commercial, political, and foreign exchange coverage to the exporter; government export guarantee programs do the same, as well as sometimes providing a portion of funds lent to the buyer on a nonrecourse basis (i.e., the exporter is not liable for repayment if the buyer defaults). Government-sponsored insurance programs also provide coverage to banks for export loans. In virtually all cases, however, the guaranteeing or insuring party requires coinsurance or cofinancing by the exporter or lending bank as a means of inducing the latter to act in a prudent fashion in extending credit.

Third-Party Risk

Under a confirming house arrangement, a bank in the buyer's home country confirms, as a principal, orders placed by the foreign buyer with the exporter. The bank is thus liable for payment to the exporter without recourse on evidence of shipment of goods; the exporter bears no liability in the event of the buyer's default. This arrangement can also call for either immediate or delayed payment. One example is a commercial letter of credit, covered in more detail below.

Under a buyer credit arrangement, a third party (usually either a commercial bank or a government export credit agency) provides a loan directly to the buyer, who in turn uses this to pay the exporter. The exporter therefore has no liability to the lending party in the event of buyer default. Under an export leasing arrangement, the manufacturer sells her product (usually some form of capital goods best suited to long-term financing) to a leasing company for cash. The leasing company, in turn, will then lease the goods to the foreign user, although it will often require a bank in the importer's country to guarantee the outstanding lease rentals. Finally, the exporter can attempt to reduce her risk by demanding cash payment in advance from the buyer.

ALTERNATIVES TO STRAIGHT BANK FINANCING

Three of the most common alternatives to straight bank financing (i.e., direct loans to either buyer or seller) are discounting, forfaiting, and factoring.

Discounting and Drafts

International trade finance transactions calling for delayed payment generally also involve the use of promissory notes or drafts. The former are simply a formal undertaking by one party to make a series of payments to the other party at specified future dates. With a draft, on the other hand, there are usually three parties: the drawer (in this case the exporter or her sales agent), the payee (or the party who is to receive payment, usually the exporter), and the drawee, who is the party promising to make payment (e.g., the buyer's bank in the case of a letter of credit). The draft may be either a sight or a time draft; the former calls for immediate payment, the latter for payment at a specified future date. This date determines the maturity of the draft, often referred to as its tenor or usance. When the draft is presented to the buyer, he "recognizes" it; this is done formally by stamping "accepted" on the back of the draft and endorsing it.

The time draft thus accepted by the drawee becomes a trade acceptance; in cases involving letters of credit where the bank issuing the credit also recognizes the draft, it becomes a bankers' acceptance. In either case, the acceptance (or bill of exchange, the name commonly used during the 19th century) is now a negotiable financial instrument. The exporter can then sell it to a local commercial bank at a discount from face value; the discount incorporates both the credit risk of the buyer (or the buyer's bank) and the buyer's country as well as the time value of money up to the payment date. If the buyer's credit rating is good, trade acceptances may then be traded in a secondary market, where they are transferred from one party to another by endorsement.

Forfaiting

Forfaiting uses free market funds to provide fixed-rate supplier credits for project financing or capital goods exports with payment periods stretching several years into the future. It is usually done on a 100% nonrecourse basis, meaning that the supplier discounts the full sale amount and is not liable in the event of buyer default. The financing arrangements involve four parties: the importer, exporter, a guaranteeing bank (generally in the importer's country), and the forfaiter. In a typical deal, the buyer pays the supplier with promissory notes or bills maturing at set intervals over a several-year period. These are then guaranteed by a bank in the importer's country; this guarantee ("aval") is usually irrevocable, unconditional, and transferable. The supplier in turn sells the guaranteed paper to the forfaiter at a discount from the face amount on the basis of the buyer's credit rating, the guaranteeing bank's creditability, and interest costs over the paper's lifetime. The greater the risk from any of these sources, the greater the discount. As the bills or promissory notes mature, they are presented to the guaranteeing bank by the forfaiter for payment. In the event the buyer or confirming bank defaults, the responsibility for collection lies with the forfaiter, or the current holder of the bill if the forfaiter has resold it via the secondary market. The exporter bears no liability. The forfait markets, centered in London and Zurich, are substantially free of government support, supervision, or regulation.

From the exporter's perspective, forfaiting has the dual advantage of separating the export transaction from both foreign political and financial risks. It protects the exporter from:

- Credit risk that the bank guarantor and/or the buyer may be insolvent
- Political risk that the bank guarantor and/or the exporter may be unable to pay for political reasons, such as war or revolution
- Transfer risk that the government in the importing country may impose regulations prohibiting remittance of foreign exchange

- Commercial risk that the buyer and/or bank guarantor may fail to pay without any valid reason

Forfaiting can have several drawbacks. First, the discount can be quite large: a 365-day, 100% nonrecourse deal with an Iraqi buyer in 1986 (Iraq was at war with Iran at the time) was done at a discount of approximately 7% over London InterBank Overnight Rate (LIBOR). In addition, the guaranteeing bank also generally charges a substantial fee and places a freeze of equal value on the buyer's account. Most importantly, however, the exporter still faces some risk. For example, she is liable (to the holder of the bill or note) if the bank guarantor and/or buyer refuses to pay on the grounds that the instrument is not binding due to some hidden legal defect, such as not being in compliance with the commercial code in the issuing country. This has led to reluctance on the part of U.S. exporters to use forfaiting and the resulting attempt by some financial institutions to develop alternative instruments.

Factoring

Factoring is a short-term financing mechanism under which a third party provides immediate cash against a company's outstanding accounts receivable; in effect it is a form of invoice discounting. Typically, the factor will advance up to 80% of the receivable, paying the balance at the time of collection. In return, the factor charges the seller interest (usually at least several points over prime) on the advanced portion of the receivable as well as a discount on the face amount of the invoice. Under this arrangement, the seller maintains liquidity and the buyer avoids the expense of having to open a letter of credit. Consequently, factoring in international trade finance is largely directed to short-term open account trading between nonrelated companies. Since it is regarded as a very expensive and risky method of short-term financing, it generally is avoided except in times of extreme cash flow pressure.

International factors have had to provide other trade services to offset this reputation and expand their customer base. In addition to receivable discounting, they handle debt collection, run overseas sales ledgers, offer protection against bad debt and currency fluctuations, and sort out delivery problems. The charge for these services normally ranges from 0.75 to 2.5% of the invoice amount handled. International factoring works as follows: the exporter approaches the factor and requests short-term financing for export sales made on open account. The factor then has an overseas correspondent verify the credit standing of the buyer. If this is deemed satisfactory, the factor then buys the exporter's outstanding receivables from that customer (up to the credit limit it sets for that customer) and takes over all dealings with the buyer after the goods are shipped. The exporter bills the customer and sends a copy of the bill to the factor; the factor in turn advances a proportion of the invoice value to the exporter. Finally, the factor then follows up on the transaction, handling any shipping problems that may arise and making sure that the buyer pays promptly for the goods.

LETTERS OF CREDIT

A letter of credit (L/C) introduces one or more financial intermediaries into a transaction between two commercial parties. It is most common when the exporter wants the buyer's promise to pay backed up by a guarantee from a bank, and the importer wants to delay formal obligation for payment until such time as the exporter actually makes shipment of the goods. As described by one authority, the letter of credit is in essence a letter addressed to the seller, written and signed by a bank acting on behalf of the buyer. In it, the bank promises the exporter it will honor drafts drawn on itself (which when recognized become banker's acceptances) provided that the exporter has complied with the specific conditions and furnished the required documents as set forth in the terms of the credit.

In a commercial L/C, the buyer informs his local bank that he wishes to open a letter of credit in a set amount for payment on a set date to the foreign exporter. The local bank that issues the L/C is then referred to as the issuing bank; it sends a telegraphic message to a correspondent bank in the exporter's home country, with the request that this second bank (referred to as the advising bank) notify the exporter that the credit has been opened. Under this arrangement, the exporter now has the commitment of the issuing bank to pay her when she makes shipment in compliance with the terms of the credit. Since the exporter, however, may not be familiar with the foreign bank, or may be concerned about its ability to pay due to sovereign risk, she may require the guarantee of a bank in her own country. In this case, the advising bank provides its guarantee or "confirmation" in exchange for a fee generally charged to the importer; the L/C then becomes a *confirmed letter of credit*. The exporter now has the commitment of the confirming bank to pay her upon presentation of evidence of shipment in compliance with the terms of the credit; all risks of default or inability to pay by either the issuing bank or the importer are now borne by the confirming bank.

Further distinctions exist among types of L/Cs. Under the terms of a *revocable letter of credit*, the buyer can cancel the L/C at any time up to shipment and credit negotiation. Under an *irrevocable credit*, on the other hand, the buyer cannot cancel the credit after it has been opened and advised to the exporter. Thus, a confirmed irrevocable L/C provides maximum coverage for the exporter and is often used when the buyer is either not well known to the supplier or is not regarded as a good credit risk. In most cases, the exporter is required to negotiate the credit (i.e., present the specified documents for collection) directly with the confirming bank. If the exporter is located in a different city, this function can be undertaken via her local bank. Under the terms of a *negotiable L/C*, on the other hand, the exporter has the right to present the documents for collection at any bank; the bank pays her (after deducting a fee) and then in turn presents the L/C and accompanying documents for collection for its own account at the confirming bank.

A *transferable L/C* allows the beneficiary (i.e., the exporter to whom the credit was opened) to transfer her rights to make shipment under the terms of the credit to a third party. Such an arrangement is only permitted when the L/C formally specifies that it is transferable. It is most commonly used when the exporter is not the actual manufacturer of the goods but a broker trading them for her own account. Since she may not have the funds to pay the manufacturer, she can transfer the credit to him in return for a commission. Two alternative trade finance vehicles in such a situation are an *assignment* and a *back-to-back letter of credit*. In the former, the exporter legally assigns a portion of the credit's value to the manufacturer but does not pass along the right for the latter to negotiate the credit directly. Under a back-to-back credit, the export broker, as the beneficiary of the credit opened by the foreign importer, offers it as security to the advising or confirming bank in order to open her own credit to the actual manufacturer. The second credit must exactly match the wording of the first, the only exceptions being the beneficiary, price, and shipment date. The two credits are then negotiated in reverse sequence as title to the goods passed from manufacturer to export broker to importer. The back-to-back credit thus fulfills the same function as the transferable L/C, providing liquidity to a capital-short export broker, but has the advantage of hiding the ultimate buyer's name and price from the manufacturer. Banks, however, are often reluctant to open confirmed back-to-back letters of credit unless additional security is provided by the export broker, because the bank is liable to pay the manufacturer irrespective of whether the exporter herself gets paid under the first credit and is able to reimburse the bank.

Documentation

Since a letter of credit is normally negotiable only upon presentation of proof of shipment, the specification of documentary requirements is critical for both buyer and seller. The most common of these is the *bill of lading* (B/L, or blading), which is issued by the shipping carrier in fulfillment of three major functions:

1. It is a contract between the carrier and the exporter for shipment of the goods from the port of embarcation to the port of debarcation.
2. It is the exporter's receipt for the goods.
3. It is the document that establishes control over the goods as they move in transit between seller and buyer.

The bill of lading is often misinterpreted as an assurance that the goods have been loaded aboard a shipping carrier and sent on their way to the buyer. However, some B/Ls are merely an indication that the shipper has received the goods. A "received for shipment" B/L, for example, merely certifies that the carrier has received the goods for shipment, not that they have actually been placed on board. An "on-board" bill of lading, in contrast, certifies that the goods have been received by the carrier and that they have actually been loaded on board the named vessel. A "clean" B/L states that the goods were received in what appeared to be good condition; if the goods were received by the carrier in what appears to be poor condition, a "fouled" B/L will usually be issued. For maximum protection, buyers usually require that only clean on-board bills of lading be negotiable under the terms of the L/C.

Since the B/L essentially provides its holder with title to the goods being shipped, important distinctions have been developed about its provisions. Under a "straight" B/L, the exporter consigns the goods directly to the importer; the straight B/L is neither transferable nor negotiable via endorsement and delivery to a third party (in the event the buyer is an import broker who does not want to take physical possession of the goods). It therefore is not good collateral for a bank that may be financing the importer. Consequently, most documentary letters of credit involve "order" bills of lading, under which the goods are consigned "to the order of" a named party, usually the exporter himself. In this manner, the exporter retains title to the goods until she endorses the B/L to another party. The importer's L/C therefore generally requires that the shipper furnish endorsed order bills of lading at the time of credit negotiation; these B/Ls are then passed on by the advising or confirming bank to the issuing bank, which in effect becomes the owner of the merchandise. The issuing bank in turn passes the B/Ls on to the buyer, who uses them to claim the goods from the shipping carrier. If the buyer does not immediately reimburse the issuing bank for the credit amount but instead takes a short-term loan to finance the new inventory, it will usually hold and sell the goods under a trust receipt from the bank and make repayment as it collects from its customers.

Letters of credit frequently require that the exporter furnish several other documents at the time of credit negotiation. The most common of these is the *commercial invoice,* in which the exporter enumerates the goods being shipped, the cost of each item, and the total amount owed by the buyer (including freight charges if the exporter is handling shipping for the buyer's account; see the term C&F in *Appendix* 2). If the contract terms specify that the exporter must pay for insuring the goods during shipment (see the term CIF in *Appendix* 2), the L/C will require that the exporter furnish an *insurance certificate* from a reputable agent stating the value and terms of coverage. If the exporter has an open or floating insurance policy (typical of most large exporters), then the exporter herself fills out the insurance certificate on a form provided by her insurance company, presenting the original with the L/C at the time of negotiation and sending a copy to her insurance company.

Many countries require that all imports be registered with their consular representative in the exporting country. This is done via a *consular invoice,* which in virtually all cases is a simple formality. The exporter draws up an invoice and presents it to the importing country's local consul to be visaed in exchange for a nominal fee. The visaed invoice is then included with the other documents presented at the time of credit negotiation. Bulk commodity shipments generally require two additional documents: a *certificate of inspection* and a *draft survey.* The former is furnished by an independent inspection firm, which samples and tests the shipped goods and describes their actual product characteristics vis-à-vis the required characteristics as specified per the L/C (e.g., protein content in the case of soybean meal or mineral composition in the case of raw iron ore). If the sampled-product characteristics are below those specified in the credit, the L/C is generally not negotiable unless the buyer formally waives the requirement (usually in return for a discount from the exporter). In some cases, however, the original contract and L/C may permit a sliding payment scale based on the product characteristics (e.g., so many dollars per ton per percentage point of protein in the soybean meal); the inspection results would then be reflected in the commercial invoice. A draft survey done by an impartial third party (the surveyor) is a statement of the weight of the bulk cargo loaded aboard a maritime vessel. The surveyor, by knowledge of the vessel's structural characteristics and visual inspection of how high it rides in the water before and after the cargo has been loaded, states the bulk weight of the cargo he believes has been loaded on board. Techniques have been developed over the years so that these are generally very accurate appraisals. The commercial invoice is then drawn up on the basis of the survey weight.

Lastly, for foodstuffs, drugs, cosmetics or other items involving consumption of or application to human beings or animals, the importer and/or the importer's government may require that the exporter furnish a *health or sanitary certificate* attesting to the quality and safety of the goods being exported. These are usually provided through the exporting country's ministry or department of health. They can be very important for imports into the United States, since the U.S. Food and Drug Administration (FDA) can prohibit importation of products that it regards as potentially harmful as well as rejecting specific shipments of permitted goods because they are deemed of substandard quality with regard to health. For this reason, L/Cs for some types of goods contain what is known as an *FDA rejection clause*. Under these terms, the exporter receives only a portion of payment when the goods are shipped; the balance of the obligation comes due only after the goods have been inspected and passed for importation into the United States by the FDA.

EXCHANGE RATE RISK MANAGEMENT

One of the most vexing problems in trade finance since the abandonment of fixed exchange rates in 1973 has been management of foreign exchange (FX) risk. The easiest solution to this problem is for the seller to require that the buyer pay in the seller's home currency. Buyers are reluctant to do this since it forces them to assume the currency risk. In international markets where multiple suppliers are competing for the buyer's order, the buyer may have some leverage in determining the currency of payment. The supplier therefore generally has to assume and manage the currency risk. One method is simply to accept payment in the foreign currency and convert it into home currency at the spot foreign exchange rate on the payment date. This leaves the exporter with a high foreign exchange exposure and is only attractive when the two currencies have a stable relationship, such as when both are part of the European Monetary System (EMS) and are required by government agreement to fluctuate within a narrow band.

The forward foreign exchange market is the traditional vehicle for managing such FX risk. Under a forward market arrangement, the exporter and a bank agree to exchange set amounts of two currencies at a prescribed rate on a particular future date. The bank maintains a bid-asked spread to assure its profit margin (e.g., it will pay US$1.00 to obtain DM 2.5000 but will require a customer to pay it DM 2.5002 to purchase US$1.00). Since most banks try to maintain a neutral foreign exchange book (i.e., a net zero exposure in any currency for each maturity), the time frame of the forward market available to firms is generally limited by the time frame of the Eurocurrency market, normally 1 year. In cases where the exporter's foreign currency revenues will occur several years in the future, some firms elect to cover forward with a 1-year maturity and then roll the coverage forward as time elapses. In attempting to manage its FX risk by a forward market transaction, however, the exporter assumes a new risk: if the buyer defaults, the exporter must still make good on her forward contract to supply the set foreign currency amount to the bank. She could therefore be forced to cover the obligation via an FX purchase at an unknown future spot exchange rate.

A currency futures contract has the same problem. The exporter still incurs the obligation to supply a set amount of the foreign currency at a set rate on a specific future date, and in the event of buyer default would either have to repurchase or cover the contract on the basis of the unknown future spot rate. Options contracts allow the exporter to avoid this exposure. In the case of a put (call) option, the exporter purchases the right but not the obligation to sell (buy) a given amount of the foreign (home) currency at a set rate on a specified future date. Premiums, however, can be quite high for currencies not actively traded in the Euromarkets, making it unprofitable to be fully hedged on low-margin items.

BONDS

Importers wanting an additional guarantee that exporters will perform as per their contract may require that suppliers post a bid or performance bond. The former is most commonly used when the importer makes a public tender, requesting that firms forward their firm offers and prices for supplying the goods enumerated in the tender. Contract awards are sometimes not announced until several weeks after the closing date for offers. The bid bond—often in the form of a confirmed irrevocable letter of credit opened by the supplier with the buyer as the beneficiary—is a penalty that the exporter will have to forfeit if she receives the contract award but fails to perform according to the terms of her firm offer. The bond's typical penalty is for 1 to 5% of the contract amount and tends to rise according to the price volatility of the commodities being supplied. Performance bonds fulfill a similar role for capital goods exports that may be made over a period of several years. Advance-payment bonds are posted by the supplier as security for prepayments made by the seller to provide working capital for the supplier while she manufactures the goods.

GOVERNMENT MOTIVATIONS FOR ARRANGING TRADE FINANCE

Most governments today take an active role in trade finance in the belief that they can increase national exports by providing loans, insurance, and subsidized credit. Justifications include foreign exchange earnings, balance of trade or payments stabilization, maintaining employment in key domestic industries, helping firms and industries gain the scale or learning effects of high-volume production, and assisting domestic infant industries to become competitive in international markets. Although each major exporting country has its own export program (see *Appendix 1* for information on several OECD members), one feature common to all systems is the assumption by the government or a government-sponsored agency of the bulk of the credit risk inherent in extending financing to foreign buyers. Insurance facilities are provided to cover exporters who provide credit to buyers, particularly where the exporter then discounts the buyer's promissory notes with a local financial institution. In cases where buyer credit is provided by a commercial bank, government agencies offer commercial and political risk guarantees on the loan. Programs that limit official support to insurance and guarantees are sometimes referred to as "pure cover." Most countries, however, also have government agencies that offer direct financing to foreign buyers for large capital goods purchases involving long-term (5- to 10-year) payment periods. In addition, these agencies also provide banks with an interest "makeup" or subsidy in compensation for the difference between the banks' (market rate) cost of funds and the OECD-sanctioned minimum lending rates.

The OECD Arrangement

In 1978, the OECD nations concluded an agreement on government-sponsored export financing, the "Arrangement on Guidelines for Officially Supported Export Credits," commonly known as the OECD Arrangement. The guidelines set terms governing the buyer's minimum allowable cash down payment, minimum interest rates (the Matrix or Consensus Rates), maximum allowable payment period, and procedures for notification and discussion when one of the signatories departed from the guidelines. Major provisions include:

- Minimum buyer cash down payment of 15% of the export value at the contract "starting point," usually defined as the date when buyer takes physical possession of the goods in his home country or when construction on a project is completed.
- Ten-year maximum repayment period.
- Establishment of minimum allowable interest rates (Matrix Rates) according to the economic status of the buyer's country, with lowest rates charged to relatively poor (Category III) countries and the highest rates to the relatively rich (Category I) ones; rates are adjusted semiannually and are set on the basis of a weighted average of the long-term bond rates for the five SDR (Special Drawing Rights) currencies.
- Differentiation of interest rates according to loan maturity, with rates becoming higher as the repayment period gets longer.
- Establishment of Commercial Interest Reference Rates (CIRRs) for the "low-interest-rate currencies," historically the Japanese yen, the German mark, and the Swiss franc; these are set at a 0.2% margin over average government borrowing costs for a 5-year fixed-rate obligation and are adjusted monthly.

By establishing the matrix interest rates on the basis of a five-currency weighted average, the high-interest-rate countries are allowed to offer government-sponsored export financing at rates below those prevailing in their domestic money markets. However, the matrix rates are above prevailing commercial interest rates

in the low-interest-rate countries (LIRCs), and it would place LIRC exporters at a competitive disadvantage if they were required to provide financing at the Matrix Rates. The CIRRs therefore serve as the minimum allowable rate for exports denominated in the low-interest-rate currencies. The Matrix Rates for the July 15, 1986, to January 15, 1977, period were:

	1–5 year credits	5–8 year credits	8–10 year credits
Category I	9.55	9.80	—
Category II	8.25	8.75	—
Category III	7.40	7.40	7.40

Under the Consensus Arrangement, 85% of any government-sponsored export financing outside the LIRCs would be priced at these rates. The subsidy component inherent in such below-market rates allows exporters from high-interest-rate countries to offer attractive currency swap arrangements to foreign buyers (see below).

Mixed Credits

Mixed credits have been one of the most contentious topics among OECD members, since they reduce the effective interest rate on project loans by bundling commercial aid with export financing. Under the terms of a mixed credit, part of the financing is provided by such conventional sources as commercial banks and government export credit agencies, with the balance coming from direct government-to-buyer financing at concessionary (i.e., foreign aid–type) interest rates. In this manner, the effective interest rate on the entire package can fall below the minimum permitted by the OECD Arrangement, providing a competitive advantage to firms from countries whose governments use mixed credits as a means of export promotion as well as foreign aid. The OECD

Arrangement prohibits mixed credits from being offered to buyers in Category I (the rich countries), and requires that mixed credits offered to middle- (Category II) and low-income (Category III) buyers must constitute at least 25 and 50%, respectively, of the total amount financed. The U.S. position has been that mixed credits distort trade by permitting evasion of Consensus Rates and has sought to increase the minimum concessionary element allowed. This would make it even more expensive for governments to match each others' mixed rate financing bids as well as forcing them to concentrate their available funds on a smaller number of deals.

Guarantees and Insurance

Virtually all major capital goods exporting countries provide credit insurance and guarantees to exporters for coverage of buyer nonpayment due to either commercial or political causes. Most programs include a coinsurance feature requiring the exporter to bear part of the credit risk as a means of avoiding moral hazard problems. Coverage is restricted, moreover, to the domestic content portion of any export. This condition has made private insurance arrangements increasingly attractive for capital goods exporters who source important components overseas; these also generally require coinsurance by the exporter.

U.S. INSTITUTIONS

The *U.S. Export-Import Bank* (ExIm) is an autonomous government agency; although it receives an annual budget allocation from the U.S. Congress, it was originally intended to be self-financing. Loans are made for the specific purpose of financing the sale of goods and services of U.S. origin only; these loans are occasionally granted at highly subsidized rates to signal U.S. government discontent with the

foreign trade practices of other major American trading partners. In evaluating any loan proposal, particularly for capital goods exports, ExIm is required by law to consider whether these might ultimately have an adverse effect on the U.S. economy or balance of payments. On occasion, ExIm has acted on the import side as well. Several years ago it offered subsidized financing to the Budd Company to help it compete against a Canadian company (Bombadier) in a bid to supply the New York City Transit System with subway cars.

ExIm provides four basic trade finance services through a variety of programs:

1. Credit insurance for political and commercial risk
2. Direct buyer financing
3. Guarantees to commercial banks for loans to foreign buyers
4. Fixed-rate financing to U.S. commercial banks for medium-term credits to foreign buyers

ExIm's direct lending program provides long-term (5 to 10 years) fixed-rate loans for U.S. capital goods exports and will match competitive government-sponsored financing where contract values exceed $10 million and involve long construction periods. In line with OECD consensus guidelines, ExIm requires that the buyer make a 15% down payment. ExIm will then lend up to 65% of the total contract value with the balance coming from a commercial bank, which in turn may be covered by an ExIm commercial and political risk guarantee. In exceptional cases, ExIm will provide direct financing for 75% of total contract value on the condition that the exporter arrange financing for the 10% allowable balance at the same fixed interest rate as the ExIm portion of the loan. Under its medium-term credit program, ExIm provides fixed-rate financing to banks for 1- to 5-year foreign buyer credits when U.S. exporters are competing with foreign firms receiving government export credit support.

The *Private Export Finance Company* (PEFCO) is jointly owned by 54 commercial banks and 7 U.S. industrial firms. It provides funds for medium- and long-term credits to foreign importers of U.S. goods. ExIm fully guarantees the repayment of these fixed-rate loans, which are all subject to its approval. PEFCO commonly provides about 20 to 25% of the total amount financed when it participates jointly with ExIm and commercial banks. Political and commercial risk insurance for export credits are available from both private firms and the *Foreign Credit Insurance Association* (FCIA), a cooperative effort among ExIm and about 50 private marine, casualty, and property insurance companies. Under a typical arrangement, the exporter assigns the proceeds of her FCIA policy to a commercial bank, which in turn purchases the foreign buyer's promissory notes from the exporter without recourse (i.e., the exporter is not liable if the buyer fails to make payment). In most cases, however, the exporter is required to provide 10% coinsurance.

How Firms Use the System

Maneuvering through the bureaucratic maze to find the right program and to qualify for export assistance can be difficult for inexperienced U.S. exporters, as ExIm's procedures for each of its programs are quite different. Under the direct loan long-term program, for example, only the borrower (i.e., the foreign importer) may apply, a time-consuming and paperwork-intensive process. In consequence, financing packages under this program can only be put in place when all the parties—exporter, commercial bank, and the importer—have agreed on all terms of the contract. In order to reduce the uncertainty involved and to enable both the exporter and foreign importer to arrange their financing plans earlier, ExIm allows the parties to apply for preliminary

commitments (PCs) which outline the amount, terms, and conditions of the financing it will extend to purchasers of U.S. products. The PC, generally issued for a 6-month period during which final contracts are to be negotiated, strengthens the U.S. exporter's competitive position by giving her the chance to offer a financing package as part of the original equipment proposal.

The PC applicant can be the U.S. supplier, the foreign customer, or a financial institution providing part of the credit for the deal. Obtaining a PC requires no cost or obligation and is usually done by means of a letter outlining a deal's general circumstances and tentative arrangements. Often this follows an unofficial approach by either company or bank representatives to an ExIm loan officer, giving experienced banks and major exporters a decided advantage in knowing how to work within the system. Applications for ExIm guarantees, on the other hand, must be made by a U.S. commercial bank on behalf of the exporter. The exporter, in turn, is required to furnish ExIm with information about the transaction, either directly or through the bank. Experts advise that the exporter's first step should be to consult her commercial bank concerning the likelihood of ExIm's furnishing the guarantee. Most large banks not only have a good idea of any proposal's chances but also have a "delegated authority" to approve (on ExIm's behalf) certain types of deals within present volumes and terms.

For very large projects involving multicompany multinational sourcing, each firm in the consortium making the bid will generally try to obtain financing from its own export credit agency for its part of the project. Since the terms offered can vary across nations, this can affect the optimal equipment specification. Alternatively, large firms that produce in a number of countries can source equipment on the same basis, using the export credit systems of the nations in which their overseas plants are located. One author[1] cites the case of the J.I. Case Company, a Tenneco subsidiary:

In Nigeria, Case markets its own brand of tractors and construction equipment from both its U.S. and Brazilian plants. Sourcing from Brazil is attractive because the Brazilian government, through Cacex (similar to the U.S. Export-Import Bank), provides better credit terms than the U.S. Under the aegis of Eximbank, U.S. banks could offer three-year financing to Case's Nigerian dealer, but the Brazilian agency is able to guarantee as much as five years of credit—at about the same interest rates.

NEW TRADE FINANCE INNOVATIONS
Electronic Letters of Credit

Banks are now attempting to devise new electronic instruments that would replace the documentary credits or notes used in trade finance. Electronic letters of credit allow importers to avoid much of the paperwork of documentary credits by opening L/Cs via a terminal in their offices; negotiation of the credit by the exporter still involves presentation of documents (e.g., bill of lading) to the advising or confirming bank. Thus, the electronic L/C expedites the credit's opening but not its negotiation. Documentation requirements have been a barrier to a system where negotiation would also occur electronically. Bills of lading, drafts, and promissory notes are all negotiable instruments, allowing the holder to transfer title to the goods; their legal status and jurisdiction are well-established. The status of an electronic instrument, with or without endorsement, is still undefined. Banks looking to generate fee income through documentary transactions have traditionally offered electronic L/Cs as part of a bundle of trade finance services. More recently, they have also been offered by banks

[1]Peter Evans, *Dependent Development: The Alliance of Multinational, State and Local Capital in Brazil*, Princeton University Press, 1979, p. 321, citing a report in *Business International*, 1976, p. 204).

as part of integrated cash management services providing a wealth of on-line financial information to bank customers.

Capital Market Instruments

One recent trade finance innovation has been to take export credits guaranteed (but not financed) by government agencies and repackage them for sale in the capital market. This appeals to commercial banks that fund their fixed-rate exports credits by borrowing at floating rates in the Euromarkets and then receiving a government subsidy or interest rate makeup. The government guarantee, in turn, enables banks to either place the credits privately or resell them to public investors seeking a low-risk, fixed-rate, medium-term instrument. The bank is thus acting as an intermediary between the foreign buyer and the local capital market. But in order to make their trade finance operations more competitive, government institutions are developing new wrinkles on traditional practices. For example, CoFACE (the French government export credit agency) recently announced a plan to guarantee bonds issued by foreign companies to finance French exports. Significantly, the plan allows for issuance of nonfranc-denominated bonds on foreign capital markets. U.S. bankers, however, express reservations about capital market placement of ExIm-guaranteed paper. "Every placement has a story," said one. "If a loan has to be guaranteed by ExIm, it already has a problem." One of the major problems with the ExIm guarantee is that it doesn't quite guarantee everything. The interest guarantee, for example, does not cover the full amount of the originally contracted interest rate, only a maximum of 1% over the Treasury Bill rate at the time of the borrower's default. Moreover, the ExIm Bank's annual 0.5% guarantee fee, normally paid by the foreign borrower, has to be paid by the lender when the borrower defaults.

Export Trade Notes

Although forfaiting has become an attractive means of packaging trade paper in Europe over the past 20 years, it has not been adopted by many U.S. exporters. Investors are trying to adapt the concept to U.S. financial market and legal requirements via the creation of export trade notes. One of the problems with forfaiting lies in its unregulated nature. Should a buyer default, the forfaiter (or subsequent holder if the notes have been resold in the secondary market) has to enforce the aval offered by the guaranteeing bank. Since this bank's legal residence is usually in the importer's country, however, the question arises as to which country's legal system is applicable. Several cases litigated thus far have not provided clear guidance. Second, the secondary market for the forfaited paper is not open to general investors. This constrains both its size and liquidity. The promoters of U.S. export trade notes seek to enhance the negotiability of the paper, opening the market to all investors, as well as mandating that U.S. (New York State) law govern all transactions. The proposed export trade notes would standardize all contract terms and conditions, increasing substitutability and tradability of the instruments. They would also be adapted so that holders would come under the jurisdiction of the Uniform Commercial Code (UCC) relating to negotiable instruments, which would formalize the exporter's nonliability for payment (to the current note holder) in the event that the buyer defaults and the guaranteeing bank refuses to make payment.

Concern with the guaranteeing bank's reliability requires that the notes obtain some credit risk enhancement from domestic U.S. sources in order to be a marketable instrument. Under one arrangement, a U.S. capital goods exporter, who holds promissary notes from her customer guaranteed by a foreign bank, purchases insurance to cover the foreign bank's guarantee; this is cheaper than purchasing insurance on the risk of the foreign buyer himself. The notes are then sold in the institutional market. They generally require some exporter coinsurance and are limited to 2- or 3-year maturities. One further option involves pooling notes before resale, spreading country and commercial risk over multiple buyers. In this manner, a market could be created (in theory) with several different layers of credit:

- Those that are acceptable in their own right (i.e., based on the commercial and country risk of the buyer and guaranteeing bank)
- Those that would require a guarantee from or insurance by a U.S. financial institution
- Those that would require the guarantee of a public-sector international financial entity (e.g., the World Bank or a national Export-Import Bank)

Currency Swaps

Currency swaps as used in trade finance enable the buyer to make repayment in a third currency and achieve a lower interest rate on the financed portion of the purchase.[2] The latter is possible when a loan at the OECD Consensus minimum rate is made in the currency of an exporting country with high interest rates. Under a currency swap, this interest rate subsidy is transferred via foreign exchange transactions into a below-market interest rate in one of the low-interest-rate currencies (LIRCs).

---

[2]There are several other uses of the term "swaps" in international finance. It can refer to an agreement between two parties to exchange the payment and repayment streams of borrowings that each has made in a different currency, much as in an interest rate swap. In the foreign exchange markets, swaps are the simultaneous sale and purchase of a given amount of currency for settlement at different value dates. For further information on both of these types of swaps, see Harvard Business School Notes 9-286-067, "Note on Foreign Exchange," and 9-286-074, "Foreign Currency Swaps."

The swap works off the presumed conditions of interest rate parity (IRP) and forward parity (FP) in the foreign exchange market. These state that given spot market exchange rates and current Euromarket interest rates, the equilibrium forward foreign exchange rate should leave an investor indifferent to holding her funds in one currency or the other. In practice, this means that the forward exchange rate should equal the ratio of compound yields in the two currencies times the current spot market exchange rate. An example of a currency swap relying on these conditions is provided in Table 1.

Assume that a U.S. exporter makes a $200 million sale to an OECD Consensus Category III foreign buyer. Under some conditions, the U.S. ExIm Bank will lend 75% of this amount at the OECD Consensus minimum rate, if the supplier provides an additional 10% of the financing at the same rate. The example therefore uses a 10-year, US$170 million loan. For simplicity it presumes a flat term structure of interest rates and assumes that forward ex-

change rates are set on the basis of long-term government bond yields. The latter were 10.74 and 6.09%, respectively, for the U.S. dollar and Japanese yen in October 1985. At that time, the OECD Consensus Rate was 9.85% and the spot yen/dollar exchange rate was 202 to 1. By contracting with a commercial bank to swap the repayment stream of the dollar-denominated loan made at 9.85% into yen using the implied forward market exchange rate, the borrower is able to achieve an effective yen interest rate of 5.24%. This is almost a full point less than the minimum 6.29% yen interest rate permitted under the LIRC provisions of the OECD Consensus Agreement.

The example abstracts from banks' normal foreign exchange bid-asked spreads, as well as from the fees and commissions they usually charge borrowers. It also ignores difficulties in setting up the entire swap transaction at the time that loan terms are established. Typically, ExIm Bank loans are made in a series of tranches, as different proportions of work are completed

TABLE ONE

DOLLAR LOAN AMOUNT: $170 MILLION
Dollar Interest Rate: 9.85%
Implied Yen Interest Rate: 5.24%

Time	U.S. interest rate, %	Compound yield on dollar investment	Yen interest rate, %	Compound yield on yen investment	Implied yen/dollar forward exchange rate	Dollar repayment amount, millions	Yen/dollar exchange rate	Value of loan in yen, billions	Yen repayment amount, billions
1985	10.74		6.09		202.00		202.00	34.34	
1986	10.74	1.1074	6.09	1.0609	193.52	27.49	193.52		5.32
1987	10.74	1.2263	6.09	1.1255	185.39	27.49	185.39		5.10
1988	10.74	1.3580	6.09	1.1941	177.61	27.49	177.61		4.88
1989	10.74	1.5039	6.09	1.2668	170.15	27.49	170.15		4.68
1990	10.74	1.6654	6.09	1.3439	163.01	27.49	163.01		4.48
1991	10.74	1.8443	6.09	1.4258	156.16	27.49	156.16		4.29
1992	10.74	2.0424	6.09	1.5126	149.60	27.49	149.60		4.11
1993	10.74	2.2617	6.09	1.6047	143.32	27.49	143.32		3.94
1994	10.74	2.5046	6.09	1.7024	137.30	27.49	137.30		3.77
1995		2.7736		1.8061	131.54	27.49	131.54		3.62

on a project, and may include repayment grace periods as well. Only after all tranches have been made is it possible to set up a fixed amortization schedule determining the exact currency amounts to be swapped.

Banks may be reluctant to provide firm long-term forward market rates unless they can hedge these via an offsetting foreign exchange transaction. Realistically, therefore, bid-asked spreads can be expected to widen with the tenor of the swap, since the longer-term foreign exchange transactions are difficult to cover in the Euromarkets. One banker described the situation, which essentially requires finding an offsetting party that wants to lock in its future foreign exchange transactions on the basis of the loan amortization schedule of an entirely unrelated export transaction, as "like holding a suit and running around looking for somebody to fit it."

APPENDIX 1

Canada

Canada's Export Development Corporation (EDC) is a government-owned, commercially self-sustaining enterprise responsible for ensuring that competitive credit facilities are available to Canadian exporters. It provides direct buyer loans for Canadian capital goods exports as well as credit insurance and guarantees for buyer financing provided by Canadian exporters and commercial banks. Coinsurance of at least 10% is generally required in addition to a minimum 60% Canadian goods and services content. Private export credits can be refinanced under three different EDC programs depending upon the transaction and type of security required. All three provide up to 85% coverage of the contract value on a nonrecourse basis, although the direct financing program is in practice usually limited to 60% of total con-

tract value. The buyer must make a 15% down payment; this can be lent to him by a commercial financial institution, but the EDC will not insure this portion of the transaction. Interest rates are fixed and are negotiated on a case-by-case basis with each exporter in compliance with OECD Consensus rates. The three facilities are:

1. Note purchase: for 3- to 5-year credits covering capital goods exports; requires complex agreements and a first-class foreign bank guarantee
2. Simplified note purchase: for 1- to 3-year credits covering quasi capital goods; requires no formal agreements, only an offer letter; no bank guarantee required
3. A forfait: note purchase with bank guarantee but less cumbersome documentation

The EDC also runs a Specific Transaction Insurance and Guarantee Program in which it unconditionally guarantees 100% of the principal and interest to banks that provide nonrecourse financing to Canadian exporters via purchase of notes from foreign buyers. The EDC as a practice will lend in either Canadian or U.S. dollars; recently, it has advanced credits in several other convertible foreign currencies as well. In 1984 it adopted an exposure fee, paid by the exporter as the funds are disbursed under its long-term buyer credit program. The rate is based on three factors: the buyer's country, whether the buyer is public or private, and the term of the financing. The EDC's newest insurance program covers exporters and financial institutions against losses incurred by failure of another consortium member to perform under the terms of an export contract which had been cross-guaranteed by bid or performance bonds.

France

The French government has traditionally been very competitive in the area of export financing, providing direct export credits through two government agencies. The Compagnie Francaise d'Assurance pour le Commerce Exterieur (CoFACE), which is jointly owned by a group of nationalized insurance companies and banks, provides credit insurance and guarantees for French exporters and financial institutions. Along with these, it also offers an interest rate makeup to cover the difference between banks' funding costs and the minimum allowable interest rates under the OECD Consensus guidelines. The Banque Francaise du Commerce Exterieur (BFCE) refinances a portion of a medium-term credits (up to 7 years) and provides direct financing for loans of 7 to 10 years. The BFCE raises funds for its operations on both the French and international money markets under a French government guarantee, which enables it to obtain a lower cost of funds.

During initial negotiation of the sales contract, the exporter applies to CoFACE for insurance cover and fixed-rate financing. If the application is approved by the Office of External Relations of the Ministry of Finance (the DREE), CoFACE then promises the exporter that it will issue a guarantee once the contract is signed. For medium-term credits, the exporter then obtains refinancing by discounting the buyer's promissory notes with a French commercial bank, which in turn discounts them with the BFCE or the Banque de France (the Central Bank). Via a rather circuitous procedure involving loans and deposits at different interest rates, the financing bank is compensated for the difference between its cost of funds and the special discount rate offered the exporter. In cases where the promissory notes extend beyond 7 years, the exporter usually discounts them directly with the BFCE at the subsidized fixed rate.

France follows the OECD Consensus Arrangement regarding the maximum 85% of contract value financing. For credits of up to 7 years, a French commercial bank will generally make credit available either directly to the importer or indirectly via the importer's (foreign) bank at the minimum allowable Consensus Rate. The French bank has its loan insured by the government and receives an interest rate makeup if necessary. For credits beyond 7 years, the BFCE will often directly finance a major portion of the loan. Funds are available in other major convertible currencies as well as French francs, but the CoFACE premium is higher. CoFACE also issues two separate insurance policies: one to the exporter, giving 90% cover during the manufacturing period, the other a guarantee to the financing commercial bank, providing 95% cover against both commercial and political risks.

Germany

Germany's successful export performance has largely been achieved without extensive direct government intervention, according to the 1985 edition of the U.S. Export-Import Bank's annual competitive report, which attributes German export competitiveness to product quality and a well-established banking community. In recent years, Germany's status as a low-commercial-interest-rate country has also helped its firms provide competitive export financing. Since most export credit financing is provided through the commercial banking sector, the government's role is limited to three areas:

1. Export insurance, provided by a private consortium of insurance companies (HERMES) acting as a government agent
2. Long-term financing from the Kreditanstalt fur Wiederaufbau (KfW) at the OECD minimum for the low-interest rate countries
3. Support of commercial banks' supplier credit facilities through a refinancing facility at the German central bank (the Bundesbank)

Commercial banks, via the Ausfuhrkredit-Gesellschaft (AKA, a 56-bank consortium restricted to export financing), provide supplier credit on both commercial lending (with recourse) and forfaiting (without recourse) bases. Under the former, the exporter assigns the benefits of her HERMES insurance on the buyer's draft or promissory notes to the lender; the lender in turn either offers financing to the exporter on a secured overdraft or a fixed-rate basis or else discounts the importer's notes. In cases of buyer credit, the lending bank insures its loan for 95% commercial and political risk cover with HERMES, which also offers exchange inconvertibility insurance as well as performance and bid bond coverage in case of cross-guarantees by consortium members. For capital goods exports to developing countries, KfW may provide minimum CIRR financing for the maximum contract value allowable under OECD guidelines. AKA will typically finance up to 85% of the allowable contract value for private foreign borrowers and slightly higher for public ones. Credits are almost always linked to HERMES coverage and are denominated in Deutsche marks. Export contracts with state-owned enterprises or state trading companies receive special coverage under a joint German government–AKA program. The exporter assigns the benefits of her HERMES insurance to AKA, which in turn discounts the buyer's promissory notes for the exporter. AKA can then refinance up to 55% of the contract value with the Bundesbank at 1.5% over the German Federal Discount Rate.

Italy

The Italian government pursues an active export promotion policy. Exports are financed at subsidized rates through the Mediocredito Centrale, a state-owned financial institution that funds itself by issuing bonds, CDs, and time deposits. It will refinance supplier export credits on either a note purchase agreement (floating rate) or at a fixed-rate discount basis. Under the former, a bank advances the amount of the credit against the exporter's presentation of the buyer's promissory notes; the exporter then designates the bank as the beneficiary of her commercial and political risk insurance. The exporter is then charged a floating interest rate until she repays the advance (i.e., usually when she receives the buyer's payment). Mediocredito subsidizes the exporter by refunding her the difference between the refinancing rate charged by the bank and the minimum allowable OECD Matrix Rate. Alternatively, the exporter can discount the buyer's promissory notes at a fixed rate with an Italian commercial bank at market rates. Mediocredito pays the bank's fees and reimburses the exporter for the difference between the market discount rate and the OECD Matrix Rate.

Mediocredito performs three roles in buyer credits. (1) It will lend directly to foreign importers for medium- to long-term credits on purchases of Italian capital goods. (2) In cases where financing is provided by other Italian financial institutions at OECD Consensus Rates, Mediocredito will provide an interest makeup as well as pay some of the bank's fees. (3) Mediocredito gives interest rate makeup in so-called triangular credits, where the financing bank is neither Italian nor domiciled in the buyer's home country.

Export guarantees and insurance are provided through the Sezione Speciale per l'Assicurazione del Credito all'Esportazione (SACE), an autonomous government agency. SACE insures or reinsures exporters and financial institutions against political and commercial risks on medium- and long-term capital goods exports. It provides 100% coverage for foreign banks providing financing in a triangular credit, and exchange risk insurance for foreign-currency-denominated credits. However, SACE coverage is limited to only 90% of the value of supplier credits financed under the note purchase arrangement, and guarantees to commercial banks for buyer credits are only available in cases where the buyer is either a foreign government entity or its debt is guaranteed by its government.

Japan

The Japanese government has historically been active in supporting and encouraging exports. According to the 1985 U.S. ExIm Bank competitive report, the Japanese government's focus on macroeconomic variables, such as low interest rates and abundant credit for major exporters, has meant not having to offer overly generous terms or actively engage in subsidies. Export support is handled through the Japanese Export-Import Bank (JEXIM), the Export Insurance Division of the Ministry of International Trade (EID/MITI), and the Overseas Economic Cooperation Fund (OECF). The amount of subsidy provided by JEXIM on any given transaction is greatly constrained by Japan's strict adherence to the OECD Consensus Guidelines. On the other hand, Japan is often accused of circumventing these limits by extensive use of mixed credits.

Because Japanese interest rates are generally among the lowest of the OECD Low Interest Rate Countries (LIRCs), the rates offered by JEXIM are in fact sometimes higher than the commercial market rates for very good credit risks. Banks, however, often are reluctant to participate in anything beyond 6-month fixed-rate financing unless JEXIM also participates; its maximum participation in a long-term (up to 10-year) supplier credit to support capital goods exports is 70%, with the balance coming from commercial banks or the exporter herself. Direct-buyer loans are offered by JEXIM in cooperation with Japanese banks. JEXIM also provides loans for foreign direct investment and overseas joint venture projects by Japanese firms. This support is seen both as a means of guaranteeing access to vital imports and as a method of reducing trade frictions with the host country.

The EID/MITI provides commercial, politi-cal, and currency risk insurance at premium rates determined by the category of the creditor; the subsidy component of these rates is minimal or nil. The insurance, however, is required for all JEXIM financing. It is available for up to 50% of the foreign content of a multicountry consortium's capital goods project as long as Japanese suppliers provide at least half the project's total value. The OECF is the government institution responsible for directing Japan's economic cooperation with foreign countries, mainly through loans on concessional terms (Overseas Development Assistance, or ODA). The program is heavily weighted toward large-scale public works and infrastructure projects in Asian countries where Japan is seeking to maintain or improve existing political and trade ties. OECF implements its policy under the guidance of the Ministries of Finance, Foreign Affairs, and MITI. The concessional terms, when coupled with commercial financing at low Japanese market rates, can lead to very low effective interest rates for buyers.

APPENDIX 2

Glossary of Trading and Shipping Terms

Goods Moving at Buyer's Risk and Cost

ex works (EXW)   Seller delivers goods at loading dock of her production facility; buyer arranges and pays for and bears all risks of loading and transporting the goods.

free carrier (FCR)   Seller delivers goods to shipping facility of carrier of the buyer's choice; ownership of goods passes to the buyer at the time of this delivery, and buyer assumes all costs and risks from that point onward; commonly used for delivery to truck terminal or railroad.

free on rail (FOR)   Seller delivers goods to the railroad at her own expense; buyer assumes all subsequent costs and risk.

free alongside (FAS) Seller delivers goods to the point where they will be loaded on maritime vessel of buyer's choice; cost of delivery to this point is borne by seller; loading charges, any export charges or duties, and all subsequent costs and risks are for buyer's account.

free on board (FOB) Seller delivers goods to a maritime vessel of the buyer's choice and assumes cost and risk of loading them on board; ownership passes to buyer once goods have been loaded and an onboard bill of lading issued; buyer assumes all costs and risks of ocean shipment.

free on board airport (FOB airport, FOA) Seller delivers goods at own expense to air carrier's point of departure; ownership and all subsequent costs and risks pass to buyer at time of this delivery.

Goods Moving at Buyer's Risk and Seller's Cost

cost and freight (C&F) Seller delivers good to maritime vessel of her choice and pays loading and freight charges to delivery port; buyer pays unloading fees and any import duties at port of arrival; risk passes to the buyer when the goods cross the ship's rail in the port of *departure.*

cost, insurance, and freight (CIF) Identical to C&F except that seller pays the cost of insuring the goods for the ocean voyage; note that this insurance covers the buyer's possible loss, since all risks pass to the buyer when goods cross the ship's rail in port of departure.

duty, carriage, paid to (DCP) Seller assumes loading and freight charges up to mutually agreed-upon point, whereupon buyer assumes all expenses; note that buyer assumes all risks once goods have been delivered by seller to freight carrier; often used in cases of multimodel transport.

freight, carriage, and insurance, paid to (CIP) Identical to the above except that insurance during transport is now paid by shipper.

Goods Moving at Seller's Risk and Cost

ex ship (EXS) Seller delivers goods to maritime vessel, pays loading and export fees as well as ocean transport charges to port of arrival, and assumes all risks of these operations; buyer pays to unload goods in port of delivery and assumes any import duties or fees; ownership passes to buyer at home of unloading.

ex quay (EXQ) Seller delivers goods to maritime vessel, pays loading charges, export duties, and ocean freight charges, as well as unloading charges in port of arrival and assumes all risks of these operations; buyer may then pick up goods at point of unloading; seller pays import duties unless contract specifies otherwise.

delivered at frontier (DAF) Seller delivers goods to the agreed-upon frontier and bears all costs and risks up to that point; buyer pays import costs and assumes all further transport costs and risk.

delivered duty paid (DDP) Seller assumes all costs and risks of transport and delivery up to the buyer's premises.

BIBLIOGRAPHY AND SOURCES OF ADDITIONAL INFORMATION

Andrews, Suzanna, "The Bold New Look in Trade Financing," *Institutional Investor,* January 1984.

Baron, David P., *The Export-Import Bank: An Economic Analysis,* New York, Academic Press, 1983.

Celi, Louis J., and I. James Czechowicz for Business International Corporation, *Export Financing: A Handbook of Sources and Techniques,* Morristown, N.J., Financial Executives Research Foundation, 1985.

Comptroller General of the United States, "Financial and Other Constraints Prevent Eximbank from Consistently Offering Competitive Financing for U.S. Exports," Washington, D.C., GPO, 1980.

Continental Illinois National Bank, "Commercial Letters of Credit," Chicago, 1981.

Czinkota, Michael, R., *Export Development Strategies: U.S. Promotion Policy,* New York, Praeger, 1984.

Emery, James J., Norman A. Graham, Richard L. Kauffman, and Michael C. Oppenheimer, *The U.S. Export-Import Bank: Policy Dilemmas and Choices,* Boulder, Col. Westview Press, 1984.

"Euromoney Trade Finance Report," various issues, London, Euromoney Publications.

Export-Import Bank of the United States, 1984 Annual Report, Washington, D.C.,

——, "Report to the U.S. Congress on Export Credit Competition and the Export-Import Bank of the

United States, for the Period January 1, 1981, through December 31, 1981," Washington, D.C., GPO, 1982.

————, "Report to the U.S. Congress on Export Credit Competition and the Export-Import Bank of the United States, for the Period January 1, 1984, through December 31, 1984," Washington, D.C., GPO, 1985.

General Accounting Office, "Report to the Secretary of Commerce and the United States Special Trade Representative: Benefits of International Agreement on Trade-Distorting Subsidies Not Yet Realized," Washington, D.C., GPO, 1983.

Gmur, Charles J. (ed.), *Trade Financing*, London, Euromoney Publications, 1981.

International Chamber of Commerce, "Guide to Documentary Credit Operations," Paris, I.C.C., 1978.

Kolde, Endel J., *International Business Enterprise*, Englewood Cliffs, N.J., Prentice-Hall, 1982.

Machinery and Allied Products Institute, *A Handbook on Financing U.S. Exports*, 4th ed., Washington, D.C., Machinery and Allied Products Institute, 1984.

Manufacturers Hanover Trust Company, "International Export Credit Financing," 3rd ed., New York, 1984.

OECD, *The Export Credit Financing Systems in OECD Member Countries*, Paris, 1982.

Philadelphia National Bank, *International Trade Procedures: An Introduction to Business Abroad*, 4th ed., Philadelphia, Philadelphia National Bank, 1977.

Shapiro, Alan C., *Multinational Financial Management*, Boston, Allyn and Bacon, 1982.

Stigum, Marcia, *The Money Market: Myth, Reality and Practice*, Homewood, Ill., Dow Jones Irwin, 1978.

PART FIVE

The Political Economy of Trade Policy

Textiles and the Multi-Fiber Arrangement

Representatives from over 50 countries gathered in Geneva in September 1981 to resume discussions about the future of trade and protectionism in textiles and apparel. For more than 20 years, developed nations had been erecting barriers to imports of Third World textiles. By 1981, 85% of global trade in cotton, wool, and man-made fiber products was regulated (see *Exhibit 6*). Since the industry was the largest source of manufacturing employment worldwide, the outcome of these trade negotiations was vitally important to all of the participants. Developing countries relied on textiles and apparel as the foundation of their industrialization strategies. Without freer world trade in this industry, these nations faced slower growth in the years ahead. Yet the developed countries, concerned about the decline of basic domestic industries, generally favored greater restrictions. The governments of the European Community and the United States were under pressure from their local industries and unions to reduce textile and apparel imports.

The Geneva discussions focused on the renewal of the Multi-Fiber Arrangement (MFA)— a multilateral treaty first signed in 1974 under the auspices of the General Agreement on Tariffs and Trade (GATT) and renewed for four years in 1977. Originally conceived as a temporary measure, the arrangement laid out the principles governing international trade in textiles and apparel. In theory, the MFA was to provide developing countries with guaranteed and growing access to markets of developed countries while allowing governments of developed countries to prevent the "disruption" of their domestic industries. In practice, the MFA was not temporary; it did not provide a guaranteed or growing market for developing countries' exports, and it did not prevent market "disruptions" in the developed countries. Thus, as the expiration date of December 31, 1981, approached, none of the parties to the current agreement was satisfied. The developed nations, and especially the European Economic Community (EEC), pointed to continuing problems of declining employment and

Assistant Professor David B. Yoffie and Research Associate Jane Kenney Austin prepared this case as a basis for class discussion rather than to illustrate either effective or ineffective handling of an administrative situation.

rising imports (see *Exhibits* 3 and 7). Developing countries complained that their economic and social development suffered, because industrialized countries were using the MFA to protect their uncompetitive industries. With little more than three months to go, the participants still disagreed on the MFA's basic objectives. Some developed and developing countries openly questioned whether their interests might not be better served by allowing the agreement to expire and taking their chances in the free-for-all that might result.

The United States, however, was concerned about the potential collapse of the MFA. For the previous 25 years, the United States had played a critical role in organizing global textile trade. Officials of the U.S. Trade Representative's Office, the State Department, and the Treasury feared that the collapse of the Multi-Fiber Arrangement could lead to an outbreak of protectionism by Europe against the Third World. Since President Reagan was promoting freer world trade, this was a disturbing prospect. Furthermore, American textile and apparel firms and unions were pressuring the U.S. government for greater restrictions. If the MFA fell apart, it would be harder for the Reagan administration to fend off protectionist pressures.

EVOLUTION OF THE MFA

The long history of protectionism in the textile and apparel industry stemmed from its critical role in the industrial performance and economic development of all nations. Textile and apparel was a fragmented, labor-intensive industry that produced yarn, fabric, and clothes. Its low capital and skill requirements, together with widely available standard technologies, suited many countries in the early stages of industrialization. Britain built its industrial base on textiles in the 19th century, the United States and European nations dominated the industry through the middle of the 20th century, and

developing countries emerged as strong international competitors in the late 1950s. As the volume and value of textile trade rose, the industry took on global dimensions.

By the end of the 1970s, textile and apparel provided 25 million jobs worldwide. In developing countries, the average share of manufacturing employment in textiles and apparel was 30%, and in some developing countries the percentage was 50% or higher (see *Table A*). For the industrial nations, textile and apparel provided 14% of manufacturing employment: American firms employed 2.1 million

TABLE A		

VALUE ADDED IN THE TEXTILE AND CLOTHIING INDUSTRIES BY SELECTED COUNTRIES, 1975

Category and signatory	Value added in textiles and clothing[a] ($ millions)	Percent of total manufacturing
Low-income countries		
India	2,484.0	30
Pakistan	704.0	43
Middle-income countries		
Egypt	561.3	34
South Korea	812.4	24
Mexico	1,628.6	14
Brazil	1.731.2	10
Yugoslavia	836.5	14
Hong Kong	1,026.1	98
Greece	638.6	27
Industrialized countries		
Italy	4,129.2	13
United Kingdom	3,150.4	9
Japan	6,423.9	7
Netherlands	650.8	6
France	2,962.8	6
West Germany	5,535.0	7
United States	21,135.6	8

[a]1970 dollars.
Source: Comitextile, Bulletin 79/5–6, 1979.

workers in 1979, while EEC firms provided 2.5 million jobs. Since textiles and apparel were among the oldest industries in industrial countries, firms were often concentrated in declining regions. The industry employed many disadvantaged workers, including the elderly and minorities. Women who were second wage earners were also employed. As a result, textile workers had few alternative job opportunities and were difficult to retrain if they lost their jobs (see *Exhibit 10*).

The three major segments of the industry—fiber production, textiles, and apparel—varied in industrial structure and characteristics. The fiber industry, for example, comprised natural fiber producers, which tended to be small and fragmented, and synthetic fiber producers, which included such large firms as Du Pont. Textile firms were similarly diverse: large manufacturers such as Burlington Industries and J.P. Stevens were *Fortune 200* companies that produced various cloths and materials in modern, relatively capital-intensive plants; at the other end of the spectrum were hundreds of small specialty firms, frequently owned and operated by single families. Finally, the apparel segment of the industry was the most highly fragmented and the area of the strongest domestic and international competition. Barriers to entry for making most clothing were extremely low: with a few sewing machines, virtually anyone could assemble a pair of pants or a shirt. Since labor content was the critical cost component, the low wages of developing countries provided a major advantage (see *Exhibits 1, 2, 4, 5,* and *8*).

The emergence of low-cost competitors in the Third World led textile and apparel producers in the industrial nations to lobby hard for protectionism. Since their numbers were large and they were widely dispersed throughout the United States and Europe, textile firms and unions had traditionally wielded political clout. As early as the mid-1950s they were able to convince their governments to erect barriers to textile imports. The roots of the MFA itself went back to 1956, when American textile interests launched a fierce attack against Japanese textiles. Even though imports were barely 2% of U.S. consumption, the American government was under great pressure to help the industry after it organized boycotts, got protectionist bills introduced into Congress, and lobbied executive agencies for tariffs and quotas.

President Eisenhower, however, did not want to give the textile industry higher tariffs or quantitative restrictions. An increase in tariffs would undercut U.S. efforts to promote freer world trade, and the use of quantitative restrictions was forbidden under the GATT. Eisenhower therefore decided to negotiate a voluntary agreement with Japan, whereby the Japanese would restrict their *cotton* textile exports to the United States for five years in return for a promise of no further restrictive actions. This so-called voluntary export restraint (VER) was announced in January 1957 and provided the model for the next 25 years of textile and apparel protectionism.

One consequence of the VER was to encourage the migration of production facilities to other low-wage countries. Soon imports from other Asian countries, Hong Kong in particular, were more than filling the market position formerly occupied by the Japanese. Faced with a proliferation of new suppliers to the American market, the United States sought a more comprehensive arrangement to control the flow of imports. In 1959 the United States called for an investigation under the auspices of GATT. Use of the GATT forum would serve to legitimize any deviations from GATT rules. When the conference convened in June 1961, the United States told the developing countries that they had two choices: face unilaterally imposed restraints by the industrialized countries or negotiate a market sharing arrangement. Under the circumstances, the developing countries had little choice. Sixteen countries signed an agreement called the Short-Term Agreement, and within one year, negotiations for a Long-Term Agreement Regarding International Trade in Cotton Textiles (LTA) were concluded.

The LTA was supposed to last five years and provide developing countries with 5% annual growth in the volume of their exports. When the LTA was extended in 1967 and 1970, dissatisfied exporters searched for ways to minimize the LTA's effects. Since the LTA restricted only *cotton* textiles—defined as 50% or more cotton by weight—countries such as Japan, Taiwan, Korea, and Hong Kong found that they could mix other fibers with cotton and increase their exports. As a result, American imports of man-made fiber products soared in the late 1960s (see *Exhibit 9*).

Textile industrialists and unions responded to the increased competition by demanding a replacement for the LTA—one that would cover all fibers. In 1971 the United States obtained a three-year bilateral agreement with Japan covering wool and synthetic textiles; and similar five-year agreements with Hong Kong, Taiwan, and Korea. Once these multifiber bilateral agreements were in place, the stage was set for a multilateral multifiber agreement. The Europeans wanted more protectionism because East Asian countries started directing their exports to Europe. The East Asian suppliers wanted an agreement to ensure against losing their market share to unrestricted countries. And the Japanese, once the champions of freer textile trade, found themselves more amenable to an international accord. In a period of two to three years, Japan had gone from the world's largest exporter of textiles to a major importer. Higher Japanese wages and revaluation of the yen in 1971 made Japanese goods uncompetitive with textiles from less developed nations.

In 1974 the first Multi-Fiber Arrangement was signed (see *Appendix 1*). Like the LTA, the MFA was designed as a global framework within which countries could negotiate separate bilateral agreements. The MFA promised devel-

oping countries 6% annual growth in the volume of their exports and considerable flexibility for filling their quotas. To tailor protectionism to their particular needs, however, industrial countries preferred to negotiate bilateral deals with the developing countries.

TEXTILE TRADE UNDER THE MFA
The EEC

Textiles and apparel had long been declining in the United States and Europe. Low income, elasticity of demand, strong foreign competition, and low levels of investment contributed to the demise of this low value-added industrial sector. Furthermore, several technical innovations in the industry had been adopted by late-entering developing countries, while the majority of European and American producers delayed making technical improvements. The supposed purpose of the MFA was to control the growth of developing countries' imports in order to phase out slowly the uncompetitive portion of the industrial countries' industries. If the market had grown 3 to 4% a year, and the developing countries had increased their share about 6% a year, then it might have been possible for an orderly decline. But within months of signing the first MFA, these assumptions had been undermined. The quadrupling of oil prices and a global recession with rising unemployment made most of the industrial governments unhappy with the MFA.

The EEC, in particular, was hard hit. Employment declined 4% annually as imports of textiles and apparel increased from 21% of the market to 44% between 1973 and 1980. Part of the problem was that the European Community had moved slowly to negotiate comprehensive bilateral agreements during the first three years of the MFA. A tradition of encouraging trade with former colonies and close ties with certain textile exporters constrained the formulation of EEC trade policy. In addition, it was difficult finding a consensus with 10 sovereign nations. Strong protectionist pressure emerged from Britain, Belgium, and France, while Germany, Holland, and Denmark pleaded for more liberal trade. For example, the Belgian government viewed protectionism as the only way to stem massive unemployment. Between 1973 and 1978, Belgium lost 32% of its clothing employment (28,000 workers). Since the industry was concentrated in slow-growth Flemish provinces, only one-third of those unemployed workers were able to find jobs. Germany, by contrast, willingly advocated free trade despite industry losses. German textile and apparel manufacturers suffered dearly after 1973, forcing the lay-off or firing of 215,000 workers. Yet by 1978, only 28,500 former textile and apparel workers were registered as unemployed, compared with 13,000 in 1973.

Despite internal battles on textile policies, European governments agreed on stronger protectionist actions in 1976. By 1977, the EEC had negotiated 22 bilaterals with major suppliers—bilaterals that were far more restrictive than allowed by the MFA. Previously, the EEC negotiated bilaterals on an ad hoc basis: each exporting country was treated individually and was allowed to negotiate the best possible deal. Under this new EEC system, called the globalization of bilateral agreements, a target for aggregate imports was set. Exporting countries were then told the size of the pie and that one nation's gain would be another's loss. Furthermore, flexibility provisions were tightened and growth rates for some categories were set as low as 0.5% annually.

When the MFA came up for renewal in 1977, the EEC sought to reconcile the restrictive provisions of its bilaterals with the MFA. The result was the insertion into the MFA of the *reasonable departures* clause:

The Committee agreed that, within the framework of the MFA, such (bilateral) consultations and negotiations should be conducted in a spirit of equity

and flexibility with a view to reaching a mutually acceptable solution . . . which does include the possibility of jointly agreed *reasonable departures* from particular elements in particular cases.

The outcome of the 1977 MFA renewal appeared to be a triumph for the EEC protectionists. But the MFA was only a framework for protection, and the EEC had no guarantee that restricting developing countries would help some of its member nations. The European Community had become the world's largest importer of textiles and clothing, buying about 45% of all imports consumed by the industrial nations and taking about 55% of those exported from the developing countries to the developed countries. Since trade among various EEC members amounted to $22 billion per year, and the United States was one of the largest external suppliers of textiles and apparel to Europe, only dramatic cuts in developing countries' imports would satisfy Britain, France, and others. (The Europeans had no leverage to negotiate a bilateral agreement with the United States, even though the United States was a larger exporter to the EEC than most developing countries. To try to stop the flood of American textiles into Europe, several European producers filed countervailing duty suits against U.S. imports of certain man-made fibers. The Europeans claimed that artificially low oil prices in the United States (before deregulation) subsidized the production of petroleum-based fibers.)

The European Community negotiated cuts in some bilateral agreements between 1977 and 1981. But to the chagrin of many of its members, the EEC found that tighter, more complex bilaterals were very difficult to implement. When the second MFA came up for renewal, the industry and protectionist countries pressed for several important changes in the MFA. A key demand was that growth levels be explicitly tied to the market growth in the importing country; a second demand called for distinctions to be made between the poorer developing countries and those that could be characterized as newly industrializing, such as Hong Kong, Singapore, and Korea. This proposal was a major departure from previous practice. Under the LTA and the first MFA, all developing countries were supposed to be treated equally. However, strong divisions remained among the EEC members even after official renewal discussions had begun within GATT. The EEC negotiators arrived with only a partial mandate, and their actions were subject to veto by the Council of Ministers.

Developing Countries

The EEC did not present an official position at the first GATT meetings, but its preliminary suggestions drew heavy fire from the developing countries' delegates. The developing countries viewed the outcome of the MFA negotiations as vitally important, and for the first time they formed a common negotiating position before discussions with the industrialized nations. In an official statement issued before the negotiations, the developing countries:[1]

. . . expressed their concern that the commitment of developed importing countries to liberalize world trade in textiles and clothing remains unfulfilled. Furthermore, the restrictive nature of the regime under the MFA has been aggravated by the unrestrained trade among developed countries, which they contend grossly discriminates against developing countries. Moreover, while developed countries severely restrained textiles and clothing imports from developing countries, they continued to expand substantially their exports to developing countries not only of textile machinery, chemicals, fibers, and related products, but also of nontextile products that affect the overall trade balance.

The participants reiterated that, for more than

two decades, developing countries that export have faced an increasingly discriminatory and restrictive regime that has derogated the normal rules and practices of the General Agreement on Tariffs and Trade. This policy regime has been renewed repeatedly and expanded in scope despite the original and specific understanding that it would be temporary. The perpetuation of this derogatory system was held to be unacceptable to developing countries. World trade in textiles and clothing must be liberalized in real terms by means of a gradual return to free trade in conformity with normal GATT rules and practices.

Despite this show of unity, no one was certain how long the common stance would last. The developing countries possessed diverse industrial capabilities, and a new MFA would have differential effects. Countries such as Hong Kong, Taiwan, Korea, and Singapore, which possessed highly competitive industries across a broad range of products, favored freer trade. Other countries, such as India, were competitive in a selected number of products but were not opposed to all protectionism. India and several other nations benefited from restrictions that locked low-wage countries out of the market. Finally, there was a group of countries with minute quotas such as Sri Lanka, which were competitive in low-quality products. These nations might benefit if tougher restrictions were placed on the more competitive countries such as Hong Kong. (Sri Lanka's situation was particularly ironic. The developed countries had financed the establishment of a textile and apparel industry in Sri Lanka through the World Bank. However, the fledgling industry was soon threatened by import restrictions instituted by its benefactors.)

Traditionally, developing countries had accepted some trade limitations to ensure access to the developing countries' markets. But the recent push by importing nations to discriminate among exporters and cut back the quotas of the largest textile producers seemed unusually threatening. All the developing coun-

---

[1]Meeting of twenty-two developing textiles exporting countries in Bogotá, Colombia, November 3–7, 1980.

tries felt that the restriction of their major exports was short-sighted. They contended that without foreign exchange earnings from textiles they were forced to make heavier credit demands on international banks. In addition, trade officials in Hong Kong, Taiwan, and Korea (known as the Big Three in textile circles) increasingly spoke out against the trends toward greater restrictions. They saw little to be gained if the MFA was renewed on EEC terms. Hong Kong, for example, decried the "unfair, false and pious arguments" used to justify trade restrictions solely against the developing countries. They said European statements such as "imports from the U.S. and other industrialized countries wouldn't be affected [by the new MFA] because those countries had comparable wage costs in living standards" were a betrayal of the principles of comparative advantage and most-favored nation. One textile official noted, "The developing countries accepted the MFA in exchange for very explicit guarantees in respect to their rights of access. They didn't accept the MFA as a gift for the major importing nations."

The United States

With the Europeans and the developing countries so far apart, the United States held the key to the future of the Multi-Fiber Arrangement. Yet the United States, like the EEC, was having difficulty reaching an internal consensus. The formation of U.S. trade policy had many similarities to the formation of trade policy within the EEC. Although the United States did not have to contend with sovereign governments, there had always been tension on trade issues within the executive branch and between the executive and legislative branches. On the one hand, the president, the State Department, the U.S. Trade Representative's Office, and the Treasury usually promoted free trade; on the other hand, the Commerce and Labor Departments, allied with Congress, usually defended the industry's protectionist position. Since the executive branch relied on the legislature for its authority to negotiate trade agreements, U.S. trade policy often reflected "horse-trading" between the two branches.

During the 1960s and early 1970s, the protectionist elements within the government were relatively successful influencing policy. As a result, the U.S. industry fared better in the mid-1970s than its European counterparts. Imports' share of the U.S. market was only 50% of the European level. Although American textile and apparel markets were hurt by the 1974–1975 recession, the added protection cushioned U.S. producers from import competition. Some segments of the American industry still worried about imports, but little sympathy was expressed for greater restrictions at high levels in the U.S. government. When the first MFA came up for renewal in 1977, the United States would have been happy with a simple extension. In the end, it agreed to European demands for the reasonable departures clause, because it felt that was the only way to keep the Europeans within the MFA guidelines.

The United States, however, did not take immediate advantage of the reasonable departures clause. The more liberal elements of the bureaucracy seemed to be in control. But in 1978, protectionist pressure came to the fore again when Congress passed legislation preventing reductions in tariffs on textiles and textile products during the Tokyo Round of GATT talks. President Carter vetoed the bill because some reductions were thought to be critical to the success of the negotiations. Yet to mollify Congress, Carter had to promise more help for the industry in meeting import competition. A program, known as the textile White Paper, was put together in time for congressional approval of the Tokyo Round. The White Paper assured better enforcement of the existing protectionism, and included a *snapback clause*, which promised that tariff reductions on textiles made during the Tokyo Round would be reversed if the MFA was not renewed, in some form, in 1981.

To fulfill its promises to Congress, the Carter administration started to use the reasonable departures clause of the 1977 MFA to tighten restrictions against Hong Kong, Taiwan, and Korea. However, the Carter administration resisted industry pressure to link aggregate import growth rates to the rate of growth in the domestic market or to globalize U.S. quotas.

Disappointed by Carter's program, the textile industry thought it found a more receptive ear in presidential candidate Ronald Reagan. During his 1980 campaign, Reagan sent a letter to Senator Strom Thurmond of South Carolina noting that "the MFA expires at the end of 1981 and needs to be strengthened by relating import growth from all sources to domestic market growth. I shall work to achieve this goal." Reagan's promise to change textile policy helped him garner the support of congressional textile interests (sometimes known as boll weevils) and win votes in the South.

Once in office, though, the new president committed his administration to freer world trade as one of the pillars of American foreign policy. In a speech to the International Monetary Fund (IMF) and the World Bank in September 1981, the president reaffirmed the "magic of the marketplace" and that the U.S. "government is committed to policies of free trade, unrestricted investment, and open capital markets." The president stressed that Third World nations could benefit by lifting themselves up through their own exports, and this could be achieved only through freer trade. Finally, the president acknowledged that aid had a role in helping the developing countries diversify their economies. Toward this end, he committed the United States to a sizable foreign aid package.

Reagan's free trade proclamations left textile policy in disarray. The industry and the congressional boll weevils felt betrayed. Intent upon a more restrictive MFA, they looked for legislation that could be blocked, forcing Reagan to support a more protectionist stance. Within the bureaucracy, Commerce and Labor also wanted the MFA tightened, while State, Treasury, and the U.S. Trade Representative's Office favored renewing the existing MFA or liberalizing it further. The bureaucrats handling textile policy were so divided in September 1981 that they couldn't present an official position. The final decision was up to the president: he would have to decide how to reconcile his free trade proclamations and his prescriptions for developing countries with congressional pressure for protectionism and the European Community's demands.

EXHIBIT ONE

BALANCE OF TRADE: NON-OIL LDCs, 1979

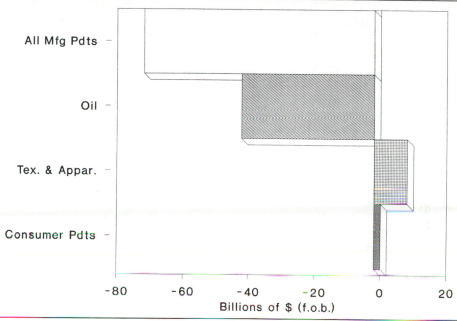

Source: IMF, World Economic Outlook 1984.

EXHIBIT TWO

1980 U.S. EXPORTS AND IMPORTS, AGGREGATE AND DEVELOPING COUNTRIES INCLUDING OPEC ($ millions)

	Aggregate			With developing countries		
	Exports	**Imports**	**Balance**	**Exports**	**Imports**	**Balance**
Total	$220,782	$244,871	$(24,089)	$81,125	$117,026	$(35,901)
Selected end-use categories:						
Food, feeds, beverages	35,310	18,100	17,210	13,635	10,678	2,957
Industrial supplies and materials including	70,527	127,061	(56,534)	22,821	77,420	(54,599)
fuel, lubricants	8,775	79,922	(71,147)	1,663	67,086	(65,423)
Capital goods	75,651	3,681	41,970	31,613	7,081	24,532
Consumer goods	28,979	57,375	(28,396)	9,623	16,864	(7,241)
Textiles and clothing	4,840	9,480	(4,640)	1,657	6,485	(4,828)

Source: U.S. Department of Commerce, International Trade Administration, *Overseas Business Reports,* November 1982 (*OBR* 82-19).

EXHIBIT THREE

PRODUCTION, EMPLOYMENT, AND PRODUCTIVITY IN TEXTILES AND CLOTHING. EUROPEAN COMMUNITY, JAPAN, AND THE UNITED STATES, 1963–1978 (1973 = 100)

	1963	1973	1975	1977	1978
European Community					
Textiles:					
Production	61	100	88	94	92
Employment		100	89	84	81
Productivity		100	99	112	114
Clothing:					
Production	67	100	95	98	94
Employment		100	89	84	NA
Productivity		100	107	117	NA
Japan					
Textiles:					
Production	49	100	83	88	89
Employment		100	87	76	71
Productivity		100	95	116	125
Clothing:					
Production	49	100	83	88	89
Employment		100	107	107	105
Productivity		100	78	82	85
United States					
Textiles:					
Production	64	100	86	96	98
Employment[a]	88	100	89	97	97
Productivity		100	97	99	101
Clothing:					
Production	78	100	92	106	108
Employment[b]	89	100	91	94	93
Productivity		100	101	113	116

[a]For 1940, the index = 116; 1950 = 124; 1960 = 91.
[b]For 1940, the index = 65; 1950 = 84; 1960 = 86.
   Source: *Textile and Clothing Production and Trade Statistics,* 1973–79, Comitextile/W/63 (Geneva: GATT Secretariat, 1970, Tables 1 and 2).

EXHIBIT FOUR

TEXTILE SPINNING AND WEAVING: AVERAGE HOURLY LABOR COSTS, SELECTED COUNTRIES

	Hourly labor cost, 1981[a]	Index U.S. = 100
United States	$7.03	100
Japan	4.90	70
Mexico	3.06	44
Brazil (São Paulo)	2.39	34
Hong Kong	1.42	20
South Korea	1.35	19
Taiwan	1.32	19
India	0.69	10
Philippines	0.43	6
Thailand	0.34	5
Sri Lanka	0.16	2
1979:		
West Germany		149
Italy		119
France		113
United Kingdom		76

[a]Includes wages and fringe costs such as paid holidays, vacation, unemployment insurance, old-age insurance, and workmen's compensation in U.S. dollars.

Source: U.S. International Trade Commission, *Emerging Textile-Exporting Countries,* Washington, D.C., 1982.

EXHIBIT FIVE

MANUFACTURING COST COMPARISON: MAN'S SPORT SHIRT, DESIGNED TO RETAIL AT $12.00 (one dozen)

	United States	Hong Kong	Thailand
Material cost[a]	$30.00	$30.00	$30.00
Direct labor hours	3.5	5.0	6.0
Payroll cost (including fringe benefits)	22.75	7.10	2.04
Manufacturing overhead (20% of payroll cost)	4.55	1.42	.40
Total manufacturing cost	57.30	38.52	32.44
Overhead and profit (25% of total manufacturing cost)	14.32	9.63	8.11
Tariff (21% ad valorem)		10.11	8.52
Freight		3.65	3.28
Other importing costs		1.00	1.00
Total cost	$71.62	$62.91	$53.35

[a]Fabric content 50% cotton and 50% polyester.

Source: U.S. International Trade Commission, *Emerging Textile-Exporting Countries,* Washington, D.C., 1982.

EXPORTS OF TEXTILES AND CLOTHING BY AREA OR COUNTRY, 1979 ($ billion)

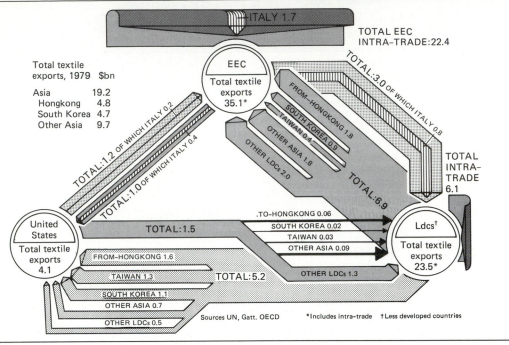

Total textile
exports, 1979 $bn

Asia   19.2
  Hongkong   4.8
  South Korea   4.7
  Other Asia   9.7

Sources UN, Gatt. OECD   *Includes intra-trade   †Less developed countries

Source: The Economist, December 12, 1981. © The Economist Newspaper Limited. Reprinted by permission.

NET TRADE IN TEXTILES AND CLOTHING IN SELECTED COUNTRIES, 1973 AND 1980 (% billion)

	Textiles		Clothing		Total	
	1973	1980	1973	1980	1973	1980
Industrialized countries						
European community (10)	2.02	0.44	(0.85)	(5.74)	1.17	(4.66)
France	0.29	(0.69)	0.45	(0.33)	0.74	(1.02)
West Germany	0.30	(0.56)	(1.63)	(5.46)	(1.33)	(6.02)
Italy	0.62	1.50	1.11	3.83	1.73	5.33
Netherlands	0.19	0.01	(0.45)	(2.01)	(0.26)	(2.00)
United Kingdom	0.19	(0.44)	(0.38)	(0.98)	(0.19)	(1.42)
United States	(0.36)[a]	1.08	(1.88)[a]	(5.72)	(2.24)[a]	(4.64)
Japan	1.32	3.45	(0.20)	(1.03)	1.12	2.42
Middle-income countries						
Yugoslavia	(0.05)	0.04	0.13	0.43	0.08	0.47
Egypt	0.14	0.21	0.03	0.02	0.17	0.23
Hong Kong	(0.48)	(2.06)	1.27	3.95	0.79	1.89
South Korea	0.14	1.79	0.74	2.94	0.88	4.73
Brazil	0.16	0.57	0.08	0.13	0.24	0.70
Mexico	0.09	0.11	0.01	(0.18)	0.10	(0.07)
Low-income countries						
India	0.68	0.92[b]	0.10	0.54[b]	0.78	1.46[b]
Pakistan	0.41	0.68	0.02	0.10	0.43	0.78
Indonesia	(0.17)	(0.17)	0.00	0.10	(0.17)	(0.07)
Colombia	0.04	0.07	0.02	0.11	0.06	0.18
Sri Lanka	. . .	(0.13)	. . .	0.11	. . .	(0.02)

[a] Imports f.o.b.
[b] 1979 data.
Source: GATT, *International Trade,* 1981/82, Table A-10, Geneva.

WORLD PRODUCTION AND TRADE OF TEXTILES AND CLOTHING

World production by areas, 1963–1981 (annual compound growth rate)

	Textiles		Clothing	
	1963–1973	1973–1981	1963–1973	1973–1981
World	5.0%	1.0%	4.0%	1.5%
Industrial countries	4.5	(1.0)	2.0	(0.5)
EEC	2.0	(1.5)	1.5	(1.5)
United States	4.5	(0.5)	2.5	0.5
Japan	7.5	(1.5)	7.5	(2.5)
Developing countries[a]	4.5	. . .	5.5	
Centrally planned economies	6.0	4.0	7.0	5.0

World trade ($ billions and annual compound growth rate)

	Exports ($ billion)			Compound growth rate	
	1963	1973	1981	1963–1973	1973–1981
World	$8.73	$35.94[b]	$94.50[b]	15.2%	12.8%
Industrial countries	6.82	25.11	63.75	13.9	12.4
EEC	4.36	16.12	53.93[c]	14.0	9.8
United States	0.58	1.51	4.87	10.0	15.8
Japan	1.10	2.82	6.43	9.9	10.9
Developing countries[a]	1.34	7.87	26.05[d]	19.4	16.1
Centrally planned economies	0.57	3.53	9.45[d]	20.0	13.1

[a]Excludes OPEC countries.
[b]Estimate.
[c]EEC exports include intra-EEC trade.
[d]1980.
Source: GATT, *International Trade,* 978, 1980/81, Geneva.

UNITED STATES IMPORTS OF TEXTILES AND APPAREL, 1961–1980

[$ Millions and Square Yard Equivalents (SYE)]

	Cotton		Synthetic		Wool		Total three-fiber only	
	$	SYE	$	SYE	$	SYE	$	SYE
1961	199	720	60	151	200	85	459	956
1965	369	1,312	193	566	357	212	919	2,090
1970	537	1,536	1,053	2,760	359	170	1,949	4,466
1975	1,000	1,281	1,773	2,470	340	78	3,133	3,829
1980	2,839	2,009	3,409	2,746	941	129	7,189[a]	4,884

[a]This figure is lower than the total imports in Exhibit 2 because of classification differences.
Source: U.S. Department of Commerce.

EXHIBIT TEN

U.S. TEXTILE AND APPAREL INDUSTRY DEMOGRAPHICS, 1980
Textile Plant Location

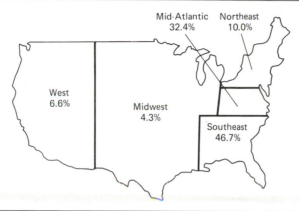

Work force characteristics, %	Textiles		Apparel	Manufacturing
Semiskilled	67%		78%	NA
Women	48		80	31%
Minorities		28[a]		18

[a]Average of textile and apparel, separate data not available.
Source: America's Textiles, August 1982. Illustration reprinted by permission.

EXCERPTS FROM ARRANGEMENT REGARDING INTERNATIONAL TRADE IN TEXTILES (MFA)

Preamble *Recognizing* the great importance of production and trade in textile products . . . and their particular importance for the economic and social development of developing countries and for the expansion and diversification of their export earnings. . . . *Desiring* within a multilateral framework . . .

Source: General Agreement on Tariffs and Trade.

to promote on a sound basis the development of production and expansion of trade in textile products. . . . *Recognizing* that, in pursuit of such action . . . the fullest account [should be] taken of . . . economic and social problems . . . in both importing and exporting countries . . . that such action should be designed to facilitate economic expansion and to promote the development of developing countries . . . by providing larger opportunities . . . to increase their exchange earnings. . . . THE PARTIES TO THIS ARRANGEMENT have agreed as follows:

Article 1 It may be desirable during the next few years for special practical measures . . . to achieve the expansion of trade . . . ensuring the orderly and equitable development of this trade and avoidance of disruptive effects in individual markets. . . .

Article 3 . . . If, in the opinion of any participating importing country, its market . . . is being disrupted by imports . . . it shall seek consultations with the participating exporting country. . . . If, after a period of sixty days . . . there has been no agreement . . . the requesting participating country may decline to accept imports. . . .

Article 4 . . . participating countries may . . . conclude bilateral agreements on mutually acceptable terms . . . to eliminate real risks of market disruption . . . in importing countries and disruption to the textile trade of exporting countries. . . . Bilateral agreements . . . shall, on overall terms, including base levels and growth rates, be more liberal than measures provided for in this Agreement. [Six percent per annum real growth per Annex B] . . . and shall include provisions assuring substantial flexibility.

Article 6 . . . it shall be considered appropriate . . . to provide more favourable terms . . .

for developing countries . . . however, there should be no undue prejudice to the interests of established suppliers or serious distortions in existing patterns of trade. . . .

Article 12 . . . the expression "textiles" is limited to tops, yarns, piece-goods, man-made articles . . . of cotton, wool, man-made fibers, or blends thereof. . . . This Arrangement shall not apply to developing country exports of handloom fabrics of the cottage industry . . . or to traditional folklore handicraft textile products. . . .

Annex A . . . a situation of "market disruption" . . . shall be determined on the basis of examination of the appropriate factors . . . such as: turnover, market share, profits, export performance, employment. . . . The factors causing market disruption . . . which generally appear in combination are as follows: (i) a sharp and substantial increase or imminent increase of imports. . . . (ii) these products are offered at prices which are substantially below those prevailing for similar goods of comparable quality in the [importing] market. . . .

Note on Free Trade and Protectionism

THE UPS AND DOWNS OF WORLD TRADE

The international trading system underwent a revolution at the close of World War II. Trade barriers were progressively lowered, institutions such as the General Agreement on Tariffs and Trade (GATT) were set up to promote trade and investment, and the volume of international transactions expanded at unprecedented rates. While the volume of international commerce had grown by only 0.5% per year between 1913 and 1948, it leaped to an annual growth rate of 7% from 1948 to 1973. Global exports and imports far outpaced the growth of production of goods and services in the world economy. Moreover, trade became an increasingly important component of gross national products. From 1950 to 1980 the arithmetic sum of imports and exports rose from 8.4% of U.S. GNP to 21.1%, from 25.4% to 57.3% for Ger-

many, and from 20.1% to 31.2% for Japan. The resulting interdependence created by this monumental shift in the world economy led many to believe that continued expansion of free trade was inevitable; too much seemed at stake to change the tide.

In the late 1970s, however, optimism turned to pessimism. An article in the *Wall Street Journal* on April 14, 1978, reflected this concern:

After three decades of immense increase in world trade and living standards, exports and imports are causing trade pressures in nearly every nation and among the best of allies. The U.S. sets price floors against Japanese steel, Europe accuses the U.S. of undercutting its paper makers, the Japanese decry cheap textiles from South Korea, French farmers have smashed truckloads of Italian wine, and AFL-CIO President George Meany rattles exporters worldwide by calling free trade "a joke."

Rather than the 1980s heralding an era of liberal trade, new and dangerous forms of protectionism seemed to be supplanting the more traditional barriers of tariffs and quotas. As the growth of international commerce slowed in the early 1980s, many questioned the future of free trade.

Assistant Professor David B. Yoffie prepared this note with the assistance of Research Associate Jane Kenney Austin, as a basis for class discussion.

THE POSTWAR POLITICS OF INTERNATIONAL TRADE

The progress toward freer international trade was slow and arduous after World War II. The 1930s had left the world with a legacy of protectionism that continued to plague international commerce through the late 1950s. Most industrial nations abolished quantitative restrictions within a decade or so after World War II, but tariffs remained quite high. And despite five attempts to reduce tariff barriers under the aegis of the General Agreement on Tariffs and Trade, success was very limited. Part of the problem was protectionist legislation in the United States. Since the 1930s American trade laws allowed tariff reductions, but only on a product-by-product basis. In addition, American industries could petition the U.S. government for higher trade barriers. If imports increased faster than domestic sales, or if any industry was considered important to national security, the president was obliged to increase tariffs or erect quotas. All of this changed in 1962 when the U.S. Congress passed the Trade Expansion Act. On the request of President Kennedy, the Congress allowed the executive branch to use a linear method of tariff cuts. Under this method, U.S. negotiators could reduce *all* tariffs by the prescribed percentage if they could bargain for reciprocal reductions by other governments. Furthermore, the Trade Expansion Act made it more difficult for U.S. firms to get protection. After 1962 industries would have to prove that imports were a cause of declining domestic production. Once this was done, the government did not have to raise tariffs; it could give aid in the form of subsidies, tax benefits, or extended unemployment compensation.

The Americans used their new powers to launch a bold attack on trade barriers under the auspices of the GATT. This so-called "Kennedy Round" of negotiations lasted from 1963 to 1967 and was a resounding success. Duties on two-thirds of the industrial countries' products were cut by 50% or more. The average tariff reductions on manufactures were about 33%. Yet the process of international negotiations was not easy; the Europeans resisted many American initiatives. Since the structure of American tariffs had more peaks and valleys than European duties, a linear tariff reduction would have the greatest impact on Europe. Moreover, there were several crises over agricultural policy when the Europeans refused to abandon their restrictive practices.[1] The EEC finally compromised, but many of its tariff and nontariff barriers remained in place.

The immediate impact of the Kennedy Round tariffs cut was an explosion in international trade. In only four years, from 1969 to 1973, world exports more than doubled. The secondary effect, however, was a resurgence in protectionism. As world trade multiplied, more and more industrial countries had problems adapting to the rapid increase in import competition. Some countries found that trade liberalization entailed considerable expense, such as retraining labor in import-competing sectors. In addition, a new variety of competitors emerged in the late 1960s—the newly industrializing countries. Nations such as Korea, Hong Kong, and Brazil started expanding their share of world manufactures at the same time that many global industries were experiencing worldwide surplus capacity. The result was that European and American firms in steel, textiles, shipbuilding, and other sectors lobbied their governments for protection. Free trade was supposed to rationalize these sectors by putting the least efficient out of business, but few countries wanted to bear the burden of adjustment.

The dilemma faced by industrial nations was that traditional protectionist devices were no longer available to address these problems. The General Agreement on Tariffs and Trade restricted its members from employing the most common barriers to trade in manufactured products. The GATT allowed an importer to impose countervailing duties if an exporter was subsidizing its goods; and the GATT sanctioned special duties if an importer could prove that another country was dumping its exports (i.e., selling below costs or below home-market value adjusted for freight and insurance). But neither of these measures would help industries confronted with more competitive foreign firms. Quotas, the most restrictive trade barriers, were only permissible under the GATT for developing countries and for advanced nations with severe balance of payments problems. And tariffs, the most widely used barrier before World War II, could only be employed under GATT Article XIX. Yet this provision of the General Agreement was so restrictive that it was rarely invoked. Article XIX required a nation to consult with other GATT members before raising tariffs and to provide affected countries with some form of tariff compensation. If tariff compensation was not provided, GATT sanctioned tariff retaliation by the affected nations.

Since countries did not want to violate the GATT, they had to find other ways to deal with unwanted competition. Their answer was to develop new forms of protectionism that were specifically designed to circumvent international rules. Instead of using tariffs and quotas to block free trade, governments found that less visible policies, such as voluntary export restraints (bilaterally negotiated quotas), public subsidies, and nationalistic procurement policies, could be equally effective in stemming imports. By the mid-1970s it became hard to distinguish national industrial policies from protectionism.

It was in this atmosphere that countries decided to launch a new round of GATT talks. The Tokyo Round, also called the Multilateral Trade Negotiations (MTN), formally began un-

der American sponsorship in 1973 and continued until 1979. Its purpose was to eliminate tariffs as a constraint to international trade and attempt to engage the problem of nontariff barriers. On the one hand, the goals of the MTN were more ambitious than all previous GATT talks; but on the other hand, most countries sought to use the MTN for classical mercantilist ends. Participants seemed interested in trade surpluses rather than a Ricardian world of maximum aggregate welfare.[2]

The outcome of the Tokyo Round reflected this diversity of goals. Six years of negotiations produced the desired reductions in tariffs but left many ambiguities in the treatment of nontariff barriers. All major industrial countries agreed that between January 1, 1980, and January 1, 1987, they would reduce the weighted average tariff rate from 7% to 4.67% on manufactured goods. On all other areas of the agreement, however, there was no simple arithmetic measure of success. Codes on subsidies, countervailing duties, technical barriers to trade, import licensing, and antidumping were subject to interpretation. A committee of signatories was to monitor the implementation, but every provision could be interpreted in liberal or restrictive ways.

In many ways the MTN was a great success. Significant strides were made to limit the impact of nontariff barriers. Never before had they even been systematically discussed at the international level. In addition, tariffs were cut by almost one-third and some special preferences were legitimized for developing countries. Yet the vague, nonbinding language of the final product left many questions for the 1980s. Some policymakers, business executives, and labor leaders started to ponder the future durability of free trade; others even wondered about its desirability. Many questioned if the assumptions of the liberal, Ricardian world were outmoded in a world where national industrial policies, state-owned enterprises, and multinational corporations were overshadowing the free market.

THE DEBATE OVER PROTECTIONISM

Arguments in favor of protectionism date back hundreds of years. During the fifteenth century, mercantilists supported protectionism as a means of raising revenue, building surpluses of gold or precious metals, and protecting domestic industries against the predatory practices of foreigners. Since that time challenges to free trade have proliferated. Some have based their defense of protectionism on purely economic grounds; others have claimed protectionism to be appropriate for social or political reasons. Whatever the rationale, protectionism has had a growing appeal since the early 1970s. Six of the most widely discussed reasons for protectionism are outlined below.

National Security

One of the most politically persuasive arguments for protectionism is that trade barriers may be necessary to protect national security. According to this line of reasoning, any country that wishes to be a major world power must maintain certain key sectors. If a nation does not have a steel industry, armament industry, and dozens of others considered to be strategic, then that country could be vulnerable in time of war.

Unfair Competition

Another politically popular position is that low wages in foreign countries constitute unfair competition. Labor-intensive industries in more developed countries have tended to be the most vocal exponents of this view. The president of the American Textile Manufacturers Institute (ATMI), for example, argued that:

If the items entering this country in such volumes were better designed or more attractive, more du-

rable or more efficiently produced, we would have little reason to object. But the vast majority of imports sell here primarily because they are cheaper; and they are cheaper for one reason only—they are made at wages and under working conditions that would be illegal and intolerable in this country.

The ATMI president contended that: "No nation can long endure the type of trend of low-wage import penetration which is assaulting the textile industry. And no nation that wants to preserve such a vital asset as this . . . should be expected to permit the import situation to get so out of hand."

Low wages, however, are only one type of unfair competition noted by advocates of protectionism. The theory of comparative advantage and subsequent refinements assumed perfect competition, free mobility of capital and labor, and ample time for markets to adjust. If the marketplace was allowed to "rationalize" production, all countries would benefit by comparative specialization. Yet in the world of the 1980s, rarely has the marketplace been allowed to operate fully. Countries with industrial policies have been able to mold comparative advantage through public policies such as special tax incentives, subsidies, and selected protection. The use of industrial policies has led many business and labor leaders to proclaim the irrelevance of Ricardian comparative advantage. The CEO of Motorola, for instance, charged that as long as Japan's government gave its firms preferential loans, subsidies for R&D, freedom to collude, and so forth, it was impossible for a single American company to compete. Thus, if only some countries play by the rules of free markets while others do not, firms in the free market economy will be at an unfair disadvantage.

Multinational Investment and Intrafirm Advantage

A third political argument in favor of trade barriers is that the growth of multinational corporate investment created a network of international trade never foreseen by Adam Smith or David Ricardo. Large corporations, with branches all over the world, have increasingly organized their production and marketing on a worldwide basis. The result, according to critics, has been that a large percentage of world trade has not been conducted on the basis of comparative advantage. Rather, trade has become a product of intrafirm transactions. No one has been able to calculate the precise figure for intrafirm trade, but as much as 25% of world trade in the early 1980s may have been between corporate subsidiaries. The United States has been the only country systematically collecting data on intrafirm trade. On the basis of that data, one scholar estimated that 48% of all U.S. imports in 1977 originated with a seller that was related by ownership to the buyer.

Labor unions, in particular, have argued that the spread of multinational investment and intrafirm trade has been a major cause of unemployment. Countries like the United States should therefore require multinationals to manufacture a large percentage of their production within the country. An official of the AFL-CIO stated the case succinctly:

The decision of executives of U.S.-based multinational . . . to export American job opportunities may be rational . . . in terms of the firm. But the interests of the U.S., as a nation, and of the American people, are not identical with the interests of the multinational firm . . . Free, competitive trade relations hardly exist any longer in this world of managed national economies, global technology-transfers, and the large-scale operations of foreign subsidiaries of U.S. companies.[3]

Infant Industry

While the above arguments have been reactions to problems in the international economy, the infant industry rationale has traditionally been a more positive approach to protectionism. Originally formulated by Alexander Ham-

ilton, the infant industry argument has been endorsed by some ardent supporters of free trade. John Stuart Mill, for example, a strong defender of Ricardian comparative advantage, wrote:

The only case in which, on mere principles of political economy, protecting duties can be defensible is when they are imposed temporarily (especially in a young and rising nation) in hopes of naturalizing a foreign industry, in itself perfectly suitable to circumstances of the country. The superiority of one country over another in a branch of production often arises only from having begun it sooner. . . . A protecting duty, continued for a reasonable time, will sometimes be the least inconvenient mode in which the nation can tax itself for the support of such an experiment.[4]

The persuasiveness of the infant industry argument led the United States to erect high tariff barriers in the nineteenth century. In the twentieth century most developing countries have defended their protectionist policies for infant industry reasons, and even advanced countries such as Japan have used the infant industry rationale for protecting high-tech industries in the 1980s.

Most economists, however, have been careful to limit the application of infant industry protection. J. S. Mill, himself, pointed out that "the protectionism should be confined to cases in which there is good ground of assurance that the industry which it fosters will after a time be able to dispense with it; nor should the domestic producers ever be allowed to expect that it will be continued to beyond the time necessary for a fair trial of what they are capable of accomplishing."[5]

Terms of Trade

A second positive reason for protection is that tariffs, under certain conditions, can improve a country's terms of trade. The terms of trade can be defined as the quantity of domestic goods that must be exported to receive an imported good. The terms of trade are favorable if a nation can sell few of its own goods while it receives a large quantity of imported goods; the terms of trade are unfavorable if a country must sell a large quantity of domestic production to buy a small quantity of imported products.

For tariffs to have desirable effects on the terms of trade, the importing country must be very large and the exported product must be very important to the producing country. If the exporter does not want to have its volume of shipments reduced by a tariff, the exporter will have to cut its price. Although this type of tariff does not afford protection to a domestic producer, it will improve a country's terms of trade by allowing the importing nation to purchase the foreign products at a cheaper price.

Income Distribution and Employment

A third positive approach to justifying protectionism relates to purely social goals. Through the use of tariffs and quotas, for example, a government can redistribute income within a country. Barriers to trade in a given product usually increase the domestic price of the product; domestic firms have little incentive to price their goods at world levels if they are sheltered from international competition. Higher prices will usually encourage more production for the protected product, which in turn increases the demand for labor. Higher demand for labor in the protected industry raises wage rates relative to other sectors in the economy, which thereby redistributes income.

A more frequently espoused social goal of protection is to maintain domestic employment and domestic living standards. Since aggregate income (GNP) is comprised of $C + I + G + X - M$, advocates of protection claim that a reduction in imports (M) will increase GNP and stimulate the domestic economy. This argument tends to be especially powerful when related to labor-intensive industries that employ workers who cannot be easily absorbed into other sectors of the economy. If a factory closes down in an isolated area, workers who are unable to relocate or are too old to retrain may never find new jobs. If imports cause this unemployment, protectionism is one way to preserve these jobs.

THE LIBERAL POLITICAL ECONOMIST DEFENSE

The above discussion of protectionism is by no means exhaustive. Almost every country and interest group has its own rationale for supporting the use of trade barriers. Some developing countries, for example, justify protection as a way to attract multinational investment and/or exclude unwanted cultural influences. Some developed countries claim that protectionism is the best way to bolster balance of payments and build industrial strength. A group of noted economists in Cambridge, England, for instance, believe that free trade strengthens the strong and weakens the weak forever. Trade barriers, they argue, are just as important for "senile" industries in Great Britain as they are for infant industries in developing nations.

Liberal political economists do not deny the rationality of protectionism in all instances. They believe that some exceptions to free trade are justified. The terms-of-trade argument is widely accepted as appropriate if a nation holds some monopoly power and wants to maximize domestic welfare at the expense of other countries. Similarly, the infant industry argument is viewed by many economists as a respectable prescription as long as the protectionism meets a number of conditions. For example, the domestic industry should have the management skills and technology necessary to become competitive on a world scale, the industry must be able to capture sufficient economies of scale to survive once the protection is removed, and the protection should not be so high as to encourage excessive expansion.

In general, however, liberal political economists argue that protectionism is a bad policy on both political and economic grounds. On the political side, they claim that protectionism, especially in large countries, tends to provoke retaliation by others. If this occurs, any short-run benefits derived from protection would be offset by a reduction in exports. The experience of the 1930s is the most frequently cited example of this phenomenon: the United States raised its average tariff levels and countries around the world retaliated. The net effect was a decline in global exports that severely aggravated the Great Depression. Political economists also point out that protectionism in democratic societies tends to be politically difficult to remove. Special interest groups that prosper behind trade barriers fight to maintain their privileged position. The history of textile protectionism in the United States is one of the most glaring instances of this problem. Begun in 1957 as a temporary measure, textile restrictions persisted into the 1980s.

Equally important to political economists are the efficiency problems associated with protectionism. While they argue that political and social objectives of a country should not be ignored, liberal economists claim that protectionism is usually the least efficient way to achieve these goals. The national defense arguments, for instance, made some sense in the days of protracted conventional warfare. In an era of thermonuclear power, however, a nation's ability to protect itself may no longer depend on steel mills. Although limited conflicts such as the Korean War remain possibilities, it seems unlikely that such wars would isolate a country from strategic materials.

In response to the "unfair" competition argument, most economists point out that wage advantages are no more unfair than the advantage of superior capital resources or sophisticated technology. Furthermore, the notion of unfair competition based on lower wages rejects the very principle of comparative advantage. Countries benefit from international trade by specializing in those products they make the best. This means that an importing country would be better off if workers in less productive sectors moved into more productive industries. If workers have difficulties finding those jobs, the government should provide retraining skills rather than protect inefficient producers.

Liberal economists also respond to arguments about the managed nature of world trade by noting that the market is usually the most efficient way to allocate resources. Multinational corporations will not remain profitable if intrafirm transactions do not reflect global comparative advantage. And even though some intrafirm trade by multinationals does export jobs, those same multinationals are often responsible for creating jobs that lead to exports.

Finally, national industrial policies are not viewed as a sound justification for protectionism, in part for efficiency reasons and in part because free trade, in the Ricardian sense, has always been a myth. Governments have always intervened in their economies, and they have always played a part in molding national comparative advantage. This makes drawing a line on many unfair trade policies extraordinarily difficult. It is clear why predatory pricing practices and subsidies devoted explicitly to exports might qualify as unfair. But if one nation has an investment tax credit for all industry, another nation has investment tax credits for selected industries, and a third directly subsidizes capital investment, which country has the unfair advantage?

While there is little agreement among liberal economists on what should be the appropriate response to a world of industrial policies, most concur that more protectionism would be a mistake. Some believe that countries without industrial policies should adopt their own national strategies; others claim that restrictions on the use of certain industrial policy tools would be a more efficient answer to these trade problems. In any case, they argue that protectionism can only aggravate the plight of the world economy. Increasing trade barriers would reduce the effectiveness of the market, hinder the adjustment of troubled industries, and lead the world back to the beggar-thy-neighbor policies of the 1930s.

NOTES

1. The Europeans remained steadfast on agricultural products because they feared that any major concessions would unravel the EEC's Common Agricultural Policy (CAP). CAP included such restrictive measures as high price supports and a variable levy that adjusted tariffs on imports daily.

2. Ricardian comparative advantage is discussed in "Kennedy and the Balance of Payments," HBS Case Services No. 9-383-073.

3. Nat Goldfinger, "A Labor View of Foreign Investment and Trade Issues," in *International Trade and Finance*, ed. Robert Baldwin and J.D. Richardson (Boston: Little, Brown & Co., 1974).

4. Miltiades Chacholiades, *International Trade Theory and Policy* (New York: McGraw-Hill, 1978), p. 526.

5. Ibid.

The Soviet Gas Pipeline

On June 18, 1982, President Ronald Reagan announced a new embargo on certain American exports. Henceforth, the United States would not allow any products of American overseas subsidiaries and foreign licensees of U.S. companies to be used in a $30 billion Soviet gas pipeline project. The restrictions would be retroactive: any firm that had already signed a contract would have to cancel.

European and Soviet officials and the American corporate executives affected by the embargo were stunned. None of these players were unaccustomed to American export controls, but the sweeping nature of these new restrictions was unprecedented in peacetime. There had been earlier controls, but all had been directed at American firms shipping their products from the United States. In 1978, for example, human

rights violations in the U.S.S.R. had prompted President Carter to restrict the sale of energy-related equipment and technology to the Soviet Union. In 1980, Carter had embargoed American grain exports to the Soviet Union because of the Soviet invasion of Afghanistan. And in December 1981, President Reagan widened the Carter administration restrictions on energy-related exports to the U.S.S.R. in response to Soviet activities in Poland. Now, however, by applying the new restrictions to American companies overseas and to foreign companies that licensed their technology from U.S. firms, President Reagan was extending jurisdiction further than ever before.

Reactions to the embargo were swift and angry. Many Europeans perceived the president's assertion of power over foreign companies as an infringement on national sovereignty. British Prime Minister Margaret Thatcher, considered a close ally of Reagan, was the first European leader to condemn the new restrictions. The governments of France, West Germany, and Italy soon joined Britain in urging companies to honor pipeline contracts in defiance of the United States. In Au-

This case was prepared by Research Assistant Sigrid Bergenstein and Assistant Professor David Yoffie, as the basis for class discussion rather than to illustrate either effective or ineffective handling of an administrative situation.

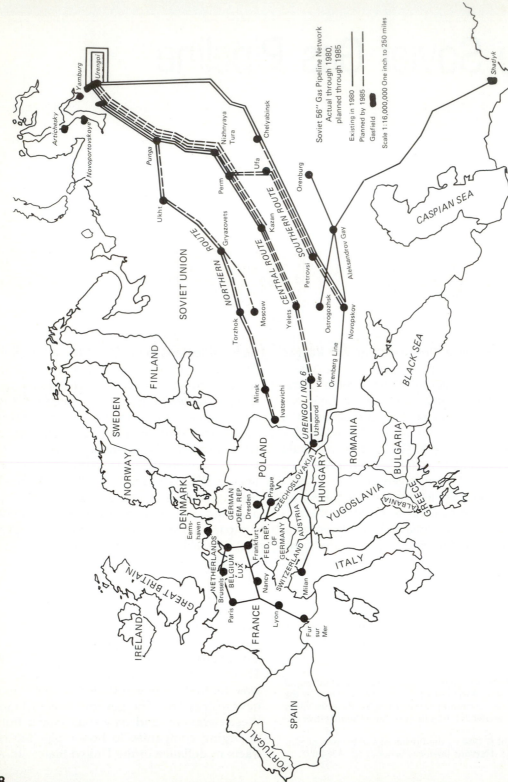

Source: Edward A. Hewett, "The Pipeline Connection: Issues for the Alliance," *The Brookings Review*, Fall 1982. Reprinted by permission.

gust 1982, the EEC lodged a formal protest with the State and Commerce Departments, claiming that the U.S. action violated international law and "constituted an unacceptable interference in EEC affairs." President Reagan nonetheless stuck to his position.

The crisis came to a head on August 23, when the French government ordered Dresser-France, a wholly owned subsidiary of Dallas-based Dresser Industries, to ship products in violation of the American embargo. This placed Dresser in the delicate position of having to decide which master to obey: if it obeyed the French government, the company could face American sanctions; if it obeyed American law, the firm's French subsidiary might face nationalization or the jailing of its executives. At the same time, France was laying down a challenge to Reagan: the president would now have to decide whether to (1) apply sanctions to America and foreign companies, (2) maintain the embargo but not apply sanctions or (3) back down in the face of European resistance.

THE URENGOY PIPELINE

In the 1960s, the Soviet Union discovered vast reserves of natural gas in Western Siberia in an area known as Urengoy (see *map*). To exploit this great resource, the Soviets decided in the early 1970s to build six gas pipelines which would stretch 20,000 km, use 14 million tons of pipe, and require more than 160 compressor stations to move the gas to consuming regions. Although the U.S.S.R. had some of the capabilities necessary to build these lines, the Soviet government planned to rely upon $25 to $30 billion of Western imports, especially Western wide-diameter pipe and large-scale turbines.

The original plans to ship some of this gas to Western Europe were initiated after the Iranian revolution in 1979. Before the fall of the Shah, the Soviets had negotiated a trilateral switch arrangement among the U.S.S.R., Iran, and certain European countries. A pipeline was

to have been built from southern Iran to the Soviet border. Iranian gas would be transported to the U.S.S.R., and an equivalent amount of Soviet gas would be delivered to the Europeans. The revolution canceled the Iranian leg of the deal, which meant that the Soviets would have to rely on the Urengoy field to fulfill their obligation to Europe and to supply the areas that would have used Iranian gas.

The Urengoy project was originally supposed to bring 60 to 75 billion cubic meters (BCM) a year to Western Europe via pipeline #6. This would have amounted to almost one-third of the EEC's natural gas consumption. Even though plans were scaled down to deliver 35 BCM/year, the pipeline would still be the largest East-West transaction to date (see *Table 1*). Deliveries of 10 BCM were to begin in 1984.

TABLE ONE	
SOVIET LARGE-DIAMETER PIPELINE EXPANSION: 1981–85 ($ U.S.)	
Urengoy #6	
Length	5000 km (3125 miles)
Diameter	1440 mm
Capacity	35 BCM/yr
Estimated completion date	1987/88
Cost of imported equipment	$5 billion
Pipe	3.2 million tons
Compressor stations	41*
Cost of Soviet inputs	$20–$30 billion
Western credits	$5B at average 7.5%
Payback period	1985–94
Estimated annual earnings	$6.5B hard currency**
Gas price	$5.70 per mmbtu guaranteed minimum

*Each compressor station required three 25-megawatt (MW) turbines; Soviet 10 and 16 MW turbines could be clustered in extra compressor stations to achieve equivalent power.

**This estimate assumed that the pipeline would run at full capacity. As of 1982, however, firm European orders for Soviet gas amounted to approximately two-thirds of full capacity.

Sources: Hewett (1982) and Stern (1982).

Given the size of the project and the Soviets' need for imported materials, most European governments and many European American firms saw the pipeline deal as a great opportunity. The biggest questions at first were how would the Soviets finance this project and who would they choose as their suppliers. Since each European government wanted to ensure large export orders for its own companies, each sought to sweeten its bid as much as possible. These divisions among the European nations allowed the Soviet Foreign Ministry to play the Europeans off against each other. Although complete financial details of the pipeline were not made public, it was widely suspected that the Soviets had used the competition to reduce prices and lower financing terms.

American government officials were highly critical of this process, in part because it directly violated international agreements on export subsidies. Industrial countries had been spending over $2 billion/year in the mid-1970s to subsidize their export trade.[1] In April 1978, 22 OECD nations tried to limit this costly competition by agreeing to a "Consensus" Arrangement on Guidelines for Officially Supported Credit. The Consensus established interest rates and repayment periods to be offered to importing countries and allowed the terms to vary depending upon income level of the importer.

When the Soviets began negotiating equipment purchases and loans for the Urengoy pipeline, the Consensus rate had increased to 8.5%. Yet in early 1980, the Soviets negotiated an open-ended line of credit with France at 7.8%, valid for five years. The French government, in other words, agreed to subsidize the discount from prevailing market rates. By November 1981 it had climbed to 11%. Because France continued to offer credit at 7.8%, other European countries felt obligated to put together similarly attractive packages. The Americans argued that this was a clear violation of the OECD agreement and an unreasonable

subsidy, especially considering the identity of the borrower.

The Europeans countered that the easy credit terms were desirable since they would be used to purchase massive amounts of large-diameter pipe, compressor stations, and pipelaying equipment. The pipeline project meant at least 1000 new jobs for Mannesmann, the leading German supplier of large-diameter pipe. Hundreds of additional jobs would be created by Creusot-Loire (an engineering firm owned by the French government) to complete a contract to supply 22 compressor stations. And despite the Soviets' selection of GE-designed 25-megawatt turbines to power the compressors, production was contracted to GE licensees in Britain, Italy, France, and Germany.* One hundred seventy-five million dollars worth of the essential rotor blades were to be supplied by GE-USA; 40 additional sets to be used as spare parts would be built by France's Alsthom-Atlantique, the only foreign company licensed to build the crucial rotor blades. The order filled most of Alsthom-Atlantique's capacity. Dresser-France got involved when it agreed to build twenty-one 50-ton centrifugal compressors. The $20 million order was 20% of its total operations and was equivalent to a substantial portion of the annual work load at Dresser-France's plant in Le Havre. The compressors were built under license from Dresser Industries' Clark Division at Olean, New York. Most of the technical data for the compressors and for drilling rigs, a product line Dresser was hoping to expand, originated in the United States.

---

*There were multiple bids for the turbine contract. GE's main competitor was the consortium of Houston-based Cooper Industries and Rolls Royce of Britain. Similarly, Caterpillar Tractor, selected to supply $90 million worth of pipelayers, faced stiff competition from Komatsu of Japan.

NATURAL GAS AND EUROPE'S ENERGY NEEDS

The "oil shocks" of 1973–74 and 1979–80 made Europeans acutely aware of their reliance on OPEC. As the current account balances of the EEC countries deteriorated in the mid-1970s, diversification of energy suppliers and a reduction in oil consumption became strategic and economic imperatives. One consequence of the oil shocks was the growing importance of natural gas. In 1973 natural gas prices were two-thirds that of crude oil on a BTU basis; by 1974–77, the gap had widened to 50%. Although gas-producing countries attempted to establish price parity with oil, the high costs of processing and transportation ensured that for the near term, gas would be discounted to remain competitive.

The attractiveness of natural gas led to major changes in Western European consumption patterns. Between 1973 and 1980, gas rose from under 10% of total energy use to an average of 14%, overall volume of consumption increased by 50%, and consumption by residential and commercial customers rose by even more. EEC analysts predicted a steady increase in both demand for natural gas and the proportions of gas in total energy consumption. They expected annual consumption to reach about 400 BCM by the end of the century, double the 1980 amount.

Since EEC natural gas production would not be sufficient to meet the new demand, the Europeans began to search for other sources of supply. Their decision on alternative suppliers was based on the cost, reliability, and potential impact on the balance of payments. From the European perspective, the only country that came reasonably close to meeting these criteria was the U.S.S.R.

The Soviets had supplied oil and gas to Europe for many years. Severe winter weather and technical problems had occasionally led to interruptions in gas deliveries, but these were always temporary. The Europeans believed that any risks inherent in increasing trade with the Communists were balanced by the Soviets' growing reliance on European exports of industrial and consumer goods. The Soviets could gain little, the Europeans reasoned, by shutting off gas deliveries. As one German put it, "Entweder sie liefern, oder sie kommen." (Either they deliver, or they invade.)[2]

Previous energy projects with the Soviet Union had been profitable for European business. Most ventures had been a type of countertrade known as compensation agreements.* Western products and know-how were exported to the Soviets, financed by Western credits. Repayments were wholly or partly in the form of counter deliveries of the resultant product or other products. One of the largest joint ventures to date was the Orenburg natural gas pipeline which had been completed in 1978. It had been constructed with German and Japanese pipe, American- and Italian-designed compressors, and a French gas-processing plant. In the period 1975–78, using gas-for-pipe deals, the U.S.S.R. imported $7B worth of pipe.

Europeans saw two other advantages to expanding business with the Soviets. First, hard currency earnings from energy sales could serve as insurance on the East European debt to Western banks ($60B in 1980). Second, economic cooperation with the Soviets was considered a sensible way of enhancing Europe's security. On the one hand, geographic proximity and historical ties seemed to dictate that Europe should work out a modus vivendi with the U.S.S.R. On the other hand, European leaders were confident that they would not become overly dependent on the Soviets. They believed that they could establish a "safety net"

---

*See "Countertrade and Merban Corporation," Harvard Business School case #9-383-116.

to counteract any danger inherent in increasing consumption of Soviet gas. Moreover, analysts predicted that Soviet oil exports would decline and therefore net European imports of Soviet energy would not rise.

THE SOVIET NATURAL GAS INDUSTRY

The accelerated development and exploitation of Siberian natural gas resources is a matter of highest economic and political priority. [Leonid I. Brezhnev, February 1981]

In the early 1980s the Soviet Union seemed to be suffering an economic crisis. The world's second largest economy was experiencing declining growth in GNP and productivity as well as a serious labor shortage. Domestic problems were compounded by the rising costs of economic and military aid to the Communist bloc. Through the 1970s, the Soviet economy had been bolstered by huge exports of oil. But by 1980, the future of the oil industry was also in question. Western analysts predicted that Soviet oil production would peak close to its 1980 level. Some suggested that by 1980 the Soviet bloc would actually go from a major exporter of oil to a net importer.

One of the bright spots in the Soviet economy was the natural gas industry. The 1981–85 plan called for production to rise to 600 BCM by 1985, a 40% jump. The Urengoy field in Western Siberia was to expand more than four-fold, accounting for most of the growth in the Soviet gas industry. With over one-third of the world's proven natural gas reserves, there was no question about the Soviets' potential for increasing gas production. But serious problems stood in the way. Infrastructure at the Urengoy field was underdeveloped: roads, electricity, labor, and gas treatment installations were in short supply. The harsh climate and physical conditions posed formidable obstacles. In addition, inefficient Soviet industry had failed to produce pipe and equipment that could match the quality of imported materials.

If the Soviets could find foreign markets for their natural gas, then future export earnings might pay for imports of pipe and compressor stations as well as defray the cost of imported technologies and consumer goods. Since the Soviets manufactured few items that were competitive in Western markets, they needed to export energy and other commodities in order to earn foreign exchange. The Soviets projected that gas exports to Western Europe might earn $10 to $15 billion in hard currency annually by the 1990s. Timely construction of the Urengoy pipeline would go far toward realizing this goal.

U.S. OPPOSITION TO THE SIBERIAN PIPELINE

Since July 1981, the U.S. government had tried to persuade the Europeans to abandon the Urengoy pipeline project. There were several reasons for this opposition. The first was that there was a widespread belief among several members of Congress and in the administration that the pipeline project was an unreasonable threat to European security. In June 1981, for example, 40 legislators wrote a letter to President Reagan urging him to review the project "in light of its potentially dangerous implications for the security and cohesion of Western Europe and the NATO alliance."[3] Several months later, a state department official presented data to a Senate subcommittee which further suggested that the pipeline represented an unacceptable danger to the energy security of Western Europe (see *Table 2*).

Even though Soviet gas would not exceed 9% of total energy by 1990, in certain regions, such as Bavaria and West Berlin, the figure could reach 90%. Moreover, since residential and commercial customers would be the majority of gas users, national governments would face strong political pressure to avoid risking an interruption. The Reagan administration also argued that Soviet gas might have been an ac-

TABLE TWO

WESTERN EUROPE: DEPENDENCE ON SOVIET GAS
% of Total Gas and of Total Energy Consumption

	1981		1990	
	Gas	Energy	Gas	Energy
West Germany	16	3	24	5
France	15	3	32	6
Italy	24	4	35	9

Source: U.S. Department of State, *Current Policy*, No. 331, October 14, 1981; U.S. Congress, Office of Technology Assessment, *Technology and Soviet Energy Availability*, 1981.

ceptable alternative to OPEC in the 1970s, but the oil problem was now less serious. OPEC, they argued, would not be a significant problem in the 1980s. Oil prices were falling in 1982, and the United States was predicting a worldwide glut.[4]

The second reason for administration opposition was that the pipeline would generate large hard currency earnings that could assist the Soviet military. Foreign exchange could be used to purchase nonessential goods, which would free domestic resources for use by the military. To Mr. Reagan and his advisors, this was the most serious threat. From their perspective, U.S. defensive capabilities had fallen dangerously behind the U.S.S.R.: the Soviets had engaged in a massive military buildup that threatened the security of the United States. As Defense Secretary Caspar Weinberger said in May 1981:

We hoped that the nuclear balance could be stabilized through arms control agreements and that the Soviet leadership shared our goal. . . . This hope has been badly disappointed. The Soviet expenditures for armaments grew more rapidly . . . during the period of "detente" than during the so-called Cold War.[5]

It was a top priority of the Reagan administration to reverse this trend in the balance of forces by spending more money on defense and by applying economic pressure against the Soviet Union.

Many members of the administration argued that export controls could help to achieve the goal of hurting the Soviets and reducing their arms buildup. Candidate Ronald Reagan had criticized President Carter's embargo on grain exports to the Soviet Union in 1980, and new President Ronald Reagan lifted the grain embargo in April 1981. Nonetheless, the administration believed that export controls could be effective under certain conditions. Grain sales, administration officials argued, were inherently ineffective because other countries would continue to sell to the Soviets. Furthermore, grain sales were in the West's interest because the Soviets had to pay for grain with scarce hard currency. If alternative forms of economic pressure could be found, the Reagan administration claimed, then the West could force the Soviet leaders to choose between guns and butter.

This strategy was a radical departure from the approach President Richard Nixon had taken 10 years earlier. Nixon and his chief advisor, Henry Kissinger, believed that the bipolar world of the Cold War had passed. The emergence of Japan and Western Europe as economic equals of the United States and the proliferation of nuclear weapons prompted Kissinger to advocate a multipolar world order in which a "web of economic interests" would reduce the likelihood of confrontation. While Kissinger sought to implement the strategic aspects of detente, Commerce Secretary Peter Peterson laid the groundwork for a new economic relationship with the U.S.S.R. Peterson maintained that there was an economic fit between the two powers: the Soviets' relative lack of technology and consumer durables offset its abundant raw materials. Peterson hoped for an expansion of joint ventures, whereby the United States would help develop Soviet resources. He said in May 1972:

I believe that these types of projects are potentially the single most important product of this new commercial relationship . . . gas projects are likely to be the largest and for that reason deserve high priority.[6]

The Reagan administration, however, regarded these views as outdated. Instead, they saw trade as part of a worldwide confrontation. As in the 1930s, the choice was either "appeasement" or "containment." Moreover, according to Richard Pipes, a Harvard professor and the president's expert on the U.S.S.R. until December 1982, economic difficulties in the Soviet Union provided leverage with which the West might promote liberalization of the Soviet political system. As Pipes put it:

What opponent of racial discrimination would recommend assisting South Africa to develop its mineral resources at preferential credit and using advanced technology unavailable to it, and then contracting to purchase the minerals thus produced for decades to come at guaranteed prices? In this case the connections between economic aid and the maintenance of apartheid would be apparent. Why then is it not apparent in the case of the Siberian pipeline that its construction with Western aid promotes the maintenance of an odious and dangerously aggressive totalitarian regime?[7]

THE POLISH CRISIS

On December 13, 1981, a new factor entered the picture when the Polish government declared martial law. This action brought to a head the long confrontation between Solidarity, Poland's independent union, and the Soviet-backed Polish government. While European leaders refrained from implicating Moscow directly in the Polish crackdown, the U.S. government blamed the Soviets and decided to take retaliatory action. On December 29 President Reagan announced new economic sanctions against the Soviet Union, including:

• No further issuance or renewal of validated licenses for export to the U.S.S.R. of high-

technology products, technical data, and oil and gas equipment and technology
• Expansion of the 1978 list of restricted oil and gas equipment exports to include oil and gas transmission and refining-related goods

The immediate implications of these sanctions were that General Electric would lose most of its $175 million contract for the rotor blades (only 23 out of 120 sets had been supplied), Caterpillar would lose its $90 million pipelayer contract, and millions of dollars in other related exports by firms such as Dresser Industries would be denied licenses.[8]

European participants in the pipeline project were not deterred by the American actions; within two weeks they expressed their intentions to proceed. Columnist William Safire questioned West German Chancellor Helmut Schmidt about his decision to proceed with the "Kremlin pipeline":

Safire: Don't you think that the billions of dollars in revenue that the Soviets get as a result of this pipeline will be used to buy Western technology?
Schmidt: No. They will be used to pay for your grain.
Safire: So the only impressive action that the United States can take in the way of a sanction would be a grain embargo?
Schmidt: Certainly, it would be the only economically weightly sanction that is thinkable. . . . But I'm not advocating it.[9]

THE VERSAILLES SUMMIT

In June 1982 President Reagan traveled to Versailles, France, for the annual economic summit of the seven industrialized democracies (the United States, the United Kingdom, France, Germany, Japan, Canada, and Italy). There were several issues on the agenda ranging from European concern about high U.S. interest rates and volatile foreign exchange markets to the top American priority of limiting credit to the

Soviets and tightening restrictions on the sale of strategic goods. Given this diversity of views going into the summit, observers were not surprised when the industrial leaders failed to reach any firm agreements. The final communiqué of the summit nonetheless tried to smooth over the differences. In a loosely worded statement, all governments agreed to take a "prudent and diversified" economic approach to the U.S.S.R. and Eastern Europe. Assuming this was accomplished, the Europeans understood from their discussion with President Reagan that he would drop the unpopular pipeline embargo.

The illusion of consensus was shattered a few days later when French President Mitterrand stated publicly that the Versailles agreements would have no effect on France's credit policy vis-à-vis the U.S.S.R. Disappointed by Mitterrand's statement, President Reagan convened a National Security Council meeting in Washington on June 18 to formulate a response. Reagan's advisors generally agreed that American efforts to pressure the Soviets and the Polish government were being undermined by European policies. Although the Cabinet was divided over the efficacy of export controls, the president decided to expand the scope of the December embargo. Under the new policy, the United States would prohibit overseas subsidiaries and licensees of U.S. firms from participating in the pipeline project. In addition, the new restrictions would apply retroactively. No matter how long ago the company signed its contract, it was required to stop work immediately on pipeline-related contracts. Since it was standard practice for licensing agreements to include clauses obligating the licensee to observe U.S. export laws, Reagan's lawyers assured the president that the restrictions were binding.

European leaders were unprepared to accept this new assertion of American jurisdiction. Some claimed that no business contract could override the right of a sovereign government to regulate business in its own country.

To counter the U.S. actions, the European governments considered a variety of options. One possibility was simply to defy the embargo by ordering companies to honor their contracts. Another possibility was to expand technical assistance to the Soviets. A third option was to retaliate against the United States by limiting imports of U.S. agricultural products or by filing a complaint with the GATT against allegedly illegal U.S. export subsidies.[10]

The Soviets were also determined to show the United States that they could complete the pipeline on time. Said one Soviet official, "Reagan's move has prompted a tide of patriotism: the gas pipeline is becoming a symbol." Soviet propaganda also tried to exploit tension in the NATO alliance: "It is well understood that the embargo is aimed not only against the U.S.S.R. but also against Germany, France and Britain who are economic competitors [of the United States]."[11] Finally, the Soviets threatened to press substantial cancellation charges on firms that failed to deliver on time.

Time for Decision

In mid-August 1982, Dresser Industries learned that the Soviets had dispatched a ship to pick up the three compressors that were completed and sitting in Dresser's warehouse in Le Havre. Dresser-France was to be the test case in the emerging conflict of wills. On August 23 the plant manager received a French government Requisition Order for Services commanding Dresser to ship the compressors and resume production on the remaining 18 units. French "actes du gouvernement" were not subject to court challenges. Defiance was a criminal offense punishable by fines and imprisonment. In addition, Dresser's headquarters in Dallas could not rule out the possibility that the French government would nationalize Dresser-France's facilities.

Dresser's dilemma was that the legal position of the Reagan administration was also strong. The 1979 Export Administration Act (EAA) had granted the president total discretion in deciding to implement export restrictions for foreign policy reasons. Only in the case of agricultural commodities was there even a provision for congressional veto. The president's policies were translated into Commerce Department export regulations; if the administration decided to enforce its threats, Dresser could be subject to a range of civil and criminal penalties (see *Exhibit 7*). Dresser-France could also be denied access to all U.S. goods and technology, including Dresser's data bank.

Dresser was convinced that whatever the foreign policy rationale behind the president's actions, he was violating the intent of the Export Administration Act by imposing sanctions that were retroactive and that extended to companies outside of U.S. jurisdiction. On August 24, 1982, Dresser appealed to a Washington District Court for a temporary restraining order that would prevent the Commerce Department from applying sanctions to Dresser-France. The judge, however, denied the motion, ruling that Dresser had failed to demonstrate irreparable harm if the compressor sale were blocked. Dresser management was not deterred. Senior Vice President Edward Luter commented, "Dresser has several options to pursue."[12] It was not entirely clear what Mr. Luter had in mind.

EXHIBIT ONE

RESERVES AND PRODUCTION OF NATURAL GAS AND CRUDE OIL, FIVE LEADING NATIONS AS OF JANUARY 1, 1982 (as % of total world)

Natural gas—estimated reserves		Natural gas—production	
1. U.S.S.R.	39.8%	1. United States[1]	34.6%
2. Iran	16.6	2. U.S.S.R.	28.1
3. United States	6.9	3. Netherlands	5.2
4. Algeria	4.5	4. Canada	4.5
5. Saudi Arabia	3.9	5 Mexico	2.5
Crude oil—proven reserves		**Crude oil—production**	
1. Saudi Arabia	24.6%	1. U.S.S.R.	22.6%
2. Kuwait	9.6	2. United States[2]	16.3
3. U.S.S.R.	9.4	3. Saudi Arabia	11.9
4. Iran	8.5	4. Mexico	5.6
5. Mexico	8.5	5. Iran	4.2

[1]1981.
[2]Includes lease condensate.
Source: American Petroleum Institute.

EXHIBIT TWO

U.S.–U.S.S.R. TRADE, 1977–1981 (U.S. $ millions)

	1977	1978	1979	1980	1981
U.S. exports: world	$120,816	$142,054	$184,473	$224,237	$236,254
U.S. exports: U.S.S.R. (FAS)					
Total	1,623	2,249	3,604	1,510	2,339
Agricultural	1,037	1,686	2,855	1,047	1,665
Nonagricultural	586	562	749	463	674
Oil & gas equipment, excluding pipe	92	83	164	51	64
Oil & gas equipment, including pipe	92	83	164	51	64
U.S. imports: U.S.S.R. (CIF)					
Total	223	540	873	453	347
Agricultural	11	13	14	8	13
Nonagricultural	212	527	859	445	334
Gold bullion[1]	—	287	549	88	22
U.S.–U.S.S.R. trade turnover (Imports plus exports)	1,857	2,799	4,477	1,963	2,686

[1]Gold bullion (monetary gold) was not included in trade statistics until 1978.

Sources: Economic Report of the President, 1983 (line 1); *Highlights of U.S. Exports,* Schedule B, Commodity by Country of Destination, U.S., Census Bureau, U.S. Department of Commerce.

EXHIBIT THREE

U.S.S.R. GRAIN PRODUCTION AND TRADE, 1975–82 (million metric tons)

Year[1]	Production	Total net imports	Imports from U.S.
1975–76	140.1	25.4	13.9
1976–77	223.8	7.7	7.4
1977–78	195.7	16.8	12.5
1978–79	237.4	12.8	11.2
1979–80	179.2	30.2	15.2
1980–81	189.2	34.3	8.0
1981–82[2]	160.0	45.5	15.4

[1]July–June.
[2]Preliminary data.
Source: U.S. Department of Agriculture.

U.S.S.R. TRADE WITH THE INDUSTRIALIZED WEST (IW)[1] AND UNITED STATES, 1977–80 (U.S. $ millions)

	1977	1978	1979	1980
Imports from IW	$12,914	$14,870	$18,114	$19,837
United States (%)	12.6	15.1	19.9	7.6
European Community (%) of which:	51.7	48.2	47.7	52.6
Manufacturers	$10,916	$12,154	$13,642	$15,113
United States (%)	5.0	3.8	4.8	2.8
European Community (%)	57.4	55.7	57.6	56.8
High Technology	$ 2,085	$ 2,345	$ 2,371	$ 2,330
United States (%)	8.8	5.6	6.5	3.6
European Community (%)	59.1	58.0	61.2	62.8
Exports to IW	$11,622	$12,888	$18,503	$23,658
United States (%)	2.0	2.1	4.9	1.9
European Community (%)	59.8	61.5	61.0	64.4

[1]Belgium-Luxembourg, Denmark, Federal Republic of Germany, France, Ireland, Italy, Netherlands, United Kingdom, Austria, Canada, Finland, Japan, Norway, Sweden, Switzerland, and the United States.
Source: United Nations data.

U.S.S.R. HARD CURRENCY EXPORTS AND IMPORTS[1] (current U.S. $ millions)[3]

	1977	1978	1979	1980	1981[2]
Total exports	$11,863	$13,336	$19,417	$23,584	$23,778
Petroleum	5,583	5,710	9,585	11,995	12,287
Natural gas	566	1,072	1,404	2,704	3,968
Coke and coal	366	295	315	366	179
Machinery and equipment	905	1,299	1,574	1,466	1,534
Ferrous metals	181	129	216	246	169
Wood and wood products	1,084	991	1,370	1,500	1,016
Chemicals	215	287	542	746	770
Agricultural products	652	447	457	454	690
Diamonds[4]	606	773	1,043	1,304	3,555
Other	1,705	2,333	2,911	2,803	
Total imports	$14,805	$17,026	$21,435	$26,070	$27,778
Grain	1,356	2,353	3,279	4,360	6,217
Other agricultural products	2,005	1,721	2,854	4,400	5,104
Machinery and equipment	5,117	5,900	6,032	6,039	4,523
Ferrous metals	1,819	2,588	3,536	3,606	3,597
Chemicals	658	815	1,190	1,545	1,590
Other	3,850	3,579	4,544	6,120	6,747

[1]Includes all countries trading with the Soviet Union on a hard currency basis as of January 1, 1981. Hard currencies refer to currencies such as the dollar, the German D.M., and the Japanese yen, which are readily accepted as a form of payment among most international trading nations.
[2]Estimated.
[3]*Source:* Official Soviet foreign trade statistics.
[4]*Source:* OECD statistics.

EXHIBIT SIX

A. RATE OF UNEMPLOYMENT (% of civilian labor force)

Period	United States	France	F. R. Germany	United Kingdom
1970	4.9	2.0	0.7	2.0
1978	6.9	5.3	4.3	5.7
1981	7.6	7.8	5.5	10.6
1982: I*	8.8	8.3	6.8	11.8
1982: II*	9.5	8.3	7.4	12.1

B. TOTAL AND PER CAPITA CNP GROWTH RATES AT CONSTANT 1972 PRICES (% change from preceding year and quarter)

Period	United States	France[1]	F. R. Germany	United Kingdom[1]
1970	−0.2	5.7	5.0	2.2
1978	5.0	3.8	3.5	3.3
1981	1.9	0.2	−0.2	−2.0

[1]Gross domestic product.
*Seasonally adjusted annual rates.
Note: Growth rates calculated from unrounded figures.
Source: IMF, *International Financial Statistics,* 1982.

EXHIBIT SEVEN

EXPORT ADMINISTRATION ACT REGULATIONS, EXCERPTS

§ 387.1 Sanctions

(A) CRIMINAL

(1) Violations of Export Administration Act

(i) General . . . whoever knowingly violates the Export Adminstration Act ("the Act") or any regulation, order, or license issued under the Act is punishable for each violation by a fine of not more than five times the value of the exports involved or $50,000, whichever is greater, or by imprisonment for not more than five years, or both.

(ii) Willful Violations Whoever willfuly exports anything contrary to any provision of the Act or any regulation, order, or license issued under the Act, with the knowledge that such exports will be used for the benefit of any country to which exports are restricted for national security or foreign policy purposes except in the case of an individual, shall be fined not more than five times the value of the exports involved or $1,000,000, whichever is greater; and in the case of an individual, shall be fined not more than $250,000, or imprisoned not more than 10 years, or both. . . .

(B) ADMINISTRATIVE

(1) Denial of export privileges

Whoever violates any law, regulation, order or license relating to export controls or restrictive trade practices and boycotts is also subject to administrative action which may result in suspension, revocation, or denial of export privileges conferred under the Export Administration Act. *(See § 388.3 et seq.)* . . .

(3) Civil penalty

A civil penalty may be imposed for each violation of the Export Administration Act or any regulation, order or license issued under the Act either in addition to, or instead of, any other liability or penalty which may be imposed. The civil penalty may not exceed $10,000 for each violation except that the civil penalty for each violation involving national security controls imposed under Section 5 of the Act may not exceed $100,000. . . .

Source: Export Administration Regulations, January 25, 1983.

EXHIBIT EIGHT

DRESSER INDUSTRIES FINANCIAL SUMMARY ($ millions except per share data)*

A. Summary of operations	Years ended October 31:			
	1977	**1980**	**1981**	**1982**
Net sales and service revenues	$2,538.8	$4,016.3	$4,614.5	$4,160.6
Cost of sales and services	1,658.5	2,704.1	3,047.1	2,728.2
Interest expense	44.9	48.4	52.7	59.5
Earnings before taxes	335.6	448.2	528.6	242.8
% of sales	13.2%	11.2%	11.5%	5.8%
% of avg. shareholders' investment	33.6%	29.2%	29.6%	12.3%
Income taxes	150.5	186.1	212.0	70.5
Net earnings	185.1	261.1	316.6	172.3
% of sales	7.3%	6.5%	6.9%	4.1%
% of avg. shareholders' investment	18.6%	17.0%	17.7%	8.7%
Total dividends paid	32.0	43.9	51.7	60.8

B. Segment operating profit				
Petroleum operations	$124.2	$248.1	$393.7	$254.3
Energy processing and conversion (including compressors and pumps)	143.1	100.5	100.6	106.9
Refractors and minerals operations	43.5	53.7	37.1	(20.5)
Mining and construction equipment	45.9	38.9	(10.0)	(10.4)
Industrial specialty products	44.1	62.4	46.2	(6.3)
Less corporate expenses, net	65.2	55.4	39.0	81.2
Earnings before taxes	335.6	448.2	528.6	242.8

*Excerpts.
Source: Annual Report, 1982, Dresser Industries, pp. 28–29.

NOTES

1. *Wall Street Journal*, February 11, 1982.
2. John P. Schutte, Jr., "Pipeline Politics" in *SAIS Review*, Summer 1982, Number 4, pp. 137–147.
3. *Congressional Record*, October 7, 1981, p. S11309.
4. "Soviet-West European Natural Gas Pipeline," U.S. Dept. of State, *Current Policy*, No. 331, October 14, 1981.
5. Department of State Bulletin #2052, Vol. 81, July 1981.
6. "US-Soviet Commercial Relations in a New Era," U.S. Department of Commerce, August 1972, p. 5. cited in Jonathan P. Stern, *Soviet Natural Gas Development to 1990*. Lexington Books, Lexington, MA and Toronto, 1980, p. 111.
7. Richard Pipes, "The Soviet Union in Crisis," 1983. Manuscript provided by author.
8. *New York Times*, December 30, 1981.
9. Ibid.
10. Interview with high-ranking EEC official, July 15, 1982. The official claimed that America's Domestic International Sales Corporation (DISC) provided tax incentives to support exports. The EEC would ask GATT for permission to retaliate against the $1.7 B DISC cost the U.S. government in 1982.
11. *Wall Street Journal*, August 3, 1982.
12. *Wall Street Journal*, August 25, 1982.

Europe 1992

The European Community (EC) reached a turning point in 1985 when its 12 member states agreed to remove all barriers to the free movement of goods, services, capital, and people by 1992. Their hope was to make Europe the largest single economy in the world, with some 320 million customers, and to provide new opportunities for growth (see *Exhibit 1*).

This objective reflected the view of many European business and political leaders that their companies and countries had not kept pace with international competition. In the words of Dr. Wisse Dekker, president of Philips:

"America will provide the world with food, Japan will provide the world with industrial products, and Europe will be their play ground." I recently heard this statement and it has certainly made an impression on me. Why? Well, perhaps it has a ring of truth about it. . . . We really have to blame our-

selves. Let us be frank. In Europe we have quite simply failed to make the best of things.[1]

It was widely believed among Europeans that the 1992 program would be a huge breakthrough. However, the shape and direction of the program depended on the resolution of several points of disagreement within the European Community. Would 1992 result in a United States of Europe, or would it be merely an incremental step in the evolution of the Common Market? Would it result in a "Fortress Europe," or would it encourage a new international climate of free trade?

THE POSTWAR BACKGROUND OF EUROPEAN ECONOMIC INTEGRATION

The destruction wrought by the Second World War gave rise to a new spirit of international cooperation that led to the creation of such institutions as the International Monetary Fund (IMF) and the General Accord on Trade and Tariffs (GATT). The former was intended to oversee a stable international monetary order; the latter, to eliminate protectionism and discrimination in international trade.

Efforts were also made to promote greater

Professor John B. Goodman and David Palmer prepared this note as the basis for class discussion rather than to illustrate either effective or ineffective handling of an administrative situation.

Copyright © 1989 by the President and Fellows of Harvard College. Harvard Business School case 9-389-206.

cooperation in war-torn Europe. In 1947, the United States announced the Marshall Plan, a massive aid package designed to promote the recovery of European economies. The act which authorized Marshall Plan aid explicitly recognized the advantages to the United States of a "large domestic market with no internal trade barriers" and noted that "similar advantages can accrue to the countries of Europe." With the backing of the United States, the GATT therefore allowed for the creation of customs unions, in which member countries eliminated internal tariffs and established a common tariff for outside nations.

Within Europe, an outpouring of sentiment in favor of European unification arose. In 1946, Winston Churchill called for a "United States of Europe." Others talked of the need for some type of European federation. Yet all efforts to create political unity, such as the Council of Europe in 1949, failed because most governments would not surrender political sovereignty.

Economic integration, on the other hand, proved more tractable. In 1951, France, West Germany, Belgium, Luxembourg, the Netherlands, and Italy established the European Coal and Steel Community (ECSC). The ECSC was essentially a customs union in coal and steel. It served to create greater efficiency and profitability in these two industries, and equally important, it fostered greater cooperation between former adversaries like France and Germany. Founders of the ECSC hoped that success on this front would eventually lead to broader economic (and perhaps even political) integration in Western Europe.

Indeed, in 1957, the six ECSC members signed the Treaty of Rome, which established the European Economic Community (EEC).* The Treaty of Rome laid out a timetable by which its members would remove all internal tariffs and establish a common external tariff by 1970 (an objective that was reached two years ahead of schedule). It also provided for the creation of a common agricultural policy; the removal of nontariff barriers to the free movement of people, services, and capital; and the harmonization of national legislation. Finally, it sought to "lay the foundations of an ever closer union among the people of Europe and . . . to preserve and strengthen peace and liberty."

After several delays, Europe moved closer to economic integration. In 1967, the European Economic Community, the European Coal and Steel Community, and the European Atomic Energy Community merged into the European Communities (more commonly referred to as the European Community or EC). A further step toward economic integration was taken with the formation of the European Monetary System (EMS) in 1979. The EMS established a system of "fixed but adjustable" exchange rates, designed to insulate intra-European trade from the effects of floating exchange rates and to promote greater macroeconomic convergence. EC membership also increased. Britain, Ireland, and Denmark joined in 1973, Greece in 1981, and Spain and Portugal in 1986, bringing the total number of member states to 12.**

Despite these steps, progress toward economic integration appeared painfully slow, and pessimism about Europe's ability to compete in world markets persisted (see *Exhibit 2* through *Exhibit 5*). Many Europeans began to see the need for a strategy geared to restoring Europe's economic vitality. In 1985, after much debate, EC member states endorsed the goal of completing the internal market by 1992.

---

*The Treaty of Rome also established the European Atomic Energy Community. Seven nations—Austria, Denmark, Noway, Portugal, Sweden, Switzerland, and the United Kingdom—remained outside the European Economic Community and formed the European Free Trade Association (EFTA).

**Norway applied to join the EC in 1973, but in a national referendum, its citizens voted against membership.

INSTITUTIONS OF THE EUROPEAN COMMUNITIES

The Treaty of Rome defined the powers and responsibilities of the four principal institutions of the EC: the Commission, the Council of Ministers, the European Parliament, and the Court of Justice.

The Commission was the executive arm of the EC. In 1988, it was directed by a president and 17 commissioners. The president was selected by all member countries (for a two-year renewable term); the commissioners were appointed by national governments (two from each of the five large countries—France, Great Britain, Italy, West Germany, and Spain—and one from each of the smaller EC countries). Commission members were supposed to represent the interests of the EC as a whole. The commissioners were supported by a staff of 2,000 "Eurocrats," who served in 22 divisions (directorates-general).

The Commission performed three main functions: It initiated EC proposals, represented the EC in international trade negotiations, and managed the EC budget. It was also responsible for overseeing national policies to ensure that they were consistent with EC policy. It investigated violations of EC treaties, issued judgments when violations were found, and had the option of referring violations to the Court of Justice.

The Council of Ministers served as the EC's main decision-making body; it could not initiate legislation but had the power to approve, amend, or reject Commission proposals. It consisted of representatives from each government but was not a permanent group. Agricultural ministers sat on the Council when it dealt with agricultural policy, trade ministers sat on the Council when it dealt with trade matters, and so on. The Council was also staffed by a Committee of Permanent Representatives of ambassadorial rank. Originally, the Council intended that decisions would be by majority vote, but in 1966 French President Charles de Gaulle insisted that they be made by unanimous consent, allowing each country to defend its "vital interests." The Council presidency rotated among member states every six months. The Council's president set the agenda, thereby giving proposals his country favored more time for discussion and a better chance of passing.

The European Parliament comprised 518 members, directly elected by voters in each nation since 1979. The Parliament did not have legislative power, and its decisions originally were not binding on the Council. It served mainly in a consultative capacity, acted as a forum for public opinion within the EC, advised the Council on proposals, and gave final approval to the EC budget. Theoretically, the Parliament could also turn out the Commission through a vote of no-confidence, although as of 1988 this power has never been exercised. Members of Parliament tended to follow the party lines of their own countries and formed groups along those lines.

The Court of Justice interpreted EC treaties and directives and sought to apply Community law in a uniform way. Thirteen judges sat on the Court, including one from each member nation. The Court based its decisions on the original provisions in the Treaty of Rome, as well as on later EC directives and regulations. Court decisions had precedence over national rulings, but in numerous cases, companies and states disregarded the Court. Between 1976 and 1986, violation of Court rulings by member states became an increasingly serious problem.[2]

EC directives (or laws) began as proposals. The process for approving proposals typically took from two to five years. Proposals were initiated by the Commission and then sent to the Council for study and debate. After approval by the Council, a proposal was sent to the Parliament, which had three months to accept or reject it. Rejection, however, had to be unanimous. Once the Parliament accepted a proposal, it became a directive. Member states were then obligated to change their national laws to conform to it.

THE OBJECTIVES OF 1992

In 1985, the Commission presented the conclusions of an exhaustive three-year study on the future of the European Community. The resulting *White Paper* specified three types of obstacles that the Commission believed needed to be removed: (1) *physical barriers*, which included intra-EC border stoppages, customs controls, and associated paperwork; (2) *technical barriers*, which involved meeting divergent national product standards, technical regulations, and conflicting business laws, and the opening of nationally protected public procurement markets; (3) and *fiscal barriers*, which mainly dealt with rates of VAT (value-added taxes) and excise duties.

The *White Paper* outlined a program to complete the internal market. It did not set any priorities. Instead, it listed nearly 300 directives (scaled down to 279 by the end of 1988), covering a variety of issues, products, services, and industries, each with its own timetable for implementation. The directives were designed to eliminate many of the costs and constraints facing European firms and thereby increase their efficiency and competitiveness. (*Appendix 1* lists the major elements and expected benefits of the 1992 program.) In the words of the *Economist*, the *White Paper* was an "adventure in deregulation" that would create a stronger and more prosperous Europe.[3] One prominent study concluded that EC market integration would add an average 4.5% to the EC's GDP, improve the EC's balance of payments by approximately 1% of GDP, deflate prices by some 6.1%, and reduce unemployment by about 1.5%.[4]

In 1985, the heads of state of EC countries passed the Single European Act, which amended key parts of the original Treaty of Rome (see *Appendix 2* for key provisions). The act replaced the requirement of unanimous consent (and hence the ability of any country to veto a Council decision) with majority rule, except for fiscal reform.* It also increased the power of the EC Parliament. Henceforth, the Parliament could pass amendments to directives and regulations by a two-thirds vote. Those amendments had to be taken into account by the Commission and the Council. Measures rejected in their entirety by the Parliament could be enacted only by unanimous vote of the Council.

ELIMINATING BORDER CONTROLS

A key component of the 1992 agenda was the elimination of border controls. These controls included tax collection (aggravated by differences in VAT and excise rates); agricultural checks (such as applications for adjustments to farm product prices); veterinary checks (which were necessitated by differing national health standards); and transportation controls. Such measures created delays and added considerably to costs. For example, a truck going from London to Milan (excluding the Channel crossing) took 58 hours, while one covering the same 750-mile distance within Great Britain took only 36 hours. Smaller companies suffered the most from border controls. Customs costs per consignment were estimated to be up to 30% to 45% higher for companies with fewer than 250 employees than for larger firms.[5]

EC governments made slow progress in eliminating border controls. In January 1988, EC member states adopted the Single Administrative Document (SAD). The SAD replaced the numerous forms used by each country with a uniform import-export declaration and transit document. Member states also agreed to cut other paperwork at national borders. Further

---

*The total number of votes in the Council was 76. Germany, Britain, France, and Italy each had 10; Spain had 8; the Netherlands, Belgium, Greece, and Portugal had 5; Ireland and Denmark had 3; and Luxembourg had 2. To pass a law required a "qualified" majority of 54 votes.

progress, however, depended upon the resolution of issues such as different national import and social policies.

The difficulties created by different import policies were evident in the case of Japanese automobiles. Italy imposed the strictest limits, maintaining a quota of 3,500 vehicles in 1988. France was similarly restrictive (see *Exhibit 6*). European governments also disagreed over the appropriate policy toward Japanese cars built within the EC. France, for example, argued that Nissan's British-built cars (expected to reach 200,000 by 1992) must be treated as Japanese until they reached an EC content level of at least 80%. The United Kingdom, on the other hand, argued that with 70% local content, these cars should be considered European products. West Germany rejected the need for any local content requirement.

Other difficulties arose as a result of differences in national customs, conditions, and priorities. For example, West Germany had strict gun controls, while France guaranteed the right to bear arms. Britain, surrounded by the sea, checked people only at its frontier ports and rejected the use of identity cards. France, on the other hand, had virtually unpoliceable frontiers; it therefore placed greater emphasis on the use of national identity cards. Eliminating border controls required a consensus on issues such as immigration and the rights of asylum, as well as greater police collaboration in guarding Europe's borders against drugs and terrorism.[6]

STANDARDIZATION

More than 100,000 different regulations and standards existed in the EC in the 1980s. These included regulations affecting health, safety, and the environment, and technical standards within industries. EC countries set their own national standards for a wide range of industries, from automobiles to food processing, from electrical products to telecommunications. Firms

were required to duplicate products and testing to sell in different national markets, which increased marketing difficulties and added to costs.

In the past, the Commission had sought to solve the problem of divergent standards and regulations by harmonizing national legislation throughout the EC (i.e., establishing similar laws in all member states). For the most part, this method limited the possibilities for greater integration given the entrenched interests in each country. The *White Paper* therefore proposed a new approach, based on the principle of mutual recognition.* As explained by Michael Calingaert:

Mutual recognition . . . means that a practice, regulation or another form of control in one member state will be recognized as valid in the other countries, even if it does not conform to such controls there. . . . The EC's role will be limited to agreeing on regulations of a general oversight nature that establish minimum conditions with which all member states must abide. . . . The net effect of [this concept] is to reduce the area over which EC-wide agreement will be necessary and thus to enhance the prospects for movement toward 1992.[7]

Thus, products lawfully produced or marketed in one EC nation would have access to all EC member states.

Progress in this area was slow; negotiations on minimum conditions remained difficult. By the end of 1988, directives had been adopted (or were close to adoption) on pressure vessels, toys, construction equipment, and electromag-

---

*The foundation for the principle of mutual recognition in the EC was the landmark *Cassis de Dijon* decision by the Court of Justice in 1979. That ruling upheld the Commission's refusal to allow Germany to block imports of a French alcoholic beverage because its level of alcoholic content fell below German standards. The Court held that a product legally produced and marketed in one member state was entitled to be sold throughout the Community, unless an importing country could show that public health and safety were at stake.

netic compatibility. The Council also adopted a directive that required member states to inform the Commission before introducing new standards in specified areas, including foodstuffs, pharmaceuticals, cosmetics, and agricultural products. The Commission's report on the directive, issued at the end of 1988, criticized several member states for not complying with this prior notification requirement.

The Case of Food Processing

Of the 279 EC directives, 103 dealt with food. Food processing was the largest employer and the greatest contributor to value-added of all EC industries. European companies operated primarily in their own national markets. Only 10% of Europe's 46 largest food-processing companies operated in four or more of the largest EC countries. Foreign multinationals played a predominant role. Eight of the ten largest food-processing companies in Europe were American, including names like General Mills and Philip Morris.

Many of the directives in this industry were designed to standardize the purity and labeling laws across the Community. In the Commission's view, such laws had often served primarily to protect national producers. Among the most disputed cases were Italy's prohibition on the use of common flour in pasta and Spain's practice of double inspection of imported spirits. Germany's beer purity law, which was justified on health grounds, created a highly protected domestic market; imports made up only 1% of German consumption. In 1987, the European Court of Justice censured this law and encouraged its repeal.[8]

The Case of Pharmaceuticals

The pharmaceutical industry was characterized by a particularly high level of government involvement, both because of its role in public health and safety and because of the government's role as a provider of health services. National standards for testing and registration of drugs varied considerably, and differences tended to create protected national markets. In addition, most EC governments intervened to influence price levels of pharmaceuticals as a matter of social policy, thereby reinforcing this protection.

The industry itself was highly fragmented. More than 600 manufacturers existed in West Germany alone. U.S. pharmaceutical manufacturers were well established in the Community. Virtually all of the major U.S. firms had European subsidiaries; they controlled about 25% of the market. Although some of the multinational firms benefited from the fragmentation of the European market because of their ability to fill particular niches and engage in price discrimination, the cost of having to seek up to 12 separate registrations for a product was substantial.

The 1992 program aimed to standardize procedures and reduce the time involved in product registration. These proposals pointed toward a larger political issue: the extent to which regulatory power should be transferred to a Community-level institution. Some EC officials advocated a single European registration agency (comparable to the FDA in the United States). National governments recognized the need for greater coordination, but their long-established social security policies represented an obstacle to creating any common EC policy.

NATIONAL PROCUREMENT

Public procurement amounted to some 15% of the EC's GDP. Public purchasing of goods and services divided into five general areas: agriculture, forestry, and fishery products (0.6%); energy products (16.3%); manufactured goods (32.7%); construction (28.6%); and market services (21.8%).[9]

EC governments purchased almost exclusively from home-based companies. By 1987, they awarded only about 2% of public contracts to firms from other EC nations; some 75% of contracts went to "national champions."[10] Protected national markets resulted in higher costs for the public sector and less competition for national manufacturing and service industries.

EC legislation, enacted in the 1970s, had sought to make procurement more competitive, but with little success. Numerous infringements of EC procurement regulations occurred. These infringements included the failure to advertise tenders, illegal exclusion of firms from other EC member states, and bid conditions incompatible with legislation. In addition, four important "strategic" sectors—energy, transport, telecommunications, and water supply—were excluded from the Community's legislation on public purchasing.

The 1992 program sought to end national protectionism for all public procurement contracts. In particular, the Commission aimed to open the four previously excluded sectors to competitive bidding. However, the Commission's proposal allowed national governments to reject products not made with 50% European content. The telecommunications industry was expected to be significantly affected by this change in procurement practices. Since PTTs were the largest European buyers of telecommunications equipment, the Commission believed that more open bidding in this sector would dramatically increase competition and efficiency throughout the industry. It proposed a phased opening of 40% of procurement contracts, with a 100% opening after 1992.

The Commission's strategy was to focus first on obtaining legislation specifying procedures for awarding procurement contracts and only later on improving its ability to enforce that legislation. According to one analyst, progress in this area was bound to be slow:

Although the Commission may well obtain approval for most of what it has proposed by 1992, innumerable vested local and national interests are likely to fight to maintain a privileged position, depressed areas will look for special treatment, economic dislocation resulting from more open tendering will create political counterpressures, many purchasing authorities will try to ignore EC rules . . . and the pursuit of legal remedies (a course of action many EC firms may be reluctant to follow) will be protracted.[11]

VAT HARMONIZATION

The 1992 program sought to end the divergence in national indirect tax rates, which encompassed both the value-added tax (VAT) and excise taxes. The VAT was a national tax, based on the difference between a firm's input costs and output receipts. Firms that exported received a rebate of the VAT. (Applications for rebates were made at the border.) Divergent VAT rates, the Commission believed, distorted trade flows by encouraging consumers to buy goods in low-VAT countries and ship them home without paying the higher VAT.

One of the problems confronted by the Commission in considering changes in the VAT was that most EC countries had two, if not three, tiers of VAT rates. The *White Paper* proposed abolishing the highest tier of VAT rates (applied in only six countries). Two tiers would then remain: a reduced rate for basic necessity goods and a standard rate for all other products. As of 1988, reduced rates in the EC ranged from 1% to 10%; standard rates varied from 12% to 25%. The *White Paper* proposed that differences within each of these two tiers be reduced—to a band of 4% to 9% for the reduced rate and a band of 14% to 20% for the standard rate. Advocates of VAT harmonization regularly cited the successful experience of the United States, where contiguous states maintained differences in sales tax of up to five percentage points without any significant distortions in trade.

To reduce the need for border controls, the *White Paper* proposed that the VAT should be applied in the country where the sale took place rather than at the border. Companies would report the value of their exports to their own governments, which would then seek reimbursement of the VAT from the government of the country where the good was sold. To make this deduction system work, the *White Paper* foresaw the need for a clearing mechanism to deal with refunds to member states. The benefits of VAT harmonization, the Commission believed, would be far-reaching, both in terms of financial impact and the psychological boost it would give to European integration.

Yet each country had its own reasons for taking issue with the Commission's proposals. Denmark, for example, estimated that its tax loss would be equivalent to 6% of its GDP if it were forced to lower its VAT rate to the level set by West Germany. To recover that loss, it would have to raise income tax rates by 13%. Luxembourg, on the other hand, had particularly low rates and therefore faced the prospect of having to raise its VAT rate. Implementing the 1992 VAT proposals, it argued, would drive prices up by 7.5% and unemployment up by 1%. For its part, Great Britain contended that the Commission's proposal represented an unacceptable intrusion on its political sovereignty.[12]

SERVICES AND THE APPLICATION OF MUTUAL RECOGNITION

In the view of the Commission, "the establishment of a common market in services [was] one of the main preconditions for a return to economic prosperity."[13] Services encompassed a variety of activities, including finance, transportation, and telecommunications. It was one of the fastest-growing and most heavily regulated sectors in Europe.

In the three key areas of finance—banking, insurance, and securities—member states agreed that some regulation was justified on the grounds of consumer protection. However, differences in national financial regulations tended to protect domestic firms, inhibit trade, and raise costs to consumers. A typical commercial insurance policy, for example, cost 250% more in Italy than in Luxembourg; home mortgages cost 90% more in France than in the United Kingdom. The 1992 program placed a high priority on creating a common financial market, as its proposals in banking illustrate.

The Case of Banking

A central element in the 1992 program was the liberalization of capital movements—what one Commission official referred to as "the life-blood of cross-frontier trade in financial services."[14] The Commission hoped that the adoption of its proposals would enhance Europe's appeal as an international financial center. During most of the 1970s, only Germany and the Netherlands permitted unrestricted capital movements.* Britain followed suit in 1979, and in the 1980s several other EC nations began to reduce their restrictions. In 1988, the Council agreed on a program of comprehensive capital liberalization. Eight member states planned to liberalize all capital movements by 1990; the remaining four states (Ireland, Greece, Portugal, and Spain) were allowed to wait until the end of 1992.

Several member states had reservations about the effects of liberalization. Some were concerned that complete freedom of capital movement would reduce their control over monetary policy; others feared that it would increase tax fraud. In response to this latter concern, the Commission proposed a Europeanwide general withholding tax and greater cooperation among tax authorities.

The second thrust of the 1992 banking program aimed to eliminate two other significant barriers found in most states: restrictions on the right of establishment (the right to set up

---

*Belgium also did not restrict capital movements but maintained a dual exchange rate.

branches or subsidiaries in another country) and restrictions on the freedom to provide services across frontiers (marketing and advertising of financial services). The Commission envisioned that the deregulation of operations would lead to a greater geographic scope of banking activity throughout the Community and thereby decrease the costs of financial products and improve the quality of service.

The Commission also wanted to change the responsibilities for banking supervision within the Community. In the past, host governments had the power to regulate branches of foreign banks operating within their territory. For example, the Paris branch of a British bank was subject to the regulations and supervision of the French government. As a result, banks operating in more than one European country had to meet as many as 12 different sets of national regulations (such as capital ratios). In the 1992 program, the Commission proposed that the principles of home country rule and mutual recognition should govern banking supervision. Thus, the Paris branch of a British bank would be supervised by the British authorities. Similarly, Britain would recognize the right of the French authorities to supervise the London branch of a French bank. Of course, since the degree of regulation differed among member states, a bank's location could become a source of competitive advantage. As a result, some observers predicted that the EC approach would inevitably lead to the convergence of banking regulation throughout the Community.

Some EC officials and bankers argued that foreign banks should not have unrestricted access to European markets. In particular, they contended that foreign banks should be denied licenses to operate in the EC if their home country's banking regulations were not as open as the Community's. The demand for reciprocity was directed at Japan, where foreign banks faced many limitations, and at the United States, where intrastate banking was prohibited. The

United States protested sharply against this proposal. As a result, the Commission announced that there would be no discrimination against U.S. banks in Europe, so long as European banks operating in the United States were treated the same as American banks.

Nonetheless, differences in EC and U.S. banking regulation remained a source of friction. The EC view was summed up by Sir Leon Brittan, EC commissioner for competition: "We are not using threats to get you to open your markets, only persuasion. So long as our banks receive the same treatment and access to markets as your own, there will be no questions of any sanctions against American banks in the European Community. But we believe that now is the time for the United States to follow the Community's open-market example in the banking sector."[15]

SOCIAL IMPLICATIONS OF 1992

The Single European Act addressed a number of social concerns that would accompany the completion of the internal market, including the rights of workers regarding health and safety, labor relations, and concerns over job security; the rights of medium and small business; and the problems of less-developed regions within the Community. The *White Paper*, however, did not directly address questions of social policy.

This gap was of particular concern to countries with strong labor movements or institutionalized forms of labor relations. West Germany, for example, opposed any plan that would allow German companies to avoid codetermination. Britain, on the other hand, opposed any compulsory worker participation schemes. Faced with this controversy, the Commission proposed a compromise: companies, it argued, should be allowed to choose between three systems of worker participation, although firms would have the choice of observing national laws where they were operating.

Labor unions generally remained skeptical that the completion of the internal market would serve their interests. Some feared that their collective bargaining power would be undermined. Deregulation also threatened to arouse worker protest. In late 1988, West German truckers staged strikes to challenge the deregulation of their industry, which they claimed would cost 10,000 jobs.

Commission President Jacques Delors sought to include such social issues in the 1992 agenda. In 1985, he initiated a series of meetings between unions and employers and aimed to develop a Community consensus on the issue of social protection. Not all members of the EC shared Delors' goals, however. British Prime Minister Margaret Thatcher, in particular, railed against those who saw "European unity as a vehicle for spreading socialism."[16]

Less-developed regions expressed concern that they might not fully benefit from the 1992 program. Indeed, their leaders argued that poor regions might simply become poorer. One Commission study concluded that the EC would have to provide assistance "to the Community's declining regions and labor affected by industrial restructuring. At the same time, the potential gains from market integration should help reinforce the concensus around the 1992 program which European employers and labor began to forge in 1985."[17]

INTERNATIONAL REACTIONS

Both Japan and the United States expressed concern that the 1992 program would result in a "Fortress Europe." Japan had benefited greatly from the liberal world trading regime of the 1960s and 1970s and was concerned by the apparent trend toward regional trading blocs. Its apprehension grew with the 1988 free-trade agreement between the United States and Canada. Already, it appeared that Euro-

pean import quotas on Japanese automobiles would become more restrictive in accordance with the policies of the most protectionist countries.[18]

Although the United States had similar concerns regarding the maintenance of a liberal trade environment, many U.S. multinational corporations welcomed the goals of 1992. Firms such as Ford and General Motors believed that they were well-positioned to take advantage of the European market, since they already had established plants and subsidiaries throughout Europe. As part of a drive to position themselves, U.S. firms sought new acquisitions in Europe, nearly tripling their takeovers from $1.3 billion in 1987 to $3.6 billion in 1988.[19]

Members of the European Free Trade Association also began to reevaluate their policies in light of 1992. Some EFTA countries, such as Austria and Norway, expressed a growing interest in joining the EC. Others, such as Switzerland, preferred to negotiate preferential arrangements with the EC.

Although 1992 was expected to promote greater European unity on trade issues, members of the European Commission denied that 1992 would result in a "Fortress Europe." As EC Trade Commissioner Willy de Clercq pointed out:

Why should the European Community—which is the number one trading power in the world, which represents more than 20% of all trade flows in the world—why should such an entity turn protectionist? When you're the biggest exporter in the world . . . that would be shooting yourself in the foot.[20]

Nonetheless, the Commission declared that it reserved "the right to make access to the benefits of 1992 for nonmember countries' firms conditional upon a guarantee of similar opportunities—or at least nondiscriminatory opportunities—in those firms' own countries."[21] *Exhibit 7* and *Exhibit 8* provide data on trade with and foreign investment in the EC.

1992 AND BEYOND

Of the 279 measures in the *White Paper*, 109 had been adopted by the end of 1988. Another 120 had been proposed by the Commission and were before the Council. In its Third Report to the Council and the European Parliament on the completion of the internal market (issued in March 1988), the Commission remarked that the 1992 objectives were "already becoming an established part of the expectations of individuals, enterprises and the governments of the member states." Nonetheless, the Commission's upbeat mid-term progress report (issued in December 1988) was qualified by disappointment at the pace of progress. The Commission had hoped to have drafted 90% of the measures in the *White Paper* (for votes in the Council) by the end of 1988 but succeeded in completing 80%.

As EC institutions and national governments sought to resolve the issues raised in the 1992 program, new differences began to emerge. To create a more level playing field for market unification, the Commission tightened enforcement of EC rules against state subsidies. In May 1988, the Commission ordered Alfa Romeo to repay $420 million in aid received from the Italian government in 1985 and 1986. It also ordered an investigation of the French government's decision to forgive $1.8 billion in debt

owed by the state-owned automaker Renault. Subsidies for other industries came under scrutiny as well. The Commission's efforts came under fire from many French, Italian, and Spanish politicians who argued that continued state subsidies were essential if their industries were to survive global competition.

Even more difficult were differences regarding the future of Europe beyond 1992. In a speech to the European Parliament, Commission President Delors stated that the EC was developing an "embryo European government," which, within 10 years, would take over 80% of the economic and social decision making from the member states. Belgian Prime Minister Wilfried Martens echoed this view. The ultimate EC goal, he argued, was "common sovereignty over foreign policy, defense and security, monetary, economic, environmental and social policy."

Such a prospect infuriated Prime Minister Thatcher. In a speech at one European gathering, Thatcher announced that she had not "rolled back the frontiers of the state in Britain, only to see them reimposed at a European level, with a European superstate exercising a new dominance from Brussels." A supranational European government, she argued, "would never come in my lifetime and I hope never at all."[22]

EUROPEAN COMMUNITY: THE SUM OF ITS PARTS

	Area (000 km)	Population (000)	Gross domestic product ($ billion)	Gross domestic product per capita
Belgium[a]	30.5	9,920	152.5	$15,376
Denmark[b]	43.1	5,130	101.3	19,751
France[b]	544.0	55,630	878.9	15,799
Greece[b]	132.0	9,990	47.2	4,722
Ireland[b]	68.9	3,540	29.4	8,313
Italy[b]	301.3	57,350	758.1	13,219
Luxembourg[c]	2.6	370	5.7	15,281
Netherlands[b]	41.2	14,660	231.2	14,540
Portugal[c]	92.1	10,210	29.5	2,893
Spain[c]	504.8	38,670	259.8	6,719
United Kingdom[b]	244.1	56,890	669.6	11,769
West Germany[b]	248.7	61,170	1,124.0	18,374
EC 12	2,253.3	323,530	4,269.2	13,195
United States[b]	9,372.7	243,770	4,497.2	18,448
Japan[b]	372.3	122,090	2,373.1	19,436

[a]1988 data.
[b]1987 data.
[c]1986 data.
Sources: IMF, *International Financial Statistics Yearbook* 1988; *New York Times,* December 12, 1988, p. 12.

GROSS DOMESTIC PRODUCT (real % change on preceding year)

	1961–1973	1974–1981	1982	1983	1984	1985	1986	1987
Belgium[a]	4.9	2.0	1.5	0.2	2.3	.9	1.9	2.0
Denmark[a]	4.3	1.2	3.0	2.5	4.4	4.2	3.3	− 1.0
France[a]	5.4	2.5	2.5	0.7	1.3	1.7	2.1	2.2
Greece[b]	7.7	3.0	0.4	0.4	2.8	3.1	1.2	(0.4)
Ireland[a]	4.4	4.3	2.3	(0.2)	4.2	1.6	(0.4)	4.1
Italy[a]	5.3	2.6	0.2	1.1	3.2	2.9	2.9	3.1
Luxembourg[a]	4.2	1.2	1.5	2.9	6.2	3.7	4.7	2.5
Netherlands[a]	4.8	2.0	(1.4)	1.4	3.2	2.6	2.1	1.3
Portugal[c]	6.9	3.0	2.2	(0.0)	(1.4)	2.8	4.3	4.7
Spain[a]	7.2	1.8	1.2	1.8	1.8	2.3	3.3	5.5
United Kingdom[d]	3.2	0.7	1.2	3.8	1.8	3.6	3.1	3.8
West Germany[a]	4.4	1.9	(0.6)	1.5	2.8	2.0	2.3	1.9
Europe(12)[a]	4.8	1.9	0.8	1.6	2.3	2.5	2.6	2.8
United States[e]	4.0	2.1	(2.6)	3.9	7.2	3.8	3.0	3.6
Japan[a]	9.6	3.7	2.8	3.2	5.0	4.7	2.4	4.3

[a]1980 prices.
[b]1970 prices.
[c]1986 prices.
[d]1985 prices.
[e]1982 prices.
Source: European Commission.

EXHIBIT THREE

UNEMPLOYMENT (as % of civilian labor force, annual average)

	1961–1973	1974–1981	1982	1983	1984	1985	1986	1987	1988[a]
Belgium	2.2	7.4	13.0	14.3	14.4	13.6	12.5	12.3	11.1
Denmark	1.1	5.9	9.3	10.1	9.9	8.7	7.5	7.6	8.4
France	1.1	5.1	8.7	8.9	10.0	10.5	10.7	10.8	10.9
Greece	—	—	—	7.8	8.1	7.8	2.8	7.4	na
Ireland	4.8	8.4	12.3	14.9	16.6	17.9	18.3	19.0	18.6
Italy	5.2	6.2	9.7	11.0	12.0	12.9	13.7	14.0	16.3
Luxembourg	0.0	0.5	1.3	1.6	1.8	1.7	1.5	1.6	1.6
Netherlands	1.3	5.7	11.8	14.2	14.5	13.3	12.3	11.5	7.5
Portugal	—	5.1	5.7	5.6	6.7	7.7	8.3	7.2	na
Spain	—	5.8	14.2	16.5	18.4	19.5	20.0	20.5	19.1
United Kingdom	2.1	5.1	10.6	11.6	11.6	11.8	12.0	10.7	8.6
West Germany	0.8	3.7	6.9	8.4	8.4	8.4	8.1	8.1	8.1
Europe (12)	—	5.1	9.4	10.6	11.2	11.6	11.7	11.6	11.2
United States	4.9	6.9	9.7	9.6	7.5	7.2	7.0	6.2	5.4
Japan	1.3	2.0	2.4	2.7	2.7	2.6	2.8	2.8	2.5

[a]1988 numbers are taken from the final two sources. These series are close to, but do not match exactly, earlier data in the chart.
Source: European Commission; Eurostat; OECD, *Quarterly Labour Force Statistics,* No. 1 (1989).

EXHIBIT FOUR

INFLATION (% change on preceding year)

	1961–1973	1974–1981	1982	1983	1984	1985	1986	1987	1988[a]
Belgium	3.7	7.8	7.7	6.7	5.7	5.8	0.4	2.2	1.2
Denmark	6.6	11.0	10.2	6.8	6.4	4.7	3.4	4.1	4.5
France	4.8	11.5	11.5	9.7	7.7	5.8	2.7	3.1	2.6
Greece	3.5	16.8	20.7	18.1	17.9	18.3	22.2	15.7	13.5
Ireland	6.0	16.6	15.3	9.2	8.1	4.5	3.9	3.1	2.1
Italy	4.8	17.6	15.9	15.0	11.7	9.3	5.8	4.8	5.0
Luxembourg	3.0	7.5	10.8	8.9	5.5	5.2	0.8	2.9	1.5
Netherlands	5.0	7.1	5.3	2.7	2.0	2.1	0.6	(3.0)	0.8
Portugal	3.4	21.7	20.2	25.9	28.7	19.8	13.5	10.2	9.6
Spain	6.6	17.5	14.5	12.3	11.0	8.2	8.7	5.4	4.8
United Kingdom	4.8	15.1	8.8	4.8	5.1	5.3	4.4	3.9	4.9
West Germany	3.6	5.0	4.7	3.2	2.4	2.1	(0.2)	0.7	1.2
Europe (12)	4.6	12.3	10.5	8.5	7.2	5.9	3.8	3.4	3.6
United States	3.1	8.4	6.0	3.5	3.9	3.1	2.2	4.2	4.1
Japan	6.1	8.4	2.6	1.9	2.1	2.2	0.5	(0.1)	0.7

[a]1988 numbers are derived from the second source. The IMF data are close to, but do not match exactly, earlier data listed in the chart.
Source: European Commission; IMF, *International Financial Statistics Yearbook,* 1988.

GAINS (+) AND LOSSES (−) OF MARKET SHARE BY THE EUROPEAN COMMUNITY IN THIRD COUNTRIES OVER THE PERIOD 1979–85 (in descending order)[a]

Branch	Loss	Branch	Gain
Electrical goods	−4.39	Leather and footwear	+5.45
Motor vehicles	−4.25	Timber, furniture	+4.86
Rubber and plastic products	−2.53	Textiles and clothing	+3.87
Industrial and agricultural machinery	−2.49	Nonmetallic minerals and mineral products	+2.47
Other transport equipment	−2.27	Food, beverages, tobacco	+2.03
Office and data-processing machines, precision and optical instruments	−2.23	Paper and printing products	+1.25
Other manufactured products	−0.84	Ferrous and nonferrous ores and metals, other than radioactive	+1.23
Metal products, except machinery and transport equipment	−0.65	Chemical products	+0.51

[a]Market share is defined as the exports of the European Community (10) to the rest of the world compared with exports of OECD countries to the rest of the world.
Source: European Economy, March 1988.

AUTOMOBILE SALES AND EMPLOYMENT IN THE EUROPEAN COMMUNITY, 1986

	Car sales	Sales of Japanese cars as % of total sales	Sales of Ford and General Motors cars as % of total sales[a]	Employees in manufacturing of motor vehicles, parts, and accessories (000)
Belgium	395,039[a]	20.8	20.4	51.6
Denmark	169,386	35.1	28.0	5.1
France	1,911,521	2.9	11.6	361.5
Greece	65,227	28.6	11.8	na
Ireland	57,781	43.4	25.1	4.3
Italy	1,825,383	0.5	7.0	271.7[b]
Luxembourg	30,174	14.7	25.2	0.3
Netherlands	560,512	24.3	26.8	20.6
Portugal	75,983[a]	9.8	18.5	na
Spain	649,361[a]	0.7	28.9	142.2[c]
United Kingdom	1,882,474	11.1	42.5	260.2
West Germany	2,829,438	15.0	25.4	706.3
Total	10,452,279	10.5	22.8	1,769.8

[a]Estimate based on new registrations.
[b]1985.
[c]1984.
Sources: Wards Automotive Yearbook, 1988, p. 85; *World Motor Vehicle Data,* 1988; Eurostat, *Employment and Unemployment* 1988, Theme S, Series C; Eurostat, *Industry Statistical Yearbook,* 1988, pp. 28–29.

TRADE FLOWS ($ billion)

	1952	1958	1973	1981	1986	1987
Total world exports	80.4	107.6	573.4	1,958.4	2,117.4	2,480.4
EC to EC	4.3	7.5	110.6	308.2	450.5	550.7
EC to non-EC	10.1	15.9	99.7	297.4	339.3	400.5
Non-EC to EC	10.1	14.1	93.6	311.9	289.6	353.3
EC to U.S.	0.9	1.7	15.7	41.1	73.8	82.7
U.S. to EC	1.8	2.4	16.4	48.6	50.3	57.2

TRADE FLOWS (compound annual growth rates)

	1952– 1958	1958– 1973	1973– 1981	1981– 1987	1986– 1987	1952– 1987
Total world exports	4.9%	11.8%	16.6%	4.0%	17.1%	10.3%
EC to EC	9.7	19.7	13.7	10.1	22.2	14.9
EC to non-EC	7.9	13.0	14.6	5.1	18.0	11.0
Non-EC to EC	7.9	13.4	16.2	2.1	22.0	10.7
EC to U.S.	11.1	16.0	12.8	12.4	12.1	13.8
U.S. to EC	4.9	13.7	14.5	2.8	13.7	10.4

Notes: From 1958 to 1972, EC included Belgium, France, West Germany, Italy, Luxembourg, and the Netherlands. From 1972, the definition of the EC also included Denmark, Ireland, and the United Kingdom. From 1986, it also included Spain, Portugal, and Greece.

All trade flows are exports (fob) and include provenance and destination reported by exporting countries.

Sources: UN data, published in various years:

For 1987–1984: UN, *Monthly Bulletin of Statistics,* June 1988, Special Table E.

For 1981–1983: UN, *International Trade Statistics Yearbook, 1984,* Special Table B.

For 1972–1980: UN, *Yearbook of International Trade Statisitics, 1981,* Special Table C.

For 1963–1971: UN, *Yearbook of International Trade Statisitics, 1972,* Table B.

For 1962: UN, *Yearbook of International Trade Statisitics, 1970–71,* Table B.

For 1952–1961: UN, *Yearbook of International Trade Statisitics, 1962,* Table B.

EXHIBIT EIGHT

FOREIGN DIRECT INVESTMENT, 1960–1987 ($ million)[a]

	1960	1965	1970	1975	1980	1985	1986	1987
U.S. foreign direct investment in EC (stock)[a]	2,645	6,304	11,516	38,773	77,153	81,337	98,474	122,247
As % of total stock of U.S. foreign direct investment	8%	13%	15%	31%	36%	35%	38%	40%
Japanese foreign direct investment in Europe (stock)[b]	na	na	na	na	na	12,541	14,471	21,047
As % of total stock of Japanese foreign direct investment	na	na	na	na	na	15%	14%	15%
EC foreign direct investment in U.S. (stock)[a]	557	na	3,528	15,633	47,107	107,105	127,221	157,710

[a]EC-6 until 1973; EC-9 until 1981; EC-10 until 1986; EC-12 1986 and after.
[b]Calculated on fiscal year basis, March to March. Definition of Europe used by the Japanese Ministry of Finance includes Switzerland.
Sources: U.S. Department of Commerce, *Selected Data on U.S. Direct Investment Abroad, 1950–76,* 1982, pp. 11, 16, 21, 26; U.S. Department of Commerce, *Survey of Current Business,* various years; Ministry of Foreign Affairs, Japan, *Statistical Survey of the Japanese Economy;* Ministry of Finance, Japan.

APPENDIX 1

Major Elements of the 1992 Program

In Standards, Testing, Certification

Harmonization of standards for:

Toys
Automobiles, trucks, and motorcycles and their emissions
Telecommunications
Construction products
Machine safety
Measuring instruments
Medical devices
Gas appliances
Cosmetics
Quick frozen foods
Flavorings
Food preservatives
Instant formula
Fruit juices
Food inspection
Definition of spirited beverages and aromatized wines
Tower cranes (noise)
Household appliances (noise)
Tire pressure gauges
Detergents
Fertilizers
Lawn mowers (noise)
Medicinal products and medical specialties
Radio interferences

New Rules for Harmonizing Packing, Labeling, and Processing Requirements

Ingredients and labels for food and beverages

Nutritional labeling

Classification, packaging, labeling of dangerous preparations

Harmonization of Regulations for the Health Industry (Including Marketing)

Medical specialties

Pharmaceuticals

Veterinary medicinal products

High-technology medicines

Implantable electromedical devices

Single-use devices (disposable)

In vitro diagnostics

Changes in Government Procurement Regulations

Coordination of procedures on the award of public works and supply contracts

Extension of EC law to telecommunications, utilities, transport

Services

Harmonization of Regulation of Services

Banking

Mutual funds

Broadcasting

Tourism

Road passenger transport

Railways

Information services

Life and nonlife insurance

Securities

Maritime transport

Air transport

Electronic payment cards

Liberalization of Capital Movements

Long-term capital, stocks

Short-term capital

Consumer Protection Regulations

Misleading definitions of products

Indication of prices

Harmonization of Laws Regulating Company Behavior

Mergers and acquisitions

Trademarks

Copyrights

Cross-border mergers

Accounting operations across borders

Bankruptcy

Protection of computer programs

Transaction taxes

Company law

Harmonization of Taxation

Value-added taxes

Excise taxes on alcohol, tobacco, and other

Harmonization of Veterinary and Phytosanitary Controls

Harmonization of an extensive list of rules covering items such as:

Antibiotic residues

Animals and meat

Plant health

Fish and fish products

Live poultry, poultry meat, and hatching eggs

Pesticide residues in fruit and vegetables

Elimination and Simplification of National Transit Documents and Procedures for Intra-EC Trade

Introduction of the Single Administrative Document (SAD)

Abolition of customs presentation charges

Elimination of customs formalities and the introduction of common border posts

Harmonization of Rules Pertaining to the Free Movement of Labor and the Professions within the EC

Mutual recognition of higher educational diplomas

Comparability of vocational training qualifications

Training of engineers and doctors

Activities in the field of pharmacy

Elimination of burdensome requirements related to residence permits

ESTIMATES OF COSTS OF BARRIERS

(Billion ECU)[a]

1. Costs of specific types of barriers

Customs formalities—1.7%–1.9% of intra-Community trade flows	8–9
Public procurement	21
Total	29–30

2. Costs of barriers in specific industries

Food—0.67%–1.5% turnover[b]	0.5–1.0
Pharmaceuticals—1%–2% turnover	0.3–0.6
Automobiles—5% turnover	2.6
Textiles and clothing—0.5%–1% turnover	0.7–1.3
Building materials—1.67% turnover	2.8
Telecommunications (equipment)—10%–20% turnover	3–4.8
Total	9.1–13.1

3. Costs of barriers in specific service sectors

Financial services—10% average prices	22
Business services—3% turnover	3.3
Road transport—5% turnover	5
Air transport—10% turnover	3
Telecommunications (services)	6
Total	38.3

[a]In 1987, 1 ECU = US$1.15.
[b]Turnover is total sales revenue of a business.
Source: European Economy, March 1988.
Note: The table records the results of special studies undertaken by consultants, except the transport cases, which rely on earlier published sources.
Adding categories 1 and 2 would imply some double counting, since some but not all the costs of customs formalities and government procurement are covered under branches in 2.

APPENDIX 2

SINGLE EUROPEAN ACT (EXCERPTS)

Common Provisions

The European Communities shall have as their objective to contribute together to making concrete progress towards European unity.

Source: Single European Act, Bulletin of the European Communities, Supplement 2/86.

Provisions Relating to Internal Markets

The community shall adopt measures with the aim of progressively establishing the internal market over a period expiring on 31 December 1992. . . . The internal market shall comprise an area without internal frontiers in which the free movement of goods, persons, services, and capital is ensured in accordance with the provisions of this Treaty. . . .

The Council, acting by a qualified majority on a proposal from the Commission, shall determine the guidelines and conditions necessary to ensure balanced progress [towards completing the internal market] in all the sectors concerned.

The Council shall issue directives, acting by a qualified majority. It shall endeavor to attain the highest possible degree of [financial] liberalization. Unanimity shall be required for measures which constitute a step back as regards the liberalization of capital movement.

Provisions Relating to Macroeconomic Policy

In order to ensure the convergence of economic and monetary policies which is necessary for the further development of the Community, Member States shall cooperate [in the setting of macroeconomic policies].

Provisions Relating to Social Policy

Member States shall pay particular attention to encouraging improvements, especially in the working environment, as regards the health and safety of workers, and shall set as their objective the harmonization of conditions in this area, while maintaining the improvements made.

The Commission shall endeavor to develop the dialogue between management and labor at a European level which could, if the two sides consider it desirable, lead to relations based on agreement.

Provisions Relating to Economic and Social Cohesion

The Community shall aim at reducing disparities between the various regions and the backwardness of the least-favored regions.

Provisions Relating to Research and Technological Development

The Community's aim shall be to strengthen the scientific and technological basis of European industry and to encourage it to become more competitive at [the] international level.

Provisions on European Cooperation in Foreign Policy

[The members of the EC] shall endeavor jointly to formulate and implement a European foreign policy . . .

Final Provisions

This Act [shall be] drawn up in a single original in the Danish, Dutch, English, French, German, Greek, Irish, Italian, Portuguese, and Spanish languages.

NOTES

1. Wisse Dekker, "Europe 1990," speech at the Centre for European Policy Studies, Brussels, January 11, 1985.
2. Michael Calingaert, *The 1992 Challenge from Europe: Development of European Community's Internal Market* (Washington, D.C.: National Planning Association, 1988, p. 36).
3. "A Survey of Europe's Internal Market," *The Economist*, July 9, 1988, p. 8.
4. Paolo Cecchini et al., *The European Challenge 1992: The Benefits of a Single Market* (Aldershot, England: Gower, 1988, p. 97).
5. Ibid., pp. 8–10.
6. Calingaert, *The 1992 Challenge from Europe*, p. 39.
7. Ibid., p. 33.
8. Michael Emerson et al., *The Economics of 1992: The EC Commission's Assessment of the Economic Effects of Completing the Internal Market* (Oxford: Oxford University Press, 1988, pp. 67–71).
9. Emerson et al., *The Economics of 1992*, p. 50.
10. Calingaert, *The 1992 Challenge from Europe*, p. 27.
11. Ibid., p. 63.
12. Ibid., pp. 42–44.
13. Commission of the European Communities, *Completing the Internal Market*, White Paper from the Commission to the European Council, Brussels, 14 June 1985.
14. European Community, *News*, No. 7/89, March 14, 1989.
15. Cited in European Community, *News*, No. 12/89, May 1, 1989.
16. *Washington Post*, October 31, 1988.
17. Cecchini, *The European Challenge*, pp. 105–106.
18. *BusinessWeek*, August 1, 1988, p. 41.
19. *Wall Street Journal*, January 17, 1989.
20. *New York Times*, October 23, 1988.
21. Ibid., October 20, 1988.
22. *Washington Post*, October 31, 1988.

PART SIX

Trade Policy and Corporate Strategy

Searching for Trade Remedies: The U.S. Machine Tool Industry, 1983

In February 1983, many of the 287 members of the National Machine Tool Builders Association (NMTBA) worried about the fates of their companies. Import penetration of the U.S. machine tool market had increased from 17% to 27% in only 5 years. The United States had experienced a trade deficit in machine tools in 1978 for the first time in over 40 years, and by 1982, that deficit had grown to half a billion dollars. The February issue of *American Machinist* magazine estimated a 67% decline in sales for U.S. producers from 1981 to 1983. The most serious competitive threat came from Japan, which became the world leader in machine tool production in 1982. Japanese penetration of the U.S. market was most dramatic in the fastest growing market segment—numerically controlled machine tools. Some U.S. producers suspected that they were suffering the consequences of Japanese "industry targeting" and proposed that the American industry consider requesting government intervention. The NMTBA needed to recommend to its CEOs if protection was desirable; which import remedy, such as tariffs, quotas, or voluntary export restraints, might be the most advantageous; and which administrative channels the association should pursue.

BACKGROUND ON THE MACHINE TOOL INDUSTRY

Machine tools were power-driven devices designed for shaping solid metal. They were customarily classified into two segments: metal-forming and metal-cutting. The former consisted of presses equipped with a movable ram that was forcefully pushed against an anvil or base. These tools were generally used to stamp or bend sheet metal into a usable shape, such as an automobile hood or fender. Metal-forming machine tools accounted for 23% of the

This case was prepared by Research Associate Richard Phelps, under the supervision of Associate Professor David B. Yoffie, as the basis for class discussion rather than to illustrate either effective or ineffective handling of an administrative situation. It is based on secondary sources, selected industry interviews, and "The Global Machine Tool Industry," HBS Case Services #9-387-087, prepared by Assistant Professor David Collis.

industry's sales in 1982. Metal-cutting machine tools included equipment which milled, planed, turned, ground, bored, or drilled. These machines removed metal, in the form of chips or shavings, most commonly through the application of a rotating cutting tool.

Traditionally, machine tools were operated by skilled machinists who loaded each piece onto the tool, fixed it in place with a jig or spindle, and then, following engineering drawings or blueprints, manually turned wheels or changed slide lengths to remove (or shape) the requisite amount of metal. In the 1950s, machine tool design and construction had remained relatively unchanged since their development during the industrial revolution. They were still, essentially, the metalworking equivalent of woodworking tools.

Machine tool technology changed dramatically with the adoption, first, of numerical control (NC) and, later, of computerized numerical control (CNC). Numerical control machines automatically followed directions from an input medium (such as punched paper tape) to produce a specific workpiece. With different instruction programs they could produce different workpieces. NC freed an operator from manually making all of the adjustments and settings required to do the machining. Productivity was substantially increased and quality was improved.

In the early 1970s, NC technology was expanded into computerized numerical control, which used a minicomputer to store and manipulate the control programs. Computer software allowed manufacturers to develop and alter instruction programs more easily. Computer hardware contained a large storage capacity for retention of various programs and could process the instructions for machining hundreds of different parts. CNC machine tools, in general, deemphasized the importance of the machinist's craft in favor of electronic expertise. CNC also led to the introduction of the machining center—essentially an expanded capability lathe—which allowed several different metal-cutting operations to be combined on a single machine tool. In CNC's most advanced form, the flexible manufacturing system (FMS), a number of machine tools could run unsupervised for several days under the control of a central computer, producing high volumes of dozens of different metal parts, in batches of various sizes.

Traditionally, machine tool manufacturers worldwide had been small in size, family owned and operated, and had specialized in one or two types of tools. As the technology for each tool was different—to develop a lathe required a different expertise from that needed to develop a grinding machine, which was different still for a drill or a boring machine—producers accumulated considerable mechanical and design expertise in their specialties. This pressure for product specialization was reinforced by two factors: learning in the manufacturing process (which remained through 1982 primarily batch production by skilled manual workers) and customer loyalty induced by the high costs to switch (due to the stocks of engineering drawings, jigs, and spare parts needed for each particular tool).

The machining center, however, required firms to have knowledge of several different types of metal-cutting technology, and so broke down the old product specialties. In FMSs, this requirement for broad expertise was taken even farther with the need for robot, automatic pallet, and system software technology. Firms competing in this part of the market could no longer be small specialists. Moreover, the R&D expense involved in each model update was now much greater, and as the technology changed rapidly, updates had to be undertaken more frequently. The average life of machine tool models had declined from over 10 years to about 5 years, with a substantial increase in the R&D component of value added. The archetype Bridgeport Series I milling machine, for example, was introduced in 1938 and was redesigned in only minor ways before the addition of NC. By contrast, over 50% of industry leader Cincinnati Milacron's sales, in 1980, were in products less than 5 years old.

More sophisticated machine tools also required more service and marketing. Historically, most machine tool breakdowns could be repaired by a user's own mechanics. This was rarely possible with CNC machine tools, where breakdowns could be caused by faults in the software or the electronics. Selling the sophisticated machines also required broad-based knowledge and different selling skills. Since CNC was expensive and would often require changing the organization of production in the factory, salespeople needed to communicate with higher-level managers as well as engineers on the plant floor.

Technological advances in machine tool design in the 1960s and 1970s thus made possible the construction of increasingly sophisticated machines and systems which altered the industry value chain (see *Exhibit 4*). The proportional value of R&D, marketing, and electronic controls had increased, while the proportional value of mechanical parts, basic manufacturing, and manufacturing labor had decreased.

During the same period, changes in purchasing behavior served to create two types of buyers for machine tools. On the one hand, many customers who once used customized machine tools switched to standard, low-cost tools. Although certain kinds of work might be done less efficiently with the simple manual or NC tool, the customer still saved money if the price was sufficiently low to outweigh the efficiency lost. On the other hand, some buyers still required customized tools—both manual and CNC—which they continued to purchase on the basis of quality, reputation, and service.

Hence, the global machine tool industry had evolved from the extremely fragmented structure of the 1950s and 1960s to an industrial sector with five distinctive segments in the 1980s. These were (1) standard manual machine tools, where low labor costs were critical; (2) standard CNC tools, where global scale was essential to take advantage of the learning curve as well as to amortize high R&D; (3) specialized manual tools, such as gear-cutting and precision tools, which dictated high-quality construction and service; (4) customized CNC tools and special-purpose machinery, which demanded high R&D combined with extensive service and local contacts; and finally, (5) FMS and systems which necessitated all the requirements associated with making special-purpose machines in addition to skills for building robots, automatic conveyor systems, etc. In 1983, the first segment was dominated by the newly industrialized countries, Japan dominated the second, German and Swiss manufacturers remained strong in the third, and the Americans remained supreme in customized CNC and FMS but were being challenged by Japan.

Other than technological change, the chief influence on the machine tool industry in the 1960s and 1970s was its globalization (see *Exhibit 1*). In the 30 years up to 1983, world production of machine tools tripled. During the same time period, world *trade* in machine tools more than quintupled. The lesson some strategic analysts took from this industrial catharsis was to get bigger in order to achieve some scale. Small firms were hard put to manage the increasing complexity of the product and the more rapid pace of technological change. Larger company size, greater financial resources, and more diversified product lines had become increasingly advantageous. At the same time, other analysis emphasized the importance of flexibility. They recommended that producers source globally for the lowest-cost components and put together packaged solutions to customer problems with whatever equipment did the job best, no matter where it came from.

Against this background, members of the NMTBA had to decide whether they should ask the government for protection in early 1983. Some of the American machine tool manufacturers had successfully capitalized on recent industry trends, but not all (see pp. 288–290). Furthermore, most American firms were concerned about the governmental practices of their major competitors, including Japan, West Germany, and the newly industrializing countries (NICs). Profiles of these practices are outlined below.

Japan

Industrial leaders in postwar Japan recognized that its machine tool industry was strategically vital to the development of its manufacturing infrastructure, but it was not internationally competitive. So, the Ministry for International Trade and Industry (MITI) designated it as one of the top group of industries for government support, and the June 1956 "Extraordinary Measures Law for the Promotion of the Machinery Industry" outlined a policy to strengthen it. The programs which followed included the provision of capital to the industry, through both loans from the Japan Development Bank (which though not large by themselves, provided implicit approval of the machine tool industry as a priority borrower from private banks) and a series of tax breaks, such as accelerated depreciation, reserve funds, and export deductions, which reduced the overall corporate tax rate by 20%.

To control imports in the 1950s and 1960s, MITI set differential tariffs on different machine tools and released foreign exchange only for purchases of the sophisticated tools that Japan did not yet produce. Moreover, MITI prohibited foreign firms from investing in Japanese plants. An industry association was formed to coordinate exports. Until the 1970s, however, exporting functioned primarily as a safety valve during recessions. Government officials tacitly acknowledged that Japanese exports were then sold at "dumped" prices in the United States and Europe.

To control the flow of technology, MITI strictly managed the approval process for the licensing of foreign products and processes. MITI tended to approve the purchase of licenses of more sophisticated technologies but tended to disapprove those for technologies it felt Japanese producers were ready to develop themselves. MITI operated, effectively, as a monopsony, preventing competitive bidding for foreign licenses. The Japanese government offered very little direct support for R&D during the 1950s and 1960s. The most successful firms were the traditional Japanese machine tool manufacturers, which were often subsidiaries of larger heavy manufacturing concerns.

In the early 1970s, MITI encouraged a shift from the production of standard machine tools (where it recognized that comparative advantage would move to the NICs) to numerical control. This mirrored a general trend in Japanese industry from resource-intense to knowledge-intense production. MITI set a goal of 50% NC output for the end of the 1970s. The government then provided R&D assistance through tax credits, subsidized loans, and a direct subsidy from the proceeds of the government monopoly of bike, motorbike, and powerboat race courses.

MITI encouraged the development of small, standardized NC machine tools which would be useful to the large number of smaller manufacturing operations in Japan. This reflected the perceived role of the machine tool industry as supplier to other manufacturing industries. Producers focused on developing simple, low-cost NC lathes and machining centers. Together, these two categories, nonexistent in the late 1960s, were to constitute 20% of world machine tool consumption by the 1980s. The industry association established industrywide standards for tool-changing mechanisms, size increments, etc. Within those guidelines, firms tended to specialize on one type of NC tool and develop simple, stripped-down modular designs. As a consequence, the number of parts in a machine tool was reduced by up to 30%, and a 10% to 40% overlap of parts between models was achieved.

In a further effort to lower costs through standardization, MITI encouraged machine tool companies to follow the NC standard set by Fujitsu FANUC. FANUC designed the simplest possible control unit for each type of machine tool and sold its models to the whole of Japanese industry. By 1971, only one Japanese tool company produced its own control unit, and FANUC commanded 80% to 90% of the Japanese NC control unit market. A FANUC-Siemens joint venture was established in the United States in 1975 to begin sales and provide service support. By 1983, this company controlled 20% of the open market sales of control units in the United States, and FANUC itself had a 50% share of the worldwide market for control units.

In the late 1960s, the United States and other trading partners exerted pressure on Japan to cut tariffs and liberalize capital flows. To accommodate these pressures, tariffs on standard drills and lathes were drastically reduced, but those on NC tools were maintained. Capital inflows were allowed so that foreign firms could establish joint ventures in Japan—but only on Japanese terms. In return for establishing factories in Japan to manufacture cheap standard manual machine tools, foreign companies had to license NC technology to their Japanese joint venture partner.

Only after 1975, however, did exports reach 20% of output and become central to the industry's development. The Japanese machine tool industry then demonstrated its international competitiveness in high-technology products, and ironically, companies in the 1980s were licensing CNC machine tool designs to the very companies from which they had licensed 25 years earlier. In the early days of this success, in 1976, MITI planned the next step— funding a $60 million, 7-year FMS research project. Small- and medium-sized firms were the intended beneficiaries.

Production of numerically controlled machine tools constituted 50% of total Japanese production by 1980, hitting exactly the target set a decade earlier. By 1982, NC constituted 54% of production, compared to 31% in the United States and approximately the same level in West Germany (see *Exhibit 2*). As a whole, the Japanese machine tool industry had grown at a compound annual rate of over 11% since 1970 (see *Exhibit 7*). The introduction of NC had shaken up the traditional industry competitors and increased industry concentration.

West Germany

West Germany alternated with the United States as the world's number one or number two producer during the 1970s and, by 1983, had been the world's leading exporter of machine tools for a quarter century. Its strong market position was founded on its specialization in grinding, gear-cutting, and metal-forming machine tools. Its machine tool industry was still made up of large numbers of small product-specialist firms that worked at the forefront of technology in those specialties.

West German machine tools in 1983 remained relatively sophisticated, requiring substantial ongoing R&D to keep manufacturers abreast of advances in technology, and were still segmented by end-use industry. Customization of gear-cutting and metal-forming machines for the auto industry, for example, placed heavy engineering demands on a supplier and demanded a closeness to the customer which engendered brand loyalty. The West German industry had been less exposed to the threat of Japanese imports because NC was less appropriate for its strongest products. Grinding, polishing, and gear-cutting were complex tasks, difficult to analyze (so, difficult to automate), and often required custom manufacture; while the one-action nature of metal-forming tools made NC irrelevant.

To support its successful industry, the West

German government, working through a strong industry association, encouraged broad cooperation in R&D, training, the setting of standards, and sales and service support in foreign markets. Through contracts with eight major technical institutes, the industry association provided research that small companies could not afford to undertake. A single firm could obtain funding from its local or federal governments for its own research projects so long as the results were published within 2 years of completion. Because of this high degree of cooperation, some described the industry as a "group of clubs."

Taiwan and South Korea

Both of these NICs used low labor cost and minimal industry regulation to produce cheap standard manual machine tools for export. In 1982, their exports constituted 2% of the world market and 9% of U.S. imports when measured by value and over 30% of U.S. imports when measured by unit volume. Each country exported more to the United States alone than to the rest of the world. Little was spent on R&D. The product lines were simple and familiar— some U.S. and Japanese producers claimed that some of the designs were pirated copies of their machines. The countries differed in two respects: in their trade policy and in the size of their machine tool firms. Korea limited imports in order to incubate its domestic industry and relied on large trading companies to effect industry development. Smaller entrepreneurial firms characterized the more open Taiwanese industry.

The United States

Other than Switzerland, the United States was the only major machine tool producer left with an industrial plant intact after World War II's devastation. Consequently, the United States dominated world production in the postwar years. As late as 1956, the United States accounted for 43% of the world production, with West Germany and Great Britain second and third with only 14% and 8%, respectively.

The United States had seen little in the way of Japanese-style industrial policy. U.S. government support of the industry tended to be more implicit than explicit, more indirect than direct. The Pentagon, for example, accounted for approximately 5% of demand in any one year. Defense Department (DOD) contracts, themselves, sometimes financed machine tool product development. A large guaranteed sale provided manufacturers a comfortable cushion to absorb risk and finance the R&D. And the military felt that it required the best technology possible at any given time. The Air Force, for example, sponsored the original project in the 1950s that developed NC machine tools. DOD contracts maintained this tradition up to 1983— encouraging U.S. machine toolmakers to develop the high-technology end of the market.

The development of simple, low-cost NC machine tools in the United States was, by and large, left to independent companies and the incentives of the marketplace. The machine tool association flirted with the idea of developing standards for control units but claimed that it felt restrained by the threat of antitrust action to attempt any form of standardization. So, the major manufacturers went ahead with in-house control unit development. By 1970, 10 machine tool companies had developed their own NC control units, in addition to the five major outside suppliers, and each was incompatible with the others. The control units each firm developed were also relatively complex and expensive.

The U.S. machine tool industry supplied equipment to a wide range of large and small metal-working companies. This demand was highly cyclical. Industry folklore believed that sales occurred only when capacity utilization in all manufacturing industry exceeded 80%.

To smooth production, the industry allowed delivery times to lengthen during booms and to shorten during recessions. (Imports also tended to move cyclically, taking advantage of excess demand during booms.) Cyclical demand imposed severe cash flow problems on firms in funding R&D and capital expenditures. During a boom, cash was squeezed by the heavy working capital buildup required to meet increased demand, but as working capital was freed in the downturn, economic conditions looked unfavorable for investment.

During the late 1970s, downsizing by auto firms and good business in aerospace and farm equipment led to a boom in machine tool orders and profits (see *Exhibit 9*). As backlogs of American machine tool firms lengthened (see *Exhibit 5*), imports, especially from Japan, increased dramatically (see *Exhibit 6*): Japan's share of the U.S. market for NC tools rose from 5% to over 50%. By the early 1980s, many small U.S. firms which had targeted the low end of the NC market were going out of business.

Larger U.S. companies continued their emphasis on high-technology custom-designed special products and, increasingly, on systems. These firms spent heavily on R&D and began to acquire other machine tool companies. Just as they had left production of manual machine tools in the 1960s, in the 1970s they ceased designing and manufacturing their own low-cost NC machine tools. Instead they sourced such machine tools from the Japanese, opened joint venture plants in Japan for supplying U.S. demand, or manufactured them in the United States under license from the Japanese to sell under their own brand names. For a few full-line American suppliers, key segments of their product lines were Asian imports.

In 1981 and 1982, there was a spate of merger and acquisition activity. Larger firms merged in order to rationalize excess capacity and compete with the potential threat of General Motors and IBM in FMS. They also felt threatened by the Japanese advances in FMS, where it was believed that even if the United States had a technological lead, cooperative R&D and closer links between Japanese producers and Japanese users (which were often the same company) gave them the lead in installation of FMSs.

SEARCHING FOR TRADE REMEDIES

Historically, American machine tool builders were fiercely independent entrepreneurs who sought to avoid government intervention in their business. One of the first cracks in this tradition occurred in 1977 when concerns over rising imports led the NMTBA to look into alleged Japanese dumping. After the Japanese announced a voluntary price floor for their exports, the U.S. Justice Department seized the NMTBA records. Justice was concerned about possible collusion between American and Japanese manufacturers to fix prices. This effectively stalled any further action by the NMTBA until 1980, when the case was dropped.

The next effort to seek government intervention came from Houdaille Industries, one of the makers of the NC machining centers bearing the brunt of the Japanese invasion. Fearing the permanent loss of market share and its own demise, Houdaille petitioned the federal government for relief from imported machine tools, claiming unfair competition from a government-subsidized Japanese cartel. Desiring a quick response, Houdaille avoided the better-known legal avenues toward import relief which mandated studies or hearings and routed the petition through slow, deliberative bodies, such as the International Trade Commission (ITC). Rather, Houdaille called upon Section 103 of the Internal Revenue Act of 1971 to deny investment tax credits for purchases of imported machine tools, submitting the brief in June 1982. Fees for the 714-page brief alone cost Houdaille half a million dollars, and Houdaille's president, Philip A. O'Reilly, devoted considerable personal effort stumping for the cause.

Section 103 had never before been used. It allowed that the president could exclude foreign goods from eligibility for the investment tax credit if the foreign government had engaged in discriminatory acts. Houdaille argued that the Japanese practice of "industry targeting" constituted due discrimination. Houdaille chose to use Section 103 because, unlike more commonly used remedies in U.S. trade law, it left enforcement entirely up to the discretion of the executive, which meant, theoretically, that the president could act on it immediately. Unfortunately for Houdaille, President Reagan decided to defer action indefinitely. Observers speculated that by early 1983 Reagan had decided to reject the Houdaille petition and was simply waiting for the most opportune moment to do so publicly.

The expected failure of the Houdaille petition put the responsibility for a trade initiative back into the hands of the NMTBA. There was considerable debate among the members about whether the industry should request trade restrictions at all. If they did, what kind of trade barriers would be most beneficial to the industry, and which administrative routes offered the most promising prospects for success?

PRODUCTION, EXPORTS, AND TRADE BALANCES

(All figures in $ million or in percentages)

	World production	World production (1982 $)	E/P[a] ratio (%)	United States			West Germany			Japan			Taiwan		
				Share world production	Share world exports	Net trade balance	Share world production	Share world exports	Net trade balance	Share world production	Share world exports	Net trade balance	Share world production	Share world exports	Net trade balance
1955	$ 2,438	$ 8,963	23%	40.4%	22.7%	NA	14.1%	24.5%		0.6%	0.5%				
1960	3,244	8,993	27	24.3	23.8	NA	17.4	25.5		2.3	0.9				
1965	5,000	14,793	30	29.2	16.3	185	16.7	27.1	303	5.4	2.4	(16)			
1970	7,804	18,581	34	18.5	11.7	173	19.0	30.6	587	14.2	3.5	(70)	0.2%	0.1%	(7)
1975	13,640	23,002	44	17.3	9.4	250	17.6	30.3	1,607	7.8	5.2	168	0.2	0.2	(18)
1976	13,387	21,216	43	15.9	8.9	201	18.3	30.5	1,528	7.9	7.4	300	0.3	0.5	(6)
1977	15,107	22,447	43	16.1	6.6	26	17.4	28.2	1,503	10.7	9.5	532	0.4	0.8	14
1978	19,088	26,438	42	15.8	6.9	(155)	17.8	26.3	1,660	12.3	12.6	896	0.7	1.2	36
1979	22,925	29,167	42	17.7	5.8	(155)	17.5	26.2	1,888	12.6	12.9	1,073	0.9	1.5	53
1980	26,501	30,923	42	18.2	6.6	(565)	17.8	25.2	1,955	14.5	13.1	1,228	0.9	1.6	52
1981	26,398	28,083	40	19.4	9.0	(482)	15.0	23.3	1,851	18.2	16.0	1,470	0.9	1.7	83
1982	22,694	22,694	42	16.8	6.3	(580)	15.7	24.2	1,718	17.0	13.9	1,053	0.8	1.4	44

[a]World exports as a percent of production.
Sources: *American Machinist, Iron Age,* NMTBA.

COMPETITION IN THE U.S. MARKET IN 1982 (prices in $ thousands)[a]

Metal cutting	U.S. shipments[b]				Japanese imports				West German imports		Taiwanese imports	
	Total units	Avg. unit price	NC units	Avg. unit price	Total units	Avg. unit price	NC units	Avg. unit price	Total units	Avg. unit price	Total units	Avg. unit price
Boring	994	195.0	231	479.2	96	165.0	13	440.2	—	—	2	42.00
Drilling	22,936	4.6	449	149.0	1,007	3.8	11	37.3	304[d]	13.4	399,957	0.07
Gear cutting	445	194.4	—	—	15	111.6	—	—	97	112.1	—	—
Grinding/polishing	58,284	7.9	495	85.1	3,213	7.8	31	139.7	11,729	2.9	1,492	3.19
Lathes (turning)	10,758	48.1	1,489	218.5	2,799	70.1	2,350	75.7	516	55.4	5,978	2.64
Milling	7,803	38.9	1,037	170.9	1,877	8.7	184	58.3	487	44.6	4,767	2.89
Sawing	5,258	16.1	—	—	—	—	—	—	835	5.9	50,374	0.13
Maching centers	1,265	268.5	1,265	268.5	1,728	95.7	1,728	95.7	—	—	48	46.00
Other	33,828	24.5	1,412[c]	61.0	51,472	0.4	—	—	366	49.4	1,216[e]	0.86
Total	141,571	20.6	6,378	180.0	62,208	7.2	4,317	84.5	14,334	14.1	463,834	0.16

[a]Exchange rates: $1 = 2.4266 DM = 249.05 yen = 39.0 NT$.
[b]Includes exports.
[c]Projected 1983 figures.
[d]Combined with miling.
[e]Includes NC metal-forming tools.
Sources: NMTBA and casewriter's estimates.

ANNUAL PRODUCTION VOLUMES OF MACHINE TOOLS[a]

	U.S.	Japan	W. Germany
CNC lathes	240	1500	360
Machining centers	180	480	120
Special-purpose machinery	48	24	24

[a]These numbers represent the approximate number of units produced annually by the median firm within each country.

Source: Adapted from Sciberras and Payne, *Machine Tool Industry: Technical Change and International Competitiveness* (Essex: Longman 1985)

MACHINE TOOL INDUSTRY VALUE CHAIN (%)

	1982	1955
R&D		
R&D	5%	2%
Custom engineering	5	5
Components		
Metal parts	13	19
Electrical equipment	14	13
Controls	8	3
Manufacturing		
Payroll	34[a]	38
Depreciation	2	3
Marketing		
Selling (including service)	12	10
Advertising	1	0
G&A	6	7
	100%	100%

[a]Of which 10 is direct labor.

Source: "The Global Machine Tool Industry," HBS Case Services #9-387-087, prepared by Assistant Professor David Collis.

EXHIBIT FIVE

ORDER BACKLOGS

End-of-year

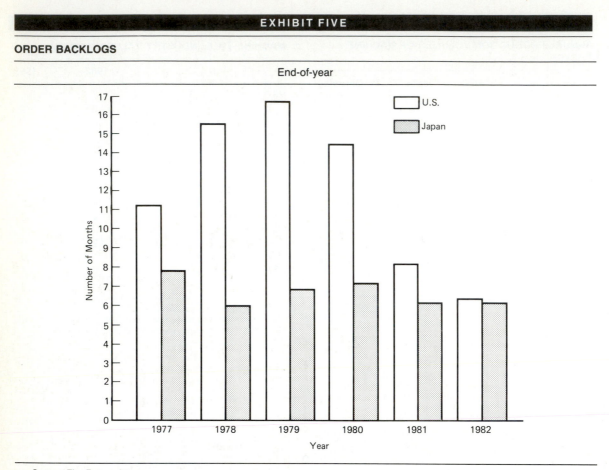

Source: The Economist.

EXHIBIT SIX

MACHINE TOOL IMPORTS AS A PERCENT OF DOMESTIC MACHINE TOOL CONSUMPTION, 1964 TO DATE

Year	U.S.A.	Japan	United Kingdom	West Germany
1964	3.5%	21.3%	28.5%	17.2%
1970	9.5	13.6	28.7	23.8
1971	10.1	15.5	28.8	20.6
1972	10.0	12.2	29.6	22.1
1973	10.3	8.0	32.5	21.3
1974	13.4	11.6	34.1	23.7
1975	14.5	14.2	37.7	27.8
1976	16.1	9.3	40.8	27.7
1977	16.5	8.0	34.2	30.0
1978	21.5	8.2	38.3	29.9
1979	23.3	9.2	47.4	29.8
1980	23.6	8.5	45.3	32.8
1981	25.6	6.6	73.9	28.4
1982	27.4	8.0	70.0	25.4
1983(P)	35.3	7.0	72.0	26.7

P = projections.
Source: National Machine Tool Builders' Association and respective machine tool trade associations.

EXHIBIT SEVEN

MACHINE TOOLS IN USE IN SEVEN INDUSTRIAL NATIONS[a] BY NUMBER AND AGE (thousands)

Country	Year	Total	Percent of total		
			Under 10 years	10–20 years	Over 20 years
United States	1976–78	2,631	31%	35%	34%
West Germany	1977	1,480	37	37	26
United Kingdom	1976	891	39	37	24
Japan	1973	825[b]	61	21	18
Canada	1978	211	47	35	18

[a]*American Machinist,* March 1977, indicates this total is for plants with over 100 employees.
[b]Machine tool age classifications are as follows: under 11 years, 11 to 20 years, over 20 years.
Source: NMTBA.

EXHIBIT EIGHT

SIZE AND GEOGRAPHIC DISTRIBUTION OF THE U.S. MACHINE TOOL INDUSTRY IN 1982

Region	Establishments Total	Establishments With >20 employees	Number of employees[a]	Value of shipments[b]
New England	166	52	14,590	1,139
Middle Atlantic	178	53	12,100	751
East North Central	565	228	39,200	3,551
West North Central	104	37	6,810	182
South	71	22	1,630	129
West	165	32	2,910	223
U.S. total	1,392	455	77,600	5,869

[a]Estimates.
[b]Casewriter estimates based on Census Bureau data.
Source: NMTBA.

EXHIBIT NINE

MACHINE TOOL INDUSTRY FINANCIALS, 1967 TO DATE

Year	Net income as percent of sales — All manufacturers	Net income as percent of sales — Machine tool manufacturers[a]	Net income as percent of assets — All manufacturers	Net income as percent of assets — Machine tool manufacturers	New capital expenditures $ millions — Machine tool manufacturers
1967	8.3%	12.1%	10.9%	16.6%	n.a.
1970	6.8	3.8	8.3	4.8	72.7
1971	7.0	(2.7)	8.7	(2.7)	39.1
1972	7.4	(1.3)	9.5	(1.4)	52.7
1973	8.0	4.3	11.0	4.8	65.9
1974	7.7	5.6	10.7	7.2	93.3
1975	6.7	8.9	8.8	12.7	76.1
1976	7.8	9.3	10.6	12.3	93.5
1977	7.8	7.6	13.5	12.8	132.4
1978	7.8	7.4	10.7	11.8	142.4
1979	7.5	12.0	11.1	16.9	199.4
1980	6.7	12.9	9.5	19.4	241.0
1981	7.4	12.2	10.5	18.0	296.2
1982	5.3	5.0	6.7	6.1	190.3
1983(P)	6.3	(9.6)	7.9	(8.7)	132.9

[a]Data based on the machine tool activities of 111 companies and divisions.
P = projected.
Source: NMTBA.

United States Trade Law

This note examines the evolution of U.S. trade law and policy in the post-World War II period. The first half of the note emphasizes trade in manufactured goods and services as well as the relationship between the Executive and the Legislature. The second half of the note describes the key features of U.S. trade law, how those laws affect U.S. firms, and the actions required for firms to invoke specific sections of U.S. trade legislation.

EVOLUTION OF U.S. TRADE LAW

United States trade policy up to the early twentieth century was synonymous with tariff policy. Tariffs, set by the Congress under the powers provided by the founding fathers in the Constitution, were used as a revenue instrument and as a mechanism for protecting domestic industry. Since the tariff was the exclusive domain of the Legislative branch, the Executive branch played only a peripheral role in trade policy.

As early as 1790, there were groups within the United States that disagreed with the protectionist philosophy that pervaded the country. In a 1790 U.S. congressional debate, a delegate noted:

We up in Massachusetts do not want that duty upon molasses, we trade our fish for molasses, and if you shut out molasses you shut in fish.

In the early twentieth century opponents to protectionism and the high tariffs of the period began to emerge in greater numbers. Many who advocated free trade also proposed that the Executive, rather than the Legislative branch, set tariffs. The Legislative branch, they contended, was more susceptible to political pressures from domestic industries. The Congress, however, was reluctant to delegate its power to set tariffs, even though tariffs became less important as a source of government revenue after the passage of an income tax in 1913. The tariff-set-

This note was prepared by Research Assistant Alvin G. Wint and revised and updated by Research Associates Richard Phelps and David Dobrowolski, and Associate Professor David B. Yoffie, as the basis for class discussion.

Copyright © 1987 by the President and Fellows of Harvard College. Harvard Business School case 9-387-137.

ting power of the Congress was most vividly demonstrated in 1930, when it enacted the Tariff Act of 1930 (Smoot-Hawley Act). Smoot-Hawley inflated tariff rates so that an average dollar's worth of dutiable American imports paid a tariff of about 60 cents. (See *Exhibit 1*.) Many trading partners retaliated, which contributed to a reduction in America's share of world trade from 16% to 11% between 1930 and 1935.

The 1934 Reciprocal Trade Act

Crisis in the American economy and the deteriorating fortunes of U.S. goods on world markets prompted a major change in U.S. trade policy for manufactured goods and services. In 1934, Congress enacted the Reciprocal Trade Act. This legislation reversed the balance of power between the Executive and Legislative branches on trade policy. It allowed the president to negotiate bilateral tariff-reduction agreements that did not require congressional ratification. Congressional restrictions stipulated that the president could cut tariffs from Smoot-Hawley levels by no more than 50% and limited the duration of the president's tariff-cutting power to three years. The president's authority to set tariffs was renewed by the Congress in 1937, 1940, 1943, and repeatedly since then. By 1945, the United States had negotiated 32 bilateral trade agreements under this act. These agreements granted tariff reductions on 64% of all dutiable imports and reduced tariff rates by an average of 44%.

The General Agreement on Tariffs and Trade

In the postwar period the United States moved toward multilateral, rather than bilateral, tariff negotiations. In 1945 Congress updated the president's authority to negotiate tariff reduc-

tions. This enabled the president to participate in negotiations leading to the General Agreement on Tariffs and Trade (GATT) in 1947. The United States joined the provisional GATT, even though the Senate did not accord the GATT treaty status.

The articles of the GATT promoted free trade among nations. Protection was to be a controlled exception to the general principle of free and liberal trade. To this end, the GATT's objectives included the elimination or reduction of tariffs and quantitative restrictions. The GATT institutionalized multilateral tariff negotiations by promoting the unconditional most-favored-nation (MFN) principle, a principle the United States had been following since 1922. Under MFN, a tariff reduction given to one trading nation had to apply to all other trading nations that were signatories to the GATT. In addition, the GATT provided a framework within which the United States and its major trading partners could settle disputes and enter into global negotiations.

The first five negotiating rounds sponsored under the GATT extended from 1947 to 1960. The first round in 1947 yielded broad and deep tariff cuts. The next four rounds, however, were less effective, stifled by the fact that tariff negotiations were handled on an item-by-item basis and governed by the rule of "principal supplier." (The principal supplier rule stated that countries needed to negotiate only with the largest exporter of a particular product.) Congress also slowed the momentum of trade liberalization by granting single rather than multiyear extensions of presidential negotiating authority and by instituting procedures that made it fairly easy for industries to qualify for trade relief. The main procedure, called the escape clause (later codified in Section 201 of the 1974 Trade Act), allowed an affected industry to appeal for temporary import relief if it could prove injury resulting directly from trade concessions.

The 1962 Trade Expansion Act

In 1962, President John F. Kennedy success-fully persuaded Congress to enact the Trade Expansion Act, which gave his administration sweeping authority to negotiate tariff reductions, particularly with member countries of the European Economic Community. The Trade Expansion Act also codified and revised the escape clause. A domestic interest group seeking relief now had to demonstrate that an increase in imports due to U.S. tariff concessions was "a major cause of serious injury" (major cause meant greater than all other factors combined). If an industry met this test, the president then had a choice of whether to recommend higher trade barriers or trade adjustment assistance (TAA). Under TAA, firms or workers hurt by imports could be given financial, technical, or retraining assistance. This plan was designed to liberalize trade by providing an alternative to import restrictions and defuse labor's opposition.

Coincident with granting the president wide-sweeping authority to liberalize trade in the 1962 Trade Expansion Act, Congress also required that the responsibility for international trade policy be shifted from the State Department to a new Office of the Special Trade Representative (in the 1970s, the name was changed to the United States Trade Representative, or USTR). Congress wanted the USTR to be more independent than either the State or Commerce departments. Accordingly, Congress established that the USTR would answer directly to the president and not to specific domestic or international constituencies. Congress also granted the president broad authority to retaliate against unfair foreign trade practices.

The Kennedy Round

The Kennedy Round of multilateral tariff negotiations under the GATT began in 1964 and was completed in 1967. Unlike the four previous rounds, the Kennedy Round was highly successful in reducing tariffs. The major industrial countries agreed on a target of an across-the-board cut of 50% in all tariff rates. Each country could propose to except some of its tariffs from the cut. These exceptions were generally cases where unacceptable injury to domestic industries would result. The major industrial nations bargained over the size of the exceptions lists, rather than the target 50% cut. Eventually, they agreed to weighted-average tariff cuts of about 35%. The extent and scope of these tariff cuts made the Kennedy Round one of the most sweeping sets of tariff reductions in the history of world trade.

In 1973, the effect of the tariff reductions of the Kennedy Round was evident in the low tariff levels of the major industrial nations. U.S. tariffs on dutiable imports averaged 8.9%, those of the European Economic Community countries 9.0%, Japan 11.2%, and Canada 14.2%.

During the Kennedy Round, the participants also discussed nontariff barriers (NTBs) for the first time. To address the problem of NTBs, the contracting parties in the Kennedy Round negotiated an Antidumping Code. This code, however, was not ratified by the U.S. Congress. Observers blamed poor coordination between the Executive and the Legislature for the failure.

The Trade Act of 1974

The deterioration in the world trading and economic system following the OPEC oil increases led to the resurgence of protectionist sentiment within the United States. In response, the Trade Act of 1974 legislated several important changes: It gave the U.S. Tariff Commission (the agency primarily responsible for administering U.S. trade law) more independence from the president and renamed it the International Trade Commission (ITC), it required the president to submit any agreements on reducing NTBs to a majority vote of the Congress, and it created an elaborate advisory system to work with the USTR in multilateral trade negotiations. Congress intended with this legislation to limit the freedom of the president in reducing tariffs and NTBs. The act did, however, represent the first time the president was given any authority to negotiate reductions in NTBs.

The 1974 Trade Act also made it easier for American firms to appeal for protection by weakening the legal tests required for escape clause relief. Section 201 of this act required that instead of imports being a "major cause" of injury (as described in the 1962 Act), relief would be granted if domestic interest groups could prove that imports were a "substantial cause of serious injury." (Substantial injury was defined to mean not less than any other cause.) Section 201 also waived the requirement that such injury had to result from specific U.S. tariff concessions. In addition, the 1974 legislation relaxed the eligibility criteria for adjustment assistance by dropping the causal link that had previously been required between an increase in imports and previous trade concessions.

Other provisions of the 1974 Trade Act gave the Executive branch power to negotiate reductions in duties of up to 60% of existing rates, or down to zero duty if the existing rate was 5% or less, and authorized the president to grant tariff preferences to developing countries. This authority coincided with the "Generalized System of Preferences" (GSP) adopted by the GATT in 1971, which allowed any GATT signatory to provide preferential treatment to developing countries.

The Tokyo Round

The significant reduction in tariff rates and the elimination of most quotas on manufactured goods prompted many industrial countries to substitute NTBs for tariffs and global quotas during the late 1960s and 1970s. These barriers were especially difficult to manage since they were less transparent than tariffs, and the GATT was not empowered to deal with them.

The Tokyo Round of GATT negotiations, from 1974 to 1979, represented the first concerted attempt to eliminate a wide array of NTBs. Nontariff barriers of concern to the participants in the Tokyo Round included subsidies and countervailing duties, dumping and anti-dumping duties, discriminatory government procurement practices, import licensing schemes, methods of customs valuation, prohibitive product standards, abuses in the trade-remedy laws, interventionist foreign investment regimes, and restrictive agreements providing for "voluntary" export restraints (VERs) and "orderly marketing arrangements" (OMAs).

In the Tokyo Round the Antidumping Code initially negotiated during the Kennedy Round was revamped and subsequently accepted by the United States; a Subsidies Code was also negotiated. The Subsidies Code distinguished between export subsidies, which prejudiced the trade and production interests of other countries and were therefore subject to countervailing duties, and production subsidies. Production subsidies, defined as subsidies designed for the promotion of domestic and social economic policy objectives such as redeploying industry to backward regions, were not expressly prohibited under the code. In the aftermath of the Tokyo Round only a minority of GATT signatories formally joined the Subsidies Code; this group, however, included the United States, the European Community countries, Japan, Canada, Hong Kong, India, Brazil, and South Korea.

The Trade Agreements Act of 1979

The 1979 Trade Agreements Act represented the beginning of an attempt to change the way trade policies were made in the United States. Previous acts were widely viewed as biased against protectionism. Even in cases of illegal dumping or proven subsidies, the trade laws had provided significant discretion to the Executive branch, allowing it to ignore industry pleas for assistance and relief in the name of the national interest. The 1979 Trade Act attempted to redress this perceived bias by shifting authority for dumping and countervailing duty cases from the free trade–oriented Treasury Department to the more protectionist-oriented Commerce Department. This act also included other measures designed to reduce the discretion afforded the Executive branch in trade policy. For instance, tighter time limits were set reducing the time foreign firms and governments had to develop complicated countercases. In addition, the new law gave a labor union or a trade association the right to appeal a trade relief decision even if it had not initiated the case. Finally, the requirements for invoking the escape clause (Section 201) were expanded: firms could petition if they were "threatened" with substantial injury rather than waiting until they were injured.

The Trade and Tariff Act of 1984

The Trade and Tariff Act (TTA) of 1984 continued the legislative trend toward a more protectionist-oriented trade policy. The act was divided into three main areas: authority for the Executive branch to negotiate with, and retaliate against, U.S. trading partners; the operation of the trade-remedy laws; and measures relating to specific products, for example, steel.

The TTA departed from previous laws by providing the president with the authority to negotiate bilateral free trade zones. Unlike all other authorities granted since 1934, the TTA mandated that any tariff reductions granted in bilateral negotiations would not be automatically extended to other countries that would normally have been entitled to them under unconditional MFN policy. The president used this authority to negotiate a free trade area with Israel in 1985 and initiate similar negotiations with Canada, which led to the U.S.-Canada free trade agreement in 1988.

Within the ambit of the TTA, the Congress also made it an objective of U.S. trade negotiations to reduce or eliminate barriers to international trade in services, in addition to renewing the GSP program until 1993. With this renewal, GSP products from the more competitive beneficiary countries (for example, some of the newly industrializing countries) were subject to "graduation"; their products would no longer be eligible for preferential treatment. GSP could also be suspended under other conditions, such as expropriation of American property. Another amendment included in the TTA codified and tightened the application of a practice called upstream subsidization. This practice subjected finished goods containing subsidized inputs to countervailing duties, whether or not the goods themselves had been subsidized.

The Omnibus Trade and Competitiveness Act of 1988

Large U.S. trade deficits (see *Exhibit 2*) and a growing perception of a decline in U.S. competitiveness made trade an important issue in the 1988 presidential campaign. Representative Richard Gephardt (D-Mo) gained prominence during the primaries with vocal advocacy of greater protectionism. Meanwhile, the Reagan administration tried to co-opt pressures for more trade barriers by pushing foreign countries, especially Japan, Korea, and Taiwan, to open their markets.

Protectionist sentiment abated somewhat as the value of the U.S. dollar declined and export volumes began to rise. Nevertheless, Capitol Hill was determined to change the course of U.S. trade policy. A three-year legislative effort finally culminated in the Omnibus Trade and Competitiveness Act of 1988. While the administration effectively watered down or removed most protectionist provisions, the massive 1200-page legislation introduced many changes into U.S. trade law. Yet the real effect of the bill would depend on how it was implemented by the Bush administration. Congress made it more costly for the president to refuse industry requests for protectionism or retaliation against "unfair trade practices," but Congress continued to give the president discretion.

The principal features of the bill included enhanced and expedited ("fast track") negotiating authority for the president in bilateral and multilateral (GATT) agreements, a $1 billion worker readjustment program, reinforced Section 301 provisions against unfair foreign trade practices ("Super 301" described below), improved intellectual property protection, less burdensome export controls, a reduction in the scope of the Foreign Corrupt Practices Act, and implementation of the Harmonized System of tariff nomenclature. The bill also included sanctions against Toshiba Corporation and its subsidiary Toshiba Machine Co. The sanctions were a response to the illegal sale of sophisticated propeller milling machines to the Soviet Union that U.S. officials claimed enabled the Soviets to build quieter submarines. On December 28, President Reagan signed an executive order implementing the sanctions, which banned imports from Toshiba Machine (and Kongsberg Trading Company) for three years. In addition, Reagan banned government procurement from both firms, and their parents, for three years.

The Uruguay Round

While U.S. trade policy in the 1960s had emphasized multilateralism, American trade policy in the 1980s had become increasingly unilateral (exemplified by U.S. trade sanctions in machine tools, semiconductors, and elsewhere) and bilateral (exemplified by the free trade areas [FTAs] negotiated with Israel and Canada). Multilateral efforts, however, re-

mained an important part of the U.S. trade agenda. A new round of trade talks began at Punta del Este, Uruguay, in the fall of 1986 and were scheduled to continue for four years through the GATT in Geneva.

The Midterm Review of the Uruguay Round was held in Montreal in December of 1988. As of that date, framework agreements were achieved in 11 of the 15 negotiating groups, including rules for trade in services, the functioning of the GATT system, dispute settlement, an agenda for trade-related investment measures (TRIMS), nontarrif measures, tropical products, and a target amount for tariff reductions at least as ambitious as that achieved in the Tokyo Round. The four remaining issues were agriculture, intellectual property, textiles, and safeguards. The stalemate between the United States and the European Community over farm trade effectively put on hold the progress achieved in the other areas. The differences over agriculture were exacerbated by a bilateral trade dispute involving a Community ban on hormone-treated meat.

As 1988 came to a close, U.S. trade policy seemed to be in a state of flux. There was a new administration in Washington, an unfinished set of multilateral trade talks, and a comprehensive new trade law awaiting implementation. Yet elements of continuity were also present. While the Omnibus Trade and Competitiveness Act of 1988 modified many important sections of U.S. trade law, the ultimate significance of these changes was in doubt.

STRUCTURE OF U.S. TRADE LAWS— AS OF JANUARY 1989

U.S. trade legislation at the end of the 1980s was an amalgam of various laws enacted at various times. While the Trade Act of 1974 introduced the most sweeping changes up to that time, other laws in active use were first introduced in the nineteenth century. In common trade parlance, the laws were identified by the section numbers of the act that introduced or most significantly updated them. The main items of U.S. trade legislation were Section 201 (1974 Trade Act), Section 301 (1974 Trade Act), Section 337 (1930 Tariff Act), Section 303 (1930 Tariff Act), and Section 731 (1930 Tariff Act). Several of these acts are summarized in *Exhibit 3.* All of the above acts were modified by the Omnibus Trade and Competitiveness Act of 1988 (OTA).

Section 201—Import Relief under the Escape Clause

Section 201 of the 1974 Trade Act, also known as the escape clause, provided for relief from injury caused by import competition. The escape clause provision first appeared in a Reciprocal Trade Agreement with Mexico in 1943. Since then, it has appeared in many other bilateral treaties and in the multilateral General Agreements on Tariffs and Trade. It was codified in the Trade Expansion Act of 1962 and then appeared as Section 201 of the Trade Act of 1974. Over time, the general principle behind the escape clause has remained the same; i.e., domestic firms have a right to relief if they are injured by import competition. The scope and execution of the clause has, however, evolved with changes in the trade policy and philosophy of the Legislative and Executive branches. The latest modification (OTA) to Section 201 encouraged efforts by domestic industries to make "a positive adjustment" to import competition.

Circumstances under Which the Law Was Invoked. Section 201 was invoked when a group (for example, a trade association, firm, or union) representing a domestic industry submitted a petition to the U.S. International Trade Commission (ITC). The petitioner was required to present information showing that increased imports were the "substantial cause" of, or threatened to cause, "serious injury" to

the domestic industry. The Trade Act of 1974 set out the following criteria that the ITC had to use in determining whether or not the industry had suffered "serious injury": a decline in sales; a higher and growing inventory; and a downward trend in production, profits, wages, or employment in the particular domestic industry. The 1984 amendment to Section 201 stipulated that the ITC could not conclude that a domestic industry had avoided serious injury simply because of the absence of one indicator. After the ITC determined that the domestic industry had suffered serious injury, it had to establish that imports were a "substantial cause" of this injury. U.S. law defined "substantial cause" to mean a cause which was important and not less than any other cause.

Investigating and Monitoring Agencies. The ITC investigated the request for relief, primarily by applying the injury test, and voted on whether relief should be granted and, if granted, the form that the relief should take. In making its decision the ITC collected information from the affected domestic industry, government agencies, domestic importers, foreign producers, trade associations, and other interested parties. The ITC's report had to be presented to the president within six months of the filing of the petition. The president then had 60 days to decide whether to accept, reject, or modify the commission's recommendations. Section 201 stated that the president should provide relief, unless he determined that such relief would not be in the national economic interest. If the president rejected an ITC recommendation, the Congress had 90 days to override the decision. If the United States did invoke the escape clause, its trading partners were entitled to compensation under GATT rules throughout the period relief was provided.

The 1988 amendment changed some of the ITC procedures. It created a two-step process by which the injury determination was to precede the remedy recommendation. An injury finding was due within 120 days of the petition. The remedy report deadline remained at six months. The voting procedures within the ITC were also modified. Only those commissioners who had voted affirmatively on injury could vote on the remedy. In addition to these procedural changes, the language of the 1988 amendment made it more difficult for the president to reject an affirmative finding. It stated that the president should "take all appropriate and feasible action within his power" to promote positive adjustment of the domestic injury.

Remedies Available under Section 201. Relief might take the form of import duties, quotas, quantitative restrictions, or any combination of these measures. As an alternative to import relief, the commission could recommend that trade adjustment assistance be offered to the workers and firms that suffered from import competition. The president could also choose to negotiate orderly marketing agreements (joint agreements to limit shipments of goods) with the principal suppliers of the goods in question. The 1988 amendment expanded the scope of remedies available to include auctioned quotas, the initiation of international negotiations, and legislative proposals.

Section 232—Safeguarding National Security

Section 232 of the 1962 Trade Expansion Act, also known as the national security clause, provided the president with broad power to adjust imports of any article if it was determined that its import threatened to impair the national security. The 1962 Act assigned investigatory responsibility to the director of the Office of Emergency Planning, a now-defunct office. The role was transferred to the secretary of the Treasury in the 1974 Trade Act and, finally, to

the secretary of Commerce in the 1979 Trade Act.

Circumstances under Which the Law Was Invoked. An immediate investigation was to be made upon request of the head of any department or agency, or upon application of an interested party, to determine the effects on the national security of imports of the subject article. Consideration was to be given to domestic production needed for projected national defense requirements; the capacity of domestic industries to meet such requirements; existing and anticipated availabilities of the human resources, products, raw materials, and other supplies and services essential to the national defense; the growth requirements of the industries and supporting suppliers; and the impact of imports, as measured by their qualities, availabilities, character, and use, which would affect the capacity of the domestic industry to meet national security requirements.

The investigation was also to consider that a weakened domestic economy could impair national security. So, the adverse impact of foreign competition on the economic welfare of domestic industry was to be measured in a wide variety of ways, including a decrease in government revenues, a loss of skills or investment, or the displacement of domestic products.

Investigating and Monitoring Agencies. The secretary of Commerce was responsible for the investigation and for determining whether or not the item was being imported into the United States in such quantities or under such circumstances as to threaten to impair the national security. If the investigation revealed such a threat, the secretary was to advise the president promptly. The president then determined whether or not the threat was valid. Through 1988, the president had no deadline on his decision. The OTA of 1988 shortened the time for the Commerce Department report from one year to 270 days and imposed time limits on the presidential determination (90 days) once the report was received.

Remedies Available under Section 232. The president could take whatever action, for whatever time period, that was deemed necessary to adjust imports.

Section 301—Retaliation

Section 301 of the 1974 Trade Act, also known as the presidential retaliation authority, gave the president the authority to take all appropriate action to remove foreign trade barriers. This authority was first given to the president in the 1962 Trade Expansion Act. The 1974 Act strengthened the presidential authority, giving the president more flexibility to retaliate against unfair foreign trade practices.

Before the Reagan administration, however, 301 was used sparingly. Although Reagan had actively approved actions under 301, the OTA of 1988 transferred authority to determine whether a practice was unfair from the president to the USTR. The USTR could then decide, "subject to presidential direction," what action to take. The authority transfer was designed to give more leverage to the USTR in market access negotiations.

The legislative history of Section 301 revealed a pattern of increasing scope. The 1974 act dealt primarily with the problems faced by U.S. exporters and investors. In the Trade and Tariff Act of 1984, the law was amended to allow direct retaliation against countries that denied U.S. firms the right to invest in their service sectors. Other amendments codified in the 1984 Act provided for retaliation against export performance requirements that adversely affected the economic interests of the United Strates and against specific countries by sector if sectorial reciprocity in bilateral tariff and NTB negotiations was not achieved. While 301 actions were industry-specific prior to 1988,

the OTA added a "Super 301" provision which mandated that the USTR identify priority unfair practices and priority *countries* to be targeted for negotiations. If trade talks failed, the USTR had authority to retaliate.

Circumstances under Which the Law Was Invoked. Section 301 could be invoked independently by the USTR, by a formal petition of U.S. firms, or by other domestic interest groups, requesting the USTR to initiate Section 301 proceedings in order to pursue a complaint against foreign governments. This law gave the Executive broad retaliatory authority so the domestic interest group could complain about any activity by a foreign government that appeared to be "unjustifiable, unreasonable, or discriminatory and burdened or restricted U.S. commerce." In 1988 additional practices were defined as "unreasonable" and therefore actionable under 301. These included export targeting, foreign cartels, and the denial of workers' rights.

Investigating and Monitoring Agencies. The Trade Act of 1974 gave the USTR almost complete control over Section 301 cases. If a domestic firm petitioned the USTR, the petition had to explain the nature of the foreign practice that allegedly violated U.S. rights and had to indicate whether the policy involved unfair import restrictions or export practices. The USTR then had 45 days to determine whether to initiate an investigation. In making this determination, the USTR often consulted with other agencies through an interagency Section 301 committee, chaired by the USTR. One or more participants on the committee were responsible for quantifying the burden or restriction to U.S. commerce. Once that step was accomplished, a list of products or services was drawn up to be targeted for possible retaliation. The retaliation list gave the foreign producers an incentive to lobby their government to reform its unfair practice. Another step in the 301 process usually involved an opportunity for public comment for all parties concerned, often through the forum of a public hearing.

The law set deadlines during which the USTR either had to resolve the dispute through negotiation or bring the investigation to the action stage. The 1988 amendment reduced some time limits for action and imposed others. Consultations were to be initiated with the foreign government on the day the investigation was initiated (with some provisions for delays). The USTR was required to request dispute-settlement proceedings if consultations were not concluded within 5 months. The USTR was required to make the unfairness determination and decide what, if any, action to take within 12 months in subsidy and nontrade agreement cases and within 18 months in trade agreement cases other than subsidies. Action was to be implemented within 30 days (with delays up to 180 days in certain cases). Before 1988, the deadlines were slightly different (see footnote in *Exhibit 3*) because of the separation of the investigatory report (the USTR) from the action decision (the president).

Remedies Available under Section 301. Section 301 gave the president (and after 1988 the USTR, subject to the direction of the president) broad scope for retaliatory action. The Executive branch could suspend or withdraw any previous trade concessions granted to the foreign government or impose duties or other import restrictions on the products and services of the foreign country in question. (The 1988 amendments required the USTR to give preference to duties over other import restrictions). It could retaliate against countries that restricted investment in their service sectors and against governments that imposed export performance requirements that forced firms producing in their country to export. The retaliation could be applied to all countries on a nondiscriminatory basis, to a single country or group of countries on a discriminatory basis, or to specific sectors within one or more coun-

tries. Further, the retaliation could be directed against goods and services other than those identified in the original petition. The 1988 amendment made (unspecified) retaliation mandatory for foreign trade agreement violations. It was not unusual through the 1980s for measures to be threatened or imposed and then dropped through negotiated settlements.

Section 337—Unfair Trade Practices and Intellectual Property Rights

Section 337 of the Tariff Act of 1930 was also known as the "Unfair Trade Practices Act." Most of the actions under this act involved infringement of U.S. intellectual property laws—patent, copyright, or trademark; theft of trade secrets; and passing off or violation of the antitrust laws of the United States.

In 1986, the Reagan administration sought passage of an Intellectual Property Rights Improvement Act that would amend the 1930 Act. The Omnibus Trade and Competitiveness Act of 1988 incorporated this initiative and amended Section 337 by removing hurdles that stood in the way of innovators' ability to get protection from the ITC. In these intellectual property rights cases, the "injury test" was eliminated. U.S. industries would not have to show that an import substantially injured the industry in order to obtain relief. They only needed to prove patent infringement. Prior to these changes, protection under Section 337 was considered "cumbersome and costly" (text of the 1988 amendment). The 1988 amendment stated that the U.S. persons who relied on this protection were "among the most advanced and competitive in the world."

Circumstances under Which the Law Was Invoked. Section 337 was usually invoked when a domestic interest group petitioned that it faced unfairly traded imports. The type of unfair imports most frequently considered under this act were counterfeit goods that infringed on registered U.S. patents or trademarks. The domestic parties whose patents, copyrights, or trademarks had been infringed could petition to the Office of Unfair Import Investigations of the ITC for relief.

Investigating and Monitoring Agencies. The investigating agency, the ITC, had to determine within 30 days of the filing of a petition whether to initiate an investigation. Prior to 1988, the criteria used to determine whether an investigation was appropriate was if there was evidence that the unfair trade practices destroyed, substantially injured, or threatened to destroy or injure a domestic industry. In addition to eliminating the injury criterion, the 1988 amendment relaxed the "industry requirement" to include foreign licensing as well as domestic production under the patent. If the ITC began an investigation, it had to be completed within one year, and the president then had 60 days in which to approve or disapprove the ITC's determination. The 1988 amendment also required the USTR to identify countries that did not adequately protect U.S. copyrights and patents and to initiate unfair trade cases in the most harmful instances.

Remedies Available under Section 337. The ITC could direct that the goods which were imported unfairly into the United States be excluded from entry, or it could issue cease and desist orders that demanded that the companies listed in the petition stop violating U.S. patents or trademarks or stop engaging in other unfair trade acts.

Section 303—Countervailing Duty; and Section 731—Antidumping

Countervailing Duties (CVDs). Section 303 of the Tariff Act of 1930 was also known as the Countervailing Duties Act. The first U.S. countervailing duty law was enacted, in a form very similar to its current one, in 1897. The original act required the secretary of the Treasury to assess a duty on any import that had benefited from a subsidy or grant from a foreign government. The duty was supposed to nullify the effect of the subsidy. The countervailing duty law was codified in Section 303 of the Tariff Act of 1930, which, in the mid-1980s, remained the basic antisubsidy law of the United States. In the Trade Act of 1974 the substantive text of the law remained intact, but many procedural changes were made designed to limit the scope of discretion of the Executive branch. The Trade and Tariff Act of 1984 made additional changes, such as relaxing the injury test, designed to assist petitioners in countervailing duty cases. The Omnibus Trade and Competitiveness Act of 1988 made further changes by clarifying the application of the countervailing duty law to domestic subsidies. Procedures for the Commerce Department to follow in the analysis of this gray area were made more specific. The USTR was also given the authority to revoke the injury test if a country violated the GATT's Subsidies Code commitment to the United States.

Antidumping (AD). The first U.S. antidumping statute was enacted in 1916. This statute was later amended and became the Antidumping Act of 1921. This act provided that when a foreign company dumped merchandise in the United States, the Treasury Department would levy antidumping duties equivalent to the dumping margins. Under this law, the two requirements for a dumping finding were a determination that sales in the U.S. market were at less than fair value and a determination that these sales resulted in injury to domestic interests.

The antidumping law was codified, with very few amendments, in Section 731 of the Tariff Act of 1930. In the Trade Act of 1974 and the Trade Agreements Act of 1979, the antidumping law was amended. These amendments, however, were generally procedural rather than substantive. In the Trade and Tariff Act of 1984 the antidumping laws, like the countervailing duty laws, were subjected to significant procedural amendments that were generally expected to benefit petitioners. Further changes were made in 1988 under the OTA. Some of these included new provisions with respect to imports from nonmarket economies, third-country dumping, and expedited procedures for short-life-cycle products.

Circumstances under Which the Laws Were Invoked.   The countervailing duty (CVD) and antidumping statutes (AD) had similar implementation procedures. Both were invoked when a petition was filed with the ITC and the International Trade Administration of the Commerce Department (ITA) by an interested domestic party. The ITA could also independently initiate a petition. The petitioner had to show that a foreign company was dumping goods in the United States or was the beneficiary of export subsidies from its government and that these unfair trade acts were causing or threatened to cause "material injury" to a domestic industry. The threat of material injury might be indicated by increases in production capacity or existing unused capacity in the exporting country, rapid increases in U.S. market penetration, or substantial increases in U.S. inventories.

Investigating and Monitoring Agencies. The ITA and the ITC were responsible for monitoring the AD and CVD laws. The ITA determined the existence and amount of any subsidy or dumping margin, negotiated any agreements intended to offset these practices, imposed duties, reviewed the effectiveness of the remedy, and determined when to terminate or modify the remedy. The ITC applied an injury test to determine whether subsidized or dumped imports caused, or threatened to cause, material injury to domestic parties. The

injury test was applied in all AD cases but was selectively applied in CVD cases. The United States applied the injury test in CVD cases only when the country adhered to the GATT Subsidies Code or assumed commitments to the United States substantially equivalent to code obligations. If a country was not entitled to the injury test, then the ITA had total responsibility for investigating the petition.

After a petition was filed by an interested party, the ITA had 20 days to determine whether the petition was sufficient for the initiation of an investigation. If the ITA determined that an investigation was warranted, the ITC had 45 days after the filing of the petition to determine whether there was reasonable indication of material injury.

If the ITC's preliminary determination was negative, the proceedings were terminated. If, however, there was a preliminary determination of injury by the ITC, the ITA continued its own investigation. ITA investigators would send questionnaires to foreign and domestic parties requesting financial and other information. They would then verify the responses through on-site visits and audits. In AD cases, the ITA determined the fair market value of the product (usually the price of the product in the exporting country) and compared that value with the U.S. price, the difference being the dumping margin. Occasionally prices of the goods in third markets or imputed production costs would be used to determine the dumping margin. In CVD cases, the ITA attempted to establish the extent, if any, of foreign export subsidies.

On the basis of its investigation, the ITA would make a preliminary finding. If the ITA reached an affirmative finding, the foreign producer was assessed a preliminary fine based on the estimated dumping margin or subsidy and was required to post a security deposit pending final resolution of the case. If the preliminary finding was negative, the ITA continued its investigations, but imports could still enter without the foreign producer having to post a security deposit.

If the ITA's final determination was negative, then the case was terminated and any securities posted after the preliminary determinations were returned.

Remedies Available under Sections 303 and 731. If the ITA's final determination indicated that the AD or CVD statutes had been infringed, then it would issue antidumping or countervailing duty orders against the imported merchandise. The orders were equal to the final dumping margin or subsidy amount, as estimated by the ITA. Typically, the importer was required to deposit the estimated duties for the next 12-month period. If the dumping or subsidy stopped, the deposit would be returned. In 1988, Commerce was authorized to prevent circumvention of AD or CVD orders through minor alterations of merchandise. Monitoring procedures for assessing impact of duties on downstream products were also added.

EXHIBIT ONE

UNITED STATES AVERAGE IMPORT DUTIES (1792–1978)

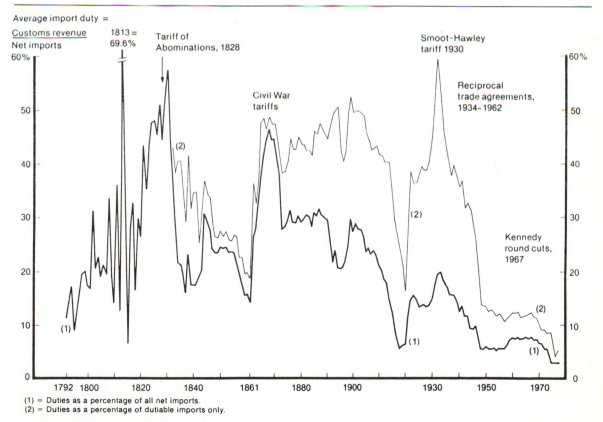

Average import duty =

$$\frac{\text{Customs revenue}}{\text{Net imports}}$$

1813 = 69.6%

Tariff of Abominations, 1828

Civil War tariffs

Smoot-Hawley tariff 1930

Reciprocal trade agreements, 1934–1962

Kennedy round cuts, 1967

(1) = Duties as a percentage of all net imports.
(2) = Duties as a percentage of dutiable imports only.

Source: Peter H. Lindert and Charles P. Kindleberger, *International Economics,* 6th ed. (Homewood, Ill.: Richard D. Irwin, 1982, p. 232.) Figures are from the U.S. Bureau of the Census.

EXHIBIT TWO

U.S. TRADE STATISTICS: 1946–1986 ($ millions)

Year	Merchandise		Trade net	Services net	Balance on goods/ services	Balance on C/A
	Exports	Imports				
1946	11,764	−5,067	6,697	1,110	7,807	4,885
1950	10,203	−9,081	1,122	1,055	2,177	−1,840
1955	14,424	−11,527	2,897	31	2,928	430
1960	19,650	−14,758	4,892	240	5,191	2,824
1965	26,461	−21,510	4,951	3,334	8,378	5,431
1970	42,469	−39,866	2,603	3,022	5,773	2,331
1975	107,088	−98,185	8,903	13,826	22,984	18,116
1980	224,269	−249,749	−25,480	34,430	9,466	1,873
1981	237,085	−265,063	−27,978	42,350	14,344	6,884
1982	211,198	−247,642	−36,444	36,700	278	−8,679
1983	201,820	−268,900	−67,080	30,270	−36,766	−46,246
1984	219,900	−332,422	−112,522	17,480	−94,975	−107,077
1985	215,935	−338,083	−122,148	22,000	−100,093	−115,103
1986	223,969	−368,516	−144,547	21,020	−123,520	−138,828
1987	249,570	−409,850	−160,280	19,740	−140,519	−153,964
1988	322,300	−459,600	−137,300	−3,880[a]	−143,300[a]	−155,500[a]

[a]Estimate based on reported data for quarters I, II, and III.

Sources: Economic Report of the President—1989 (Washington: U.S. Government Printing Office), Table B-102; and *International Economic Conditions* (St Louis: Federal Reserve Bank, 1987). "Net services" 1981–1988 were obtained from *International Financial Statistics* (Washington: IMF, Feb. 1989).

EXHIBIT THREE

SUMMARY OF MOST COMMONLY USED U.S. TRADE LAWS

	Escape clause	National security clause	Retaliation	Countervailing duties	Antidumping
U.S. law	Section 201 1974 Trade Act	Section 232 1962 Trade Act	Section 301 1974 Trade Act	Section 303 1930 Tariff Act	Section 731 1930 Tariff Act
Modified	1979, 1984, 1988	1974, 1979, 1988	1984, 1988	1974, 1984, 1988	1974, 1979, 1984
Rule	Increased imports cause or threaten to cause substantial injury	Imports threatened to impair national security by weakening vital domestic industry	Barriers restrict U.S. commerce No injury test	Export subsidy causes or threatens to cause material injury	Price below "fair market value" causes or threatens to cause material injury
Penalty	Duty, quota, OMA or trade adjustment assistance, or other action	At president's discretion	Determined by USTR, subject to direction of president[a]	Tariff which offsets subsidy, or negotiated settlement	Tariff which raised price to fair market value, or negotiated settlement
Investigating agency	ITC	Commerce (ITA)	USTR	Commerce (ITA) and ITC	Commerce (ITA) and ITC
Recommendation due	6 months	270 days[b]	12–18 months[a]	160–300 days	235–420 days
Decision maker	President, based on ITC's proposed remedy	President	USTR, subject to direction of president[a]	Commerce (ITA)	
Decision due	60 days	No deadline	Included in recommendation, 30-day implementation limit[a]	Upon recommendation	
Congressional override	Yes, within 90 days if president rejects	No	No	No	No

[a]In 1983, penalty was determined by the president, who was the decision maker in 301 cases. The USTR's recommendation was due between 9 and 14 months, depending on the nature of the unfair practice. The decision was due 21 days after the USTR's report to the president. The OTA of 1988 gave this authority to the USTR.

[b]In 1983, recommendation was due in 12 months.

EXHIBIT FOUR

RECORD OF PETITIONS UNDER U.S. TRADE LAW

Type of action	Year included	Number of petitions	Successful	Success rate	Unsuccessful[c]	Pending as of most recent year
201 Escape clause	(1958–1977) (1975–1984)	87 53	15 18	.17 .34	72 35	1
232 National security	(1962–1983)	14	3	.21	11	0
301 Foreign trade barriers	(1975–1987)	43[a]	32[b]	.74	6	4
303 Countervailing duty	(1979–1984)	235	27	.11	189	19
731 Antidumping	(1979–1984)	175	48	.27	127	60

[a]Twenty-six agricultural cases were excluded.
[b]In 20 cases, a negotiated settlement was reached; in 12 cases the president retaliated.
[c]Cases that were withdrawn by petitioners after the investigation began were coded as unsuccessful; these included 51 antidumping cases, 64 CVD cases, 3 foreign trade barrier cases, and 1 national security case.
Sources: USTR; Commerce Department: Judith Goldstein, "The Political Economy of Trade: Instutitions of Protection," *American Political Science Review*, March 1986; Robert Stern, *U.S. Trade Policies in a Changing World Economy*, MIT Press, 1987; and casewriter estimates.

BIBLIOGRAPHY AND SOURCES OF ADDITIONAL INFORMATION

Baldwin, Robert, "The Changing Nature of U.S. Trade Policy since WWII," in Robert Baldwin and Anne Krueger, *The Structure and Evolution of U.S. Trade Policy* (Chicago: University of Chicago Press, 1983).

Baldwin, Robert, *The Political Economy of U.S. Import Policy* (Cambridge, Mass.: MIT Press, 1986).

Business America, Text of Remarks by President Reagan to Business Leaders and Members of the President's Export Council and Advisory Committee for Trade Negotiations (*Business America*, September 30, 1985).

Caves, Richard E., and Ronald W. Jones, *World Trade and Payments: An Introduction* (Boston: Little Brown, 1981).

Cline, William (ed.), *Trade Policy in the 1980s* (Washington, D.C.: Institute for International Economics, 1982).

Dam, Kenneth W., *The GATT: Law and International Economic Organization* (Chicago: University of Chicago, 1970).

Destler, I. M., *American Trade Politics: System under Stress* (New York: The Twentieth Century Fund, 1986).

Hufbauer, Gary Clyde, and Joanna Shelton Erb, *Subsidies in International Trade* (Cambridge, Mass.: MIT Press, 1984).

Jackson, John H., *Legal Problems of International Economic Relations* (St. Paul, Minn.: West Publishing, 1977).

Kindleberger, Charles, *The World Depression, 1929–1939* (Berkeley: University of California Press, 1973).

Krugman, Paul (ed.), *Strategic Trade Policy and the New International Economics* (Cambridge, Mass.: MIT Press, 1986).

Lande, Stephen L., and Craig Vangrasstek, *The Trade and Tariff Act of 1984: Trade Policy in the Reagan Administration* (Lexington, Mass.: Lexington Books, D.C. Heath, 1986).

Lawrence, Robert Z., and Robert E. Litan, *Saving Free Trade: A Pragmatic Approach* (Washington, D.C.: The Brookings Institution, 1986).

Pastor, Robert A., *Congress and the Politics of U.S. Foreign Economic Policy* (Berkeley: University of California Press, 1980).

Rugman, Alan M., and Andrew Anderson, *Administered Protection in America: Implications for United States-Canadian Trade Policy* (New York: Crown Helm, 1987).

Scott, Bruce, and George Lodge (eds.), *U.S. Competitiveness in the World Economy* (Boston: Harvard Business School Press, 1984).

Yoffie, David B., *Strategy, Structure and American Trade Policy*, Harvard Business School note, #9-786-028.

Yoffie, David B., *Power and Protectionism: Strategies of the Newly Industrializing Countries* (New York: Columbia University Press, 1983).

Zysman, John, and Laura Tyson (eds.), *American Industry in International Competition* (New York: Cornell University Press, 1983).

The Cummins Engine Company in the Soviet Union

In October 1987, Henry B. Schacht, chairman and CEO of the Cummins Engine Company, traveled to the Soviet Union. There he met with senior officials from six industrial ministries to discuss the commercial opportunities for Cummins to sell engineering and management services as well as products to Soviet enterprises. The Soviets, under the leadership of General Secretary Mikhail Gorbachev since 1985, were attempting a large-scale reform of their economic system. As part of this effort, they were actively seeking Western technology to improve their industrial equipment, including diesel engines. These engines powered equipment serving the largest single mining, oil and gas, rail, marine, and agricultural equipment market in the world. Cummins had been selling a small number of engines and parts to the Soviets for years, but much more was now at stake. Several specific project proposals were before Henry Schacht in the spring of 1988, and it was time for him to decide whether the company should widen its involvement in the Soviet Union. The questions Schacht posed were:

- What are the short-term and long-term opportunities for Cummins to develop profitable business ventures in the Soviet Union, and what forms can and should these ventures take?
- Should an American firm do business with a country some considered to be an enemy of the United States?
- What rules has the U.S. government established to regulate trade with the Soviets, and what role should Cummins play in the policymaking process?

CUMMINS CORPORATE STRATEGY

Since the 1950s, Cummins had been recognized as one of the premier producers of heavy-duty diesel engines in the world (see *Exhibit 1*). Every major North American truck manufacturer offered Cummins' engines as standard or op-

Research Associate Ralinda Young Lurie prepared this case under the supervision of Associate Professor David B. Yoffie as the basis for class discussion rather than to illustrate either effective or ineffective handling of an administrative situation.

tional equipment, and its off-highway customers included major equipment manufacturers in the construction, mining, and agricultural industries.

Cummins' product line and business portfolio had changed significantly in the 1980s. Slower growth, increased demand for smaller, lighter-weight engines, and greater foreign and domestic competition had challenged the company's dominant position in North America at the end of the 1970s (see *Exhibit 2*). The company responded to the changing business environment by restructuring. In 1979, an ambitious product development program was begun. Over the next six years, Cummins invested $700 million to upgrade its product line and another $300 million to develop a series of lower horsepower engines.

About three years into this project, Cummins instituted a "New Standards of Excellence" program to cut costs by at least a third in real terms. It focused on improving volume and production efficiencies, lowering employment levels, decreasing manufacturing floor space, and cutting materials costs by increasing purchases from offshore suppliers. In 1984, while Cummins continued lowering its cost structure, Japanese engine manufacturers tried to increase their presence in the U.S. market for medium-truck engines by quoting prices as much as 40% below those of Cummins. Proclaiming, "We're not going to let them in," the company reduced its prices to be competitive worldwide. Cummins also diversified its business portfolio in the mid-1980s by acquiring several component manufacturers. As a result, Cummins' three nonengine business groups contributed almost one-third of the company's sales in 1987.

This restructuring yielded significant results (see *Exhibit 2*). The company could boast that its upgraded engine models and three new engine families offered the most advanced diesel engine technology available. Cummins' standard engines had been improved substantially

in reliability, durability, and fuel economy. Its new engines had become the performance leaders in their respective classes and had gained acceptance in markets where Cummins had not had a significant presence in the past. Real costs were down more than 15%, and Cummins' pricing strategy had proved to be an effective defense against Japanese competitors. But the restructuring process was incomplete. Cummins' profitability objective of 5% return on sales was still a goal and not a reality (see *Exhibits 3* and *4*). Cummins' new products had not yet achieved target margins. The company's nonengine business acquisitions were profitable but still incurred substantial start-up costs. Its cost reduction program also continued as Cummins worked to eliminate production inefficiencies resulting from production line moves and plant closings. Its employment levels had declined as employees took advantage of Cummins' early retirement program. But the loss of experienced engineers and technical personnel had led to greater training costs as demand levels rose in 1986 and 1987.

Management believed that Cummins' differentiated products were the key to their leadership position in the increasingly competitive business environment and remained committed to a high level of research and engineering expenditures for their commercial customers. In addition, U.S. government sales and regulations required the company to maintain its commitment to technology. Not only did Cummins work closely with the U.S. military on advanced engine and vehicle projects, it sold approximately $100 million in engines to the U.S. government in 1986. With stringent emission requirements for the U.S. on-highway truck market to take effect in 1991 and again in 1994, Cummins also had to commit engineering time and talent to redesigning its engines to conform to these standards. Cummins' engineers already had figured out how to meet the 1991 standards, but the emission requirements for 1994 were widely believed to be "10 times more difficult." In 1987 alone, several million dollars had been spent on this effort, and a number of Cummins managers were concerned about the amount of financial and technical resources that might be necessary to meet the deadline only a few years away.

Although Schacht firmly believed that Cummins was on the right track, the opinion on Wall Street was mixed. In his March 1988 research report, Timothy S. Drake of McDonald & Company Securities wrote, "After struggling for several years as a result of restructuring activities, price decreases on many products and a major shift in engine mix, the view ahead is beginning to brighten. We believe Cummins will continue to outpace the market as investors recognize the tremendous earnings power that has been buried in the past several years."[1] Cummins' stock price, however, was down substantially as investors remained uncertain of the company's outlook. As John E. McGinty of First Boston put it in his February 1988 report on Cummins, "[the company] is oversold because it disappointed Wall Street one too many times."[2]

Looking ahead, the state of the U.S. economy would continue to be the dominant influence on Cummins' business outlook. Domestic markets still represented more than 70% of its total sales and two-thirds of its profits. With only modest growth in demand forecast for the heavy-duty truck market in North America, Cummins' international operations offered many of its most promising opportunities.

OVERSEAS OPERATIONS AND OPPORTUNITIES

Cummins' involvement overseas began in the 1940s. The company's engines powered World War II army trucks throughout Europe and equipment for the oil, mining, and construction industries which had been exported from the United States. In company founder Irwin Miller's words, "We had to be international to provide service wherever our diesel engines were employed."[3] Starting in the 1950s, Cummins established wholly owned subsidiaries and manufacturing facilities in the United Kingdom, Canada, France, and Brazil. Through license agreements and joint ventures, the company also manufactured engines and engine components in China, India, Indonesia, Mexico, South Korea, and Turkey. In most of these countries, diesel engines were of significant economic importance, and foreign firms were required to make direct investments or run assembly operations. In addition, Cummins' products were sold through export houses in the United States and Western Europe and were handled by 115 distributors and 5,000 dealers in more than 100 countries. Cummins also competed internationally through engine sales to truck manufacturers and producers of industrial equipment in Europe and Japan.

One of the strategic objectives for Cummins was "to become a key player in all of the major markets of the world." On average, 25% of its sales already was being generated from international operations. By 1987, the company held a 26% share of the heavy-truck market in the United Kingdom, supplied over 95% of the heavy-truck diesel engines for automotive applications in Mexico, and had captured one-third of the mid-range truck market in Turkey. Its joint venture in India had developed during its 27-year history into one of the most profitable manufacturing companies in that country. In addition, it served as a manufacturing base for commodity componentry which Cummins shipped to the United States, Japan, and Western Europe.

Cummins also was among the first Western companies to sign licensing agreements with the Chinese. In Schacht's view, "the first one in is the last one in" in the diesel engine industry. Under the terms of these agreements, Cummins' engines were assembled in China, with the local content of each engine increasing over time. Cummins hoped to maintain its long-term relationship with the Chinese. Preliminary steps had been taken to convert these agreements to joint ventures, but the negotiations had been difficult.

The establishment of manufacturing facilities in developing countries was an important part of the company's worldwide strategy. This strategy called for low-volume components to be assembled, tested, and manufactured close to the customer. High-volume components were to be purchased from the location with the lowest costs. Facilities in developing countries, particularly Brazil, India, and China, provided Cummins with a good source of low-cost componentry for the company's plants throughout the industralized world.

New opportunities also were evident in Africa and the Eastern bloc. In a March 1987 internal memo, R. S. Campbell (vice president—International) discussed the sales potential for Cummins' engines in Hungary, where he thought it was possible that the company could generate $20 million in annual revenues; Algeria, where Campbell was hopeful that Cummins could displace one of its biggest competitors; and the Soviet Union. On the basis of his recent visits to Eastern Europe, Campbell wrote, "There is a wind of change blowing in all the Socialist countries of the world. China's success has accelerated the movement towards a more pragmatic, slightly more market-oriented, more profit-oriented, economic approach. All countries desperately want to modernize their facilities. They want Western technology and they must export in order to afford the modern technology."

THE SOVIET UNION

On the basis of their own experience and knowledge of foreign diesel engine manufacturers operating in the U.S.S.R., Cummins' managers estimated that the company could achieve $100 million in annual revenues in the Soviet market. Moreover, recent political changes seemed to promise a more open business environment for American companies.

THE POLITICAL ENVIRONMENT

In March 1985, Mikhail S. Gorbachev assumed power as general secretary of the Central Committee of the Communist Party in the Soviet Union. Shortly before taking on his new duties, Gorbachev told the party's Central Committee, "We cannot remain a major power in world affairs unless we put our domestic house in order."[4]

Gorbachev inherited a chronically ailing economic system. The country had experienced 20 years of steadily declining growth rates, its industrial plant was dilapidated, and the quality and design of many of its products were still far below world standards. Economic reform became Gorbachev's top priority. His program of perestroika got under way with a thorough restructuring of the Politburo, the Central Committee, and the government's vast ministerial bureaucracy. Officials judged to be incompetent or viewed as hesitant to institute reform were transferred to other positions. But from all appearances, Gorbachev did not just want to do a better job of running old Russia. Many Soviet experts believed his goal was to modernize Soviet industry since "the price of radical change was less than the price of business as usual."[5] In the words of Martin McCauley, a senior lecturer at the London School of Slavonic Studies, Gorbachev's "model for the Soviet Union is to have the dynamism of the American market economy in a country run by the Communist Party."[6]

"Gorbanomics" called for factories to compete among themselves, prices to be set partly by market forces, and successful enterprises to be rewarded. But in order for the Soviet economy to be more productive, Gorbachev had to make it more accessible to foreign firms. "What he wants" said Abel Aganbegyan, his top economist, "is a Soviet economy with a new face, a more democratic one."[7] Through actions such as decentralizing economic decision making, passing foreign trade legislation facilitating joint ventures, maintaining a solid credit rating, and minimizing the pressure to accept countertrade, the Soviet leadership had taken substantive steps toward allowing greater freedom for foreign involvement in the economy.

Many American business leaders, however, were wary of the reaction of their stockholders, employees, and other constituents to fullfledged commercial relations with Moscow. Violations of human rights in the Soviet Union were a matter of concern for many Americans. The Soviets' repressive practices, including the jailing of dissidents and restrictions on Jewish emigration, had persisted while the United States had made the promotion of respect for human rights a principal goal of its foreign policy. The public relations aspect of doing business in the Soviet Union worried the business community. Numerous executives expressed concern about the uncertainty of the Soviet market given the history of bilateral political relations (see *Exhibit 9*).

Changes in the Soviet business environment also had caused some confusion within the Soviet government and troubles for Western companies pursuing business opportunities in the U.S.S.R. Problems ranged from lack of steady deliveries of equipment, to delays in decision making, to worries over production. A West German business official complained, "The main difficulty in joint venture operations in the U.S.S.R. is the desire of Soviet partners to immediately start exporting the manufactured goods—and exporting them to the very markets which we have already penetrated."[8]

RECENT UNITED STATES/SOVIET RELATIONS

In the early years of the Reagan administration, the president and his advisors perceived U.S. defensive capabilities to have fallen dangerously behind the Soviets. One of their top priorities was to reverse this trend in the balance of forces by spending more money on defense and by applying economic pressure against the Soviet Union. At the time, the Reagan administration saw trade as part of a worldwide confrontation. Richard Pipes, a Harvard professor and the president's expert on the Soviet Union until December 1982, "believed that economic difficulties in the Soviet Union provided leverage with which the West might promote liberalization of the Soviet political system."[9]

By Reagan's second term in office, the two countries had made progress in their negotiations on arms control and the prospects for greater U.S. involvement in the Soviet Union's economic development improved. Reagan and Gorbachev met three times between 1985 and 1988 to discuss arms control, human rights, superpower involvement in regional conflicts, as well as commercial and cultural matters. In the words of one Soviet expert, "The release of dissidents, the freeing up of the arts, all represent a broader policy to reorder not only industry but society as well."[10] For Gorbachev, his ambitious plans to restructure the Soviet economy required improved relations with Washington. Arms control increasingly was perceived as imperative not only for the safety of both countries but also for their economic viability. As *Newsweek* reported in 1987, "Calling a halt to the arms race . . . might give Gorbachev the economic resources and the political clout he needs to tackle the most important item on this agenda, the effort to reform the monolithic Soviet system."[11]

TRADE REGULATIONS

Fourteen members of NATO and Japan established COCOM (the Coordinating Committee on Multilateral Export Controls) in 1949 to regulate the transfer of technology with potential military applications to Soviet bloc countries.

COCOM had no official power, however, to prohibit sales of strategic or sensitive materials. While the recommendations of this voluntary organization generally were followed, each member country interpreted the regulations according to its own legal, administrative, and policy situation.

The United States adhered to COCOM regulations but imposed additional restrictions on trade and the transfer of technology. Foreign firms which signed license agreements with U.S. companies also were required to comply with stricter U.S. regulations. During President Reagan's first term in office, administration officials viewed their European and Japanese allies as too liberal in their licensing and enforcement practices and worked for a stronger COCOM. Assistant Secretary of Commerce Lawrence J. Brady commented, "Some of our technology is our first line of defense. We are not going to allow the transfer of technology that can be converted to military use. . . ."[12]

In the United States, commercial goods and technical data, including diesel engines and related commodities, were subject to export licensing controls administered by the U.S. Department of Commerce in consultation with the Department of Defense and other agencies. Many exports could be made without specific authorization under general licenses. Cummins had registered its hardware with the U.S. Department of Commerce and received authorization to export under a general destination (G-DEST) license. Standard Cummins diesel engines and related parts, therefore, did not require advance specific approval by the U.S. government for commercial transactions with Soviet customers.

Other exports required prior specific approval from the U.S. government to qualify for a validated export license. This included technology which could contribute to Soviet economic development. The issuance of a validated export license could be influenced by foreign availability considerations (i.e., the

probability that the Soviets could and would legally obtain comparable technology from other Western nations). Although the technology related to Cummins' hardware was subject to this export licensing control, diesel engines and diesel engine technology was available, with only some technical variation, throughout the Western world. The State and Defense departments also were empowered to refuse, without explanation, any application for the transfer of technology for reasons of national security. This included any cooperative work which would enhance the Soviet Union's capacity to continue up the technology learning curve independent of outside help.

Cummins abided by U.S. export regulations but viewed them as setting minimum guidelines for the company. It also issued its own policy statements to establish standards for Cummins' business conduct in specific areas. For example, in 1988 Cummins drafted a policy statement on South Africa. In this statement, the company reviewed the history of its involvement in South Africa and its position with regard to that country's policy of apartheid (see *Exhibit 5*). In 1979, Cummins elected not to participate in a manufacturing program sponsored by the South African government even though Cummins' engine was favored. The company estimated it lost sales in the range of $15 million per year over the following seven years as a result of this policy. Cummins also had developed a defense sales policy in 1979. This policy set the parameters for the sale of its products to be used in military applications and established an approval process for those sales (see *Exhibit 6*).

One exception to the general U.S. trade regulations was a separate, foreign policy–based export control which specifically prohibited exports of technical data and equipment to the Kama River and ZIL truck plants in the Soviet Union. The Kama Motor Vehicle Plant (KamAZ) was a fully integrated truck production and diesel engine facility built in Brezhnev on the banks of the Kama River 1,000 miles east of Moscow. Americans who had been there considered it to be a drab company town supporting a lower standard of living than they were accustomed to in the West. Completed in 1976, Kama River was the world's largest heavy-duty truck plant with 3 million square meters under roof, including an engine plant, a forging plant, a tool and repair plant, a transmission plant, a frame-pressing plant, a foundry, and a vehicle assembly plant. In the 1970s, at least 35 U.S. firms negotiated arrangements with the Soviets to provide machinery for KamAZ and to construct production facilities at the site. Almost one-third of the Soviets' original $3.5 billion investment in KamAZ went to companies from the United States, Western Europe, and Japan. Cummins was among the companies invited to bid on the Kama River project but declined the opportunity to participate. As Schacht recalled, "We didn't know how to do it and we didn't know how we were going to get paid." After the plant was completed, a series of heavy-duty trucks were built for domestic use in the Soviet agricultural, mining, and construction industries.

In 1980, trucks built at KamAZ were used in the Soviets' invasion of Afghanistan. This provoked the U.S. government to revoke all outstanding licenses authorizing exports to the KamAZ facility. The controls also applied to the ZIL plant, which produced vehicles for the Soviet military. Since that time, there had been no further involvement of any U.S. company at either plant. According to the Commerce Department's *1987 Annual Foreign Policy Report to the Congress*, ". . . the control is effective in restricting U.S.-origin equipment used in truck production from Soviet military use. The relaxing of these controls would indicate a shift in U.S. opposition to the Soviet invasion of Afghanistan and such a shift would conflict with U.S. foreign policy interests. Negotiations with other allied governments have not resulted in the imposition of similar controls,

nonetheless the purpose of restricting certain U.S.-origin equipment from military use is effectively achieved."[13] However, approximately 20 companies from Italy, West Germany, and the United Kingdom continued to work with the Soviets at KamAZ through the 1970s and 1980s to expand the facility, improve its production processes, and further develop the technology of its trucks and engines.

As political relations with the Soviet Union improved during the 1980s, Cummins sensed increasing pressure on the U.S. government to liberalize its trade regulations with the Soviets. But while calls were being made for greater economic cooperation, it was discovered that the Toshiba Machine Company of Japan had shipped sophisticated propeller-milling equipment to the Soviet Union for almost two years. This equipment enabled the Soviets to build submarines that ran quieter and were harder to detect. Japan responded to this violation of COCOM regulations by instigating legal proceedings against Toshiba. In the meantime, the U.S. Senate voted to prohibit Toshiba from selling any of its products in the United States for two to five years. Although this action was subject to further debate in conference committee meetings, it clearly expressed the anger of congressional officials for Toshiba's violation of COCOM regulations. As one Cummins manager remarked, "There are few in Washington right now that want to be seen as helping upgrade the Soviets' capability."

THE COMPETITIVE ENVIRONMENT IN THE SOVIET UNION

Cummins had identified 4 diesel engine producers, 13 diesel engine component manufacturers, and 51 OEMs (original equipment manufacturers) utilizing diesel engines from 13 countries who were active in the Soviet market for diesel engines and related equipment and technology in the mid-1980s. A number of the company's principal Western Europe and Japanese competitors had established long-term relationships in the Soviet Union. For example, Daimler Benz/MTU of West Germany, Klockner-Humboldt-Deutz of West Germany, and Wartsila-Marine of Finland all had signed product license and facility development agreements with Soviet enterprises during 1987 which would provide each firm with an estimated $150 to $250 million in revenue from a combination of hardware and software sales over a 5- to 10-year period.

Although Cummins was the technological leader in the diesel engine industry, other firms offered fairly comparable products, often at lower prices. Cummins had observed that Western European and Japanese companies which sold engineering and management services to the Soviets also had sold significant amounts of hardware, despite the limited hard currency available for hardware sales. Consulting services, in particular, were known to be potentially very profitable. Campbell told Schacht that he knew of no other single country in Eastern or Western Europe that could match the sales potential of the Soviet Union.

OPPORTUNITIES FOR CUMMINS IN THE SOVIET UNION

Cummins had sold modest volumes of engines and parts to the Soviets for more than 25 years. Initially, the company's engines were sold exclusively through several Western European and Japanese OEMs. They powered almost 10,000 dump trucks, dozers, loaders, and logging trucks in the U.S.S.R., manufactured by Komatsu, Fiat-Allis, Clark Michigan, and International Hough Dresser. By 1984, OEMs were having trouble getting spare parts to service their equipment, and Cummins' engines were not working well. Cummins was concerned about maintaining the reputation of its products as well as its competitive position in the Soviet marketplace. As a result, the company started its own engine service operation in the U.S.S.R. Three years

later, Cummins also established a spare parts depot in the Soviet Union to service its OEM customers and entered into a direct supplier relationship with three Soviet trade organizations to sell engines and service parts to large mining end-users.

Cummins generated $24.6 million in revenues from its operations in the Soviet Union during 1986. The profitability of this business was comparable to the company's overseas parts sales and above the returns from Cummins' domestic business. The company had built an excellent reputation with the Soviets based on its performance in the mining and construction industries where Cummins had its largest concentration of heavy-duty engines outside of North America.

In the past, Schacht had been skeptical of the commercial viability of Soviet business opportunities despite Cummins' long-standing involvement in the Soviet Union. Over the years, Soviet ministers had approached Cummins on numerous occasions about doing additional business, acknowledging that their country was deficient in diesel engine technology and needed help. The Soviets were interested in purchasing technology and usually proposed a licensing agreement which allowed them to pay Cummins with the products resulting from the integration of this technology into their facilities in the Soviet Union. By contrast, Cummins was looking for opportunities to sell its products directly to the Soviets, since licensing its technology would allow the company little, if any, control over its use by the Soviets.

One such licensing agreement was proposed in 1974. At that time, the Soviets were interested in acquiring the technology to produce high-horsepower engines to power mining trucks manufactured at the Cheboksary tractor plant. Even though the Soviets also were considering the engines produced by one of the company's West German competitors (MTU), Cummins decided that transferring the technology for its new K series engines was not appropriate since production of the engines had just started. Five years later, the Soviets again approached Cummins about licensing the K series engines. This time, Cummins scheduled a delegation to visit the Soviet Union in early 1980 to discuss the proposal. At the end of 1979, however, deteriorating political relations between the United States and U.S.S.R. made the trip impossible.

Late in 1985, the Soviet Ministry of Tractor and Agricultural Machinery again invited Cummins to bid on the same Cheboksary truck project. Although the German press had reported that Daimler Benz/MTU might have already won the contract, Cummins submitted a proposal. In company documents prepared for a Department of Defense briefing, Cummins stated its position: "From a short-term point of view, this is a large, profitable business. We expect around $250 million in sales over several years. It would enhance our capability to support and service our engines in one of the world's largest markets and we need to begin establishing business relationships that will lead to future competitive export success." Daimler-Benz/MTU did win the contract for the Cheboksary project. The Soviets acknowledged that their most recent invitation for Cummins to bid was issued too late.

Cummins' Cheboksary proposal led to additional inquiries from middle-level Soviet officials regarding the establishment of working relationships with the company on other engine-related projects for the commercial transport industry. Improving relations between Moscow and Washington had given the Soviets some hope that an American company could be a reliable, long-term business partner. What interested some Cummins' managers was not only the nature of these projects but also the Soviets' acceptance of the economic requirements for doing business with an American firm. The Soviet officials, looking to build long-term relationships, appeared willing to deal with Cummins on a basis that it would find worth-

while. In addition, Cummins found itself dealing with a very different group of officials. The company historically had conducted all of its business through the Soviet Ministry of Foreign Trade, which represented the interests of the variouos operating ministries. As part of Gorbachev's restructuring program, the production ministries and some individual enterprises had been given the right to work directly with foreign firms. Although these officials were not familiar with the commercial terms of foreign trade, their technical competence and market awareness helped to further the discussions. Consequently, serious talks took place during 1986 and 1987 between Soviet officials representing the automobile, oil and gas, tractor and agricultural machines, and heavy transport ministries and Cummins representatives.

In March 1987, Cummins sent a technical delegation to the U.S.S.R. to talk about opportunities for cooperation in the diesel engine industry. Schacht chose the individuals composing the delegation for both their technical expertise and their healthy skepticism about pursuing new business ventures with the Soviets. Schacht noted that most of the group felt that any commercial dealings with the Soviets would be "so long range, so unlikely and so fraught with emotions as to not be interesting." By the time the delegation returned to Cummins' Indiana headquarters, they had developed a surprisingly favorable impression of the prospects for doing business in the Soviet Union and the people managing the ministries. Campbell wrote in his report to Cummins' Management Group, "We were impressed by the people we met in the Automotive Industry. They are all new; the top people are under 50 years of age. We speak the same language. They are much more concerned with producing quality product than they are with politics."

A follow-up trip was made in May 1987 by W. D. Schwab, a member of Cummins' board of directors and the retired head of the company's research and engineering operations, along with six other Cummins executives. This time the members of the delegation returned with preliminary project proposals (see *Exhibit 7*). These projects presented a number of options for Cummins which ranged from providing short-term technical assistance to working jointly with the Soviets to develop new products on a long-term basis. Each project required a different level of commitment from Cummins in terms of technical and managerial talent and capital investment and offered different financial returns. Several of the most interesting projects involved the politically sensitive Kama River Truck Plant.

In the fall of 1987, Henry Schacht accepted an invitation from the Soviets to travel to Moscow to meet with senior officials. Schacht also met with the general manager of the KamAZ facility, whom he found to be "down to earth, fact oriented and a friendly and outgoing person." By the end of his four-day stay, Schacht acknowledged that "unless we were badly fooled, these are people with whom we have a common language, common experiences and common challenges—engines."

Shortly after his return to the United States, Schacht made a follow-up trip to Washington, D.C. The purpose was to debrief government officials on his experience in the Soviet Union and to get a better sense of the prevailing opinions within the Reagan administration on technology sales to the Soviets and the Kama River export controls. Schacht, along with other U.S. business leaders, had been invited to meet with General Secretary Gorbachev at the Washington summit in early December, where economic issues were scheduled to be discussed. With the third summit only a few weeks away,

administration officials were very interested in the project proposals Cummins had received from the Soviets and Schacht's impressions of the business environment in the Soviet Union.

TIME FOR DECISION

Cummins' managers were expected to evaluate developmental projects on the basis of the company's commercial return requirements and its ethical standards (see *Exhibit 8*). These issues had been debated within the company for many months. A number of these discussions had been heated, and some strong feelings had been expressed. Schacht knew that a large number of émigrés from Eastern Europe were employed throughout Cummins and that some of these employees felt betrayed by the company even considering greater involvement with the Soviet Union.

By the spring of 1988, Reagan and Gorbachev had set a date for their fourth summit meeting and the Soviets had reached a preliminary agreement for the withdrawal of its troops from Afghanistan. It was time for Cummins to resolve the commercial and ethical issues outstanding and decide whether or not to expand its presence in the Soviet Union. As Henry Schacht wrote in a March 10 memo to Campbell, "I am convinced from my discussions in Washington . . . that our friends will expect us to move very quickly in the Soviet Union if they give us the 'go' signal. I'm not sure we have all our thoughts together on this within the company. We should use this period to sort out the issues internally and come to an agreement on if and how we should proceed. . . ."

EXHIBIT ONE

DIESEL ENGINE MANUFACTURERS WORLDWIDE MARKET SHARES 1986

Manufacturer	Horsepower				
	0–50[a]	51–200[b]	201–400[c]	401–1000[c]	Total
Fiat	8.5%	6.1%	3.6%	12.1%	6.4%
Daimler-Benz/MTU	0.2	7.6	8.6	5.7	6.3
Cummins	0.4	0.5	18.4	16.6	1.9
Detroit Diesel	0.0	1.9	5.8	6.5	1.9
Caterpillar	0.0	0.7	10.4	19.5	1.3
Volvo/White	0.6	0.5	10.6	1.6	1.3
Komatsu	0.0	0.6	1.6	7.8	0.6

[a]0–50 HP engines are used in electrical generators and in automotive, industrial, and mobile refrigeration applications.
[b]51–200 HP engines are used in light- and medium-duty trucks, agricultural equipment, and construction applications.
[c]201–400 HP engines are used in heavy-duty trucks, buses, and industrial, agricultural, and construction applications.
[d]401–1000 HP engines are used in generator sets and industrial, construction, mining, and marine applications.
Source: Excerpted from company documents.

EXHIBIT TWO

CUMMINS' PENETRATION RATE: NORTH AMERICAN HEAVY-DUTY TRUCK MARKET

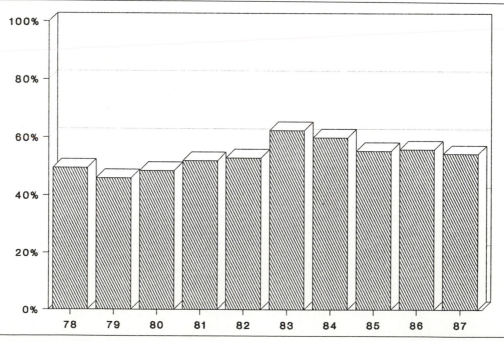

Source: Cummins Annual Report, 1987.

EXHIBIT THREE

SUMMARY INCOME STATEMENT[a] ($ millions)

Year ending December 31	1979	1982	1984	1986	1987
Net sales	$1,770.8	$1,587.5	$2,325.7	$2,303.7	$2,767.4
Cost of goods sold	1,255.8	1,158.7	1,548.9	1,713.7	2,071.4
Gross profit	$ 515.1	$ 428.4	$ 776.9	$ 590.0	$ 696.0
SGA and R&E expense	408.1	429.7	483.9	585.3	617.0
Operating profit	$ 107.0	$ (0.9)	$ 293.0	$ 4.7	$ 79.0
Interest expense	22.9	34.5	31.6	44.8	51.7
Other (income)/expense[b]	1.4	(14.8)	17.0	116.9	(7.0)
Pretax profit/(loss)	$ 82.8	(20.6)	$ 244.4	$ (157.0)	$ 34.3
Net profit/(loss)	$ 57.9	$ 7.7	$ 187.9	$ (107.3)	$ 13.9

[a]All figures are rounded.
[b]Unusual charges are included in the 1983 and 1985 figures.
Source: Cummins' 1987 annual report.

EXHIBIT FOUR

SUMMARY BALANCE SHEET[a] ($ millions)

Year ending December 31	1979	1982	1984	1986	1987
Cash and marketable securities	$ 27.9	$ 29.1	$ 159.5	$ 162.1	$ 76.8
Accounts receivable	248.2	178.3	257.3	365.9	356.7
Inventories	316.0	250.4	314.8	350.4	413.3
Investments and other assets	98.8	242.4	204.5	241.6	235.6
Net fixed assets	398.1	570.6	567.4	840.6	909.7
Deferred charges and intangibles	13.5	11.0	2.0	29.3	27.3
Total assets	$1,102.6	$1,281.8	$1,505.5	$1,989.9	$2,019.4
Loans payable	$ 49.2[b]	$ 31.4	$ 34.0	$ 105.2	$ 51.6
Current maturities of long-term debt	—	6.4	11.5	20.4	20.1
Accounts and income taxes payable	158.4	110.1	168.1	197.8	265.0
Accrued expenses	160.6	192.0	244.6	339.2	313.2
Long-term debt	186.7	279.4	221.4	319.9	332.6
Other liabilities	71.7	128.0	176.7	237.0	171.7
Total liabilities	$ 626.6	$ 747.3	$ 856.3	$1,219.5	$1,154.2
Shareholders' investment	476.0	534.5	649.2	770.3	865.2
Total liabilities and shareholders' investment	$1,102.6	$1,281.8	$1,505.5	$1,989.9	$2,019.4

[a]All figures are rounded.
[b]Includes current maturities of long-term debt.
Source: Cummins' annual reports.

EXHIBIT FIVE

DRAFT POLICY STATEMENT ON SOUTH AFRICA

January 25,1988

The company in September 1986 made the decision to close its Johannesburg sales office, which was the company's only investment in South Africa. The office was closed by December 31, 1986. The company now has no assets, equity, or employees in South Africa.

The closing of the company's Johannesburg office should be viewed in the context of a progressive downscaling of Cummins' activities in South Africa. Prior to 1979, Cummins held a strong position in the diesel engine market in South Africa with a market share in excess of 20%. In 1979 we were invited by the South African government to participate in a joint venture in which we would have licensed our technology for production by a government-controlled engine manufacturer. Cummins declined to participate in the venture because we were unwilling to supply our product to the South African government and risk the strong likelihood that our engines would be used by the military and police to power vehicles to enforce apartheid. The South African government proceeded to develop the project with a West German competitor of Cummins. As a result, the government venture now supplies the bulk of our former South African market, and Cummins' market share is now less than 2%.

Since the early 1980s, the company operated its business in South Africa in voluntary accord with the rec-

ommendations of the Commission on United States Policy Toward South Africa. . . . The company observed the Commission's recommendations that it make clear its fundamental opposition to the system of apartheid, commit itself to a policy of nonexpansion in South Africa, commit a generous proportion of its resources to improve the lives of black South Africans, and subscribe to the Statement of Principles for South Africa, formerly the Sullivan Principles. In addition, the company refused to sell to the South African military or police and did not sell its products for use which the company believed could advance or support apartheid. . . .

Cummins' primary remaining business in South Africa is with a distributor which has been independently owned for more than 20 years. In the spirit of the Principles, the distributor is active in promoting, training, and financially supporting the nonwhite labor force which is represented in all areas of the business. The distributor has contravened the local job reservation laws by promoting nonwhites to supervisory positions, demonstrating the fourth amplification of the (then) Sullivan Principles. . . .

In 1987, sales of the company's products in South Africa were less than $7 million, which is less than one-half of 1% of the company's total sales. Over half of the sales is attributable to service parts for engines sold in the past. . . .

Source: Excerpted from company documents.

EXHIBIT SIX

CUMMINS PRACTICE: DEFENSE SALES POLICY

April 6, 1979

I. Practice

A. While Cummins manufactures and markets engines primarily for commercial civilian applications, various product lines are adaptable for use in military applications as well. Cummins regards these military applications as a legitimate market and wishes to pursue them.

B. At the same time, Cummins recognizes that sales of defense products can in some circumstances have harmful consequences, by supporting military aggression or repression, by provoking wasteful international arms competition, or by contributing to international tensions. Such consequences are not likely to result from the sale of engines for use in military trucks or military construction equipment. They are, however, a serious concern in the sale of engines for combat vehicles and other items on the United States munitions list.

C. Cummins accordingly believes that it should aggressively approach sales opportunities for non-munitions-list applications, while at the same time following a prior approval process for munitions-list items which recognizes their sensitive nature.

D. Cummins will therefore deal with defense sales opportunities in the following way:

1. Cummins will pursue defense sales of products not on the United States munitions list without reservation. . . . (The United States munitions list *excludes* most varieties of military trucks, construction equipment, and military support equipment.)

2. . . . Cummins will pursue defense sales of products which are on the United States munitions list only after corporate approval. . . .

3. Corporate approval is not required for sales of munitions-list products directly to:

a. The national government of a country in which Cummins owns or licenses a manufacturing facility or

b. A manufacturer of fully assembled military equipment within such country

Cummins believes that its responsibility to a host country is to sell without restrictions as it does in the United States. If the company is not willing to do this, it should not establish a manufacturing facility in that country.

II. Responsibility and procedure

A. Corporate approval process

1. Sales . . . requiring corporate approval will be addressed by the following approval process:

a. The Group Head . . . will:

(1) Gather . . . [needed] information . . . [on the prospective sale] and

(2) Prepare a briefing document and recommendation to the President and the Chairman of the Board

b. The President and the Chairman of the Board will grant or withhold corporate approval.

2. Separate approval is required for each sales project.

3. . . . corporate approval will authorize the solicitation of business, sales of engines and/or parts, and provision of technical support over the life of the project.

B. Approval criteria

Issues to be addressed in the approval process . . . include:

1. Cummins' ability to identify the national government ultimately receiving the product

2. The likely use of the product, in view of the recipient government's foreign and military policies, its domestic police policies, and its military export policies

3. The likelihood of product resale by the recipient government

4. The effect of the sale on:

a. Regional tensions

b. United States policy objectives

c. Cummins commercial objectives in the relevant country

5. The effect of Cummins' decision on the local Cummins distributor. . . .

Source: Excerpted from company documents.

EXHIBIT SEVEN

APPROACH TO OPPORTUNITIES IN THE SOVIET UNION

COMMERICAL OPPORTUNITY IN THE SOVIET UNION

Cummins Engine Company has a commercial opportunity to sell engineering and management services for the analysis, design, manufacture, and application of engines, engine components, power systems, and related equipment to enterprises and design institutes in the Soviet Union. Cummins would sell a variety of services to Soviet organizations, which would enhance the value of existing Soviet commercial equipment or result in designs for new commercial products.

OVERVIEW OF POSSIBLE PROJECTS

The engineering and management services which Cummins could offer fall into five commercial project categories.

1. Redesign of existing Soviet engines and components
   Cummins would critique current Soviet product designs and recommend changes to improve performance, durability, reliability, and applicability. Cummins would provide technical assistance with the intent of enhancing the commercial capabilities of a Soviet diesel engine without requiring significant additional capital investment in plant and equipment. Cummins design changes would target improvements in fuel consumption and durability.

2. Engine application and installation assistance
   Cummins would critique the installation of both Soviet and Cummins engines in Soviet equipment for domestic and export sale and recommend application engineering changes to improve performance and salability. Possible projects include:

   - Improvement of bus engine applications—The Soviet automobile industry produces buses with which customers are dissatisfied. Soviet industry is cooperating with foreign companies to improve bus and engine installation. Cummins could install engines in these vehicles.

   - Installation of Cummins engines in heavy dump trucks—The Soviets produce heavy dump trucks for both domestic use and export. Cummins is working with truck component suppliers to package a complete power module for such trucks which would improve their export marketability. Cummins also could supply K series engine kits for assembly in the Soviet Union and support engines at its 5,000 worldwide service points.

3. Joint venture or license to produce existing Cummins products
   Possibilities include:

   - Joint venture or license of the Cummins L-10 engine—Cummins would license the L-10 engine for production by an enterprise under the Soviet automobile ministry. This enterprise might be structured as a joint venture. The L-10 engines would be used for transit buses and coaches. The license would include the transfer of technical information, such as blueprints and process specifications, the sale of components, training at Cummins manufacturing sites, and technical assistance at the Soviet sites in using Cummins technical data and manufacturing the engine. A separate contract could include technical consultation on the purchase and installation of machine lines.

   - Joint venture or license of Holset turbochargers—Holset Engineering (a Cummins subsidiary) would license turbochargers for manufacture in the Soviet Union.

   - License of the Cummins K Series engines—Cummins would license the K Series engines for production by a Soviet enterprise or joint venture. These engines would be used in dump trucks and in other applications. The license would include the transfer of technical information, the sale of components, training, on-site technical assistance, and consultation in the development of manufacturing facilities.

4. Joint design of new products
   Possibilities include:

   - Joint design of an advanced fuel system—Cummins would work with a Soviet fuel system producer to incorporate new fuel system designs into future Soviet engines. This offers the Soviets the best opportunity to obtain world-class engine performance in terms of specific power output, lower fuel consumption, and low emissions.

5. Purchase and export of products manufactured in the Soviet Union to Cummins' specifications
   Cummins would provide designs, specifications, and other assistance necessary to manufacture products such as fuel pumps, consumable machine tools, and castings.

Source: Excerpted from company documents.

EXHIBIT EIGHT

CUMMINS PRACTICE; ETHICAL STANDARDS

October 1, 1980

. . . the following discussion and policies elaborate on our traditional policy in order to provide personal guidance and to establish procedures for problem resolution. . . .

I. Practice

  A. For Cummins, ethics rests on a fundamental belief in people's dignity and decency. Our most basic ethical standard is to show respect for those whose lives we affect and to treat them as we would expect them to treat us if our positions were reversed. This kind of respect implies that we must:

    1. Obey the law.

    2. Be honest; present the facts fairly and accurately.

    3. Be fair; give everyone appropriate consideration.

    4. Be concerned; care about how Cummins' actions affect others, and try to make those effects as beneficial as possible.

    5. Be courageous; treat others with respect even when it means losing business. . . .

  B. The reason for such behavior is that, in the long run, nothing else works. If economies and societies do not operate in this way, the whole machinery begins to collapse. No corporation can long survive in situations where employees, creditors, and communities don't trust each other. Since a corporation lives by society's consent, it must plan on earnings and keeping that consent for the duration. Successes we have today . . . are in major part made possible by the fact that others have learned to expect that Cummins will deal with them fairly. What we do today will maintain or undermine that legacy.

  C. Our aim is that Cummins—its individual members, each of its distributors, and their people—all be known worldwide as trustworthy in all respects. . . . We can't operate by one set of standards internally and by another set externally. We can't say one thing and do another. Our ethical standards shouldn't tolerate split behavior.

  D. On numerous occasions the company has reiterated its commitment to fundamental ethical standards. There are, however, reasons for more specific statements:

    1. As we grow larger, we have to set down in writing those standards which have informally guided our action in the past.

    2. Not only do we have to make these statements formal and written, but they must be expressed in policy statements to ensure that all management employees have easy access to them.

    3. Finally, general statements are important for setting the tone and character of a company, but specific policies are required in addition to make the intent of the general principles clear to each person.

  E. Accordingly, all employees are expected to understand and subscribe to the following general standards of corporate behavior.

    1. Cummins Engine Company, Inc., competes on a straight commercial basis; if something more is required, the company is not interested.

    2. Cummins employees do nothing in search of business that they should not reveal willingly and publicly to *any* other member of the Cummins family or to *any* government official in any land.

    3. Cummins neither practices nor condones any activity that will not stand the most rigorous public ethical examination.

    4. If an employee has *any* doubt about the appropriateness or morality of *any* act, it should not be done. . . . The company is prepared to help any employee resolve a moral dilemma and to ensure that no employee is put at a career disadvantage because of his or her *willingness* to raise a question about a corporate practice or *unwillingness* to pursue a course of action which seems inappropriate or morally dubious. . . .

COUNSEL

  The Chairman should be consulted for any advice needed concerning this practice.

Source: Excerpted from company documents.

CHRONOLOGY OF MAJOR EVENTS IN U.S./U.S.S.R. TRADE RELATIONS

Cold War

1949	The United States develops economic containment policy and pressures European allies to support a larger number of embargoed strategic items. The Export Control Act is passed to control exports of U.S. goods and technology and to regulate exports to Communist countries.
1951	The Korean conflict leads Congress to revoke the most-favored-nation (MFN) tariff treatment for Communist countries and empowers the president to deny all U.S. assistance to countries shipping strategic goods to Communist countries.
1962	In the aftermath of the Cuban missile crisis, Congress eliminates presidential discretion to restore MFN treatment to Eastern countries and prohibits export of commodities and technical data contributing to the economic and military potential of countries threatening U.S. security.
1968	The expansion of East-West trade is opposed by members of Congress as Soviets support North Vietnam and invade Czechoslovakia.
1969	The Export Administration Act (EAA) endorses trade in peaceful goods between U.S. firms and countries with which the United States has commercial relations and authorizes the Commerce Department to control normal commercial exports of U.S.-origin commodities and data.

Détente

1972	Congress amends the EAA, removing unilateral controls if controlled items are available without restriction from sources outside the United States in significant quantities and comparable quality.
	At the first Moscow summit, President Nixon and General Secretary Brezhnev issue a statement that both countries will actively promote the growth of commercial and economic ties to strengthen bilateral relations.
	The U.S./U.S.S.R. Trade Agreement is signed, providing for (1) the Soviets to place large orders in the United States, (2) government commercial offices to be opened in Moscow and Washington, (3) both governments to cooperate to avoid disruption of domestic markets through exports of products from the other country, and (4) exports from each country to be treated in a nondiscriminatory fashion.
1974	Congress amends the EAA, requiring the involvement of the Defense Department for export licenses. Congress amends the U.S./U.S.S.R. Trade Agreement, banning MFN status and subsidized loans to countries discouraging emigration. This results in Soviet abrogation of the Agreement.
1978	President Carter retaliates for sentences given Soviet dissidents by broadening export licensing requirements in the petroleum sector.
1979	Congress instructs the Commerce Department to approve licenses for export of items readily available from other sources and sets deadlines for license decisions.

Renewed tension

1980	In response to the Soviet invasion of Afghanistan, the Carter administration institutes sanctions against the Soviet Union including (1) the imposition of license controls on agricultural commodities and embargo on shipment of agricultural commodities, (2) an embargo on export of phosphatic rock, acid, or fertilizers, (3) the suspension of shipment of goods under outstanding validated licenses and the suspension of processing of applications for new validated licenses, and (4) a bar on U.S. participation in the Moscow Olympics and the export of related goods and technology.
1981	Reagan announces new sanctions in response to the Soviet Union's role in imposition of martial law in Poland including (1) suspending the processing of applications for validated export licenses, (2) expanding the list of oil and gas equipment requiring validated licenses, (3) closing the Soviet Purchasing Commission in New York City, (4) postponing negotiations on long-term grain agreement, and (5) declining renewal of exchange agreements on space, energy, science, and technology.
1982	President Reagan drops 1981 sanctions.

Renewed efforts at cooperation

1987	Soviets announce plans to withdraw from Afghanistan, and President Reagan and General Secretary Gorbachev sign an INF Treaty eliminating a class of medium- and shorter-range missiles.
1988	The United States, its Western allies, and Japan agree to fewer, more rigorously enforced curbs on exports to the Soviet Union.

NOTES

1. Timothy S. Drake, McDonald & Company Securities, Inc., March 14, 1988.
2. John E. McGinty, First Boston, February 22, 1988.
3. *Industry Week*, September 26, 1977.
4. *Time*, January 4, 1988.
5. *Fortune*, September 28, 1987.
6. *Newsweek*, December 14, 1987.
7. Ibid.
8. *Boston Globe*, April 1988.
9. Richard Pipes, "The Soviet Union in Crisis," 1983. Manuscript provided by the author.
10. *Business Week*, February 2, 1987.
11. *Newsweek*, December 14, 1987.
12. *Fortune*, December 28, 1981.
13. *1987 Annual Foreign Policy Report to the Congress*, United States Department of Commerce.

Airbus versus Boeing (A): Turbulent Skies

On September 21, 1985, Indian Airlines, India's rapidly expanding domestic carrier, signed a letter of intent with Airbus Industrie, the European consortium jointly owned by France, West Germany, Great Britain, and Spain, to purchase nineteen A-320 aircraft (each seating 162 passengers) with delivery in 1989 and the option to purchase twelve more in 1990. The total value was estimated at $1.6 billion including spare parts. Immediately following this announcement, the U.S. embassy in New Delhi, acting on advice from Washington, lodged a formal complaint with the Indian Ministry of Aviation.

The previous June 1984, Boeing, the U.S.-based private commercial aircraft manufacturer, received a letter of intent and a refundable deposit of $800,000 from India Airlines for the purchase of twelve 757 aircraft (each seat-ing up to 208 passengers) and the option to purchase thirteen more. The initial order was worth $560 million including the price of the twin engines. According to a Commerce Department official, Boeing, acting in "good faith," had begun by September 1985 to build aircraft to meet the deadlines specified in the letter of intent.

In October of 1984, Airbus managed to re-open the negotiations, offering the new A-320 in place of the originally offered A-310 (seating 220 passengers). After several rounds of price cutting, Airbus dropped its price from $31 million per plane to $24 million (or, $148,000 per seat capital cost) and offered to cover the years 1985 to 1989 with Boeing 737s and A-300s on lease (twelve in all) for payments which would be deducted from the price of the A-320. The "free" leasing alone was valued at $60 million. All totaled, Airbus offered financing to cover 85% of the cost, an amount permissible under an international agreement signed by the principal aircraft producing nations. Boeing countered by dropping its price per plane from $42 to $34 to $27 million ($130,000 per seat capital cost). Boeing also offered to buy back the 757s in 1992 and replace them with an advanced aircraft called the 7J7. At the time of negotiations, Indian Airlines already owned ten A-300s, twenty-five Boeing 737s, and nineteen smaller aircraft.

The U.S. embassy's complaint claimed that India did not examine a fresh bid made by Boeing at the end of August 1985 with the same interest and attention it gave when Airbus reopened negotiations in October of 1984. In addition, Airbus was accused by Boeing and U.S. government officials of undercutting the price substantially, violating Article 6 of GATT which required pricing to be based on reasonable expectation of recoupment of all costs. Indian Airlines officials were quoted by Reuters as insisting that "the decision was made at the highest levels of Indian government" and went so far as to claim that the decision to switch the order from Boeing to Airbus was taken personally by Mr. Rajiv Gandhi, India's Prime Minister. Visits by top officials of both the United States and France near the height of the negotiations were noted in the press.

Back in the United States, the *Wall Street Journal* reported that a Boeing top official urged President Reagan to take prompt, informal action against Airbus Industrie to force it to compete fairly for passenger aircraft sales around the world. Although visibly angry, Mr. Dean Thornton, president of Boeing's commercial airplane unit, stopped short of asking Mr. Reagan to file unfair trade practices charges with the U.S. trade officials against the European consortium. He openly accused the Airbus Industries' national owners of having pumped an estimated $10 billion into the group without regard to profit and urged Washington to pressure France, West Germany, and Great Britain to disclose fully how much they subsidize Airbus and the financial results of the consortium. Mr. Thornton was quoted in the *Wall Street Journal*: "Unless our government takes action, and unless other governments involved decide to account more openly for their costs and ac-

tions, international competition is going to become bitter and unproductive."

Exhibit 1 summarizes the details of the deals offered by Boeing and Airbus, and *Exhibit 2* displays the family of aircraft for Airbus and Boeing. On a per seat capital cost basis, the Boeing deal appeared less costly. In addition, the Boeing 757 was immediately available, allowing the airline to bring them into service faster. The A-320 wouldn't be available until 1989 and would be untested, compared to the proven capabilities of the Boeing aircraft. Yet, the 757 required a more powerful engine, which would have resulted in a higher fuel burned per seat cost compared to the A-320. Roughly speaking, the tradeoff for Indian Airlines appeared to be as follows: Airbus offered a $3,000 per seat per year savings in operating costs over Boeing, while Boeing offered an $18,000 per seat savings in capital costs over Airbus. Thus, it would take Indian Airlines 6 years to offset the higher capital cost associated with an Airbus purchase; this appeared to be above the industry norm of a 3:1 capital-to-operating cost tradeoff. Finally, Indian Airlines was already flying near a 100% load factor, which would have implied a preference for a slightly larger airplane both in terms of passengers and cargo capacity.

This was not the first incident where the European consortium was accused of unfair competition through price cutting or political interference. When in 1978 Airbus sold to Eastern Airlines the A-300 aircraft, the financial agreement was based on a "Deferred Seat Plan" whereby twelve of the twenty-three aircraft were paid for as though they had only 71% of the 240 seats. This discount plan was designed to continue for up to 4 years or until load factors exceeded a certain level. The deferral was interest-free, and Eastern was given use of four A-300s for a 6-month trial period without a lease payment to Airbus.

As for incidents of "political leverage," certain Airbus aircraft sales were obtained through such political horse trading as trade agreements, route rewards, landing rights and frequency rule adjustments,[1] military weapons support, and economic or regional assistance.[2] Large sales in the Middle East, for example, followed closely on the heels of French President Giscard d'Estaing's pro-Arab policy statements. Finally, with initial sales of the A-300 very slow, pressure was placed by the participating governments early in 1975 on their national carriers to "buy national": France's Air France, West Germany's Lufthansa, Spain's Iberia, and Belgium's Sabena all followed suit, according to testimony before the House of Representatives Subcommittee on International Economic Policy and Trade of the Committee on Foreign Affairs.

Airbus felt that these charges—and others related to alleged government subsidies—were false and misleading. Indeed, the European government had its own list of charges about the U.S. government's support of its civilian aircraft industry. All these charges and countercharges were to become the agenda of informal consultations concerning trade in civil aircraft among the governments of the Federal Republic of Germany, France, the United Kingdom, and the United States, held on March 20–21, 1986.

THE BUSINESS OF MAKING AND MARKETING AIRFRAMES

Launch Economics

Commercial airframe manufacturers tended to be in the business for the long haul. A large investment of time and money was needed before production began and even longer before revenues were seen. Launch investment costs typically fell into three categories: 40% for development, 20% for tooling, and 40% for work-in-process and overhead costs. The total amount, spent over 5 years, was necessary to develop and certify the aircraft and set up a production line, all in advance of any assessment of its success in the market. Naturally, the manufacturers' aim was to book as many launch orders as possible, but never have there been enough to ensure break-even profitability prior to the launch date. As a measure of investment risk, Boeing's combined investment in the 1970s for its new 757 and 767 aircraft totaled more than the company's net worth.

The development period began with the aircraft design known as the "paper airplane," a three-way view model with estimates of performance and operating costs. The manufacturer used them to demonstrate new technology and, most importantly, to assess the response of potential buyers. Typical was an interactive process between the manufacturer and key airlines as adaptations were made and options incorporated into the prototype. Often these airlines became launch customers, guaranteeing a minimum volume while sending a signal to the marketplace that the aircraft would likely succeed. The reputation of these launch customers was important for subsequent sales.

Once sufficient backing was achieved, in the form of either orders received from a group of airlines or financial commitments from supporting government bodies to allow the program to proceed, full-scale development began. The design and development phase faced built-in costs such as regulatory approval and costly and time-consuming flight tests, in addition to prototype construction and assembly.

The majority of the tooling costs were associated with the construction jigs, which were expensive to build and required very accurate specifications. Work-in-process and general administration costs were relatively large because the producer was required to start production of a new model long before it was certified; otherwise there would be a delay of 12 to 24 months (the length of the manufacturing cycle) before any aircraft were delivered. The initial inventory was equivalent to about forty aircraft, although this total could be offset partly by customer progress payments and subcontractor credits. All in all, launch costs could total up to $20 million per seat, as inferred from estimates of the launch investment of $2.5 billion for Airbus' A-320. In addition, any upgrades or derivatives, a normal part of the development phase for long production runs, could add 30% to 40% to the overall investment.

The sales price of an aircraft typically included purchased parts, direct expenses (labor and supplies), plus the launch investment. With normal 25% gross margins, the break-even point to recover launch costs was 400 units, often 12 to 14 years after the decision to launch the program. The realization of profits followed the traditional learning curve such that as more were produced, the marginal cost to produce each unit decreased. Yet, not every manufacturer faced the exact same curve; in Airbus' case with the A-320, it was more likely that 600 units were needed to break even. However, none of the twelve European jetliners that had entered service since 1952 ever reached 300, and only five out of eleven American models— the Boeing 707, 727, 737, and 747 and the McDonnell Douglas DC-9—had ever generated over 600 shipments each.

Added to high break-even requirements was the cost of capital required to produce a minimum of forty aircraft per year. In 1983, for example, only the Boeing 737 and 767 and the MD-80 produced forty or more annually. With inflation, the cost increased the hurdle rate. With a 7- to 8-year lag between the investment decision and revenue stream, airlines found it ever more expensive to purchase the equipment and more economical to keep the planes in service longer.

Civil aircraft selling was a long-term business. The sales force and designers worked closely with the airline during the development phase. The manufacturer also found it critical to provide service worldwide, with minimum delay, as it supported a broad customer base

which facilitated additional sales to new and repeat customers. Neighboring airlines found it advantageous to have access to one another's spare parts and maintenance services. Since operational and maintenance efficiency dictated that airlines not mix directly competitive types of aircraft or engines in their fleets, an initial order tended to establish an airline's fleet composition for the aircraft or engine type for a decade or more. With an aircraft's normal service life of 22 years, a lost sale could easily have a ripple effect of 15 to 20 years. In addition to mounting the hurdle of launching costs, suppliers needed to sell several jetliners at the outset to a few large customers in order to avoid far higher "customer introductory costs" of marketing these initial units to a cluster of small airlines. The intensity of competition could depress the sales price to a point at which costs were not covered and the manufacturer was no longer able to resist pressure to make available a major variant that was really unaffordable to produce. If a manufacturer were desperate, it would drive the deal down to a "sacrificial price" just to move down the learning curve. Mr. Harry Colwell of Chase Manhattan Bank has said, "The manufacturer feels that he has to win each competition. It becomes so important as to be obsessive—a kind of phobia."[3]

Aircraft Life Expectancy

The rate of aircraft replacement was determined by the airlines' ability to pay for new equipment and the costs of keeping old equipment in service. Indeed, as the upkeep costs became more costly, eating into the cash flow benefits of accelerated depreciation taken on new aircraft, the airlines found it more economical to hold onto their aircraft longer. Other factors that affected the replacement life were the resale value of old aircraft, availability of funds, and routes to be served. All of this implied a gradual and evolutionary improvement in efficiency. The focus was more on the engines, which paced fuel economy improvements. Furthermore, compared to airframe improvement, engine progress was more costly, gradual, and slower; simultaneously, their share of the initial selling price increased from 15% to 20% in the early jet age to 20% to 30%.

Airlines were not always in control of the longevity of their aircraft. As of January 1, 1985, the first-generation jetliners like the Boeing 707 and the DC-8 were no longer able to serve the U.S. markets because of noise regulations. The positive news for the airlines was that the more modern narrow-bodied and wide-bodied types followed a slower replacement cycle since they could be in service up to 50 years.

Future Demand

Demand for new aircraft was driven by traffic growth and fleet replacement. As of 1985, 6,441 aircraft with over 1 million seat capacity were in service. Of these, 1,036 were between 16 and 25 years old. Since deregulation in the United States, average load factors improved from 57.2% in 1973 to 62.3% in 1983. Forecasts indicated a further gain in load factors of only 1% to 2%. The industry's world market projection for future air travel growth was 5% through the end of the century, slightly faster for non-U.S. carriers and slightly slower for U.S. carriers. In terms of value, in 1985 dollars, between 1985 and 1995 the aircraft demand would be worth over $130 billion. Implied was a demand and average output through the 1980s of 58,500 seats annually or 355 aircraft.

The growth regions—Asia, the Middle East, and Latin America—reflected the growing importance of international orders. Between 1982 and 1985, 60% of Boeing's orders were to non-U.S. airlines, and overall, between 1971 and 1984, non-U.S. carriers accounted for 61% of aircraft deliveries compared to 37% between

1958 and 1970. Of these, many were ordered by small airlines, most of which were government-owned and tended to place small orders. For example, seventeen international companies ordered eighty-eight aircraft in the same year that nine U.S. companies ordered 236. On average, the American order size was fourteen in contrast to five for non-U.S. carriers.

As of 1984, the average age of an aircraft was 18.5 years. In 1985, many airlines continued to postpone aircraft retirement, causing the average age to be at an all-time high. Replacement of old generation jetliners, though, saved the airlines fuel (24% of operating cost) and labor (two instead of three in the cockpit), which represented 35% of operating cost. It was expected that the near-term replacement demand would come from U.S carriers since the average age was 11 years compared to 8.8 for non-U.S. carriers and the replacement cycle of foreign carriers lagged that of the U.S. by 8 to 10 years. As estimated by Goldman, Sachs & Co., and First Boston Corporation, the average replacement demand per year through the end of the decade was 50 aircraft, bringing total demand to 400 aircraft per year through 1990, rising in the 1990s to 500 to 600 annually.

Aircraft Manufacturing and the National Interest

National economic health was inextricably intertwined with the rate of growth of the aircraft industry because of the effect on a country's merchandise trade account, the technology developed, and the impact on employment. In the United States, for instance, civil aircraft, engines, and parts accounted for more than 10% of all U.S. exports of manufacturers, with Boeing heading the list. *Exhibits 3, 4, 5,* and *6* reveal the magnitude of aircraft sales in the United States and abroad. The $12.6 billion trade surplus in 1985 for all aerospace products as compared to the total merchandise trade deficit of $148.5 billion ($49.7 billion with Japan and

$27.4 billion with Europe) indicated the importance of these products to the U.S. economy. Of the total $11.4 billion civil aircraft shipments in 1985, large transports constituted $9.6 billion. Research and development expenses for the U.S. aerospace industry in 1985 totaled $18.3 billion, the highest outlay of domestic industries.

The Europeans also viewed the airframe industry as serving their national interest. Commercial benefits flowed from the high technologies developed; in some countries nearly 50% of the balance of trade was derived from aircraft exports. Also observable was the enhanced prestige and political presence of supplier countries through sales of jetliners abroad.

Both the United States and European countries claimed that $1 billion in sales lost cost 40,000 jobs for that year, with secondary effects due to loss of salaries and governmental revenues such as taxes. But U.S. and European aircraft manufacturers faced vastly different labor laws and practices. Briefly stated, U.S. firms could lay off and rehire (within limitations) to expand or contract the labor force as demand and output fluctuated. In Europe, the labor force was fairly stable since their number did not grow or diminish much, due mostly to the large sums governments had to pay to laid-off workers in either publicly or privately owned enterprises (90% of wages for a year plus comprehensive health and welfare benefits in France, for example). The need for backlog orders to ensure continuous production became paramount. According to figures provided by Airbus Industrie, in 1985 there were 166,000 skilled workers in the Airbus partners' labor force, of which 27,000 were directly employed on Airbus work. In the United States, 602,000 were directly employed in aircraft-related work in 1985, with nearly 1.3 million in the total aerospace work force.

It was not unusual to observe government involvement in the commercial aircraft industry. The fierce rivalry among the Airbus consortium and America's McDonnell Douglas with its DC-10 for roughly the same market revealed the competitive nature of national policies in support of high-technology industries for economic purposes. The American companies complained that the foreign governments were heavily subsidizing their competitors. Their complaints were not without basis. Historically, Great Britain and France have been concerned about the adequacy of their high-technology industries and have financed the development and subsidized the production of particular aircraft designs aimed explicitly for a civilian market. In addition, British and French aircraft manufacturers were given access to low-cost credits and protection from imports and were guaranteed commercial procurement orders. However, it is also clear that America's postwar commercial aircraft business would not have flourished without military R&D and government procurement contracts.

International Collaboration

Success in the commercial aircraft industry had become more dependent upon multinational joint ventures by the mid-1980s. Such collaboration (see *Exhibit 7* for examples) reduced market and technological uncertainties by sharing the risks of the development costs and changes in the market requirements. Complementary resources were shared more efficiently as each partner contributed its comparative advantage to the program and allowed a project to fill out its production lines without making major investments. Subcontractors shared more of the risk in return for larger potential profit. Because access to export markets was often influenced by government policy and international politics, multinational joint ventures had a better chance of appearing politically acceptable in many major industrialized countries. For example, the European governments involved in the Airbus programs pursued policies and attitudes that some third world countries found more congenial than America's. Consequently, the Arab nations and Brazil, for instance, switched their airplane purchases from Boeing to Airbus. From their vantage point, security was linked to the United States, so weapons were purchased from the United States. Yet, these governments also found it advantageous to hedge their bets politically by ordering a high visibility aircraft from another source.

With overcapacity in the industry, joining actual or potential competitors tended to be preferable to competing in a market too small for all to survive. Both Lockheed and, to a lesser extent, McDonnell Douglas suffered in this overcrowded market and lost out to Airbus as strong competitors to Boeing. In addition, multinational joint ventures tended to discourage potential competitors from launching independent programs, a contributing factor for Boeing's arrangements with Japan. The Ministry of International Trade and Industry (MITI) identified the aerospace industry as one in which the Japanese firms needed to develop domestic capabilities and provide access to government-funded subsidies for joint ventures in which Japanese participation in manufacturing met certain conditions.

Governmental Role in Marketing Efforts

Except for the United States, nearly all airlines were owned by governments. It became necessary for successful aircraft selling to negotiate with both the management and owners of the airline companies. Typically, the former were civilians and the latter government officials exemplified by the airliner's Chairman of the Board being a Minister of Transportation or Finance. As a result, ambassadors from all countries were often sent to promote the product on behalf of the manufacturers when the deals reached the government level. However, the purchase decision was not always harmonious since gov-

ernment priorities could differ from those of the operators. For instance, country or countries of origin of the equipment best suited for the routes served might not be the most preferable to trade with, given the current trade balance between the seller's and purchaser's governments. Also, not unusual were negotiations for other purchases of equipment (energy-related, military, etc.) that would occur at the same time discussions were held about aircraft sales. Linkages of aircraft sales to nuclear power plants or, for instance, to the offer, during the Indian Airlines deal, by the French government to promise French technical assistance in cleaning up the Ganges River; to lend support in the World Bank for securing soft loans for India and in the United Nations for India's aim of establishing a nuclear-free zone for the Indian Ocean; and to accelerate delivery schedules of French Mirage jets to India were rumored but difficult to substantiate.[4] There was little question, however, that the French made heavy use of sending ambassadors on multiple-purpose sales calls.

Trade Agreements in Civil Aircraft

The GATT Agreement on Trade in Civil Aircraft, summarized in *Exhibit 8*, set forth the general policy objectives of an international framework governing the conduct of trade in civil aircraft. Highlights included elimination of duties and technical barriers to trade components for civil aircraft, airlines' freedom from governmental interference on sales or purchases, avoidance of disruptions in trade including fair pricing, and establishment of a committee to address relevant issues pertaining to the agreement. In the 5 years since its inception, many of the agreed-to objectives were achieved, confirming the Agreement as effective. As an example, the Committee described in Article 8 was established, meeting under GATT in Geneva two to three times a year. Their meetings were attended by all the Signatory members and nonparticipatory observers who were part of GATT but not party to the Agreement. The Committee also established one technical subcommittee which sought to address those relevant aircraft items not already covered by the Agreement. Their proposed additions to the Agreement product list were presented to and accepted by the full Committee and converted into the annex of applicable items to reflect the changed picture of trade and technology.

Not all Signatories appeared to be fully in accordance with Articles 4 and 6. Some governments, such as those in the European Airbus consortium, continued to pressure their national airlines to purchase certain aircraft. Some U.S. suppliers claimed that European government officials had intervened in the sales of the A-320. One U.S. government representative, party to the aircraft agreement, observed that it was hard to control political linkages; not everything was visible. Doubts were often cast as to whether Airbus was actually pricing its aircraft to cover costs, implying heavy subsidization from their partner governments.

One other trade agreement, the *Harmonization of Officially Supported Financing for Large Commercial Jet Aircraft*, was a multilateral agreement among the officials responsible for government-supported export credits in the United States, West Germany, France, and Great Britain. It originated from an exchange of letters, in the spring of 1982, between the Export-Import Bank and U.S. Treasury and the officials of the three other governments. The focus was on sales and leases to third markets, namely to markets other than West Germany, France, United Kingdom, and the United States. The objectives were (1) not to compete on financial terms; (2) to establish minimum interest rates, i.e., 12% for dollar financing, 11.5% for franc financing, etc.; (3) to limit maximum financing percentage of the total price of the aircraft, i.e., 85%; and (4) to establish payment schedule guidelines. The aircraft covered by the arrange-

ments were all the Airbus models; the Boeing 727, 737, 747, 757, and 767; the McDonnell Douglas DC-9, DC-10, and MD-80 series; and the Lockheed L-1011.

The agreement was supplemented in July 1985 by the *Large Aircraft Sector Understanding*. Its formation was viewed as part of a comprehensive Organization of Economic Cooperation and Development (OECD) civil aircraft agreement, aiming to establish a balanced equilibrium in all markets by (1) equalizing competitive financial conditions between participants, (2) neutralizing finance by participants as a factor in the choice among competing aircraft, and (3) avoiding distortions of competition. The essence of the new agreement was an adjustment to the minimum interest rates. It contained a complex formula for determining interest rates in each of the partner currencies and the European Currency Unit. The formula was based on 10-year government bond yields and changed every 2 weeks, a departure from the earlier system of fixed rates.

AIRBUS INDUSTRIES

Government Ownership and Management

Airbus Industrie was formed in 1970 as a GIE (Groupement d'Intérêt Economique), a French entity, which provided for the pooling of mutual economic interests and an increase in the extent of the contributors' current activities to enable its members to increase the profitability of their own enterprises. GIE itself does not exist to make a profit. Reflective of this, all of the financial accounts associated with the Airbus programs were incorporated into the partners' own accounts. Each participant's profit depended upon its own costs, and the costs of one participant were not borne by the others. In effect, profits were not shared. Initially, the two members were France's Aérospatiale and West Germany's Deutsche Airbus (M-B-B being the major manufacturer). Discussions emanated from the fact that, at the time, over 60% of the world's airline traffic flew routes less than 2,500 nautical miles[5] and that the short-to-medium-range airliner market was virtually untapped. Furthermore, the partners were anxious to overcome the U.S. dominance in this industry and to improve their own disappointing national efforts in the past. The opportunity to consolidate respective resources appeared as a viable way to launch and compete effectively and cost efficiently in a commercial aircraft program.

France, Great Britain, and West Germany focused their discussions around the development of the A-300, the world's first twin-engine wide-body aircraft, seating 240 to 345 passengers. Disagreements over size and choice of engine, coupled with President De Gaulle's rejection of Great Britain's entry into the Common Market, led to Britain's withdrawal. Later in 1970, Fokker of the Netherlands joined the A-300 program as an associate member and CASA of Spain joined as a consortium member. In January 1979, British Aerospace finally rejoined as a full member, and later, in May of that year, Belairbus of Belgium joined as an associate member. *Exhibit 9* lists the manufacturing contribution of each member.

Airbus Industrie was responsible for managing the development, production, marketing, and after-sales service of the A-300, A-310, A-320, and subsequent commercial aircraft programs. Functions specifically associated with the engineering, production, and program finance, while coordinated by Airbus Industrie, were primarily executed by the partner companies. The aim was to combine effectively the technical strength of the participating companies without locking up large capital sums which members needed for all their non-Airbus work. Flexibility in the structure to ensure the ability to react quickly to the needs of its customers and members was among the criteria established to be a global player. The aim was to keep Europe in the technical forefront in com-

mercial aviation and in related industries to bolster exports and provide employment in a key sector. Indeed, the participating nations each considered their contribution to the Airbus programs as important national projects.

The costs of the programs were financed on a national basis by the participants, partially backed by government loans. The loans were repaid by an agreed share of the proceeds of aircraft sales, transferred by Airbus Industrie to the partners. Delivery of 360 A-300s was needed to repay the initial loans. A similar number was determined for repayment on the loans for the A-310. The major portion of the funds were bank loans, made on commercial terms to the member companies to enable them to finance work in process. Responding to U.S. allegations that the Airbus-related governments unfairly subsidized the aircraft programs, the chairman of Airbus North America, Inc., Mr. Alan Boyd, stated that "government support is legitimate as long as it does not distort the market." In fact, he continued, "Boeing's market position and earnings are better than before Airbus entered the market."

The total European content value in the Airbus programs was roughly two-thirds for the A-300 and A-310 and three-quarters for the A-320 (the French contributed less than one-third the value of the A-320). The remaining was provided by U.S. companies, which supplied components and replaceable parts, primarily the engines. Pratt & Whitney and General Electric, either alone or part of a joint venture, were the suppliers of engines to all the Airbus family.

The first two aircraft manufactured by Airbus Industrie, the A-300 and A-310, were short-to-medium-range and medium-to-long-range twin-aisle, twin-engine wide bodies, covering up to 3,800 nautical miles, offering state-of-the-art technology, expanded cargo capacity, lower noise levels, and greater fuel efficiency than existing wide-body trijets. These aircraft also allowed for the first two-pilot operation of a wide-body aircraft. The next addition was the A-320, a 150-plus-seat, short-to-medium-range, single-aisle twinjet. In its category it offered greater fuel efficiency, advanced design concepts, and increased cargo capacity. The A-320 was the first to offer a narrow-body twinjet. Market forces leading to the development of the A-320 included deregulation, which had allowed new carriers to enter the market, many of which operated at lower cost, offered discounted fares, yet required smaller seating capacity. Also, scheduling patterns were focused around the "hub and spoke" pattern, whereby short-haul routes fed into major airports for connection with longer-haul segments of the trip.

According to forecasts provided by the consortium, Airbus Industrie expected to capture 26% of the single-aisle short-to-medium-range market with its A-320; 35% of the twin-aisle short-to-medium range with its A-310, A-300-600, and A-330; and 17% of the long-range market with its A-310-300 and A-340—with a total 25% expected share of large commercial transports by the end of the century. Airbus' only mid-1980s significant market position was in the twin-aisle short-to-medium-range category. *Exhibit 9* gives the status of sales, deliveries, and backlog orders as of December 31, 1985.

Role of Creditors

The three largest partners offered export credits, loans, and guarantees for the purchase of aircraft outside the consortium countries through their government-owned institutions. France's Compagnie Francaise d'Assurance du Commerce Extérieur (COFACE) along with the Banque Francaise du Commerce Extérieur (BFCE) provided insurance and financing up to 85% of the total purchase at the interest rates set out by the *Large Aircraft Sector Understanding*. Great Britain's Export Credit Guaranty De-

partment (ECGD) performed both roles, insurance and banking, under the international guidelines. West Germany's Hermes, a private insurance agency owned by a consortium of large commercial banks but acting on behalf of the government, provided export credit guarantees for Deutsche Airbus. Conditions offered were reportedly in accordance with the agreements.

BOEING COMPANY

The Boeing Company, founded in July 1916 in Seattle, Washington, was the world's largest private commercial aircraft manufacturer and the largest American exporter. In 1985, new commercial orders totaled 390 aircraft valued at $14.9 billion and deliveries were 203 aircraft compared to 146 in 1984. Boeing also produced military aircraft, bringing 1985's revenues to $13.64 billion, up from $10.35 billion in 1984, and earnings to $566 million, up from $390 million.[6] Within the three major reporting segments approximately 58% of the revenues were attributed to commercial aircraft sales, 29% to military sales, and 9% to aerospace sales. Boeing forecasted deliveries through 1989 of 935 commercial aircraft, 375 satisfying replacement demand and 560 meeting increased traffic. However, Mr. Frank Shrontz, Boeing's CEO, was not content: "I don't think we have yet achieved the level of profit we need for product development which will still have a fair return for our stockholders."[7] According to *The Economist*, Mr. Shrontz's idea of a fair return was 20% on stockholders' equity, which compared with the 14% achieved last year (1985) and the 17% of the aerospace sector as a whole. See *Exhibit 10* for Boeing's range of models, orders, balance sheet, and income statement.

Boeing, like McDonnell Douglas and Lockheed, had its roots in military production, which promoted the development of new technology and their applications. The military programs absorbed heavy early costs of the commercial airplanes and engines, which enabled the companies to move down the learning curve. For example, with a break-even point of 300 aircraft for early models, the military ordered 600 KC 135s, thereby ensuring profitability for the derivative Boeing 707.

Boeing was the first to recognize the advantages of a global strategy. Its stated goal was to dominate every segment of the commercial transport market, and by early 1985, it was close to doing so with nearly a 60% share of the large transport aircraft market, followed by Airbus' 19%, based on cumulative 1980–1984 orders valued at $45.7 billion. To accomplish the goal, Boeing identified several strategies. First, it had to be a technological leader, spending billions on research and development programs for new commercial aircraft and derivatives, costing annually 4% to 8.6% of sales. Underscoring this commitment, Boeing was nearly pushed into bankruptcy because of the large expense of developing the 747. Survival demanded a drastic retrenchment in Boeing's work force, from a peak of 101,000 in 1968 to 37,000 in 1971. Second, Boeing needed to develop a basic model for every segment, from which derivatives were to be developed to expand the market and to extend the model's life cycle. Boeing aligned itself with a few key airlines worldwide to ensure close developmental relationships.

Third, Boeing built a strong, well-coordinated marketing team on a global basis which hoped to identify potential sales earlier than its competitors and respond quickly and effectively to rivals' actions. Fourth, Boeing attempted to be a low-cost producer by pursuing manufacturing efficiency through a tightly controlled and centrally coordinated R&D manufacturing system. Fifth, marketing and services were to be centrally coordinated from the corporate headquarters to maintain high standards and consistency worldwide. Several of the early models, in particular the 727, were very successful, which enabled the company

to generate a stream of cash flows to fund the implementation of its strategy.

Consequently, Boeing boasted of an enormous customer base: 4,500 commercial aircraft delivered to more than 400 different operators. Its marketing techniques evolved to compete against Airbus, which was rooted in a different political and social system, financed by public funds, and committed to a fundamental goal different from its own. Boeing set up a new organization to refurbish and sell used or new aircraft taken in part-exchange deals to make easier new aircraft sales. For instance, in November 1984, Boeing bought three new (i.e., never-flown) A-310s from Kuwait Airways in order to sell the airline its own Boeing 767s. As reported in the *Financial Times:*

This curious situation emanates from the searing competition between Boeing and Airbus. . . . Aircraft manufacturers have long been purchasing used aircraft, their own and rival makes, in order to sell new ones. But buying up the competitors' brand new airliners marks a new stage in the sales battle.[8]

Boeing, it was reported, also bought five Airbus A-300s from Singapore Airlines in exchange for selling the airline Boeing 747s and 757s.

Furthermore, Boeing renegotiated a labor contract in 1983 which set up a two-tier labor agreement with International Association of Machinists. Boeing paid its new workers a 26% lower wage rate than existing workers and eliminated cost-of-living increases for some workers. Concerning product and capacity, Boeing was considered the only civil aircraft producer with a genuine range of aircraft meeting the demands of most large continental and intercontinental flights. In addition to offering a large and growing assortment of jetliners, Boeing had the capacity to produce 400 aircraft per year, putting it in the position to single-handedly meet the world's aircraft demand.

Soon after the launches of the Boeing 757 and 767, Airbus announced its newest entrant, the A-320, which would fill an untapped niche. Faced with capital tied up in large program costs and the risk of a new model that could cannibalize sales of existing lines, Boeing attempted to persuade Airbus to delay the launch of the A-320, stressing the financial risk of such a launch. Yet, Boeing boldly sent a signal that it would be prepared to match the action by Airbus, if the consortium proceeded ahead with it. Preaching to the airliners, Boeing stressed market and technological uncertainties coupled with the danger of prematurely committing to a jetliner which could quickly become obsolete. Boeing encouraged its customers to buy or lease existing airplanes with proven technology while they explored the optimum design of its version of the new aircraft. Boeing was able to introduce major derivatives of its 737, a close rival of the A-320, for $300 to $400 million instead of $2 billion required to launch the A-320 and sell them at lower prices. After much deliberation, Boeing announced it would develop a new aircraft, the 7J7, to compete in the 150-seat short-to-medium-range segment.

The 7J7 program would be different from previous ones. Three major Japanese aircraft manufacturers and Boeing agreed to collaborate on the development and production of the 7J7, with the Japanese firms sharing a 25% stake and participating as full partners. It was agreed that the Japan Aircraft Development Corporation would be the overall management and coordinating agency for the Japanese involvement. The companies would participate in the manufacturing, design, marketing, and product support as well as share the investment, revenues, and risk in proportion to their equity shares. The 7J7 was intended to enter service in 1992 and use a new type of engine called a prop fan, utilize new lightweight structural materials, and provide more advanced technology than the A-320. Boeing was also betting that its December 1985 purchase of Havilland

Aircraft of Canada would aid its entry into the smaller aircraft market.

Role of the Export-Import (Ex-Im) Bank

The Ex-Im Bank, counterpart to the European creditor agencies, was a government lending and guarantee-granting institution which, in its promotion of sales of U.S. products abroad, extended or guaranteed loans up to 85% of the total price for purchases by foreign carriers of American-made airlines and engines. Under certain circumstances the Ex-Im Bank helped American "sellers" by matching the financing which agencies of other governments may have offered to American carriers. The Reagan administration, seeking ways to reduce the federal budget, attempted to cut back the funds available to the bank on the grounds that the chief recipients were companies such as Boeing and General Electric, America's number one and two exporters, which, because they were large and profitable, did not need the federal support. Nevertheless, Congress rejected the budget cut and left the Ex-Im Bank intact.

THE BATTLEGROUND HEATS UP

On March 20 and 21, 1986, European and American officials met for informal talks in Geneva, Switzerland, at the German Mission to discuss charges from both sides of unfair competitive practices. The meeting's roots came from an autumn 1985 press conference held by President Reagan, where he delineated alleged violations of trade agreements by trading partners. Airbus was number three on the list. Concerned about reports in the press that Congress was considering a Section 301[9] case against Airbus, the three largest European governments involved in the Airbus program wrote in December to Mr. Clayton Yeutter, the U.S. Trade Representative, requesting a forum to respond to questions and clear up any disagreements. The request was granted, and an agenda was agreed upon. All the subjects discussed were covered by the GATT agreement.

The U.S. delegation was headed by Mr. S. Bruce Wilson, assistant U.S. trade representative, and supported by Mr. Steve Falken, assistant to Mr. Wilson, Mr. Crawford Brubaker and Ms. Sally Bath of the Commerce Department, Ms. Ann Hallick and Mr. Robert Deutsch of the State Department, Mr. Richard Larm of the Department of Justice, and Mr. Christopher Hawkins of the Department of Labor. Nonparticipatory advisers were Mr. Ray Waldman, a lobbyist for Boeing, Ms. Michelle Olivo from McDonnell Douglas' marketing department, and Ms. Celia Sherbeck, an economist at the Aerospace Industry Association. The latter two were members of the industry Sector Advisory Committee (ISAC) on the aerospace equipment industry.[10] The European delegation was headed by Dr. Dieter Wolf of West Germany's BMWI (Ministry of Economics and Trade) and supported by Mr. Michael Lagorce of France's DGAC (Ministry of Transportation) and Under Secretary Mr. John Michell of the U.K.'s Department of Trade and Industry in the Air Division. Also present in Geneva, but not at the meetings, were company representatives from Airbus, Boeing, and McDonnell Douglas. Excerpts of the press releases are found in *Exhibits 11* and *12*.

Highlights of some of the accusations included an Airbus claim that American manufacturers have benefited from extensive research subsidies from NASA for aerospace development and large defense contracts, from which commercial aircraft derived. Boeing was accused of selling its unique 747 expensively

in order to discount the price of the 767, the most recent competitor to the A-310 and A-320. Aware that the United States claimed that the Europeans pressured their national airlines and former colonies to buy Airbus, Airbus officials made clear that there was limited evidence of such pressure on former colonies and that, to date, neither British Airways nor France's UTA owned any Airbuses and Lufthansa owned more Boeings than Airbuses.

Boeing, too, made claims against Airbus, asserting that Airbus "swings deals simply because 'certain directors seem to have the power to commit the company to guaranteeing that money is available at certain rates.' "[11] Boeing argued that Airbus could offer much more liberal discounts and incentives to potential customers than Boeing, since Boeing was private and performance was judged by the bottom line. Also, Airbus had the ability to mobilize political influence and pressures and, as such, was eager to escalate sales negotiations to the political level whenever possible. Additionally, the national governments supporting Airbus allegedly provided large public subsidies that, according to Boeing, created distortions in the trade of civil aircraft. Further concern was that the exact amount of the subsidies was unknown, which led government and industry officials to use the term "transparencies" to describe the issue at the March 20/21 meeting. Another part of Airbus' success was tied to undue influence placed on Air France by the French government, an action which ran counter to the GATT Agreement. Finally, the loss of the Indian Airlines deal over extreme price cutting, in September, heightened the tension between the two rivals.

INDIAN AIRLINES DEAL, 1985

Competitive products	Seating capacity	Range	Type	Price per seat (000s)
Boeing				
737	100–140	S-M	N	@ 138 seats $145–$181
757	180–224	M	N	@ 208 seats Original: $202 Final: $130
Airbus				
A-310	210–220	S-M	W	@ 220 seats $173–$219 (case writer's estimate)
A-320	150–162	S	N	@ 162 seats Original: $191 Final: $148

S = Short.
M = Medium.
N = Narrow-body.
W = Wide-body.

FAMILY OF AIRCRAFT[a]

Airbus		Boeing	
		737-200	Seats: 115 Range: 1,600–2,000 nmi
A-320	Seats: 150 Range: 1,750 nmi[b]		
		757-200	Seats: 180 Range: 3,500 nmi
A-310	Seats: 210 Range: 3,255–4,150 nmi		
		767-200	Seats: 211 Range: 3,200–5,600 nmi
A-300	Seats: 260 Range: 3,150–3,350 nmi		
		747-200	Seats: 440 Range: 5,500–6,000 nmi

[a]Seating given for typical layouts.
[b]nmi = nautical mile. One nautical mile equals 6,076 feet.

U.S. CIVIL AIRCRAFT SHIPMENTS AND EXPORTS (1978–1985)

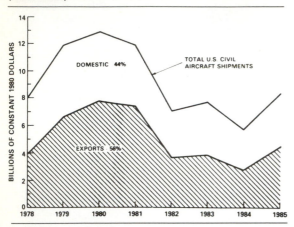

Source: Commerce Department. ITA: TD/Aerospace.

U.S. EXPORTS OF CIVIL AIRCRAFT (1978–1985)

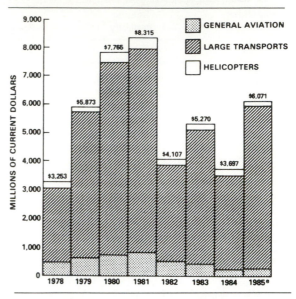

● Estimated.
Source: Commerce Department. ITA: TD/Aerospace.

U.S. IMPORTS OF CIVIL AIRCRAFT (1978–1985)

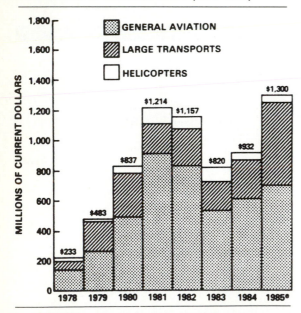

● Estimated.
Source: Commerce Department. ITA: TD/Aerospace.

U.S. TRADE BALANCE IN HIGH-TECH INDUSTRIES (1980–1985)

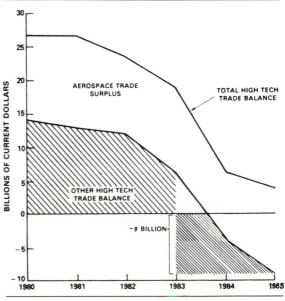

Source: Department of Commerce. ITA: TD/Aerospace.

MULTINATIONAL VENTURES IN COMMERCIAL AIRCRAFT AND ENGINE MANUFACTURING, 1984

Name of venture[a]	Aircraft or eninges manufactured	Partners and home countries	Nature of relationship among partners
Airbus Industrie	A-300, A-310, A-320 jet aircraft	Aerospatiale (France) Duetsche Airbus (West Germany) British Aerospace (United Kingdom) Construcciones Aero-Nauticas-CASA (Spain)	Airbus is a Groupement d'Intérêt Economique under French law and exercises management control over the project. Engineering and manufacturing were handled by member companies, but marketing was done by Airbus. Shares in the A-300/A-310 were Aerospatiale (37.9%), Deutsche Airbus (37.9%), British Aerospace (20%), CASA (4.2%). On the A-320 they were as follows: Aerospatiale (36%), Deutsche Airbus (31%), British Aerospace (27%), CASA (6%).
	Boeing 767 jet aircraft	Boeing (United States) Japan Commercial Aircraft Corporation (Japan) Aeritalia (Italy)	The Japanese and Italian participants were risk-sharing subcontractors to Boeing. Each manufactured major airframe structures accounting for approximately 15% of the cost of the airframe and major structures. Japan Commercial Aircraft Corporation is a government-sponsored partnership of Mitsubishi Heavy Industries (40%), Kawasaki Heavy Industry (40%), and Fuji Heavy Industry (20%). Boeing handled all basic design and marketing and supervised the detailed engineering. Final assembly was done by Boeing.
CFM International	CFM 56 jet engine	General Electric (United States) SMECMA (France)	Development and manufacturing were split equally between the two partners. Each partner built major sections of the engines, which were assembled and tested in both the United States and France. CFM International, a jointly owned company, handled sales and overall administration. Revenues were shared equally. (Often used by Airbus.)
International Aero Engines	V2500 jet engine	Rolls Royce (United Kingdom) Pratt & Whitney (United States) Japanese Aero Engines Corp. (Japan) Motoren-und Turbinen-Union (West Germany) Fiat Aviazione (Italy)	A jointly owned company, JAE managed the project, with equity shares divided as follows: Rolls Royce (30%), Pratt & Whitney (30%), JAEC (19.9%), MTU (12.1%), Fiat (8%). Engineering and manufacturing work was split as follows: Rolls Royce (30%), Pratt & Whitney (30%), JAEC (23%), MTU (11%), Fiat (6%). JAEC is a government-sponsored partnership of Ishi Kawajima-Harima Heavy Industries, IHI (60%), Mitsubishi Heavy Industries, MHI (15%), and Kawasaki Heavy Industries, KHI (25%). JAEC handled the marketing. (Offered with Airbus' A-320.)
	General Electric CF 6-80C2	General Electric (United States) Rolls Royce (United Kingdom)	The two partners participated in 15% of the investment, profits, and production of each other's engines. No separate company or joint programs were created. Each produced parts for and did final assembly of each other's engine.

[a]In some cases no separate entity was created, so no name was given.
Source: Columbia Journal of World Business, "Multinational Ventures in the Commercial Aircraft Industry," Summer 1985, p. 56.

SUMMARY OF GATT AGREEMENT ON TRADE IN CIVIL AIRCRAFT

Signatories to the Agreement were Austria, Belgium, Canada, Denmark, EEC, West Germany, France, Ireland, Italy, Japan, Luxembourg, Netherlands, Norway, Romania, Sweden, Switzerland, the United Kingdom, and the United States.

PURPOSE

1. Achieve expansion and ever-greater liberalization of world trade through the progressive dismantling of obstacles to trade.
2. Maximize freedom of world trade.
3. Promote technological development.
4. Ensure fair and equal competitive opportunities.
5. Affirm importance in civil aircraft sector.
6. Recognize aircraft sector as a particularly important component of economic and industrial policy.
7. Eliminate adverse effects on trade in civil aircraft resulting from governmental support in civil aircraft development, production, and marketing while recognizing that such governmental support, of itself, would not be deemed a distortion of trade.
8. Accept that civil aircraft activities operate on a commercially competitive basis and government-industry relationships differ widely among them.
9. Provide for international notification, consultation, surveillance, and dispute settlement procedures.
10. Establish an international framework governing conduct of trade.

Key articles the Signatories agreed to:

1. Product list.
2. Eliminate all customs, duties, and other charges as of January 1, 1980, on imports, repairs, maintenance, modification, or rebuilding, and provide an end-use system of customs administration to ensure duty-free or duty-exempt treatment that is comparable to the treatment provided by other Signatories.
3. Eliminate technical barriers to trade.
4. Ensure airlines' freedom from governmental pressure to select suppliers on the basis of commercial and technological factors; purchase of products covered by this Agreement should be made only on a competitive basis; avoid attaching inducements of any kind to the sale or purchase of civil aircraft from any particular source which would create discrimination against suppliers from any Signatory.
5. No application of trade restrictions such as import quotas, import licensing requirements, or export licensing requirements to restrict imports or exports.
6. Avoid adverse effects on trade in civil aircraft, and take into account the special factors which apply in the aircraft sector, in particular the widespread governmental support in this area, their international economic interests, and the desire of producers of all Signatories to participate in the expansion of the world civil aircraft market; pricing should be based on a reasonable expectation of recoupment of all costs, including nonrecurring program costs, identifiable and prorated costs of military research and development on aircraft, components and systems subsequently applied to the production of such civil aircraft.
7. Not to require or encourage regional and local governments and other bodies to take action inconsistent with provisions of this Agreement.
8. Establish a Committee on Trade in Civil Aircraft to afford Signatories the opportunity to consult on any matters relating to the operation of this Agreement, to determine whether amendments are required to ensure continuance of free and undistorted trade, and to examine any matter for which it has not been possible to find a satisfactory solution through bilateral consultations; the committee may establish subsidiary bodies in order to ensure a continuing balance of mutual advantages, reciprocity, and equivalent results; recognize the desirability of consultations with other Signatories in the Committee in order to seek a mutually acceptable solution prior to the initiation of an investigation to determine the existence, degree, and effect of any alleged subsidy; the Committee may issue such rulings or recommendations as may be appropriate.

The Agreement was signed April 12, 1979, in Geneva and went into effect January 1, 1980.

Source: GATT Agreement on Trade in Civil Aircraft.

EXHIBIT NINE

AIRBUS INDUSTRIE PARTNERSHIP AND ORDERS, 1985

Consortium members

- Aérospatiale of France produced the flight deck, forward fuselage sections, center fuselage/wing box section below the cabin floor, engine pylons, and lift dumpers.
- Deutsche Airbus of West Germany, owner of Messerschmidt-Bolkow-Blohm (M-B-B), produced the major fuselage sections, fin, rudder, tail cone, flaps, spoilers, and flap track fairings. It was responsible for the assembly and equipment of the complete wing and the entire interior of the aircraft.
- British Aerospace of Great Britain produced the main wing box.
- Construcciones Aeronautics SA (CASA) of Spain produced the tail plane, elevators, nose landing gear doors, and forward cabin entry doors.
- Fokker of Netherlands and Belairbus of Belgium participated as associates in production, with Fokker producing the ailerons, wing tips, main landing gear doors, and leg fairings, and Belairbus producing the slats.

Assembly and testing was centralized in Toulouse, France.

Cumulative orders	A-300	A-310	A-320
Sales	275	117	90
Deliveries	258	72	—
Backlog	17	45	90

Source: Airbus Industrie.

EXHIBIT TEN

BOEING FAMILY AND ORDERS, 1985

Model	Range	Seating capacity	Sales	Deliveries	Total ordered to date
737	S-M	110–140	282	117	1,535
747	L	331–496	41	24	683
757	M	180–224	45	38	182
767	M-L	211–290	22	24	189
7J7	S-M	150 (proposed)	—	—	—

CONSOLIDATED BALANCE SHEET, 6/30/85 ($ millions)

Assets		Liabilities and shareholders' equity	
Cash and equivalent[a]	$1,842.0	Short-term debt[b]	$ 200.0
Other current assets	4,569.0	Other current liabilities	3,115.0
Total current assets	6,411.0	Total current liabilities	3,315.0
Property, plant, and equipment, net	1,719.0	Long-term debt	32.0
		Deferred taxes	1,317.0
Investments and other assets	603.0	Deferred investment credit	131.0
		Shareholders' equity	3,938.0
Total assets	$8,733.0	Total liabilities and shareholders' equity	$8,733.0

[a]$2,275 as of September 30, 1985.
[b]$18 as of September 30, 1985.

INCOME STATEMENTS, 6/30/85 ($ millions)

Consolidated revenues	$6,304.0
Operating profits	245.0
Other income	135.0
Interest expense	11.0
Pretax income	369.0
Income taxes	121.0
Other expense	2.0
Net income	$ 246.0

Source: Goldman, Sachs & Company.

EXHIBIT ELEVEN

EXTRACTS FROM THE PRESS COMMUNIQUÉ BY THE GOVERNMENTS OF THE FEDERAL REPUBLIC OF GERMANY, FRANCE, AND THE UNITED KINGDOM, MARCH 21, 1986

Delegations of the governments of the Federal Republic of Germany, France, the United Kingdom, and the U.S.A. met on the 20/21 of March in Geneva to open informal consultations concerning matters of the aircraft industry. They discussed the competitive environment in the civil aircraft industry, government support of that industry, government inducements and other influences on the sale of aircraft, procurement decisions of national airlines, and the selection of component vendors by airframe manufacturers.

In their letter to the USTR C.K. Yeutter, they [the trade ministers of the three European countries] referred to his report to Congress on U.S. trade estimates wherein doubts had been expressed about the consistency of government support for Airbus with the GATT rules. [The trade ministers] feel concerned that this might be a source of a controversy harmful to economic relations in general and to desirable cooperation in the aerospace section in particular. In their opinion there is a need for strong competition in large civil aircraft and the avoidance of monopolistic structures. Were it not for the Airbus, such competition would not be assured. In one important segment of the market, airlines complain about the excessive price of the only aircraft presently offered (long range). A policy based on free competition has, of course, enabled United States aircraft manufacturers to sell their products successfully and in large numbers in Europe (more than 1,000 aircraft in operation), whereas the Airbus share of the United States market has thus far been substantially smaller (no more than 56 aircraft). The American competitors of Airbus continue to derive benefit from a wide range of government support, including public contracts as well as publicly funded programs. According to estimates, the combined aeronautics expenditure by DOD, NASA, [and] Department of Transport over the last 15 years exceeds $47.5 billion. Tax forgiveness on the switch over to Foreign Sales Corporation has saved Boeing $397 million and McDonnell Douglas well in excess of $300 million. . . .

The representatives of the Airbus partner countries took great care to describe the competitive environment in the civil aircraft industry. They held it necessary to promote competition and technological progress. With the Airbus, the European industry had concentrated its potential and achieved a high market acceptance. In order to reach the conditions of their U.S. competitors who have built up their strong base in many decades, the Airbus program needs front-end investment, of course, but the results already achieved have proved that this is a commercially viable concept. The recent launch aid advanced for the development of the Airbus 320 is repayable and has been provided only after a careful evaluation of the economics of the project and its market potential, which in between has been proved by 250 orders and options even years before the first delivery. The GATT agreement on trade in civil aircraft does not preclude government support as such—it recognizes that such support is widespread in this industry and, of itself, would not be deemed a distortion of trade and that government-industry relationships in the individual countries differ widely—but asks for the governments to seek to avoid adverse effects on trade in civil aircraft. In this respect the European representatives draw attention to the fact that the U.S. aircraft manufacturers enjoy a predominant position in the market of around 90% within the existing fleets of large turbine-powered aircraft and maintain strong order books, last year having been one of the best in their history.

All delegations agreed that efforts should be intensified to come to a joint understanding of the rules of the GATT agreement on trade in civil aircraft and to strengthen the fruitful cooperation between the European and United States aerospace industries.

The commission of the European Communities was represented as an observer at the talks.

EXHIBIT TWELVE

EXTRACTS FROM THE AMERICAN PRESS RELEASE, MARCH 21, 1986

During the meeting, the United States expressed its concern over the effectiveness of the provisions in the GATT Aircraft Agreement. Specifically, the United States was concerned that direct program subsidies by the three large governments are leading to trade distortions in large transport aircraft. The United States believes that continued support of this type will result in increased trade tensions in the area of civil aircraft—a sector that has generally been one of cooperation in trade. The United States requested information on the subsidies given in order to clarify the situation.

In particular, the United States asked the Airbus governments to provide information about their launch aid, support for nonrecurring investments, and production subsidies provided to companies that are partners in Airbus Industrie. The United States also asked for information on the terms and conditions for recoupment of these subsidies and the amount of recoupment received to date. Although the Airbus governments provided some publicly available information in response to this request, they were reluctant to provide additional information in the absence of what they considered were necessary explanations about why this information was relevant to the functioning of the Aircraft Agreement.

With respect to the European argument that the United States subsidizes indirectly its commercial aircraft industry through DOD and NASA programs, the United States replied that there were no direct supports from these programs and that there was only negligible indirect flow through to U.S. civil aircraft manufacturers.

On the question of inducements, it is the U.S. view that all sides in the consultations recognized that there were problems in this area. The United States put forward its position that governments should avoid inducements and politicized marketing in civil aircraft competitions, as provided in Article 4 of the GATT Aircraft Agreement. It was the sense of the U.S. delegation that this was a view also shared by its European counterparts and that progress could be made in the near future on this issue.

The United States also expressed its concern about the need to ensure that airline procurement decisions and component vendor selection by manufacturers are made strictly on the basis of commerical and technical considerations and without government intervention. . . .

Another meeting was scheduled for early June 1986. . . .

NOTES

1. Such examples were Korean landing rights in Paris, Iberia's frequency agreement in European routes, and Swissair traffic rights offered but not delivered in France, West Germany, and Great Britain.

2. Such examples were atomic power plants to Iran and joint venture deals including a French investment in a petrochemical plant in Kuwait and Kuwaiti investments in some Paris real estate. All the examples were cited in *Overview of U.S. International Competitiveness: Hearings Before the Subcommittee on International Economic Policy and Trade*, Washington, D.C., U.S. Government Printing Office, 1983, p. 273.

3. Quoted in John Newhouse, *The Sporty Game* (New York: Alfred A. Knopf, 1982, p. 21).

4. *International Herald Tribune*, October 31, 1985.

5. One nautical mile = 6,076 feet.

6. 1984's stated earnings did not include the $397 million for Domestic International Sales Corporation (DISC) earnings, which represented the adjustment of prior years' federal tax provisions. DISCs were established in 1971 to encourage export sales by allowing up to 42.5% of a DISC's qualified export income to be deferred from taxation as long as the income was retained and used to develop exports. The Tax Reform Act of 1984 forgave all accumulated deferred taxes as part of the Foreign Sales Corporation (FSC) provisions. FSCs replaced the DISCs and became the new export incentive mechanism. The FSC was allowed tax exemption for a manufacturer's qualified export income, while the DISC was allowed only a tax deferral.

7. *The Economist*, May 3, 1986, p. 23.

8. "Why Boeing Is Putting New Airbus Airlines on Ice," *Financial Times*, November 6, 1984, p. 5.

9. Section 301 refers to the section of the Trade Act of 1974 which gave the president the power to take action to enforce the rights of the United States under any trade agreement and to obtain elimination of unfair trade policies by a trading partner.

10. ISACs were created under the Trade Act of 1974 and were composed of members from the private sector, to consult with and advise American trade policy negotiators. The executive branch was mandated to listen to the ISACs and incorporate their recommendations into American trade policy. Each committee was required to submit a summary report of its proceedings to Congress.

11. "Turbulence on Two Fronts for Europe's Airbus," *Financial Times*, February 5, 1985, p. 24.

Motorola and Japan

Japanese industry promotion policies have evolved in form over the last 30 years. They remain effective in semiconductors, telecommunications, and computers. In other words, the Japanese government is continuing to target as a national priority all of Motorola's major businesses.

Motorola Executive

In late 1981, Motorola executives held a series of meetings at their headquarters in Schaumburg, Illinois, to hammer out a response to intensifying Japanese competition. To date, all of Motorola's efforts to gain significant sales of semiconductors and mobile telecommunication products in Japan had been disappointing. Moreover, Motorola's management had evidence that some Japanese manufacturers were dumping telecommunication products in the American market. Bob Galvin, Motorola's

chairman and CEO, knew that something had to be done, but what?

BUSINESS LINES

Motorola in 1981 was balanced on an integrated technology triad of semiconductors, communications, and computers. Motorola's products included two-way radios, pagers, cellular telephones, and other electronic communications systems; semiconductors; defense and aerospace electronics; automotive and industrial electronic equipment; and data communications and information processing hardware and software. In 1981 the company registered sales of $3.5 billion (see *Exhibit 1*). Galvin was pleased with the structure of the company, noting that "we like to perform all the functions of our business under our own aegis. We control our own designs, our own processing and manufacturing and our own distribution and marketing, which includes service and sales. If we were heavily in consumer products we would be at the mercy of retailers."[1]

Motorola had long been considered a pow-

This case was prepared by Associated Professor David B. Yoffie and Research Associate John Coleman as a basis for class discussion rather than to illustrate the effective or ineffective handling of an administrative situation.

erhouse in land-mobile communications, and in 1980 it was one of the largest supplier of two-way radios and assorted mobile electronic communications equipment in the world, with market share estimates of 65% to 75%. Motorola, General Electric (GE), and E. F. Johnson controlled about 85% of the U.S. two-way radio market, with the remainder going to very large, diversified Japanese firms such as NEC, Matsushita, and Fujitsu. In some categories, such as communications gear for police departments, Motorola accounted for approximately 90% of the total U.S. market. The company expected major growth to come from cellular radio. Bell Weisz, the vice chairman and chief operating officer, estimated that by 1983 Motorola would spend about $150 million in developing the technology, and he expected it to bring in $1 billion worth of revenues before 1990. About half of this total would come from equipment for major stations that would transmit the radio signals and half from the smaller terminals that individuals would use to communicate with one another.

The primary customers for Motorola's communications products included public safety agencies, utilities, transportation companies such as taxicab operators, and institutions such as schools and hospitals. Product development pressures in communications were high and increasingly stressed the use of advanced electronic components. Competitive factors facing communications firms included price, product performance and quality, and quality and availability of service and systems engineering. Because the equipment configurations demanded by its customers were diverse, Motorola found that none of these factors was dominant overall.

Motorola's product sales and leasing took a number of forms: mostly through a company distribution force, but also through independent distributors and commission agents, and through licensing of independent companies. One important variable affecting the firm's telecommunications operation was government regulation. In the United States, the Federal Communications Commission's allocation of frequencies could significantly affect the two-way radio business, particularly in congested urban areas.

The semiconductor industry was a rapidly growing, highly fragmented industry. Motorola faced intense competition from domestic firms, which were largely small (under $1 billion sales) merchants,[2] and larger vertically integrated Japanese firms. Motorola's semiconductors were used in a variety of products, including mass-market video and audio receivers, computers, automotive controls, industrial automation systems, and defense equipment. Like most companies in the industry, Motorola's sales were heavily oriented toward original equipment manufacturers and were typically channeled through both in-house distribution forces and independent distributors. Chips were supplied to other operating units within the company, a common practice at other diversified companies. Although its semiconductor sales tended to be sharply cyclical, Motorola had one of the most diversified semiconductor product lines in the industry. Alongside of its advanced line of microprocessors and memory products, almost one-third of Motorola's semiconductor sales consisted of relatively stable discrete components.

RESTRUCTURING AND ORGANIZATION

Motorola's early history strongly emphasized consumer products. Founded as the Galvin Manufacturing Corporation in 1928 by Paul V. Galvin, 2 years later the firm introduced the first commercially manufactured car radio under the brand name Motorola (Motor + Victrola = Motorola) and subsequently (in 1947) adopted that name for the corporation. Over the next 40 years the company was involved in several consumer lines (as well as its communications and semiconductor businesses), including car and home radios and televisions. But starting in the early 1970s the company's focus shifted to high-technology industrial electronics, including advanced mobile telecommunications (e.g., cellular phones) and advanced semiconductors (e.g., microprocessors).

Motorola's leap from the consumer electronics field was unusual. As one business analyst noted, "What must be appreciated is that Galvin did this proactively. There was no crisis at Motorola; the company and the industry appeared to be in good shape. Galvin did something highly unusual for an American executive—he anticipated the need for future change even though the company was not in any imminent trouble."[3] Galvin decided, in effect, to "bet the company" and make Motorola number one in semiconductors and retain the top spot in two-way communications over the next 10 years. The overhaul at Motorola involved putting in place a mix of high-growth businesses, decentralizing the company, allowing each division substantial autonomy while building up internal controls, establishing a long-term oriented New Enterprises operation, introducing new personnel programs, and committing employees to very high quality—the formal goal was zero defects.

The company was run by the triumvirate of Galvin, Weisz, and John Mitchell, the president and chief operating officer. These three men retained independent spheres of authority with responsibility to make any decision that had to be made in the corporation. If conflicts reached a stalemate, Galvin tipped the scales one way or the other. But the company had a democratic flair and had traditionally been a first-name organization. New employees were told to call the CEO "Bob." Galvin noted that "my style is a participative one. I relegate a good deal of the operation today to others who are clearly more expert in certain details of operation than I am and put my emphasis on what I call leading the institution."

EVOLUTION OF MOTOROLA IN JAPAN

In the 1950s President Eisenhower advised American business to increase its business dealings with Japan. Galvin took Eisenhower's suggestions seriously and encouraged Motorola to purchase electronic components from Japan and help Japanese companies set standards and improve quality in consumer electronic businesses such as car radios, home radios, and televisions. But things had changed drastically by the late 1970s. Motorola officials had witnessed strong Japanese inroads in the electronic components, portable radio, stereo system, car radio, brand name television, and citizens' band radio industries. "We can see the writing on the wall," one said, and "we know that the firm's survival will depend on how we confront the Japanese challenge. Japan has the second largest market in the world for our products [semiconductors and telecommunications] and some of the biggest and best competitors." Yet Motorola had run into one road block after another in Japan in the 1970s. Each division had attempted for years to sell into the Japanese market, but thus far they had little success.

Telecommunications

By the end of the 1970s, changes in U.S. regulatory policies ended the prohibition against plugging non-AT&T equipment into the U.S. telecommunications system. This shift in policy led to increasing inroads by foreign firms into the U.S. telecommunications market at a time when foreign countries retained strict clamps on their telecommunications sectors. To redress the growing trade imbalance in telecommunications equipment, the U.S. government negotiated a bilateral agreement with Japan in December 1980. The basic point of the agreement was that NTT, Japan's state-owned telecommunications monopoly, would "for each proposed procurement, invite applications from the maximum number of domestic and foreign suppliers consistent with the efficient operation of the procurement system." The agreement stated that foreign firms responding to requests for proposals (RFPs) would "be treated in a manner no less favorable than those domestic [firms] responding to the NTT-issued RFPs."[4] NTT was also obligated to supply complete information on both the product and the procurement process in the RFP and in supplemental documentation. A bilateral dispute settlement mechanism was set up to enforce the agreement, and the United States agreed not to bring any disputes to an international forum.

Galvin decided in 1979 that Motorola had to do all it could to enter the Japanese pager market—a market thought to be growing by as much as 10% a year. Before the bilateral agreement was penned, Motorola had made inquiries to NTT. Motorola was the worldwide market share leader in pagers, so company officials were certain they had the highest volume and probably the lowest cost in the world. Galvin also recognized that telecommunications systems were part of the lifeblood of advanced industrial countries, but pagers were a modest technology which NTT could not object to on grounds of national security.

Initially, Motorola's telecom group was unable to schedule an appointment to see the people at NTT and had to ask the U.S. Trade Representative to send cables just to get the appointment. The first meeting was not fruitful and convinced people at Motorola that they were going to need additional assistance from the American government. "We had no idea what the specifications were, how to make a proposal, or how to sell a product to NTT, and NTT wouldn't tell us," Motorola's vice president of communications reported. Even after the bilateral agreement was signed, he reported, things did not get any easier:

A senior NTT executive told us we were wasting our time, because the U.S. wouldn't be satisfied with any NTT agreement with Motorola. He said that such a deal wouldn't even fit into the bilateral agreement. Even after [Secretary of State] Cyrus Vance personally confirmed that a pager deal would fall within the bilateral, NTT still hedged. We were told the specifications were considered proprietary and, in fact, they weren't even written down, they were just worked out with the manufacturers. If we wanted to get a bid we'd have to work with NTT for several years, talk with them, get to know the specifications, and relay all specific questions to them. But it's a bit difficult to ask specific questions when you're starting from ground zero.

When the specifications were eventually released, company officials soon discovered that NTT emphasized product design as well as product performance and expected designs to be followed explicitly, regardless of whether there were alternative ways to do the same thing. When Motorola originally proposed to change the electrical current used from the battery in pagers, NTT refused. After prolonged negotiation, this change was eventually allowed. Motorola ran into another problem because it used a microprocessor that recirculated a timing mechanism every 11 times the pager performed a certain task rather than every 10 as listed in the specifications. NTT considered the request to allow such an exemption a very poor reflection on Motorola and was firm in its opposition despite the negligible influence the change would have on the pager's performance.

The communications division ultimately received a contract for $9 million worth of pagers in late 1981, 18 months after the first contact. The initial NTT contract was for 50,000 to 60,000 units. After providing NTT with an acceptable product, Motorola still had to undergo long negotiations on price and share. Historically, NTT reserved 60% of the market for NEC and Matsushita, the prime suppliers. Four other firms were to divide the remaining 40%.

Motorola had experienced other problems in entering the telecommunications market. Middle managers didn't want to "buy American" because they looked to retire to the big "family firms" like NEC, Fujitsu, Oki, and Hitachi. Moreover, NTT made no multiyear purchases. This was important because Japanese companies would enter a nominal bid to design a particular product, being reasonably certain that if they got that one contract from NTT, they would get subsequent business. But a U.S. firm had neither an assurance that there would be follow-up work nor a commitment on future prices if they got a design contract. Companies had to take NTT on faith. Motorola was willing to take the risk because of its commitment to sell to NTT. For example, Motorola set up a separate pager production line for selling to NTT, at a significant cost. (Japanese specifications for telecommunications products frequently differed from worldwide standards.) Indeed Motorola expected it would take several years to show a profit with the pagers.

The company also had a long history of difficulties with the Ministry of Post and Telecommunications (MPT), which disallowed some of the services offered in other countries around the world. Japanese companies on MPT committees were not interested in rocking the boat by pushing for changes in the frequency allocation. Another problem was that standards tended to be set by MPT and a committee of Motorola's competitors, and MPT wouldn't allow competition on standards. This process gave Motorola's competitors a year's edge in getting from design to manufacturing.

Motorola had found it extremely difficult to crack other markets. While there were few discriminatory barriers, a major problem was that advanced products were regulated out of the market. This included products such as alphanumeric display pagers, digital voice privacy radios, "intrinsically safe" portable radios, and portable computer terminals with built-in modems. Several of these products had higher frequencies than the frequencies allowed in Ja-

pan. In product areas that were permitted, Motorola salespeople also found that strong social pressure and pressure from Japanese companies were placed on organizations considering foreign goods.[5] Motorola had achieved a very substantial share of the U.S. market in police two-way radios, but its police radios were invisible in Japan, despite extensive sales efforts.

Semiconductors

Disputes in semiconductors dated back to the mid-1970s, starting with the founding in the United States of the Semiconductor Industry Association (SIA) in 1977. Articles such as "The Japanese Spies in Silicon Valley" charged the Japanese with using unethical means to gather intelligence on U.S. production methods and set a bitter tone early on.[6] Later, American producers complained that while the U.S. share of the Japanese market had remained mired at about 10% for over a decade, the Japanese had managed to increase their share of the American market steadily in a few years, rising to over 12% of the noncaptive U.S. market in 1981.

One major difference between Japanese and U.S. firms was that Japanese semiconductor manufacturers tended to be very large and diversified while their U.S. counterparts were more likely to be specialized semiconductor companies. In fact, the Japanese firms challenging Motorola in semiconductors were for the most part the same firms challenging it in telecommunications. In semiconductors, however, firms such as NEC, Matsushita, Fujitsu, and Hitachi were major customers of Motorola as well as major competitors (see *Exhibit 2*).

Semiconductor Manufacturing

Motorola decided in 1979 to buy a Japanese company as a way to advance its position in the Japanese semiconductor market. Local manufacturing in semiconductors would serve two purposes: it would provide local support for local problems, and it would help promote an image that Motorola's products were Japanese products. According to Mitchell, the further down the technology curve in the semiconductor industry the more important it was that manufacturing be done in a local market. Customers were increasingly demanding that there be local manufacturing in order to support their local production operations. Texas Instruments (TI), the foreign market-share leader in Japan and Motorola's major U.S. challenger in semiconductor components other than microprocessors, had four Japanese factories and publicly expressed satisfaction with its access to Japanese customers (see *Exhibit 3*).[7]

Galvin, Weisz, and Mitchell shared a general preference for a wholly owned strategy because the company had bad experiences with joint ventures in earlier years in a number of countries. In 1980 Motorola's head of strategic planning identified Toko as a potential company in which Motorola might get involved. Toko had a semiconductor subsidiary (Aizu—Toko) involved in MOS wafer processing but didn't have the financial resources to fund these operations. A joint venture agreement was reached in November 1980 that included buyout options for both partners. Motorola was responsible for design and manufacturing, the Japanese were responsible for people matters, and both firms were to share sales and finance responsibility. However, by the end of 1981, it was already becoming clear that Toko was not going to be able to contribute its 50% of the capital spending.

Motorola's vulnerability to Japanese competition was becoming most apparent in D-RAMs in 1981. While Japan's share of global semiconductor sales rose from 20% in 1975 to 30% in 1981, in 64K D-RAMs the Japanese had 70% world market share.

THE PROBLEM IN THE U.S. MARKET

Motorola executives were concerned about the effects of Japanese industry-promotion policies on competition in the United States. The Japanese policies that most concerned Motorola were identified by Weisz as a "set of differences, the sum of which gives them a major competitive advantage that can't be matched by U.S. companies." Weisz considered differences in three categories to be especially crucial: government-supported activities, the Japanese financial system and environment, and the actions of the industrial companies themselves (see *Exhibits* 5 and 6). Weisz noted that Japanese firms' willingness to use marginal-cost pricing and cross subsidies to push those products was becoming particularly problematic in 1981. Motorola had collected evidence that Japanese firms were dumping in the United States. A year earlier, Motorola supported the successful dumping suits filed by E. F. Johnson in CB radios; and in mid-1981, it was filing its own case on copyright and patent infringements against Japanese pagers. Motorola executives also believed that two Japanese firms were now dumping pagers (simple beepers) in the United States. However, the appropriate response was unclear. Japanese price-cutting was leading to a rapid deterioration in market share, but at the same time, Motorola was still negotiating with NTT over its own pager contract.

GALVIN'S DILEMMA

Motorola had been one of the most successful American firms in mobile telecommunications and semiconductors over the previous two decades. For every previous problem, ranging from the company's consumer radio business to color TVs, Motorola had devised a strategy to remain independent and profitable. But Galvin sensed that this Japanese challenge was different. So he called together his entire top management team, asking "what are the range of strategic options, and how should Motorola respond?"

EXHIBIT ONE

FINANCIAL DATA FOR MOTOROLA, 1977–1981 ($ millions)

	1981	1980	1979	1978	1977
Net sales	$3,336	$3,086	$2,700	$2,212	$1,850
Cost of sales	2,028	1,545	1,625	1,340	1,140
SG&A expenses	855	773	672	549	426
Depreciation	173	145	111	83	73
Net interest expense	28	37	22	19	19
Income tax	77	88	105	95	85
Net earnings	175	186	154	125	107
R&D expenditures	229	200	167	133	NA
Semiconductor sales	1,278	1,209	991	718	582
Semiconductor operating profit	131	187	170	107	80
Semiconductor capital expenditure	184	177	159	72	53
Comunications sales	1,422	1,257	1,118	965	823
Communications operating profit	162	144	140	111	131
Communications capital expenditure	88	78	57	46	55
International sales	1,213	1,181	1,056	816	598
International operating profit	58	76	65	50	41
Total assets	2,399	2,112	1,903	1,657	1,420
Working capital	773	743	709	620	567
Long-term debt	352	336	296	198	200
Stockholder equity	1,288	1,152	1,004	886	788
Current ratio	2.25	2.42	2.35	2.20	2.47
Return on equity (%)	14.3	17.3	16.3	15.0	14.3
Return on sales (%)	5.3	6.0	5.7	5.7	5.8
Year-end employment (000)	76	72	75	68	68

Source: Annual and 10-K reports.

EXHIBIT TWO

FINANCIAL DATA FOR SELECTED COMPETITORS ($ millions)

	1981	1980	1979	1978	1977
NEC[a]					
Net sales	$ 4,433	$ 3,637	$ 3,712	$ 3,450	$ 2,396
Net income	93	62	36	35	29
R&D expenditures	214	186	162	108	70
Total assets	4,869	4,176	4,269	4,131	3,032
Long-term debt	798	734	931	949	737
Equity	736	550	453	431	321
International sales	1,338	1,080	943	935	612
Communications sales[b]	1,581	1,367	1,363	1,311	923
Semiconductor sales[c]	1,023	781	627	580	443
Matsushita					
Net sales	$14,563	$12,304	$10,827	$10,296	$ 7,280
Net income	661	526	451	428	291
R&D expenditures	538	428	389	369	257
Total assets	12,432	10,458	9,801	9,073	6,370
Long-term debt	150	248	312	96	166
Equity	5,381	4,609	4,224	3,973	2,734
International sales	6,662	4,911	2,782	2,781	1,982
Communications sales	1,831	743	636	563	374
Semiconductor sales[d]	1,321	522	433	398	284
Fujitsu					
Net sales	$ 2,931	$ 2,114	$ 2,021	$ 1,859	$ 1,225
Net income	114	66	49	39	35
R&D expenditures	239	208	212	212	NA
Total assets	2,804	2,115	2,027	1,931	1,444
Long-term debt	303	507	498	507	397
Equity	855	542	521	467	349
International sales	443	335	296	228	140
Communications sales[e]	556	495	501	444	285
Semiconductor sales[f]	426	240	131	97	45
General Electric					
Net sales	$27,240	$24,959	$22,461	$19,754	$17,909
Net income	1,652	1,514	1,409	1,230	1,088
R&D expenditures	1,690	1,600	1,440	1,270	1,156
Total assets	20,942	18,511	16,645	15,036	13,697
Long-term debt	1,059	1,000	947	994	1,284
Equity	9,128	8,200	7,362	6,587	5,943
International sales	10,190	9,597	4,997	4,379	3,973
Consumer products[g]	4,202	3,998	5,448	4,865	4,215

(continued)

EXHIBIT TWO

CONTINUED

	1981	1980	1979	1978	1977
Texas Instruments					
Net sales	$ 4,206	$ 4,075	$ 3,224	$ 2,550	$ 2,047
Net income	109	212	173	140	117
R&D expenditures	373	344	134	111	96
Total assets	2,311	2,414	1,908	1,494	1,255
Long-term debt	212	212	18	19	30
Equity	1,260	1,165	953	821	724
International sales	1,984	1,498	1,494	1,127	873
Semiconductor sales	1,532	1,899	1,527	1,192	958
Intel					
Net sales	$ 789	$ 855	$ 663	$ 401	$ 283
Net income	27	97	78	44	32
R&D expenditures	116	96	67	41	28
Total assets	872	767	500	357	221
Long-term debt	150	150	0	0	0
Equity	488	433	303	205	149
International sales	191	233	245	141	60

[a]One yen-dollar exchange rate used for each year to translate yen into dollars for all three Japanese companies. May not match exchange rate used to translate yen figures in individual company annual reports.

[b]Telecommunications.

[c]Electron devices.

[d]Lighting equipment, tubes, and semiconductors.

[e]Communication, measuring, and special equipment.

[f]Telephone exchanges and telephone set plus radio and carrier transmission equipment.

[g]Includes communications products, excludes major appliances.

[h]All sales from semiconductors.

Sources: Annual and 10-K reports.

EXHIBIT THREE

**1980's TOP TEN SEMICONDUCTOR MERCHANTS
WORLDWIDE**

	Rank in $ millions		
Company	1980 rank	1975 rank	1966 rank
Texas Instruments	1	1	2
Motorola	2	4	3
Philips/Signetics	3	5	4
NEC	4	NA	NA
National	5	3	NA
Toshiba	6	NA	NA
Hitachi	7	NA	NA
Intel	8	5	NA
Fairchild	9	2	1
Siemens	10	NA	NA

Source: Office of the Secretary of Defense, "Report of the Defense Science Board Task Force on Semiconductor Dependency—Action Memorandum," December 31, 1986, p. 51; *Electronics,* April 2, 1987, p. 60.

EXHIBIT FOUR

HISTORY OF MOTOROLA IN JAPAN

1960	Tokyo office opened as Motorola's first office in Far East.
1961	Motorola Service Company Ltd. established as Consumer Products Division purchasing office. Automotive Products Division pruchasing functions added in following years.
1967	Automotive Products Division/Alps joint venture established to manufacture automotive radios.
1968	Motorola Semiconductors Japan Ltd. established.
1969	Osaka branch sales office opened.
1973	Communications Division's two local representatives added to Motorola Service Company's payroll. Semiconductor Products Division/Alps joint venture established and began construction of N-MOS plant at Morioka.
1974	Consumer Products Division's television business sold to Matsushita.
1975	Motorola/Alps semiconductor joint venture dissolved, Motorola semiconductor production in Japan suspended, and Morioka facility sold to Alps Electric Co. Motorola Communications Japan was established and assumed responsibility for sales operations.
1976	In November the new Motorola Semiconductor Japan started.
1978	CODEX Tokyo office opened in January (Information Systems Group, data-processing hardware). Motorola/Alps auto radio joint venture dissolved in August. Asia/Pacific Design Operations began.
1980	Motorola/Tokyo joint venture etablished as Aizu-Toko Corporation Inc. for MOS wafer processing capability.

Source: Company documents.

EXCERPTS FROM JAPAN'S PUBLIC LAW NO. 84, JULY 1978

ARTICLE 1. PURPOSES

The purposes of this law are to develop specific machinery and information industries by promoting, among other things, improvement of manufacturing technology and rationalization of production thereof, and thus to contribute to the sound development of the national economy and improvement of national standards.

ARTICLE 3. ADVANCEMENT PLAN

The competent minister must set up a plan concerning advancement . . . with respect to the following industries. . . : (a) those industries manufacturing such electronic machines and tools specified by government order, the manufacturing technology of which has not yet been established in Japan and which especially require the promotion of experiment and research. . . ; (b) those industries manufacturing such equipment and tools specified by government order, the industrial production of which is not conducted in Japan or the production quantity of which is extremely small, and which especially require the promotion of the commencement of industrial production or increase of production quantity; (c) those industries manufacturing such electronic machines and tools specified by government order, which especially require the promotion of rationalization of production, such as improvement of performance or quality or reduction of production costs, etc. . . .

Matters to be set forth in the Advancement Plan for those industries described in (a) include content of the experimentation and research and the target year of its completion; matters concerning funds necessary for the experimentation and research. . . . With respect to the industries in (b), such matters which are fundamental for the promotion of the commencement of industrial production or increase of production quantity, including . . . the production quantity for the final target year; the kind and numbers of facilities to be newly established. . . . With respect to industries in (c), such matters which are fundamental for the promotion of rationalization of production, including target of rationalization, such as target of performance or quality, production costs, etc., for the final target year; kind and number of facilities to be newly established; matters including proper scale of production, introduction of cooperation of the business or specialization of the kinds to be produced; matters concerning funds necessary for rationalization; and other important matters concerning promotion of rationalization.

ARTICLE 5. PROCUREMENT OF FUNDS

The government shall make efforts to procure the necessary funds set forth in the Advancement Plan.

EXHIBIT SIX

EXTRACT FROM BILL WEISZ MEMO, 1981

Specific actions, differences by the Japanese—past and present

1. Higher tariffs (some recently reduced)
2. Prohibition on almost all 100% non-Japanese ownership or acquisition of a Japanese company for many years (some now allowed but culture is very anti)
3. Cartelization of Japanese companies promoted and required (Public Laws #17 and #84)
4. Japanese government support of direct commercial activities
5. Protection of Japanese "infant" industries
6. Joint research by various means
7. Focused countrywide goals and targeted industries for worldwide dominance
8. Low-interest loans to industry, many never repaid
9. Rebate of excise tax on exports
10. Japanese companies allowed a deductible "overseas market development reserve"
11. "Old boy" network in government and industry
12. No external pressure on companies for substantive earnings
13. Low profit margins acceptable, 10% to 20% dividend rate on *par* value of stock acceptable
14. High debt-to-equity leverage
15. Bank and government support of big companies, substantially eliminating risk of their failure and providing a continuous effectively guaranteed flow of capital
16. Industrial groupings with interlocking ownerships, including banks who own about 60% of industrial companies' shares
17. Low-interest financing on exports
18. Alleged division of customers among Japanese companies
19. Alleged use of incremental pricing/dumping in order to increase penetration of markets and sustain export growth. Examples:

Past

Citizen Band Radio—Reckless price reduction killed the market for all. U.S. ITC action found injury to U.S. industry and raised tariffs, but too late to save companies.

TV Dumping—Most Japanese companies found guilty *years* ago and fines levied but none paid to date. The appeal process continues.

Current

Semiconductors

16K RAMS—Price collapse
64K RAMS—Price collapse on new product just *beginning* its life cycle

Communications

Radio Paging—35% price reductions overnight

20. Massive continuing increase in certain semiconductor manufacturing capacity even though world-over capacity is estimated by independent observers
21. Restricted access to NTT's market (recently improving)
22. NTT's past favored-supplier concept provided closed market that allowed build-up of competence and volume by the suppliers
23. Difficulty of foreign companies to hire, for employment in Japan, experienced Japanese people (also difficulty of foreign companies to hire on Japanese college campuses)

NOTES

1. *International Management*, March 1978, p. 113.
2. Several large U.S. companies were involved in the manufacture of semiconductors exclusively for internal use, including GE, GTE, Rockwell, Western Electric, and IBM. These so-called captive producers posed no direct competitive threat to Motorola's semiconductor business lines.
3. James O'Toole, *Vanguard Management: Redesigning the Corporate Future* (Garden City, N.Y. Doubleday & Co., 1985, p. 91).
4. Cited in Stefanie Ann Lenway, *The Politics of U.S. International Trade: Protection, Expansion, and Escape* (Boston: Pitman Publishing, 1985, p. 188).
5. The owner of a trucking company told Motorola salespeople that "we could not buy a pager unless [Prime Minister] Nakasone himself called me and said it was worthwhile."
6. *Fortune*, 27 February 1978.
7. TI invested in Japan before all other American manufacturers (1968). However, TI paid a high price for its rights to produce locally. The Japanese government demanded, and TI agreed to provide, licenses to all Japanese companies for some of its leading-edge technology.

Trade in Services and American Express

On issues of trade in services, American Express is one of the most sophisticated actors.

High-Level OECD Official
Summer 1982

For several years, American Express had actively encouraged companies, governments, and international organizations around the world to oppose the rising protectionism against trade in services. One of the company's principal objectives was the creation of a set of international trade rules for services, comparable to those for trade in goods. American Express was especially concerned because its basic businesses—traveler's checks, charge cards, investment services, and insurance—were service businesses vulnerable to trade barriers. Moreover, these businesses depended on the rapid transmission of sophisticated computer and te-lecommunication networks to transfer large amounts of data across national borders. Such transborder data flows were increasingly threatened by protection.

American Express' efforts seemed to be bearing fruit in 1982. The U.S. Trade Representative announced that liberalized trade in services would be one of the key elements of U.S. trade policy in the 1980s. In 1982, he appointed James Robinson, chairman of American Express, to be one of six private sector members of the American delegation to an upcoming meeting of the General Agreement on Tariffs and Trade (GATT). At the GATT meeting, which was the first such meeting in almost a decade, member nations issued a communiqué recommending national studies on service trade and the exchange of findings through the GATT.

When he returned from Geneva, Robinson asked Harry Freeman, senior vice president for Corporate Affairs and Communications, to review American Express' activities. He wanted a complete assessment of the company's past political strategy and advice on what the company should do in the future.

This case was prepared by Assistant Professors David B. Yoffie and Joseph L. Badaracco, Jr., as the basis for class discussion rather than to illustrate either effective or ineffective handling of an administrative situation.

THE GROWTH IN THE SERVICE ECONOMY

The premise of American Express' overall service strategy was that the service sector was too important for the American government and the world community to ignore. Harry Freeman told a U.S. Senate subcommittee in 1981 that "trade in services is the major trade issue of the 1980s. The U.S. has become a service economy and service exports have become the most dynamic part of U.S. trade. It is time for us to recognize this reality. . . . It is time for us to concentrate on the trade problems of today and tomorrow instead of the problems of the past." Freeman believed that the world was changing, and it was time for policymakers to catch up with economic reality.

The basic problem, according to Joan Spero, vice president for International Corporate Affairs, was that governments underestimated the importance of services in the international economy. Although services, which ranged from transportation to financial services to communications, were becoming the backbone of economic output, government policies were biased toward the other sectors of the economy—manufacturing, construction, and mining. Top management feared that the results of the misunderstandings and the antiservices biases would be bad for the world economic situation and worse for American Express.

American Express' argument rested on several facts. First, services had grown to 67% of gross domestic product in the United States in 1981; even after excluding government, services represented 55% of total economic activity (see *Table 1*). Second, the services sector employed 66 million people—70% of the work force. And again, after the public sector was excluded, services employed 50 million people, or 66% of nonfarm private sector labor. Third, services were relatively recession-proof busi-

TABLE ONE

COMPOSITION OF GROSS NATIONAL PRODUCT 1981

Millions of current dollars

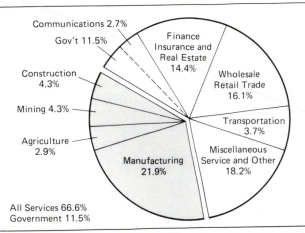

All Services 66.6%
Government 11.5%

Source: U.S. Dept. of Commerce, Bureau of Economic Analysis, Survey of Current Business, July 1982, p. 78.

nesses and acted as a stabilizing force in the economy. Finally, the standard complaints about stagnant U.S. productivity did not apply to services. Overall, the service sector had twice the productivity gains of manufacturing: from 1967 to 1979, it experienced a 20% increase in labor and capital productivity versus 10% growth for manufacturing.

Freeman perceived a similar lack of appreciation for the importance of services on international economic issues. Few policymakers recognized that the world market for services had expanded dramatically in the past decade. Trade in global services rose from $85 billion in the early 1970s to approximately $620 billion in 1980 (see *Exhibit 6*). And in recent years, exports and imports of services had grown more

than twice as fast as international trade in goods. The United States held the dominant share of international service trade. The closest competitors to the United States in services were France and the United Kingdom, but American service exports exceeded those of the two countries combined (see *Exhibit 3*).

The importance of services to the United States' position in the world economy was evident from the balance of payments accounts. Service exports expanded at an average annual rate of 18% in the 1970s—twice the pace of the previous decade and much faster than world trade as a whole. Service exports, including the receipt of income in U.S. assets abroad, generated over $135 billion in 1982 and added at least $54 billion net income to the U.S. current

---

TABLE TWO

U.S. BALANCE OF TRADE IN GOODS AND SERVICES

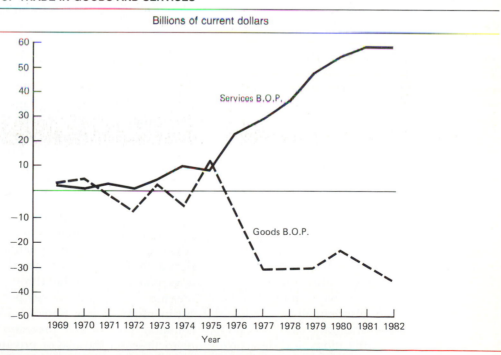

Billions of current dollars

Source: U.S. Dept. of Commerce, Survey of Current Business, Feb. 1983, Table 4.1 (unpublished).

account (see *Exhibit 2*). In the meantime, trade in merchandise goods was nearly $28 billion in deficit in 1982 (see *Table 2*).

The lack of recognition of services' vital contribution to U.S. competitiveness traditionally meant that services were neglected in international trade policy. Every major trade initiative in the postwar period focused on the problems of trade in manufactured goods and agricultural products. And despite the positive contribution of services to the balance of payments, the vast majority of American incentives to stimulate exports were tailored toward the manufacturing and agricultural sectors. The danger of this policy void, according to Freeman, was that services "are not being ignored by the world's protectionist forces." In a letter published by *The Economist*, Freeman wrote:

While our economies are being transformed and service exports are growing, barriers to those exports are becoming higher and more dangerous.

Moreover, Freeman contended that protectionism in services was not only bad for companies like American Express but also bad for world trade in goods. Hampering services such as shipping, aviation, communications, banking, and insurance would make the exchange of manufactured goods or farm products more difficult.

The barriers to international trade in services varied from country to country and from service industry to industry. The variety of the restrictions was so great that the Office of the U.S. Trade Representative required 230 pages just to inventory the barriers. In Argentina, for example, American accounting firms were limited in the number and type of audits they could perform. In Germany, foreign banks were prohibited from offering or providing services; only representative offices were allowed in the country. Japan had discriminatory licensing practices, standards, tariffs, and a host of other barriers to telecommunications and data processing services. The United Kingdom required

foreign air transportation companies to pay landing fees. And the list went on.

Although American Express was concerned about virtually all of these barriers—since it had interests in travel services, banking, stock brokerage, and insurance—the company asserted that rising barriers to transborder information flows and data processing were the greatest threat (see pages 372–374 for a description of American Express' business). The origin of the threat was in the merger of the computer and telecommunications technology. Computer communications allowed companies to draw upon data banks located around the world and exchange information in seconds. The results were new information systems through which businesses could link their worldwide operations. In the last several years, multinational corporations have come to depend on transborder data flows (TDF) to coordinate marketing, production, and finance, and to facilitate global planning, inventory control, and sales. In addition to supporting international manufacturing operations, TDF has become essential to international banking, financial services, retailing, and tourism. Without access to electronic funds transfers, for instance, much of the world banking community would grind to a halt. According to Bank of America's telecommunications director, "It's simple; if we can't have information, we go out of business." Thus, TDF not only opened the door to greater efficiencies but also created a new and dangerous form of dependence for multinationals.

The growing importance of information industries led many foreign governments in both advanced and developing nations to erect barriers to the electronic movement of data. These governments hoped that through protectionist measures they could develop national expertise in information technology. One of the most common types of TDF protectionism involved restrictions on the use of private leased communications lines. These are telephone lines or satellite circuits that companies valued because of their economical fixed rates and because they were more secure, more flexible, and technologically superior. Government-controlled telecommunications authorities in countries such as Japan, Germany, and France had moved to restrict usage of leased lines and thereby force multinationals to use more expensive volume-sensitive public networks. Such protectionist policies increased the operating costs and reduced the competitiveness of services offered by foreign firms. American Express, for example, spent $10 million per year on leased lines. With some of the changes proposed by foreign authorities, American Express could be faced with increased costs of as much as $7 million.

Restrictions on TDF have included a large variety of classical nontariff trade barriers: local content laws, discriminatory pricing, limits on the equipment available to nonresident users, the imposition of incompatible technical standards, and outright denial of access to national markets. Brazil, for example, required corporations to maintain and process computer data within the country.

THE RATIONALE FOR PROTECTION

American Express gave several reasons for growing protectionism in services. Generally, governments have traditionally been very sensitive to financial services such as banking and national communications systems. In fact, outside the United States, these latter have been dominated by government-owned or -controlled postal, telephone, and telecommunications administrations (PTTs). The most widely cited rationale for protection was that services deal with finance and communication, which were important to national defense and diplomacy. Just as countries maintain a steel, textile, or automotive industry for reasons of national security, some governments felt compelled to protect and control service industries, particularly banking, transportation, and communications.

A second rationale for protection was the traditional infant industry argument. Foreign governments said that the United States was far ahead of the rest of the world in the service sector, especially in the fast-growing areas of telecommunications and information services. If countries not as advanced as the United States lowered their barriers to service trade, competition from American companies might overwhelm local "infant" industries. Governments also erected barriers to safeguard employment. According to one high official in the OECD, European nations measured the importance of services not only in economic terms but as a public good.

All of these arguments, and others, were applied to transborder data flows. In August 1977, the Canadian minister of state for science and technology gave a speech in which he outlined five potential dangers related to the free flow of information:

1. The potential of growing dependence rather than interdependence
2. The loss of employment opportunities
3. An addition to the balance of payments problem
4. The danger of loss of legitimate access to vital information
5. The danger that industrial and social development will largely be governed by the decisions of interest groups residing in another country

In 1981, a high-level French official summed up the problem of TDF with the statement, "Information is power and economic information is economic power." And indeed, the Europeans discovered this to be the case in 1982. In June, President Reagan announced an embargo on the export of American technology for a Soviet-European gas pipeline and ordered Dresser Industries to end all technical communications with its French subsidiary—a subsidiary making large compressors for the project. With the flick of a switch in Pittsburg, Dresser France was without critical design information, financial data, and inventory listings.

One widely cited rationale for regulation of TDF was related to the issue of privacy. The information revolution made it possible for governments and corporations to amass huge amounts of data on individuals. As in George Orwell's *1984*, it was possible to aggregate a citizen's personal history—family, education, employment, financial records, and so on—in a single data bank and retrieve the information with the push of a button. As a result, privacy codes have been established in numerous countries. Typically, these laws required a firm to notify a government that it was maintaining information on individuals who, in turn, must be allowed to examine and correct this information. In addition, authorities had to approve the export of certain types of information. Frequently, export approval would be contingent upon whether or not the data were being sent to a country that has similar data protection laws. This trend was potentially dangerous for American Express. One of American Express' largest data processing facilities was in the United Kingdom—a country without strict privacy laws and considered by many to be a data haven. Should European nations restrict the flow of data to the United Kingdom, it would be difficult or costly for American Express to authorize simple credit card charges or process traveler's checks.

AMERICAN EXPRESS

In 1982, American Express earned $581 million on revenues of $8.1 billion. The company was organized into four major business units. These were the Fireman's Fund Insurance Companies, the Travel Related Services Company, the American Express International Banking Corporation, and Shearson/American Express, Inc. American Express and Warner Communica-tions were also 50% owners of Warner-Amex Cable Communications. *Exhibit 5* provides basic financial data on these businesses.

American Express had been a service company from its inception. For the first 30 years, between 1850 and 1880, it carried gold, bank notes, mail, and general goods throughout the East, Midwest, and Far West. In 1891, the company introduced the first traveler's check and launched what became one of the company's most profitable businesses. In 1982, American Express had an average of $2.5 billion in traveler's checks outstanding. These were available in American and Canadian dollars, Swiss francs, German marks, French francs, British pounds, and Japanese yen. The business press estimated that American Express had roughly a 50% share of what was a $40 billion annual business. Its checks were sold through more than 100,000 authorized outlets around the world. During 1982, the company completed its Worldwide Travelers Cheque Operations and Communication Center in Salt Lake City. This "information factory" used the latest data processing technology to handle the annual clearing and payment of 350 million traveler's checks and the replacement of lost or stolen checks. Replacements were available at over 90,000 worldwide locations.

The American Express Card was another of the company's major travel-related services. More than 15 million cards were in use in 1982, and they were issued in 25 currencies, including Thai baht and Brazilian cruzeiro. More than 500,000 establishments around the world accepted the American Express card. These establishments, the cardholders, and American Express itself all demanded extremely fast and accurate authorization whenever a cardholder wanted to charge a purchase above specified amounts. Authorization required communication with a central data bank that contained the cardholder's up-to-date credit record. In 1982, American Express performed more than 150 million authorizations. Disruption of the data and telecommunication systems used for authorization could inconvenience thousands or even hundreds of thousands of cardholders and establishments. Such disruptions would also undermine one of American Express' principal ways of marketing its cards: the theme of trust and reliability implicit in the words "Don't Leave Home Without It." Once a charge was authorized, American Express relied on its data facilities to process it as quickly as possible. On average, the company carried $4 billion in receivables from its cardholders during 1981. As retail establishments that accepted the American Express card and checks became linked to the American Express network via computers, the company was able to reduce losses from stolen traveler's checks, speed the processing of cardholders' charges, and reduce financing costs.

Other parts of American Express also depended on the effective management of enormous data flows. The Fireman's Fund Insurance Companies, whose business was principally domestic, processed nearly 60 million premium and claim transactions each year. The 1,000 American Express travel offices worldwide relied on global reservation networks for air travel, accommodations, car rentals, and so forth. Shearson/American Express had data systems capable of accommodating daily volumes of 110 million shares for sustained periods. The ability to process data efficiently meant better cost control, better service to customers, and better cash management. All in all, American Express and its subsidiaries operated 70 major computer systems and 230 smaller systems around the world. Their development, operation, and cost exceeded $400 million a year.

The 1981 annual report reflected American Express' reliance on data management as part of its long-term strategy:

American Express Company is one enterprise created from several interrelated businesses. The mission of these businesses—individually and in total—is to deliver services that help customers to better manage their financial assets and to enjoy more secure, convenient and satisfying lives at home and when they travel.

. . . new businesses will be built upon the competitive advantages we already enjoy:

- The internationally recognized and respected name of American Express;
- Our traditional ability to meet the demands and expectations of clearly defined market needs; and
- A global data processing and telecommunications network that is the foundation for our delivery systems and a key to keeping us an efficient, low-cost producer.

The theme of "one enterprise" and the reliance upon integrated data systems were apparent in several of American Express' major business commitments. By far the most important was the integration into American Express of Shearson Loeb Rhoades, one of the largest brokerage houses and investment banks in the United States, which was acquired in 1981 for about $1 billion. This merger was one of several combinations of traditional and nontraditional financial service organizations that had taken place in the last few years. American Express planned to use the combination of its own resources and Shearson's to build the world's premier financial service institution. Each company brought to the merger its own affluent clientele; jointly, the new entity could offer these individuals services ranging from payment systems, property and life insurance, and international banking to securities trading, financial planning, tax-advantaged investments, retirement funds, and trust services. Eventually, many of these products and services would be available through expanded distribution channels, including the two-way cable offered by Warner-Amex.

Three steps in this direction were taken during 1982 and early 1983. First, 3,600 brokers of Shearson/American Express began offering Fireman's Fund Life Insurance. Later, they introduced the Shearson Financial Management

Account (FMA), which makes available computerized cash and investment management services to 2 million holders of the American Express Gold Card. Like Merrill Lynch's Cash Management Account, the FMA permitted card and check withdrawals from an investment account. Merrill Lynch, however, had encountered significant operational problems with its account because of the time-consuming customer inquiries directed to its brokers. The company eventually had to hire several hundred clerks for the program. American Express officials believed they could avoid these difficulties. American Express' computer systems and staff already handled hundreds of thousands of customer inquiries every year. A third step toward creating the world's premier financial service institution was the acquisition of the Trade Development Bank of Geneva in January 1983. By adding the highly profitable bank with its wealthy depositors, AmEx executives hoped to expand the company's worldwide client base.

In offering these services and seeking to create "one enterprise," American Express faced serious challenges. The principal challenge arose from greatly increased competitive pressure. Both VISA and MasterCard already had more than five times as many cardholders as American Express. VISA was aggressively challenging American Express' franchise among the affluent with a major advertising campaign based on the theme "We all know you can leave home without it." The competition also included several other nontraditional financial combinations such as Prudential Insurance and the Bache Group, Sears and Dean Witter Reynolds, and Bank-America and Charles Schwab, a large discount broker. Merrill Lynch's 900,000 Cash Management Accounts represented over 80% of the market, and the company would soon offer its accounts in four countries overseas.

A second challenge for AmEx was also a possible opportunity. The U.S. government was in the midst of deregulating financial services in the early 1980s. *The Economist* described this process as a "chaotic development of new types of banks in America" (February 4, 198). Intense political debate among the finance committees of Congress, government agencies,[1] and trade associations created a great deal of uncertainty about the final laws and regulations which would govern competition. Extensive deregulation might permit nonbanks like American Express to offer services such as deposit privileges and could permit commercial banks to offer insurance and to underwrite certain securities. According to a McKinsey banking consultant, "Banking strategies will be driven by the sequence of deregulation. For example, if major money-center banks are given permission to expand their banking services geographically before nonbank financial institutions (e.g., American Express) are permitted to offer new products such as checking privileges, money-center banks will emerge in a stronger position following deregulation than would have been the case had the sequencing been reversed." American Express' earlier moves to compete in this market had already drawn fire. Dee W. Hock, the president of VISA International, had recently charged that "to anyone knowledgeable about electronic-payment systems and the direction banking is going worldwide, it's apparent American Express is already functioning as a worldwide consumer bank."

THE POLITICAL STRATEGY OF AMERICAN EXPRESS

American Express executives did not believe in sitting idly by while their environment was undergoing rapid change. Part of their response to these changes was an active political

---

[1] These included the Federal Reserve Board, the Comptroller of the Currency, the FDIC, the SEC, the Department of Justice, the Federal Home Loan Bank Board, and state bank departments.

strategy, which Joan Spero described as a "Vince Lombardi" strategy:

The best defense was a good offense. The company did not want to be a passive observer of events. On the contrary, the fundamental principle guiding American Express' actions was that "if you don't like the environment, you should try to change it."

Harry Freeman told *Business Week* in late 1982:

If you see a cannon being aimed at you, you don't wait until the first shot is fired to take action.

Underlying this approach was the view of top management that the company was, in important respects, unique. Most firms, especially in traditional manufacturing industries, could rely upon trade associations to handle their governmental affairs. American Express, however, believed it could rely neither on trade associations nor on the whims of governments. Several of the major businesses of American Express were not represented by trade lobbies in Washington through the late 1970s. Credit cards, traveler's checks, and those firms concerned with transborder data flows had little or no organization to represent American Express' concerns. This meant that the company had "to fight its own battles" or else be adversely affected by an unattended environment. Hence, the company decided in the mid-1970s to take a leading role among service firms. This required an effort to mobilize the service industry and to influence government policies at home and abroad.

American Express said its principal goal was the creation of a new international regime that would govern and help liberalize trade in services. In particular, the company wanted GATT nations to negotiate a set of codes or rules that would curtail protectionism in services. "We need to bring services within the established framework for international trade negotiations, which until now have dealt almost entirely with trade in goods," noted James Robinson. If the problems of the service sector could be brought under GATT supervision or perhaps the supervision of another international organization, then it might be possible to stem the rise in protectionism.

The company pursued its objectives through a variety of channels. James Robinson spent a sizable portion of his time making speeches and attending meetings with congressional representatives, agency officials, and cabinet secretaries. Its government affairs office, which in the mid-1970s consisted of a single representative in Washington, D.C., was expanded to three offices with a staff of 11. Harry Freeman was responsible for managing their activities. American Express also formed a political action committee, but it was small compared to most other PACs. Finally AmEx introduced a companywide privacy code. Before AmEx started to lobby for data protection laws overseas, Harry Freeman "wanted to be sure that we had our own house in order."

The effort to draw attention to service trade issues inside and outside the company was enhanced by the extensive public activities of several top American Express officials. As part of this "strategy of illumination," they gave literally hundreds of speeches on the need for an international regime to govern trade in services. In the months before the November 1982 GATT Ministerial, American Express personnel could read weekly quotes by James Robinson, Harry Freeman, and Joan Spero in *The Economist, Fortune, Business Week,* the *New York Times,* the *Washington Post,* and other publications.

These highly visible activities were just part of the overall American Express effort. To help develop the U.S. agenda for the Ministerial, Robinson, as chairman of the Services Policy Advisory Committee, spent long hours working with top U.S. trade officials, chief executives, and labor leaders on the committee. Robinson also flew to the United Kingdom for a week-long meeting with senior trade officials from GATT countries to prepare for the Ministerial.

American Express, along with Bechtel, Peat Marwick, Citibank, and other firms, helped establish the Coalition of Service Industries (CSI) in January 1982. Its objective was to encourage the U.S. government to develop a coherent approach to communications and information policy. At least 15 government bodies—including the finance committees of both houses of Congress; the Federal Communications Commission; the State, Commerce, Defense, and Treasury departments; and the Office of the U.S. Trade Representative—had a hand in the formulation and implementation of these policies. Robinson wanted the government to develop an integrated policy that would strengthen the U.S. hand for negotiations with other governments and their centralized telecommunications authority.

While these activities were under way in the United States, AmEx also played a role in getting companies in other countries to organize: several major British service companies, such as Midland Bank and Lloyd's of London, established counterparts to the Coalition of Service Industries, called the Liberalization of Trade in Services Committee, or LOTIS. With the encouragement of LOTIS, the British government issued a white paper on services in 1982 and was planning to propose legislation.

American Express' idea of organizing companies and governments to negotiate on trade in services had its skeptics. Both inside and outside the United States, one heard that the world had too many serious problems with trade in goods to start worrying about a new, complex area such as services. *The Economist* suggested that services were beyond the competence of GATT. Any attempt to put services on the agenda, it said, would run the risk of being "too broad, too ambitious, and too vague." It argued that the world should focus on the problems of protectionism in textiles, steel, agriculture, and other goods, rather than services (see *Exhibits 6* and *7*).

A related criticism was that talks on services had a low probability of success because the issue was too sensitive for most countries. A study by two economists concluded that:

This category of trade is too vast and complex to interpret and negotiate. It has also proved throughout history to be a much more sensitive policy question than goods, often seeming to intrude upon cultures and societies. Service activities are at the very core of national development strategies and are intimately related to policies on technology, banking, and foreign investment.

This position has been seconded by countries such as Brazil, which did not understand how it could gain through liberalizing trade in services. A third argument put forth by skeptics was that if the United States pushed to liberalize services, it must mean that American companies, like American Express, had much to gain—and therefore, non-American companies had something to lose. In addition, many other countries wondered what the United States could give up to achieve an agreement on services. In past trade negotiations, the United States had its own tariff and nontariff barriers to exchange for other countries' lowering their barriers. In services, the United States had fewer barriers than other nations, and those few barriers were difficult to dismantle. Banking and insurance, for example, were regulated by 50 separate states. Under these conditions, the federal government's leverage would appear to be limited.

Beyond these broad issues of liberalizing services, some Europeans wondered if American Express' strategy was not counterproductive. An OECD official thought that American Express had attracted too much attention to its business activities by taking a high-profile political position. The result, this official postulated, was that European governments became more aware of the competitive threats of American Express. Moreover, when U.S. government officials raised issues of trade in services, there was the possibility the issue would be viewed as an American Express "special interest" issue. Some highly successful European service companies also hesitated to join American Express' efforts to liberalize services. They thought it was best to minimize the role of government; if problems arose, these companies preferred to deal with them privately, quietly, and through their own networks.

American Express responded to these criticisms by pointing out that the service economy was essential to the United States and the world. Joan Spero said that American Express was "fighting the future war" to avert disaster. While she understood that many companies did not want to run the risk of alienating foreign governments with a high-profile strategy, she felt that complacency could only hurt in the long run. Companies and governments alike were failing to recognize that rising barriers to services could seriously damage corporate, national, and international interests. A protected market for services, like a protected market for goods, "raises costs, decreases efficiency, and lowers technical quality for domestic companies and local citizens." It would seem logical that if countries benefit from lowering barriers to trade in goods, there should be gains from lowering barriers to trade in services. Harry Freeman stressed that someone had to "get the ball rolling," otherwise governments and corporations around the world would not systematically confront the growth in protectionism.

Moreover, American Express also believed its activities had helped its worldwide business interests. In one case, the company used what it considered an American-style approach in response to a difficulty in Japan. The members of a national credit card association had started discussions on the development of joint technology for point-of-sale terminals in restaurants and small shops. These terminals would have allowed instant authorization for credit card charges. Initially, American Express had been excluded from the association and the discussion. If American Express were to be excluded from access to the technology, it would

be excluded from the market. The company responded by asking the U.S. Trade Representative to raise the issue very informally in ongoing trade discussions with the Japanese government. It later sent Joan Spero to Japan for several weeks, during which time she made more than 30 speeches, several of which were well-publicized, on the importance of free trade and cooperation on service issues. She also met with company and government officials. In the end, the credit card association agreed to let American Express join the association and participate in the discussions.

Joan Spero's trip was just one of many cases in which American Express had made use overseas of its U.S. strategy of high company visibility and vigorous publicity for the issues of service trade and data flows. A consequence of this approach, according to Harry Freeman, was that "if anyone picks on American Express, it will automatically become a public matter." The approach was intended to be a kind of preventive medicine. In the process, American Express was also building networks of private relationships with government officials, companies, and trade associations, and these could prove useful as the company pursued liberalization of services trade and dealt with specific problems, such as the one in Japan.

In general, Freeman was satisfied with the company's political activities. Thus far, the company had avoided major problems with the sale of its services overseas and the transmission of data. The difficulties that arose in Japan had been resolved. Overall, the strategy of deterrence seemed to be working.

In the United States, Freeman could point to the enthusiasm of U.S. Trade Representative William Brock for liberalizing services. From the outset of the Reagan administration, Brock chose the negotiation of an international regime in services as one of his top priorities. At his first meeting with OECD nations in 1981, Brock persuaded the OECD to endorse the idea of rules for services. In February 1982, Brock argued strongly with the Europeans that services should be on the negotiating agenda at the GATT Ministerial the following November. And Brock asked the Senate Subcommmittee on Trade to provide the president with powers to curb barriers to American services, investment, and high-technology products.

American Express officials were also satisfied with the results of the GATT Ministerial in November 1982. This was only the third such meeting of trade ministers and high-level officials[2] since the creation of GATT. The two previous meetings both led to important negotiations that moved the world toward freer trade—the Kennedy Round of tariff reductions (1963–1967) and the Tokyo Round (1973–1979).

The climate for the November Ministerial was dramatically different. Originally, the Americans wanted to launch a work program covering a wide range of issues, including services. As the Ministerial approached, bitter disputes over the Reagan administration's restrictions on pipeline technology, over proposals for quotas on shipments of European steel to the United States, and over EEC subsidies for agricultural exports led the U.S. delegation to lower its expectations. In the words of one diplomat, "The purpose is to stop the hemorrhages in the present system." Trade volume had stagnated in 1980, fell in 1981 and 1982, and economists estimated that as much as half of world trade was taking place outside the GATT framework through barter deals and disguised protectionism. The paramount U.S. concern became that of stemming the strong protectionist tide. Nevertheless, services remained on the short list of key U.S. interests to be pursued at the Ministerial.

The overall result of the Ministerial meeting was a broad pledge by all 88 member countries to avoid new trade restrictions and to begin dismantling existing ones. Some observers thought the outcome was a significant achievement, considering the world recession and strong pressures for protection. Others called the meeting a "near fiasco." The final communiqué, which all 88 participating countries acknowledged, included a commitment to negotiate an accord on nontariff barriers such as voluntary export restraints and orderly marketing agreements and the establishment of a special committee to study subsidies of agricultural exports.

The final paragraphs of the communiqué dealt with trade in services. It said:

The contracting parties decide:

1. To recommend to each contracting party with an interest in services of different types to undertake, as far as it is able, national examination of the issues in this sector.
2. To invite contracting parties to exchange information on such matters among themselves, inter alia through international organizations such as GATT. The compilation and distribution of such information should be based on as uniform a format as possible.
3. To review the results of these examinations, along with the information and comments provided by relevant international organizations, at their 1984 session and to consider whether any multilateral action in these matters is appropriate and desirable.

To Robinson, Freeman, and Spero, the GATT communiqué represented a triumph. Since services had been ignored by the GATT for the previous 35 years, they felt that this statement by the international organization was a step forward. Where American Express should go from here was an open question.

---

[2]For example, the U.S. Delegation included numerous senators and congressional representatives.

EXHIBIT ONE

U.S. GROSS NATIONAL PRODUCT BY SECTOR, 1940–1980

In billions of constant 1972 dollars

	Total GNP	Goods	Structures	Services
1940	344.1	171.7	32.5	139.9
1945	560.4	278.5	18.8	263.0
1950	534.8	261.5	65.9	207.4
1955	657.5	316.7	80.7	260.1
1960	737.2	335.8	89.5	312.5
1965	929.3	422.6	116.0	390.7
1970	1,085.6	486.9	116.3	482.4
1975	1,233.9	549.2	108.3	576.4
1976	1,300.4	588.9	116.0	595.6
1977	1,371.7	628.8	124.6	618.2
1978	1,436.9	655.9	132.1	649.0
1979	1,483.0	674.5	130.6	678.0
1980	1,480.7	665.2	119.8	695.7

Source: U.S. Dept. of Commerce: *Survey of Current Business,* April 1981; historic data prior to 1979 summarized in *Economic Report of the President,* January 1981, Table B-7.

A. DEFINITIONS

TRAVEL

Travel includes transactions in a variety of services and related goods by individuals residing for less than one year in a foreign country for business, education, vacation, or other personal reasons. Transactions of U.S. government personnel stationed in the U.S. are excluded, but transactions of government and international organizational personnel on official travel are included. The types of services and goods most likely to be purchased by travelers are lodging, meals, entertainment, transportation within the country or area visited, gifts, souvenirs, and articles for personal use, except automobiles.

ROYALTIES AND FEES

Royalties and fees consist of receipts and payments of royalties and licensing fees for the use of intangible property rights—copyrights, trademarks, patents, techniques, processes, formulas, designs, franchises, manufacturing rights, etc.—and other fees. Other fees consist of net charges between parent companies and their affiliates for services rendered, research and development expenditures, assessments, rentals for the use of tangible property, and other expenses allocated by the home office.

PRIVATE MISCELLANEOUS SERVICES

Private miscellaneous services include, among exports, contractors' receipts for technical services; reinsurance; communications; and services and goods provided to foreign government agencies and international organizations located in the U.S. Among imports, the major transactions are reinsurance; communications; and wages paid to temporary resident aliens.

TRANSPORTATION

The transportation estimates primarily consist of international transactions of vessel and airline operators. Exports include receipts of U.S. vessel and airline operators for the transportation of U.S. export freight from the U.S. port of export to foreign destinations, and for the transportation of foreign freight between foreign ports.

PASSENGER FARES

Passenger fares consist of the earnings of vessel and airline operators for the transportation of persons. Exports include receipts of U.S. operators for the transportation of foreign residents (a) between the U.S. and foreign countries and (b) between foreign countries. Imports include payments by U.S. residents to foreign operators for transportation to and from the United States.

INVESTMENT INCOME

U.S. receipts (exports) of investment income consist of income derived from U.S. residents' ownership of foreign assets; U.S. payments (imports) consist of income derived by foreign residents from their ownership of U.S. assets. Investment income—both receipts and payments—is classified as income related to direct investment, other private income, and U.S. government income.

Source: The International Operations of U.S. Service Industries: Current Data Collection and Analysis, Final Report, The Economic Consulting Services, Inc., Washington, D.C., June 1981.

CONTINUED

B. SERVICES IN THE U.S. BALANCE OF PAYMENTS, 1960–1980: SUBTOTALS, SELECTED INTERNATIONAL TRANSACTIONS; SHARES IN TOTALS FOR GOODS AND SERVICES (in $ millions, except where indicated otherwise)**

Receipts	1960	1970	1976	1978	1980
Travel	919	2,331	5,742	7,186	9,985
Passenger fares	175	544	1,229	1,603	2,582
Other transportation	1,607	3,125	6,747	8,306	11,041
Fees and royalties	837	2,331	4,353	5,840	6,993
Other private services	570	1,294	3,584	4,217	4,645
Subtotal private services	4,108	9,625	21,655	27,152	35,246
Income on investment*	3,001	7,663	20,258	29,660	56,589
Total receipts for private services and investment*	7,109	17,288	41,913	56,812	91,935
Total export of goods and services	28,861	65,673	171,630	221,036	340,887
Services (excluding receipts of investment income) as percent of total exports of goods and services	14%	15%	13%	12%	10%
Services (including receipts of investment income) as percent of total exports of goods and services	25%	26%	24%	26%	27%

Payments					
Travel	−1,750	−3,980	−6,856	−8,475	−10,384
Passenger fares	−513	−1,215	−2,568	−2,896	−3,533
Other transportation	−1,402	−2,843	−6,852	−8,912	−10,981
Fees and royalties	−75	−225	−482	−607	−757
Other private services	−593	−827	−2,006	−2,566	−2,980
Subtotal private services	−4,333	−9,090	−18,764	−23,456	−28,635
Income on investment*	−731	−4,058	−7,132	−10,816	−25,145
Total payments for private services and investment*	−5,064	−14,138	−25,896	−34,272	−53,780
Total imports of goods and services	−23,729	−60,050	−162,248	−230,240	−333,810
Services (excluding payments of investment income) as percent of total imports of goods and services	18%	15%	12%	10%	9%
Services (including payments of investment income) as percent of total imports of goods and services	21%	22%	16%	15%	16%

Net					
Travel	−813	−1,649	−1,114	−1,289	−339
Passenger fares	−338	−671	−1,339	−1,293	−951
Other transportation	205	282	−105	−606	60
Fees and royalties	762	2,106	3,871	5,233	6,236
Other private services	−23	467	1,578	1,651	1,665
Subtotal private services	−225	535	2,891	3,696	6,611
Income on investment*	2,270	3,605	13,126	18,844	31,544
Balance on private services and investment*	2,045	4,140	16,017	22,540	38,155
Official and other transactions**	−1,805	−1,119	2,671	2,015	−3,724
Balance on merchandise trade	4,892	2,603	−9,306	−33,759	−27,354
Balance on goods and services	5,132	5,642	9,382	9,204	7,077

*Includes interest, dividends, branch earnings, and other private payments or receipts. Excludes reinvested earnings of foreign incorporated affiliates of U.S. firms or of U.S. incorporated affiliates of foreign firms, as well as U.S. government receipts or payments of investment income.

**Includes transfers under U.S. military agency sales contracts; direct defense expenditures; U.S. government receipts/payments for miscellaneous services and of income on U.S. assets abroad/foreign assets in the United States; and net reinvested earnings of incorporated affilitates.

Data Source: U.S. Department of Commerce, Bureau of Economic Analysis, Survey of Current Business, March 1981 (for 1979–80 data) and June 1980 (for 1960–78 data).

Prepared by: Economic Consulting Services, Inc.

EXHIBIT THREE

NATIONAL BALANCES OF INVISIBLE TRADE, 1969, 1977, AND 1978

SDR (special drawing rights) million

Country	Transport			Travel			Investment income			Other services			Total		
	1969	1977	1978	1969	1977	1978	1969	1977	1978	1969	1977	1978	1969	1977	1978
United Kingdom	19	336	270	84	1,744	1,460	1,197	300	1,279	1,093	2,511	3,255	2,383	4,891	6,264
United States	−433	−1,630	−1,480	−1,330	−1,110	−940	5,800	15,440	17,210	2,251	4,990	5,700	6,288	17,690	20,490
France	−70	−175	−89	128	395	1,308	312	566	1,141	66	1,868	3,050	436	2,654	5,410
West Germany	−202	−420	−730	−986	−6,010	−7,690	38	220	1,810	−1,118	−2,740	−2,730	−2,268	−8,950	−9,340
Canada	−187	−334	−327	−198	−1,341	−1,230	−1,149	−3,559	−3,822	−453	−834	−785	−1,987	−6,068	−6,164
Japan	−921	−2,050	−2,010	−93	−1,480	−2,580	−287	100	690	−720	−2,280	−2,630	−2,021	−5,710	−6,530
Brazil	−139	−836	−809	−49	−149	−149	−344	−2,939	−3,380	−89	−311	−359	−621	−4,235	−4,697
Mexico	−95	−231	−327	528	802	937	−617	−1,899	−2,229	113	482	603	−71	−846	−1,016

Source: Ronald Kent Shelp, *Beyond Industrialization, Ascendancy of the Global Service Economy*, pp. 30–31, N.Y.: Praeger Publishers, 1981.

EXHIBIT FOUR

A. THE PROBLEMS OF DATA ON SERVICES

Although there has been a growing interest in trade in services in recent years, research on the subject has been severely hampered—even discouraged—by lack of adequate data. The U.S. Government Work Program on Trade in Services calls for a review of U.S. statistics on trade in services for the purpose of improving official data.

What are the problems with official data on trade in services? Generally speaking, there are two basic problems:

1. Trade in services is not sufficiently recorded in light of the growing importance of services in the U.S. economy.
2. Existing methods of reporting data on trade in services are not entirely adequate for the present needs of policymakers.

THE RECORDING OF DATA ON SERVICES

A number of international transactions in services are simply not recorded. This is in many instances because the services are either relatively new or only recently significant in international commerce. Services which are not recorded include exports of data processing and information services and a wide array of consulting and professional services.

In addition to the problem of the substantial amount of service exports going unrecorded, there appears to be a need to reevaluate the present procedures for recording certain types of international transactions in services. For example:

• Services or service contracts (often accompanying high-technology exports) provided in conjunction with trade in goods are usually recorded in the U.S. balance of payments entirely as merchandise trade.
• Repatriation of royalties and fees for services rendered by a parent corporation to a foreign subsidiary are recorded as investment income (return on investment).
• The insurance of U.S. exports shipped c.i.f. (costs, insurance, and freight) is not recorded as a U.S. export of insurance even though the importer pays for the insurance (under c.i.f., the U.S. exporter purchases cargo insurance, normally from a U.S. insurer, and passes the cost to the importer).

The result of these deficiencies in U.S. data collection on services is that U.S. statistics on services greatly underestimates the true volume of U.S. service exports. It has recently been estimated that the actual volume of U.S. exports of services for 1980 was $60 billion—almost double the amount shown by official statistics. (See Exhibit 4B.)

Source: International Services Newsletter, January–June 1981.

B. ESTIMATED FOREIGN REVENUES OF U.S. SERVICES SECTOR, 1980

Service industry	Foreign revenues[1] (billions dollars)
Accounting	$ 2.35
Advertising	2.05
Banking	9.10
Business/professional technical services	1.07
Construction and engineering	5.36
Education	1.27
Employment	0.55
Franchising	1.26
Health	0.27
Information	0.60
Insurance	6.00
Leasing	2.35
Lodging	4.60
Motion pictures	1.14
Tourism	4.15
Transportation	13.93
Subtotal, 16 service industries	$56.05
Miscellaneous financial services, communications, etc.	4.00 (estimate)
Total of U.S. services sector[2]	$60.00 billion

[1]Quantities being considered as "foreign revenues" vary from industry to industry; for example, because of the characteristics of international services performed by the banking industry, the estimated "foreign revenues" are *net* of overseas offices' interest payments (which, if they were included here, would raise total order-of-magnitude for U.S. services sector to nearly $100 billion).

[2]Includes 16 designated service industries plus communications, nonbank financial services, and miscellaneous services.

Source: The International Operations of U.S. Service Industries: Current Data Collection and Analyis Final Report, The Economic Consulting Services, Inc., Washington, D.C., June 1981.

EXHIBIT FIVE

FINANCIAL PERFORMANCE ($ millions)

	Travel services	Insurance	Investments	International banking	Other and adjustments	Total
1982						
Revenue	$2,516	$3,356	$1,318	$1,025	$(122)	$8,093
Net income	247	244	124	60	(94)	581
1981						
Revenue	2,175	3,104	1,106	1,068	(72)	7,291
Net income	209	231	114	47	(77)	524
1980						
Revenue	1,661	2,914	922	930	(1)	6,426
Net income	177	210	90	41	(52)	466

GEOGRAPHIC OPERATIONS[1]

	U.S.	Europe	Asia/ Pacific	All other	Adjustments	Total
1982						
Revenue	$6,111	$ 786	$ 409	$ 838	$(51)	$8,093
Pretax income*	699	59	22	127		907
1981						
Revenue	5,441	834	399	704	(87)	7,291
Pretax income*	711	39	30	66		846
1980						
Revenue	4,818	746	287	609	(34)	6,426
Pretax income*	597	32	17	63		709

[1]*Note:* The breakdown between U.S. and overseas revenue may not fully reflect the importance of international operations to American Express. A large fraction of total American Express purchases with cards and traveler's checks takes place outside the United States. Nevertheless, all revenue from the float on traveler's checks sold in the United States and from annual fees for U.S. American Express cards is recorded as U.S. revenue. Furthermore, revenues generated from Americans using their American Express cards overseas are allocated to both the United States and the country in which the card is used.

*Before general corporate expenses.

EXHIBIT SIX

WORLD EXPORT OF GOODS AND SERVICES, 1980 (percentages of world trade)

Source: *The Economist,* December 25, 1982.

EXHIBIT SEVEN

SELECTED INCIDENCE OF MAJOR NONTARIFF BARRIERS IN SELECTED INDUSTRIAL COUNTRIES IN 1980*

	Agriculture	Industry	Total
Discretionary licensing			
France	13%	82%	74%
Germany, Fed. Rep. of	4	—	1
Japan	29	11	14
United States	19	—	2
Global quota			
Germany, Fed. Rep. of	13	—	2
Japan	11	—	1
United Kingdom	2	3	2
United States	13	1	2
Tariff quota			
Benelux	9	4	5
Germany, Fed. Rep. of	14	4	6
Denmark	9	5	5
Ireland	7	5	5
United Kingdom	16	5	6
United States	2	—	—
Quota of unspecified kind			
France	14	36	33
Italy	6	29	26
Japan	32	14	16
United States	29	4	6

*The shares of imports covered by individual nontariff barriers are not additive because a given commodity may be subject to more than one type of nontariff barrier. For Community members, only the nontariff measures applied by the individual member countries are included.

These categories also do not include (1) Europe's variable levy, which covers almost 50% of the EEC's agricultural imports; (2) the Multifiber Agreement, which regulates $100b in world trade; and (3) less visible trade barriers such as product standards and discriminatory procurement policies.

Source: Data provided by the UNCTAD Secretariat.

PART SEVEN

Review: International Trade and the Global Semiconductor Industry

The Global Semiconductor Industry, 1987

In 1947, William B. Shockley and a team of Bell Laboratory engineers devised the solid state transistor, ushering into being the semiconductor industry—one of the most technologically dynamic industries of modern times. Over the next 40 years, semiconductor products would shrink in size, grow in power, and diminish in price. Semiconductors had become so pervasive in industrial and consumer products that they were being called the "crude oil of the 1980s." In 1987, however, the industry was in transition. After more than two years of global depression which led to $6 billion in corporate losses worldwide, demand and profits were finally picking up. In the meantime, the structure of the industry was evolving as new leaders emerged.

Associate Professor David B. Yoffie prepared this case with the assistance of Research Assistant Alvin G. Wint as the basis for class discussion.

HISTORY AND EVOLUTION OF THE SEMICONDUCTOR INDUSTRY

After Shockley's team invented the transistor, companies focused on developing an efficient manufacturing process. Production was complicated because transistors, then made of germanium, were easily susceptible to contamination. In 1954, Texas Instruments discovered how to make transistors out of silicon, which quickly catapulted the company to a position of leadership. However, the power of transistors remained limited despite several further advances in production methods: scientists knew how to design a powerful computer circuit that would use 500,000 transistors, but wiring each circuit together was expensive and unreliable. The solution to this problem was discovered in late 1958 and early 1959 when TI and Fairchild independently filed patents for the integrated circuit (IC). The invention of the IC was of enormous importance. By putting transistor circuits directly on semiconductor material, elements no longer had to be wired together. As a result, it became possible to make highly complex and reliable electrical circuits.

The first marketable chips were not produced until 1961, but they were so expensive compared to transistors that they had no commercial market. Nonetheless, the timing was fortuitous. President John F. Kennedy had just committed the United States to landing a man on the moon by the end of the decade. The new ICs would be critical to the space program's success and related military technologies. The U.S. government, and especially the Department of Defense, became the first major chip customer and constituted the entire market for ICs until 1964.

The willingness and ability of the government to purchase chips in quantity at premium prices allowed a growing number of companies in the industry to refine their production skills and develop elaborate manufacturing facilities. These improvements resulted in the continuous increase in the number of elements contained on a single IC, coupled with significant decreases in price. More than any other product in America's industrial history, the production of ICs benefited from an amazingly steep learning curve. In 1964, a chip containing about 64 components was priced at around $32. By 1971, the price of a chip containing over 1,000 components was about $1. (See *Exhibit 1*.)

Another set of revolutionary innovations occurred in the late 1960s when Robert Noyce and another eminent scientist, Gordon Moore, left Fairchild to start Intel. In 1971, the firm introduced an IC that permitted random access to information. This device, which could store 1,024 bits in memory, was dubbed a 1K RAM (or random access memory). In the same year, Intel made yet another breakthrough: the company created a single IC chip that performed all the central-processing-unit functions of a simple computer and could therefore be programmed for a variety of jobs. This chip developed into Intel's first microprocessor, which ultimately led to the birth of personal computers. These plus other Intel inventions made the founders very wealthy and the firm an industry leader by the late 1970s.

The industry continued to generate increases in IC memory. The 1970s spanned two generations of chip technology: in the early part of the decade, a 4K RAM was introduced, ushering in the era of large-scale integration; and in the mid-to-late 1970s, the production of 16K RAMs followed by 64K RAMs began the period of very-large-scale integration (VLSI). These increases in chip memory continued into the 1980s. By 1987, the 256K RAM was the standard: 1,000K or 1-megabit RAMs were in volume production, and many firms had announced plans for 4- and 16-megabit chips.

SEMICONDUCTOR PRODUCTS

At the most general level, semiconductor technology in the mid-1980s could be divided into two broad groups: discrete semiconductors and ICs. (See *Exhibit 2*.) Discrete devices performed only one function and included products such as transistors and diodes. Demand for discrete devices was relatively stable, although industry experts considered the whole segment to be in the mature or decline phase of its life cycle.

ICs were the dynamic growth segment of the industry. There were literally thousands of different IC types that could be distinguished by their speed of operation, function, size, power consumption, and cost. Typically, ICs could be divided into two classes: bipolar ICs and metal-oxide semiconductors (MOS). These two types of ICs differed in their operational characteristics and the way in which they were manufactured. The bipolar technology was older but operated at very fast speeds. The MOS technology generally produced slower chips but required less power. A special form of MOS technology, known as CMOS, was growing in popularity because it produced ICs almost as fast as bipolar chips but still consumed little power.

Both bipolar and MOS ICs could also be divided into analog and digital ICs. Analog or linear ICs accepted and returned signals over a continuous range. Their principal applications were in radios, televisions, and communication receivers. Digital ICs, which acted as on/off switches, could be subdivided into memory and logic. Memory devices stored information and were composed of large numbers of identical elements. The most popular memory ICs were DRAMs—chips which stored data that could be erased from memory simply by interrupting the flow of electrical current to the circuit's memory cells. Static RAMs (SRAMs), chips which performed similar functions, were growing in popularity in 1987 because they were faster than DRAMs. However, greater speed came at the cost of more complexity, more expense, and less storage capacity than a similarly sized DRAM. A third popular memory, called an EPROM (erasable programmable read-only memory), could be erased by exposure to ultraviolet light and made available for reprogramming.

Logic ICs were capable of processing information rather than only storing it. Simple logic chips were used in products such as watches and calculators and were programmed to run a predetermined set of specific functions. A more complicated logic chip could be programmed to perform different tasks under varying conditions. For instance, a logic chip might be used to regulate the air-fuel mixture of an automobile engine. Finally, the most complex logic ICs were microprocessors. While most logic devices were designed for specific functions, microprocessors were programmable—software engineers could compose a variety of programs that would run on a particular chip.

Most memory devices were functionally in-terchangeable with other memory chips[1] and met certain industrywide standards (e.g., all 256K RAMs should be capable of storing the same amount of information). However, different company logic products were only indirect substitutes. Two companies' logic devices could perform similar functions, but each might require a unique set of instructions. Since every family of microprocessors required its own operating language to run a program, they were the most differentiated of the logic products. It was hypothetically possible for software to duplicate the microcode embedded in a logic chip, but once a company designed a microprocessor into its machine, it could be costly to switch to another firm's product. This was especially true in the personal computer business. By 1987, more than $10 billion of software had been written to run exclusively on the Intel family of microprocessors which powered IBM PCs. If IBM switched to a non-Intel microprocessor, future IBM PCs would lose compatibility with IBM's previous machines.

Rivalry in the industry was complicated by the possibility that buyers could find a variety of substitutes within any product segment. For example, within a product category such as a 1-megabit DRAM, buyers could choose companies that offered varying options with respect to speed, power consumption, and often quality and reliability. It was also cheaper for a computer company in 1987 to buy four 256K DRAMs at $2.50 a piece rather than a 1-megabit chip at almost $20. The four chips would per-

---

[1]This meant that a 16K DRAM could typically be switched with any other 16K DRAM, and a 16K EPROM with another 16K EPROM. However, a 16K DRAM was functionally distinct from a 16K EPROM. Occasionally, similarly sized memory products could be made incompatible. A DRAM might have a different pin structure which could not be plugged into another DRAM slot, and electrical input signals could vary.

form the exact same function, but a single 1-megabit semiconductor took up less space, which could lower the computer system's cost.

One of the most widely discussed trends of the 1980s was customization. The market for custom and semicustom chips, known as ASICs (application specific integrated circuits), had grown from virtually nothing in 1980 to $6 billion in 1987. (See *Exhibit 3*.) Firms were also finding in the mid-1980s that product life cycles were shortening, especially in commodity memory products. The 4K RAM was in production for almost ten years; the 256K RAM was likely to be in production for only three to four years.[2] Finally, technological advances were producing chips so powerful that they were accounting for larger and larger shares of the total value of end products. A 16-bit microprocessor, selling for under $100 in 1987, had the power of a 1970 mainframe computer that sold for $500,000.

Designing Integrated Circuits

Circuit design was the first important step toward making an IC: it was also the most time-consuming, skill-intensive, and costly phase in the production process.[3] Since engineers with the requisite skills tended to be in scarce supply, they commanded premium wages. However, despite the high costs, American firms found it difficult to keep designs proprietary. It was common for an American engineer with an idea for a new design to leave a firm and start his or her own company. These start-ups would frequently license their designs to established domestic and foreign merchants in exchange for capital or access to a particular market. Many of these fledgling companies would produce one moderately successful product and then go out of business. Chip designs spread rapidly for two further reasons: it was relatively simple to copy and commercialize a product with impunity, since patent protection was weak; and established manufacturers widely cross-licensed their technology. In areas where firms held significant patent positions, most managers viewed cross-licensing as a way to avoid costly, counterproductive court battles. Japanese firms, however, were able to license technology in the 1960s and early 1970s even when they lacked distinctive innovations. American companies that wanted to sell or invest in the rapidly growing Japanese market were required by Japan's government to license key technologies. The continual revolutions in technology through the 1970s made innovating firms confident that by the time licensees exploited the technology, a new generation would be in vogue.

Rising costs and complexity as well as the problems of pirated designs were leading to significant changes in the mid-1980s. To make the design phase of production more cost-effective and reduce design time, most firms in the United States and Japan were moving to automated tools such as computer-aided design (CAD) equipment. To prevent piracy, companies were turning toward the court. Protecting intellectual property had become more important for product segments such as ASICs because customers were choosing suppliers partly based on the quality of their chip designs and on the size of their design library. It had also become easier to protect chip designs. The passage in the United States of the Chip Protection Act of 1984 and a few landmark court cases forced some firms that were occupying designs to discontinue sales or pay substantial

---

[2]While life cycles were generally moving toward shorter lives, some products, such as the 8-bit microprocessor, continued to have longevity. In addition, it was possible for some firms to revise old designs for new application, which would, in effect, lengthen the life cycle.

[3]Costs varied with the complexity of the chip. Three engineers could design a memory in a few months; dozens of engineers could take a few years to design a microprocessor.

royalties. In 1987, analysts were predicting much more litigation over intellectual property.

Manufacturing Integrated Circuits

Producing ICs has been described as one of the most complex mass manufacturing processes in the industrial history of the world. The first stage was wafer manufacturing, which was usually performed by large diversified chemical companies. By 1987, most wafer manufacturers were located in Japan, with TI and IBM the only U.S. firms making wafers for in-house use and Monsanto the only U.S. firm selling wafers. Wafer manufacturers grew silicon or gallium arsenide[4] crystals of high purity and then "pulled" the crystals into ingots which were sliced into thin wafers. Finally, the wafers were polished and coated with a layer of silicon dioxide. The standard wafer size in 1987 was six inches in diameter, but all semiconductor manufacturers were in a race to increase that size. The larger the wafer, the more chips that could be produced during a manufacturing cycle.

The next step was for engineers to transfer an IC design to a set of masks to be used in two lithography processes which imprinted the circuit patterns, layer by layer, onto a silicon wafer. The wafers had to be handled in a dust-free environment, otherwise dust particles could contaminate the products. As semiconductor devices shrunk in size, even the smallest particle of dust could ruin a chip. This became especially problematic as the line width between circuits was being reduced to under one micron by the mid-1980s. To create a dust-free environment, firms built "clean rooms" with

special air ducts to filter out impurities in the air, used special water supplies, and required workers to wear special clean room attire. The sensitive nature of the process led many IC manufacturers to automate their plants in the 1980s to reduce human interference.

The next stage in production involved testing to find defects and then separating each chip from the wafer. Finally, the chips were packaged so that their circuitry could be connected to external outlets. This labor-intensive process was frequently done in low-wage countries. By the mid-1980s virtually all U.S. semiconductor firms and most Japanese firms had low-cost assembly operations in developing countries. The final stage of IC manufacture involved performing a battery of computerized tests to ensure reliability.

The complexity and difficulty in manufacturing chips led to long lead times for plants to come on-stream. American and Japanese firms needed as much as 18 to 24 months to "ramp up," i.e., build the plant, install the equipment, and qualify the product's quality and performance.

ECONOMICS OF THE INDUSTRY

One of the most striking characteristics of the semiconductor industry was that production costs for most products would decline by 30% for every doubling of cumulative volume. One of the reasons that learning produced such dividends was that semiconductor manufacturing routinely yielded more defective than sound products. For new products, yields as low as 10% for inexperienced manufacturers and 25% for experienced manufacturers were quite common. For more mature products, however, yields could be as high as 90%. The need to raise yields led firms to manufacture high-volume products that could act as "technology drivers." It was generally believed that skills learned in manufacturing large volumes of a simple product could be transferred to lower-

---

[4]Gallium arsenide, a material only recently commercialized for IC production, promised to be up to ten times faster than silicon. However, despite significant R&D efforts, this material had limited applications in 1987 because it was brittle and very difficult to use.

volume, higher-value-added devices and help "drive" the firm down a very steep learning curve. The production of DRAMs was particularly well-suited for this task because they had a less complex structure than other ICs, which allowed firms to distinguish quickly between a flaw in the design and a flaw in the manufacturing process. Some industry experts believed that other high-volume products, such as EPROMs and static RAMs, could also serve as technology drivers.

Although semiconductor manufacturing was clearly capital-intensive, it was difficult to calculate minimum efficient scale (MES) because of the enormous variations in yield. Nonetheless, many industry analysts estimated in 1987 that MES was at least 1,000 and probably closer to 2,000 wafer starts per week; at a cost of about $25,000 per wafer start for a state-of-the-art one-micron plant, this represented an initial capital outlay for the fabrication facility of $40 to $45 million. Since the plant required another $40 to $60 million in equipment, total costs ranged from $80 to $105 million. The rapid obsolescence of equipment (which was often outdated within two to three years) also led to huge ongoing capital investments. In the mid-1980s, most large firms were building new IC fabrication facilities that cost over $150 million. Analysts estimated that a firm needed about 3% of the market to justify building a fab in the late 1970s, while a 6% share was necessary in 1987. While it remained possible in the 1980s to build low-volume plants for as little as $20 million, these were only useful for specialized producers that could charge big premiums for their unique chips.

Rising complexity of products and plants altered semiconductor firms' cost structure. Worldwide, the average semiconductor firm was projected to spend 15% of sales on R&D in 1987, a percentage that had been rising steadily for a decade. In addition, as much as 30% of sales was spent on capital equipment to prevent obsolescence. In the meantime, raw material costs were dropping: a polished wafer that cost $30 in the early 1980s could be purchased for only $6 to $10 by 1987, labor costs were falling with the rise in automation, and distribution and transportation costs were tiny (1% to 2%). The entire production of the world's semiconductors in 1986 could fit in ten 747 jets.

The chip industry was highly cyclical. (See *Exhibit 8*.) Excess capacity and the practice of forward pricing ICs, especially by the Japanese, contributed to the enormous industry losses of the mid-1980s. Industry analysts estimated that between 1985 and 1986, U.S. companies lost about $2 billion, Japanese companies lost about $2 billion, and Korean and European companies lost approximately $1 billion each.

BUYERS

The continuous increases in IC memory and computing power combined with reductions in power consumption and price made ICs an essential component for all electronic and many industrial products. As a result, there were literally tens of thousands of chip buyers in all major markets, ranging from producers of computers and telecommunications equipment to car and VCR manufacturers.

The structure and growth of user industries varied by country. (See *Exhibit 4*.) The United States had been the largest market for chips from the industry's inception. But demand in the United States slowed in the early 1980s while Japan's growth climbed through 1985. Although Japanese consumption fell in 1986 when measured in local currency, a 40% appreciation in the value of the yen made Japan the world's largest dollar market for chips. Analysts were predicting 10% to 15% growth in consumption in the industrial markets for the late 1980s, while the countries outside of the United States, Japan, and Europe were expected to grow by more than 50%.

When deciding on whose chips to buy, users of semiconductors focused on different factors.

For commodity memory chips, price was the overriding variable. It was easy for users to shop for discounts because manufacturers would usually publish a list price for standard products, and there were always multiple suppliers of any product. Occasionally, a buyer might purchase limited quantities of commodity products at higher prices in order to maintain or build a relationship with a particular vendor or simply for the convenience of one-stop shopping. In more advanced and specialized chips, relative performance was the crucial factor. One American computer buyer stated that "price is irrelevant when you want to get performance leaders. In a specialty memory product, such as ECL [emitter coupled logic memory], I'm willing to pay a higher price. There are only two suppliers for this chip that excel in density and speed, as opposed to several sources of satisfactory DRAMs."

In addition to price and performance, buyers were very sensitive to quality and delivery. For many electronics products, production lines would have to be shut down if chips were unavailable. Furthermore, the failure of a $300 microprocessor would render a $5,000 to $10,000 computer unusable. Even the failure of a $2 chip could significantly reduce a machine's power: if the defect was not detected initially, it could cost up to $50 to $100 to repair. Fearful of shortages, buyers frequently ordered in excess of their needs. It was also common for buyers to cancel bookings abruptly if their inventories swelled. Most users of chips were also well-informed. The Japanese reputation for delivering higher reliability gave them a significant edge in the early 1980s. U.S. firms subsequently focused attention and resources on improving quality and lowering the number of defects per shipment. By the mid-1980s, most buyers could not distinguish differences in quality based on national origin.

ICs were particularly important for computer companies. In early 1985, a personal computer costing $1,250 to manufacture included $300 of ICs. By 1988–1989, ICs were projected to account for 33% to 38% of the manufactured cost of a PC. The centrality of ICs led some users to backward integrate. (See *Exhibit 5.*) While most big electronics firms in Japan built a large percentage of their ICs for internal use as well as for sale on the merchant market, the few American OEMs (original equipment manufacturers) that built ICs did so for in-house consumption only.[5] IBM, for instance, which bought more than $2.5 billion worth of semiconductors in 1985, was the world's largest producer. Most captive manufacturers generally produced state-of-the-art customized chips for their own use and bought commodity semiconductors on the open market. IBM and AT&T were also on the forefront of DRAM technology: both were global leaders in design, and IBM, in particular, was among the most advanced in process technology.

Although there were thousands of buyers for a firm's chips, a large computer or telecommunications company would buy volume purchases directly from the manufacturer, and it might account for 10% or more of a merchant's sales.[6] (See *Exhibit 5.*) In the early stages of the industry, these large buyers often required their suppliers to create second sources for products. If a small or unproven semiconductor firm wanted to sell a new product, the buyer insisted that the innovating firm license specific firms, either in the United States or abroad, to be second sources in the event of production problems or capacity shortages. Large customers also sought to avoid sole sources, es-

---

[5]There were exceptions. In the mid-1980s, for example, AT&T announced its intention to become a merchant semiconductor house. However, AT&T was not a low-cost producer and had not become a major merchant player. In 1987, for instance, AT&T was only the ninth largest DRAM supplier.

[6]Thirty percent of all semiconductors were sold via distributors. Distributors kept large inventories for immediate delivery, mostly for small customers.

pecially from small young companies. In some cases, second sourcing arrangements significantly reduced the innovator's revenues and profitability. Intel, for instance, was the world leader in microprocessors. But the company's second sources received more than 70% of the revenue from Intel's enormously successful 8086 microprocessor, which powered IBM and IBM-compatible PCs.

The existence of larger merchants and the emergence of ASICs promised to change second sourcing practices in the 1980s. Buyers were becoming interested in ASICs for at least five reasons: (1) a customized chip could be designed to perform the duties of many chips, thereby saving space; (2) using fewer chips could also result in cost savings; (3) ASICs could be designed to use less power than standard chips, thereby saving energy; (4) fewer chips would allow for more extensive diagnostic and quality testing; and (5) customized chips could be proprietary, which was significant for users trying to differentiate their end products.

Most buyers used single sourcing for their ASIC purchases. Buyers often wanted their ASICs delivered in three to four weeks after an order versus the industry norm of four to five months; and many chips were simply not available from more than one supplier. Price was generally less important in the ASIC market as buyers sought extensive service, reliability, and advanced technology—both in the supplier's hardware for designing the products as well as in the designs themselves.

In the early 1980s, buyers relied heavily on specialty ASIC houses which excelled in service and design. By 1987, buyers' choices were growing. (See *Exhibit 3*.) There were four generic types of ASICs, and much of the demand was moving toward chips called gate arrays—chips that could be made in vast quantities and then specialized close to the last step in production. Rather than developing a chip from the ground up with a vendor, a buyer could, in a sense, "connect the wires" on a standard

gate array to meet any number of requirements. With many analysts predicting that the worldwide gate array market would grow to $8 billion by 1992, more than 100 gate array suppliers were sacrificing profits in 1986 and 1987 in order to build market share.

The attitudes of large buyers toward semiconductor merchants were showing signs of change in the late 1980s. Users were seeking to build stronger relationships with sellers by creating longer-term contracts with a smaller number of vendors. However, a buyer from one U.S. computer firm noted that there was really no long-term ordering. While the company might sign a statement of intention to deal with a vendor for five years, it was not a binding contract: "Building a relationship is more important than the actual contract. I'm willing to pay a little more for a product on occasion if it helps to cement a relationship and gets the semiconductor vendor to think of us as being important."

INTERNATIONAL COMPETITORS

Globally, there were 150 to 200 firms making semiconductors in the mid-1980s. Total market sales of semiconductors, excluding those chips made by vertically integrated firms for their own in-house use, were approximately $27 billion in 1986. The top 50 merchant firms accounted for more than 90% of global merchant sales; and the top 10 almost 60%. American firms held the world's largest market share through 1985. However, the United States fell into second place in 1986; U.S. share of the world semiconductor sales dropped to 43%, down from about 60% in 1980, while Japan's share rose from 33%, to 45% over the same period. (See *Exhibit 6*.)

The U.S. Semiconductor Merchants

In the United States, there were four types of competitors: independent merchant companies, whose product lines were dominated by large-volume products sold to OEMs; design houses, which specialized in chip designs and subcontracted the manufacturing to foundries; process specialists, which specialized in narrow tasks, such as preparing masks or testing circuits; and semicustom houses, which focused exclusively on products such as ASICs. In the late 1970s, a few large diversified firms had bought successful merchants. These combinations, however, had not worked well in the United States. Mostek, for example, was a leading DRAM manufacturer in the 1970s but went bankrupt and was resold after being bought by United Technology; and Fairchild, an industry leader in the 1960s, lost money and market share after being purchased by Schlumberger and was resold to National Semiconductor.

Despite the large number of firms in the industry, only five American merchants had been significant players in the wholesale market for chips since the mid-1970s: Texas Instruments (TI), Motorola, Intel, National Semiconductor, and Advanced Micro Devices (AMD) accounted for 37.5% of U.S. merchant sales in 1986. The top four firms are briefly profiled below.

Motorola   Motorola was the largest American semiconductor merchant (30% of corporate sales) in 1986, one of the world leaders in mobile telecommunications equipment (40% of sales), and a manufacturer of computers and defense electronics. Motorola's semiconductor product line was among the most diversified in the industry: it was the world leader in discrete products (30% of semiconductor sales), second in microprocessors (advanced logic was 20% of sales), and a growing player in ASICs (10% of sales). TI and Motorola were the only American companies with 100%-owned manufacturing facilities in Japan. Although Motorola had abandoned the DRAM business in 1985, it entered a joint venture with Toshiba in 1986

which involved trading Motorola's microprocessor technology for Toshiba's DRAM process and product technology as well as greater access to Japanese customers. (See *Exhibit 7*).

Texas Instruments (TI)   TI, the world leader in semiconductors until 1985, had fallen to fifth place in 1987. In addition to semiconductors (merchant sales of $1.8 billion and in-house sales of $300 million), the company produced defense electronics ($210 million in earnings on $1.7 billion in sales) and digital products such as computers and electronic calculators. Although TI was a minor player in microprocessors, it was considered by industry analysts to be technologically innovative and a broad-line, quality-oriented supplier with one of the lowest cost positions among American firms. TI typically sold standard volume products and was the only large American manufacturer of DRAMs. Although the company had slipped from first to sixth among DRAM producers, it was seeking to regain leadership. In 1987, TI was the first to announce an operating 4-megabit DRAM.

TI's strategy was to continue focusing on defense electronics but also meet the Japanese challenge by becoming a leader in customer service, design automation, and manufacturing processes. As part of this strategy, it was agressively targeting ASICs by increasing its capital expenditures on design tools and trying to build strong customer relations. In July of 1987, TI entered into an alliance with Intel to swap their libraries of chip designs. TI also had a unique position in Japan: in 1968 it was the first U.S. firm to establish Japanese production facilities, and by 1987 its four Japanese factories had sales of $377m, making it that country's tenth largest semiconductor company.

Intel   Long considered the most technologically innovative company among the large merchants, Intel had pioneered many of the industry's standard products. Intel had dropped out of DRAMs, but in 1987 it remained the world leader in its two dominant product lines: EPROMs and microprocessors. About two-thirds of Intel's revenues were derived from semiconductors, and one-third was systems (e.g., computer boards and other assembled components). The company had a reputation as a relatively high-cost producer with poor customer service. Reversing that reputation became the company's top priority. Major actions included large layoffs and heavy investments in manufacturing and marketing. To bolster its small share of the ASIC business, Intel invested more than $100 million in CAD equipment and entered into agreements with IBM and TI to swap chip designs. Intel had various other alliances, including ones with Japan's Mitsubishi (for second sourcing EPROMs), Korea's Samsung (which supplied DRAMs that Intel marketed), and AMD (which second sourced many Intel products, including microprocessors). In 1987 Intel decided to discontinue its second sourcing policy for its most advanced microprocessors. AMD sued Intel, while IBM negotiated a deal which allowed it to make a substantial portion of its own demand for advanced microprocessors by the early 1990s.

National Semiconductor Before National bought Fairchild in 1987, it was the fourth largest American producer of ICs with 72% of all sales coming from semiconductors. The company had a broad portfolio of products in memory, logic, and optoelectronic devices. National was largely a follower in product innovation. Although it was the first company to introduce a 32-bit microprocessor in 1984, it was still a distant third in the microprocessor market by 1987. National's reputation had been built on producing "jelly bean" ICs—i.e., standard high-volume parts. Historically the firm had been weak in customer service, but compared to its American competitors, National was thought to be a relatively low-cost producer. In 1987, National was seeking a stronger custom IC

business and greater leadership in design. For example, it signed a long-term deal with Xerox to provide ASICs in 1986. Xerox provided the system expertise, while National provided chip design, manufacturing, and packaging. National made two further strategic moves in 1987: it was expanding its presence in Japan through international alliances, including contracting with a Japanese firm to manufacture and sell selected products; and by purchasing Fairchild, it became the largest supplier of semiconductors to the U.S. government. The merger with Fairchild was only the second time American merchants joined forces, and both mergers took place in 1987.

Small American Players The large merchants had captured the lion's share of industry sales for more than a decade, but competition began changing in the early 1980s. The growing cost of IC designs and software combined with increased availability of venture capital contributed to an explosion in start-ups specializing in the design or production of custom ICs. Excess capacity, especially in Japan, led many start-ups to subcontract their manufacturing, thereby avoiding huge investments in fixed assets. These factors produced niche players like LSI Logic, which grew from nothing in 1980 to over $200 million in 1987. Founders of the successful start-ups often became multimillionaires.

The Japanese Semiconductor Industry

Japan was a late entrant into semiconductors, initially relying heavily on American technology. Two actions in the mid-1970s gave Japan its initial foothold in the U.S. market. First, U.S. firms cut their capacity expansion plans during the 1975 recession, while Japanese companies continued to invest. When the market turned up in 1976–1977, American firms were caught short. Second, Japanese firms took the risk of investing in large-scale commercial production of MOS circuits for desktop calculators at a time when U.S. companies were largely committed to bipolar technology. Over the next decade, Japanese firms became the global sales leaders and low-cost producers, dominating the commodity segments of the business, especially DRAMs and SRAMs. In 1987, the rising yen and intense Korean competition were pushing Japanese firms away from volume products toward more creative research in artificial intelligence, new materials, and new system architecture.

Most Japanese competitors followed strikingly different strategies compared to their American counterparts. In manufacturing, for instance, U.S. firms historically emphasized pushing products to their technological frontiers while Japanese companies focused more heavily on raising yields and reducing costs. Japanese firms also organized their factories differently and spent more money on plant and equipment. By 1986, Japanese firms had more automation and higher average yields; two-thirds of their plants could produce state-of-the-art chips (line width under two microns), while only 50% of U.S. plants had that capacity.

Large Japanese manufacturers were highly diversified compared to American merchants. On average, around 50% of Japanese semiconductor production went to large captive markets, while semiconductor revenues averaged only 9% of corporate sales. Virtually all of the top semiconductor firms in Japan had big consumer electronics divisions, which used enormous volumes of ICs. In addition, a chip which did not meet the high performance standards for a computer or industrial product might find a market in the firm's consumer electronics division. For instance, a chip that was inadequate for a computer could be suitable for a TV.

Like the U.S. industry, only a few firms dominated Japan's domestic market: five Japanese suppliers accounted for 60.3% of domestic sales. The four largest firms are profiled below.

Nippon Electric Company (NEC)   NEC, a member of the Sumitomo group, was a diversified firm that was the largest merchant semiconductor company in the world. Although the company's principal areas of competitive strength were in semiconductors and communication equipment, NEC was a big player in personal computers, consumer electronics, and selected industrial electronics. In semiconductors, NEC was considered a broad-line supplier of standard parts, an aggressive leader in process innovation, and a low-cost producer with a strong customer service orientation. NEC's multiple plants in the United States enhanced its service focus in the American market. Even though NEC was usually a follower in technology, it was the first Japanese company to design its own microprocessor. After second sourcing Intel's microprocessor, the company pioneered its V series chips in 1984.[7]

Hitachi   Hitachi was a highly diversified, vertically integrated manufacturer of a full line of consumer, electronics, and heavy industrial products. A $32 billion company in 1986, it was often compared in size and product mix to the General Electric Corporation. In semiconductors, Hitachi was the second largest manufacturer in the world, deriving 9% of its revenues from chips. Analysts considered the company to have superior technological abilities, a strong low-cost position, and a moderately broad product line serving consumer, industrial, and automotive markets. In 1987, Hitachi was the world's largest DRAM supplier. The company had licensing arrangements with Motorola and

---

[7]In 1985, Intel filed a suit claiming that NEC's V 20 microprocessor had infringed Intel's copyright on its 8086 microprocessor. In early 1987, a U.S. court agreed with Intel that microcode was copyrightable. At that time, no decision had been made as to whether NEC had infringed Intel's copyright. A loss in this case could ban all of NEC's V 20 series microprocessors from the U.S. market.

Texas Instruments and had long-term supply contracts with Olivetti and BASF. It also had offshore assembly plants in many developing and developed countries, including a plant in Texas. In 1986, the company announced a co-operative venture with Fujitsu to build a 32-bit microprocessor that company officials hoped would become the industry standard. Hitachi also had a five-year cross-licensing agreement on software with IBM.

Toshiba   Toshiba, the second largest general electrical and electronic Japanese equipment manufacturer, after Hitachi, was a member of the Mitsui group. Toshiba was also affiliated with the General Electric Co., which owned about 10% of its shares, and had strategic ties with LSI Logic, Siemens, Olivetti, Hewlett-Packard, and Motorola. Semiconductors averaged 10% of the company's sales, consumer electronics 31%, heavy-electric machinery 26%, and machinery and materials 10%. Toshiba was the Japanese industry leader in CMOS technology and was second only to NEC in total MOS production. It was also a leading producer of discrete devices. Toshiba developed one of the first chips based on gallium arsenide technology. In 1987, Toshiba stated its intention to become the world's largest ASIC vendor. (See *Exhibit 3b.*) The company signed agreements with CAD makers and six different semiconductor firms to build its software capabilities and a library of chip designs. Toshiba was also rumored to be giving away design tools to customers to entice them to buy their ASICs.

Fujitsu   Japan's largest computer manufacturer, Fujitsu, was the second largest manufacturer of telecommunications equipment and the fourth largest IC manufacturer. The company oriented its semiconductor production toward computer and communications applications. It was a leading producer of memory ICs with competitive strength in both dynamic and static RAMS. The company had pioneered research on high-speed switching techniques as part of the cooperative Japanese effort to develop a supercomputer. Fujitsu was considered to have a strong low-cost position and a major commitment to customer service. Fujitsu was a major second source for Motorola's 8-bit microprocessor family and Intel's microprocessors and microcomputers. In 1986, Fujitsu announced its intention of acquiring Fairchild Semiconductor from Schlumberger. Negotiations progressed until 1987, when Fijitsu abruptly withdrew its offer after U.S. government officials indicated their opposition to the merger.

Other Competitors

Several European and East Asian firms were also involved in the production of semiconductors. By the mid-1980s, Korea, in particular, was emerging as a potent competitor in commodity businesses. Korean firms gained access to state-of-the-art designs and technology by reverse engineering or through licenses from U.S. and Japanese companies. Once the Koreans had the designs, they benefited from low labor and overhead costs, a supportive government, and the rising Japanese yen. Government subsidies, fewer safety and environmental standards, and low construction costs allowed the Koreans to "ramp up" a new plant in six months at considerably lower cost than the Americans or the Japanese. In 1987, Korea had 6% to 7% of world semiconductor production capacity but only 2% to 3% of world market share. None of the five major Korean manufacturers, Samsung, Gold Star, Korean Electronics, Hyundai, or Daewoo were operating at or near capacity. In April 1986, Korea launched a Semiconductor Cooperative Research Project. Funded largely with government funds, this private-public partnership targeted $119 million toward producing 4-megabit DRAMs and entry into the logic markets, especially microprocessors and ASICs. Observers believed that Korea had some of the most modern fabs in the world and could capture 10% of the world market by 1990.

European firms had traditionally concentrated on discrete and optoelectronic devices, although in the mid-1980s, some European firms were making inroads into the custom design segment of the world market. The industry consisted of a few large, vertically integrated, diversified electronic equipment manufacturers. Major firms included Philips, Siemens, Thomson-CSF, and AEG-Telefunken.

SUPPLIERS OF SEMICONDUCTOR MANUFACTURING EQUIPMENT

The rapid growth of the semiconductor industry spawned the growth of semiconductor equipment (SME) firms. The SME industry, which included wafer processing, testing, and assembly, was generally a low-volume business, where scale economies were relatively unimportant. In the United States, the SME industry was not very concentrated in the mid-1980s with fourteen firms accounting for 56% of the sales. For certain important machines, however, there may have been only one or two suppliers. Most of the manufacturers had sales in the $10 to $50 million range.

Timely delivery of state-of-the-art equipment was critical for all semiconductor manufacturers. Any new equipment which could increase yield or reduce downtime could be an important source of competitive advantage. Historically, however, relations between U.S. chip and equipment companies were strictly at arm's length and usually adversarial. In boom times, SME firms would charge premiums; and in downturns, the merchants were quick to cancel orders and demand steep discounts. This began to change in the United States after the economic downturn in the industry in 1985 put several American SMEs on the verge of bankruptcy. Fearing dependence on Japanese equipment suppliers, many U.S. semiconduc-

tor merchants started seeking greater cooperation. For instance, the SEMATECH project, discussed below, included several equipment manufacturers.

The United States dominated the world SME industry, but the Japanese were making substantial inroads. The Japanese SME industry consisted of about 500 firms producing wafer processing, testing, and assembly equipment. Despite the many firms in the industry, it was fairly concentrated with twelve firms accounting for 75% of sales. In some critical areas in 1987, such as steppers made by Nikon Camera, Japanese firms held virtual monopolies. Whereas the U.S. equipment manufacturers had historically been independent of the chip manufacturers, many important SME producers in Japan were subsidiaries of, or were financially linked to, Japanese chip manufacturers.

GOVERNMENT POLICY

Governments around the world had been active in their semiconductor industries. European governments had intervened extensively through subsidies and joint R&D efforts. In 1987, for instance, Germany and Holland were in the midst of a $2 billion project to give Philips and Siemens an edge in the 4-megabit DRAM and 1-megabit SRAM market. By contrast, the U.S. government provided little direct support to the industry during the heyday of U.S. dominance. The major exceptions were the military's procurement program in the early years of the industry and the Very High Speed Integrated Circuit program, established by the Pentagon in 1979 to provide R&D funding ($300m) for the development of advanced ICs designed to meet specific military needs.

The U.S. government played an additional role by allowing the industry very limited antitrust exemptions. This led the Semiconductor Industry Association (SIA) to establish the nonprofit Semiconductor Research Cooperative in 1982 to fund basic research at American universities. In 1983, a group of 21 firms created the Microelectronics and Computer Technology Corporation to sponsor long-term applied research. By the mid-1980s, however, neither effort had made a significant contribution to the competitive balance between Japan and the United States.

In 1986–1987, the U.S. government started to become more active. Japan's share of the U.S. market had reached almost 20% in the summer of 1986 when the United States negotiated a trade agreement with Japan. The accord required individual Japanese firms to stop dumping chips in the United States and third markets and specified that America's share of the Japanese market would more than double to 20% by 1991. After apparent violations of the agreement, the Reagan administration retaliated against Japan in April 1987. In the fall of 1987, Congress allocated $100 million to support a consortium of computer companies, chip makers, and semiconductor equipment manufacturers. SIA firms made an equal monetary contribution, while IBM and AT&T donated advanced proprietary chip designs for DRAMs and SRAMs, respectively. The consortium would be called SEMATECH, and its goal would be to produce state-of-the-art manufacturing techniques to help U.S. companies reestablish dominance in mass-memory-chip production.

The Japanese government was more actively involved in semiconductors, targeting the industry very early. Government support for the industry began in the 1950s in the form of financial assistance, R&D assistance, and a lib-

eral antitrust policy. Japan's MITI (Ministry of International Trade and Industry) orchestrated the government support, beginning with the administration of a series of laws, codified in 1957, that exempted the computer and semiconductor industries from antitrust prosecution. Government support of the industry continued throughout the 1970s and 1980s. It is estimated that between 1976 and 1982, the Japanese government provided at least $500 million in direct subsidies and loans to the industry.

The Japanese government also played a role in coordinating competitive strategies. In the mid-1970s, MITI targeted DRAMs and selected the five largest vertically integrated electronic firms for the project. While 60% of the budget came from the companies, MITI supported the effort with interest-free loans, government scientists, and a protected domestic market. Although quantitative restrictions on imports were eliminated in 1974 and tariffs reduced to zero in 1985, American firms believed that they did not have free market access. In addition, government R&D support came from NTT, the government telephone monopoly prior to its privatization in 1985. Over the 1976–1980 period NTT invested $350 million in VLSI research, the results of which were available to all Japanese semiconductor manufacturers. In 1987, MITI was also guiding firms to cut production and increase purchases of American chips in order to comply with the U.S.-Japan semiconductor accord.

EXHIBIT ONE

INDUSTRY EXPERIENCE CURVE IN DRAM ACROSS PRODUCTS (68% curve slope)

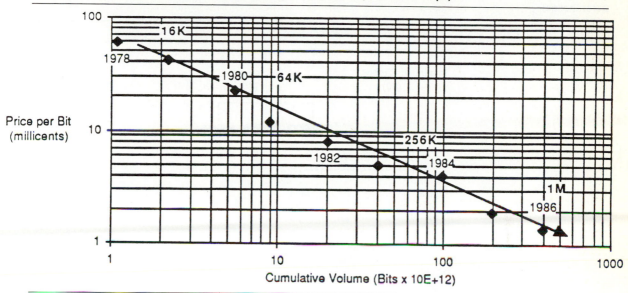

Source: HBS field study, Spring 1987.

EXHIBIT TWO

FAMILY TREE OF SEMICONDUCTOR PRODUCTS (approximate percentages of consumption in the mid-1980s in parentheses)

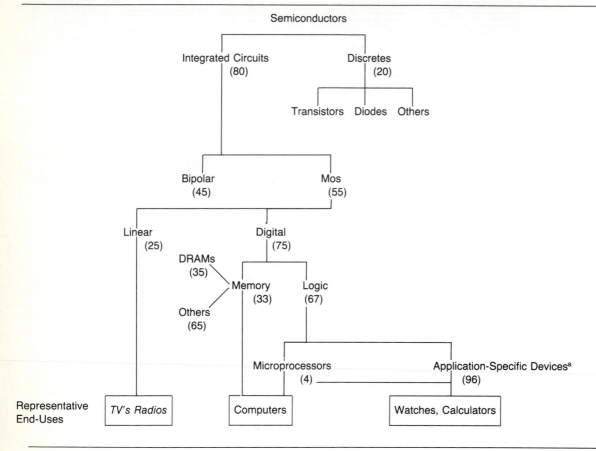

[a]Includes all standard, custom, and semicustom ICs. The nonstandard "ASIC" portion of this category was very small in the mid-1980s.

EXHIBIT THREE

A. ESTIMATED WORLDWIDE ASIC CONSUMPTION ($ billions)

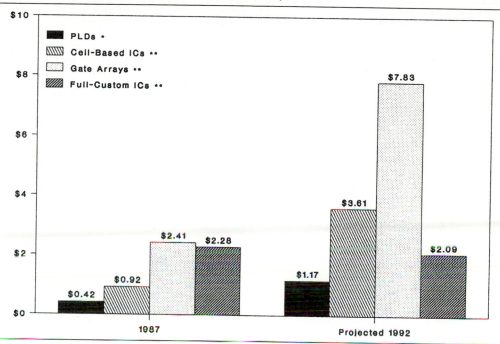

*PDLs are logic chips that can be programmed with software by the user. PDLs are the cheapest and fastest ASIC to design (usually within a few days), but the least versatile ASIC.

**Gate Arrays (GA) and Cell Based Devices (CBD) are ASICs designed by the semiconductor manufacturer in collaboration with the user. A GA, which can be designed in only 2–4 weeks, has fixed circuits (transistors, resistors, and capacitors) which the ASIC designer interconnects to fulfill user specific applications. In a CBD, an engineer selects standard semiconductor cells from a firm's library and then designs the chip to maximize efficiency and minimize space. CBDs are more versatile and efficient but require up to 16 weeks to design. Full custom chips are the most efficient ASICs, but require up to 12 months to design and have the highest design costs.

Source: Adapted from Dataquest, January 1988.

EXHIBIT THREE

CONTINUED

B. TOP TEN ASIC VENDORS WORLDWIDE IN 1986 ($ millions)

Company	% growth 1985–1986	1986	Approximate revenues by segments		
			Gate array	Cell-based	PLDs
1. Fujitsu	43.0%	$ 359.2	$309	$ 50	—
2. LSI Logic	38.9	194.3	$192	—	—
3. AT&T	26.8	183.1	—	183	—
4. MMI/AMD[a]	19.3	176.7	—	—	$172
5. NEC	55.9	151.2	145	—	—
6. Toshiba	152.3	132.6	120	—	—
7. TI	40.0	99.7	38	42	20
8. Motorola	20.9	94.7	92	—	—
9. Hitachi	35.6	78.8	79	—	—
10. Signetics	3.7	76.0	—	—	50
Top 10 vendors	38.8%	$1,546.3			

[a]MMI (Monolithic Memories) merged with AMD (Advanced Micro Devices) in 1987.
Source: Adapted from Dataquest, *JSIS Newsletter,* May 1987.

EXHIBIT FOUR

A.   ESTIMATED 1987 SEMICONDUCTOR CONSUMPTION BY APPLICATION MARKET

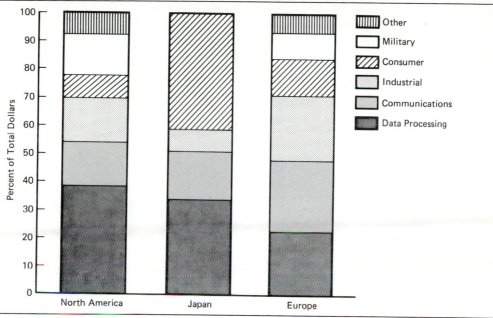

Source: Instat, Inc.

EXHIBIT FOUR

B.   TOTAL SOLID STATE CONSUMPTION WORLDWIDE (ICS AND DISCRETES) ($ millions)

	1982	1983	1984	1985	1986	1987[a]
U.S.A.	$ 6,259	$ 7,763	$11,599	$ 8,091	$ 8,509	$ 9,823
Japan	3,985	5,534	8,034	7,598	10,451	11,117
Europe	2,998	3,319	4,738	4,541	5,344	6,387
R.O.W.	822	1,152	1,586	1,250	2,052	2,496
Total world	$14,064	$17,767	$25,956[b]	$21,479[b]	$26,355[b]	$29,823
% growth	NA	26.3%	46.1%	−17.2%	22.7%	13.2%

[a]Estimate.
[b]Instat estimates are lower than Dataquest estimates reported in Exhibit 7.
Source: Instat, Inc.

A. GLOBAL COMPUTER LEADERS, 1986 ($ millions)

Mainframes		Minicomputers		Microcomputers	
Company	Revenues	Company	Revenues[a]	Company	Revenues
1. IBM	14,450	IBM	3,000	IBM	5,650
2. Fujitsu Ltd.	2,470	DEC	2,000	Apple	1,781
3. NEC Corp.	2,275	H-P	1,100	Olivetti SpA	1,267
4. Unisys Corp.	2,200	Wang	805	Tandy Corp.	997
5. Hitachi Ltd.	1,372	Toshiba Corp.	766	Unisys Corp.	800
6. Groupe Bull	822	Fujitsu Ltd.	620	NEC Corp.	697
7. Honeywell Inc.	740	Unisys Corp.	600	Compaq	625
8. Siemens AG	583	Olivetti SpA	493	AT&T	600
9. Cray Research Inc.	526	Mitsubishi	475	Toshiba	582
10. Amdahl Corp.	498	Data General	450	Zenith	548

[a]Revenue figures may understate corporate sales because of *Datamation*'s narrow industry segmentation.
Source: Datamation, June 15, 1987, pp. 30–31.

B. ESTIMATED SEMICONDUCTOR PRODUCTION OF U.S. CAPTIVE MANUFACTURERS ($ millions)

Company	1981	1982	1983	1984	1985
IBM	1,500	1,680	1,932	2,318	2,600
AT&T	675	720	755	980	600
Honeywell	60	76	90	95	81
Delco	68	75	80	95	111
DEC	47	61	65	80	71
H-P (IC only)	116	118	134	165	180
Subtotal	2,466	2,730	3,056	3,733	3,643
Others	250	275	300	370	395
Total captive	2,716	3,005	3,356	4,103	4,038
Total merchant[a]	7,607	7,694	9,509	14,244	11,103

[a]Excludes intracompany sales of merchant firms, which averaged 5% from 1981 to 1985.
Source: Dataquest, July 1986.

C. ESTIMATED SEMICONDUCTOR USERS PURCHASING MORE THAN $100 MILLION

Year	Number of companies	Total semiconductor consumption (billions of dollars)	Percent of total semiconductor consumption
1976	1	$0.11	2%
1978	5	$0.69	8%
1980	12	$1.80	17%
1982	23	$3.90	26%
1984	36	$5.80	28%
1985	46	$7.10	31%

Source: Adapted from Dataquest, *SUIS Industry Trends*, March 1987.

EXHIBIT SIX

A. TOP FIVE SUPPLIERS ACROSS TECHNOLOGICAL GENERATIONS

1955 (vacuum tubes)	1955 (transistor)	1965 (semiconductor)	1975 (IC)	1985 (VLSI)
RCA	Hughes	TI	TI	NEC
Sylvania	Transitron	Fairchild	Fairchild	Motorola
GE	Philco	Motorola	National	TI
Raytheon	Sylvania	GI	Intel	Hitachi
Westinghouse	TI	GE	Motorola	Toshiba

Source: Richard N. Foster, *Innovation. The Attachers' Advantage* (New York: Summit Books); Dataquest.

(*continued*)

B. PRELIMINARY 1986 WORLD SEMICONDUCTOR MARKET SHARE RANKING ($ millions)

1986 rank	1985 rank	1984 rank	Company	1984	1985	1986	Percent change '85–'86
1	1	3	NEC	2,251	1,984	2,638	33.0%
2	4	4	Hitachii	2,052	1,671	2,305	37.9
3	5	5	Toshiba	1,561	1,468	2,261	54.0
4	2	2	Motorola	2,320	1,830	2,025	10.7
5	3	1	Texas Instruments	2,480	1,742	1,820	4.5
6	6	6	Philips-Signetics	1,325	1,068	1,356	27.0
7	7	9	Fujitsu	1,190	1,020	1,310	28.4
8	10	12	Matsushita	928	906	1,233	36.1
9	11	10	Mitsubishi	964	642	1,177	83.3
10	8	8	Intel	1,201	1,020	991	−2.8
11	9	7	National Semiconductor[b]	1,263	925	990	7.0
12	12	11	Advanced Micro Devices[c]	936	615	629	2.3
13	14	15	Sanyo	455	457	585	28.0
14	13	13	Fairchild[b]	665	492	510	3.7
15	22	29	Sony	177	252	475	88.5
16	15	16	Siemens	450	420	457	8.8
17	16	20	Sharp	354	329	456	38.6
18	17	22	Thomson-Mostek[a]	301	324	436	34.6
19	19	19	Oki	362	307	427	39.1
20	23	24	Rohm	252	249	379	52.2
21	20	21	SGS	335	300	370	23.3
22	18	17	RCA	402	310	370	19.4
23	21	25	ITT	250	270	312	15.6
24	24	23	Harris	275	247	264	6.9
25	25	26	Analog Devices	210	226	232	2.7
26	31	32	Sanken	162	155	220	41.9
27	29	33	Telefunken Electronic	161	170	219	28.8
28	26	28	Hewlett-Packard	182	206	217	5.3
29	36	35	TRW	142	125	213	70.4
30	30	30	Fuji Electric	176	156	213	36.5
31	28	27	Monolithic Memories[c]	200	172	210	22.1
32	27	18	General Instrument	362	201	205	2.0
33	32	47	LSI Logic	84	140	192	37.1
34	41	57	Samsung	60	95	183	92.6
35	42	39	Seiko Epson	115	93	167	79.6
36	44	55	Honeywell	64	88	157	78.4
37	33	31	American Microsystems	164	140	155	10.7
38	34	38	International Rectifier	115	128	145	13.3
39	38	42	Siliconix	97	110	126	14.5
40	39	49	Plessey	82	99	112	13.1
41	48	53	VLSI Technology	69	78	110	41.0
42	n/a	n/a	Powerex	n/a	0	95	n/a
43	49	n/a	Burr-Brown	n/a	78	95	21.8
44	40	41	Ferranti	105	98	95	−3.1
45	45	48	Sprague	84	87	94	8.0
46	43	40	Unitrode	106	89	90	1.1
47	37	36	General Electric	136	118	89	−24.6
48	52	n/a	Precision Monolithics	n/a	68	81	19.1
49	46	34	Inmos	146	85	80	−5.9
50	50	46	NCR	85	75	80	6.7
Top 50 total				26,507	21,928	27,651	26.1%

[a]Mostek and Thomson revenues are aggregated in 1986 but not in 1984 or 1985.
[b]National and Fairchild merged in 1987.
[c]AMD and MMI merged in 1987.
Source: Dataquest, January 1987.

FINANCIALS OF NINE LEADING PRODUCERS[a] ($ millions)

	1986	1985	1984	1983
Motorola				
Net sales	5,888	5,443	5,534	4,328
Semic. sales	1,880	1,728	2,240	1,612
Net income/(loss)	194	72	387	244
Semic. operating profit/(loss)	87	(37)	373	205
R&D expenses	492	457	489	392
Semic. capital expenditures	250	325	412	174
Total assets	4,682	4,370	4,194	3,236
Long-term debt	334	705	531	262
Equity	2,754	2,284	2,278	1,948
Return on sales (semi.)	4.6%	(2.1%)	16.7%	12.7%
Semi. cap. exp./semi. sales	13.3%	18.8%	18.4%	10.8%
Texas Instruments				
Net sales	4,974	4,924	5,742	4,580
Semic. sales	2,065	2,041	2,740	1,885
Net income	29	(119)	316	(145)
Semic. operating profit	23	(89)	516	236
R&D expenses	406	402	367	301
Semic. capital expenditures	232	281	472	232
Total assets	3,337	3,076	3,423	2,713
Long-term debt	191	382	381	225
Equity	1,727	1,428	1,540	1,203
Return on sales (semi.)	1.1%	(4.4%)	18.8%	12.5%
Semi. cap. exp./semi. sales	11.2%	13.8%	17.2%	12.3%
Intel				
Net sales	1,265	1,365	1,629	1,122
Net income	(173)	2	198	116
R&D expenses	228	195	180	142
Total capital expenditures	155	236	388	145
Total assets	2,080	2,152	2,029	1,680
Long-term debt	287	271	146	128
Equity	1,275	1,421	1,360	1,122
Return on sales (semi.)	(13.7%)	0.2%	12.2%	10.3%
Semi. cap. exp./semi. sales	12.3%	17.3%	23.8%	12.9%
National Semiconductor				
Net sales	1,478	1,787	1,655	1,210
Semic. sales	842	1,156	1,107	788
Net income	(91.5)	43	64	(14)
Semic. operating profit	(129)	62	110	10
R&D expenses	222	205	158	115
Semic. capital expenditures	69	322	224	65
Total assets	1,295	1,410	1,156	847
Long-term debt	123	226	24	149
Equity	717	681	619	336
Return on sales (semi.)	(15.3%)	5.4%	9.9%	1.3%
Semi. cap. exp./semi. sales	8.2%	27.9%	20.2%	8.3%

(continued)

CONTINUED

	1986	1985	1984	1983
LSI Logic				
Net sales	194	140	84	35
Net income	4	10	15	13
R&D expenses	22	14	12	4
Capital expenditures	70	40	NA	NA
Total assets	451	372	318	211
Long-term debt	107	82	67	21
Equity	251	232	206	176
Return on sales (semi.)	2.1%	7.1%	17.9%	37.1%
Semi. cap. exp./semi. sales	36.1%	28.6%	NA	NA
Fujitsu				
Net sales	11,072	7,870	6,444	5,149
Semic. sales	1,375	1,051	1,259	928
Net income	92	181	366	285
Semic. operating profit	(204)	(153)	222	136
R&D expenses[b]	1,099	730	547	438
Semic. capital expenditures	197	335	473	NA
Return on sales (semi.)	(14.8%)	(14.6%)	17.6%	14.7%
Semi. cap. exp./semi. sales	14.3%	31.9%	37.6%	NA
Hitachi				
Net sales	32,086	23,302	20,630	18,583
Semic. sales	2,586	1,953	2,222	1,532
Net income	671	698	864	711
Semic. operating profit	(257)	(130)	444	226
Semic. capital expenditures	211	428	494	NA
Return on sales (semi.)	(9.9%)	(6.7%)	20.0%	14.8%
Semi. cap. exp./semi. sales	8.2%	21.9%	22.2%	NA
NEC				
Net sales	16,224	10,860	9,292	7,498
Semic. sales	3,125	2,051	2,453	1,809
Net income	184	126	272	191
Semic. operating profit	(204)	(33)	329	136
Semic. capital expenditures	362	572	531	NA
Return on sales (semi.)	(6.5%)	(1.6%)	13.4%	7.5%
Semi. cap. exp./semi. sales	11.6%	27.9%	21.7%	NA
Toshiba				
Net sales	21,230	15,668	13,757	11,519
Semic. sales	2,217	1,391	1,523	1,013
Net income	217	274	354	251
Semic. operating profit	(207)	(140)	198	72
R&D expenses[b]	1,316	884	720	600
Semic. capital expenditures	428	572	560	NA
Return on sales (semi.)	(9.3%)	(10.1%)	13.0%	7.1%
Semi. cap. exp./semi. sales	19.3%	41.1%	36.8%	NA

[a]Semiconductor sales figures reported by firms in their annual reports will not always correspond to Dataquest estimates in other exhibits. Most corporate fiscal years, for instance, do not correspond to the calendar years reported by *Dataquest*.
[b]Corporate R&D; semiconductor R&D figures were not available.
Source: Prudential Bache Securities, 1986; Dataquest, *JSIS Newsletter,* December 1986; and annual reports.

EXHIBIT EIGHT

A. GROWTH IN U.S. SEMICONDUCTOR CONSUMPTION VS. U.S. GNP GROWTH
(year-to-year percentage change)

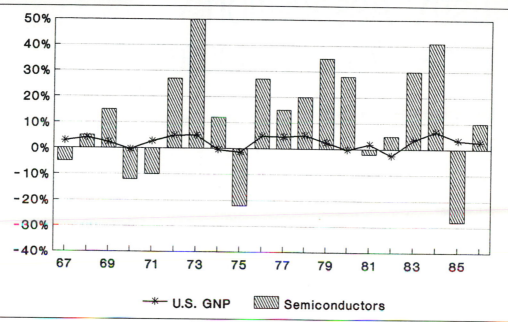

— ✳ — U.S. GNP   ▨ Semiconductors

Source: Dataquest, March 1987.

EXHIBIT EIGHT

B. CAPACITY UTILIZATION AND GROWTH IN DEMAND IN U.S. SEMICONDUCTOR MARKET, 1966–1985

Period	Annual growth rate	Capacity utilization wafer fabrication
1966–71	0	n/a
1971–74	31%	n/a
1974–75	(18)%	70
1975–79	25%	80
1979–82	7%	64
1982–84	31%	77
1984–85	(29%)	50

Source: Semiconductor Industry Association, *Performance of the U.S. Semiconductor Industry,* 1986.

The Semiconductor Industry Association and the Trade Dispute with Japan (A)

Semiconductor firms do well politically because we tell a good story. We have never paid a dividend, we have contributed significantly to the growth of employment, we have desirable jobs and a good mystique. Also, our naïveté has been one of our major advantages: We have few lobbyists; the CEOs go directly to Washington. You have to remember that the whole semiconductor industry is small compared to General Motors.

Robert N. Noyce, Vice Chairman
Intel Corporation

The U.S. government decided several trade cases in the American semiconductor industry's favor in the first half of 1986, most significantly an unfair trade practices case filed by the Semiconductor Industry Association (SIA) under Section 301 of the Trade Act of 1974. In July

1986, the Japanese and American governments inked an agreement that promised foreign firms (as a group) a doubling of their Japanese market share and elimination of any Japanese dumping into U.S. and third country markets. But now, in March 1987, member firms of the SIA were convinced that the Japanese were violating the agreement. Industry officials had to decide what the SIA and the government should do next.

The decision on an appropriate response would come from the SIA's Public Policy Committee (PPC), headed by George Scalise. Scalise, chief administrative officer of Advanced Micro Devices (AMD) and a 30-year semiconductor industry veteran, played an important role in the SIA's political activities after assuming the PPC chair in 1982. He considered the forging of consensus to be perhaps his most important task as head of the PPC and believed that achieving internal agreement had allowed the SIA to take on controversial issues and move fast and effectively. Yet finding a consensus on whether and how the United States should retaliate against Japan would be no easy task.

THE SEMICONDUCTOR INDUSTRY ASSOCIATION

Consisting of five members when founded in 1977, the SIA had 48 firms on its membership rolls in 1985 (see *Exhibit 1*). Collectively, these firms produced 95% of the semiconductors fabricated annually in the United States. Although the association's primary objective was to coordinate the political action of the semiconductor industry, the SIA was engaged in a number of other activities as well. These activities included the collection of statistics related to occupational health and safety, the environment, and industry market trends. This latter project, known as the Worldwide Semiconductor Trade Statistics program, assembled and analyzed data submitted voluntarily by most American, European, and Japanese semiconductor companies. The SIA also published several monographs relating to economic aspects of the industry. Politically, the SIA's agenda included trade concerns, export controls, intellectual property rights, capital formation, research and development, and antitrust issues.

Unlike most trade associations, the SIA was not staff-driven. Only six professionals ran the association, two handling government affairs. Instead, the SIA relied on the initiative of the people in the individual companies who sat on the various SIA committees. CEOs and high-level executives, whether on the committees or not, played a very important role in defining and promoting industry positions in Washington. The SIA also tried to leverage outside expertise. For instance, Scalise believed that the SIA had a good idea of what the government would and wouldn't do for the industry because of the real-world experience of the SIA's outside legal counsel.

This combination of maximizing company involvement, leveraging outside expertise, and using the SIA staff to coordinate a common front to the government resulted in a number of successes. Of six goals set in 1983, five clear victories were obtained over the next three years. The SIA won an amendment to the Trade Act of 1974 which made clear that "denial of fair and equitable market access" could be the subject of a trade petition. The SIA also successfully eliminated semiconductor duties in the United States and Japan. Passage of the Semiconductor Chip Protection Act, which offered intellectual property protection to chip designs and encouraged foreign countries to reciprocate, was another achievement. The National Cooperative Research Act eased antitrust restrictions on joint R&D projects. An amendment to the Export Administration Act helped streamline export licensing procedures. Finally, one partial success was the 1986 extension of the R&D tax credit, which would have otherwise been phased out.

THE SECTION 301 CASE

Firms in the SIA had thought about what trade actions to adopt for many years before actually filing the 301 case in 1985.[1] The central American charge was that Japan was a protected market. This protection prevented U.S. firms from improving their position in Japan, gave the Japanese the opportunity to dump chips abroad, and altered the industry's pricing

---

[1]Section 301 cases considered trade practices deemed to be "unfair": acts, policies, or practices of a foreign government that violated or denied benefits to the United States under a trade agreement or were considered unjustifiable, unreasonable, or discriminatory and a burden or restriction on U.S. commerce. Unlike the more judicial proceedings used to decide antidumping and countervailing duty cases, Section 301 cases were notable for their political orientation. The flexibility given to both the U.S. special trade representative (who need not investigate a submitted petition) and the president (who could fashion almost any, or no, response to a finding of unfair practices) differed sharply from the more structured procedures for antidumping and countervailing duty cases.

structure dramatically. The American firms argued that their share of the Japanese market in no way approximated their overall position in the world semiconductor market (see *Exhibits* 2 and 3).

Early Activities

From 1979 to 1983, the association informally urged the government to take trade action of some sort against Japan. At the same time, however, the SIA was internally divided over the exact tactics and demands to employ. A 1979 International Trade Commission probe of the U. S.'s semiconductor position in Japan and Europe, which was encouraged by the U.S. industry, declared that the United States would maintain its lead in semiconductors despite targeting and trade barriers. In 1982, Motorola asked the government to conduct an informal study of Japanese pricing policies in 64K DRAMs, with a view to possible antidumping action. The SIA was split on whether to participate in a 64K DRAM dumping case, with Motorola and IBM the primary proponents of the pro and con views, respectively. Ultimately, the SIA did not approve any particular plan to combat Japanese marketing practices in 64K DRAMs.

The idea of a 301 suit was first discussed in 1982. When the possibility of a 301 action was mentioned to U.S. Special Trade Representative (USTR) Bill Brock in 1982, he advised against it, suggesting that the case did not seem strong. Instead, Brock pursued a route of negotiations by pressing for the formation of a U.S.-Japan High Technology Working Group (HTWG). The HTWG agreement reached in 1983 called on the Japanese government to promote actively the purchase of U.S. semiconductors.

For the first half of 1984, the HTWG agreement seemed to work. American sales in Japan increased faster than the overall increase in the Japanese market, pushing the U.S. market share over 12%. The U.S. share of the Japanese market was 10.1% and 10.8% in 1982 and 1983, respectively. But this increase was at least partly due to the shortage of chips in Japan during the unprecedented boom of 1983–1984. By late 1984 worldwide demand for semiconductors was decreasing. The U.S. share in Japan for 1984 finished at 11.4%, and in 1985 it returned to its pre-HTWG rate of about 10%. The severity of the market decline made the lack of penetration of Japan even more costly. Semiconductor sales dropped 20% in the world market in 1985, with a 30% drop in the United States. At this point, according to the SIA's legal counsel, "the decision to file a 301 case was largely a tactical decision in response to the violations of the HTWG agreement. Firms had no patience for any further negotiations."

Deciding to File a Section 301 Case

George Scalise thought a 301 case would validate the SIA's claims about the Japanese market, show that it was willing to commit real resources to prove its point, and establish a way to deal with similar issues in the future. From January to June 1985 Scalise sought to build a consensus within the SIA for a 301 petition. The first step was estimating the costs of a case as accurately as possible, because the SIA was resource-constrained and any 301 action was going to be paid by a special assessment on SIA members. Another important step was getting the support of major semiconductor consumers within the association. Scalise noted that companies such as IBM, Hewlett-Packard, and Digital Equipment Corporation (DEC) were important enough within the SIA that they could have vetoed a decision to move forward. Ultimately, "these companies passed the word that 'we won't stand in the way.'"

The SIA also had to work out a common position among firms with different inclinations toward political involvement and different economic interests. Intel, AMD, Motorola, DEC, Rockwell International, and Harris were among the firms most active politically. On the other extreme was Texas Instruments (TI), which had declined to even join the association until 1984.[2] While firms such as IBM wanted to move cautiously, a few, including Motorola, were much more aggressive. By the time the semiconductor boom of 1984 had turned into the bust of 1985, many firms within the SIA had moved closer to Motorola's position.

Economic factors differentiated the firms as well. Merchant firms had proposed embargoes on certain products, such as EPROMs, and the imposition of high tariffs and fines. Semiconductor customers within the SIA, including IBM and DEC, opposed any embargo. TI, a major customer and producer, opposed the imposition of any tariffs or quotas. The SIA ultimately reached a consensus that asked for (1) an increase in the U.S. firms' market share in Japan somewhat more commensurate with their worldwide performance and (2) a monitoring procedure that would ensure that Japanese chips were not being dumped in the United States or in third countries.

Scalise also tried to build consensus for the case outside the SIA. One important endorsement came from the American Electronics Association (AEA). The effort to gain AEA support highlighted some of the concerns customers had about the 301 case. Customers in the AEA noted that (1) less market share did not necessarily mean discrimination, (2) there might be competition in some semiconductors but not others, (3) any kind of required market percentages could not be enforced, and (4) U.S. semiconductor firms were perhaps not as vigorous as they needed to be in the Japanese market. "But there was absolute agreement that there was lack of fair access," an AEA official noted, "and most of our members felt that something should be done to send the Japa-

nese a message." The AEA ultimately wrote a letter to the USTR supporting the SIA's objectives in the 301 case.

The SIA submitted its 301 petition in June 1985, organizing its evidence around four central themes: Japanese market barriers, the structure of the Japanese market, Japanese government policies, and the promotion of a positive environment for dumping. Speaking specifically about market share, one of the key SIA players in Washington described the industry's position this way: "Despite changes in the dollar/yen ratio, despite changes in tariffs, despite new product introductions by American firms, there was at no point a change in market share over a ten-year period between the United States and Japan" (see *Exhibit 4*). The association stressed that the U.S.'s relative position in almost all product areas was trending downward. The vaunted job-creating ability of high-tech industries was also portrayed as vulnerable: 65,000 U.S.-based chip company positions were lost worldwide by the end of 1985.

Political Strategy and Tactics

According to Scalise, the SIA's 301 case had two overriding strategic goals. First, the SIA wanted to build the broadest case possible in order to enhance its bargaining position. Second, the chip firms wanted to ensure that the case did not disadvantage any of their customers in any of their markets. "If the customers were hurt," Scalise noted, "no one would win."

Within these broad strategic goals, the SIA employed several political tactics. The SIA decided to focus considerable energies on the Congress, much in contrast to the track followed by the Japanese industry's representatives in Washington; the Japanese industry focused its attention and energy almost exclusively on the executive branch. Because U.S. trade deficits with Japan (and overall) were at his-

---

[2]TI subsequently became quite active in the 301 case.

torical peaks, interest in trade issues on Capitol Hill was growing. New and tougher trade bills were introduced almost weekly, and some political observers suggested that if one of these bills were to pass, a presidential veto stood a strong chance of being overridden.

To establish a base in Congress, the SIA formed the Congressional Support Group, a group of sympathetic legislators consisting of ten representatives, ten senators, ten Republicans, and ten Democrats. The SIA wanted to use this group to "energize" the executive branch by sending letters and making phone calls. All twenty of the group signed a letter to Brock's successor as USTR, Clayton Yeutter, requesting that his office become more involved in the semiconductor case. Eventually, five of the group met with Yeutter. This group of legislators was often needed simply to get access to cabinet-level and sub-cabinet-level people. The SIA got 180 members of Congress to write letters to the executive branch, including entire delegations from California, Illinois, New Mexico, Arizona, and Texas. The California delegation also met with the Japanese ambassador to the United States (see *Exhibit 5*).

Although the SIA's political tactics were channeled predominantly through the Congress, the SIA did not form a political action committee to contribute to congressional campaigns. And while member companies made some candidate endorsements, the SIA did not attempt to encourage grass-roots or constituency (employees, shareholders, etc.) letter writing. Scalise worried that these tactics "might taint the legitimacy of our arguments a little bit. Representatives and senators are smart enough to know that most voters would have very limited understanding of and interest in this issue."

Scalise believed that going through the Congress provided, ironically, the best way for the industry to express its case to the administration. He was concerned about the attitudes within the executive branch. He found the most

resistance initially coming from within the State Department and the Defense Department, although other agencies were opposed as well. State and Defense were eager to shore up the U.S.-Japan relationship as allies and saw cases of this kind as a threat to bilateral cooperation. Indeed, the SIA's legal representative noted that "one big problem with a 301 case is that it is quite dependent on the president taking action, and that means you risk raising larger foreign policy questions unintentionally." Indeed, the SIA found that raising these larger questions brought a number of executive agencies into the decision-making process. Scalise found it necessary to hold interagency progress meetings covering developments in the Departments of Defense, Labor, Treasury, State, and Commerce, in addition to the Central Intelligence Agency, the National Security Council, the Council of Economic Advisors, and the Office of Management and Budget.

Despite the opposition of State and Defense and the wavering of the USTR, segments of the administration were supportive. When the SIA managed to get some time with Secretary of State George Schultz, Schultz took particular interest in a page of comparative pie charts showing the dominant U.S. market share in the United States, Europe, and the rest of the world and the relatively meager market share gained by U.S. firms in Japan.[3] "This tells me all I need to know," he reportedly declared as he tore the sheet from a bound document. "The cash registers have to start ringing over there [in Japan]." The SIA also had some success dealing with the working-level people in the Commerce Department but had trouble with higher-ranking free-trade economists in other

---

[3]The United States heavily outsold Japan in all regions other than Japan. Between 1982 and 1986, the United States averaged 53% of Europe's market and 47% of all other markets, while Japan averaged only 10% and 28%, respectively.

agencies. "It was frustrating," Scalise sighed, "trying to convince them that you can't have free trade without a free market."

Another step in the SIA political plan was to maintain good relations with the press by distributing literature and holding briefings for major national media and local media in Silicon Valley. The SIA also distributed basic background information on the issues to a wide array of groups and hired a public relations firm based in Washington to help get media contacts, write press releases, and so on. Scalise felt that the industry's educational campaign "started in a good position because we had already been discussing these issues in an incremental, nonextreme way for more than three years before the 301 petition was even filed." The SIA allocated less than $1 million annually to cover legal expenses and other operating costs associated with the 301 campaign. More significant than the financial cost, however, was the contribution of time. Three to four labor years were devoted to the case by the staffs of Motorola, Intel, and Rockwell. George Scalise spent roughly one-third of his time on the project. And the CEOs and high-level executives of several SIA companies—including AMD, National Semiconductor, TI, Intel, and Motorola—devoted much time to speeches, testimony, and interviews on the subject.

Other Trade Actions

Trade action against Japan in semiconductors was not limited to the 301 case. By the end of 1985, three suits had been filed charging Japanese firms with selling semiconductors in the United States below their cost of production. In late June, soon after the 301 petition was filed, Micron Technology charged Japanese semiconductor firms with dumping 64K DRAMs. Then, in late September, Intel, AMD, and National Semiconductor claimed that Japanese firms were dumping EPROMs. (TI, a large

EPROM firm, declined to join this suit.) Finally, in a rare move, the Department of Commerce "self-initiated" a case in early December and charged Japanese firms with dumping 256K and up DRAMs. Although most U.S. firms had already abandoned the 256K DRAM market, this case held particular importance for Texas Instruments, the last major U.S. merchant producer. In all three cases, the petitioners argued that Japanese prices had fallen far too sharply in short periods of time to be explained by superior production methods (see *Exhibit 6*).

All three petitioners recognized that their dumping suits would interact indirectly with the Section 301 case. Intel felt that the EPROM case and the 301 case increased American bargaining power and hoped that the Japanese would want to settle everything at once—the 301 and the EPROM dumping suit. Intel officials also hoped they could get specific provisions on EPROMs built into an agreement; they believed that such a specific provision was highly unlikely without the pressure of the dumping suit. (Intel executives noted that the United States could supply enough EPROMs to make up for any embargo on Japanese EPROMs coming into the United States, thereby minimizing any inconvenience to users.) Intel proposed that financial penalties paid by Japan go to the Semiconductor Research Corporation, an organization that distributed research funds to U.S. universities. The concern for Intel, AMD, and National was that they retain EPROMs as their "technology driver," that is, a chip they could produce in high quantities that would encourage both design innovations and manufacturing efficiencies. Intel absorbed the financial costs of the case, while Scalise spearheaded the issue in Washington.

U.S.–JAPAN SEMICONDUCTOR NEGOTIATIONS

Once the USTR announced in early 1986 that he supported the SIA's position in the 301 case,

President Reagan had until July 1, 1986, to determine a U.S. response to the unfair trading practices (later extended to July 30). Once the positive finding in the 301 case was issued, U.S. and Japanese government negotiators began meeting to work out a solution to the trade problems in semiconductors. The U.S. position was strengthened considerably by preliminary positive findings during Spring 1986 on all three of the dumping suits that prescribed dumping duties of up to 188%.[4] Scalise explained that "those decisions gave us some bargaining leverage. The Japanese firms knew that dumping duties would be imposed as a result of the three dumping cases. The preliminary margins were already published, and their application was automatically provided for in the trade laws. Furthermore, sanctions could be imposed because of the 301 case itself. At a time of sharp trade tensions, they couldn't just assume that these sanctions would be weak. They could already see that we had built some high-level support in the administration."

During the negotiations no actual figure for the Americans' desired Japanese market share was specified by the SIA, but the industry argued that in the absence of trade barriers the U.S. semiconductor industry should have had between 20% and 30% of the Japanese market.[5] As one company official noted, "The key became that the Japanese had to guarantee a market share in the 20's. It had to have 'a two' in front of the number in order to be acceptable."

In August 1986 the United States and Japan announced that the two countries had reached an accord on semiconductor trade.[6] The Japanese agreed to increase their purchase of foreign-made chips to slightly over 20% of the Japanese market over a five-year period, effectively doubling U.S. semiconductor sales in Japan. Japan intended to establish an organization that would provide sales assistance for foreign semiconductor manufacturers. The Japanese also agreed to have the Ministry of International Trade and Industry (MITI) monitor export prices on a wide range of semiconductor products—including EPROMs, 256K DRAMs, and 8-bit and 16-bit microprocessors—to prevent Japanese chipmakers from selling at less than fair market value in the United States or in third countries. The United States reserved the right to add or drop products from this list in the future.

The U.S. Commerce Department was responsible for determining the foreign market values (FMVs)[7] for each Japanese company's chips and monitoring production costs and prices of Japanese-made chips. These prices varied for each firm depending on their costs of manufacture (see *Exhibit 7*). (In their rebuttals to the SIA stance during the 301 case, the Japanese firms sharply criticized the "cost-price" method of determining fair selling values, arguing that it overlooked market conditions). Firms were prohibited from selling chips below the specified price in the United States and third country markets. Prices in Japan were not bound to the FMVs, but Japanese firms were expected not to "undercut" the agreement in Japan. Chips produced in the United States

---

[4]The margins were 11% to 35% of the retail price in 64K DRAMs, 21% to 188% in EPROMs, and 19% to 108% in 256K and up DRAMs. The duties levied varied by firm.

[5]The SIA kept an industry advisory team available to the negotiators for assistance in technical negotiations. Available on site for consultation, this team could tap a network of experts. Aside from the assistance in technical matters, the government found the quick industry feedback on its reactions to various proposals to be helpful in its negotiations.

[6]The announcement of the agreement was one week prior to a scheduled House of Representatives vote to override President Reagan's veto of the Jenkins Bill—a bill that would have significantly cut textile imports.

[7]The term "fair market values" was used during dumping proceedings. The term "foreign market values" was employed after the signing of the 301 agreement.

were not subject to the FMVs, even if produced by the subsidiary of a Japanese firm. The FMVs were to be adjusted quarterly. This specific targeting of individual Japanese companies was highly unusual; the more common procedure was to issue one overall ruling for a country as a whole and let the foreign government work out the details of implementing the policy company by company.

For its part, the United States agreed to suspend the existing dumping suits against Japan and the 301 case. The United States retained the right to reactivate the suits if Japanese firms were found guilty of selling at less than fair value. For the dumping suits, this meant that duties could be reimposed; for the 301 case, President Reagan would have to determine the U.S. government's response. If either country were concerned about possible violation of the agreement or other matters pertaining to the agreement, immediate consultations would be held and would last for a maximum of two weeks.

Reaction to the agreement in the press and among some semiconductor customers was strongly negative. Scalise was taken aback by the vociferous opposition the pact had engendered. Press reaction predominantly portrayed the agreement as protectionism instigated by an American industry that no longer wanted to accept the verdict of the marketplace. Some customers argued that U.S. producers had caused their own troubles by misreading the market in the late 1970s and early 1980s and by failing to keep pace with Japanese improvements in manufacturing. Others saw the agreement as effectively charging customers a premium in order to make the U.S. industry competitive again. In Japan, firms and MITI were unhappy with the agreement but contended that they would abide by the new regulations. European manufacturers accepted the antidumping provisions for the U.S. market but expressed concern that the U.S. industry was being granted discriminatory access to the

Japanese market. The European manufacturers submitted a complaint with GATT that the accord violated multilateral international trade agreements. Scalise spent time in Europe explaining the trade case to major customers and attempting (unsuccessfully) to get the GATT complaint withdrawn. He felt that it was important that the Europeans knew that the agreement called for "foreign capital affiliated firms" to get 20% of the Japanese market, not just U.S. firms.

In early September 1986, several semiconductor customers met with Commerce Department representatives to argue that the semiconductor agreement was forcing them to consider moving production overseas. These customers reported that prices of 256K DRAMs in the United States had risen anywhere from two to eight times the preagreement price and argued that these prices would make U.S. computers and other electronic products noncompetitive in world markets. Indeed, many member firms in the AEA, especially the smaller firms, reacted negatively to the trade agreement and predicted tremendous offshore movement by U.S. companies. In response, the SIA set up a subcommittee within the AEA to deal with user concerns. Scalise felt that the greatest opposition came from firms that did not make their own semiconductors and were not in the SIA.

One AEA official noted that the organization supported the negotiated agreement but was "appalled" by the FMVs issued by Commerce in August. Expressing surprise at the prices, he noted that "we thought they'd use high FMVs as a negotiating tactic, but we never imagined they'd actually put them into effect." Anger in the user community, he reported, was aimed primarily at the price of DRAMs; users had much less trouble with the EPROM prices. Tempers cooled somewhat when the FMVs were adjusted in October. And by March 1987, managers in charge of semiconductor purchasing at several larger computer firms reported that the revised FMVs were not too far off what the market itself would have produced. While they could live in the existing environment, however, several reported that they were "determined to see that things don't go any further."

IMPACT OF THE AGREEMENT

In March 1987, seven months after the chip accord was signed, SIA members were convinced that the Japanese were violating the agreement by selling below fair value in third countries and failing to increase purchases from U.S. semiconductor manufacturers (see *Exhibit 10*). They charged that chips were being bought up cheaply in Japan and then resold in "gray markets." Moreover, they argued that despite substantial commitments by U.S. companies to the Japanese market, both before and after the agreement, there was little impact on sales.[8] The question facing the SIA was what to do next.

Political Environment

The U.S. semiconductor industry seemed surrounded by bad news since the signing of the agreement. In 1986, for the first time, the Japanese market for chips was actually larger than the American, and Japanese firms in total had a larger worldwide semiconductor market share than the Americans.[9] A Japanese firm was the world's largest semiconductor merchant for the first time in 1985, and by 1986 the top three firms were Japanese. Japanese firms held seven of the top ten spots in 1986, up from five in 1982.

The U.S. Congress had become increasingly concerned in the early months of 1987 about the country's trade "competitiveness" and the growing U.S. trade deficits, particularly with Japan. Tension over the alleged violations of the semiconductor agreement was especially high: semiconductor trade had become one of the dominant issues confronting the United States and Japan. A major trade bill which toughened several trade provisions but still retained presidential flexibility in implementing penalties was working through committee hearings. In more focused actions in early March, the House of Representatives voted unanimously and the Senate voted 93–0 to encourage the administration to apply sanctions on Japanese chips.

In the executive branch, the Defense Department's Defense Science Board issued a report in early February that pointed with alarm to the declining U.S. competitiveness in semiconductors and in semiconductor manufacturing equipment. The report called for $1 billion to be provided over five years to shore up American manufacturing ability in semiconductors and painted the loss of the American semiconductor industry as a major national security issue. Another $1 billion was recommended for semiconductor laboratory research. Cabinet-level officials were scheduled to meet to decide what action, if any, to take.

The response from the Japanese govern-

---

[8]Dataquest's *User Update* reported in October 1986 that expected FMVs of $2.50 to $4.00 for 256K DRAMs were apparently undercut in Taiwan, where "prices have remained at $2.00 or less." An SIA memo noted that "the average U.S. share in the first month of a quarter in 1986 (i.e., January, April, July, and October) was 7.9%, a level equal to the January 1987 level. Similarly the gain in share in February 1987 over January 1987 was consistent with the pattern observed within a quarter in 1986. These figures are consistent with our belief that there has been no gain in U.S. market access in Japan."

---

[9]These changes were attributable partly to actual growth in Japan and partly to foreign exchange fluctuations caused by the sharp decline of the dollar in relation to the yen.

ment to the U.S. concerns was mixed. On one hand, MITI requested two reductions in Japanese semiconductor production—the first by an average of 10% and the second by another 11%.[10] These requests were designed to increase prices in Japan in an effort to thwart the gray market (see *Exhibit 8*). On the other hand, the Japanese government also argued that the American firms were not realistic about how quickly their sales in Japan could increase. Moreover, USTR Yeutter, while supporting the U.S. industry's position, noted that the Japanese had become particularly aggressive in trade disputes, largely because of the damaging effects a rapidly rising yen was having on production, sales, and employment. Hints in the press suggested that the Japanese might retaliate if the American government took new measures in semiconductors.[11] The Japanese were also known to be concerned about the pricing threat in memory chips by firms in South Korea and Singapore.

Determining the SIA's Response

Scalise believed the SIA needed to move quickly in this environment of high trade tensions, especially since he felt that the press was now largely in favor of the SIA's position. In early March, the SIA Board approved plans for a multifirm collaborative project known as SEMATECH. Spearheaded by Charles Sporck, president of National Semiconductor, and strongly supported by IBM, SEMATECH was conceived as a laboratory and small production facility where American manufacturing processes could be enhanced and then distributed to the member firms. The SIA Board feared that the United States was falling behind in semiconductor technology, primarily because of deficiencies in process technology (see *Exhibit 9*). Funding of SEMATECH in the SIA plan was to be 50% industry and 50% government. Annual costs were expected to reach $200 million.

The SIA still faced the issue about what to do next in its trade dispute with the Japanese. Several decisions needed to be made. One decision was whether to propose a tariff (duty), a quota, or an embargo. These policies could be applied to semiconductors themselves, to products containing semiconductors produced by the highly diversified Japanese semiconductor companies, or even to unrelated products. If products containing semiconductors were selected, there remained a choice between mass-market items such as videocassette recorders and color televisions, which the Japanese dominated, and markets such as mainframe computers, where they were seeking to build market share. Even the party to target with retaliatory action was not clear. Should the SIA favor company-specific penalties against Japanese firms or propose instead that an overall penalty be imposed on Japan?

Scalise believed the association should act quickly: he was concerned about Reagan's upcoming meeting with Japan's Prime Minister Nakasone within six weeks and the yearly summit talks among the largest industrial nations scheduled for early June. In addition to weighing the pros and cons of these specific choices, Scalise, as head of the Public Policy Committee, had to determine the answers to several more general questions: What would the U.S. government accept? What types of action would lead the Japanese to enforce the agreement? And what would be an acceptable consensus among SIA members?

---

[10] The reductions reflected comparisons to the previous quarter. The 10% cut recommended for the first quarter of 1987 resulted in an actual production cut of nearly 23%. The 11% cut was for the second quarter of 1987.

[11] *New York Times*, 24 March 1987, p. D5.

SIA MEMBERS, 1985

	Represented on[a]		Products[b] sold	Projected sales ($ mil)
	Board of directors	Public policy comm.		
Merchant producers				
Advanced Micro Devices	x	(2)	IC	500–1000
AT&T			Both	N/A
California Devices			IC	10–50
Cherry Semiconductor			IC	10–50
Digital Equipment		x	IC	10–50
General Electric			Both	100–300
General Instrument			Both	100–300
General Semiconductors			D	10–50
GigaBit Logic			IC	<10
Gould AMI	x		IC	100–300
GTE Communication Systems			IC	10–50
Harris	x	(2)	IC	300–500
Intel	x	x	IC	>1000
Int'l Microelectronic Prod.			IC	10–50
International Rectifier		x	D	100–300
ITT			Both	100–300
Linear Technology			IC	10–50
LSI Logic			IC	50–100
Microwave Semiconductor			D	10–50
Monolithic Memories	x		IC	100–300
Mostek	x	x	IC	N/A
Motorola	x	(3)	Both	>1000
National Semiconductor	x	(2)	Both	>1000
NCR			IC	50–100
NEC			IC	500–1000
Precision Monolithics			IC	50–100
Raytheon			Both	N/A
RCA			Both	300–500
Rockwell International	x	(2)	IC	100–300
Siemens Components			Both	10–50
Signetics		x	IC	500–1000
Silicon Systems			IC	50–100
Solid State Scientific			IC	50–100
Sprague Electric			Both	50–100
Telmos			Both	N/A
Texas Instruments	x	x	Both	>1000
Thomson-CSF Components			Both	10–50
Unitrode			Both	100–300
VLSI Technology			IC	50–100
Westinghouse			D	10–50
Xilinx			IC	>10
Zilog			IC	50–100
ZyMOS			IC	10–50
Captive producers				
Burroughs				
Control Data				
Hewlett-Packard	x	(2)		
IBM	x	x		
Northern Telecom				

[a]Numerals represent the number of representatives on the committee. An x indicates one representative.
[b]IC = integrated circuits; D = discrete semiconductors.
Source: Semiconductor Industry Association, *1985–86 Yearbook and Directory.*

EXHIBIT TWO

U.S.-BASED SEMICONDUCTOR COMPANIES' WORLDWIDE SALES ($ billions)

1975	1976	1977	1978	1979	1980	1981	1982	1983	1984	1985	1986
2.6	3.4	3.9	4.8	6.6	8.4	7.8	8.0	9.6	14.0	10.6	10.7

Pretax income as percent of sales

1975	1976	1977	1978	1979	1980	1981	1982	1983	1984	1985	1986
NA	NA	NA	NA	NA	13.4	4.7	−0.1	7.9	15.0	−6.5	−6.0

Percent worldwide market share—U.S.-based firms

1975	1976	1977	1978	1979	1980	1981	1982	1983	1984	1985	1986
61	57	62	55	60	61	57	57	55	54	50	43

Percent worldwide market share—Japan-based firms

1975	1976	1977	1978	1979	1980	1981	1982	1983	1984	1985	1986
20	26	25	29	27	28	30	33	36	37	40	45

Source: World Semiconductor Statistics.

EXHIBIT THREE

U.S. SHARE OF JAPANESE MARKET VERSUS JAPANESE SHARE OF U.S. MARKET

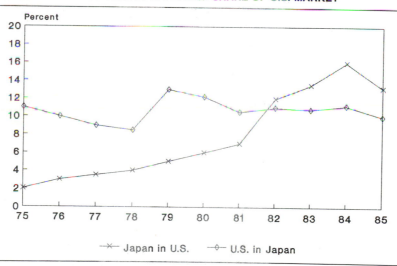

—×— Japan in U.S.   —◇— U.S. in Japan

Source: Adapted from Dataquest, August 1987.

"LIBERALIZATION" MEASURES, U.S. INVESTMENT ATTEMPTS, AND YEN APPRECIATION HAVE HAD LITTLE EFFECT ON U.S. MERCHANT FIRMS' PENETRATION OF THE JAPANESE MARKET

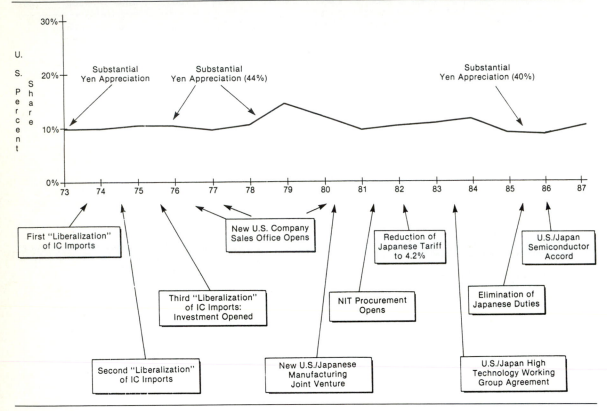

Source: SIA.

° EXHIBIT FIVE

U.S. SEMICONDUCTOR EMPLOYMENT, 1984

State	Percent of total U.S. semiconductor employment	Semiconductor industry employment (1000s)
Arizona	11.5	31.7
California	32.4	89.0
Florida	3.2	8.7
Massachusetts	4.2	11.5
New Jersey	2.2	6.0
New York	9.6	26.2
Oregon	3.0	8.2
Pennsylvania	5.3	14.5
Texas	14.1	38.8
Utah	3.2	8.7
Vermont	3.2	8.7
12 other states (<2% each)	7.1	21.9
Industry total	100	274.0
Total merchant	46	127.0
Total captive	54	147.0

Source: U.S. Census of Manufacturers, 1982; U.S. Bureau of Labor Statistics.

EXHIBIT SIX

256K DRAM REGIONAL PRICING

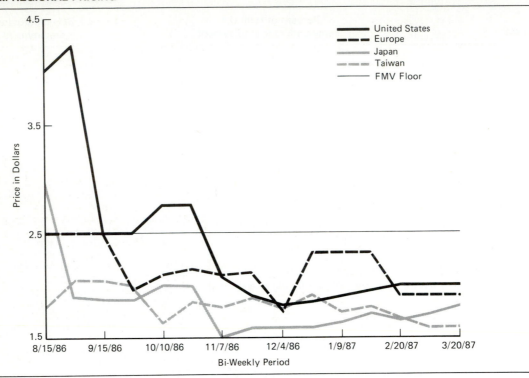

Source: Dataquest.

EXHIBIT SEVEN

DETERMINATION OF FOREIGN MARKET VALUES

The Department of Commerce used a formula to construct the quarterly foreign market values (FMVs). This formula (A + B + C + D = foreign market value) was made up of the following four parts:

A. Material costs, including some R&D
B. Fabrication costs
C. General sales and administrative expenses, including some R&D (not less than 10 percent of the above two costs)
D. Profit (not less than 8 percent of the above three costs)

The formula was applied on a company-by-company basis using proprietary cost information to determine the minimum price of each company's products. This method used real-time fabrication cost data in determining FMVs. The capacity utilization of a given company at a given time determined in large part what that company's FMV would be. A company running at 80 percent capacity would have lower fabrication costs per unit than a company running at 50 percent capacity. The initial capacity utilization rate used could determine which companies would be continually competitive and which would continue to be uncompetitive, since a profit always had to be added to a higher manufacturing cost.

Source: Excerpted from Dataquest, *User Update*, October 1986.

EXHIBIT EIGHT

STORY ON KYODO (JAPAN) NEWSWIRE

Japanese Strongly Concerned About Senate Call On Chips

Tokyo, March 20, 1987—Japan has reacted with strong concern about the U.S. Senate resolution calling for retaliation against Japan for failing to honor the bilateral pact on orderly trade in semiconductors. Hajime Tamura, Minister of International Trade and Industry, personally asked representatives of 10 major Japanese chipmakers to ensure there are no exceptions to the agreement which calls for chip prices to be maintained at fair market prices in Japan, the U.S., and third countries. He said allegations of dumping in third countries at well below the Japanese and U.S. prices must not be allowed and he called on presidents, vice presidents, and managing directors of 10 major Japanese users of microchips to step up their own buying of semiconductors from U.S. manufacturers. The 10 represent some 40% of the Japanese market for semiconductors.

Prime Minister Yasuhiro Nakasone also stepped into the fray and ordered Tamura to ensure there are concrete results from the pact. . . . MITI is to announce a guideline on April–June chip production in Japan soon and is expected to call for a 20% to 30% reduction in Japanese output. Japanese chipmakers also expressed concern about the Senate resolution which passed 93–0 and indicated they will follow MITI production guidelines when they are set, probably next week.

EXHIBIT NINE

STATUS AND TRENDS OF U.S. SEMICONDUCTOR TECHNOLOGY RELATIVE TO JAPAN

	Japan lead	U.S.–Japan parity	U.S. lead
Silicon products			
DRAMs	<		
SRAMs	<		
KPROMs		●	
Microprocessors			<
Custom, semicustom logic			<
Bipolar	<		
Nonsilicon products			
Memory	<		
Logic	<		
Linear			●
Optoelectronics	<		
Heterostructures	<		
Materials			
Silicon	<		
Callium arsenide	<		
Processing equipment			
Optical lithography		<	
E-Beam lithography			<
X-ray lithography		<	
Ion implantation technology			
Chemical vapor deposition		●	
Deposition, diffusion, other		●	
Energy-assisted processing	<		
Assembly		●	
Packaging	<		
Test	<		
CAE		●	
CAM		<	

< U.S. position declining.
● U.S. position maintaining.
Source: Interagency working Groups on Semiconductor Technology.

EXHIBIT TEN

U.S. SALES IN JAPAN, CALENDAR YEAR 1986

	Q1	Q2	Q3	Q3	Total
U.S.-based sales	178,730	223,960	241,890	230,800	875,370
Japan market	2,235,00	2,563,000	2,905,000	2,769,000	10,472,000
U.S. share	8.0%	8.7%	8.6%	8.3%	8.4%

Source: World Semiconductor Trade Statistics; Japanese Ministry of International Trade and Industry; Japanese Ministry of Finance.

Intel Corporation 1988

Sitting in one of the standard Intel cubicles, Andy Grove, Intel's president and CEO, told a newly hired consultant that "our most important challenge is how to use our momentum to continue our growth. Success must be based on a vision of the future, a strategy to optimize growth in promising areas." The consultant's job would be to assess Intel's present position and to offer recommendations on the company's future. The key question was: How should Grove position the firm for long-run growth vis-à-vis its more diversified and vertically integrated American and Japanese competitors?

The following account is a synopsis of the major issues in the consultant's report. In addition to reviewing company documents and interviewing key executives, she talked with customers, investment bankers, and competitors. Particular attention was given to the sys-

tems business, estimated by investment analysts to gross almost $800 million in revenue in 1988. The consultant thought that Grove and Intel management needed to address the future of the systems division and its relationship with the rest of Intel.

THE HISTORY OF INTEL

Intel was founded in 1968 by Robert Noyce and Gordon Moore, both pioneers in the semiconductor industry. Intel's original business mission was to "design, develop, manufacture, and market advanced memory circuits for digital equipment." Intel was one of the first companies to develop and commercialize the industry's three primary memory devices. In 1969, Intel introduced its first product, a static random access memory (SRAM) chip. Also in that year, Intel announced a 64-bit random access memory chip, and shortly thereafter, 256-bit and 1024-bit chips. Although Intel was not the first to introduce dynamic RAMs (DRAMs) in 1970, its DRAMs quickly gained a major share and became the industry standard. Within two years, Intel's DRAMs had become the largest

This case was written by Research Associates Ralinda Lurie and Ben Huston and Associate Professor David B. Yoffie as a basis for class discussion rather than to illustrate either effective or ineffective handling of an administrative situation.

selling semiconductor component in the world. In 1971, Intel introduced the first erasable programmable read-only memory (EPROM) chip. Although the true significance of this innovation did not become apparent for several years, EPROMs could be reprogrammed and thus provided an alternative for cost-effective means of storing information. Intel led the market for programmable memory devices with each successive generation of EPROMs. This high-volume product also helped the company to refine its manufacturing techniques and served as technology and process drivers for its future family of logic products.

While Intel continued to innovate in memory chips, its next important technological breakthrough was a logic product—the microprocessor. In the early 1970s, Intel proclaimed that its programmable microcomputer on a chip had "ushered in a new era of integrated electronics." Although these new microprocessors were clearly revolutionary, there were no existing markets for the products. Intel's response to the uncertainty in the marketplace was to educate the technical community and to manufacture board-level products which made microprocessors easier to use. Intel's second generation microprocessor, the 8080, led to the most successful microprocessor product families of the 1980s: the 8086 and 8088. Along with Intel's technological success came substantial financial returns. Starting with sales of $2,672 in 1968, both revenues and profits grew at compounded annual growth rates of nearly 65% from 1971 to 1980. (See Exhibit 1.) Intel became one of the fastest-growing and most profitable merchant semiconductor firms in the world.

After more than a decade of continued prosperity, however, Intel's financial results suffered. Intel's initial strategy was to be the first mover, continually introducing new products for which it could demand premium prices. Intel would then withdraw from mature markets where products had become commodities.

This strategy worked as long as the company had developed revolutionary products every few years. During the 1980s, however, Intel introduced fewer revolutionary products and the company had made some mistakes. For instance, after failing several times to produce a competitive 256K DRAM, Intel fell so far behind Japanese chipmakers that it decided to withdraw from DRAMs.[1] A few years later, Intel stumbled in the application specific integrated circuits (ASIC) business. ASICs—which included gate arrays (GAs), cell-based integrated circuits (CBICs), and programmable logic devices (PLDs)—were expected to be a $9 billion market by 1989. These were all semicustom chips which customers would create using Intel design tools and proprietary "cells" as building blocks. After an enthusiastic but late start in 1985, Intel signed a number of technology exchange agreements with other firms attempting to enter the business. Citing competitive pressures and the problems of being a late entrant, the company withdrew from the merchant gate array business in April 1988 and integrated its PLD and CBIC businesses into the logic division.

INTEL IN 1988

Although the early 1980s were difficult, Intel made record profits in 1988. Most semiconductor firms also reported healthy profits during the year. (See Exhibits 2 and 3.) After a significant pruning of product lines and restructuring of manufacturing operations in 1985–1986, Intel had rededicated itself to being the leading "microcomputer" company. Featured on the cover of Business Week in September 1988, Intel was proclaimed by the press and the in-

---

[1] Intel management estimated in 1988 that the cost of reentering the DRAM market, which would include rehiring designers and building fabrication facilities, could be as much as $400 million.

vestment community to be one of the premier American manufacturers of "electronic building blocks" used by original equipment manufacturers (OEMs).[2] Even the CEO of AMD proclaimed 1988 the "glory year for Intel." Intel's biggest market was the computer industry, and its biggest customers included IBM (14.5% of Intel's sales), Ford Motor, and Compaq Computer. Although the company's Product Guide listed well over 300 different product lines, these lines could be divided into three distinct groups: memory components, which manufactured EPROMs; logic products, such as microprocessors and microcontrollers; and systems, which included everything from boards to supercomputers. About one-third of Intel's revenues came from sales to electronics distributors who resold to tens of thousands of customers. Intel serviced its biggest customers directly with one of the largest technical sales forces in the industry (over 650 field engineers and salespeople worldwide). Since 1985, Intel also sold add-in products for personal computers through a network of over 1500 retail computer stores.

Memory Products

In 1988, Intel was active in only one type of memory products—EPROMs. The company, along with the entire semiconductor industry, had lost money in EPROMs and other memory segments since 1985. The July 1986 trade agreement between the United States and Japan in which the Japanese firms agreed not to dump semiconductors had a beneficial effect on EPROM prices. During 1987, Intel maintained its position as the world's number one supplier of EPROM's, with a market share ranging from 16.0% to 39.0% across the density spectrum.

In March of 1988, Intel entered into a three-year marketing agreement with U.S. manufacturer Micron Technology to market DRAMs stamped with the Intel trademark. In the short run, Intel planned to sell these commodity products through its distribution channels. One analyst commented that "before this move, Intel was like a supermarket without a dairy section." Intel had signed a similar marketing agreement for memory products with Samsung Electronics, a Korean firm, in 1987.

Logic Products

While memory accounted for 90% of Intel's revenues in 1972, logic products accounted for approximately 90% of chips sales in 1988. Intel's strongest logic products were microprocessors—a business which took off after IBM chose Intel's 8088 for its personal computers in 1980. Intel's position as the industry standard was reinforced when IBM adopted the 80286 for its PC AT and the 80386 chip for its high-end PS/2 computers. In 1982, IBM went so far as to acquire a 20% interest in Intel to help ensure its survival. In 1987, however, IBM sold the last of its remaining shares in the company. By that time, the IBM and IBM-compatible PCs had grown to approximately 5.5 million units. Each of these computers incorporated one of three different types of Intel-based microprocessors, with approximately 46% using the 8088 (or a slight variant, the 8086), 49% using the 80286 chip, and the remaining 5% using the relatively new 80386 chip.

National Semiconductor, Motorola, and AT&T successfully introduced 32-bit micropro-

---

[2]Intel's reputation, symbolized in the *Business Week* cover story, was that the company had brilliant leadership at the top and many of the best chip designers in the world. However, investment analysts as well as some insiders expressed concern about the depth of Intel's management, especially since Andy Grove planned to retire in a few years, Gordon Moore had reduced his active management role, and Bob Noyce had left to run SEMATECH. Intel's strong internal culture—which emphasized decentralized responsibilities, openness, and constructive confrontation—created a familylike environment for insiders. This made it difficult for the company to assimilate newcomers at a very high management level.

cessors up to two years before Intel, but the 80386 chip quickly captured the momentum. Produced over a four-year period at a total cost of about $200 million, the 80386 was becoming the new PC standard. As a member of Intel's 86 architectural family, the 386 ran all the software available for its 8- and 16-bit microprocessors, which amounted to $10 billion worth of programs by 1987. The 386 could also handle multiple tasks at one time and run Microsoft's DOS and OS/2 as well as AT&T's UNIX.

Historically, the company was pressured by its customers, including IBM, to provide second sources for its microprocessors: by 1987, there were 12 second sources for the 8086, leaving Intel with less than a 30% share of the chips' revenues and profits. Royalties received by Intel for transferring this technology were insignificant compared to the lost revenues. For the 80286, Intel had limited the number of second sources to only four firms and, consequently, had achieved 75% of the revenues and profits. While it had granted IBM the sole license to manufacture the 80386 (ASP $250) for its own captive demand, Intel desired to maintain tight control over the manufacturing and marketing of its 386 chip. Intel also introduced a low-cost version of the 386 in 1988, known as the 80386SX (ASP $150).[3] Ultimately, Intel's decision to maintain a proprietary sole source position on the 80386 chips meant that the company would have to dedicate a significant portion of its existing production capacity to meet market demand. This included building new front-end fabrication facilities, which cost up to $200 million each.[4]

Intel's next-generation superchip design, the 80486, was expected to lead the new age of "personal mainframes." Produced at an estimated cost of around of $300 million, the 486 was targeted to be the high-end workstation and mainframe markets. (See *Exhibit 3*.) In July of 1988, a major trade journal reported that the company's new 80486 CPU would have 1 million transistors versus 275,000 for the 386, be fully compatible with 386, include a math coprocessor (which increased a computer's computational capabilities), operate at speeds up to two to three times the 386, and run DOS, OS/2, and UNIX operating systems. The microprocessor's initial high price, estimated by analysts at close to $1,000, would restrict its use for the mass market. Desktop products using the 486 would probably sell for about $20,000. However, industry experts expected the price eventually to fall low enough for use in the broader desktop market. Small quantities of the 486 were projected to be available in mid-1989.

Systems

Intel developed, manufactured, sold, and supported a broad line of subsystem- and system-level products built largely around its microprocessor technology and sold through the corporate sales force. The consultant concluded that corporate management had mixed

[3]The 386SX—which could run OS/2, DOS, and UNIX— was compatible with 16-bit PCs. This made a system with an SX microprocessor cheaper to design and manufacture. Intel hoped that its 286 chip, which ran at 12 MHz (ASP $25), would be used for the very low end of the PC market; and the SX, which ran at 16 MHz, would compete successfully with AMD's 16-MHz 80286 (ASP $75). In late 1988, the verdict was still undecided.

[4]Analysts estimated that 386 sales accounted for 30% to 40% of total Intel revenues in 1988. Corporate profits were even more dependent upon the 386. When the company announced in November 1988 that supply had caught up with demand, customers who had been hoarding 386s immediately cut their bookings. Intel had overexpanded capacity, and fourth-quarter profits headed lower. One analyst speculated that "it looks like every dollar of sales [that Intel won't make on the 386] is a dollar of lost profit." (*Wall Street Journal*, 11/21/88, p. B4.)

feelings about the systems division, which included four relatively distinct businesses in 1988: OEM systems, which included boards, OEM PCs, and software and hardware tools (analysts estimated sales to be around $400 million in 1988); PCEO (personal computer enhancement operations, with estimated retail sales of $200 million); a start-up operation in supercomputers; and a service business, which primarily serviced Intel's systems (approximately $100 million sales). Although top management had stated for several years that systems should be 50% of corporate revenues, there remained considerable differences about the appropriate mission for systems, its general lack of visibility in the end-user market, and its lack of independent momentum. While systems, along with the rest of Intel, had a spectacular year in 1988, its growth was less than that for components.

OEM Systems The primary thrust of the system business had been to provide semiconductor technology to OEM customers at any level of integration. One departure from this strategy came in 1972 when Intel acquired Microma, a small firm that had a prototype digital watch. Intel executives thought they had a sufficient repertoire of relevant production, technology, and assembly capabilities to compete in this market. However, the company soon exited because it lacked distribution channels, consumer marketing expertise, and the money needed to develop the requisite skills. Gordon Moore still wears his Microma watch. He claims that "it is to remind me, if I ever find myself thinking of getting into other consumer products, of the trouble we'd be getting into."

To encourage sales of its 8080 microprocessor, Intel pioneered what some industry experts considered the world's first "personal computer," the Series 2 development system. Introduced in 1977, these systems, which were similar to the early Apple computers and sold for comparable prices, were primarily used for

hardware design and software development. In the mid-1980s, Intel was selling its systems (prices ranging from $8,000 to $30,000) to customers who were designing the 8086 microprocessor into their end products. At its peak in 1984, analysts estimated that the development system business generated more than $200 million a year. By 1988, however, the commercialization of PCs, workstations, and other alternative design techniques led to the virtual disappearance of this business.[5]

Microcomputer products for the OEM market represented the largest segment of the systems business. Intel offered bus products, real-time computers for system OEMs, and building blocks for other computer OEMs. Intel's board business, for instance, enabled its customers to reduce development time for new products that incorporated Intel microprocessors and other related chips. According to Les Vadasz, general manager of the systems group, "We were so early in both semiconductor memories and in microprocessors that many of our customers did not have the ability to use them. They didn't have the technical capabilities, nor could they really afford it. So we saw a business opportunity by moving up to board-level products." One of the company's most successful board-level products was its "bus" business. Intel's MULTIBUS products, which were boards

---

[5]Another "missed opportunity" cited by insiders was the systems group's foray into database processing and transaction processing systems. Like the development system, this product was closer to a building block than an integrated system which fully satisfied customer needs. In addition, one of the managers of the project noted that Intel "was late to market," had "lousy execution, with an inferior product and technology, and used the wrong sales approach." The manager went on to explain that the systems group continually felt hamstrung by the component group and corporate management. "Santa Clara [corporate headquarters] is so concerned not to step on the toes of its major customers," he said, " that the systems group is like a fighter entering arenas with one hand always tied behind his back."

that allowed the components of a system (central processing unit, input-output, peripherals, and memory) to be connected to one another, had become the industry leader in the OEM market.

One of Intel's largest OEM product lines was a recent offering: the 386 platform introduced in 1987. (See *Exhibit 6*.) The 386 platforms were computers without screens or keyboards. Sold at both the board and box levels, OEMs turned these platforms into finished computer products for end-user applications. Essentially a commodity business where high sales volume was critical, this type of operation required little manufacturing investment relative to the semiconductor business. By the early 1990s, the total market for 386 platforms was expected to be 2 million units (ASP $1,500). Vadasz hoped that he could win 30% of this business, and according to the press, Intel had won very large OEM contracts from Unisys and AT&T.

Although the systems group was not treated differently from other customers of Intel's component division, Vadasz thought that he had two potential competitive advantages: economies of scale, which could be realized in platforms, and close personal ties with Intel's microcomponent personnel. If systems engineers worked closely with component engineers, they could get board-level products to market up to six months before many competitors.[6] Thus when Intel announced the 80386, the systems group was the first to introduce a myriad of board-level 386 products.

PCEO   PC enhancement products were another major product segment within the systems group. Started as an entrepreneurial venture in 1984, PCEO sold add-in boards and components directly to end users. PCEO's major product lines, which often included no Intel silicon, were memory expansion boards and math coprocessors (80387s). Management attributed the success of PCEO to Intel's strong name recognition among computer specialists and the company's ability to work with software vendors to establish its products as industry standards.

Service and Supercomputers   Intel's systems group had two other divisions in 1988: a service business, whose primary function was to maintain the installed base of Intel's OEM systems[7] and an experimental development program, launched in 1986, in the supercomputer business. The company had designed fast computers that combined hypercube interconnect and parallel processing technologies with Intel 286 and 386 microprocessor technologies. The company's ultimate goal was to develop a new market for this class of computer, which would reach at least $100 million in revenue by the 1990s. By 1988, the supercomputer operation has broken even, and Intel could boast the largest installed base of hypercube parallel processing supercomputers.

---

[6]Relations between the components and systems were not always smooth. Several managers interviewed from the systems group, which was located in Portland, Oregon, complained that customers such as Compaq and IBM often got better information and delivery. In addition, they complained that systems had a much harder time getting resources than its semiconductor counterparts. In the meantime, a few executives in the component division in Santa Clara, California, expressed a lack of confidence in the systems group and concern that systems was competing with its customers. While the two divisions operated at arm's length, the systems group bought chips from the component group at its "best customer" price. Each division had its own P&L, and performance was assessed by various measures of profitability, with the most recent focus on return on assets.

[7]About 25% of the service business revenue came from maintaining Intel's development systems; about 40%, from servicing platforms sold to the U.S. army; and the remainder, from networking and servicing Intel supercomputers, other PCs, and mainframes.

CONFUSION IN THE DESKTOP PRODUCTS MARKET

For buyers, 1988 was one of the most uncertain periods in the history of the personal computer business. Both hardware and software standards were proliferating.[8] In September of 1988, for instance, nine IBM PC clone manufacturers joined forces to make an unprecedented challenge on IBM's efforts to establish the design standard for future personal computers with its new PS/2 model. The focus of their challenge was the announcement of an alternative bus to IBM's new Micro Channel, which was an electronic conduit that moved data within the PC. Intel's components group (operating totally independent of the systems group, which had its own bus product) had participated in this new effort by implementing in silicon the design for the new bus standard. More than 80 companies expressed their support for this rival conduit.

The software market was also jammed with vendor choices for DOS, OS/2, and various flavors of UNIX. Some analysts were speculating that Intel's PC dominance could be threatened by the obsolescence of DOS, or software compatibility bridges, technically known as emulation and binary recompilation. One possibility was that software vendors might write new operating systems which would replace DOS, become the new industry standard, and run on most microprocessors. If new versions of major application software, such as Lotus 1-2-3, were written for such an operating system, and the user was able to import all his or her data, the costs of switching to a new system would be reduced. A more direct threat, but technically very difficult, was emulation. It was hypothetically possible for a chip manufacturer to design a system with non-Intel-architecture processors and still have access to the PC software base with acceptable performance. Finally, binary compilation allowed existing programs to be translated into another processor's machine language while losing little of the efficiency of the original implementation. This would make it theoretically possible to convert PC programs to run at much higher speeds on a non-Intel architecture. By November of 1988, Motorola had announced a new software product, called XDOS, which was pioneered by a third party vendor. XDOS enable UNIX workstations and other departmental computers designed around the Motorola's 68000 and 88000 family of microprocessors to run programs written for IBM and IBM-compatible personal computers. Since nontechnical users did not have the expertise to take advantage of XDOS, it was still a highly inefficient way to compete with Intel architecture. Motorola nonetheless claimed that popular PC programs could be converted into UNIX programs and run with comparable speed.

RISC TECHNOLOGY

In 1988, new battle lines were being drawn in the microprocessor market. RISC, or reduced instruction set computing, began to gain momentum in the market. RISC, a revolutionary microprocessor design technique first investigated by IBM in the 1970s, increased speed by streamlining the number of "hard-wired" instructions that a semiconductor must process. RISC technology was said to compute faster than traditional CISC (complex instruction set computing) microprocessors, such as the 386. By 1988, applications for this new breed of chip could be split into two distinct markets: application-specific embedded processors/controllers[9] and engineering workstation/business

---

[8]An elaboration of many of these trends may be found in "Note on Microcomputers: Overview of PCs and Workstations," #9-389-136.

[9]Microcontrollers were used for controlling and monitoring equipment and real-time events. A typical application would be to control the fuel mixture in a car engine.

computer systems. Dataquest predicted that RISC's share of the worldwide 32-bit microprocessor market would grow from 9% in 1988 to nearly 39% by 1992. By and large, desktop systems designed using a RISC chip were entering the market with UNIX operating systems. A growing number of U.S. semiconductor and systems vendors—including Motorola, Sun Microsystems, and MIPS Computer Systems—were betting that workstations built around RISC semiconductor technology would take over that market within two years.

One of the greatest impediments to more rapid growth in RISC microprocessors was the lack of a software base. During 1988, several commercial RISC vendors had formed consortiums to recruit large software companies to write programs for their chips. While several other systems vendors had developed their own proprietary RISC CPU designs for internal consumption, the commercial RISC contenders were hoping that their RISC microprocessor chips would ultimately become the new industry-standard hardware platforms in a new age of fast computing.

In late 1988, Intel planned to introduce two of its own RISC chips, one for the embedded controller market and one for the high-end technical workstation market. The RISC processor designed for technical workstations would not be DOS compatible or compatible with the 86 family architecture, but it would outperform other RISC chips presently available.

COMPETITIVE ENVIRONMENT

By 1988, Intel was the eighth largest semiconductor company in terms of revenue and the third largest manufacturer of MOS ICs.[10] (See

---

[10]MOS (metal oxide silicon) was a process for making ICs which produced chips that consumed less power than major alternative bipolar processes.

Exhibit 4.) In her report to Intel, the consultant noted several important structural characteristics and trends in the industry that could affect Intel's future prospects. The first of these trends was the growing market for MOS chips in Japan (see Exhibit 5) and the improved competitive position of vertically integrated Japanese electronics companies. Although the semiconductor industry began in the United States and was dominated by American firms for its first three decades, Japanese production surpassed the United States in dollar value in 1986. Japan had targeted the semiconductor industry as a strategic means for achieving dominance in a variety of downstream markets such as consumer electronics and computers.

Initially, Japanese companies licensed semiconductor technology. But as product innovations became more evolutionary rather than revolutionary, their skill at making incremental improvements in older technologies appeared to give the Japanese firms an increasing advantage in the mid-1980s. They had also set the standards in manufacturing efficiency by focusing on high-volume production, channeling significant financial resources to the development of production expertise, using dedicated instead of multiple-line plants, and continually innovating process technology. In the words of one Intel executive, ". . . Japanese firms make investments in production technology that often cannot be justified on an ROI basis. They are often able to build larger plants that are more organized with larger clean rooms and more automation. Success in this industry is made easier when a company has a cash cow that can support leading edge investments."

The consultant also noted that the biggest American firms, Motorola and Texas Instruments, were more horizontally integrated than Intel. Motorola's main business sectors included communications and semiconductor products for the commercial, industrial, nonprofit, governmental, and consumer markets. Motorola applied its expertise as an electronic end-equipment manufacturer in distributed data systems, advanced military electronics systems and equipment, computer-based radio/telephone systems, and information processing equipment and components for the automotive, industrial equipment, and major appliance industries. It was rumored that Motorola was preparing to enter the engineering workstation market in 1989 using its own RISC technology.

Texas Instruments focused on its semiconductor and defense electronics businesses, with semiconductors serving as the foundation for its other business activities. Recently, the company had invested in knowledge-based systems, industrial automation, and computer-aided software engineering. Through an agreement with Apple Computer, TI planned to deliver artificial intelligence capabilities to desktop computers. One observer argued that the company's objective was to "build on the synergy between its semiconductor and defense electronics businesses" in order to integrate its silicon and systems expertise.

Another persistent trend in the semiconductor industry was the formation of alliances. According to Dataquest, "The adversarial, contractual relationships of merchant semiconductor companies has tended to promote fragmentation and instability in the industry. Cooperation of buyers and sellers of products all along the product chain has become essential, and the concept of 'virtual vertical integration' has come into vogue. Its advocates urge that product development alliances be extended into joint-manufacturing agreements, long-term purchase contracts, and other relationships that help justify capacity expansions." In order for both component and systems companies to compete in this new business environment, many chose to combine their resources with other firms that could offer the necessary expertise. For instance, DEC signed joint technology agreements for network computing with Apple and Compaq in 1988, both

established competitors in the personal computer market. In another example, Sun Microsystems was one of the first players in the systems business to design and commercialize its own RISC microprocessor chip. Sun subcontracted the manufacturing of the silicon to merchant semiconductor houses. AT&T had also agreed to a partnership with Sun Microsystems to improve its UNIX operating system. Intel's most recent alliance was its formation of a joint venture in computers with Siemens.

THE INTEL/SIEMENS ALLIANCE

In 1988, Intel announced the formation of a new company, BiiN (pronounced "bine") Partners, jointly owned (50%-50%) with Siemens AG, a West German electronics conglomerate. Analysts estimated that Intel and Siemens each spent more than $100 million on the joint venture as well as committed hundreds of design and engineering staff personnel to BiiN's Portland, Oregon, headquarters.[11] BiiN was to manufacture and market fault-tolerant computer systems for mission-critical markets, such as CAD/CAM, military applications, computer-integrated manufacturing, and on-line transaction processing (OLTP). (Fault-tolerant computers were specially designed to never crash or go down.) Intel and Siemens believed that existing computer architectures were inadequate for such tasks and that the base technology existed to create a new architecture that met the market's requirements. The BiiN series of secure multiprocessing systems were based on a flexible building-block approach to hardware and software.

---

[11]Both Siemens and Intel planned for BiiN to be self-sufficient and independently operated. There would be little or no transferring of people between companies, and all transactions were done at arm's length. No provisions were made for personnel who left Siemens or Intel for BiiN to return to their original jobs.

The OLTP market segment alone was approximately $16 billion in 1987 and was presently dominated by IBM, DEC, Stratus, and Tandem Computers. The largest segment was estimated to be on-line transaction processing, followed by computer-integrated manufacturing, battle management, and medical systems. The most optimistic analyst projections were that BiiN would break even in two to three years and sell $500 million annually by 1992.

BiiN utilized proprietary microprocessor technology from Intel (that would not be sold to third parties). Although the volume was low, Intel had high yields on these microprocessors because they were manufactured with the same process and on the same lines as the 386. Eventually BiiN expected to develop its own design and technological capabilities. BiiN also anticipated significant benefits from its access to Siemens' European distribution and service network. As one analyst described BiiN: "Intel has been in the high-performance systems business for 12 years, but people still think of them as a chip company. This is another move in (expanding toward) that direction." BiiN shipped its first computers in the fall of 1988.

EXHIBIT ONE

INTEL CORPORATION, HISTORICAL FINANCIAL STATISTICS

In millions

	1978	1979	1980	1981	1982	1983	1984	1985	1986	1987[b]	1988
Net revenues	$399	$661	$855	$789	$900	$1,122	$1,629	$1,365	$1,265	$1,907	$2,875
Cost of sales	196	313	399	458	542	624	883	943	861	1,043	1,506
Research & development	41	67	96	116	131	142	180	195	228	260	318
Marketing/general administration	76	132	176	184	199	217	316	287	311	358	456
Operating income (loss)	85	149	183	30	28	139	250	(60)	(195)[a]	246	594
Net income (loss)	44	78	97	27	30	116	198	2	(173)	248	453
Cash & short-term investments	28	34	128	115	85	389	231	361	373	630	930
Long-term investments[c]										204	422
Inventories	52	79	91	97	122	152	219	171	198	236	366
Net investment in plant & equipment	160	217	321	412	462	504	778	848	779	891	1,123
Total assets	357	500	767	872	1,056	1,680	2,029	2,152	2,080	2,499	3,550
Short-term debt	44	19	12	32	75	81	66	89	112	195	200
Long-term debt	—	—	150	150	197	128	146	271	287	298	479
Shareholders' equity	205	303	433	488	552	1,122	1,360	1,421	1,275	1,276	2,080
Capital expenditures	$104	$97	$156	$157	$138	$145	$388	$236	$155	$302	$362
Number of employees	10.9	14.3	15.9	16.8	19.4	21.5	25.4	21.3	18.2	19.2	20.8
Average ROE	25.0%	30.6%	26.3%	5.9%	5.8%	13.9%	16.0%	0.1%	n.m.	19.7%	27.0%
Market valuation[d]	607	1,065	1,658	1,400	1,454	3,656	3,692	1,420	n.m.	4,725	5,025
Book value[e]	206	303	283	487	552	1,126	1,363	1,420	1,275	1,304	1,838

[a] Includes $60 million for "restructuring of operation" in 1986.
[b] Among *Fortune* 500 companies in 1987, Intel ranked as follows: 200th in sales, 91st in profits, and 43rd in earnings per share.
[c] Long-term investments are primarily liquid and are stated at cost, which approximates market value.
[d] Market valuation = average stock price * # shares outstanding.
[e] Book value = book value/share * # shares outstanding.
Source: Intel Corporation annual reports and *Value Line*.

EXHIBIT TWO

A. ESTIMATED REVENUES BY PRODUCT LINE ($ millions)

Intel revenues	1983	1984	1985	1986	1987	1988E	1989E
Semiconductor							
Microprocessor							
8-bit, incl. 8086	315.8	418.5	95.2	24.4	11.7	4.5	2.0
80186/80286	27.7	282.2	444.4	410.9	475.5	450.0	334.2
80386	—	—	1.9	42.9	349.1	1,100.0	2,295.4
Subtotal	343.5	700.7	541.5	478.2	836.3	1,554.5	2,631.6
MOS memory							
EPROM	236.6	210.7	180.2	185.8	203.2	310.5	416.7
DRAM	66.2	61.1	25.1	—	—	—	—
SRAM	13.3	54.7	49.0	48.2	40.5	—	—
Other	18.9	65.6	58.0	25.3	23.0	24.0	24.0
Subtotal	335.0	392.1	312.3	259.3	266.7	334.5	440.7
Telecomm, ASIC, and other semiconductor	123.3	209.2	206.1	208.3	250.0	276.0	334.0
Total semiconductor	801.8	1,302.0	1,059.9	945.8	1,353.0	2,165.0	3,406.3
Systems	321.2	327.3	319.0	329.6	550.1	800.0	n.a.

Source: Prudential Bache Securities and case writer's estimates; 1988 numbers slightly overestimated revenues.

EXHIBIT TWO

B. ESTIMATED PROFITABILITY BY PRODUCT LINE ($ millions)

Intel operating profits	1985	1986	1987	1988E	1989E
Semiconductor					
Microprocessor					
8-bit, incl. 8086	− $4.0	− $0.5	$0.0	$0.0	$0.0
80186/80286	14.1	5.5	92.4	79.9	76.0
80386	− 11.5	− 8.5	96.6	431.0	713.0
Subtotal	− 1.4	− 3.5	189.0	510.9	789.0
MOS memory	− 65.4	− 123.7	3.4	30.0	54.0
Telecom, ASIC, and other semiconductor	3.6	− 4.8	15.1	32.9	56.9
Total semiconductor	− 63.2	− 132.0	207.5	573.8	899.9
Systems	3.0	− 0.8	38.5	76.5	n.a.

Source: Prudential Bache Securities and case writer's estimates.

EXHIBIT TWO

C. ANNUAL REVENUES AND EARNINGS FOR YEAR ENDING DECEMBER 1988

Company	Revenue	Net income
	($M)	($M)
AMD[a]	1,126.9	8.5
Cypress Semiconductor[b]	122.5	18.5
Intel	2,875.0	453.0
Motorola[c,d]	8,250.0	444.8
National	2,469.8	50.0
Siliconix	127.3	3.1
Texas Instruments[c,d]	6,300.0	323.2
VLSI Technology[c]	221.4	6.8
Western Digital	768.2	42.9

[a]Earnings reflect a $17.5 million nonrecurring charge for restructuring in 4Q88.
[b]Results reported for year ending September 1988.
[c]Estimates.
[d]Semiconductor revenues accounted for less than half of total revenues.
Source: Standard & Poor's, *Value Line,* 1988.

EXHIBIT THREE

PRODUCT EVOLUTION: MICROPROCESSORS VS. APPLICATION

Transistors/Chip

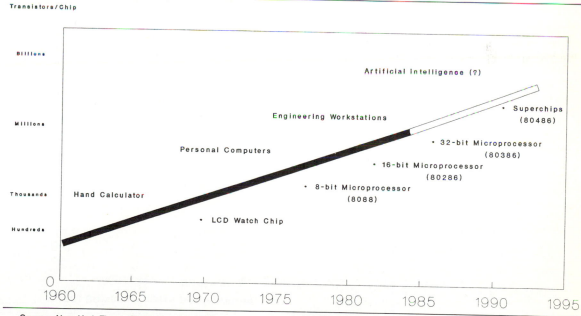

Source: New York Times, September 14, 1988.

EXHIBIT FOUR

TOP TEN MOS MANUFACTURERS

Worldwide revenues					
1976	**$MM**	**1981**	**$MM**	**1987**	**$MM**
TI	135	Intel	491	NEC	2,006
Intel	132	NEC	438	Toshiba	1,566
NEC	74	Motorola	372	Intel	1,473
Gen'l Inst.	68	TI	350	Hitachi	1,236
National	67	Hitachi	288	Fujitsu	1,014
Hitachi	63	National	255	Motorola	986
AMI	59	Toshiba	250	Mitsubishi	811
Mostek	56	Fujitsu	218	TI	784
Motorola	55	Mostek	210	Matsushita	593
Rockwell	50	Gen'l Inst.	141	OKI	566

Source: Dataquest, 1987.

EXHIBIT FIVE

MOS[1] MICROCOMPONENT CONSUMPTION BY REGION (% shares)

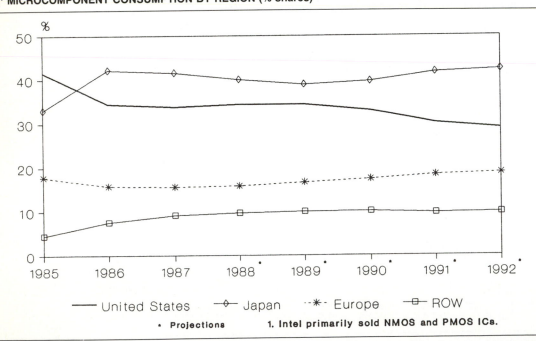

— United States   ◇ Japan   *··* Europe   □ ROW

• Projections   1. Intel primarily sold NMOS and PMOS ICs.

Source: Dataquest, 1987.

INTEL'S OEM PC

INTEL 25 MHZ 80386 PERFORMANCE IN A PC AT COMPATIBLE

Running at 25 MHz, the Intel 80386 based MicroSystem/AT 302 offers OEM's state-of-the-art performance in a PC AT compatible design. A 64K Byte cache provides effective 0 wait state execution, without the high cost of fast access main memory. Memory capacity is extensive, beginning with 4M Bytes on-board, expandable to 24M Bytes via two 32-bit expansion slots. Additionally, the 302 is designed to pass FCC B and VDE B levels of EMI/RFI regulations, a significant test at 25 MHz.

Based upon the PC AT architecture, the MicroSystem/AT 302 is compatible with such software products as MS-DOS, OS/2, and UNIX*. Furthermore, PC AT hardware products from a multitude of vendors plug into 8 I/O expansion slots. If your application runs on a PC today, it will run on the 302.

STANDARD FEATURES:

- Intel 80386 running at 25 MHz
- 64K Byte cache (0 w.s. performance)
- 4M Byte Main Memory (Customer expandable to 8M Byte)
- Phoenix Technologies ROM BIOS
- High Reliability Chassis
- 8 I/O expansion slots

- 220 watt power supply
- 2 32-Bit I/O Expansion Slots
- 2 Serial Ports
- 1 Centronics Parallel Port
- 5 Half-Height, 5¼" Peripheral Bays
- FCC Class B/VDE Level B
- UL/CSA/TUV

OPTIONS:

- Intel 80387 Running at 25 MHz
- 2M Byte Main Memory Option
- Zero Main Memory Option
- 1.2M Byte Floppy Drive

- 8-16M Byte Extended Memory
- 40M Byte Winchester Drive

Note on Microcomputers: Overview of PCs and Workstations

HISTORY OF COMPUTING

One of the first electronic digital computers was developed in 1941 and kept in absolute secrecy by a joint team of scientists from the United States and Great Britain. The ENIAC (electronic numerical integrator and computer) was a mainframe used in cryptology applications for deciphering enemy communication codes during World War II. The original ENIAC system weighed 30 tons, took three years to build, and cost nearly $500,000 to develop (in 1943 dollars). It contained 70,000 resistors, 20,000 vacuum tubes, and 3000 neon lights.

Since the ENIAC, computers moved through a series of radical improvements in technology. The mainframes of 1950s were followed by minicomputers in 1962, microcomputers and supercomputers in the 1970s, and workstations and personal computers (PCs) in the 1980s. (See Exhibit 1.) During 1988, information processing amounted to over $150 billion in annual revenues, while expenditures in the technology sector accounted for over 40% of U.S. corporate capital spending. In its fifth decade of existence, the computer industry was the third largest in the United States, after only automobiles and petroleum.

Product Classification

Historically, computers have been classified by product features that include processing speed, materials technology, input/output performance, centralized versus distributed computing, memory capacity, number of users, and price. Traditional industry segments could be neatly categorized and broadly defined, as there were clear distinctions between mainframes, minicomputers, and microcomputers.

Mainframes Mainframes were large-scale, batch-processing computers capable of supporting more than 128 concurrent users. Mainframes handled the central data processing

Research Associate Ben Huston prepared this note under the supervision of Associate Professor David B. Yoffie as the basis for class discussion.

needs of a large organization or the needs of a smaller number of users performing computational-intensive applications. These computers usually required the service and support of dedicated maintenance personnel. By 1988, unit pricing for a mainframe typically exceeded $500,000.

Minicomputers Minicomputers were first developed in 1961 by the Digital Equipment Corporation (DEC) and ushered in the era of distributed computing (the simultaneous sharing of computer resources). These systems supported up to 64 concurrent users and served the data processing needs of a large department within an organization or the central data processing needs of a small organization with similar computing power requirements. These systems required limited service and support personnel and ranged in price from $100,000 to $500,000.

Microcomputers The development of the microprocessor in the 1970s eventually led to the high concentration of computing power packed in small machines that would make up a new broad class of systems. Microcomputers were generally single-user systems that were originally dedicated to a limited number of applications. These systems were typically priced below $100,000 and required little on-site maintenance service.

By the mid-1980s, the long-standing definitions of the three major industry classifications were less clear. As semiconductors and microprocessors became more powerful and less expensive to manufacture, computer makers were increasingly able to build machines that performed across a broader spectrum of price and performance features. Technological advances in hardware, software, and connectivity eventually led to new systems that defied easy classification. The remainder of this note will focus on two of the newest computer systems: PCs and workstations.

PERSONAL COMPUTERS

Both PCs and workstations were desktop machines powered by microprocessors. Originally, PCs were designed with 8- and 16-bit CPUs (central processing units), while workstations processed data 32 bits at a time. PCs had commonly been employed in a wide variety of office automation roles and were primarily used for word processing, spreadsheet, and database management applications. Workstations were used in more highly specialized and complex tasks such as financial modeling, computer-aided design, and scientific calculation.

The personal computer industry's hardware product cycles could be most readily identified with four generations of microprocessors[1]: (1) 1978, 8-bit Apple; (2) 1981, 8/16-bit IBM PC (8088); (3) 1984, 16/32-bit IBM PC AT (80286) and Apple's Macintosh (68000); (4) 1987, 32-bit COMPAQ Deskpro 386, IBM PS/2 Model 80 (80386), and Macintosh II (68020). (See *Exhibit 2.*)

Worldwide sales of personal computers for 1988 were close to $40 billion, up from $30 billion in 1985. Greater than 60% of the personal computers sold in the domestic market were priced between $1000 and $5000, and business users accounted for a majority of unit and sales volumes. PC manufacturers sold through five main channels. (See *Exhibit 3.*) A survey of corporate volume buyers of PCs conducted by *PC Week* found that compatibility was most highly valued. (See *Exhibit 4.*) Knowledgeable users realized that hardware prices represented about 25% to 30% of the cost of supporting a PC, while software, training, and maintenance costs were the major expenses.

---

[1]The 68XXX family of microprocessors was designed and manufactured by Motorola; the 80XXX family of microprocessors was designed and manufactured by Intel Corporation.

Manufacturing

High-volume, low-cost manufacturing had become critical in the PC business. This was particularly true for IBM PC clone makers that sold computers at the low-end of the market, where markets became rapidly saturated and product life cycles were short. Most IBM PC-compatibles were highly price competitive. Two-thirds of the cost of bringing a PC to market was tied up in advertising, distribution, and other overhead expenses. Materials and assembly costs accounted for the other third. Long production runs and automated assembly techniques characterized the manufacturing process. Manufacturers attempted to locate low-cost sources of reliable components from semiconductor and materials vendors anywhere in the world. Industry experts estimated that each dollar saved in manufacturing could amount to a $4 advantage in the retail channels.

Vendors

IBM In the late 1970s, IBM viewed microcomputers as a growing threat to its mainframe and minicomputer businesses. When IBM finally introduced its PC in 1980, the company departed from its traditional strategy of designing systems with proprietary technology. The first IBM PC used merchant semiconductor components and included the Intel 8088 microprocessor. Microsoft Corporation's MS-DOS was selected as the standard operating system for IBM PCs. As a late entrant in the personal computer business, IBM published a detailed description of its system architecture in order to encourage independent application software and peripherals developers to support the IBM PC. This strategy allowed IBM to leverage its financial resources and reputation to dominate the growing market for personal computers. By 1984, the company claimed 71% of the total market for microcomputers.

In 1988, IBM remained the dominant, worldwide, full-line producer of computers, with an estimated $60 billion in revenues and 400,000 employees. The company had an extensive sales and service organization, and its personal computers had a strong reputation for quality and reliability. IBM's domestic microcomputer hardware sales (PCs and workstations) accounted for $4.9 billion in revenues during the last four quarters ending in June of 1988. The company was one of the three manufacturers (in addition to Apple and Compaq) firmly established in computer retail channels. IBM was also the dominant vendor to large companies. In 1987, its share of PCs in *Fortune* 1000 firms was 72%, while its closest competitors, Compaq and Apple, supplied 5% and 4%, respectively.

During 1987, IBM introduced a new generation of personal computers called the Personal Systems/2 (PS/2). Five out of six models in the PS/2 line incorporated a new, proprietary micro channel bus architecture (MCA), and each model ran Microsoft's OS/2 extended edition operating system. Models at the low end of the PS/2 line were designed with the Intel 80286 chip, while high-end models used the 80386 microprocessor. For example, IBM's PS/2 Model 80 was an 80386-based microcomputer, could run MS-DOS and Unix, and offered multiuser high-end graphics capabilities. Some industry analysts predicted that the MS-DOS operating system would remain the dominant standard through the early 1990s because of its broad base of experienced users and existing software libraries. However, as users' needs shifted to graphics-intensive applications, OS/2 was eventually expected to outsell MS-DOS. IBM intended to market the PS/2 to installations with large investments in IBM PCs and compatibles. By the third quarter of 1988, micro channel PCs accounted for nearly 25% of business PC sales through computer specialty stores.

One year prior to the PS/2 introduction, IBM's

RISC[2] technology (RT) workstations were unveiled as the company's first entry into the technical workstation market. These relatively inexpensive systems were designed with IBM's proprietary 32-bit RISC microprocessor chip and were targeted for engineering and scientific installations seeking to distribute technical computing down to the desktop level. Most industry observers agreed that the RT's performance was not competitive with other available workstations. IBM's share of the U.S. workstation market was 4% in 1987.

Apple Computer   Apple Computer offered an innovative product line of peripherals and personal computers. The year 1988 marked the beginning of Apple's second decade in the computer business and featured the company's first billion-dollar revenue quarter. Total revenues in 1987 accounted for nearly 9% of the worldwide PC market. The company's proprietary Macintosh computers, accounting for 60% to 65% of Apple revenues in 1987, were designed using Motorola's 68000 family of microprocessors. The Macintosh product line featured a "friendly" graphics user interface that gave it the ability to represent information and programming with icons and symbols. The graphics user interface was similar and consistent across most software application packages. This helped to reduce the learning time required when users shifted from one program to another. A majority of Apple customers used the Macintosh for its high-end graphics capabilities in desktop publishing applications.

AppleTalk, the company's proprietary communications network, had been installed on nearly 10% of the 2.2 million Macs in use in 1988. AppleTalk linked Macs to laser printers and was usually restricted to connecting only a few machines within a single department. During 1988, however, Apple was making acquisitions and developing software to link Macs with IBM and Digital Equipment Corporation systems. Apple and DEC, for instance, were developing a product that would enable Apple users to exchange documents with DECnet users. Apple also acquired Orion Network Systems, whose software let Macs work with IBM mainframes.

Apple held a 12% share of the office/professional market sector in 1988, up from only 6% in 1986. The company maintained a strong position in the dealer channel. (Until 1988, Apple had sold almost exclusively through retailers.) Apple planned to become a more significant player in the business PC market and was expanding its direct marketing efforts. Apple's corporate goals were to reach a 20% share of the business PC market in the next few years and to more than double the company's revenues from an estimated $4.1 billion in 1988 to $10 billion by the early 1990s.

Compaq Computer   Compaq was another company whose PCs could typically be found on computer retailers' shelves. During 1988, revenues were expected to increase by greater than 60%, to nearly $2 billion, which would account for nearly 9% of the U.S. PC market. The company also expected record earnings in 1988. (See *Exhibit 6.*) Compaq had a strong brand name, particularly among buyers that had remained faithful to the MS/DOS operating system. Compaq's success could be partly attributed to its marketing skills and its early mover strategy. Compaq had often been the first player in the PC business to use Intel's most advanced or newest microprocessors, such as the 80386 and 80386SX chips. Compaq's product strategy consisted of a two-pronged offensive against IBM's PS/2 computers. First, Compaq underscored its commitment to the original IBM PC

---

[2]IBM pioneered much of the early research for reduced instruction set computing (RISC).

AT architecture in 1987 by introducing the Compaq Deskpro 386/20, based on the Intel 20-MHz 80386 microprocessor, and an 80386-based portable computer. Both products were designed to keep Compaq at the high-profit, high-performance range of the personal computer market. Compaq products were priced well above the clones, demonstrating the company's confidence in its technology. Second, Compaq was attempting to convince customers that Microsoft's OS/2 operating system could run just as well on its machines as on IBM's PS/2 systems that utilized the micro channel architecture. Industry observers suggested that Compaq was also capable of producing a PS/2 clone in the event that customer demand developed.

Others There were over 200 IBM PC clone makers worldwide. Most of these second-tier suppliers reported disappointing sales and earnings in 1988. Since the new generation of 32-bit PCs was designed to work more closely with mainframes and other computers on corporate networks, customers had become increasingly reluctant to rely on smaller suppliers. In addition, the industry had begun to mature, and distribution channels were saturated. Together, IBM, Compaq, and Apple accounted for nearly 66% of all personal computer sales through U.S. computer stores. Second-tier players had to compete on price (e.g., Wyse Technology with IBM clones) or look for a niche market (e.g., Toshiba with laptops).

Although independent computer stores handled nearly half of all PCs sold in the United States, there were other ways to reach customers. Zenith, for example, bid on large government PC contracts and competed aggressively in the OEM (original equipment manufacturers) and university markets with its high-end laptop computers. Dell Computer used direct mail channels to become a $250 million company in less than five years. Also, Tandy

used its own Radio Shack outlets to build a billion-dollar PC clone business and had strength in the small business market.

Most Japanese and Korean computer companies served as OEMs to domestic subsidiaries and independent U.S. computer makers that manufactured low-cost IBM PC clones. In 1988, Japanese producers were estimated to hold less than 30% of the U.S. personal computer market.

Trends in the PC Business

Analysts estimated that by 1990 more than $50 billion worth of personal computers would be in U.S. homes, offices, and classrooms. About 29 million PCs would be installed in offices by the end of the decade, compared with only 9 million in 1985. At the beginning of 1988, penetration of the U.S. business PC market was nearly 25% and was expected to reach 60% by 1992. (See *Exhibit 5*.). Also, international sales were becoming a significant factor in the overall PC industry picture. In 1988, nearly 10 million PCs, over 60% of the worldwide total, were estimated to be shipped in the United States. European shipments were 4 million units, while Japan and the rest of the world accounted for 2 million units each.

In 1988, there was heavy pressure on R&D expenses because of the transition to a more complex type of networked computing. Many of these R&D expenses were either directly or indirectly related to software development. Industry observers considered the development of integrated information networks to be the next major challenge for the PC industry. For example, IBM had been working on a design project called systems application architecture (SAA) since 1986. SAA's twin goals were to provide links to other manufacturers' products and to integrate IBM's own diverse computer lines for the first time. In 1987, 10% of the installed base of U.S. business PCs were networked. That figure was estimated to rise to

60% of an installed base of 37 million units by 1992.

Confusion over hardware standards continued to plague PC customers in the late 1980s. IBM's original AT system bus design had become an industry standard architecture (ISA) for all 80286-based PCs. In 1987, however, IBM attempted to establish a new standard with its MCA-based PS/2 line. Soon after the MCA introduction, other computer vendors indicated that they would legally try to clone the machine. Yet, by mid-1988, most of these cloning plans were put on hold. The continued success of the "classic" AT bus led IBM's competitors to conclude that they might be able to establish an alternative standard. In September of 1988, a group of companies led by Compaq Computer announced the extended industry standard architecture (EISA). EISA, expected to be first shipped in late 1989, was a 32-bit extended AT-compatible bus design that would provide vendors and users with another alternative to MCA. Companies supporting the EISA standard cumulatively shipped more than 60% of all worldwide business PCs in 1988. To hedge its position, IBM introduced a PS/2 Model 30 in late September of 1988 that was a low-end PS/2 with a data bus similar to the AT-bus standard.

The role of the PC was also changing. Personal computers had traditionally been sold for office automation and productivity applications. By 1988, however, high-performance personal computers—such as IBM's PS/2, Apple's Macintosh II, and Compaq's Deskpro 386—were becoming an accepted part of the technical workstation market. Segmentation of the workstation and PC markets below the $15,000 level was becoming increasingly difficult. The software base for both markets continued to grow, and fewer technical differences separated the two groups. Industry observers believed that PCs' increasing speeds, functional capabilities, and low unit prices were threatening sales of technical workstations. Also, an abundance of third-party add-on hardware and software had turned high-end PCs into tools for such demanding tasks as product design, simulation, and scientific problem solving.

WORKSTATIONS

Workstations were high-performance microcomputers built to accommodate complex applications processing in scientific, engineering, and commercial environments. Most of these machines featured powerful 32-bit microprocessors and ran either proprietary operating systems or versions of the UNIX operating system.[3]

The market for workstations had grown rapidly since their initial introduction by Apollo Computer in 1980. (See *Exhibit 7.*) Many former PC users were migrating upward from less powerful systems to machines capable of delivering more computational power, storage, and display capabilities. The increasing demand for workstations could also be attributed to a downward migration from centralized data processing to distributed microprocessor-based systems. Individual workstations were endowed with the power of multiuser systems. By distributing demanding applications to networks of desktop and deskside systems, users had access to more processing power and throughput for department and workgroup-specific applications.

Product Strategy and Distribution

According to Dataquest, the workstation market was $4.1 billion in 1988, and the number of workstations installed worldwide was

---

[3]UNIX was a preferred operating system of choice because it was a readily available systems tool and was easy to license from AT&T, saving vendors the expense of developing a proprietary operating system. Also, UNIX had intrinsic features well suited to software development, a task for which workstations were originally employed.

450,000, which was more than three times the 1986 installed base. As competing systems began to proliferate, workstation vendors faced a number of critical product design and marketing decisions.

Compatibility, a function of the system architecture, was a key issue for both workstation vendors and their customers. Some workstation vendors elected to design and offer "closed systems," or workstations that incorporated system architectures made up of hardware and software components and proprietary technology unique to their products. Closed-systems manufacturers could protect their intellectual property through patents and copyrights but were often willing to license their technology to other vendors for a royalty fee. Maintaining compatibility across computer systems in a heterogeneous or multivendor computing environment was difficult. Many closed-system customers had significant investments tied up in hardware and software and were often reluctant to abandon them.

However, a growing number of vendors chose to build workstations for an "open-systems" environment, using off-the-shelf hardware and software components that either adhered to industry standards, were widely employed in the marketplace, or were already available for use on a variety of system architectures or products. The use of merchant components enabled the vendor to reduce manufacturing and delivery costs. Research and development time and expense could also be reduced, enabling these vendors to pass along those economies to the users. Many workstation customers wanted nonproprietary solutions: open systems would reduce system migration and applications porting costs when moving to or from another hardware platform, increase the available base of applications software, standardize computing across the organization, and provide a degree of compatibility among systems in the increasingly prevalent multivendor or multiple-architecture comput-

ing environment. Software sales for open-systems (DOS, OS/2, and UNIX) were expected to increase from 34% of the U.S. market in 1987 to over 48% by 1991.

Throughout the 1980s, the average selling price (ASP) of workstations continued to drop. The increasing use of microprocessor chips such as the Intel 80386 drove the power of personal computers up into the technical workstation range. In response, high-performance workstation leaders—such as Sun Microsystems, Apollo Computer, and Digital Equipment Corporation—significantly dropped the cost of entry-level desktop workstations so that prices were comparable with those of the so-called technical PCs. Some of these workstations were priced below $7500, while others were below $5000 in a diskless configuration.

Traditionally, workstation customers were frequently volume buyers. Machines were configured as networks or sold into a departmental computing configuration. As workstations were increasingly designed and supported to serve a variety of applications, they were expected to move through broader channels of distribution in order to reach new customers. By 1987, direct sales accounted for nearly 60% of their revenues. (See *Exhibit 8.*) Workstations were also commonly sold through value-added resellers (VARs) and OEMs. As selling prices continued to drop, industry analysts expected that several workstation vendors would be pushing their products through retail channels by 1989.

Workstation Vendors

Sun Microsystems Founded in 1982 by four young Stanford graduates with virtually no prior business experience, Sun Microsystems was one of the fastest growing companies in the computer business. By the end of 1988, Sun claimed a 30% share of the workstation market and nearly $1 billion in annual revenues. (See *Ex-*

hibit 9.) Sun offered a broad product line of workstations and servers, and targeted market segments within the business, professional support, and scientific computing sectors. The company's innovative product design, aggressive pricing strategy, and large network of value-added resellers contributed to Sun's success in the marketplace.

Sun's emergence as the leader in the workstation business could be attributed in large part to its open-systems computing approach. While the company built systems that adhered to existing software and hardware standards, it was also successful in getting many of its proprietary solutions accepted as new industry standards. Examples included its open network computing (ONC) platform and a RISC-based scalable processor architecture (SPARC) microprocessor chip. ONC software communication tools allowed Sun workstations to interact with IBM and IBM-compatible PCs, workstations, departmental computers, and host systems that employed the Ethernet networking standard.

Sun was the first computer company which aggressively sought to establish its internally developed microprocessor chip as a standard for other hardware competitors. Sun targeted its RISC-based SPARC chip for the workstation market and licensed the technology and manufacturing rights to several merchant semiconductor vendors. Industry observers speculated that the company's long-term goal was to establish its systems as the workstation industry standard of the 1990s. In January of 1989, Solbourne Computer (a U.S. company with majority ownership held by Matsushita Electric of Japan) introduced the first clones of the Sun-4 family of workstations based on SPARC microprocessor technology. Solbourne computers were the first of many Sun-compatible machines expected to be announced during 1989.

To tap the low-end workstation/high-end PC markets, Sun introduced its 386i workstation in 1988. Rather than use its SPARC chip, the 386i was an Intel 80386-based machine with an 80387 math coprocessor and high-resolution graphics displays. The 386i boasted three critical capabilities: (1) all networking was preinstalled and fully automatic, (2) the graphic icon-based interface insulated the user from cryptic UNIX commands, and (3) the 386i ran DOS applications software in separate windows and could even run more than one simultaneously.

Apollo Computer Apollo Computer, an industry pioneer, had once dominated the workstation market. By 1987, the company held second place behind Sun Microsystems with a 22% market share. In the early 1980s, Apollo targeted design automation and manufacturing applications as its primary market sectors. The company's workstation architectures were once almost exclusively proprietary. This closed-system approach made it difficult for users to port applications over from other vendors' systems, to connect other computers for information distribution, and to find appropriate software application systems for specific processing tasks.

By 1988, however, Apollo had redefined its product strategy, responded to customer calls for systems with commonly available facilities, and repositioned its workstation line to compete in the business applications and software development markets. The Domain Series' distinguishing factor was its networking capabilities. In addition, the company had challenged Sun Microsystems and Hewlett-Packard in the superworkstation market sector with its Series 10000 workstation that incorporated an internally developed parallel RISC-based multiprocessing (PRISM) architecture.

Digital Equipment Corporation Digital Equipment Corporation, the number two computer maker after IBM, entered the workstation market in 1984 and sold a variety of proprietary systems products. The VAXstation 2000, 3000, and 8000 workstations were designed to appeal to DEC's large installed base of VAX[4] minicomputer users that wanted to add power at the desktop and workgroup levels. A number of these systems provided connectivity features as well as hardware and software compatibility that enabled smooth integration into existing VMS[5] operating environments. During 1988, DEC's low-end VAXstation 2000 was the best-selling workstation in the industry based on unit volume. However, Sun and Apollo workstations had typically been purchased over DEC systems where standard UNIX requirements were specified.

In January of 1989, DEC's announcement of a low-priced, powerful workstation line designed to operate in an open-systems computing environment marked a significant change in business strategy for Digital. The DECstation 3100 used a high-speed RISC microprocessor designed by MIPS Computer Systems and ran the industry-standard UNIX operating system. At the same time, DEC also introduced the VAXstation 3100 to run its proprietary operating system. The VAXstation 3100 was estimated to operate over two times as fast as the VAXstation 2000.

Others Several Japanese companies—including Hitachi, Sony, NEC, Mitsubishi, and Toshiba—had entered the workstation business by 1988. Most of these machines were based on Motorola microprocessors, and many used various versions of the UNIX operating system. Most Japanese vendors emphasized that these machines would serve an important role in the future of engineering networks. In 1989, Motorola announced its own technical workstation line, with products ranging in price from $28,000 to $80,000. Motorola's offering was based on its recently introduced RISC processor, which the company hoped would create a new standard.

---

[4]VAX, or virtual address extension, was DEC's proprietary hardware platform.

[5]VMS was DEC's proprietary operating system designed to run the VAX hardware platform.

EXHIBIT ONE

COMPUTER MAKERS' SHARE OF WORLD MARKETS BY GEOGRAPHY, 1988

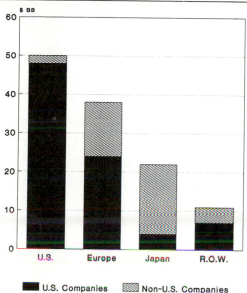

■ U.S. Companies ▨ Non-U.S. Companies

COMPUTER MAKERS' SHARE OF WORLD MARKETS BY PRODUCT LINE, 1988

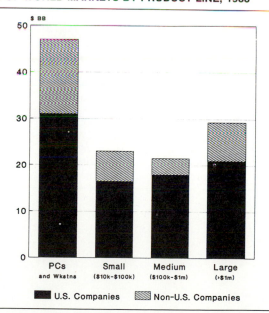

■ U.S. Companies ▨ Non-U.S. Companies

Source: Reprinted from *Business Week,* March 6, 1989 by special permission, copyright © 1989 by McGraw-Hill, Inc.

EXHIBIT TWO

WORLDWIDE PERSONAL COMPUTER MARKET (millions of units)

	1981	1982	1983	1984	1985	1986	1987	1988
Total PCs								
Units shipped	1.7	5.4	9.0	11.7	11.5	12.6	14.6	17.4
Installed base	3.0	7.9	16.4	27.0	36.8	46.4	56.8	68.4
Intel micro-based								
Units shipped	0.0	0.2	1.0	2.6	3.4	4.5	6.3	8.0
Installed base	0.0	0.2	1.2	3.7	7.1	11.4	17.4	25.1
8088								
Units shipped	0.0	0.2	0.9	2.4	2.8	2.9	2.7	2.4
Installed base	0.0	0.2	1.1	3.5	6.3	9.1	11.7	13.8
80286								
Units shipped	0.0	0.0	0.0	0.1	0.4	1.4	3.1	4.4
Installed base	0.0	0.0	0.0	0.1	0.5	1.9	4.8	9.2
80386								
Units shipped	0.0	0.0	0.0	0.0	0.0	0.0	0.3	1.0
Installed base	0.0	0.0	0.0	0.0	0.0	0.0	0.3	1.3
Motorola micro-based								
Units shipped	0.0	0.0	0.0	0.5	0.7	0.9	1.1	1.5
Installed base	0.0	0.0	0.1	0.5	1.2	2.1	3.2	4.6

Source: Infocorp, 1988.

EXHIBIT THREE

U.S. MICROCOMPUTER UNIT SHIPMENTS—BY DISTRIBUTION CHANNEL (thousands)

	Mass merchants	Computer retailers	Wholesale distribution	OEM/VAR	Direct sales
1983	2,332	1,626	867	434	163
1984	2,367	2,360	879	676	473
1985	2,085	2,641	765	834	626
1986	2,101	2,852	750	976	825
1987	2,037	3,097	815	1,141	1,059

Source: IDC, 1985.

EXHIBIT FOUR

PC BUYING CRITERIA

	Volume buyers of PCs	
	386 PCs	**286 PCs**
Compatibility	94%	95%
Reliability	94	94
Vendor support	80	77
Performance	79	75
Documentation	77	75
Reconfigurability	74	75
Relative price	74	77
Easy to install	72	71

Source: PC Week, 1988.

EXHIBIT FIVE

U.S. BUSINESS PC MARKET PENETRATION

By end-user type, 1988, millions of units

End user	Total available market[a]	Number of installed PCs	Market opportunity[b]
Large company	10	3.2	6
Medium company	25	6.2	15
Small company	18	4.3	11
Home offices	4	0.5	2
Government	4	0.8	2
Total	61	15	36

[a]Defined as total number of white-collar employees.
[b]Market opportunity figures are estimated.
Source: Businessland, 1988.

SELECTED FINANCIAL STATISTICS—1983–1988 ($ millions, except ratios and stock prices)

	Wyse Technology[b]				Apple[f]			
	1988[e]	1987	1986	1985	1987	1986	1985	1984
Revenues	457	260	166	78	2,661	1,902	1,918	1,516
Net income (loss)	28	18	13	8	217	154	61	64
Liquid assets[a]	391	292	111	50	1,872	1,617	1,159	803
Total assets	383	229	108	51	1,478	1,160	936	789
Long-term debt	116	86	5	3	0	0	0	0
ROS	6.1%	7.0%	7.6%	9.6%	8.2%	8.1%	3.2%	4.2%
ROA	8.4	10.8	13.9	14.7	16.4	14.6	7.0	9.4
ROE	10.1	22.0	21.9	41.5	28.3	24.6	11.9	15.1
Stock prices ($/share)								
High	26	40	19	15	60	22	16	17
Low	7	13	11	7	20	11	7	11
P/E ratio	4	21–7	12–7	12–6	16–12	36–12	18–9	31–14
Market valuation[c]	107	n.a.	n.a.	n.a.	4,223	1,744	1,367	
Book value	167	94	64	25	1,188	836	693	552

	Compaq[f]				Zenith[d]			
	1987	1986	1985	1984	1987	1986	1985	1984
Revenues	1,224	625	504	329	2,363	1,892	1,624	1,716
Net income (loss)	136	43	27	13	(19.1)	(10.0)	(7.7)	63.6
Liquid assets	813	317	317	217	1,110	969	694	698
Total assets	901	378	312	231	1,373	1,235	927	909
Long-term debt	149	73	75	0	315	272	165	172
ROS	11.1%	6.9%	5.3%	3.9%	NM	NM	NM	3.7%
ROA	19.8	12.3	9.8	7.2	NM	NM	NM	7.7
ROE	43.2	26.6	21.5	12.7	NM	NM	NM	15.5
Stock prices ($/share)								
High	79	22	14	15	34	30	25	29
Low	19	12	6	4	10	18	16	20
P/E ratio	22–5	14–8	15–6	31–7	NM	NM	NM	13–7
Market valuation	1,515	421	257		NM	NM	NM	NM
Book value	400	183	137		478	432	437	

a Includes cash plus current assets.
b Results reported for year ended 3/31/88.
c Market value = average stock price * # shares outstanding.
d Zenith had 26 million common shares outstanding in 4Q88.
e Estimated using stock price @ $7 1/4 per share on 11/28/88.
f Estimated book value and market value for Apple at year-end 1988 were $1.2 BB and $5.0 BB, respectively; and for Compaq at year-end 1988, they were $0.8 BB and $2.3 BB, respectively.
Source: Value Line, 1988.

EXHIBIT SEVEN

TECHNICAL WORKSTATION MARKET: 1985–1989

Year	Revenues ($000)	Unit ASPs ($)
1985	$ 938	$28,400
1986	1,563	25,500
1987	2,700	22,700
1988E	4,100	17,200
1989E	n/a	13,000

Source: Dataquest, 1988 and 1989.

EXHIBIT EIGHT

TOP FIVE WORKSTATION VENDORS

Market share and distribution channels (%)

Vendor	1987 market share	Direct sales	OEM	VAR/vendor	Distribution
Apollo	21%	50%	49%	1%	—
DEC	20	55	35	1	9
Hewlett-Packard	12	65	33	2	—
IBM	4	70	15	15	—
Sun	29	58	41	1	—
Others	14				

Source: Electronic Business, 1988; IDC, 1988.

EXHIBIT NINE

SELECTED FINANCIAL STATISTICS: 1983–1988 ($ millions, except ratios and stock prices)

	Sun Microsystems[b]					Apollo				
	1988	1987	1986	1985	1984	1988	1987	1986	1985	1984
Revenues		1,052	538	210	115		554	392	296	216
Net income (loss)		66.4	36.3	11.9	8.5		21.7	9.6	(1.5)	23.9
Liquid assets[a]		660	613	183	95		333	293	169	216
Total assets		757	524	182	84		447	367	258	217
Long-term debt		125	127	4	7		117	117	29	1
ROS		6.3%	6.8%	5.7%	7.4%		3.9%	2.4%	NM	11.1%
ROA		10.1	9.7	9.7	14.8		5.3	3.0	NM	15.2
ROE		21.1	19.3	16.4	25.4		10.4	5.1	NM	19.4
Stock prices ($/share)										
High		41	46	24	NA		25	18	31	29
Low		27	22	11	NA		9	9	9	16
P/E ratio		23–15	41–20	53–24	NA		41–14	68–34	NM	39–21
Market valuation[c]	1,261	1,107	209	NA		352	654	480	NM	
Book value	379	234	104	34		241	225	190	174	

	DEC[b]					IBM				
	1988	1987	1986	1985	1984	1988	1987	1986	1985	1984
Revenues		11,475	9,389	7,590	6,686		54,217	51,250	50,056	45,937
Net income (loss)		1,306	1,137	617	447		5,258	4,789	6,555	6,582
Liquid assets[a]		9,094	8,319	7,217	5,718		37,987	35,006	31,692	24,737
Total assets		10,112	8,407	7,173	6,369		63,688	57,814	52,634	42,808
Long-term debt		124	269	333	837		3,858	4,169	2,955	3,269
ROS		11.4%	12.1%	8.1%	6.7%		9.7%	9.3%	13.1%	14.3%
ROA		14.1	14.7	8.8	7.4		8.7	8.7	13.7	16.4
ROE		18.9	19.1	11.6	10.3		14.6	14.5	22.5	26.4
Stock prices ($/share)										
High		145	200	109	69		176	162	159	129
Low		86	105	66	43		102	119	117	99
P/E ratio		15–9	23–12	23–14	18–11		20–12	21–15	15–11	12–9
Market valuation	17,225	16,038	8,783	5,992		71,260	86,562	85,277	80,768	
Book value	7,512	6,293	5,727	4,554		40,563	38,263	34,377	31,990	

[a]Includes cash plus current assets.
[b]Year ended September 30.
[c]Market value = average stock price ∗ # shares outstanding.
[d]Estimated book value = book value/share ∗ # shares outstanding.
Source: Value Line, 1988.